SINATRA

SINATRA

ROBIN DOUGLAS-HOME

GROSSET & DUNLAP Publishers
NEW YORK

First published in England by Michael Joseph Ltd.
Photographs by Robin Douglas-Home
Some material in this book first appeared in *The Queen Magazine*
Manufactured in the United States of America

CHAPTER 1

The first time I ever heard the name Frank Sinatra was at Eton in 1945. The boy who lived in the room next to mine had pinned up on the door of his bureau the photograph of a grinning youth with a thin face dominated by large eyes and a tiered coif of hair. Pinned up on my own I had pictures of Lauren Bacall and Charlie Smirke, representing my two main interests at the time – brunettes and betting. But this grinning youth was unknown to me.

'Who's that?' I asked my neighbour.

'Frank Sinatra,' he said.

'What does he do?'

'Sing.'

'Oh yes,' I said and passed on to more interesting subjects.

The next nine years yield no conscious memory of the thin singer's existence. I suppose I must have read the newspapers, but the reportage of his matrimonial troubles left no impression whatsoever . . .

The next time I remember his name cropping up was one night in Egypt in 1954. I was duty officer with the Perimeter Defence Company, guarding the vast arms and ammunition dump at Tel-el-Kebir. This involved sitting awake most of the night in the command post hut at the centre of the 17-mile perimeter and waiting for the Very light signal that indicated trouble with looting Egyptians. I used to spend the time fiddling with a powerful Army wireless set that was used at certain hours for contact with our battalion headquarters a few miles away, but for the rest of the time for picking up music from European disc-jockey programmes. As I twiddled the knob and dreamed of all the pleasures of the flesh I was foregoing by being incarcerated inside a barbed-wire fence in the middle of the Egyptian desert, the sound of a brassy swing band came through the earphones. The tune was 'The Birth of The Blues' and it was being sung in the most dynamic manner by a lean male voice. I will never forget hearing that song blaring rather tinnily from the earphones: it gave substance to my reveries in an extraordinarily potent way.

'Who was that singing?' I asked the duty signaller, who happened to be the platoon Tin Pan Alley expert.

7

'Frank Sinatra, sir,' he answered with a look suggesting I had asked him what my own name was . . .

There is another gap of two years, and then, one afternoon some six months after being demobbed, I was walking down Knightsbridge in the rain. I was in the throes of a wild romance at the time, and walking in the rain without a coat or umbrella seemed exactly the right activity for my mood. There was a little record shop on the north side of the road just where the grass of Hyde Park joined Knightsbridge, and in the window in a place of prominence was an eye-catching long-playing record sleeve bearing the title 'Songs For Swingin' Lovers.' Underneath the title in smaller letters was the name Frank Sinatra. The only records I owned at that time were a collection of scratched 78's of the Hot Five and Muggsy Spanier – the buying of long-players was (and still is) an expensive pursuit, for which I did not have sufficient spare money. Anyway, regardless of this consideration, and regardless of the fact that I knew no more about Frank Sinatra than what I had learned from my room-neighbour at Eton and the duty signaller that night in Tel-el-Kebir, I walked straight in and bought that record without even looking to see what the songs were or asking to hear it first.

I took it straight home and put it on the gramophone. The effect was electric – I sat mesmerised, scarcely noticing my mother's entry during Juan Tizol's wild trombone solo in 'I've Got You Under My Skin' and her muttered 'What a *terrible* noise – must we have it so loud, darling?' For the next year I don't suppose a day went by without my playing that record at least five times – while shaving in the morning or while lying in bed at night. It seemed to capture the essence of my mood at the time, the essence of that time of life, the essence of a youthful romance that could only end as the lyrics of 'I've Got You Under My Skin' so succinctly forecast: 'Don't you know, little fool, you never can win – use your mentality, wake up to reality . . .'

Even now, after hearing it more than two thousand times, that record has never lost its spine-tingling freshness and inexplicable magic for me. I have only had one other comparably powerful musical experience, and that was hearing Louis Armstrong play 'The Gipsy,' at a distance six feet away from me, in a cellar in Kensington High Street.

8

From 1956 onwards I bought every Sinatra record available, and absorbed every note he recorded, in an attempt to analyse the man's unique power of communication. I read all the so-called profiles on him in British and American publications, but my search for an explanation of his particular talent was invariably fruitless; every writer seemed far more concerned with what girl he was dating at the moment than with an analysis of his professional approach, his artistic ability, or his unique lyric interpretation. Here was the only really exceptional voice in contemporary popular music, and all that the chroniclers of the day could find to report about him was his readiness to pick a fight or his fondness for girls. So what? Both were tediously normal characteristics for any artist, especially a hypersensitive and volatile one, as I imagined this man must be.

His refusal to kow-tow to the press or allow journalists to interview him was well known; I assumed that this policy so pricked the vanity of that too-often embittered body of men and women that they indulged in denigrations of him in print as a kind of reprisal, as if to say, 'So you think you can get on without *us*, do you, Frankie boy? Well, we'll show you.' His own behaviour cannot have helped his press relations, but he is under no obligation to give interviews or to pander to the insistent demands of reporters unless he wants to. The counter-argument that without the press he would still be serving hot dogs in a Hoboken Hamburger Heaven cuts no ice at all – you have only to hear that voice to be instantly affected by it, and the press does not propagate the sound of his voice. Of course this bad-boy image built up by the press may have helped sell a lot of his records: it gives him a fascinating public appeal. But it is nonsense to say that he would be nowhere but for the press.

In 1959 I decided there was only one thing for it – to get to Sinatra and find out for myself what made this extraordinary talent tick. The fact that he had never been authoritatively and comprehensively profiled in print made the challenge all the more stimulating, the reward of success all the more attractive – if I ever *had* success. I found out the name of his publicity agent and wrote a long letter explaining my aim. I received a prompt and courteous reply thanking me for my interest but regretting that 'Mr Sinatra's schedule is so tight for the immediate future that he regrets he will not be able to spare the time for an interview along the lines you suggest.'

9

So I then wrote to Sinatra himself. After three weeks the same reply came from his publicity agent, to whom the letter had been passed.

A year passed but the intention remained in the back of my mind. It was a question of waiting for a lucky break – the lucky break I had a naïve hunch would eventually turn up out of the blue.

Sure enough it did. In June 1960 I suddenly and unexpectedly found myself at dinner sitting next to two people who knew Sinatra well: they were Michael and Gloria Romanoff – he is the famous owner of Romanoff's Restaurant in Beverly Hills and a great character. I nervously put my plan to them and they kindly promised to relay the idea to the singer himself.

'But don't bank on anything,' they emphasised again and again. 'You never can tell with *him*.'

I got a letter from them some months later saying they had mentioned the plan to him but that no real progress could be made unless I came out to California myself and tried pot luck. This was a gamble that appealed to *me*, but unfortunately not to my bank manager nor the managing director of the firm where I worked at the time from 9.30 to 5.30. And I could see their point.

Then came the second lucky break – Nelson Riddle, whose orchestrations contributed so much to Sinatra's recordings during the late 'Fifties, came to London. I found out where he was staying, telephoned him and said I wanted to interview him. He, incidentally, was another key figure in the popular musical field whose talent and working methods had never been analysed or explained in any publication – in fact, he told me he had never been interviewed on the subject before! What an indictment of the journalist profession.

I spent several evenings with Riddle, and watched him at work at the piano in Elstree Studios. The result was published in *The Queen* magazine in July 1961, and I sent a copy to the Romanoffs asking them if they thought it might help matters if they showed it to Sinatra and explained that that was the kind of approach I wanted to use with him – i.e. focused on his personality and his music rather than his relationships with the opposite sex.

Two weeks later I received a letter from Gloria Romanoff saying, first, that she had shown the Riddle article to Sinatra; secondly, that Sinatra was arriving in London the next week and would I please call him as soon as he arrived.

Eight days later I walked into a room on the first floor of Claridges and shook hands with a lean, dapper man with piercing blue eyes who said in the terse voice of Pal Joey: 'That article you did on Nelson was a gas.'

CHAPTER 2

Two qualities of Sinatra immediately struck me at that first meeting. The first was the exceptional sharpness and directness of his eyes – very blue with a dash of gun-metal grey, they stabbed rather than saw, challenged rather than looked.

The second quality was his courtesy. He was scrupulously observant about those oft-forgotten details like offering and lighting cigarettes, getting up and opening the door for women, watching for an empty glass or a length of ash on a cigarette. Where was this vandal, this uncouth Philistine I had so often read about in the columns of the popular press and the pulp magazines? Or was he just on his best behaviour?

He was smartly dressed in a dark blue suit, dark tie, white shirt, red silk handkerchief in his breast pocket, fat gold signet ring on his left little finger. Perfectly kept finger-nails. The appearance neat and wiry, the movements quick and graceful, the walk athletic. He certainly did not look forty-five years old: the only trace of age was the balding patch on his crown.

He drank Jack Daniels and water – not too much water ('Water rusts you'). He smoked Lucky Strikes, and when he lit one he cocked his head to one side and cupped the gold Dunhill lighter with one hand.

We dined at the Mirabelle. The party included Dean Martin and Michael Romanoff. Sinatra took a great delight in helping everyone to choose their menus and an even greater delight in choosing the wine, which eventually turned out to be Château Margaux '47. He became worried by any mess on the table-cloth: if anyone spilt the minutest amount of cigarette-ash outside an ash-tray he immediately summoned a waiter to brush it up.

His conversation was fluent, intelligent – on movie-making, war, women – and above all humorous. But the only subjects on which he talked passionately were music – his plans for new record albums – his family, and the press, particularly the British press. I felt he assumed that everyone else *expected* him to be entertaining, and that he was definitely not going to let them down. But he looked considerably less relaxed in a public place than in the privacy of his hotel suite: his glance flicked a trifle apprehensively round the room from time to time, and the continual

12

movement of his hands suggested a frantically churning metabolism and a considerable inner tension.

The reason for this air of nervous apprehension became more apparent later. After he had mixed vodka stingers for everyone at the table, and had complimented the head waiter on the excellence of the dinner, we moved to a basement nightclub where the atmosphere was very different from the discreet good taste of the Mirabelle. First of all, the doorman and the waiters nearly had a stroke when they saw him come through the door. Then, in spite of genuine requests to be allowed to sit in a dark corner incognito, the cabaret was interrupted with a fawning announcement about his presence and a spotlight turned on him. I could see him sink down into his chair as the spotlight wavered about in its efforts to locate him. This was no act of false modesty, as subsequent events proved. Because, instead of him being able to sit in peace drinking his vodka stingers and talking to his party, from that moment on he was besieged by a queue of autograph-hunters and inquisitive fans standing and staring at him from a few feet. Some of the autograph-hunters were either half or wholly drunk, and the women would hang round his neck and mouth incoherent sentences at him; others were downright offensive. I know many quiet, tolerant, well-educated, English so-called 'gentlemen' whose reaction to this parade would have been either to punch one of the loud-mouthed insulters hard on the nose or to have walked angrily out of the club in the first few minutes. Sinatra's reaction was to ignore the drunken remarks and the obvious attempts to get fresh with him and just sign 'Best Wishes Frank Sinatra' on the proffered diaries, note-pads, menu-cards, envelopes and even paper napkins. But after that there was no chance of a relaxed evening. I could only too easily understand the chemistry behind those ridiculously over-publicised and wildly exaggerated incidents in his past that had grown to distort the public image of the man into a fight-provoker and a cantankerous rough-houser. But on that occasion the provocation and the cantankerousness came from everyone but him, and I was surprised at the even-keeled manner in which he gently ignored it. What the incident emphasised, however, was the tremendous nervous strain of appearing in a public place when your name is Frank Sinatra. Dean Martin, for instance, had none of these problems – a few autographs, but none of the lip. Clearly, Sinatra has an uncannily electric effect on people who suddenly find themselves near him in the flesh, especially when they are warmed by alcohol: the women become overtly coquettish, the men overtly jealous and aggressive.

At about 2 a.m. I said to Sinatra: 'I'd like to come to Hollywood to do a musical biography of you. Would that be possible?'

'I'll never have the time,' he said rather embarrassedly. 'It would mean hours of talking to you and I've got too much on just now. I tell you what – I've got a record session on September 11 – 8.30 in the evening. Why don't you come over for that, see how we work?'

Next morning I applied for three months leave from my job and booked an air passage to Los Angeles on September 11. My chips were down.

CHAPTER 3

I arrived at the recording studio in Hollywood at 8.25 p.m. on Monday evening, September 11. A uniformed janitor at the door suspiciously asked what I was doing. I gave my name and found that I was expected.

Inside the studio itself about forty musicians were standing and sitting in a large semi-circle with a rostrum at the centre. Microphones sprouted amongst them like a straggly bed of misshapen steel tulips. The conductor-arranger for the session was Axel Stordahl, famous for the arrangements behind Sinatra that first established him as a solo singer after both had left Tommy Dorsey's band in the 'Forties.

It was an impressive array of musical talent. In the violin section there were four symphony orchestra concert-masters; the French horn-players were the three leading players in the American classical music field; there was Pete Candoli in the trumpet section, and Ted Nash in the saxophone section, Al Viola on the guitar, and many other famous names from the world of jazz.

The atmosphere was relaxed. The bass-player was smoking a cigarette through a long white holder. A trombone-player was surreptitiously following a ball-game on a transistor radio earplug. Buzz of talk, smoke rings, violin squeaks, drum thuds, horn blasts, trumpet trills, flute whistles.

Suddenly the cacophony died to a whisper and all heads turned to the door. In sauntered Sinatra. He wore a well-cut dark grey suit; a dark grey felt hat crowned him jauntily; a red and yellow silk handkerchief peeked perkily from his breast-pocket; the black bows on his patent leather pumps winked from under the knife-edge creases. His face was alert, purposeful, a shade nervous – the ice-blue eyes moved here and there rather more restlessly than when he had been in London . . . but a twinkle was either in them or a split-second away.

He waved a greeting to the orchestra, cracked a few crisp jokes to the most familiar faces, picked up the vocal score for the first number, undid his top shirt-button and loosened his tie. A brief discussion with Stordahl, a practice run-through by the orchestra (neither Sinatra nor they had heard it before) during which he followed the song on his own score and sang quietly to himself as he walked about the open space behind Stordahl.

15

Then a signal to the man in the control room behind the glass panel – and a voice boomed through the vast loudspeakers: '3526 Master E Take One.'

Sinatra stood away from the orchestra, facing Stordahl's back, surrounded on three sides by a screen. The microphone hung down over the lectern in front of him, an austere-looking stool behind him. The orchestra drowned his voice, so I watched rather than listened . . .

I saw complete and utter involvement with the song he was singing – involvement so close that one might feel he was in the throes of composing both tune and lyric as he went along. When he controlled his breathing he shuddered, almost painfully – shoulders shook, neck muscles twitched, even his legs seemed to oscillate. His nostrils dilated and his eyes closed dreamily, then opened again as sharp as ever as he watched a soloist, then closed again and his face contorted into a grimace, and his whole frame seemed to be caught up in a paroxysm, quivering all over as he expressed a key note or word like the 'November' in 'September Song.'

His mouth, sometimes hardly a centimetre from the microphone, widened into a sort of canine snarl, and he cocked his head now on one side, now on the other, like a puppy listening to the squeak of a toy mouse, like the dog in the His Master's Voice trademark.

He was putting so much into that song, giving so much of himself that it drained my own energy just to watch him – without hearing a note he was singing; left me so limp at the end that I felt I had actually been living through some serious emotional crisis.

At the end of the song there was silence as the whole studio waited for the playback. Sinatra walked over to the rostrum, lit a cigarette, leaned on one elbow, gazed intently at the floor. '3526 Master E Take One' boomed again through the speakers, this time on tape and at maximum volume. This time I listened . . .

The song was a slow, nostalgic ballad of unrequited love, a bitter-sweet hymn to a very special girl who somehow got away. The voice I heard was that of an insecure man, alone, calling for understanding from the depths of a cold private wilderness . . . of a vulnerable child, almost, crying itself to sleep in the secrecy of his room. The pathos and dejection in that voice struck a range of hidden chords in my memory, bringing back vivid and searing fresh those moments, deep-buried and long-forgotten, when a cold hand gripped the ardent heart of young love – when her telephone call

16

did not come on the promised hour, when the longed-for letter never came, when you saw her dancing happily, or leaving the party, with someone else.

The words were ordinary words, words used daily in speech by millions of lovers. And when they are used they sound hollow, embarrassing, anything but poetic. Yet in the larynx of this man these banal phrases become poignant, pointful and even beautiful. How does it happen? What is the chemistry of this extraordinary power of communication?

It comes primarily from the unique timbre of his voice. It has all the mellow tone of a 'cello, yet somewhere there too is an edge of toughness, of rawness, that kills any hint of sugariness. How can I express it in metaphors of taste – a mouthful of Château Mouton Rothschild '49 chased by a teaspoon of celery salt and a sprinkling of cayenne pepper, or a spoonful of Hymettus honey washed down with the dryest of dry vodka martinis . . . Whatever it is, however it may be described, this vocal quality injects a vital force, a more profound meaning into quite mundane sentiments. And this, surely, is something only the rare and real creative artist can achieve.

His phrasing has a lot to do with it, too. You feel he understands and *means* every syllable of the lyric. He seems to be recounting a personal experience each time. He sings as if he *knows*. His phrasing is final, absolute, definitive – so logically and inevitably do the phrases follow each other that, after hearing him sing a song, that song never sounds quite right sung by anyone else. He phrases more as if he is speaking to someone: the intervals, word stresses, note values and rhythms are changed to fit in more with the cadences of colloquial speech. Add the breath control, the slurs, chopped notes, grace notes and held notes that have been his trademarks for almost twenty years and you have the basic ingredients that give that natural, effortless credibility to every word he sings.

He has, too, the instinctive good taste of a natural jazz artist. When he bends a melody a little, when he shuffles the lyrics, when he adds a favourite word, just that extra element of surprise glints, that extra dash of colour flares up, in the scene painted.

Again like the natural jazz artist, he has an uncanny sense of rhythm. Even in his handling of a slow ballad it shines, but the lonely rejected introspector is but one half of the man: turn over the coin and you find the bouncy, cock-a-hoop, wise-cracking, riproaring fellow whose charm is irrepressible, irresistible – and who knows it. The devil-may-care, swashbuckling rebel who roots for the underdog and flies the Jolly Roger from his topmast.

Take a jump at yourself, fink convention – he seems to be saying. *Spin on, world, we're doing fine, baby. Things are swinging and let's keep it that way. Shrug a shoulder, toss a curl, wink an eyelid, snap a finger. Gather ye those broads while ye may. Time's running on, baby. Life's a gasser. Make whoopee. Ring-a-ding-ding. Yup . . .*

This is the mood he can capture in his singing as accurately as its converse, with that same unrivalled combination of tone and phrasing but mainly with his hell-for-leather rhythm.

Yet, with the musician as with the man, in spite of all the brashness, still detectable under that bold brassy front – and surprisingly near the surface – was the old vulnerability, the nagging insecurity, the scars from the intimate acquaintance with rebuff and disillusionment that he sings of in his slower songs. And I could not fail to get the impression that under that nonchalant, sophisticated façade lay a heart that was far more sensitive and far easier hurt than the protective layer of thick-skinned cock-a-hoopery tried to suggest. This impression, suggesting the reverent, star-struck idolater, was confirmed in hard cold reality many times over during the following weeks.

Back to the recording session. One vibrant gut-breaking track after another. The magnetism of the man at the microphone acted on the assembly like an electric current. His hat was the barometer of his feelings – pulled down over his eyes when he was concentrating, pushed back on his crown when he was relaxing between takes. A staccato flow of suggestions, directions and wisecracks punctuated the breathing spaces, keeping the atmosphere alive and humorous – yet totally in earnest.

No note escaped his ears, however buried it might be in the total sound of the orchestra.

To the violins: 'How about playing a triplet in bar forty?'

Or to the brass: 'A little less volume in bar three. Fairly fat in front, then skinny it up.'

Or to his pianist Bill Miller, whose face is as pale as parchment: 'Hey, Suntan Charlie – you'll have to give me a note there.'

Or to the lady harpist trying to get a difficult glissando exactly to his liking: 'Make like you're killin' time, baby. Like you're likin' it and want it to last longer.' She grins, blushes, tries it again and this time gets it right:

'*That's* my girl!'

Or to the whole orchestra: 'Let's have it a shade brighter, maybe a hair-breadth.'

Wisecracks like: 'We'll dedicate the next song to Ben-Gurion and call it 'There Will Never Be Another Jew.'

Or after a strenuous finish: 'I think I broke my gadarum.'

Or after a fluffed note: 'I got a broken mirror in my throat. Let's have a jigger of brandy; it's cold up here. And some coffee to make it legitimate.'

Or after a passionate lyric: 'That record may get everyone here arrested.'

Or after stumbling three times on the same word: 'Anyone who says I can't sing this song's got a busted reed.'

When one of the musicians played a wrong note and they all had to start again at the beginning, which happened several times, there was no irritation. The only moment that the atmosphere got tense was when the man in the control room said he wanted to re-record an improvised passage on the piano by Bill Miller, put in at Sinatra's suggestion. 'Why?' asked Sinatra.

'I don't like it,' a voice boomed through the speakers.

'Well, I do. Next tune,' answered Sinatra. And that was that.

At 11.45 the last playback came to the final chord. There was a moment of silence which, after the tremendous volume of noise, gave one the strange feeling of being left suspended in mid-air. Then the orchestra started clapping. Sinatra turned away pretending to be unaware of the applause, and occupied himself by busily buttoning his shirt and straighten-ing his tie. He eventually raised an arm and said 'Thank you, fellers,' and walked towards the door. There was a disorderly shout of 'Night, Frank,' then the scores were folded, the instruments packed away, and in no time at all the studio was empty and quiet. Quiet except for the echo of a song which, through the medium of a twelve-inch circle of black acetate, was destined to awaken a million sensibilities the world over . . . to float on the sound-waves of the darkness and the dawn and make countless hands reach out for each other, eyes soften, spines tingle.

19

One man and his voice – with more power than all the uranium in the world . . .

At the door I was told: 'Mr Sinatra is expecting you for dinner. At Romanoff's.'

CHAPTER 4

'My old man thought that anyone who wanted to go into the music business must be a bum. So I picked up and left home for New York. I quit high school to do it, too.'

Thus Sinatra described to me the first step that led him to the unique position he now occupies in the entertainment world. The home he left was in Hoboken, New Jersey. He was born there on December 12, 1915, and christened Francis Albert. His birth was a difficult one, and the left side of his neck still bears savage scars from the doctor's clumsy forceps. 'People have suggested to me I ought to hide those scars,' he said. 'But no. They're there, and that's that. Why bother?'

He was an only child, son of Martin Sinatra, captain of the Hoboken fire department and a locally respected character of Italian ancestry (the name Sinatra is in fact Sicilian and can be traced back through centuries of Sicilian history), and Natalie, a dominating lady with piercing blue eyes and the nickname of Dolly. Mrs Sinatra was a busy woman in local affairs and when Frank was six months old she turned him over to his grandmother to bring up.

It is clear from certain remarks he made to me that his early home life was not happy. Undoubtedly psychiatrists would say that his great need for affection from others and his deep urge to give affection *to* others could spring from an emotional starvation or lack of affection as a child. He talked occasionally of gang escapades with his High School friends and his work after graduation as copy-boy on a local newspaper. But he plainly preferred to recall even his adolescence within a musical framework.

'I used to sing in social clubs and things like that,' he said. 'We had a small group. But it was when I left home for New York that I started seriously. I was seventeen then, and I went around New York singing with little groups in road-houses. The word would get around that there was a kid in the neighbourhood who could sing. Many's the time I worked all night for nothing. Or maybe I'd sing for a sandwich or cigarettes – all night for three packets. But I worked on one basic theory – stay active, get as much practice as you can. I got to know a song-plugger called Hank Sanicola – he's now my personal manager – and he used to give me fifty cents or a dollar some weeks to buy some food. For some reason he always had terrific faith in me.'

For five years it was a long grind of song-plugging, radio shows and club-dates for ten or fifteen dollars a week if he was lucky. But he had one sure source of support and comfort – a pretty dark-haired, brown-eyed girl from Jersey City called Nancy Barbato. On February 4, 1939 Miss Barbato became Mrs Frank Sinatra.

His marriage was not the only major change in routine that took place in that year. One night he was singing at the Rustic Cabin, a small club in New Jersey, and Harry James looked in. James, leader of one of the top big-bands which were enjoying their heyday in the wild hectic days of the late 'Thirties, booked Sinatra as his vocalist there and then. On July 13, 1939 the Sinatra voice, even then markedly individual, was captured on disc for the first time, singing a song called 'From The Bottom Of My Heart.'

The demigod of the band-leaders then was the bespectacled trombonist Tommy Dorsey. Dorsey was more than a top band-leader: he was one of the most talented, colourful and dynamic men ever to make his living by music, a tough-minded personality who would stand no nonsense from anyone. In retrospect it seems inevitable that Sinatra would soon be on the same bandstand as Dorsey, for they are two characters surprisingly similar – ruthless perfectionists, dedicated, controversial, emotionally extreme.

Sure enough, early in 1940 Dorsey's singer Jack Leonard was suddenly called up for military service and Dorsey was at once in pursuit of the skinny young singer whose success with the Harry James band had been reported to him from all sides. Dorsey offered him 125 dollars a week to start right away. There was only one snag – Sinatra had signed a long contract with James.

'When I told Harry about Tommy's offer and said I wanted to leave, he just tore up my contract there and then and wished me luck,' Sinatra told me. 'That night the bus pulled out with the rest of the boys at about half-past midnight. I'd said goodbye to them all, and it was snowing, I remember. There was nobody around and I stood alone with my suitcase in the snow and watched the tail-lights disappear. Then the tears started and I tried to run after the bus. There was such spirit and enthusiasm in that

22

band, I hated leaving it. For maybe the first five months with Dorsey I missed the James band. There was a group of Jack Leonard's fans in the band and they sort of resented a newcomer in his place. So I kept to myself. But then I've always been a loner – all my life. Eventually I shared a room with another loner, Buddy Rich, who was drummer with the band.

'Funny thing is that about three years before, I'd been out dancing with Nancy at a Dorsey band-show and I was cocky, you know, and I pointed up to where Jack Leonard was sitting on the stand and said to her: "See that singer guy? One day I'll be sitting where he's sitting." And sure enough I was.

'I'd sung in front of Dorsey once a few years before I'd joined him, though. Or rather I *hadn't* sung! It was an audition, and I had the words on the paper there in front of me and was just going to sing when the door opened and someone near me said "Hey, that's Tommy Dorsey." He was like a god, you know. We were all in awe of him in the music business. Anyway, I just cut out completely – dead. The words were there in front of me but I could only mouth air. Not a sound came out. It was terrible. When he eventually did send for me and ask me to join his band, the first thing he said was "Yes, I remember that day when you couldn't get out those words." '

To start with, Dorsey made Sinatra a member of the Pied Pipers, the band's vocal group, which featured Jo Stafford. But Dorsey noted the extraordinary effect that his 'skinny kid with big ears' had on the women in the audience and quickly promoted him to soloist. Sinatra recorded his first song with the Dorsey band and the Pied Pipers on February 1, 1940. It was called 'The Sky Fell Down.' Between then and the end of the year he recorded over forty more numbers. The hesitant quality, the tentative unsureness of his voice with the James band quickly gave way to a more positive, surer timbre; gradually the tone, the flair for phrasing and lyric interpretation developed under the tutorship of Tommy and his trombone. There was no actual instruction: it was merely through listening to Dorsey play. For Dorsey had an uncanny way with a melody, tying phrases together in a smooth progression that somehow gave the melodic line a new dimension, and his breath control was amazing. Night after night up on the bandstand, Sinatra noted his leader's example and translated the skill into vocal terms.

23

The professional example of Dorsey was to prove the keystone and the spark-plug of Sinatra's singing style and feel for showmanship, but it was their personal relationship that helped this close musical rapport to flourish.

Sinatra told me: 'Tommy was a very lonely man. He was a strict disciplinarian with the band – we'd get fined if we were late – yet he craved company after the shows and never really got it. The relationship between a leader and the sidemen, you see, was rather like a general and privates. We all *knew* he was lonely, but we couldn't ask him to eat and drink with us because it looked too much like shining teacher's apple.

'Anyway, one night two of us decided to hell with it, we'd ask him out to dinner. He came along and really appreciated it. After that he became almost like a father towards me – and this in spite of the fact that, being by nature a John Rebel, I was always the guy who had to pass on the beefs of the boys in the band.

'One time there was a lot of unrest in the band because of travelling all night in Greyhound buses without any refreshments. So I went to Tommy and said: "Look, the boys are unhappy – hard seats, no air, no refreshments. When they come on the stand, they're *out*. You won't get the best out of them like this." After that there were always twelve cases of Coke on every bus – till Joey Bushkin introduced the band to Pernod and all the Coke suddenly went green.' (Bushkin played piano in the band and wrote the melody of 'Oh, Look at Me Now' – one of Sinatra's 1940 record hits with Dorsey which he re-recorded in 1956 on the LP, 'A Swingin' Affair.' The 1940 version is available on the LP 'Frankie and Tommy.')

'I'd sit up playing cards with Tommy till maybe 5.30 every morning. He couldn't sleep ever: he had less sleep than any man I've ever known. I'd fall off to bed about then, but around 9.30 a.m. a hand would shake me awake and it'd be Tommy saying, "Hey pally – how about some golf?" So I'd totter out on to the golf course. Tommy bought a baby-carriage one day, filled it with ice and beer and hired an extra caddie to wheel it round after us. We'd have a beer after each shot. After nine holes, imagine – we were *loaded*.

'Tommy was great at showcasting soloists and singers. Look who he had in the band then – Bunny Berigan, Ziggy Elman, Joe Bushkin, Buddy

24

Rich – and each had their own group of fans. Tommy's presentation was superb; he'd pace and plan every band show from start to finish. I certainly learnt everything I know about phrasing and breath control from listening to the way he played that trombone.

'It was a wonderful life, they were great days. I can remember every detail of them even now. But it was hard work; nine shows a day of forty-five minutes each, in which I'd sing maybe twelve songs. There were no problems, though. No warm-up even; I had real strong pipes in those days.'

But with as shrewd a sense of timing as he shows in his singing, Sinatra decided at the age of twenty-six that the only road on which he could further progress was the lonesome one of the solo singer. Judging by the warmth with which he reminisced of those days under the wing of the great Tommy, the decision to leave the band must have cut deep. Legend has it that it cost him 60,000 dollars to buy himself away from Dorsey, but he told me this was quite untrue. His decision to leave evidently cut deep into Dorsey, too.

'Tommy was very angry when I said I wanted to leave him and start out on my own. I gave him a whole year's notice, but even so he refused to speak to me for months. He just couldn't understand why anyone should want to leave him. Years after we did a one-night stand together at the Paramount Theatre, once again the best of friends.'

Obviously the shrewd Dorsey, hurt rather than angry, had secretly known all the time that if his skinny singer had postponed that departure by a year, or perhaps even by months, there might not have been a next chapter of the Sinatra story worth telling today, almost twenty years later.

He recorded his last song with Dorsey on July 2, 1942.

I asked what had convinced him that his right course at that moment was to give up the security and prestige of being the Dorsey band-singer for the hazardous road of a soloist, long before he had securely established himself as a bill-topper.

'I'll admit, it was a very big gamble for me leaving Tommy,' he said, 'but I guess I must have had someone watching over me from the day I was born, because I seem to have made the right move every time. You see, I figured that no one had seriously challenged Bing Crosby since 1931. There

25

were two other guys coming up and if they had got the edge on me by even a few months, I might never have made it. When I left Tommy, I had Sanicola with me. Then I hired Axel Stordahl from Tommy to do my arranging. Tommy had paid him 150 dollars a week – I paid him 650, and Tommy got even madder with me then!'

CHAPTER 5

On the morning of New Year's Eve 1942 Frank Sinatra stepped on to the stage of the Paramount Theatre in New York and began what was to turn out to be the most remarkable individual career in the history of show business.

'That day at the Paramount,' he told me, 'I'll never forget it. It was the day things got really started. It was my first real engagement after leaving Tommy, and the Paramount was at that time the Mecca of the entertainment world. Benny Goodman was playing there with his band and there was a Crosby picture showing, so the kids were really being pulled in. Benny had the top band in the world then and it was the first time I'd sung with him. He'd never heard anything about me, and when he introduced me he just said kind of matter of fact: "And now – Frank Sinatra."

'Now Benny lived in a complete world of his own. All he was conscious of was his clarinet and his orchestra – nothing else. A true musician through and through. He never knew anything about new up-and-coming singers or anything like that. Anyway, when he introduced me I stuck my head and one foot out through the organdie curtains – and *froze*! The kids let out the loudest scream you ever heard. I couldn't move a muscle – I was as nervous as a son-of-a-bitch. Benny had never heard the kids holler before and he froze too – with his arms raised on the up-beat. He looked round over one shoulder and said, to no one in particular, "What the —— was that?" That somehow broke the tension and I couldn't stop laughing for the first three numbers. But for that remark of Benny's, I think I'd have been too nervous to sing at all.

'There's one story I must tell you about Benny. As I said, he lives only for his clarinet. One night I remember the boys in the band took a hotel room and gave a dinner for him – you know, invited along a small group to play for dancing and so on. This was was long before Benny was married, so they invited a good-lookin' broad along for him. The boys had never seen him dance before; he'd always been too busy with his clarinet. But eventually he thought he'd better ask this broad to dance, so the two of them got on the floor and, after a few steps, all the boys broke up laughing – Benny's right hand was unconsciously playing the clarinet fingering of the tune up and down this broad's spine . . .'

27

In the weeks after this historic date at the Paramount with Benny Goodman, the acclaim of the bobby-soxers exploded into idolatry. More and more girlish knees buckled, pulses raced, throats grew hoarse. Nurses had to be in attendance at his concerts to tend the swooning fans. Pursuers of his shirt, or tie, or trousers, or even his hair, became more and more violent. 'The Voice' had become a legend. And in less time than it normally takes to become a new name on a publicity handout.

'I had to hire a guy to keep my name out of the papers,' Sinatra continued. 'I was afraid things were getting saturated publicity-wise. Then the factions started. The Bing faction would throw up their arms and say: "Who does this new guy Sinatra think he is?" And my faction would scream: "Crosby's finished – our guy'll go further!" There were fist-fights in bars and things. Bing and I had a real war going. We'd say things about each other to stir things up, but through it all and ever since, in fact, we've been the best of friends.

'I remember my first club date in New York. Still 1942. At the Rio Bomba. I had to open the show walking round the tables and singing. There was no stage or anything and the dance-floor was only as big as a postage-stamp. I was as nervous as hell again, but I sang a few songs and went off. Walter O'Keefe was the star of the show and he was to do his act last. That night he just walked on and said: "Ladies and gentlemen, I *was* your star of the evening. But tonight, in this club, we have all just seen a star born." And he walked out without saying another word. I hadn't really been conscious of any great reception or anything during my act – maybe because I was so nervous – but next day there was a big explosion in all the papers and all round. Dean Martin followed me at that club, I remember, but it closed three days after he started – not his fault as he hadn't had too much experience, he was young, and anyway the club people figured, wrongly, that boy singers were coming in.'

From then on it was one big explosion after another, culminating in the cataclysm in Times Square on Columbus Day, 1944, when 30,000 Sinatra fans practically razed the Paramount Theatre to the ground. 'Psychologists tried to go into the reasons with all sorts of deep theories,' said Sinatra. 'I could have told them why. Perfectly simple; it was the war years and there was a great loneliness, and I was the boy in every corner drug-store, the boy who'd gone off drafted to the war. That's all. It's directly in the troubadour tradition of the old days. Forget all this nonsense about everyone wanting to "mother" me – they more likely wanted to jump on my bones ... Anyway, my gamble in leaving Tommy paid off. The first year on my own I made $650,000; the second, $840,000; the third, $1,400,000.'

That Columbus Day, 1944, was to turn out to be the peak of the first two clear cycles in this turbulent career. During the late 'Forties the cohorts of swooning bobby-soxers dwindled; 'The Voice' became more of 'a voice.' There was the occasional hit like 'Try a Little Tenderness' and 'Time After Time.' But sales of Sinatra records fell away to a fraction of their former volume.

He appeared in a number of films for MGM, none of which established him as a fully-fledged actor, mainly because he was hopelessly miscast as a vapid good-for-nothing, usually in a sailor-suit. His appeal at the cinema box-office slumped.

And then came the break-up of his home. He and Nancy had by now had three children – 'little Nancy' born in 1940, 'young Frank' born in 1944, and Tina born in 1948. But in spite of the children all had not been well for some time in the Sinatra home. On October 30, 1951, Nancy Sinatra obtained a divorce on grounds of cruelty and was awarded custody of the children and one-third of Sinatra's earnings.

Eight days later, Frank Sinatra married Miss Ava Gardner in Philadelphia. But instead of this being the start of a new spell of success, it turned out to be the prelude to still greater disasters for Sinatra. He broke with MGM and made a film for RKO; he made another film for Universal-International and two special CBS Television series – all four projects flopped.

A new strong-willed director of artists and repertoire called Mitch Miller arrived at Columbia Records, and there was friction there over what songs Sinatra should record.

His throat started haemorrhaging; he looked iller and iller. In late 1952 he was out of work, so he flew to Africa to be with his wife while she was on location for the film 'Mogambo.' He was finished, they all said, and on the available evidence they had plenty of justification for this pronouncement. But they had radically misjudged the man they were so glibly committing to oblivion. One day in early December 1952 the wheels started turning on the comeback that has become a classic fable of show business.

The decision that set those wheels in motion looked at first glance like the wild grasp of a drowning man at a floating stick; he offered to play the part of Private Maggio in the scheduled film *From Here To Eternity* for nothing – he had just read the book – and flew back to Hollywood from Africa for a screen test. Two weeks later he returned to his wife in Africa to wait for the result of the screen test. No word came, and he fell back into his old state of depression. Then a cable arrived saying he could have the part for eight thousand dollars. He flew back to Hollywood a few days later to begin work on the film.

Ten months later, on October 27, 1953, MGM formally announced that Sinatra and Miss Gardner had separated and that she would seek a divorce. It was the end of a marriage, but ironically it was also the beginning of a whole new era of success. Something had told him he *had* to play the part of Private Maggio, come hell or high water – the more everyone said he was finished, the more determined he grew to prove them wrong, and he was convinced that Maggio was the character who could help him succeed. His conviction, as instinctive as the conviction that told him to leave Tommy Dorsey in 1942 and stride out on his own, proved gloriously right; he won an Oscar for his sensitive, almost intuitive performance as a tough underdog who somehow wins through against overwhelming odds, and then dies gloriously in a stockade.

After Maggio there came a succession of film parts – in *Guys and Dolls*, *The Man With the Golden Arm*, *Pal Joey*, *High Society*. All were highly successful films and he bloomed quickly to become, if not as unique an actor as he is singer, at least one of the most popular, dynamic and engaging characters on the screen. Sometimes he has not had to act very hard: it has merely been a question of playing himself. But he is the first to admit this. One evening we were discussing his latest film role – as Captain Ben Marco in Richard Condon's thriller *The Manchurian Candidate* – and he said: 'I'm more excited about this part than any other part I've played. I'm saying kinds of things in this script that I've never had to speak on the screen before. Never had to speak at all, for that matter. Long wild speeches. For instance, my first words in the film are a long speech about the different note value systems on the clarinet. Sometimes before I've even ad-libbed for three whole pages of script, just been myself talking as I would do normally. But this is different. Very very different.'

The main reason that his script is so 'different' is because George Axelrod, script-writer and co-producer of the film, has taken some of Condon's narrative and turned it into dialogue. 'I thought it would be terrific to have that marvellous, beat-up Sinatra face giving forth long speeches on Boehm and his clarinet fingering. It's so incongruous,' Axelrod told me.

The Manchurian Candidate occupied, I suspect, a good deal more of Sinatra's interest and energy than most of his recent films. In Palm Springs, when he was meant to be relaxing and preparing for a fortnight's engagement at the Sands Hotel, he would appear at breakfast with the script and delightedly read out long passages; for the rest of the day that script would rarely be out of his reach. Stanley Kramer, the film director, once said: 'If Sinatra really prepared for a role, researched it, he'd be the greatest actor in the world.'

But Sinatra is under no illusions about his less arduous film ventures like *Ocean's Eleven* or *Sergeant's Three*, which are in essence more a good time and a good laugh with his friends than serious attempts to make movie history.

'Of course they're not *great* movies,' he told me. 'No one could claim that. But every movie I've made through my own company has made money, and it's not so easy to say that. *Ocean's Eleven* has grossed millions of dollars, and *Sergeants Three* is already well on the way to doing the same. *Manchurian Candidate* could make a lot of money, too – it could be a *great* movie. The whole business of making movies fascinates me. But the movie business is in a very bad state, and I hate to see it that way. I would love to do anything in my power to rectify the situation. The real necessity is to make good movies that make money – and recently that just has not been done. The way I see it is that Pay-TV has got to come. It could give the film industry a terrific shot in the arm. I can see us making one picture a year, taking six months to do it, doing it really properly. Spend ten or fifteen million dollars on it, lavish as you can make it. But it's got to be a *good* product as well as lavish, of course. Then you show it on colour TV to forty million people at, say, fifty cents a head. Do that three times – pow pow pow – and you're really in business.'

I asked him about his own philosophy as a film actor.

'I always try to remember three things as a movie actor,' he said. First you must know *why* you are in the movie, understand all the reactions of the man you are playing, figure out *why* he's doing what he is doing. Secondly, you must know the script. Some actors are crammers – they cram the night before and just learn their lines for the following day. I don't do it that way. I keep a script in my office, my car, my bedroom, by the telephone, even in the john. And I read the whole script maybe fifty or sixty times before shooting even starts. Then, when it comes to shooting a particular scene, you just have to glance at the script to remember the lines and, more important, you know how that scene fits into the picture as a whole.

'Thirdly, you must learn and listen to the lines of others; it's no good just learning your own. With Spencer Tracy, for instance, you don't get time between his lines and yours to think out your next. There's only one thing about making movies that really irritates me: this business of miming songs to the vision afterwards. With all the advance in microphone equipment you'd think they could have worked out some way of recording at the same time as filming. I never sing a song exactly the same way twice, so when I come to mime I find it very hard. Somehow miming seems to take away a lot of the spontaneity, and I find myself unconsciously thinking of different ways I might sing the song.'

But to return for a moment to 1953. Without doubt his decision to play the part of Private Maggio had been the mainspring of his comeback. But there was another decision he took which turned out to be no less important – he switched his recording contract from Columbia Records to Capitol Records. And it was at Capitol that he first met a pensive, aloof man called Nelson Riddle, who had once played second trombone beside a certain bespectacled trombonist-bandleader.

Out of this meeting came several recorded tracks of voice and orchestra which not only put a very different complexion on sales of Sinatra records compared with their sales over the previous six years: those tracks qualify as examples of contemporary classics, embodying the essential spirit of the time, epitomising the Age of Romantic Cynicism as exactly as Chopin epitomised the Age of Romantic Idealism.

CHAPTER 6

Like Sinatra, Nelson Riddle was born in New Jersey. He was the son of a commercial artist, and his grandparents were Dutch, Irish, Spanish and French: this could account for the individual mixture of colour, humour, efficiency and subtlety in his music.

Like Sinatra, too, he spent his apprenticeship under the dynamic baton of Tommy Dorsey, joining the Dorsey trombone section in 1945. But his front teeth turned bad a year later and he had to give up trombone-playing and concentrate on arranging. He did some arrangements for Bing Crosby and Nat King Cole.

'My first really big break was in the early 'Fifties with the backing for Nat's "Mona Lisa" which was a million-plus seller. This set me well up with Capitol records,' Nelson Riddle told me when he was in London writing the score for the film *Lolita*.

It was at Capitol Records early in 1953 that Riddle first met the man whom he somehow helped transform from a down-and-out ex-crooner into the most magnetic musical communicator and the ace mood-pitcher of the era. What sparked the mutual inspiration?

'There was no particular magic about my first meeting with Frank,' said Riddle over his favourite vodkatini and a chain of tipped cigarettes. The voice was lazy and the eyes a trifle weary, but there was no mistaking the tension that hummed under the casual exterior.

'Frank had just switched labels from Columbia to Capitol and by then I was on Capitol's books as an arranger. Part of the facilities, you might say. Someone said to him, "If you want to do some records, why, we have a man here called Riddle we'd like you to use – if you'd feel comfortable." '

Comfortable – I love this use of the word. Such a magnificently under-stating epithet to describe the most dynamic musical partnership of the decade.

'Frank undoubtedly brought out my best work,' Riddle went on. 'He's stimulating to work with. You have to be right on mettle all the time. The man himself somehow draws everything out of you. He has the same effect on the boys in the band – they know he means business so they pull everything out. Frank and I both have, I think, the same musical aim. We

C

know what we're each *doing* with a song, what we want the song to say. The way we'd work is this – he'd pick out all the songs for an album and then call me over to go through them. He'd have very definite ideas about the general treatment, particularly about the pace of the record and which areas should be soft or loud, happy or sad. He'd sketch out something brief like, "Start with a bass figure, build up second time through and then fade out at the end." That's possibly all he would say. Sometimes he'd follow this up with a phone call at three in the morning with some other extra little idea. But after that he wouldn't hear my arrangement until the recording session. He reads a lyric very carefully, too. Sometimes we'd be working on a project and he'd come up and mention something completely different which we weren't scheduled to do for months. Yes, he's a spur-of-the-moment man, I would think. No – I suspect he *poses* as a spur-of-the-moment man but all the time he's been thinking about it pretty heavily. He'd never record before 8 p.m. and we'd knock off sometime after 11.0. We'd get about four numbers finished at a session with an average of three takes a number. I suppose over our eight years of partnership he threw out an average of about one arrangement a year – not bad going. But there'd never be any anger – after the first time through he'd just say "Let's skip that one" and go straight on to the next. He'd never give out any compliments, either. If he said nothing, I'd know he was pleased. He just isn't *built* to give out compliments and I never expected them. He expects your best – just that.'

How did Sinatra's technique differ from Ella Fitzgerald's?

'I don't think Ella gives as much thought to a lyric as Frank. He is a more canny person – he sizes up a song this way and that. He uses all the tricks of the trade – Ella uses hardly any except those that come automatically to her.

'In working out arrangements for Frank, I suppose I stuck to two main rules. First – find the peak of the song and build the whole arrangement to that peak, pacing it as he paces himself vocally. Second – when he's moving, get the hell out of the way; when he's doing nothing, move in fast and establish something. After all, what arranger in his right mind would try to fight *against* Sinatra's voice?

'Our best albums together were "Songs For Swingin' Lovers," "A Swingin' Affair" and "Only The Lonely." Most of our best numbers were

34

in what I call the tempo of the heartbeat. That's the tempo that strikes people easiest because, without their knowing it, they are moving to that pace all their waking hours. Music to me is sex – it's all tied up somehow, and the rhythm of sex is the heartbeat. I always have some woman in mind for each song I arrange; it could be a reminiscence of some past romantic experience, or just a dream-scene I build in my own imagination. But to me a score for a vocalist to sing a song is like the soundtrack to some film sequence in which this imagined woman figures. In my mind's eye there is some action clearly going on. If the lyrics don't conjure up this picture on their own, I think deeply about the melody and let *it* supply the picture. So my arrangement becomes a complement to this sort of mental film sequence.

'One other thing – I usually try to avoid scoring a song with a climax at the end. Better to build it about two-thirds of the way through and then fade to a surprise ending. More subtle. I don't really like finishing by blowing and beating in top gear. I figure that the other way fits in more with the normal pattern of a person's day, or in a larger sense a person's lifetime.'

From 1954 onwards the Sinatra-Riddle albums whizzed off the presses in their hundreds of thousands. The Voice was back, charged with more power, more panache, more kilowatts of emotional content than ever before.

One night in Hollywood Sinatra talked to me at length on the subject of Nelson Riddle and the intricate anatomy of a long-playing record success.

'Nelson is the greatest arranger in the world,' he said emphatically. 'A very clever musician, and I have the greatest respect for him. He's like a tranquilliser – calm, slightly aloof. Nothing ever ruffles him. There's a great *depth* somehow to the music he creates. And he's got a sort of steno-grapher's brain. If I say to him at a planning meeting, "Make the eighth bar sound like Brahms," he'll make a cryptic little note on the side of some scrappy music sheet and, sure enough, when we come to the session the eighth bar will be Brahms. If I say, "Make like Puccini," Nelson will make exactly the same little note and that eighth bar will be Puccini all right and the roof will lift off. Nelson's quality of aloofness and way of detachment gives him a particular kind of disciplinary air at sessions and the band respect him for it.'

Then with a suddenly sharper gleam in his eye and a more intense tone in his voice: 'You know, I adore making records. I'd rather do that than almost anything else. You can never do anything in life quite on your own, you don't live on your own little island. I suppose you might be able to write a poem or paint a picture entirely on your own, but I doubt it. I don't think you can ever sing a song that way, anyway. Yet, in a sort of a paradoxical way, making a record is as near as you can get to it – although, of course, the arranger and the orchestra play an enormous part. But once you're on that record singing, it's you and you alone. If it's bad and gets criticised, it's you who's to blame – no one else. If it's good, it's also you. With a film it's never like that; there are producers and script-writers and hundreds of men in offices and the thing is taken right out of your hands. With a record, you're IT. But I must admit something – I'd never argue with someone like Nelson on a record date. It's *his* date, he's the leader.'

I asked Sinatra how he planned a long-playing album. 'First,' he said, 'I decide on the mood for the album, perhaps pick a title. Or sometimes it might be that I had the title and then picked the mood to fit it. But it's most important there should be a strong creative idea for the whole package, so to speak. Like "Only The Lonely" or "No One Cares," for instance. Then I get a short list of maybe sixty possible songs, and out of these I pick twelve and record them.

'Next comes the pacing of the album, which is vitally important; I put the titles of the songs on twelve bits of paper and juggle them around like a jigsaw until the album is telling a complete story lyric-wise. For example, the album is in the mood of "No One Cares" – track one. Why does no one care? Because there's "A Cottage For Sale" – track two. (That song's the saddest song ever written, by the way – it depicts the complete break-up of a home.) So on right through to the last track, which might be "One For My Baby And One More For The Road" – the end of the episode. We did in fact end the "Only The Lonely" album with that song, and something happened then which I've never seen before or since at a record session. I'd always sung that song before in clubs with just my pianist Bill Miller backing me, a single spotlight on my face and cigarette, and the rest of the room in complete darkness. At this session the word had somehow got around and there were about sixty or seventy people there, Capitol employees and their friends, people off the street, anyone. We had kept this

36

song to the last track of the session. Dave Cavenaugh was the A and R man and he knew how I sang it in clubs, and he switched out all the lights bar the spot on me. The atmosphere in that studio was exactly like a club. Dave said "Roll 'em," there was one take, and that was that. The only time I've known it happen like that.

'Anyway, to get back to pacing an album – Tommy Dorsey did this with every band-show he played. Paced it, planned every second from start to finish. He never told me this; it just suddenly came to me as I sat up on that stand night after night. But this is what I've tried to do with every album I've ever made.'

During the late 'Fifties Sinatra's Capitol albums also featured the arrangements of Billy May – their 'Come Dance With Me' LP sold over a million copies and won them a Golden Disc – and of Gordon Jenkins. I asked him how the methods of May and Jenkins compared with those of Riddle.

'Recording with Billy May is like having a cold shower or a bucket of cold water thrown in your face,' said Sinatra. 'Nelson will come to the session with all the arrangements carefully and neatly worked out beforehand. But with Billy you sometimes don't get the copies of the next number until you've finished the one before – he'll have been scribbling away in some office in the studio right up till the start of the session.

'Billy works best under pressure. So does Nelson, in fact, but not quite such hot pressure. I myself can't work well except under pressure. If there's too much time available, I don't like it – not enough stimulus. And I'll never record before eight in the evening. The voice is more relaxed then.

'Billy handles the band quite differently from Nelson or Gordon. With Nelson, for instance, if someone plays a wrong note, he'll hold up his hand and stop them and say quietly, "Now in bar sixteen you'll see it says the brass come in half a note after the woodwinds" or something like that. But Billy – there he'll be in his old pants and sweat-shirt, and he'll stop them and he'll say "Hey, cats – this bar sixteen. You gotta go oompa-de-da-da-che-Ow. OK? Let's go then, cats." And the band will go. Billy is driving, Nelson has depth, with Gordon Jenkins it's all so beautifully simple that to me it's like being back in the womb. That "No One Cares" album I did with Gordon is the hell of an album.'

In 1958-9 the intrinsic quality of recorded Sinatra, compared with the

'55-57 vintages, seemed to me to falter and weaken. His Capitol albums were still of far greater artistic and musical merit than those of any other male singer, but some of the old mystique and verve had gone, some vital spark was missing. I expressed this feeling to him.

'Yes, I think it fair comment,' he answered, 'Some of my recent work for Capitol has lacked some of the spark it might have had. It's a long story that I don't particularly want to go into. But you're a writer and I'll bet you can't give your best when you're not happy with the people you're writing for. I wasn't happy during that period with Capitol and I'm afraid some of those later albums show it – definitely they do. I had said I wanted to quit Capitol and even if it meant not recording at all for two years until the contract ran out. But they let me go on condition I cut four more albums for them to wind up the deal. I wanted to form my own record company and run it along my own ideas.' He would not go into further details of the reasons for his unsatisfactory relationship with Capitol. But a statement made not long after he left Capitol by Alan Livingston, Vice-President of Capitol Creative Services, explains a lot. Livingston said that the output of the record industry today, including that of his own company, was 'a wasteland composed of unneeded, unwanted, unworthy discs' making up a 'flood of substandard products that could choke the industry to death.' Livingston blamed the 'Big Business' frame of mind now running the big record companies which paid little attention to creative ideas and planning; 'The ratio of best-selling albums to total output is one in twenty-two. The implication is clear: we are making too many records, worthless records, bad records.'

Against this background it is easy to see why Sinatra wanted to form and run his own company, quite apart from any financial benefit it might bring. For he is now in a position where it is far more important to him to produce high-quality albums than money-spinning singles that make the Hit Parade.

He formed his own record company in January 1961 and christened it Reprise – 'to play and play again.' Predictably, by July there was a feud with Capitol over his second Reprise album which he wanted to call 'Swing Along With Me.' The feud burst into the open with full-page advertisements in two Hollywood trade papers and copy reading: 'Now – A newer, happier, *emancipated* Sinatra ... untrammelled, unfettered, unconfined . . . On Reprise.' More clues as to what went on behind the scenes at Capitol!

Capitol filed an 'unfair competition' suit against Sinatra and everyone connected with the release of the album, charging that the record 'closely resembles in concept, type of repertoire, style, accompaniment and title' an album already recorded by Sinatra and released by Capitol under the title of 'Come Swing With Me.' The suit demanded that Sinatra be permanently restrained from further distribution of the Reprise album. Eventually Reprise were ordered to change the title and cover before releasing any more copies, and the album became 'Sinatra Swings.'

Apart from this minor setback, the Reprise label is booming. By the end of its first year its catalogue of artists included, as well as Sinatra, Dean Martin, Sammy Davis Jr, The Hi-Los, Mort Sahl, Jimmy Witherspoon, Ben Webster, Calvin Jackson, Joe E. Lewis and daughter Nancy Sinatra, now married to another singer Tommy Sands. Several other big record names are expected to switch to Reprise as soon as their present contracts with other companies expire.

The Reprise method of operation is unique for a record company – all artists retain ownership of their master recordings, and the company simply presses, packages, distributes and advertises the discs; the artists themselves organise the recording sessions; they are free to work for any other label if they wish; and, most important, all artists own stock in the company.

The Sinatra albums already released on Reprise reveal a new exuberance, a new punch in his voice. He has used some new talent for his orchestrations; on 'Ring-A-Ding-Ding,' the first Reprise album he cut, the arrangements and conducting were by Johnny Mandel, a young ex-Basie trombonist mainly known for his composition of the jazz-flavoured score for the film *I Want To Live;* 'Sinatra and Strings' features the arrangements of Don Costa; Neal Hefti, ex-Basie arranger and new chief artists – and – repertoire man with Reprise, has provided the orchestrations for another album; and on 'I Remember Tommy,' a tribute to Tommy Dorsey, Sinatra engaged Sy Oliver who used to play in the trumpet section and arrange for Dorsey in the late 'Thirties and early 'Forties. This Dorsey album is probably his most whole-hearted and successful album for Reprise; the advertisements call it with justification 'a collector's item before it was recorded' and the trade advance order in the States was 200,000.

'This order was something of a record figure in my experience,' said Sinatra. 'It makes me laugh when I think back to when we started Reprise. The buyers all thought it was a joke, you know – the boys getting together for a laugh. They treated us pretty carefully at first, but now we're well under way.

'But this Dorsey album – I really think it has some of the best work I've ever done. I feel sentimental over Dorsey even after twenty years. I tried to sing the songs as he used to play them on his trombone. But we didn't put a trombone solo on the record because nobody has ever been able to re-create Tommy's particular sound. Instead we feature a trombone quartet. Sy Oliver's orchestrations are brilliant, full-blooded things. They're all Tommy's special songs, too: I haven't sung songs like these for years. They were a real lesson in elocution and diction: if I breathed in some of those long lyric lines I'd have wrecked the whole thing. The extraordinary thing is I have never heard anyone else sing Tommy's theme song "I'm Getting Sentimental Over You," maybe because it's such a hell of a difficult song to sing. One day I think I'm going to do another album called "I Still Remember Tommy"!'

I asked him if he had any special new album ideas up his sleeve, any pipe-dreams he might be able to put into practice now he had his own company.

'Well, musically speaking,' he said, 'do you know what I really am? A frustrated conductor. I've been saying to Nelson for two years: "Give up all this popular stuff. Give it up for six months and I'll commission you to write a complete concerto for the Spanish guitar so I can conduct it. Feature it in new settings, give it new sounds." Nelson is always very interested – he'd do it better than anyone. But so far we've both been too busy to do anything more about it.'

It looks as if, for the immediate future anyway, he will continue to be 'too busy' to fulfil his long-held musical pipedream. For the last year or so, imperceptibly but quite steadily, Sinatra the troubadour has been giving way to Sinatra the tycoon. The musician is becoming the business magnate. With him, there are no vain histrionics at the prospect of only a few more years in top vocal condition: he faces the inevitable waning of his singing power with unruffled, objective realism.

40

3 a.m., The Sands Hotel, Las Vegas. In casual get-up, Sinatra rehearses for his
opening performance that night

A signal to the orchestra to play pianissimo.   The centre spread is a view of the whole stage.

Now the rehearsal is over and he is facing his first audience of the engagement. The lights go down low, the cigarette smoke curls and he sings 'It was Just One of Those Things . . .'

More and more of his talent and interest is being channelled into the business rather than the entertainment side of the entertainment business. Apart from owning Reprise Records, with its 4-million dollar sales in the first year of its existence, he owns Essex Productions, a film production company which produces films for other stars and producers as well as Sinatra. He runs four music publishing companies. He is co-partner with Danny Kaye in a string of radio stations in the Pacific North-West. He has bought and restyled a hotel-casino near Reno, Nevada. He is Vice-President and a major stockholder in the Sands Hotel, Las Vegas. He makes sporadic investments in real estate, banks and loan societies. His various projects are said to gross somewhere around twenty million dollars a year.

The control-room for this complex network is Suite 512 of the City National Bank Building, a new all-glass tower that stands on the ridge of Sunset Boulevard and dominates many square miles of sprawling Los Angeles. There is no plaque on the door of Suite 512, no imposing lettering – just a pair of antique brass door-knockers. His work-room is more like a modern country-mansion sitting-room than an office. Two walls are almost entirely taken up by windows with white muslin curtains. Couches, small stools, a grand piano, a large round table with chairs, a bowl of fresh red apples, boiled sweets in jars, magazines, plants in bowls, antique ornaments and *objets d'art*. On the piano stands a framed colour portrait of President Kennedy bearing the handwritten inscription: 'For Frank. With the warm regards and best wishes of his friend.' The books in the shelves are reference books like Fowler's *Modern English Usage*, or art books like Picasso's *Picasso*. Telephones are in every corner of the room.

The only indication that the room is an office is the United Press International teletype machine ticking out its news flashes in one corner.

There is no desk: instead, Sinatra uses a small elegant table. Behind it, set into the wall, is a mirror-lined bar stocked with rows of glasses and bottles. One door leads into a small but beautifully finished bathroom and shower. The other door leads into the office of his personal secretary and confidante Gloria Lovell.

Every month in Suite 512 there is a brain-storming session attended by Sinatra and his lieutenants. It starts sharp at 10.30 a.m. and can last late into the evening without a break. Lunch is sent up from Romanoff's and the discussions continue over the buffet. The aim is for every man in the Sinatra empire to know about and perhaps give his views on the problems of each other man. Sinatra himself is a master of delegation with complete faith in his colleagues and advisers. He lays down the basic policy and philosophy of his organisation and leaves his employees to interpret his will in matters of detail.

The metamorphosis from king entertainer to business magnate is no easy one: the qualities that make up a successful performer are at first glance far divorced from those required by a successful entrepreneur. The extraordinary feature of the Sinatra story is not merely the ease with which he is making this metamorphosis: he even admits that he is getting as much pleasure from moving around pieces on his business chess-board as he gets from being the principal piece himself.

'I'm lucky because I have good people working for me,' he told me. 'I wouldn't trust my own judgment without advice from people who've worked among financial and business problems all their lives. Hire the right people – that's the trick. Eventually I want to be less and less the public entertainer and more and more in the background. As a singer I'll only have a few more years to go – as an actor maybe a few more than that but not many. I've been performing out front for nearly thirty years now and frankly I'm getting a bit tired. Now I want to do more and more behind the scenes, using my head. Finance fascinates me.'

CHAPTER 7

On November 4, 1961 I flew to Las Vegas in Sinatra's private aeroplane. It is a twin-engined Martin called 'Eldago' and can take fifteen passengers. The interior decoration was conceived by Sinatra himself, and shows the extraordinarily detailed way in which his mind works: everything specially fitted, right down to tiny details like ash-trays and the wash-basin fittings. There is a bar, an electric piano, a tape machine, a banquette seat, and an instrument panel in the shape of a clock; there is a conference room which can double as a card-room, and a rest-room with telephone and couch. The décor is in functional good taste and the lighting is obviously designed by someone with stage experience.

Sinatra was concerned at the press comment about the plane. 'There must be thousands of guys with private planes in the country,' he said resignedly, 'but as soon as I go and get one there's all hell let loose. It's a sound business proposition, apart from anything else. When we're not using it, we'll hire it out to selected business corporations for taking around their top executives.'

He was due to start a fortnight's engagement at The Sands Hotel the next evening: that night was Sammy Davis' last night. Half-way through Davis' act, Sinatra walked unannounced on to the stage, and there followed half an hour's worth of hilarious, spontaneous comedy and singing, ending in Davis being carried bodily off-stage for allowing his act to go on too long and 'stopping the customers gambling.'

Davis' act finished at about 1.45 a.m. At 2.30 a.m. Sinatra was due to start rehearsing. I sat among the empty tables and watched. As the orchestra filed in and arranged their chairs among the crop of microphones, platoons of waiters scurried among the tables, clearing them, brushing the floor underneath, changing tablecloths, and doing all the hundred-and-one little chores that waiters have to do in the wake of several hundred diners and in preparation for several hundred more the next day. Tables were being shifted, or stacked on top of each other; there were men on step-ladders painting a new back-drop; electricians were climbing round on ledges and clambering all over the stage, putting new microphones on stands among the orchestra, hanging new microphones down from the ceiling, shouting at each other like a pack of raucous monkeys; the orchestra was tuning up; the conductor Tony Morelli was shouting directions at the stage manager.

Into the midst of this bedlam, just before 2.30 a.m., walked Sinatra. He wore a white soft hat, an orange button-up cardigan, casual trousers and slippers embroidered with his initials. He did a quick tap-dance, asked Al Viola the guitarist if his stool was high enough, asked Johnny Markham the drummer if the sound of the vibes would get through, helped a lady violinist to move her chair round to face the conductor, and said: 'For Chrissakes, there are more microphones here than at the Communist Congress.'

A selection of some twenty songs was sung, discussed, put in order, paced, played and replayed till the orchestra was note-perfect and he himself word-perfect – he had some difficulty remembering the lyrics of his more recent songs, like 'Granada,' and when the words failed him he made up a crazy replacement of his own, much to the amusement of the orchestra. But I could see that it did not really amuse him, that he secretly felt embarrassed at what in fact was a failure on his part.

The rehearsal ended just before 4 a.m. Sinatra went straight to bed. He was clearly nervous, as uncertain of himself as if it was his first public engagement. He had not been smoking or drinking at all for over a week so that his throat and lungs would be in perfect shape; for hours at a stretch he had been playing over his latest recordings, reminding himself of the orchestrations and the lyrics, or swimming under water to improve his breath-control. He had been going early to bed, too, which is a rare practice for him.

He rose late the next afternoon, had a steam-bath and a massage, sent some crisp orders to conductor Morelli about some last-minute changes in order and pacing of songs which he had worked out during the night, and put on his dinner-jacket. His usual flow of alert conversation was completely dammed; he looked pensive, anticipatory, preoccupied, sometimes even angry. To think that, after the countless public performances he had given in the last twenty years, this man still had first-night nerves and was as concerned about the quality of his offering as a young actor whose whole future hung on his performance that night!

He need not have worried, but I can understand why he did. If he had *not* worried, he would not be the unique artist he is today. As the compère announced him from the stage, a roving spotlight picked him up walking through the packed tables. The band blared out 'Ring-A-Ding-Ding' but the deafening applause drowned the music. A cool look at the audience, a snap of the finger, a toss of the head, and he was away, into 'The Lady Is A Tramp.' Nobody in the audience moved – they just sat, staring with absorbed attention, at the man with the microphone whose voice rasped, flowed, blared, tip-toed, hovered, and swooped through a score of songs – from the poignant torch song, with just a piano and a single spotlight on his face and cigarette, to the exultant show-stoppers with full forty-piece orchestra and full floodlights. His singing electrified that audience . . . The only criticism of his total act was that he spent too much time being the comedian and not enough time singing; all the tension fades during his monologues, the atmosphere sags, and the audience starts coughing and shuffling their feet. Later I asked Bill Miller, his pianist for the last fourteen years, why Sinatra included so much talk in his act. Miller answered: 'Well, it could be to help his voice not to get too tired, which it might do if he sang non-stop. But I think it's mainly because he started as a singer, took up acting, and conquered the acting field. He's never content to stop, so now he wants to do the same thing in the comedian field. I'd much prefer myself for him to cut out a lot of the jokes. I've told him so, but he won't listen.'

Sinatra's public appearances at Las Vegas are not confined to the stage of the Sands Hotel. Whenever he appears outside the Presidential Suite, in the sitting-room of which there is a constant flow of visitors, he is, so to speak, on show. As Billy Wilder once said, 'When Frank is in Las Vegas, there is a certain electricity permeating the air. It's like Mack The Knife is in town and the action is starting.' Extra security guards are on duty in the gambling rooms to control the extra crowds milling round either to see the show or in the hope of seeing Sinatra gambling. It is easy to see where he is in the long, low room full of roulette tables, one-armed bandits, crap tables and chemmy tables, by the huddled crowd craning their heads over the massive shoulders of the guards to watch him try his luck. He prefers playing baccarat, staking anything from 500 to 2,000 dollars a hand. Sometimes he takes over a blackjack table and deals himself – to five excited women who, by virtue of some skilful sleight-of-hand on the part of the dealer, usually end the evening with considerably more money than they started with. But Sinatra is a vice-president of the Sands, and any money that he pays out while acting as dealer is debited to his own account. That is why he only deals to women, and usually women he knows.

During his fortnight's engagement he slips away to bed soon after his second show has finished somewhere around 1.45 a.m. But when he is simply visiting the Sands, perhaps to attend the opening night of a close friend such as Dean Martin, he usually sits in the cocktail lounge in a large group, drinking and talking and occasionally sallying forth to gamble, until the sun's rays are streaming through the glass doors.

One of the essential but little-known qualities of the man was revealed one night in Las Vegas. It happened to be the birthday of a member of his party. Unbeknown to everybody, he planned a celebration dinner, organised the menu, and personally – not through an aide or a secretary – bought the presents. They were no ordinary presents and must have cost several hundred dollars.

Later in the evening a close friend of Sinatra explained it thus: 'One of the few big kicks he gets out of life is from giving people things that they could never hope to get themselves. Even when he was down and out in the early 'Fifties these fantastic presents would go on arriving. He even gave someone a Cadillac. But the funny thing is – he hates being given anything himself.'

Giving presents to less wealthy friends is one outlet for his generosity. Another is his work for charity, especially charities for children, in which he is taking more and more interest. One night in Las Vegas he told me: 'Last year I took Nelson and forty musicians to Mexico. What a wild time we had! This was nothing to do with the Government – this was out of my own pocket, to help some rehabilitated children down there. Hospitals, things like that. We planned to do one show, ended up by doing five. This was really an experience for us all. They gave me a medal, and a boy came up on the stage to pin it on me. He had no hands, only metal claws, and he took it out of the box, unclasped it and pinned it on to my coat. Five thousand people were sitting in that place and you could have heard a pin drop. I can tell you – there was a big lump in my throat ... Then when we left there were maybe five hundred people at the airport, at nine in the morning. They all sang "La Golondrina" – that's their farewell

46

song – with guitars. The President of Mexico invited me to lunch and told me he wished the United States would send twenty-one performers round all the other states of Latin-America; it would do so much good. And he's right, you know. I'm sure trips like that do a tremendous lot for good-will between countries and for international relations generally. I'd like to do more of them. But I'm getting older, and less ambitious. And a bit lazy, too, I suppose . . .'

But there was nothing lazy about the task that Sinatra set himself during April, May and June 1962.

CHAPTER 8

On April 15, 1962 Frank Sinatra, describing himself as 'an over-privileged adult,' set out from his home in Coldwater Canyon to conquer the world – on behalf of the world's underprivileged children.

His aim was clear-cut – to raise a million dollars for children's charities. His route – from Los Angeles to Los Angeles via Tokyo, Hong Kong, Tel Aviv, Athens, Rome, Milan, Paris, Monte Carlo, London and New York. His party – Bill Miller and a sextet featuring two veterans of many a Sinatra recording session: Al Viola on guitar and Irv Cottler on drums; his personal photographer, Ted Allan, and a ciné team (the plan being to make a 60-minute film of the tour's highlights and sell it to American TV for the benefit of American children's charities); his manager Henry Giné; his valet George Jacobs; his two personal pilots, who flew his plane 'Eldago' straight to Europe to meet him there; a press relations aide, to move in advance of the main group; and last, but probably most important to him of all, his close friends Michael and Gloria Romanoff.

His method – to foot the whole bill for the tour himself, so that every ticket sold would be clear profit for the charities.

First stop Tokyo, and the wild excitement that fired the Japanese capital was a forerunner of the greeting awaiting him in every port of call. They rushed to hear him in their thousands; 8,000 seats for one show were sold in less than thirty minutes. One afternoon he gave an open-air concert for children and charged an optional entrance fee – anything they liked to pay, but they had to pay something. Hundreds of smiling Japanese children dropped their one-yen pieces into the boxes and sat round him wide-eyed, some even climbing the high trees round the auditorium to perch among the branches like silent monkeys. Later he was presented with the Key of the City and an orphanage was named after him.

In Hong Kong a host of handicapped children sang and waved and weaved garlands of flowers for him.

In Israel he sang outside Tel Aviv in a huge sports stadium packed with 80,000 people, visited Jerusalem and Nazareth where they named a youth centre after him, was presented with a silver-embossed Bible and had a long talk with Prime Minister Ben-Gurion.

After a few days of rest and recharging his vocal batteries aboard a yacht in the eastern Mediterranean, the Sinatra magic thrilled thousands first in Athens, then in Rome, where he was mobbed so wildly after one concert that he had to lock himself inside his car and drive out through a solid mass of fans. At least fifty of them were clinging to his car so tightly that it was impossible to see out of any window except through a tiny area of windscreen!

Milan, Paris, London – it was the same story everywhere, the same frenzy and wild acclaim wherever he went. In the early morning of June 2, he made his début on the stage of the Royal Festival Hall in front of Princess Margaret and a star-studded audience which had bought its tickets several months previously, on the day the concert was first announced.

'In a way the whole tour has been leading up to this night,' he told me the afternoon before. 'This is the climax to the whole tour. I want London to remember this night. I'm going to give them the full treatment, throw everything at them.'

He did. He sang for over an hour and a half, from 1 a.m. till 2.40 a.m. I have a tape of that concert, and from the first slightly brittle notes of 'Goody Goody' right through to the last, by then slightly tired, notes of 'Come Fly With Me' he had that audience in the palm of his hand – you can tell this by the tone and the alertness of the applause and by the way the reception quickly relaxes him. From songs two and three ('Imagination' and 'At Long Last Love') onwards he gives what could be the finest hour's worth of concert singing of his career. During the last few songs the accumulated strain of six hard weeks' singing is beginning to show through, but he never loses his touch or his pace, never becomes indifferent.

'What a night for me that was,' he said to me afterwards. 'It's a marvellous place to sing in. Acoustically it must be perfect. You can hear your voice coming back at you and when it sounds good it helps you on further. If I never sing another note, I'll always remember that night as something special.'

After three more concerts in London cinemas and visits to the children's homes belonging to the chosen charities, Sinatra flew to Monte Carlo to sing for Princess Grace's Red Cross Ball in the famous Sporting Club. The last concert of the tour – and he was singing under the stars. To hell with the tea and the honey in the cup on stage that night; it was a good old-fashioned glass with some good old-fashioned whisky in it. And the potency of his act increased accordingly.

Then back to London for five days, for the only non-charity singing task of the tour – cutting a long-playing album. This was no routine album, however. This was the first in a new series in which he planned to record the twelve best songs of one particular country using orchestrations, musicians and recording facilities *in* that country; for the sleeve he planned, if possible, to use a definitive painting of that country by one of its own great artists. For this album Sinatra wanted a picture by Sir Winston Churchill; Sir Winston's permission was sought but, alas, not granted.

The album's title – 'Great Songs From Great Britain.' The arranger – Robert Farnon. For a long time Nelson Riddle had admired the work of Bob Farnon, a Canadian arranger-composer now living in the Channel Islands, and it was mainly on Riddle's recommendation that Sinatra chose Farnon. The songs – 'If I Had You,' 'The Very Thought Of You,' 'A Garden In The Rain,' 'I'll Follow My Secret Heart,' 'London By Night,' 'The Gipsy,' 'A Nightingale Sang In Berkeley Square,' 'We'll Meet Again,' 'Now Is The Hour,' 'Roses of Picardy' and 'We'll Gather Lilacs.' The orchestra – a 38-piece group featuring most of Britain's top session musicians and a few well-known jazz artists.

The session took place from 8–11 p.m. on June 12–14 in London. Farnon's arrangements went down well. Riddle, who was in London at the time on a separate tour of his own, came to the first of the three sessions to lend his exceptional experience of Sinatra record dates if it should be needed. But from the beginning the Sinatra-Farnon partnership was 'a natural,' both personally and musically.

'My, he's certainly some writer,' Sinatra said to me about Farnon, shaking his head in awe. My own taste is for something richer and more brassy behind a nostalgic Sinatra than Farnon's arrangements – he uses brass in only two tracks – but the album's overall mood is relaxed, relaxing and pleasant – and surprisingly British in character, which was, after all, the intrinsic aim of the series.

But the session was not without its difficult moments. Normally, when Sinatra is scheduled to cut an album, he more or less goes into purdah for a week or so beforehand. He cuts down radically on his smoking and

50

drinking, goes to bed unusually early, practises scales, learns lyrics, and has several meetings with Bill Miller and the arranger to go over strategic details – the tactical ones are left till the session. In the case of 'Great Songs From Great Britain' this routine was impossible. And Sinatra clearly found the precise business of recording a considerable strain after six weeks of hard live singing and a good many late nights in between. After a few fluffs, 'holes in my reed' and 'clams in my throat,' Sinatra summed matters up on the second night by saying resignedly: 'My old man warned me about nights like these. But then he was a drinking man and he wouldn't know the difference.' Or again, with a puzzled look at the ceiling: 'Don't just sit there watching me. *Do* something.'

There was one final task ahead of Sinatra during his last two days in London – to 'sneak-preview' the first edited version of *The Manchurian Candidate* in a London cinema to test audience reaction.

'Apart from a few little things here and there, confusion at the beginning, things like that, we're very pleased,' he told me. 'But we'll easily edit those things out and then we should be in business.' Judging from the audience reaction, that was a distinct understatement.

On June 17 Sinatra and his party returned to the United States. Around the world in just under eighty days. What had the tour achieved?

It certainly caused the world's press to look at Sinatra with more focused eyeballs, and thus brought a lot of the world's readers nearer to the real Sinatra. Even *Time* magazine, his printed Enemy Number One over the years, was noticeably knocked off balance by the whole business. Under the sarcastic heading of 'Innocent Abroad,' it first tried in a heavy-handed way to rake up the old muck: 'His new friends in Israel and Japan called him "a nice gentle guest" and "a tough dandy." Back home, his old friends were only left to wonder: Who is this prince of charity, this prophet of peace, this generous, sober, chaste diplomat, this new Frank Sinatra?' That was the last thing his real friends were wondering. But then, after implying that the tour was primarily a stunt to 'camouflage his unappealing Rat Pack image' and 'his receding hairline,' and to impress President Kennedy, *Time* continued: 'His friends insist that there is no new Sinatra, that the new innocent abroad is only the old Sinatra with the old resentments stripped away.' And finally, grudgingly, through a disdainfully curling lip: 'And overseas the tour's inspiration matters less than the good it does.'

The tour certainly gave Sinatra a whole new purpose in life. A new dignity, too. In his own words: 'I found out a lot of things I didn't know before. It was a revelation. I hope to do the same thing every year or eighteen months. It's a most gratifying experience.'

What else? The tour cost him personally, excluding the lost income from not working for two months, something over half a million dollars.

Oh – one final thing. The tour *exceeded* his aim. It raised *more* than a million dollars for the world's underprivileged children.

CHAPTER 9

What makes this vivid and uncompromising character tick? What *is* the secret ingredient of his unique appeal to the world, of his Orpheus-like ability to charm, to fascinate, to intrigue, to communicate a deeply meaningful message to millions?

Before attempting to answer this, let me describe the personality and way of life of the man as it appeared after spending almost two months in his company. Perhaps then the question will partly answer itself.

His presence is unusually powerful; when he is in a room, he somehow manages to dominate it, whatever he is doing. He emits a curious sort of electricity, a peculiar galvanism probably generated by the kinetic war that must continually rage between the paradoxes of his inner self.

A flamboyant extrovert, yet huntedly introspective; to watch him in a group of friends, or to listen to much of the conversation, one would imagine him to be the most self-confident man in the world. But in a group of people whom he does not know so well, he keeps to the outer fringe, or perhaps sits in a corner, with the clear air of someone who is not entirely sure of himself. And always he has need for reassurance from people, that his act went well, or that his recording was up to standard, or that his gift was the right one – although he does his best to hide the fact that he *does* need this reassurance and would never lay himself so open that he had to ask for it outright.

Brash, yet hypersensitive; much of his conversation suggests that he has the hide of an elephant, that a slight or an insult would run off him like water off a duck's back, that he couldn't care less what people said or thought of him. But it does not take long to realise that this is a defence, an outer layer to protect the man underneath who minds very much indeed what people think of him.

Ruthless, yet sentimental; I suspect that to those who abuse his trust or try to play dirty with him he would be a terrifying enemy who would stop at nothing to bring them down. Equally, to those who do him a favour or who work for him there is nothing he will not do in return, no limit to the extent he will back them up. And in a way, he lays himself open to hurt by this blind loyalty.

53

'More than anything I expect and hope for from other people is kindness,' he told me once, 'and if I don't get it, it really upsets me. But then, I suppose, it always has.'

An imperious and gregarious leader, yet a lonely man who craves company round him, who cannot bear to be left on his own, greedy for genuine affection. For, as fame and public adulation have snowballed, so in direct proportion has the need for that brand of friendship which the many attendant parasites loudly profess to offer, but which only the handful of real, understanding friends can actually give.

A defier of convention who seemingly delights in flaunting the rules and customs of accepted social behaviour – yet a staunch upholder of those details that have come to be labelled old-fashioned.

For instance, for all his much-publicised unpredictability, he has remained a family-man first and foremost; nothing comes before his first wife's home and their children. He telephones them sometimes several times a day, refuses to let them make any move without his advice and consent. Much of his conversation is on the subject of his children, whom he obviously adores. He invited his ex-wife Nancy to his opening night in Las Vegas and in his speech after his first song he picked out all the celebrities in the audience and thanked them for coming. At the end he said: 'And finally, the mother of my children, Mrs Nancy Sinatra . . .'. The applause for her was far louder than for any of the famous names he had previously mentioned. But she deserved every clap, this loyal and sensible lady who has refused to capitalise on her difficult but exploitable position in spite of all the temptations to do so, and who instead has concentrated on preserving a home for her three children.

Yet, for all his strong instincts as a father and family man, he is too mercurial a being ever to be able to fit into the confines of a conventional home. But then, as I said, he is built of paradoxes.

Experienced in the ways of the world, and in the reactions of the men and women who live in it – yet sometimes surprisingly naïve about the inevitable illogicalities and injustices of life.

Effervescent, yet profound – he likes to act the devil-may-care swashbuckler who snaps his finger at all the deeper issues of life, but in rare moments of relaxation the mask slips off to show that all the time he has been giving quite serious thought to problems of religion, nuclear war or international politics.

Furiously prejudiced about certain people and certain beliefs, yet quite unbelievably generous and unquestioning where his own trust is invested.

In an age of stereotype and conformism, he is an anachronism – yet his appeal is as contemporary as the Hully-Gully.

A symptom of this conflict between the paradoxes of his nature is his restlessness. He gets easily bored, quickly claustrophobic; for instance, he dislikes riding in lifts, being squashed by a crowd, or being touched by a stranger.

He does not like sitting still in one place for very long. Nor does his mind stay on the same subject for more than the time it takes him to come to a conclusion on it – which is not long either. His conversation flits from fallout shelters to baseball to the problems of bringing up teenage children to the ill-fitting of one of his evening shoes to anti-trusts to Richard Nixon to the vintage of the wine for dinner to the position of Jupiter at 11 o'clock that night.

But this apparent restlessness can be misleading. Sometimes he appears not to be listening to a particular conversation, yet minutes or perhaps days later he will quote it word for word. He has a tape-recorder memory for dialogue; he injects the maximum drama into his narratives and anecdotes, mainly by the use of verbal camera-angles that exaggerate effect but not substance.

When he talks, the phrasing is more staccato and the tone more resonant than I expected. His sentences are pithy, terse, definite, interlaced with mimicry – Bogart, Cagney, Jackie Gleason, Louella Parsons – and with snatches of his songs twisted in wholesome ribaldry: 'Don't cry, Joe – it will grow, it will grow,' or 'Granaaaaaada, what makes your big head so hard . . .?' or 'Entratter, stay away from my door' (Jack Entratter is boss of the Sands Hotel, Las Vegas, and watches Sinatra's appearances with an eagle eye).

When he laughs, which is often, the tanned skin creases over the pronounced cheekbones and the teeth glare white, and the sides of his mouth turn down as he leans forward smacking his knees. He uses his hands and arms to emphasise a point. Between gestures he fiddles with the gold signet ring on his left little finger, or with the pipe that he smokes when he is at home.

His hands are neat, well-cared for. But then the whole appearance is always scrupulously neat and well-cared for. The clothes-sense is colourful, the wardrobe exotic and apparently inexhaustible, the cut immaculate.

As a host, his manners are impeccable, and he seems to enjoy entertaining as his house is always full. He takes particular interest in arranging the menus, although he himself eats very little – yet what he does eat and drink is ordered and consumed with fastidious discrimination. More often than not, it is a Chinese or Italian dish followed by a piece of chocolate cake, washed down with a light white wine.

He has two houses on the West Coast. He spends his weekdays in Coldwater Canyon, Beverly Hills, where he had a bungalow built on a hilltop overlooking the whole of Hollywood on one side and the San Fernando Valley on the other. At the entrance to the drive, there is an electrically controlled gate, and a notice-board that greets uninvited visitors thus: 'You'd better have a damn good reason for ringing this bell.' A policeman and a St Bernard called Charlie are on permanent duty by the front door. The house itself was built, he says, round a hi-fi installation; special gravel was packed into the main wall containing two vast loudspeakers just under the ceiling; the control panel, built flush into the far wall of the sitting-room, looks – with its switches, dials and lights – as intricate as the dashboard of a jet airliner. Above the panel a small plaque reads: 'Designed by Frank Sinatra.'

The décor is in what he calls 'Italian Japanese style,' but it was designed for him by a decorator and so lacks the characteristic touch of the man himself.

Outside the french windows, steps cut into the rock lead down past an illuminated kidney-shaped swimming pool to a private cinema with a log fire and wall-to-wall murals that slide back at the touch of a switch to reveal a cinemascopic screen and projection window. Evenings chez Sinatra usually include one, if not two, private showings of still unreleased films.

For the weekends he slips away to his desert hide-away in Palm Springs. It is here that the décor more accurately echoes his real self. And it is significant that he is far more relaxed there. Armchairs and sofas are arranged round a large grey stone fireplace in which burns a real, English manor-type log fire. A card table and an upright piano stand in one corner;

56

The profile that a famous American sculptor once likened to that of Abraham Lincoln

Before a wild finale, Sinatra sings a selection of old 'saloon songs,' as he calls them – sings them so poignantly that many eyes in the audience show traces of tears

At his Palm Springs swimming-pool, relaxing after the exhausting fortnight at Las Vegas. Here he tries out a model nuclear submarine

Even at the pool, the telephone is at hand. The call is probably fixing some million dollar deal

Nelson Riddle, arranger of some of Sinatra's greatest song-hits, at work at the piano. 'Frank certainly brought out my best work', says Riddle

one wall is solid glass leading out to the sun terrace, swimming pool and tennis court; in the other corner stands a remote control television cum tape recorder cum record player cum bookcase, all in one unit.

There are books everywhere – in shelves, on ledges, on tables: Simenon, Keats, Kennedy, Ustinov, Shelley, Henry Miller, dictionaries of quotations, books on science, politics, war and astronomy. Magazines, too, and as many daily papers as he can get hold of. He reads insatiably; he does not need much sleep and so reads until dawn, sometimes later. Hence his preference for work in the afternoon and early evening and his refusal to record until after 8 p.m.

He is fascinated by mechanical gadgets. A scale model of the new Thunderbird coupé sits on the piano. The construction kit for a model nuclear submarine, battery-powered, which dives and surfaces and fires a plastic missile, lies on the card table. He is always dreaming up new plans for his own radio transmitter, or a heliport on his front lawn – this, he says, would cut his car-commuting time by over half. Now, as he sits in a traffic jam, he whiles away the minutes of unwelcome enforced inactivity by calling a disc jockey friend on his car telephone and reporting the traffic flow, who then in turn can broadcast hold-ups to other car commuters in the area.

His taste in paintings reflects himself – sharp lines, vivid colours, strong contrasts. But he hates tilted frames . . .

The background music, usually on tape: Ray Charles, Oscar Peterson, Count Basie, Harry James, Les Brown, Benny Goodman, Victor Young, Vaughan Williams. He doesn't talk during Vaughan Williams, except about Vaughan Williams. Last thing at night, way into the wee small hours, he will perhaps put on one of his own slower albums like 'No One Cares' or 'Only the Lonely,' and point out to his listening guests the special little tricks of orchestration that catch his fancy.

His way of life is outwardly extravagant, but the extravagance seems as much to give pleasure to others as to himself. And, after all, with a gross earning of several million dollars a year, a man is entitled to be extravagant. He is not careless with money, though – in fact, he is surprisingly careful about small purchases, and if he thinks he is being taken for a ride he becomes a very difficult customer. He tips generously but surreptitiously.

'I've been rich twice and poor twice,' he told me one evening in Palm

Springs. 'That's evens. I wonder which way it'll work out in the end. I couldn't face myself poor now. Not because I'm frightened of the elements of poverty. But once you've been privileged to all this luxury . . .' Then he checked, as if he had suddenly become aware that he was letting the devil-may-care façade drop a little further than usual.

Probably the predominant facet of his public image is his intransigence and his quick temper. During all the time that I was with him he only lost his temper once, and that was caused by an incident that would have evoked a flare-up from most men. Even then, he did not rant and scream and hurl abuse around in the manner that his public image would suggest; he just sat in a corner, seething and incommunicado, chewing on his pipe, occasionally muttering curses.

On one other occasion I saw him get very angry, but he did not lose his temper, although there was plenty of provocation. It was around midnight in Palm Springs. He was driving his Buick Station-wagon, approaching a T junction where there was one-way traffic due to roadworks. Past the bonnet of his car, missing it by centimetres, hurtled a car at about 80 m.p.h. through the built-up area. He tooted furiously. The speeding car braked abruptly, did a 180-degree turn through a barrier saying 'No Entry' and drove back up the strip of road under construction. Out stepped a belligerent-looking giant, all of 240 lb. Sinatra jumped out and gave the giant a five-minute lecture on dangerous driving, liberally spattered with observations on his apparent mental ability, parentage and so on. The resigned comment of song writer Jimmy Van Heusen, Sinatra's long time friend and writer of many Sinatra hit songs such as 'Come Fly With Me' and 'All The Way': 'Do you know how many of these things I've been in with him? Eight thousand. In how many has he been right? Eight thousand. He is incapable of letting any injustice get by unchallenged. You or I – either we'd have cursed and done nothing, or we'd have seen the size of the driver and cleared out fast. But not him. Oh, no!'

One afternoon I asked Sinatra about his reputation for intransigence. 'Well now, let's take criticism first,' he said. 'People say I won't be criticised. It's not that I mind being criticised, for Chrissakes. I don't mind criticism so long as the people doing the criticism know their stuff, their facts. What infuriates me is that most of our so-called "music critics" have got nothing in here' (points to his head). 'No, worse still – in here' (points to his ear). 'What I've forgotten about music they haven't learned yet. But the real trouble comes from a few embittered columnists. I have consistently maintained that they have absolutely no right to question me on my private life if I don't want to answer their questions. Just because I am a public entertainer, I do not become the property of the Press. I do get angry with the Press because they will not accept this. They badger, badger, badger. And another reason I get angry is because they are so fantastically inaccurate.

'One magazine did a so-called "profile" on me which had twenty-seven major inaccuracies in it. Is that right? And I just don't think there is any excuse at all for doing what the British press do: follow me around in packed cars sprouting with telephoto lenses and things. No. I refuse to grovel to that sort of treatment. I will continue to stand up to it. While the Press behave like that, they will get nothing out of me and I want nothing out of them. You must fight back, hit them where it really hurts – like with advertising revenue. I remember one guy who wanted to interview me sent me a three-page telegram. Hundreds of words, must have cost him all of thirty dollars. I couldn't understand it, but I gathered he was explaining to me why I needed the publicity. I sent him back a telegram with one word – WHAT? – and that was the last I heard from him. There – I've made my speech about the Press. Now let's forget it, shall we? Of course, I admit – the trouble with me is that I get impatient. I've always been that way. You know, I might do some great things if only I could learn not to be impatient. For instance, I admire someone who can walk away after being needled, quietly ignoring the whole thing. I really do admire them. But I can't do that myself. I'm too much of a volatile man. Yet if someone comes up and tells me I stink to my face, I respect them for it. One night in New York there were screaming bobbysoxers all round the stage door, and a young feller came up to me and said "Are you Frank Sinatra?" I said yes. "Well, you *stink*," he said and walked off. Anyone who takes that sort of trouble and has that sort of courage has my respect. It's the little snidey jibes that I hate. And needling. Needling's quite a different matter. It's then I start getting angry. Really angry. But then I've always been a rebel, always fought to do what I thought right or best. I shall feel very rewarded if some of what I've done musically rubs off on some youngster in the future. Part of the whole thing is never to accept anything without ques-

59

tion: never ignore an inner voice that tells you something could be better even when other people tell you it's OK . . .'

This is not the place for a detailed exposition of Sinatra's long running battle with the Press. Knowing him to be a man of extremes who will not tolerate any interference that he considers unwarranted, and having experienced some of the Press's methods of obtaining and reporting information, I am not at all surprised that this particular battle has been running for so long. On at least three occasions while I was with Sinatra, items appeared in the columns referring to something he was meant to have said or done the previous evening – annoying items that certainly did not show him up in a favourable light. Yet I knew for a fact that those items were not based on any fact whatsoever, as I had been with him during the evenings in question.

On another occasion, Sinatra was dining in Romanoff's bar. A man – obviously a reporter – came up, leaned over the table at Sinatra, and started making aggressive remarks about the failure of his projected yachting holiday in the Mediterranean. Sinatra ignored him at first, then the man began to ask pointlessly irritating questions and gripped Sinatra's arm. Luckily the incident ended with the intruder being ushered out by waiters. The same thing happened with a newsman in New York, when Sinatra was again out with a private party. While he is exposed to this kind of treatment, it is unreasonable to expect Sinatra to go out of his way, or indeed to go any way at all, to co-operate with the Press. His view of columnists is best summed up by his own classic epigram on the subject: 'All day long they lie in the sun. And after the sun goes down, they lie some more.'

Thus, with the Press relationship as it is, and has been for some years, is it surprising that Sinatra's public image has been grossly distorted? That his faults have been blown up to be mammoth vices and his misde-meanours to be unspeakable crimes? Punching a reporter may seem to be a foolish and ineffective way of handling the situation, but to someone in Sinatra's position it has simple and uncomplicated appeal. The vicious circle spins, and, having spun, spins on . . .

Accurate first-hand comment on Sinatra, the *real* Sinatra, is so rare that when an example comes to light it is worth noting. Such an example is contained in a recent letter to *Downbeat* magazine from Lee Castle, now leader of the Jimmy Dorsey band and one-time trumpeter in the Tommy Dorsey band while Sinatra was the band's vocalist. This shows that, however switch-backed Sinatra's career, his personality has remained constant. The letter is worth quoting at some length:

'I'm tired of all the criticisms of Frank Sinatra. Everywhere I go I hear: "Is he really as bad as they say?" People remember that article about him that appeared in (a prominent picture magazine) a while back. Or else they've heard that Sammy Davis criticised him on that radio show in Chicago recently and that Sinatra cut Davis off his list of friends for it. Doesn't that show what a hard man Sinatra is to get along with?

'Not that I can see. Davis shouldn't have said what he did about a friend. And anyway, the quarrel is all patched up now. Unfortunately you won't hear about that part of it. You only hear one side of the Sinatra story.

'I guess I've known Frank, as an acquaintance, nearly as long as anyone in the business. When I was with Tommy Dorsey years ago, Tommy said one day: "Lee I've got another Italian boy coming on the band. Make him feel at home." We were playing at the Palmer House in Chicago at the time. The new boy was Frank Sinatra. He was my room-mate for a couple of days.

'Even then, you could see that this boy was tough. If you crossed him, you were dead. And he couldn't stand phonies. But if you were friends, that was it.

'Over the years we all watched him go up, and it's no secret that today he's the favourite singer of just about any musician you can name. But a lot of people liked him for personal reasons, too. He's always been the most generous guy in the world, whether it's with his time or his money. For some reason, he apparently doesn't like to take credit for what he does. But he does it, just the same.

'I know that right now he does an enormous amount to help the City of Hope on the west coast. He just gave a very large sum to the Combined Jewish Appeal. He does a lot for Catholic charities and cancer research. And he's generous to individuals, too. I could give you the names of a number of singers he's helped – his own competitors, if you want to look at it that way. Sometimes he'd give them money, shake hands, and forget it.

'Frank is terrifically loyal to his friends. Jack E. Leonard, the comedian, one of the funniest men alive, told me after he'd been so sick: "If it wasn't for Frank's phone calls from the coast to cheer me up, I wouldn't be here today."

'If you were out of work, Frank would get up at 2 a.m. to help you.

61

Once when I *was* out of work, I found out that Sinatra was doing a record date with Axel Stordahl. I phoned to see whether I could get on it. Axel said he'd check. He called back twenty minutes later and said: "You're on."

'Only recently I was talking to Hank Sanicola. Sanicola is a business associate and friend of Sinatra. Hank said: "I've been with Frank twenty years, and the only contract we've ever had is a handshake."

'If all this is true (and it is), how does Sinatra get the name he has? Well, it's like Tommy Dorsey used to say about him: "One thing he won't do: let anyone push him around." Then, too, when you're a name, somebody's always trying to get at you.

'I remember once eating in a restaurant in New York with Sanicola and Sinatra. Some wise guy walked in just as a piece of macaroni slipped off Sinatra's fork. The wise guy said: "How do you like the big shot? He doesn't have the strength to hold a piece of macaroni." Frank stood up and told the guy, "I'll flatten you." The guy left, quick. If that makes Sinatra a bad guy, what does it make the other guy?

'All right, people say, so that's what Sinatra used to be like. What about now?

'I'll tell you something that happened only a couple of weeks ago. I got the story from Tony Zoppi, the columnist at the Dallas *News*. Tony was playing blackjack with Sinatra in the lounge of the Sands Hotel at Las Vegas. The game was still going at 8 a.m. and they heard a baby crying. Sinatra said, "What that baby needs is a gem to keep it warm." Don't ask me to translate. That's what he said, according to Tony. Anyway, the baby cried again, and they then realised there was a woman sleeping in the lounge with her baby. Sinatra stood up and said "I'll be back."

'He came back twenty minutes later, carrying a teddy bear about five feet high. He woke the woman up, pulled out a roll of bills, pushed it into her hand, and called her a taxi. Then he came back to the table and went back to the game, and never said a word.

'If that's what a hard guy is like, I wish there were more of them in this world.'

I saw an instance of the kind of 'terrific loyalty' that Castle mentions – indeed that several musicians and show business people mentioned to me in Las Vegas and Hollywood, citing examples too intricate to be listed here. One night in New York Sinatra took his party to a small bar on Broadway and West 58th, the owner of which was a friend of his. Sitting at the next table alone, was a short, middle-aged man, who looked in the depths of depression. He saw Sinatra and came over. Sinatra greeted him as a long-lost friend and introduced him as Rube Bloom, the song-writer with 'Day In, Day Out' and 'Maybe You'll Be There' to his credit. Bloom, it turned out, had not had much success recently; his songs were 'too good' for the current taste for cacophony, and he was rapidly losing heart. 'One needs encouragement to write songs, you know,' he told me sadly.

The first thing Sinatra did was ask the piano-player to play 'Day In, Day Out.' Next, he asked Bloom to come over to the West Coast as his guest. Then, a few weeks later, Reprise Records took the odd step of releasing a record of Frank Sinatra singing the Twist. But it was no ordinary Twist tune – it was a refurbished version of that old standard 'Truckin',' with new Twist lyrics. The original writer of 'Truckin'?' Rube Bloom.

Jimmy Van Heusen put his finger on it that night in Palm Springs when he said Sinatra was 'incapable of seeing any injustice' without doing something to rectify the situation, even if it is only to hit someone. He has a passionate affinity with the underdog – hence his wild fury at anything that smacks of racial intolerance or repression of minority groups. He loathes segregationists, Nazis, Fascists, dictators, anyone associated with the denial of the small man's freedom or the abuse of power. His hatred of gossip-columnists could well spring from this phobia. I do not subscribe to the theory that he dislikes columnists because he fears that they will show up his weaknesses, because in his dealings with the Press both his strength and his weaknesses are only too apparent already – although the myopic members of that profession mostly choose to ignore the strength and hang on the weakness.

I asked him late one night what it was like to have the power he had, to be able to do more or less anything he wanted. He looked at me with a twinkle in those direct, incontestable blue eyes: 'So you think I could have anything I wanted, do you? Well, I'll tell you something. For years I've nursed a secret desire to spend the Fourth of July in a double hammock with a swingin' red-headed broad. But I never could find me a double hammock...'

There seemed to be something very symbolic about that hammock.

What, then is the explanation for this man's unique, almost universal appeal – for his magnetic hold over millions of people? It cannot come

63

from his looks alone, nor from his acting, nor yet merely from his singing – although his singing must undoubtedly be the predominant quality.

The fact is that he is far more than an entertainer. He has, by the peculiarly potent chemistry of his nature and image, become the living symbol of an ideal that millions subconsciously would like to emulate, but consciously realise that it would never work out in practice. He is every-man's dreamland alter ego and everywoman's dreamland paramour. The paradoxes in his make-up are all part of it – the swashbuckling toughness together with the poignant tenderness, the idolised hero yet simultaneously the small boy underdog, the family man yet the emancipated charmer of the world.

In the many facets of Frank Sinatra, everyone can find ground for self-identification: he represents every mood in the spectrum of emotion. And he represents them honestly, passionately, vitally.

This honesty, this passion, this vitality, forms the essential element of his singing, which is, after all, the part of himself that he makes his main public offering. It is there, in the songs that he sings and in the way that he sings them. His style is intrinsically a natural one; no man could contrive something as unphoney-sounding as his treatment of a song, be it the maudlin ballad or the exultant hymn.

It all makes sense. Total commitment like that simply cannot be rigged up in a recording studio. The whole secret of his power as an artist is in the sincerity and reality of his performances. They are *him*, laying himself bare as few artists have dared to do, or would achieve anything by doing even if they dared.

So, to find the real nature of the man, I would say simply this: listen. Listen to the vibrations in the diaphragm of your gramophone loud-speaker, and accept what they and your own ear tell you.

For that is an unmasked, undistorted self-portrait, as revealing and as unlying as an X-ray.

A self-portrait of the man Sinatra.

ALABAMA

Past and Present

Bridget Heos

rosen publishing's
rosen
central®

New York

For my English teachers, Carol Lynn, Bernie VanArsdale, and Pat Dunlay

Published in 2010 by The Rosen Publishing Group, Inc.
29 East 21st Street, New York, NY 10010

Library of Congress Cataloging-in-Publication Data

Heos, Bridget.
Alabama: past and present / Bridget Heos.—1st ed.
   p. cm.—(The United States: Past and Present)
Includes bibliographical references and index.
ISBN 978-1-4358-3518-4 (library binding)
ISBN 978-1-4358-8486-1 (pbk)
ISBN 978-1-4358-8487-8 (6 pack)
1. Alabama—Juvenile literature. I. Title.
F326.3.H456 2010
976.1—dc22

                                                   2009021850

Manufactured in the United States of America

CPSIA Compliance Information: Batch #LW10YA: For Further Information contact Rosen Publishing, New York, New York at 1-800-237-9932

On the cover: Top left: Alabama miners' company town near Birmingham around 1935. Top right: Lake Tuscaloosa Islands. Bottom: The Marshall Space Flight Center in Huntsville.

Contents

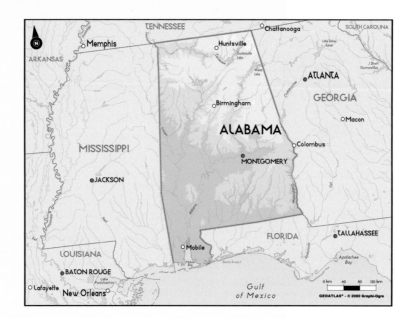

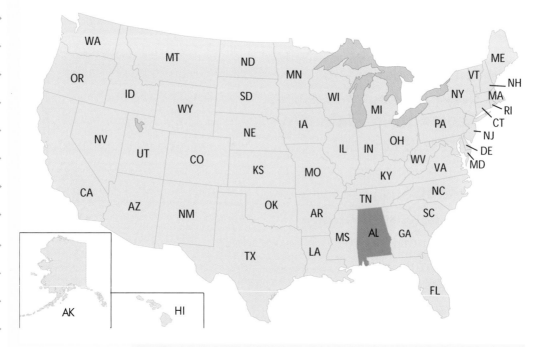

The state of Alabama is bordered by Tennessee, Georgia, Mississippi, Florida, and the Gulf of Mexico.

Introduction

In Alabama, kids say, "Yes, sir," and "No, ma'am." Men hold doors open for ladies, and people say hello to strangers on the street.

A mix of English and African cultural traditions, manners are important in the South. Alabama, part of the Deep South, is no exception. Here, residents from the Gulf Coast and central plains to the northern uplands live in a spirit of helpfulness, hospitality, and politeness.

There is also a fighting side to Alabama. The state was a battleground during both the Civil War and the civil rights movement. For decades after the Civil War, the state government maintained segregation laws. By the 1950s, many Alabamans—led by Martin Luther King Jr.—were protesting these laws. By staging sit-ins, boycotts, and marches, they forced Southerners and Northerners alike to address their prejudices and move forward as a united country.

They accomplished that goal but couldn't erase the past. Today, Alabama is America's seventh poorest state, due in large part to the lasting economic wounds of slavery and inequality. Nevertheless, many Alabamans are thriving thanks to urban industry and, in rural areas, rich natural resources and vibrant specialty businesses, such as fish farms and peanut farms.

Alabama is home to rich and poor, black and white, corporate planters and small family farmers. As diverse as its people are, they share one thing: From their good manners to their hard-earned resilience, Alabamans are distinctly Southern. This is the story of their state.

THE LAND OF ALABAMA

Alabama spans from the Gulf Coast to the foothills of the Appalachian Mountains and encompasses beaches, swamps, forests, and fertile plains. The state has some of the richest and most beautiful land in America. And to think, for millions of years it was all underwater.

In prehistoric times, the state was covered by ancient seas and coastal swamplands. When animals—from the microscopic to the enormous—died in this sea, their skeletons sank to the ocean floor and eventually became limestone and chalk. These rocks, along with shale and sandstone, make up Alabama today.

When sea levels dropped, the rocks were exposed. Wind and rain eroded them, and, at the surface, they became soil. In the middle part of the state's central plains, grass and cane grew. The plants died and decomposed, making the soil richer. Soon it became black clay. There, prairie grasses and wildflowers grew.

Alabama's first residents found this land difficult to farm. They chose to clear brush and trees instead and planted crops in the sandier soils, which were easier to work.

When Europeans settled in Alabama, they recognized the prairie as perfect for cash crops such as cotton. Plantations—dependent on slave labor—arose.

Standing 2,407 feet (734 meters) above sea level, Cheaha Mountain marks the highest point in Alabama. It is located in the Cheaha State Park and Talladega National Forest.

Spanning several Southern states, this region became known as the Black Belt, first because of the color of the soil, and later because of the predominantly African American population. Once known for its rich soil, poverty abounds in this region today. Plantation farming left deep socioeconomic wounds. Now, efforts are being made to bring economic growth to the Black Belt. Some residents have built ponds for catfish, crawfish, shrimp, and tilapia farms. Others have planted pine trees, giving rise to a large pulp and paper industry.

In addition to the Black Belt, other areas of the coastal plain include:

- The Gulf Shore. The thirty-two mile (fifty-one kilometer) shoreline located in the southwestern corner of the state (west of the Florida panhandle and east of Mississippi) attracts tourists seeking white-sand beaches and warm water. The beautiful coast is prone to hurricanes, and after storms, such as Hurricane Ivan in 2004, much rebuilding was done.
- The Southwestern Plains. Here, forests cover much of the land. Peanuts, cotton, pecan trees, and many other crops are grown here, too.
- Upper Coastal Plain. On this hilly land, peach trees and vegetables are grown.
- Smaller areas of geographical interest include the salt springs in the southwest, which ooze salty water, and the pitcher plant bogs in the lower coastal plains. These soggy, spongy lands are named for an insect-eating plant, one of the many unique elements in the ecosystem.

Alabama has a wide range of flora and fauna and hosts many native animals, including the bobcat, red fox, American alligator, copperhead, freshwater jellyfish, largemouth bass, armadillo, and several bat, skink, and tree frog species. Alabama waters contain eighty-three species of crayfish—more than any other state. As in much of America, wildlife has been threatened by land development, and conservation efforts are underway.

The Uplands

In the northern half of Alabama, the coastal plains slope upward into the foothills. These uplands make up the southern edge of the Appalachian Mountains.

The Black Belt

Past . . .

In 1860, Alabama was known as the Cotton State. That year, 989,955 bales of cotton were grown on approximately one million acres of land, much of it in the Black Belt.

Early nineteenth-century newcomers from Georgia and North and South Carolina had first settled on land by the rivers. When that filled up, they moved inland to the Black Belt, where the sticky black soil was ideal for growing cotton—a crop dependent on slave labor.

By 1860, there were nearly as many slaves as free men in Alabama. Although less than 25 percent of white Southerners owned any slaves at this time, the largest plantations worked 250 men, women, and children—who labored sunup to sundown, lived in cramped cabins, and were treated harshly.

The Civil War ended slavery, but a similar system arose: sharecropping. Through this arrangement, former slaves and poor whites grew cotton on plantation land, giving landowners half to two-thirds of their crop, leaving barely anything for themselves.

Present . . .

By the 1960s, cheap labor had been replaced by new farm machinery, and many sharecroppers had taken industrial jobs in the city.

Alabama is now eleventh among the seventeen cotton-producing U.S. states. Through the years, landowners have diversified their crops to contend with the boll weevil, an insect that devastated crops in 1915, and to maintain healthy soil.

The Alabama cotton farms that still exist are no longer clustered in the Black Belt. To some extent, cotton picking here has been replaced by other agricultural endeavors, including fish farms, forestry, and cattle ranches.

However, many of Alabama's poorest counties are in the Black Belt. Government and local leaders are trying to take advantage of the region's fertile soil and natural beauty to restore wealth to Black Belt residents—this time, all of them.

Compared to other mountains, the Appalachians are very old. In their youth, they stood as high as the Rocky Mountains but have since eroded. The mountains formed about 270 million years ago, when present-day Africa collided with present-day North America. At that time, the continents drifted together to form a supercontinent, called Pangaea. As Africa and North America collided, masses of rock piled up to the west, forming the Appalachians. When the continents split up, the Appalachians remained. Today, the range spans much of the eastern United States and parts of Canada.

Many animals, including this baby armadillo, dwell in Alabama. A range of habitats are home to diverse wildlife in the state.

In Alabama, the highest point of the Appalachian foothills is Cheaha Mountain. Named *Chaha,* or "high point," by the Creek Indians, it stands 2,407 feet (733 m) above sea level and is in the Talladega National Forest.

Many early European settlers chose Alabama's hilly, wooded uplands to farm. The soil wasn't as fertile as it was to the south, but it was cheaper. Here, poor and middle-class farmers eked out a living by raising hogs or cattle, and growing crops such as corn and beans for their families.

For years, cotton was king in Alabama. Today, crops are more diverse. However, cotton is still grown on a large scale and harvested with machines, such as this combine harvester.

Today, poultry farms and cattle ranches make up much of this region. In the Tennessee River Valley, which cuts through northern Alabama, cotton is still grown on a large scale.

State climate varies somewhat from the north to south. For instance, Mobile, on the Gulf Coast, averages 62 and 48 degrees Fahrenheit (16 and 8 degrees Celsius) for its winter high and low, whereas Birmingham, farther north, has a seasonal high and low of 55 °F and 34 °F (12 °C and 1 °C). Overall, the state enjoys mild winters, beautiful springs and falls, and hot and humid summers.

Chapter 2

THE HISTORY OF ALABAMA

Alabama became America's twenty-second state in 1819. As Native Americans were pushed off the land, settlers flocked to the state during a period known as "Alabama Fever." Wealthy landowners from other Southern states bought prime government acreage, while impoverished families squatted on poor land in hopes of buying it when it came up for sale.

French colonists and other settlers had already introduced slavery to Alabama. Now, the number of slaves increased. Alabama led the nation in cotton production, and Mobile, from where the textile was shipped to Europe, was America's third busiest port.

Plantation owners, powerful in government, believed slavery to be essential to cotton production. They believed Abraham Lincoln, a Republican, would abolish slavery. Lincoln was elected in 1860. The next year, Alabama joined other Southern states in seceding from the United States to form the Confederate States of America. The capital was in Montgomery, Alabama.

In 1861, Union and Confederate armies began fighting the Civil War, the deadliest conflict in U.S. history. The heaviest fighting occurred outside the state, but many Alabamans were soldiers. About one hundred thousand men from Alabama fought—most for the

On August 5, 1864, the Union forced the Confederate Navy to surrender during a battle in Mobile Bay. Currier & Ives illustrated the fight in this print, published around the same time.

Confederacy, but some, particularly hill country residents and slaves from the Tennessee Valley, for the Union. Many never came home.

Outnumbered and underfunded, the South suffered during the war. Although its strong military tradition allowed the Confederacy to fight long and hard, food and supply shortages plagued the army.

As the fighting dragged on, morale among Confederate soldiers and citizens faded. People in the hill country were starving. Soldiers wanted to go home to help their families on the farm.

In 1865, the Confederate Army surrendered. By that time, 620,000 Americans had died, mostly from sickness and disease. The crops,

Barbecue

Past . . .

Slow-cooked meat drenched in delicious sauce—that's barbecue, and in Alabama, it's as much an art form as a part of history.

As the story goes, the natives in southeast North America and nearby islands smoked their meat over low heat. In the Caribbean, the structure they rested the meat on was called a "babracot." "Barbecue" may be an adaptation of that word.

Colonials adopted this style of cooking pigs, but basted the meat with vinegar or butter so that it wouldn't be too dry. Barbecues were popular get-togethers even in those days, with George Washington himself attending a "'cue" or two.

African slaves from the Caribbean brought a new tradition with them—they cured the pork with red pepper. When the butter, vinegar, and spice combined, barbecue sauce was born. (Tomatoes were believed to be poisonous at the time and were added only later.) Slaves also started the tradition of making lesser cuts of meat—which they were stuck with—taste delicious through barbecuing.

When African Americans migrated north, and others became cowboys in Texas, they brought barbecue with them. Over time, regional styles developed in the South and up into Missouri.

Present . . .

Borrowing from neighboring states, Alabama barbecue includes vinegar, tomato, and mustard-based sauces. Big Bob Gibson's Bar-B-Q invented a unique sauce involving mayonnaise and apple cider vinegar.

Famous barbecue restaurants in Alabama are Dreamland Bar-B-Que, Bob Sykes Bar-B-Q, and Golden Rule Bar-B-Q. (The way people spell barbecue is as much a matter of taste as the type of sauce they like.)

Whether eaten in a restaurant or at a family party, barbecue doesn't require a lot of money. It requires time, which reminds people to slow down.

the animals, and the fertile land of the South were decimated, and one in every four Confederate soldiers lay dead.

Slavery was abolished, and 440,000 Alabamans were freed. Through an 1868 constitution created under a then-Republican state government, black men gained the right to vote. Several African Americans held political office. This postwar period is known as Reconstruction.

Then in 1874, things changed for the worse. Alabaman Democrats, also known as "Redeemers" and "Bourbons," took control of the state legislature. They still believed in the premises of slavery and wanted to keep power in the hands of white property owners.

In 1901, the Bourbons wrote laws that allowed poll workers to turn down voters for illiteracy, inability to pay a poll tax, and other insufficient reasons. Blacks and poor whites would be denied the right to vote for decades to come.

Soon fleeing racial injustice, rural poverty, and the Ku Klux Klan—a white supremacist terrorist group—many African Americans headed north, where industrial jobs were plentiful. This became known as the Great Migration.

Northern states weren't immune to racial prejudice, however, and for the blacks who stayed in Alabama, their fight for civil rights would reso-nate throughout the country.

The Great Depression made things even worse for poor farm workers, such as the two photographed here in 1935 Boone County, Alabama.

Civil Rights

Alabama's blacks and poor whites faced extreme poverty during the Great Depression, but World War II brought change. Women became trained workers during the war. Many men went to college on the GI Bill. The middle class grew. The status quo was changing. However, the state government, run by the Dixiecrat Party, clung to old laws.

Formerly Democrats, the Dixiecrats broke off from the party in protest of President Harry Truman's support of civil rights. Truman advocated for a federal antilynching law, the abolition of the poll tax, and desegregation. Truman won reelection, but segregation continued in the South.

Soon the state became a battleground for civil rights across the United States.

The modern civil rights movement began in 1955, when Rosa Parks refused to give up her seat on a Montgomery, Alabama, bus, sparking a year-long boycott by forty thousand blacks. Montgomery minister Martin Luther King Jr. led the protest and went on to head the civil rights movement.

King advocated peaceful protest, but state and local officials often responded with force. In 1963, when Birmingham residents protested segregation in downtown department stores, Public Safety Commissioner Bull O'Connor directed police to arrest and use high-pressure water hoses against them.

The Sixteenth Street Baptist Church, a black church where organizers of the Birmingham protest met, was bombed soon after the protests. Four girls were killed: Denise McNair, eleven; Addie Mae Collins, fourteen; Carole Robertson, fourteen; and Cynthia Wesley, fourteen.

When Rosa Parks refused to give up her bus seat, the civil rights movement began. Here, she is fingerprinted by police lieutenant D. H. Lackey in Montgomery, Alabama.

The civil rights advocates didn't back down. The harder the state government pushed for racial discrimination, and the more violent terrorist groups became, the harder the advocates fought—and the more battles they won.

George Wallace was elected governor in 1962, promising, "Segregation now, segregation tomorrow, segregation forever." The next year, he tried to prevent black students from entering the University of Alabama.

This and other injustices led to the 1963 March on Washington, where King gave his "I Have a Dream" speech. Soon after, the U.S. Congress passed the 1964 Civil Rights Act.

In 1965, King led thousands of protesters in the Selma-to-Montgomery march for voting rights. As a result, the U.S. Congress adopted the Voting Rights Act.

Ultimately, change did occur throughout the nation and at home in Alabama. By the 1980s, Alabama and Mississippi led the country in the number of black elected officials. Even George Wallace changed his mind about segregation. After an attempted assassination in 1972, he apologized for his racism during the civil rights movement.

Today, you can learn about Alabama's role in the civil rights movement at the Birmingham Civil Rights Institute.

Chapter 3

THE GOVERNMENT OF ALABAMA

The state government of Alabama has three branches: the executive, the legislative, and the judicial.

The Executive Branch

The executive branch includes the governor, who plays a role similar to the U.S. president, only on a state level. After the Alabama House and Senate vote on a new bill, the governor can sign it into law or do the opposite—veto it. In Alabama, the governor's veto power is fairly weak. The House and Senate can reverse the governor's veto with a majority vote. Because it takes a majority vote to pass the bill in the first place, the likelihood of a governor's veto being reversed is high.

The governor appoints members to certain state boards. Other members of state boards and commissions, such as the board of education, are elected by the people of Alabama.

Besides the governor, elected officials in the executive branch include the attorney general, lieutenant governor, commissioner of agriculture and industry, state treasurer, state auditor, and secretary of state. All are elected to four-year terms.

These officials employ staff members to help them because they have many responsibilities. For example, the attorney general, as

This Montgomery home was built in 1907, but it didn't become the Alabama Governor's Mansion until 1950.

head legal counsel for Alabama, represents state agencies and officials in cases brought against the state. The attorney general also brings cases to enforce state law and prosecutes some state criminal cases. Finally, the office supports bills that will strengthen law enforcement capabilities in the state.

The Legislative Branch

The legislative branch is made up of thirty-five state senators and 105 members of the House of Representatives. Elected to four-year terms, the 140 Alabama legislators work together to make new laws.

First, either a senator or representative introduces the bill to the Senate or House. Let's say a senator introduces it. The bill is read to the Senate. Next, the Senate president gives the bill to a committee for study. After meeting, the committee makes a recommendation to the Senate. The Senate debates the bill and finally votes on it. If passed, the bill goes to the House of Representatives, where the entire process is repeated. If the House passes the bill, the governor may sign it into law or veto it. If the governor vetoes it, the legislature votes again, with a majority vote making the bill a law.

In Alabama, the House and Senate have several differences. For one thing, each senator represents an area with approximately 125,000 residents, whereas House members each represent about forty thousand people. The House is considered the "voice of the people." The Senate is considered the more deliberative body of government, as they tend to debate bills longer. In the Senate, if there is a tie, the lieutenant governor votes as the tiebreaker.

The Alabama State Capitol, in Montgomery, is where the Senate and House debate bills and make laws.

The Judicial Branch

The state courts make up the judicial branch of the Alabama government. Where the legislative branch makes laws, the judicial branch interprets them.

Schools

Past . . .

The Alabama State School System was established in 1854. Until then, schools existed only on a local level. Many students didn't attend but instead worked as brick-layers, painters, or dressmakers—all poorly paid jobs. In Mobile in 1851, 42 percent of white children did not attend school. For slave children, school didn't exist at all.

Like much of nineteenth-century America, rural Alabama schools were held in one-room schoolhouses, where the teacher taught several ages. Schools closed during harvesttime so that students and teachers could help on the farm.

Schools weren't well funded in Alabama, so, at the time, they fared worse than in other parts of the country.

Through the mid-1900s, Alabama schools were segregated. This was legal under the claim that black and white schools were "separate but equal." In fact, black schools received as little as half the funding as white schools. In the 1954 *Brown v. Board of Education* case, the U.S. Supreme Court ruled that "separate but equal" schools were unconstitutional. Schools throughout the country needed to integrate, but Alabama refused to comply.

In 1957, a group of black parents sued the Birmingham school district, and in 1963, the courts ordered the schools to integrate. To stop this, Governor Wallace closed the schools, organized a petition, and sent state troopers to stop black students from entering school. In the end, Alabama schools integrated.

Present . . .

Today, schools are integrated by law, but in practice, some are still predominantly white or black, as is the case in other states, too.

In terms of school performance and funding, Alabama ranks average among other states. Through the years, graduates of Alabama schools have included Rosa Parks, novelist Harper Lee, actress Courtney Cox, author and journalist Rick Bragg, and *American Idol* winner Ruben Studdard.

The court system has a hierarchy, meaning higher courts can overturn the decisions of lower courts. Say you were accused of stealing something—but you didn't do it. If you lost your case in circuit court, you could ask the court of criminal appeals to hear your case.

The lowest level of the hierarchy includes the municipal court, which handles city ordinances; district court, which handles small claims and misdemeanors; and probate court, which handles wills and family matters. Alabama has 273 municipal courts, sixty-seven district courts, and sixty-eight probate courts.

The State of Alabama Supreme Court hears cases that have been appealed to the highest level. It is made up of nine justices.

Above them are the state's forty-one circuit courts. The circuit court can hear appeals from the lower courts or hear a case being tried for the first time.

Circuit court cases can be appealed to the court of civic appeals or court of criminal appeals. A civic case involves a plaintiff suing a defendant for a loss. A criminal case involves a person being prosecuted by the state for a crime. There is only one of each court of appeals, with five judges each. The court can choose to hear or not hear an appeal.

Finally, cases can be appealed to the Alabama Supreme Court, the highest court in the state. There are nine justices on the state supreme court. In Alabama, court of appeals judges and supreme court justices are elected to six-year terms by the people.

Not all courts in Alabama are state courts. Some are federal. These courts handle cases involving federal law—criminal, such as bank robbery; civil, such as bankruptcy; or cases in which a person believes a state law is in violation of the U.S. Constitution.

National Representation

Like all U.S. states, Alabama has two U.S. senators. It has seven members of the U.S. House of Representatives, which is decided based on the state population. In general, House members vote according to the wishes of the people in their district. They are reelected each year. Senators traditionally vote for the nation as a whole, not just their constituents. Often, a bill makes it through the U.S. House of Representatives only to stall in the U.S. Senate, which debates matters more thoroughly.

THE INDUSTRY OF ALABAMA

Alabama's economy is historically rooted in agriculture. Today, farming, ranching, and forestry continue to be an important part of the state's economy. Farm sales total about $4 billion annually, and approximately 15 percent of that is exported to other countries.

Once known as the Cotton State, Alabama is now more agriculturally diverse. Though cotton is still grown, particularly in the Tennessee River Valley, the top export is poultry, followed by cotton, wheat, and peanuts.

Peanuts have an interesting history in Alabama. They were brought to the American South by African slaves. (If you've ever heard peanuts called "goobers," it's because the Bantu word for the food is *nguba*.)

For years, peanuts were considered poor people's food. Then, during the Civil War, troops desperately in need of food turned to the peanut. Americans in the South and North grew to like the snack.

Snacking alone didn't create enough demand for goober peas. In Alabama, cotton was still king. This was a problem for many reasons:

- Plantation owners depended on cheap labor to turn a profit.
- Cotton stripped the soil of nutrients.
- If insects attacked, farmers didn't have an alternative crop to rely on.

George Washington Carver, photographed in about 1935, invented hundreds of products made with peanuts and sweet potatoes.

In the early 1900s, George Washington Carver, an African American botanist in Alabama, encouraged farmers to rotate their cotton crops with peanuts. To create an increased market for the crop, he invented food and nonfood products that could be made with peanuts. Soon, they became a popular crop in the South. Today, half the peanuts grown in the United States are harvested within 100 miles (160 km) of Dothan, Alabama.

Other agricultural operations include cattle ranches, fish farms, peach and pecan orchards, and pine plantations.

Today, industrial farmers employ only a few workers and use machinery in place of most labor. Many small family farmers have second jobs. Many are contract farmers, meaning they raise crops or animals for a larger company. For instance, in the upland, families raise chickens for a large poultry outfit. They are given the chickens, the feed, and the veterinary medication. Once the chickens are raised, the farmers give them back to the company to be packaged as chicken dinners.

By and large, industry jobs have replaced agriculture jobs in Alabama, just as they have in much of the country.

"Hell's Half Acre" was a row of houses on the edge of Avondale, Alabama. While factories provided an alternative to rural poverty, workers faced new hardships in the city.

Industry in Cities

During the Civil War, demand for weaponry and supplies caused industrial cities to grow. Industrialization continued after the war, and Alabama, rich in minerals, became part of this booming economy.

Birmingham was founded in 1871 amid a hill country cornfield. While rich in the supplies needed to make iron—coal, iron ore, and limestone—the region had been left alone because, with no nearby rivers, there was no way to transport the supplies. Railroads changed that, and Birmingham became a boomtown.

Music

Past . . .

African slaves brought to America a traditional style of music that they sang while working. It eventually evolved into blues. First using the banjo, an African instrument, musicians eventually added the guitar and piano, which are European instruments.

Blues became rhythm and blues, an early form of rock and roll. Alabama's Willie Mae "Big Mama" Thornton famously recorded "Hound Dog," a song Elvis Presley later sang.

Percy Sledge added a gospel sound, recording soul music, such as "When a Man Loves a Woman." Soul music became part of the Motown Sound in the 1950s and '60s.

Meanwhile, Scots-Irish settlers brought to Alabama a tradition of fiddle music, ballads, and lullabies. With the addition of the African banjo, string bands formed. Eventually, this evolved into country music. In the 1940s, Hank Williams of southern Alabama brought this "hillbilly" music to a national audience. His music contained both Alabama country and blues.

Present . . .

Country and R&B music continue to share popularity in Alabama. Several number-one country songs were written by Alabamans, and *American Idol* winner and R&B singer Ruben Studdard hails from Birmingham.

Worldwide, the most famous artist to come out of Alabama is probably Lionel Richie, former Commodore and father of reality TV star Nicole Richie. In America, his solo albums were big hits in the 1980s. U.S. reporters working in the Middle East say that, today, he is still the most popular singer in that region.

Once, while he was walking in Libya, a group of children began following him. He turned around and said, "Hello there." They answered, "Hello, hello, is it me you're looking for?" which are lyrics to one of his songs.

VB   #202 10-03-2013 4:11PM
 Item(s) checked out to Furchert, Amy.

TITLE: Hurricanes
BRCD: 30613001137383
DUE DATE: 10-24-13

TITLE: Alabama
BRCD: 3 0613 00172 6615
DUE DATE: 10-24-13

TITLE: Alabama : past and present
BRCD: 30613002368177
DUE DATE: 10-24-13

          Bayport-Blue Point Library
               (631) 363-6133

People from all over America and Europe came to Birmingham to live and work, as did rural Alabamans.

Miners and mill employees worked hard and lived in "company towns," meaning they rented their houses and bought their food from their employers. Strikes were met with violence. In the city, sanitation and overcrowding were problems. But people saw it as a better alternative to sharecropping and rural life, and Birmingham grew.

Today, Birmingham is the largest city in Alabama. About one million people live in the greater metro area. Steelmaking

The Marshall Space Flight Center became NASA's first field center in 1960. Alabamans are involved in many aspects of the space program.

is still a big business, but the health care, biotech, technology, construction, engineering, and banking industries, and the University of Alabama at Birmingham, are also major employers.

Alabama's oldest city is Mobile. Founded by the French, the city became a major Southern port city during the days of cotton. Cultural diversity set it apart from many other Southern cities. Today, it continues to be a major port.

Montgomery is the capital of Alabama and its second largest city. It was once the heart of the cotton industry. Today, about 25 percent of the population is employed by government offices here.

The tourism industry is another major employer here. The state's warm climate, history, and natural beauty—including 32 miles (51 km) of beaches—make Alabama a popular tourist attraction. Visitors can also explore the lives of the state's most intriguing people, including Helen Keller, Hank Williams, and Rosa Parks. Like many Alabamans, they overcame amazing obstacles to change not only their own lives, but also history.

Huntsville is home to perhaps the most exciting industry in the state: space exploration. Here, the George C. Marshall Space Flight Center created the rockets that flew astronauts to the moon. Currently, workers at the center are testing Einstein's theory about the structure of the universe. The city is also home to Space Camp, a popular learning destination for kids.

Chapter 5

PEOPLE FROM ALABAMA: PAST AND PRESENT

Many Alabamans, some of them against all odds, have become not just good in their fields but the absolute best. For instance, of ESPN's top fifteen athletes of all time, five of them are from Alabama: Jesse Owens, Willie Mays, Joe Louis, Carl Lewis, and Hank Aaron. Here are some of the state's greats.

Athletes

A star in the Negro Leagues, Hank Aaron played for the Atlanta Braves after Major League Baseball integrated. There, he lobbied for equality in the management offices and inched closer to Babe Ruth's 714 career home runs. This made him unpopular with racist fans, who threatened him and his family. Undeterred, Aaron shattered Ruth's record with 755 career home runs and later became vice president of player development for the Braves.

The son of sharecroppers in Oakville, Alabama, Jesse Owens was a sickly child. Prone to pneumonia, he barely survived childhood. By age six, however, he was walking several miles to school with his siblings. After attending Ohio State University, Owens went on to win four gold medals at the 1936 Berlin Olympics, shattering the myth of the superior Aryan race for Hitler's Nazis.

Mia Hamm was born in 1972 in Selma, Alabama, but moved often because her dad was an Air Force pilot. After helping her team win the World Cup in 1991, and gold medals at the 1996 and 2004 Summer Olympics, she was considered one of the greatest soccer players of all time.

Musicians and Entertainers

Singer and pianist Nat King Cole, a Montgomery native, recorded hits such as "Straighten Up and Fly Right" and "Unforgettable." His daughter Natalie Cole became a popular R&B, pop, and jazz singer.

Hank Aaron comes up to bat in the 1960s. He played for the Atlanta Braves from 1954 to 1974 and shattered Babe Ruth's home run record.

Raised in Mobile, Alabama, Jimmy Buffett grew up sailing with his dad, a naval architect. Mixing country and Caribbean sounds, he became a top touring act. His hits include "Cheeseburger in Paradise" and "Margaritaville," which now both have restaurants named after them.

Best known for her role as Monica on *Friends*, Courtney Cox grew up in a wealthy family in Birmingham, Alabama. Soon after high school, she worked for the Ford Modeling Agency. Hitting her stride in the 1990s, she costarred in *Ace Ventura: Pet Detective*, *Friends*, and

Scream. Recently, she was in *Bedtime Stories.*

Writers

Harper Lee grew up in Monroeville, Alabama, where she befriended Truman Capote. Both would become renowned writers. Lee's father was a lawyer, as was Atticus Finch, the father in her famous novel, *To Kill a Mockingbird.* Lee briefly attended law school before deciding to be a writer. In addition to

Harper Lee, author of *To Kill a Mockingbird,* visits a courthouse in her hometown. The novel was published in 1961.

her acclaimed work of fiction, she helped Truman Capote with his nonfiction book *In Cold Blood.*

Having grown up in a poor family in the uplands of northeastern Alabama, Rick Bragg became a Pulitzer Prize–winning reporter for the *New York Times.* He now writes autobiographical books about life in the South.

Civil Rights Leaders

A member of the NAACP, Rosa Parks refused to give up her bus seat to a white passenger on December 1, 1955, leading to a 381-day bus boycott in Montgomery. Although she was arrested at the time, Parks later received the Congressional Medal of Honor.

Raised in Atlanta, Georgia, Martin Luther King Jr. became pastor of a Montgomery Baptist church in 1954. The following year, he led

Alabama Football

Past . . . .

In 1970, the University of Alabama Crimson Tide was an all-white football team. The 1954 verdict in the Supreme Court case *Brown v. Board of Education* required schools to integrate, and in 1963, the University of Alabama finally complied. However, the football team didn't follow suit. Although professional sports and college programs elsewhere in the nation had integrated, teams in the Southeastern Conference had for the most part clung to segregation. They even avoided playing teams with black players.

Coach Paul "Bear" Bryant watched top athletes leave the region to play on integrated teams.

All that changed in 1970. Bryant invited the University of Southern California Trojans to play the Crimson Tide at its season opener. Integrated for years, one-third of the Trojans' team was black. USC defeated Alabama 42–21.

The next year, Alabama signed its first black player, John Mitchell, who was from Mobile. With integrated teams, the Crimson Tide dominated college football throughout the 1970s.

Present . . . .

Today, Bear Bryant's legacy in terms of integration is debated. Some say he should have integrated his team earlier. They say his status would have allowed him to stand up to the state's segregationists.

Others believed Bryant when he said the racial climate in Alabama didn't allow that. They think he scheduled the USC game knowing his team would lose, thus proving to Alabamans the need to integrate in order to compete on a national level.

John Mitchell was the first black player for the Crimson Tide. He eventually became a defensive line coach for Alabama under Bryant. Now, he is a Pittsburgh Steelers defensive coach.

Today, Alabama is considered one of the best teams in the nation.

the Montgomery Bus Boycott. Afterward, he traveled the country, giving more than 2,500 speeches. He advocated peaceful protest but was arrested many times and assaulted four times. On April 4, 1968, he was shot and killed. His wife, Coretta Scott King, and children carried on his legacy.

Educators and Public Figures

The son of a slave, George Washington Carver left a Missouri plantation after the Civil War to explore the world alone. He was ten years old. In his twenties, he received a high school education, and in his thirties he graduated from college. Afterward, he went to work at the Tuskegee Institute in Alabama. There, he encouraged Southerners to replenish the soil on their farms by planting peanuts and sweet potatoes. To create a market for these, he invented three hundred product uses for peanuts and 118 for sweet potatoes, changing Southern agriculture forever.

As first principal of the Tuskegee Institute in Alabama, Booker T. Washington led the African American school in becoming a major center for education and research. His 1901 autobiography, *Up from Slavery*, describes his life before and after the Civil War.

Born in 1880 in Tuscumbia, Alabama, Helen Keller lost her hearing and sight at nineteen months due to illness. At age seven, she learned to read, write, and speak with the help of tutor, Anne Sullivan. Keller graduated from college and wrote an autobiography, *The Story of My Life*, on which a movie, *The Miracle Worker*, was based.

Political and Military Figures

Condoleezza Rice was born in Birmingham to a Presbyterian minister and a music teacher. After high school, she pursued a doctorate in

Benjamin O. Davis, *(left)* and Edward C. Gleed, *(right)* stand next to an airplane at a base in Rametti, Italy. They were two of the 994 African American Tuskegee Airmen trained in Alabama.

political science. In the mid-1980s, she became an international affairs fellow in Washington, D.C. In 2004, she was appointed secretary of state, an office she held until the end of the Bush administration.

Trained at the Tuskegee Army Airfield in Alabama during World War II, the 994 Tuskegee Airmen were America's first black military airmen. They faced racism in the military but also became war heroes.

Timeline

1702	Mobile, Alabama's oldest city, is founded as the capital of French Louisiana.
1803	The United States claims Mobile as part of the Louisiana Purchase.
1812	After the War of 1812, the Creeks cede 40,000 square miles (64,373 km) of their land to the U.S. government.
1819	Alabama becomes America's twenty-second state.
1836–1838	Most Native Americans are forced out of Alabama.
1860	Abraham Lincoln is elected president; some white Southerners are worried he will abolish slavery.
1861	Alabama secedes from the Union. Montgomery becomes the capital of the Confederate States of America. On April 12, the American Civil War begins.
1865	Almost exactly four years later, the Confederate Army surrenders to the Union Army, ending the Civil War.
1901	A new state constitution denies the right to vote to blacks and poor whites.
1910	The Great Migration, during which blacks left the South for industrial jobs in the North, begins.
1948	The Dixiecrats, a segregationist political party, form and hold their first convention in Birmingham.
1955–1956	The Montgomery Bus Boycott marks the beginning of the civil rights movement.
1964	The Civil Rights Act is passed.
1965	The Selma to Montgomery March brings attention to voting rights.
1994	Heather Whitestone McCallum of Alabama becomes the first Miss America with a disability. She is deaf.
2002	Birmingham native Vonetta Flowers becomes the first African American to win a gold medal in the Winter Olympics.
2005	Hurricane Katrina devastates the Gulf Coast in Alabama and other states.
2007	*To Kill a Mockingbird* author Harper Lee is awarded the Congressional Medal of Freedom.

Alabama at a Glance

State motto	"We dare defend our rights"
State capital	Montgomery
State flower	Camellia
State bird	Yellowhammer
State tree	Southern longleaf pine
Year of statehood	December 14, 1819 (the twenty-second state)
State nickname	Heart of Dixie, the Cotton State, the Yellowhammer State
Total area and U.S. rank	52,423 square miles (83,685 km); thirtieth largest state
Population	4,447,100
Length of coastline	32 miles (51 km)
Highest elevation	2,407 feet (733 m), at Cheaha Mountain
Lowest elevation	Sea level, where Alabama meets the Gulf of Mexico
Major rivers	Tombigbee River, Alabama River, Tennessee River, Chattahoochee River
Major lakes	Guntersville Lake, Wilson Lake, Martin Lake, West Point Lake, Lewis Smith Lake

State Flag

State Seal

Hottest temperature recorded	112°F (44°C), on September 5, 1925
Coldest temperature recorded	-27°F (-32°C), on January 30, 1966
Origin of state name	French settlers called a tribe of native people Alibamons after the Choctaw word for "thicket clearers"
Chief agricultural products	Poultry and eggs, cattle, greenhouse and nursery products, cotton
Major industries	Service industries, such as health care and engineering; manufacturing of chemicals, paper products, metals, and heavy machinery; space industry

Yellowhammer

Camellia

Appalachians The mountain range spanning from Quebec to Northern Alabama.

Black Belt A region in central Alabama formerly known for its cotton plantations. First named for its black soil, it has come to refer to the predominantly African American population living there.

boll weevil A small beetle that decimated Alabama's cotton crops beginning in 1915, forcing farmers to turn to alternative plants, such as the peanut.

civil rights movement The collective efforts to end segregation, gain voting rights, and attain equal opportunities for African Americans.

Civil War A war fought from 1861 to 1865 between the (Northern) Union and the (Southern) Confederacy. It resulted in the abolishment of slavery.

coastal plains The land in Alabama that begins at the base of the Appalachian Mountains and continues to the Gulf Coast.

Confederacy Alliance of the eleven Southern states that seceded from the Union in 1860 and 1861. They included Alabama, Arkansas, Florida, Georgia, Louisiana, Mississippi, North Carolina, South Carolina, Tennessee, Texas, and Virginia.

cotton A shrubby plant native to the tropics and now grown in the American South. The soft white fibers in its seedpods are used to make clothing.

Deep South U.S. states considered the most rooted in Southern tradition, including Georgia, Alabama, Mississippi, and Louisiana.

Dixie A nickname for the Southern states of the United States, derived from the name of a character in a minstrel play.

Dixiecrats A political party that broke off from the Democrats in protest of Harry Truman's civil rights platform.

Great Migration The movement of several African Americans from Southern to Northern states beginning around 1910.

secession The withdrawal of the eleven Confederate states from the United States.

slavery The act of forcing people to work without pay.

Union In the Civil War, the Northern troops and states.

Alabama Music Hall of Fame

P.O. Box 740405

Tuscumbia, AL 35674

(800) 239-2643

E-mail: info@alamhof.org

Web site: http://www.alamhof.org

This state-sponsored museum honors music greats such as Lionel Richie, Hank Williams, and Jimmy Buffett.

Alabama Sports Hall of Fame

2150 Richard Arrington Jr. Boulevard N

Birmingham, AL 35203

(205) 323-6665

E-mail: info@ashof.org

Web site: http://www.ashof.org

This museum celebrates Alabama's best athletes.

Birmingham Civil Rights Institute

520 16th Street

Birmingham, AL 35203

(866) 328-9696

Web site: http://www.bcri.org

This museum and institute documents the civil rights movement in Birmingham. It also provides a forum on civil rights throughout the world.

Landmark Park

P.O. Box 6362

Dothan, AL 36302

(334) 794-3452

Web site: http://www.landmarkpark.com

Landmark Park is Alabama's official agricultural museum.

Tuskegee University

1200 West Montgomery Road

Tuskegee, AL 36088

(334) 727-8011

Web site: http://www.tuskegee.edu

This is a historically African American university in Alabama. Its Web site also provides historical resources.

University of Alabama

203 Student Services Center

Box 870132

Tuscaloosa, AL 35487

(205) 348-6010

Web site: http://www.ua.edu

UA is Alabama's oldest public university.

U.S. Space & Rocket Center

One Tranquility Base

Huntsville, AL 35805

(800) 63-SPACE (637-7223)

Web site: http://www.spacecamp.com/museum

Home of Space Camp, this museum shows the history of space exploration and the role Huntsville, Alabama, played in the space race.

Web Sites

Due to the changing nature of Internet links, Rosen Publishing has developed an online list of Web sites related to the subject of this book. This site is updated regularly. Please use this link to access the list:

http://www.rosenlinks.com/uspp/alpp

FOR FURTHER READING

Barra, Allen. *The Last Coach: A Life of Paul "Bear" Bryant.* New York, NY: W.W. Norton, 2006.

Brinkley, Douglas. *Rosa Parks: A Life.* New York, NY: Penguin, 2005.

Capote, Truman. *A Christmas Memory.* New York, NY: Knopf Books for Young Readers, 2006.

Feeney, Kathy. *Alabama* (From Sea to Shining Sea). Chicago: IL: Children's Press, 2008.

Fleischman, John. *Black and White Airmen: Their True History.* Boston, MA: Houghton Mifflin, 2007.

Fradin, Dennis. *The Montgomery Bus Boycott* (Turning Points in U.S. History). New York, NY: Benchmark Books, 2009.

Greenburg, David. *A Tugging String: A Novel About Growing Up During the Civil Rights Era.* New York, NY: Dutton Juvenile, 2008.

Lee, Harper. *To Kill a Mockingbird.* New York, NY: Harper Perennial, 2006.

Keller, Helen. *The Story of My Life.* New York, NY: Modern Library, 2004.

Key, Watt. *Alabama Moon.* New York, NY: Square Fish, 2008.

Madden, Kerry. *Harper Lee* (Up Close). New York, NY: Viking Juvenile, 2009.

Norrell, Robert J. *Up from History: The Life of Booker T. Washington.* Cambridge, MA: Belknap Press, 2009.

Schapp, Jeremy. *Triumph: The Untold Story of Jesse Owens and Hitler's Olympics.* Boston, MA: Houghton Mifflin, 2008.

Shirley, David, and Joyce Hart. *Alabama* (Celebrate the States). Tarrytown, NY: Marshall Cavendish Children's Books, 2009.

Sullivan, George. *Knockout! A Photobiography of Boxer Joe Louis.* Des Moines, IA: National Geographic Children's Books, 2008.

BIBLIOGRAPHY

Al.com. "Alabamania." Retrieved March 22, 2009 (http://www.al.com/alabamiana).

Alabama.gov. Retrieved February 20, 2009 (http://www.alabama.gov/portal/index.jsp).

Alabama Peanut Producers Association. "Peanut Facts." Retrieved February 18, 2009 (http://www.alpeanuts.com/consumer_interest/articles.phtml?articleID=102).

Alabama Unified Justice System Structure. February 12, 2008. Retrieved March 9, 2009 (http://www.alacourt.gov/CourtStructure.aspx).

American Peanut Council. "Teacher's Guide." Retrieved February 18, 2009 (http://www.alpeanuts.com/consumer_interest/PDFs/3-5/teachersguide.pdf).

Bernhard, Blythe. "The Game That Changed the World." *Orange County Register*, September 13, 2007. Retrieved March 29, 2009 (http://www.ocregister.com/articles/danehe-usc-alabama-1845545-football-team).

Biography.com. "Booker T. Washington." Retrieved March 25, 2009 (http://www.biography.com/search/article.do?id=9524663).

Biography.com. "George Washington Carver." Retrieved March 25, 2009 (http://www.biography.com/search/article.do?id=9240299).

Biography.com. "Helen Keller." Retrieved March 25, 2009 (http://www.biography.com/search/article.do?id=9361967).

Biography.com. "Mia Hamm." Retrieved March 25, 2009 (http://www.biography.com/search/article.do?id=16472547).

Birmingham News. "Alabama's Public Schools Meet the National Average, but There are Troubling Signs for the Future." January 10, 2009. Retrieved March 15, 2009 (http://www.al.com/opinion/birminghamnews/editorials.ssf?/base/opinion/1231578922295720.xml&coll=2).

Cole, Bruce. "Civility in a Democracy: A Conversation with Miss Manners." *Humanities* 26, no. 1 (January/February 2005). Retrieved Feb. 30, 2009 (http://www.neh.gov/news/humanities/2005-01/civility.html).

Country Music Television. "Jimmy Buffett." Cmt.com. Retrieved March 20, 2009 (http://www.cmt.com/artists/az/buffett_jimmy/bio.jhtml).

Encyclopedia of Alabama. Retrieved February 18, 20, 23, 24, 26; March 2, 3, 6, 9, 12, 23, 26 (http://encyclopediaofalabama.org/face/Article.jsp?id=h-1387).

FindLaw. "Federal vs. State Courts: Key Differences." Retrieved March 9, 2009 (http://public.findlaw.com/library/legal-system/fcourts-vs-scourts.html).

Halberstam, David. "Just a Coach, Not a Leader." ESPN.com. Retrieved March 29, 2009. (http://espn.go.com/page2/s/halberstam/021220.html).

Hume, Lucille Bayon. "Bridging the Great Culinary Divide." *Country Roads*, May 2007. Retrieved March 12, 2009 (http://www.countryroadsmagazine.com/ViewArticle. php?articleid = 126).

Internet Movie Database. "Courteney Cox." Imdb.com. Retrieved March 15, 2009 (http://www.imdb.com/name/nm0001073).

Jesse Owens Museum. "Biography." Retrieved March 20, 2009 (http://www.jesseowens-museum.org/index.cfm?fuseaction = bio_1936).

Johnson, Griff. "The Decline of Pitcher Plant Bogs of Alabama." *Outdoor Alabama*. Retrieved February 23, 2009 (http://www.outdooralabama.com/watchable-wildlife/ Watchablearticles/pitcherplant.cfm).

MCADCafe. "Alabama Manufacturing: Plants Up 54; Jobs Down 1.1 Percent." April 19, 2006. Retrieved March 3, 2009 (http://www10.mcadcafe.com/nbc/articles/view_ article.php?articleid = 262669).

Moody, Bradley. "The Alabama Executive Branch: Responsibility in Search of Power." Alabama University Web site (Retrieved February 20, 2009. http://sciences.aum. edu/popa/execbran.htm).

Nat King Cole Society. "Biography." Retrieved March 21, 2009 (http://www.nat-king-cole. org/biography.html).

Nelson, David. "The Origins of Alabama's Black Belt Prairies." *Outdoor Alabama*. Retrieved February 23, 2009 (http://www.outdooralabama.com/watchablewildlife/ Watchablearticles/prairies.cfm).

Netstate. "Alabama." Netstate.com. Retrieved March 25, 2009 (http://www.netstate.com/ states/geography/al_geography.htm).

NobelPrize.org. "Biography." Retrieved March 23, 2009 (http://nobelprize.org/nobel_ prizes/peace/laureates/1964/king-bio.html).

NPR. "Lionel Richie: The Key to Peace in the Middle East." *Day to Day*, December 4, 2006. Retrieved March 1, 2009 (http://www.npr.org/templates/story/story. php?storyId = 6576395).

PBS. "The Civil War and Emancipation." *Africans in America*. Retrieved March 1, 2009 (http://www.pbs.org/wgbh/aia/part4/4p2967.html).

Puma, Mike. "Bear Bryant: 'Simply the Best There Ever Was.'" ESPN.com. Retrieved March 29, 2009 (http://espn.go.com/classic/biography/s/Bryant_ Bear.html).

Rosa and Raymond Parks Institute for Self Development. "Rosa Louise Parks Biography." Retrieved March 23, 2009 (http://www.rosaparks.org/bio.html).

Schwartz, Larry. "Owens Pierced a Myth." ESPN.com. Retrieved May 23, 2009 (http://espn.go.com/sportscentury/features/00016393.html).

Southern Foodways Alliance. "A Southern Food Primer." Retrieved March 12, 2009 (http://www.southernfoodways.com/images/SouthernFoodPrimer.pdf).

Steelers.com. "John Mitchell." Retrieved March 29, 2009 (http://news.steelers.com/team/coach/49264).

Teacher's Domain. "Segregated Schooling in Alabama." Retrieved March 15, 2009 (http://www.teachersdomain.org/resource/iml04.soc.ush.civil.alaseg).

Todd, Bruce. "Salt Springs." *Outdoor Alabama*. Retrieved February 23, 2009 (http://www.outdooralabama.com/watchable-wildlife/Watchablearticles/saltsprings.cfm).

Tuskegee Airmen, Inc. "Who Were the Tuskegee Airmen?" Retrieved March 24, 2009 (http://tuskegeeairmen.org/Tuskegee_Airmen_History.html).

USDA. "Trade and Agriculture: What's at Stake for Alabama?" September 2008. Retrieved February 18, 2009 (http://www.fas.usda.gov/info/factsheets/wto/states/al.pdf).

USGS. "Southern Appalachian Mountains: Brief Geologic History." Retrieved February 26, 2009 (http://vulcan.wr.usgs.gov/LivingWith/VolcanicPast/Places/volcanic_past_appalachians.html).

York, Jake Adam. "The Southern Barbeque Trail." Southern Foodways Alliance. Retrieved March 12, 2009 (http://www.southernbbqtrail.com/introduction.shtml).

Yuhasz, Dennis. "Hank Aaron Biography." 755HomeRuns.com (Baseball Almanac). Retrieved March 19, 2009 (http://www.755homeruns.com/biography.shtml).

INDEX

About the Author

A former newspaper reporter, Bridget Heos is now the author of six children's nonfiction books. She enjoys writing about states because, even though they are united, each has a unique history and culture. Her favorite authors are from the South, and she enjoyed researching Southern history for this book. She lives in Kansas City, Missouri, with her husband and three sons.

Photo Credits

Cover (top, left), pp. 1, 13, 27, 36 Library of Congress Prints and Photographs Division; cover (top, right) © www.istockphoto.com/Edward Todd; cover (bottom) © 2009 U.S. Space & Rocket Center; pp, 3, 6, 12, 19, 21, 25, 31, 37, 39 Wikipedia; p. 4 © GeoAtlas; p. 7 © Joe Miller; p. 11 Andy Sacks/Stone/Getty Images; p. 15 Ben Shahn/Private Collection © DACS/Peter Newark Western Americana/ Bridgeman Art Library; p. 17 © AP Images; p. 20 © Phillip Tucker; p. 23 © Donnie Shackleford; p. 26 Hulton Archive/Getty Images; p. 29 NASA Marshall Space Flight Center; p. 32 Focus on Sport/Getty Images; p. 33 Donald Uhrbrock/ Time & Life Pictures/Getty Images; p. 38 (right) Courtesy of Robesus, Inc.

Designer: Les Kanturek; Editor: Bethany Bryan;
Photo Researcher: Amy Feinberg

THIR-
TEEN   BONDS PAYABLE, LEASES, AND OTHER LIABILITIES   440

PREFACE

This second edition of *Financial Accounting* is designed as a one-semester introduction to accounting. It is suitable for courses of three to four semester-hours' credit; or in the case of schools on the quarter system, for courses of four to six quarter-hours' credit.

The reduction in length from the conventional introductory accounting text has been accomplished by concentrating upon financial accounting as a unified body of knowledge. We have emphasized the responsibility of the modern corporation to do an adequate job of financial reporting to investors and others outside the corporate entity. However, management's use of accounting data is by no means neglected.

A new edition provides authors with an opportunity to add new material, to condense the coverage of topics that have declined in relative importance, to reorganize portions of the book to improve instructional efficiency, and to refine and polish the treatment of basic subject matter. We have tried to do all these things in this second edition.

New features of this edition

Among the many new features of this edition are *business decision problems*, increased use of *demonstration problems*, an appendix of published financial statements of well-known corporations, and the integration into the text discussion of pronouncements by the Accounting Principles Board and the Securities and Exchange Commission.

Many of the new topics discussed are issues that appear daily in national news headlines; as for example, the impact of inflation upon accounting standards, inventory profits, and the "quality of earnings."

Business decision problems

A *business decision problem* has been designed for each of the 17 chapters. These problems are realistic, imaginative, and provocative.

They require the student to arrive at a business decision or to make a recommendation to management. They are not procedural.

Demonstration problems

A *demonstration problem immediately followed by a complete solution* appears at the end of every chapter. By studying the demonstration problems and their solutions, students will strengthen their ability to apply theoretical concepts to business situations. Also, students will rapidly add to their skill in organizing the various elements of a problem into a useful format.

Abundance of problem material

In addition to a demonstration problem and solution at the end of every chapter, and the business decision problem, the reader will find a wealth of problem material: review questions, exercises, and problems of varying length and difficulty. A number of long problems have been shortened or eliminated, and emphasis has been placed on short- and medium-length problems. All problems have been thoroughly class-tested.

New or extensively revised chapters

As in the first edition, the accounting cycle is presented in the first four chapters. Chapter 6 ("Accounting Systems: Manual and EDP") has an expanded discussion of EDP accounting systems in simple, understandable terms. Emphasis is placed on practical EDP applications and the internal controls necessary to create a reliable computer-oriented information system. A new section deals with computer service centers and time-sharing.

Chapter 8 ("Corporations: Earnings and Dividends") includes a section on reporting the results of operations completely rewritten to reflect the concepts of *APB Opinion No. 30.* Expanded coverage is given to forms of income statements and explanatory notes accompanying the financial statements. New, more extensive treatment of earnings per share correlated with *APB Opinion No. 15* is provided, and new sections are included on the reporting and disclosure practices of corporations.

In Chapter 10, receivables and payables are treated as a single unit for efficiency and to illustrate the present-value concepts set forth in *APB Opinion No. 21.*

Chapter 11 ("Inventories") has been updated to reflect *Accounting Research Study No. 13,* "The Accounting Basis of Inventories," and to discuss the impact of inventory valuation methods on the "quality of earnings." In Chapter 12, the discussion of the problem of depreciation and asset replacement has been expanded in the context of continued inflation. The discussions of research and development costs and goodwill have been expanded and reflect the impact of *ARS No. 14,* "Accounting for Research and Development Expenditures," and *APB Opinion No. 17.*

Included in Chapter 13 ("Bonds Payable, Leases, and Other Liabilities") are major new sections on lease obligations and pension plans. Chapter 14 ("Accounting Principles") contains a short conceptual discussion of business combinations which replaces the detailed full-chapter presentation in the previous edition. A new section presents a thorough but introductory-level coverage of adjusting financial statements to reflect changes in the general price level. The organization of the Financial Accounting Standards Board is discussed along with reference to important controversial issues under consideration by the Board.

Chapter 15 ("Statement of Changes in Financial Position: Cash Flows") is a completely new chapter incorporating provisions of *APB Opinion No. 19,* and a "direct" approach to measuring sources and uses of working capital.

Chapter 16 ("Analysis of Financial Statements") has been significantly revised to include discussion of the quality of earnings and quality of assets. The impact of inflation on financial statements is also considered. A summary of key ratios and their relevance concludes the chapter.

In Chapter 17 ("Income Taxes and Business Decisions"), the discussion of tax planning has been expanded. A new section is devoted to interperiod and intraperiod income tax allocation. Increased attention is given to the impact of income taxes on business decisions.

Supplementary materials

A full assortment of supplementary materials accompanies this text. These materials include:

1. A set of four *Achievement Tests* and a *Comprehensive Examination.* Each test covers four or five chapters; the *Comprehensive Examination* covers the entire text, and may be used as a final examination.

2. A *Study Guide.* Written by the authors of the textbook, this *Study Guide* enables the student to measure his progress by immediate feedback. The *Study Guide* includes an outline of the most important points in each chapter, an abundance of objective questions, and several short exercises for each chapter. In the back of the *Study Guide* are answers to questions and solutions to exercises to help the student evaluate his understanding of the subject. The *Study Guide* will also be useful in classroom discussions and for review by students before examinations.

3. *Working Papers.* A package of *partially filled-in working papers* for the problem material is published separately from the text. On these work sheets, the problem headings and some preliminary data have been entered to save students much of the mechanical pencil-pushing inherent in problem assignments.

4. *Practice Set.* A practice set, in which the model firm is a corporation, is designed for use after covering the first six chapters of the book. Also available is a computer-based practice set, *Computers and the Accounting Process,* by Robert F. Meigs. It uses a single proprietorship as a model, and is suitable for use after Chapters 1 through 7 have been covered.

5. *Check List of Key Figures.* This list is available in quantity to instructors who wish to distribute key figures to students. The purpose of the check list is to aid students in verifying their problem solutions and in discovering their own errors.

6. *Transparencies of Problem Solutions.* A visual aid prepared by the publisher for the instructor who wishes to display in a classroom the complete solutions to most problems.

In the development of problem material for this book, special attention has been given to the inclusion of problems of varying length and difficulty. By referring to the time estimates, difficulty ratings, and problem descriptions in the *Solutions Manual,* the instructor can choose problems that best fit the level, scope, and emphasis of the course he is offering.

Contributions by others

We want to express our sincere thanks to the many users of the preceding edition who offered helpful suggestions for this revision.

Especially helpful was the advice received from James R. Morton, The University of Alabama; Vernon Kam, California State University, Hayward; Mohamed E. Moustafa, California State University, Long Beach; Donald R. Simons, Marquette University; Anita I. Tyra, Bellevue Community College; William E. Kimball, Eastern Michigan University; C. W. Lee, California State College, Dominguez Hill; Theodore J. Mock, University of Southern California; James W. Pratt, University of Houston; Robert W. Hill, California State University, Hayward; Richard Savich, University of Southern California; and Farhad Simiar, California State University, Northridge.

The assistance of Judi Takagaki, Edie Trimble, Larry Wolfe, Martin Kubota, Richard Fell, and June Jensen was most helpful in preparation of the manuscript.

We acknowledge with appreciation permission from the American Institute of Certified Public Accountants to quote from many of its pronouncements.

WALTER B. MEIGS
A. N. MOSICH
ROBERT F. MEIGS

ONE

ACCOUNTING THE BASIS FOR BUSINESS DECISIONS

Accounting has often been called the "language of business." People in the business world—owners, managers, bankers, stockbrokers, attorneys, engineers, investors—use accounting terms and concepts to describe the events that make up the day-to-day existence of every business, large or small. Since a language is a man-made means of communication, it is natural that languages should change to meet the changing needs of society. Accounting, too, is a man-made art, one in which changes and improvements are continually being made in the process of communicating business information.

We live in an era of accountability. Although accounting has made its most dramatic progress in the field of business, the accounting function is vital to every unit of our society. The individual must account for his income. The federal government, the states, the cities, the school districts, all must use accounting as a basis for controlling their resources and measuring their accomplishments. Accounting is equally essential to the successful operation of a university, a fraternity, a church, or a hospital.

In every election the voters must make decisions at the ballot box on issues involving accounting concepts; therefore, some knowledge of accounting is needed by every citizen if he is to act intelligently in meeting the challenges of our society. Finding solutions to such problems as inflation, pollution, poverty, and crime will require the imaginative use of accounting concepts in areas beyond traditional boundaries.

THE PURPOSE AND NATURE OF ACCOUNTING

The underlying purpose of accounting is to provide financial information about any economic entity. In this book the economic entity which
we shall be concentrating upon is a business enterprise. The financial
information provided by an accounting system is needed by managerial
decision makers to help them plan and control the activities of the
economic entity. Financial information is also needed by *outsiders*—
owners, creditors, investors, the government, and the public—who
have supplied money to the business or who have some other interest
that will be served by information about its financial position and
operating results.

A system for creating accounting information

In order to provide up-to-date financial information about a business,
it is necessary to create a systematic record of the daily business
activity, in terms of money. For example, goods and services are
purchased and sold, credit is extended to customers, debts are incurred, and cash is received and paid out. These *transactions* are
typical of business events which can be expressed *in monetary terms,*
and must be entered in accounting records. The *recording* process may
be performed in many ways: that is, by writing with pen or pencil, by
printing with mechanical or electronic equipment, or by punching holes
or making magnetic impressions on cards or tape.

   Of course, not all business events can be measured and described
in monetary terms. Therefore, we do not show in the accounting
records the appointment of a new chief executive or the signing of
a labor contract, except as these happenings in turn affect future
business transactions.

   In addition to compiling a narrative record of events as they occur,
we *classify* various transactions and events into related groups or
categories. Classification enables us to reduce a mass of detail into
compact and usable form. For example, grouping all transactions in
which cash is received or paid out is a logical step in developing useful
information about the cash position of a business enterprise.

   To create accounting information in a form which will be useful to
the people who use the information, we *summarize* the classified information into financial reports, called *financial statements.* These financial statements are concise, perhaps only two or three pages for a large
business. They summarize the business transactions of a specific time
period such as a month or a year. Financial statements show the
financial position of the business at the time of the report and the
operating results by which it arrived at this position.

   These three steps we have described—recording, classifying, and
summarizing—are the means of creating accounting information. Thus
one part of accounting is a system for creating financial information.

USING ACCOUNTING INFORMATION Accounting extends beyond the process of *creating* records and reports. The ultimate objective of accounting is the *use* of this information, its analysis and interpretation. The accountant is always concerned with the significance of the figures he has produced. He looks for meaningful relationships between events and financial results; he studies the effect of various alternatives; and he searches for significant trends that may throw some light on what may happen in the future.

Interpretation and analysis are not the sole province of the accountant. If managers, investors, and creditors are to make effective use of accounting information, they too must have some understanding of how the figures were put together and what they mean. An important part of this understanding is to recognize clearly the limitations of accounting information. A business manager, an investor, or a creditor who lacks training in accounting may fail to appreciate the extent to which accounting information is based upon estimates rather than upon precisely accurate measurements.

THE DISTINCTION BETWEEN ACCOUNTING AND BOOKKEEPING Persons with little knowledge of accounting may also fail to understand the difference between accounting and bookkeeping. *Bookkeeping* refers to the mechanical aspects of accounting, such as recording and classifying transactions. This is only a small part of the field of accounting, and probably the simplest part. *Accounting* also involves much *analytical* work, which is far more complex than bookkeeping. For example, the design of accounting systems; preparation of budgets, income tax services, audits, computer applications to accounting processes; and interpretation of accounting information as an aid to making business decisions are all areas of accounting which are beyond the scope of bookkeeping.

The work of accountants

Accountants tend to specialize in a given subarea of the discipline just as do attorneys and members of other professions. In terms of career opportunities, the field of accounting may be divided into three broad areas: (1) the public accounting profession, (2) private accounting, and (3) governmental accounting.

Public accounting

Certified public accountants are independent professional persons, comparable to attorneys or physicians, who offer accounting services to clients for a fee. The *CPA certificate* is a license to practice granted by the state on the basis of a rigorous examination and evidence of practical experience. All states require that candidates pass an examination prepared and administered on a national basis twice each year by the American Institute of Certified Public Accountants. Requirements as to education and practical experience differ somewhat among the various states.

AUDITING   The principal function of a CPA is auditing. To perform an audit, the certified public accountant makes a careful review of the accounting system and gathers evidence both from within the business and from outside sources. This evidence enables him to issue a report expressing his professional opinion as to the fairness and reliability of the financial statements. Persons outside the business, such as bankers and investors who rely upon financial statements for information, attach great importance to the annual *audit report* by the CPA. The *independent* status of the CPA retained to make an annual audit is just as important as his technical competence in assuring outsiders that the financial statements prepared by management disclose all relevant information and provide a fair picture of the company's financial position and operating results.

TAX SERVICES   An important element of decision making by business executives is consideration of the income tax consequences of each alternative course of action. The CPA is often called upon for "tax planning," which will show how a future transaction such as the acquisition of new equipment may be arranged in a manner that will hold income taxes to a minimum amount. The CPA is also frequently retained to prepare the federal and state income tax returns. To render tax services, the CPA must have extensive knowledge of tax laws, regulations and court decisions, as well as a thorough knowledge of accounting.

MANAGEMENT ADVISORY SERVICES   Auditing and income tax work have been the traditional areas of expertise for CPA firms, but the field of management advisory services has recently become a rapidly growing new area. When CPA firms during the course of an audit discovered problems in a client's business, it was natural for them to make suggestions for corrective action. In response, the client often engaged the CPA to make a thorough investigation of the problem and to recommend new policies and procedures needed for a solution.

Public accounting firms gradually found themselves becoming more involved in management consulting work. Although this work often concerned accounting and financial matters, sometimes it dealt with organizational structure, statistical research, and a wide variety of problems not closely related to accounting. In recent years many CPA firms have created separate management advisory service departments which are staffed with mathematicians, industrial engineers, and other specialists as well as accountants. The experience, reputation, and independence of the CPA firms have placed them in an advantageous position to render advisory services to management over a broad range of administrative and operating problems. For example, these services might include study of the desirability of a merger with another company, the creation of a pension plan for employees, or the researching of a foreign market for the company's products.

Private accounting

In contrast to the CPA in public practice who serves many clients, an accountant in private industry is employed by a single enterprise. The chief accounting officer of a medium-sized or large business is usually called the *controller,* in recognition of the fact that one of the primary uses of accounting data is to aid in controlling business operations. The controller manages the work of the accounting staff. He is also a part of the management team charged with the task of running the business, setting its objectives, and seeing that these objectives are met.

The accountants in a private business, large or small, must record transactions and prepare periodic financial statements from accounting records. Within this area of general accounting, or in addition to it, a number of specialized phases of accounting have developed. Among the more important of these are:

DESIGN OF ACCOUNTING SYSTEMS   Although the same basic accounting principles are applicable to all types of businesses, each enterprise requires an individually tailored *financial information system.* This system includes accounting forms, records, instruction manuals, flow charts, computer programs, and reports to fit the particular needs of the business. Designing an accounting system and putting it into operation are thus specialized phases of accounting. With the advent of electronic data processing equipment, the problems that arise in creating an effective financial information system have become increasingly complex. However, computers compile information that would be too costly to gather by hand methods and also increase the speed with which reports can be made available to management.

COST ACCOUNTING   Knowing the cost of a particular product, a manufacturing process, or any business operation is vital to the efficient management of that business. The phase of accounting particularly concerned with collecting and interpreting cost data has come to be known as *cost accounting.* Determining the cost of anything is not as simple as it appears at first glance, because the term *cost* has many meanings and different kinds of costs are useful for different purposes.

BUDGETING   A budget is a plan of financial operations for some future period, expressed in monetary terms. By using a budget, management is able to make comparisons between *planned operations* and the *actual results achieved.* A budget is thus an attempt to preview operating results before the actual transactions have taken place. A budget is a particularly valuable tool because it provides each division of the business with a specific goal and because it gives management a means of measuring the efficiency of performance throughout the company.

TAX ACCOUNTING As income tax rates have gone up and the determination of taxable income has become more complex, both internal accountants and independent public accountants have devoted more time to the problems of taxation. Tax accounting includes planning business operations in order to minimize the impact of taxes, as well as computing taxable income and preparing tax returns. The term *tax avoidance* includes all legal means of minimizing tax payments; the term *tax evasion* indicates illegal actions. Business managers have the responsibility of operating a business profitably and should therefore have an obligation to plan operations with the objective of *avoiding* income taxes. Although many companies rely largely on CPA firms for tax planning and the preparation of tax returns, larger companies also maintain their own tax departments.

INTERNAL AUDITING Most large corporations maintain staffs of internal auditors with the responsibility of seeing that company policies and established procedures are being followed consistently in all divisions of the corporation. The internal auditor, in contrast to the independent or external auditor, is not responsible for determining the overall fairness of the company's annual financial statements.

MANAGEMENT ACCOUNTING We have already discussed the way business concerns sometimes call upon CPA firms to render management advisory services. In larger companies, however, we can also recognize *management accounting* as a specialized field of work by the company's own accounting staff. First, we need to emphasize that the accounting system provides information for both external and internal use. The external reporting function of the accounting system has already been touched upon in our discussion of audits of annual financial statements by CPA firms. The internal reporting function of an accounting system gives managers information needed in planning and controlling day-to-day operations; it also gives managers information needed for long-range planning and for major decisions such as the introduction of a new product or the closing of an older plant.

Management accounting utilizes the techniques of both cost accounting and budgeting to achieve its goal of helping executives formulate both short-range and long-range plans, to measure success in carrying out these plans, to identify problems requiring executive attention, and to choose among the alternative methods of attaining company objectives. At every organizational level of a company, specific problems arise for which accounting information is needed to help define the problem, identify alternative courses of action, and make a choice among these alternatives.

Governmental accounting

Government officials rely on financial information to help them direct the affairs of their agencies just as do the executives of private corporations. Many governmental accounting problems are similar to those applicable to private industry. In other respects, however, accounting for governmental affairs requires a somewhat different approach because the objective of earning a profit is absent from public affairs. Universities, hospitals, churches, and other nonprofit institutions also follow a pattern of accounting that is similar to governmental accounting.

INTERNAL REVENUE SERVICE   One governmental agency which performs extensive accounting work is the Internal Revenue Service (IRS). The IRS handles the millions of income tax returns filed by individuals and corporations, and frequently performs auditing functions relating to these income tax returns and the accounting records on which they are based. Also, the IRS has been called upon to administer certain temporary economic controls, such as wage and price controls. These temporary controls have involved extensive and complex financial reporting by businesses, which is then reviewed and audited by the IRS.

SECURITIES AND EXCHANGE COMMISSION   Another governmental agency greatly involved in accounting is the Securities and Exchange Commission (SEC). The SEC reviews the financial statements of corporations which offer securities for sale to the public. Also, the SEC has the legal power to require specific accounting methods and standards of financial disclosure for these companies.

Other governmental agencies employ accountants to prepare budgets and to audit the accounting records of various governmental departments and of private businesses which hold government contracts. Every agency of government at every level (federal, state, and local) must have accountants to carry out its responsibilities.

Two primary business objectives

The management of every business must keep foremost in its thinking two primary objectives. The first is to earn a profit. The second is to have on hand sufficient funds to pay debts as they fall due. Profits and solvency are of course not the only objectives of businessmen. There are many others, such as providing jobs for people, providing protection of the environment, creating new and improved products, providing more goods and services at a lower cost. It is clear, however, that a business cannot hope to accomplish these objectives unless it meets the two basic tests of survival—operating profitably and staying solvent.

A business is a collection of resources invested by an individual or group of individuals, who hope that the investment will increase in value. Investment in any given business, however, is only one of a number of alternative investments available. If a business does not earn as great a profit as might be obtained from alternative investments, its owners will be well-advised to sell or terminate the business and invest elsewhere. A firm that continually operates at a loss will quickly exhaust its resources and be forced out of existence. Therefore, in order to operate successfully and to survive, the owners or managers of an enterprise must direct the business in such a way that it will earn a satisfactory profit.

Business organizations that have sufficient cash to pay their debts promptly are said to be *solvent.* In contrast, a firm that finds itself unable to meet its obligations as they fall due is called *insolvent.* Solvency must be ranked as a primary objective of any enterprise, since a business that is insolvent may be forced by its creditors to close its doors and end its existence.

Accounting as the basis for management decisions

How does a business executive know whether his company is earning profits or incurring losses? How does he know whether the company is solvent or insolvent and whether it will probably be solvent, say, a month from today? The answer to both these questions in one word is *accounting.* Not only is accounting the process by which the profitability and solvency of a company can be measured but it also provides information needed as a basis for making business decisions that will enable management to guide the company on a profitable and solvent course.

Stated simply, managing a business is a matter of deciding what should be done, seeing to it that the means are available, and getting people employed in the business to do it. At every step in this process management is faced with alternatives, and every decision to do something or to refrain from doing something involves a choice. Successful managers must make the right choice when ''the chips are down.'' In most cases the probability that a good decision will be made depends on the amount and validity of the information that the manager has about the alternatives and their consequences. It is seldom that all the information needed is either available or obtainable. Often a crystal ball in good working order would be helpful. As a practical matter, however, information which flows from the accounting records, or which can be developed by special analysis of accounting data, constitutes the basis on which a wide variety of business decisions should be made. For specific examples of these decisions, consider the following questions.

What price should the firm set on its products? If production is increased, what effect will this have on the cost of each unit produced? Will it be necessary to borrow from the bank? How much will costs increase if a pension plan is established for employees? Is it more profitable to produce and sell product A or product B? Shall a given part be made or be bought from suppliers? Should an investment be made in new equipment? All these questions call for decisions that should depend, in part at least, upon accounting information. It might be reasonable to turn the question around and ask: What business decisions could be intelligently made without the use of accounting information? Examples would be hard to find.

In large-scale business undertakings such as the manufacture of automobiles or the operation of nationwide chains of retail stores, and even in enterprises much smaller than these, the top executives cannot possibly have close personal contact with and knowledge of the details of operations. Consequently, these executives must depend to an even greater extent than the small businessman upon information provided by the accounting system.

We have already stressed that accounting is a means of measuring the results of business transactions and of communicating financial information. In addition, the accounting system must provide the decision maker with *predictive information* for making important business decisions in a changing world.

Internal control

Throughout this book, the fact that business decisions of all types are based at least in part on accounting data is emphasized. Management, therefore, needs assurance that the accounting data it receives are accurate and dependable. This assurance is provided in large part by developing a strong system of *internal control.* A basic principle of internal control is that no one person should handle all phases of a transaction from beginning to end. When business operations are so organized that two or more employees are required to participate in every transaction, the possibility of fraud is reduced and the work of one employee gives assurance of the accuracy of the work of another.

A system of internal control comprises all the measures taken by an organization for the purpose of (1) protecting its resources against waste, fraud, and inefficiency; (2) ensuring accuracy and reliability in accounting and operating data; (3) securing compliance with company policies; and (4) evaluating the level of performance in all divisions of the company.

When a CPA conducts an audit of a company, he will judge the adequacy of internal control in each area of the company's operations. The stronger the system of internal control, the more confidence the CPA can place in the integrity of the company's financial statements and accounting records. Consequently, his audit work can be performed more rapidly, with less detailed investigation of transactions, when internal controls are strong. The internal auditor also regards the study of internal control as a major part of his work. If internal controls are weak, the usual consequences are waste, fraud, inefficiency, and unprofitable operations.

Forms of business organization

A business enterprise may be organized as a *single proprietorship,* a *partnership,* or a *corporation.* The single proprietorship and partnership forms of organization are common for small retail stores and shops, for farms, and for professional practices in law, medicine, and public accounting. Nearly all large businesses and many small ones are corporations. The dominant role of the corporation in our economy is based on such advantages as the ease of gathering large amounts of money, transferability of shares in ownership, limited liability, and continuity of existence.

Accounting principles apply to all three forms of business organization, but are most carefully defined to aid corporations in making satisfactory financial reports to public investors. In this book we shall use the corporate form of organization as our basic model, along with some specific references to single proprietorships and partnerships.

For an individual to start a small business of which he is the sole owner requires no legal formalities. The organization of a partnership requires only an agreement (written or oral) among the persons joining together as partners. (A written agreement is highly desirable in order to lessen the chance of misunderstanding and disputes.) The formation of a corporation, however, does entail some legal formalities. Application must be filed with state officials for a *corporate charter.* The application for a charter is often referred to as the *articles of incorporation.* After payment of an incorporation fee to the state and approval of the articles of incorporation by the designated state official, the corporation comes into existence. A charter, which may be merely the approved application, is issued as evidence of the company's corporate status. The incorporators (who have subscribed for capital stock and therefore are now stockholders) hold a meeting to elect directors and to pass bylaws as a guide to the conduct of the company's affairs. The directors in turn hold a meeting at which officers of the corporation are appointed to serve as active managers of the business; capital stock certificates are issued to the subscribers; and the formation of the corporation is complete.

FINANCIAL STATEMENTS: THE STARTING POINT IN THE STUDY OF ACCOUNTING

The preparation of financial statements is not the first step in the accounting process, but it is a convenient point to begin the study of accounting. The financial statements are the means of conveying to management and to interested outsiders a concise picture of the profitability and financial position of the business. Since these statements are in a sense the end product of the accounting process, the student who acquires a clear understanding of the content and meaning of financial statements will be in an excellent position to appreciate the purpose of the earlier steps of recording and classifying business transactions.

The major financial statements are the *balance sheet* and the *income statement.* Together, these two statements (each a page or less in length) summarize all the information contained in the hundreds or thousands of pages comprising the detailed accounting records. In this introductory chapter and in Chapter 2, we shall explore the nature of the balance sheet, or statement of financial position, as it is sometimes called. Once we have become familiar with the form and arrangement of the balance sheet and with the meaning of technical terms such as *assets, liabilities,* and *owners' equity,* it will be as easy to read and understand a report on the financial position of a business as it is for an architect to read the blueprint of a proposed building.

The balance sheet

The purpose of a balance sheet is to show the financial position of a business as of a particular date. Every business prepares a balance sheet at the end of the year, and many companies prepare one at the end of each month. A balance sheet consists of a listing of the assets and liabilities of a business and of the owners' equity. The following balance sheet portrays the financial position of the Westside Cleaning Company at December 31.

WESTSIDE CLEANING COMPANY
Balance Sheet
December 31, 19__

	Assets		Liabilities & Stockholders' Equity		
	Cash	$ 1,500	Liabilities:		
	Accounts receivable	3,000	Notes payable		$ 6,000
	Land	7,000	Accounts payable		4,000
	Building	15,000	Total liabilities		$10,000
	Office equipment	1,000	Stockholders' equity:		
	Delivery equipment	2,500	Capital stock	$15,000	
			Retained earnings	5,000	20,000
		$30,000			$30,000

Balance sheet shows financial position at a specific date (margin note)

Note that the balance sheet sets forth in its heading three items: (1) the name of the business, (2) the name of the financial statement "Balance Sheet," and (3) the date of the balance sheet. Below the heading is the body of the balance sheet, which consists of three distinct sections: assets, liabilities, and the stockholders' equity. The remainder of this chapter is largely devoted to making clear the nature of these three sections.

We can tell from the illustrated balance sheet that Westside Cleaning Company is a corporation, because the ownership section is listed as *stockholders' equity* and shows that capital stock of $15,000 has been issued. A corporation is the only form of business organization which issues capital stock, or in which the owners are called stockholders.

THE BUSINESS ENTITY The illustrated balance sheet refers only to the financial affairs of the business entity known as Westside Cleaning Company and not to the personal financial affairs of the owners. Individual stockholders may have personal bank accounts, homes, automobiles, and investments in other businesses; but since these personal belongings are not part of the cleaning company business, they are not included in the balance sheet of this business unit.

In brief, *a business entity is an economic unit which enters into business transactions that must be recorded, summarized, and reported.* The entity is regarded as separate from its owner or owners; the entity owns its own property and has its own debts. Consequently, for each business entity, there should be a separate set of accounting records. A balance sheet and an income statement are intended to portray the financial position and the operating results of a single business entity. If the owners were to intermingle their personal affairs with the transactions of the business, the resulting financial statements would be misleading and would fail to describe the business fairly.

Assets

Assets are economic resources which are owned by a business and are expected to benefit future operations. Assets may have definite physical form such as buildings, machinery, or merchandise. On the other hand, some assets exist not in physical or tangible form but in the form of valuable legal claims or rights, examples are amounts due from customers, investments in government bonds, and patent rights.

One of the most basic, and at the same time most controversial, problems in accounting is the assignment of dollar values to the assets of a business. Two kinds of assets cause little difficulty. Cash and amounts due from customers represent assets that either are available for expenditure or will be in the near future (when the customers pay their accounts). The amount of cash on hand is a clear statement of the dollars that are available for expenditure. The amount that customers owe the business (after taking into account that some receivables may prove uncollectible) represents the dollars that will be received in the near future.

Other assets such as land, buildings, merchandise, and equipment represent economic resources that will be used in producing income for the business. The prevailing accounting view is that such assets should be accounted for on the basis of the dollars that have been invested in these resources, that is, the *historical cost* incurred in acquiring such property or property rights. In recording a business transaction, it is the transaction price that establishes the accounting value for the property or service received. In accounting terms, therefore, the "value" or "valuation" of an asset ordinarily means the cost of that asset to the entity owning it.

For example, let us assume that a business buys a tract of land for use as a building site, paying $40,000 in cash. The amount to be entered in the accounting records as the value of the asset will be the cost of $40,000. If we assume a booming real estate market, a fair estimate of the market value of the land 10 years later might be $100,000. Although the market price or economic value of the land has risen greatly, the accounting value as shown in the accounting records and on the balance sheet would continue unchanged at the cost of $40,000. This policy of accounting for assets at their cost is often referred to as the *cost principle* of accounting.

In reading a balance sheet, it is important to bear in mind that the dollar amounts listed do not indicate the prices at which the assets could be sold, nor the prices at which they could be replaced. One useful generalization to be drawn from this discussion is that a balance sheet does not show "how much a business is worth."

WHY SHOW ASSETS AT COST RATHER THAN PRESENT MARKET VALUE?
It is appropriate to ask *why* accountants do not change the recorded values of assets to correspond with changing market prices for these

properties. One reason is that the land and building used to house the business are acquired for use and not for resale; in fact, these assets cannot be sold without disrupting the business. The balance sheet of a business is prepared on the assumption that the business is a continuing enterprise, a "going concern." Consequently, the present estimated prices at which the land and buildings could be sold are of less importance than if these properties were intended for sale.

Another reason for using cost rather than market values in accounting for assets is the need for *objectivity* in accounting information. Objectivity refers to using amounts which are determined, as much as possible, on a definite factual basis rather than by personal opinion. For example, the cost of land, buildings, and other assets purchased for cash can be determined quite objectively. After the business has owned these assets for a while, however, the market value of the assets is largely a matter of personal opinion. Of course, at the date of acquisition of an asset, cost and market value are ordinarily the same. The bargaining process which results in a sale serves to establish both the current market value of the property and the cost to the buyer. In later periods, however, cost is still objectively determinable, whereas market value often is not.

Although the cost of many assets can be determined in an objective manner as the result of a cash purchase, the measurement of cost in some cases may be rather difficult. For example, when a factory machine is purchased, a question arises as to whether the cost basis of the machine should include (1) the charges for transporting, installing, and testing it and (2) the salary paid the purchasing agent and engineering employees, who may have devoted considerable time to making a choice among various competing machines on the market. Another common example is that of a manufacturing concern which constructs a building for its own use. Identifying and measuring all the costs to be included in the total cost of the building will require many borderline decisions.

The decline in the purchasing power of the dollar in recent years has raised serious doubts as to the adequacy of the conventional cost basis in accounting for assets. Proposals for adjusting recorded dollar amounts to reflect changes in the value of the dollar, as shown by a general price index, are receiving increasing attention.[1] Balance sheets showing assets at current appraised values rather than at historical cost are also being advocated by some accountants. Accounting concepts are not as exact and unchanging as many persons assume; to serve the needs of a fast-changing economy, accounting concepts must also undergo continuous evolutionary change. As of today, however, the cost basis of valuing assets is still in almost universal use.

[1] See *Financial Statements Restated for General Price-Level Changes,* Statement No. 3 of the Accounting Principles Board, American Institute of Certified Public Accountants (New York: 1969).

The problem of valuation of assets is one of the most complex in the entire field of accounting. It is merely being introduced at this point; in later chapters we shall explore carefully some of the valuation principles applicable to the major types of assets.

Liabilities

Liabilities are debts. All business concerns have liabilities; even the largest and most successful companies find it convenient to purchase merchandise and supplies on credit rather than to pay cash at the time of each purchase. The liability arising from the purchase of goods or services on credit (on time) is called an *account payable,* and the person or company to whom the account payable is owed is called a *creditor.*

A business concern frequently finds it desirable to borrow money as a means of supplementing the amount invested by the owners, thus enabling the business to expand more rapidly. The borrowed money may, for example, be used to buy merchandise which can be sold at a profit to the firm's customers. Or, the borrowed money might be used to buy new and more efficient machinery, thus enabling the company to turn out a larger volume of products at lower cost. When a business borrows money for any reason, a liability is incurred and the lender becomes a creditor of the business. The form of the liability when money is borrowed is usually a *note payable,* a formal written promise to pay a certain amount of money, plus interest, at a definite future time. An *account payable,* as contrasted with a *note payable,* does not involve the issuance of a formal written promise to the creditor; and it does not call for payment of interest. When a business has both notes payable and accounts payable, the two types of liabilities are shown separately in the balance sheet. The sequence in which these two liabilities are listed is not important, although notes payable are usually shown as the first item among the liabilities. A figure showing the total of the liabilities may also be inserted, as shown by the illustrated balance sheet on page 12.

The creditors have claims against the assets of the business, usually not against any particular asset but against the assets in general. The claims of the creditors are liabilities of the business and have priority over the claims of owners. Creditors are entitled to be paid in full even if such payment should exhaust the assets of the business, leaving nothing for the owners. The issue of valuation, which poses so many difficulties in accounting for assets, is a much smaller problem in the case of liabilities, because the amounts of most liabilities are specified by contract.

Owners' equity

The owners' equity in a business represents the resources invested by the owners; it is equal to the total assets minus the liabilities. The equity of the owners is a residual claim; as the owners of the business they are entitled to whatever remains after the claims of the creditors are fully satisfied. For example:

The Westside Cleaning Company has total assets of *$30,000*
And total liabilities amounting to *10,000*
Therefore, the owners' equity must equal *$20,000*

Suppose that the Westside Cleaning Company borrows $1,000 from a bank. After recording the additional asset of $1,000 in cash and recording the new liability of $1,000 owed to the bank, we would have the following:

The Westside Cleaning Company now has total assets of *$31,000*
And total liabilities are now *11,000*
Therefore, the owners' equity still is equal to *$20,000*

It is apparent that the total assets of the business were increased by the act of borrowing money from a bank, but the increase in total assets was exactly offset by an increase in liabilities, and the owners' equity remained unchanged. The owners' equity in a business is not increased by the incurring of liabilities of any kind.

The owners' equity in a corporation usually comes from two sources:

1 Investments by persons who receive in exchange shares of the corporation's capital stock and are therefore called stockholders
2 Earnings from profitable operation of the business

Only the first of these two sources of owners' equity is considered in this chapter. The second source, an increase in owners' equity through earnings of the business, will be discussed in Chapter 3.

The accounting equation

One of the fundamental characteristics of every balance sheet is that the total figure for assets always equals the total figure for liabilities (creditors' equity) and owners' equity. This agreement or balance of total assets with total equities is one reason for calling this financial statement a *balance sheet.* But *why* do total assets equal total equities? The answer can be given in one short paragraph, as follows:

The dollar totals on the two sides of the balance sheet are always equal because these two sides are *merely two views of the same business property.* The listing of assets shows us what things the business owns; the listing of liabilities and owners' equity tells us who supplied these resources to the business and how much each group supplied. Everything that a business owns has been supplied to it by the creditors or by the owners. Therefore, the total claims of the creditors plus the claims of the owners equal the total assets of the business.

The equality of assets on the one hand and of the claims of the creditors and the owners on the other hand is expressed in the equation:

Fundamental accounting equation
Assets = Liabilities + Owners' Equity

$30,000 = $10,000 + $20,000

The amounts listed in the equation were taken from the balance sheet illustrated on page 12. A balance sheet is nothing more than a detailed statement of this equation. To emphasize this relationship, compare the balance sheet of the Westside Cleaning Company with the above equation.

To emphasize that the stockholders' equity is a residual element, secondary to the claims of creditors, it is often helpful to transpose the terms of the equation, as follows:

Alternative form of accounting equation
Assets − Liabilities = Owners' Equity

$30,000 − $10,000 = $20,000

Every business transaction, no matter how simple or how complex, can be expressed in terms of its effect on the accounting equation. A thorough understanding of the equation and some practice in using it are essential to the student of accounting.

Regardless of whether a business grows or contracts, this equality between the assets and the claims against the assets is always maintained. Any increase in the amount of total assets is necessarily accompanied by an equal increase on the other side of the equation, that is, by an increase in either the liabilities or the owners' equity. Any decrease in total assets is necessarily accompanied by a corresponding decrease in liabilities or owners' equity. The continuing equality of the two sides of the balance sheet can best be illustrated by taking a brand-new business as an example and observing the effects of various transactions upon its balance sheet.

Effects of business transactions upon the balance sheet

Assume that John Green, Susan Green, and R. J. Hill organized a corporation called Greenhill Real Estate Company. A charter was obtained from the state authorizing the new corporation to issue 2,000 shares of capital stock with a par value of $10 a share.[2] John and Susan Green each invested $8,000 cash and R. J. Hill invested $4,000. The entire authorized capital stock of $20,000 was therefore issued as follows: 800 shares to John Green, 800 shares to Susan Green, and 400 shares to R. J. Hill. Each of the three stockholders received a stock certificate as evidence of his ownership equity in the corporation.

[2] Par value is the amount assigned to each share of stock in accordance with legal requirements. The concept of par value is more fully explained in Chap. 7.

The planned operations of the new business called for obtaining listings of houses and commercial property being offered for sale by owners, advertising these properties, and showing them to prospective buyers. The listing agreement signed with each homeowner provides that Greenhill Real Estate Company shall receive at the time of sale a commission equal to 6% of the selling price.

The new business was begun on September 1 with the deposit of $20,000 in a bank account in the name of the business, Greenhill Real Estate Company. The initial balance sheet of the new business then appeared as follows:

GREENHILL REAL ESTATE COMPANY
Balance Sheet
September 1, 19___

Assets		Stockholders' Equity	
Cash	$20,000	Capital stock	$20,000

PURCHASE OF AN ASSET FOR CASH The next transaction entered into by Greenhill Real Estate Company was the purchase of land suitable as a site for an office. The price for the land was $7,000, and payment was made in cash on September 3. The effect of this transaction on the balance sheet was twofold: first, cash was decreased by the amount paid out; and second, a new asset, Land, was acquired. After this exchange of cash for land, the balance sheet appeared as follows:

GREENHILL REAL ESTATE COMPANY
Balance Sheet
September 3, 19___

Assets		Stockholders' Equity	
Cash	$13,000	Capital stock	$20,000
Land	7,000		
	$20,000		$20,000

PURCHASE OF AN ASSET AND INCURRING OF A LIABILITY On September 5 an opportunity arose to buy a complete office building which had to be moved to permit the construction of a freeway. A price of $12,000 was agreed upon, which included the cost of moving the building and installing it upon Greenhill Real Estate's lot. As the building was in excellent condition and would have cost approximately $20,000 to build, it was considered as a very fortunate purchase.

The terms provided for an immediate cash payment of $5,000 and payment of the balance of $7,000 within 90 days. Cash was decreased

$5,000, but a new asset, Building, was recorded at cost in the amount of $12,000. Total assets were thus increased by $7,000, but the total of liabilities and owners' equity was also increased as a result of recording the $7,000 account payable as a liability. After this transaction had been recorded, the balance sheet appeared as follows:

GREENHILL REAL ESTATE COMPANY
Balance Sheet
September 5, 19___

	Assets		Liabilities & Stockholders' Equity	
Totals	Cash	$ 8,000	Liabilities:	
increased	Land	7,000	Accounts payable	$ 7,000
equally by				
purchase of	Building	12,000	Stockholders' equity:	
building on			Capital stock	20,000
credit		$27,000		$27,000

Note that the building appears in the balance sheet at $12,000, its cost to Greenhill Real Estate Company. The estimate of $20,000 as the probable cost to construct such a building is irrelevant. Even if someone should offer to buy the building from Greenhill Real Estate Company for $20,000 or more, this offer, if refused, would have no bearing on the balance sheet. Accounting records are intended to provide a historical record of **costs actually incurred;** therefore, the $12,000 price at which the building was purchased is the amount to be recorded.

SALE OF AN ASSET   After the office building had been moved to Greenhill Real Estate Company's lot, the company decided that the lot was much larger than was needed. The adjoining business, Carter's Drugstore, wanted more room for a parking area; so, on September 10, Greenhill Real Estate Company sold the unused part of the lot to Carter's Drugstore for a price of $2,000. Since the selling price was computed at the same amount per foot as the corporation had paid for the land, there was neither a profit nor a loss on the sale. No down payment was required, but it was agreed that the full price would be paid within three months. By this transaction a new asset in the form of an account receivable was acquired, but the asset Land was decreased by the same amount; consequently, there was no change in the amount of total assets. After this transaction, the balance sheet appeared as follows:

GREENHILL REAL ESTATE COMPANY
Balance Sheet
September 10, 19__

	Assets		Liabilities & Stockholders' Equity	
No change in totals by sale of land at cost	Cash	$ 8,000	Liabilities:	
	Accounts receivable	2,000	Accounts payable	$ 7,000
	Land	5,000	Stockholders' equity:	
	Building	12,000	Capital stock	20,000
		$27,000		$27,000

In the illustration thus far, Greenhill Real Estate Company has an account receivable from only one debtor and an account payable to only one creditor. As the business grows, the number of debtors and creditors will increase, but the Accounts Receivable and Accounts Payable accounts will continue to be used. The additional records necessary to show the amount receivable from each debtor and the amount owing to each creditor will be explained in Chapter 6.

PURCHASE OF AN ASSET ON CREDIT A complete set of office furniture and equipment was purchased on credit from General Equipment, Inc., on September 14. The amount of the transaction was $1,800, and it was agreed that payment should be made later. As the result of this transaction the business owned a new asset, Office Equipment, but it had also incurred a new liability. The increase in total assets was exactly offset by the increase in liabilities. After this transaction the balance sheet appeared as follows:

GREENHILL REAL ESTATE COMPANY
Balance Sheet
September 14, 19__

	Assets		Liabilities & Stockholders' Equity	
Totals increased by acquiring asset on credit	Cash	$ 8,000	Liabilities:	
	Accounts receivable	2,000	Accounts payable	$ 8,800
	Land	5,000	Stockholders' equity:	
	Building	12,000	Capital stock	20,000
	Office equipment	1,800		
		$28,800		$28,800

COLLECTION OF AN ACCOUNT RECEIVABLE On September 20, cash in the amount of $500 was received as partial settlement of the account receivable from Carter's Drugstore. This transaction caused cash to increase and the accounts receivable to decrease by an equal amount.

In essence, this transaction was merely the exchange of one asset for another of equal value. Consequently, there was no change in the amount of total assets. After this transaction was completed the balance sheet appeared as shown below:

GREENHILL REAL ESTATE COMPANY
Balance Sheet
September 20, 19___

	Assets		Liabilities & Stockholders' Equity	
Totals	Cash	$ 8,500	Liabilities:	
unchanged	Accounts receivable	1,500	Accounts payable	$ 8,800
by				
collection	Land	5,000	Stockholders' equity:	
of a	Building	12,000	Capital stock	20,000
receivable	Office equipment	1,800		
		$28,800		$28,800

PAYMENT OF A LIABILITY   On September 30 Greenhill paid $1,000 in cash to General Equipment, Inc. This payment caused a decrease in cash and an equal decrease in liabilities. Therefore the totals of assets and equities were still in balance. After this transaction, the balance sheet appeared as follows:

GREENHILL REAL ESTATE COMPANY
Balance Sheet
September 30, 19___

	Assets		Liabilities & Stockholders' Equity	
Totals	Cash	$ 7,500	Liabilities:	
decreased	Accounts receivable	1,500	Accounts payable	$ 7,800
by paying a	Land	5,000	Stockholders' equity:	
liability	Building	12,000	Capital stock	20,000
	Office equipment	1,800		
		$27,800		$27,800

The transactions which have been illustrated for the month of September were merely preliminary to the formal opening for business of Greenhill Real Estate Company on October 1. During September no sales were arranged by the company and no commissions were earned. Consequently, the stockholders' equity at September 30 is shown in the above balance sheet at $20,000, unchanged from the original investment on September 1. September was a month devoted exclusively to organizing the business and not to regular operations. In

succeeding chapters we shall continue the example of Greenhill Real
Estate Company by illustrating operating transactions and considering
how the net income of the business can be determined.

Effect of business transactions upon the accounting equation

A balance sheet is merely a detailed expression of the accounting
equation, Assets = Liabilities + Owners' Equity. To emphasize the
relationship between the accounting equation and the balance sheet,
let us now repeat the September transactions of Greenhill Real Estate
Company to show the effect of each transaction upon the accounting
equation. Briefly restated, the seven transactions were as follows:

Sept. 1 Began the business by depositing $20,000 in a company bank
account.

3 Purchased land for $7,000 cash.

5 Purchased a building for $12,000, paying $5,000 cash and incurring
a liability of $7,000.

10 Sold part of the land at a price equal to cost of $2,000, collectible
within three months.

14 Purchased office equipment on credit for $1,800.

20 Received $500 cash as partial collection of the $2,000 account
receivable.

30 Paid $1,000 on accounts payable.

In the table on page 23, each transaction is identified by date; the
effect of each transaction on the accounting equation is shown, and
also the new dollar balance of each item is listed. Each of the lines
labeled Balances contains the same items as the balance sheet previously illustrated for the particular date. The final line in the table
corresponds to the amounts in the balance sheet at the end of September. Note that the equality of the two sides of the equation was
maintained throughout the recording of the transactions.

CORPORATIONS, PARTNERSHIPS, AND SINGLE PROPRIETORSHIPS

The form of business organization used for illustration in this chapter
is a corporation, Greenhill Real Estate Company. A corporation is a
separate legal entity or "artificial being" chartered by the state, and
the owners' equity section of the balance sheet is called Stockholders'
Equity. If the business were a partnership of two or more persons, we
would use the caption Partners' Equity instead of Stockholders' Equity,
and would list under that caption the amount of each partner's equity.

	Cash	+ Accounts Receivable	+ Land	+ Building	+ Office Equipment	= Accounts Payable	+ Capital Stock
						Assets header / **= Liabilities + Owners' Equity**	
Sept. 1	+$20,000						+$20,000
Sept. 3	−7,000		+$7,000				
Balances	$13,000		$7,000				$20,000
Sept. 5	−5,000			+$12,000		+$7,000	
Balances	$ 8,000		$7,000	$12,000		$7,000	$20,000
Sept. 10		+$2,000	−2,000				
Balances	$ 8,000	$2,000	$5,000	$12,000		$7,000	$20,000
Sept. 14					+$1,800	+1,800	
Balances	$ 8,000	$2,000	$5,000	$12,000	$1,800	$8,800	$20,000
Sept. 20	+500	−500					
Balances	$ 8,500	$1,500	$5,000	$12,000	$1,800	$8,800	$20,000
Sept. 30	−1,000					−1,000	
Balances	$ 7,500 +	$1,500 +	$5,000 +	$12,000 +	$1,800 =	$7,800 +	$20,000

If the form of the business were a single proprietorship, the owner's equity section would consist of only one item, the equity of the proprietor. These three methods of showing the ownership equity on the balance sheet may be illustrated as follows:

For a Corporation

Equity of stockholders, of partners, and of a single proprietor

Stockholders' equity:
Capital stock $1,000,000
Retained earnings 278,000
  Total stockholders' equity $1,278,000

For a Partnership

Partners' equity:
William Abbott, capital $25,000
Raymond Barnes, capital 40,000
  Total partners' equity . . . . $ 65,000

For a Single Proprietorship

Owner's equity:
John Smith, capital . . . . $ 30,000

The preceding illustration of the ownership equity of a corporation shows that $1 million of capital was invested in the corporation by stockholders and that through profitable operation of the business an additional $278,000 of earned capital has been accumulated. The corporation has chosen to retain this $278,000 in the business rather than to distribute these earnings to the stockholders as dividends. The total earnings of the corporation may have been considerably more than $278,000, because any earnings which were paid to stockholders as dividends would not appear on the balance sheet. The term *retained earnings* describes only the earnings which were *not* paid out in the form of dividends.

Corporations are required by state laws to maintain a distinction between capital stock and retained earnings. In a single proprietorship, capital earned through profitable operations and retained in the business is merely added to the amount of the original invested capital and a single figure is shown for the owner's equity. A similar procedure is followed in a partnership, each partner's capital being increased by his share of the net income. There is no theoretical reason why the balance sheet for a single proprietorship or a partnership should not show each owner's equity divided into two portions: the amount originally invested and the earnings retained in the business, but customarily this separation is not made for an unincorporated business.

USE OF FINANCIAL STATEMENTS BY OUTSIDERS

Through careful study of financial statements, it is possible for the outsider with training in accounting to obtain a fairly complete understanding of the financial position of the business and to become aware of significant changes that have occurred since the date of the preceding balance sheet. Bear in mind, however, that financial statements have limitations. As stated earlier, only those factors which can be reduced to monetary terms appear in the balance sheet. Let us consider for a moment some important business factors which are not set forth in financial statements. Some companies have a record of good relations with labor unions, freedom from strikes, and mutual respect between management and employees. Other companies have been plagued by frequent and costly labor disputes. The relationship between a company and a union of its employees is certainly an important factor in the successful operation of the business, but it is not mentioned in the balance sheet. Perhaps a new competing store has just opened for business across the street; the prospect of intensified competition in the future will not be described in the balance sheet.

An efficient management team and an experienced staff of employees constitute a valuable element of a business entity, but as yet no means exist for assigning a dollar valuation to such resources. Efforts to develop methods of accounting for the human resources of an organization presently constitute an important area of accounting research.

Bankers and other creditors

Bankers who have loaned money to a business concern or who are considering making such a loan will be vitally interested in the balance sheet of the business. By studying the amount and kinds of assets in relation to the amount and payment dates of the liabilities, a banker can form an opinion as to the ability of the business to pay its debts promptly. The banker gives particular attention to the amount of cash and of other assets (such as accounts receivable) which will soon be converted into cash; he compares the amount of these assets with the amount of liabilities falling due in the near future. The banker is also interested in the amount of the owners' equity, as this ownership capital serves as a protecting buffer between the banker and any losses which may befall the business. Bankers are seldom, if ever, willing to make a loan unless the balance sheet and other information concerning the prospective borrower offer reasonable assurance that the loan can and will be repaid promptly at the maturity date.

Another important group making use of balance sheets consists of the credit managers of manufacturing and wholesaling firms, who must decide whether prospective customers are to be allowed to buy merchandise on credit. The credit manager, like the banker, studies the balance sheets of his customers for the purpose of appraising their debt-paying ability. Credit agencies such as Dun & Bradstreet, Inc., make a business of obtaining financial statements from virtually all business concerns and appraising their debt-paying ability. The conclusions reached by these credit agencies are available to businessmen willing to pay for *credit reports* about prospective customers.

Owners

The financial statements of corporations listed on the stock exchanges are eagerly awaited by millions of stockholders. A favorable set of financial statements may cause the market price of the company's stock to rise dramatically; an unfavorable set of financial statements may cause the "bottom to fall out" of the market price. Current dependable financial statements are one of the essential ingredients for successful investment in securities. Of course, financial statements are equally important in single proprietorships and partnerships. The financial statements tell an owner just how successful his business has been and summarize in concise form its present financial position.

Others interested in accounting information

In addition to owners, managers, bankers, and merchandise creditors, other groups making use of accounting data include governmental agencies, employees, investors, and writers for business periodicals.

Some very large corporations have more than a million stockholders; these giant corporations send copies of their financial statements to each of these many owners. In recent years there has been a trend toward wider distribution of financial statements to all interested persons, in contrast to the attitude of a generation or more ago when many companies regarded their financial statements as confidential matter. This trend reflects an increasing awareness of the impact of corporate activities on all aspects of our lives and of the need for greater disclosure of information about the activities of business corporations.

The purpose of this discussion is to show the extent to which a modern industrial society depends upon accounting. Even more important, however, is a clear understanding at the outset of your study that accounting does not exist just for the sake of keeping a record or in order to fill out social security records, income tax returns, and various other regulatory reports. These are but auxiliary functions. If you gain an understanding of accounting concepts, you will have acquired an analytical skill essential to the field of professional management. *The prime and vital purpose of accounting is to aid in the choice among alternatives that faces every decision maker in the business world.*

DEMONSTRATION PROBLEM

The accounting data (listed alphabetically) for the Crystal Auto Wash as of August 31, 19___, are shown below. The figure for Cash is not given but it can be determined when all the available information is assembled in the form of a balance sheet.

Accounts payable	$ 9,000	Land	$40,000
Accounts receivable	800	Machinery & equipment	85,000
Buildings	60,000	Notes payable	32,000
Cash	?	Retained earnings	99,400
Capital stock	50,000	Supplies	400

On September 1, the following transactions occurred:
(1) Additional capital stock was issued for $15,000 cash.
(2) The accounts payable of $9,000 were paid in full. (No payment was made on the notes payable.)
(3) One-quarter of the land was sold at cost. The buyer gave his promissory note for $10,000. (Interest applicable to the note may be ignored.)
(4) Washing supplies were purchased at a cost of $2,000, to be paid for within 10 days. Washing supplies were also purchased for $600 cash from another car-washing concern which was going out of business. These supplies would have cost $1,000 if purchased through regular channels.

Instructions
a Prepare a balance sheet at August 31, 19___.
b Prepare a balance sheet at September 1, 19___.

SOLUTION TO DEMONSTRATION PROBLEM

a

CRYSTAL AUTO WASH
Balance Sheet
August 31, 19___

Assets		Liabilities & Stockholders' Equity		
Cash	$ 4,200	Liabilities:		
Accounts receivable	800	Notes payable		$ 32,000
Supplies	400	Accounts payable		9,000
Land	40,000	Total liabilities		$ 41,000
Buildings	60,000	Stockholders' equity:		
Machinery & equipment	85,000	Capital stock	$50,000	
		Retained earnings	99,400	149,400
	$190,400			$190,400

b

CRYSTAL AUTO WASH
Balance Sheet
September 1, 19___

Assets		Liabilities & Stockholders' Equity		
Cash	$ 9,600	Liabilities:		
Accounts receivable	800	Notes payable		$ 32,000
Notes receivable	10,000	Accounts payable		2,000
Supplies	3,000	Total liabilities		$ 34,000
Land	30,000	Stockholders' equity:		
Buildings	60,000	Capital stock	$65,000	
Machinery & equipment	85,000	Retained earnings	99,400	164,400
	$198,400			$198,400

REVIEW QUESTIONS

1 Why is a knowledge of accounting terms and concepts useful to persons other than professional accountants?

2 In broad general terms, what is the purpose of accounting?

3 What is meant by the term *business transaction?*

4 Not all the significant happenings in the life of a business can be expressed in monetary terms and entered in the accounting records. List two examples of significant events affecting a business which could not be satisfactorily measured and entered in its accounting records.

5 Distinguish between *bookkeeping* and *accounting.*

6 What is the principal function of a certified public accountant? What other services are commonly rendered by a CPA?

7 Distinguish between *public accounting* and *private accounting.*

8 Define *assets.* List five examples.

9 Mint Corporation was offered $500,000 cash for the land and buildings occupied by the business. These assets had been acquired five years ago at a price of $300,000. Mint Corporation refused the offer, but is inclined to increase the land and buildings to a total valuation of $500,000 in the balance sheet in order to show more accurately "how much the business is worth." Do you agree? Explain.

10 Explain briefly the concept of the *business entity.*

11 State the accounting equation in two alternative forms.

12 State precisely what information is contained in the heading of a balance sheet.

13 The owners' equity in a business arises from what two sources?

14 Why are the total assets shown on a balance sheet always equal to the total of the liabilities and the owners' equity?

EXERCISES

Ex. 1-1 a The assets of a corporation total $1.4 million and the stockholders' equity totals $850,000. What is the amount of total liabilities?

b The balance sheet of Sky Corporation shows retained earnings of $25,000. The assets amount to $120,000 and are twice as large as the liabilities. What is the amount of capital stock?

c In the partnership of Davis & Toole, the asset total is 50% larger than the total of liabilities. The ownership equity of partner Davis is only half as much as that of Toole. If the total assets are $90,000, what is the amount of Toole's ownership equity?

Ex. 1-2 The balance sheet items of the Perez Corporation as of December 31, 19___, are shown below in random order. You are to prepare a balance sheet for the company, using a similar sequence for assets as in the illustrated balance sheet on page 12.

Accounts payable	$ 3,400	Land	$ 9,000
Accounts receivable	6,500	Retained earnings	?
Building	20,000	Office equipment	1,900
Cash	4,600	Capital stock	15,000
Notes payable	1,200		

Ex. 1-3 Indicate the effect of each of the following transactions upon the total assets of a business by use of the appropriate phrase: "increase total assets," "decrease total assets," "no change in total assets."

a Purchase of office equipment for cash

b Payment of a liability

c Borrowing money from a bank

d Investment of cash by owner

e Purchase of a delivery truck at a price of $2,500, terms $500 cash and the balance payable in 20 equal monthly installments

f Sale of land for cash at a price equal to its cost

g Sale of land on account (on credit) at a price equal to its cost

h Sale of land for cash at a price in excess of its cost

i Sale of land for cash at a price below its cost

j Collection of an account receivable

Ex. 1-4 The total assets of the Bomar Corporation amount to $1.5 million and its total liabilities to $600,000. During the five years of its existence, the corporation has been quite successful and has earned total profits equal to exactly one-half of the original capital invested by stockholders. Of the profits earned, one-half has been distributed as dividends to stockholders; the other half has been retained in the business. Prepare the stockholders' equity section of the balance sheet, including dollar amounts. Explain how you determined the amounts.

Ex. 1-5 On December 31, 1976, the total assets of the Hill Corporation amounted to $240,000. One year later the assets had increased to $300,000 and the stockholders' equity was $192,000. Liabilities were $68,000 greater on December 31, 1977, than they had been at December 31, 1976. What was the amount of the stockholders' equity at December 31, 1976? Explain the basis for your answer.

Ex. 1-6 The following balance sheet of Alaskan Corporation is incorrect because of improper headings and the misplacement of several accounts. Prepare a corrected balance sheet.

ALASKAN CORPORATION

March 31, 19___

Assets		**Owners' Equity**	
Capital stock	$ 55,000	Accounts receivable	$ 37,100
Cash	11,400	Accounts payable	13,100
Building	48,500	Supplies	1,200
Office equipment	12,900	Automobiles	16,700
		Retained earnings	59,700
	$127,800		$127,800

PROBLEMS

1-1 Prepare a balance sheet for the Kellog Corporation at June 30, 19___, from the following information:

Accounts payable	$ 9,675	Office equipment	$ 3,150
Accounts receivable	?	Notes payable	30,000
Buildings	60,000	Delivery truck	4,870
Land	30,000	Capital stock	60,000
Cash	11,220	Retained earnings	17,220

1-2 The balance sheet items for Beverly Auto Wash (arranged in alphabetical order) were as follows at August 1, 19___:

Accounts payable	$ 4,000	Equipment	$26,000
Accounts receivable	300	Land	25,000
Building	20,000	Notes payable	36,000
Capital stock	25,000	Retained earnings	13,700
Cash	?	Supplies	2,800

During the next two days, the following transactions occurred:

Aug. 2 Additional capital stock was issued for $15,000 cash. The accounts payable were paid in full. (No payment was made on the notes payable.)

Aug. 3 Equipment was purchased at a cost of $9,000 to be paid within 10 days. Supplies were purchased for $500 cash from another car-washing concern, which was going out of business. These supplies would have cost $900 if purchased through normal channels.

Instructions

a Prepare a balance sheet at August 1, 19___.

b Prepare a balance sheet at August 3, 19___.

1-3 Selected transactions of Rider Corporation for September are summarized below in equation form, with each of the five transactions identified by a letter. Write a sentence explaining the nature of each transaction.

	Cash	+ Accounts Receivable	+ Land	+ Building	+ Office Equipment	= Accounts Payable	+ Capital Stock
Balances	$ 6,000	+$18,000	+$16,000	+$42,000	+$ 6,000 =	$ 8,000	+$80,000
(a)					+1,600	+1,600	
Balances	$ 6,000	$18,000	$16,000	$42,000	$ 7,600	$ 9,600	$80,000
(b)	+1,000	−1,000					
Balances	$ 7,000	$17,000	$16,000	$42,000	$ 7,600	$ 9,600	$80,000
(c)	−400					−400	
Balances	$ 6,600	$17,000	$16,000	$42,000	$ 7,600	$ 9,200	$80,000
(d)	−600				+1,800	+1,200	
Balances	$ 6,000	$17,000	$16,000	$42,000	$ 9,400	$10,400	$80,000
(e)	+4,000						+4,000
Balances	$10,000 +	$17,000 +	$16,000 +	$42,000 +	$ 9,400 =	$10,400 +	$84,000

Column group headers: **Assets** (Cash, Accounts Receivable, Land, Building, Office Equipment); = **Liabilities** (Accounts Payable); + **Owners' Equity** (Capital Stock)

1-4 By close study of the series of balance sheets shown below, you can determine what transactions have taken place. Prepare a list of these transactions by date of occurrence. (For example, the transactions leading to the balance sheet of September 1, 19___, could be described as follows: "On September 1, 19___, Cascade Camps, Inc., issued $68,000 par value of capital stock for cash.")

(1)

CASCADE CAMPS, INC.
Balance Sheet
September 1, 19___

Assets		Stockholders' Equity	
Cash	$68,000	Capital stock	$68,000

(2)

CASCADE CAMPS, INC.
Balance Sheet
September 5, 19___

Assets		Liabilities & Stockholders' Equity	
Cash	$55,000	Liabilities:	
Land	33,000	Accounts payable	$20,000
		Stockholders' equity:	
		Capital stock	68,000
	$88,000		$88,000

(3)

CASCADE CAMPS, INC.
Balance Sheet
September 8, 19___

Assets		Liabilities & Stockholders' Equity	
Cash	$47,000	Liabilities:	
Supplies	3,000	Accounts payable	$22,000
Land	33,000	Stockholders' equity:	
Equipment	7,000	Capital stock	68,000
	$90,000		$90,000

(4)

CASCADE CAMPS, INC.
Balance Sheet
September 9, 19___

Assets		Liabilities & Stockholders' Equity	
Cash	$30,000	Liabilities:	
Supplies	3,000	Accounts payable	$16,500
Land	33,000	Stockholders' equity:	
Equipment	18,500	Capital stock	68,000
	$84,500		$84,500

1-5 Prepare a balance sheet at June 1, 1976, for Allied Company. Also prepare a separate balance sheet after each of the three transactions. Each balance sheet should reflect all transactions to date.

Accounts payable	$ 30,000	Capital stock	$200,000
Buildings	192,500	Retained earnings	168,000
Office equipment	53,000	Cash	18,000
Office supplies	?	Land	124,000

June 2 One-half of the land was sold to a contractor at a price of $62,000. A down payment of $10,000 in cash was received and the buyer agreed to pay the balance within 10 days.

June   3 A cash payment of $5,000 was made on an account payable.

June 10 Cash in the amount of $52,000 was received from the buyer of the land in final settlement of the June 2 transaction.

1-6 John Roberts and Allan Bailey own all the capital stock of R & B Property Management Corporation. Both stockholders also work full time in the business. The company is in the business of performing management services for apartment house owners, including finding tenants, collecting rents, and performing maintenance and repair work.

   When the business was organized, Roberts and Bailey invested a total of $20,000 to acquire the capital stock. At December 31, 19___, a partial list of the corporation's balance sheet items included cash of $23,600, office equipment of $5,300, and accounts payable of $24,500. The following information concerning the corporation's financial position is also available:

   (1) Earlier in 19___, the corporation purchased an office building from Roberts at a price of $15,000 for the land and $25,000 for the building. Roberts had acquired the property several years ago at a cost of $10,000 for the land and $19,000 for the building. At December 31, 19___, Roberts and Bailey estimated that the land was worth $17,000 and the building was worth $28,000. The corporation owes Roberts a $16,000 note payable in connection with the purchase of the property.

   (2) While working, Roberts drives his own automobile, which cost $5,600. Bailey uses a car owned by the corporation, which cost $3,200.

   (3) One of the apartment houses managed by the company is owned by Bailey. Bailey acquired the property at a cost of $70,000 for the land and $110,000 for the building.

   (4) Company records show a $200 account receivable from Bailey and $7,200 in accounts receivable from other clients.

   (5) Roberts has a $10,000 bank account in the same bank used by the corporation. He explains that if the corporation should run out of cash, it may use that $10,000 and repay him later.

   (6) Company records have not been properly maintained, and the amount of retained earnings is not known.

Instructions

a Prepare a balance sheet for the business entity R & B Property Management Corporation at December 31, 19___.

b For each of the notes numbered (1) through (5) above, explain your reasoning in deciding whether or not to include the items on the balance sheet and in determining the proper dollar valuation.

BUSINESS DECISION PROBLEM 1

Davis Company and Green Company are in the same line of business and both were recently organized; so it may be assumed that the recorded costs for assets are close to current market values. In both companies the notes payable are due in 60 days. The balance sheets for the two companies are as follows at October 31, 19___.

DAVIS COMPANY
Balance Sheet
October 31, 19___

Assets		Liabilities & Stockholders' Equity		
Cash	$ 4,000	Liabilities:		
Accounts receivable	8,000	Notes payable		$ 52,000
Land	80,000	Accounts payable		36,000
Building	50,000	Total liabilities		$ 88,000
Office equipment	10,000	Stockholders' equity:		
		Capital stock	$60,000	
		Retained earnings	4,000	64,000
	$152,000			$152,000

GREEN COMPANY
Balance Sheet
October 31, 19___

Assets		Liabilities & Stockholders' Equity		
Cash	$20,000	Liabilities:		
Accounts receivable	40,000	Notes payable		$ 12,000
Land	6,000	Accounts payable		8,000
Building	10,000	Total liabilities		$20,000
Office equipment	1,000	Stockholders' equity:		
		Capital stock	$50,000	
		Retained earnings	7,000	57,000
	$77,000			$77,000

Instructions

a Assume that you are a banker and that each company has applied to you for a 90-day loan of $10,000. Which would you consider to be the more favorable prospect? Explain your answer fully.

b Assume that you are an investor considering purchasing all the capital stock of one or both of the companies. For which business would you be willing to pay the higher price? Explain your answer fully. (It is recognized that for either decision, additional information would be useful, but you are to reach your decisions on the basis of the information available.)

TWO

RECORDING CHANGES IN FINANCIAL POSITION

Many business concerns have several hundred or even several thousand business transactions each day. It would obviously be impracticable to prepare a balance sheet after each transaction, and it is quite unnecessary to do so. Instead, the many individual transactions are recorded in the accounting records; and, at the end of the month or other accounting period, a balance sheet is prepared from these records.

The accounting model

You are already familiar with the use of *models* in many fields. Just as the aerospace scientist builds a model of a spaceship or an urban planner builds a model of a new city, so shall we construct a model of an accounting system. A good model is an accurate portrayal of the real world situation it represents. However, a model usually emphasizes certain key factors and relationships, while deemphasizing details which may vary without affecting the successful working of the system. The accounting model presented in this and following chapters is a miniature portrayal of the factors and key relationships that influence the accounting process in a real-world business enterprise.

Remember that accounting systems may be maintained in some businesses by one person with pen-and-ink methods, or in other companies by hundreds of people with electric accounting machines, or by large-scale electronic computers. By use of a model which emphasizes basic concepts, however, you can gain an understanding of accounting which will be useful in any one of the wide range of real-world business situations. The purpose of our rather simple model is to demonstrate how business transactions are analyzed, entered into the accounting system, and stored for use in preparing balance sheets and other financial reports. The model will enable us to study the interrelationships of the business enterprise, to determine what information is needed, by whom it is needed, how it can be gathered and classified, and how frequently the information in the system should be summarized and reported.

The use of accounts for recording transactions

The accounting system includes a separate record for each item that appears in the balance sheet. For example, a separate record is kept for the asset Cash, showing all the increases and decreases in cash which result from the many transactions in which cash is received or paid. A similar record is kept for every other asset, for every liability, and for owners' equity. The form of record used to record increases and decreases in a single balance sheet item is called an *account,* or sometimes a *ledger account.* All these separate accounts are usually kept in a looseleaf binder, and the entire group of accounts is called a *ledger.*

Today many businesses use electronic computers for maintaining accounting records, and data may be stored on magnetic tapes rather than in ledgers. However, an understanding of accounting concepts is most easily acquired by study of a manual accounting system. The knowledge gained by working with manual accounting records is readily transferable to any type of automated accounting system. For these reasons, we shall use standard written accounting forms such as ledger accounts as the model for our study of basic accounting concepts. These standard forms continue to be used by a great many businesses, but for our purposes they should be viewed as conceptual devices rather than as fixed and unchanging structural components of an accounting system.

THE LEDGER

Ledger accounts are a means of accumulating information needed by management in directing the business. For example, by maintaining a Cash account, management can keep track of the amount of cash available for meeting payrolls and for making current purchases of assets or services. This record of cash is also useful in planning future operations and in advance planning of applications for bank loans. The development of the annual budget requires estimating in advance the expected receipts and payments of cash; these estimates of cash flow are naturally based to some extent on the ledger accounts showing past cash receipts and payments.

In its simplest form, an account has only three elements: (1) a title, consisting of the name of the particular asset, liability, or owners' equity; (2) a left side, which is called the *debit* side; and (3) a right side, which is called the *credit* side. This form of account, illustrated below is called a *T account* because of its resemblance to the letter T. More complete forms of accounts will be illustrated later.

T account: a ledger account in simplified form

Title of Account

Left or debit side	Right or credit side

Debit and credit entries

An amount recorded on the left or debit side of an account is called a *debit,* or a *debit entry;* an amount entered on the right or credit side is called a *credit,* or a *credit entry.* Accountants also use the words debit and credit as verbs. The act of recording a debit in an account is called *debiting* the account; the recording of a credit is called *crediting* the account. A debit to an account is also sometimes called a *charge* to the account; an account is debited or *charged* when an amount is entered on the left side of the account.

Students beginning a course in accounting often have preconceived but erroneous notions about the meanings of the terms debit and credit. For example, to some people unacquainted with accounting, the word credit may carry a more favorable connotation than does the word debit. Such connotations have no validity in the field of accounting. Accountants use *debit* to mean an entry on the left-hand side of an account and *credit* to mean an entry on the right-hand side. The student should therefore regard debit and credit as simple equivalents of left and right, without any hidden or subtle implications.

To illustrate the recording of debits and credits in an account, let us go back to the cash transactions of the Greenhill Real Estate Company as illustrated in Chapter 1. When these cash transactions are recorded in an account, the receipts are listed in vertical order on the debit side of the account and the payments are listed on the credit side. The dates of the transactions may also be listed, as shown in the following illustration:

Cash transactions entered in ledger account

Cash

9/1		20,000	9/3	7,000
9/20	7,500	500	9/5	5,000
		20,500	9/30	1,000
				13,000

Note that the total of the cash receipts, $20,500, is in small-size figures so that it will not be mistaken for a debit entry. The total of the cash payments (credits), amounting to $13,000, is also in small-size figures to distinguish it from the credit entries. These *footings,* or memorandum totals, are merely a convenient step in determining the amount of cash on hand at the end of the month. The difference in dollars between the total debits and the total credits in an account is called the *balance.* If the debits exceed the credits the account has a *debit balance;* if the credits exceed the debits the account has a *credit balance.* In the illustrated Cash account, the debit total of $20,500 is larger than the credit total of $13,000; therefore, the account has a debit balance. By subtracting the credits from the debits ($20,500–$13,000), we determine that the balance of the Cash account is $7,500. This debit balance is noted on the debit (left) side of the account. The balance of the Cash account represents the amount of cash owned by the business on September 30; in a balance sheet prepared at this date, Cash in the amount of $7,500 would be listed as an asset.

DEBIT BALANCES IN ASSET ACCOUNTS   In the preceding illustration of a cash account, increases were recorded on the left or debit side of the account and decreases were recorded on the right or credit side. The increases were greater than the decreases and the result was a debit balance in the account.

All asset accounts normally have debit balances; as a matter of fact, the ownership by a business of cash, land, or any other asset indicates that the increases (debits) to that asset have been greater than the decreases (credits). It is hard to imagine an account for an asset such as land having a credit balance, as this would indicate that the business had disposed of more land than it had acquired and had reached the impossible position of having a negative amount of land.

The balance sheets previously illustrated in Chapter 1 showed all the assets on the left side of the balance sheet. The fact that assets are located on the *left* side of the balance sheet is a convenient means of remembering the rule that an increase in an asset is recorded on the *left* (debit) side of the account, and also that an asset account normally has a debit *(left-hand)* balance.

Asset accounts normally have debit balances	*Any Asset Account*	
	(Debit) *Increase*	*(Credit)* *Decrease*

CREDIT BALANCES IN LIABILITY AND OWNERS' EQUITY ACCOUNTS
Increases in liability and owners' equity accounts are recorded by

credit entries, and decreases in these accounts are recorded by debits. The relationship between entries in these accounts and their position on the balance sheet may be summed up as follows: (1) liabilities and owners' equity belong on the *right* side of the balance sheet; (2) an increase in a liability or an owners' equity account is recorded on the *right* side of the account; and (3) liability and owners' equity accounts normally have credit *(right-hand)* balances.

Liability accounts and owners' equity accounts normally have credit balances	Any Liability Account or Owners' Equity Account	
	(Debit) Decrease	*(Credit)* Increase

CONCISE STATEMENT OF THE RULES OF DEBIT AND CREDIT The rules of debit and credit, which have been explained and illustrated in the preceding sections, may be concisely summarized as follows:

	Asset Accounts	Liability & Owners' Equity Accounts
Mechanics of debit and credit	*Increases are recorded by debits* *Decreases are recorded by credits*	*Increases are recorded by credits* *Decreases are recorded by debits*

EQUALITY OF DEBITS AND CREDITS Every business transaction affects two or more accounts. The *double-entry system,* which is the system in almost universal use, takes its name from the fact that *equal debit and credit entries are made for every transaction.* If only two accounts are affected (as in the purchase of land for cash), one account, Land, is debited and the other account, Cash, is credited for the same amount. If more than two accounts are affected by a transaction, the sum of the debit entries must be equal to the sum of the credit entries. This situation was illustrated when the Greenhill Real Estate Company purchased a building for a price of $12,000. The $12,000 debit to the asset account, Building, was exactly equal to the total of the $5,000 credit to the Cash account plus the $7,000 credit to the liability account, Accounts Payable. Since every transaction results in an equal amount of debits and credits in the ledger, it follows that the total of all debit entries in the ledger is equal to the total of all the credit entries.

Recording transactions in ledger accounts: illustration

The procedure for recording transactions in ledger accounts will be illustrated by using the September transactions of Greenhill Real Estate

Company. Each transaction will first be analyzed in terms of increases and decreases in assets, liabilities, and stockholders' equity. Then we shall follow the rules of debit and credit in entering these increases and decreases in T accounts. Asset accounts will be shown on the left side of the page, liability and stockholders' equity accounts on the right side. For convenience in following the transactions into the ledger accounts, the letter used to identify a given transaction will also appear opposite the debit and credit entries for that transaction. This use of identifying letters is for illustrative purposes only and is not used in actual accounting practice.

Transaction (a) The sum of $20,000 cash was invested in the business on September 1, and 2,000 shares of capital stock were issued.

	Analysis	Rule	Entry
Recording an investment in the business	The asset Cash was increased	Increases in assets are recorded by debits	Debit: Cash, $20,000
	The stockholders' equity was increased	Increases in stock-holders' equity are re-corded by credits	Credit: Capital Stock, $20,000

Cash				Capital Stock		
9/1	(a) 20,000				9/1	(a) 20,000

Transaction (b) On September 3, Greenhill Real Estate Company purchased land for cash in the amount of $7,000.

	Analysis	Rule	Entry
Purchase of land for cash	The asset Land was increased	Increases in assets are recorded by debits	Debit: Land $7,000
	The asset Cash was decreased	Decreases in assets are recorded by credits	Credit: Cash, $7,000

Cash			
9/1	20,000	9/3	(b) 7,000

Land	
9/3	(b) 7,000

Transaction (c) On September 5, the Greenhill Real Estate Company purchased a building from X Company at a total price of $12,000. The terms of the purchase required a cash payment of $5,000 with the remainder of $7,000 payable within 90 days.

	Analysis	Rule	Entry
Purchase of an asset, with partial payment	A new asset, Building, was acquired	Increases in assets are recorded by debits	Debit: Building, $12,000
	The asset Cash was decreased	Decreases in assets are recorded by credits	Credit: Cash, $5,000
	A new liability, Accounts Payable, was incurred	Increases in liabilities are recorded by credits	Credit: Accounts Payable, $7,000

Cash				Accounts Payable	
9/1	20,000	9/3	7,000	9/5	(c) 7,000
		9/5	(c) 5,000		

Building	
9/5 (c) 12,000	

Transaction (d) On September 10, the Greenhill Real Estate Company sold a portion of its land on credit to Carter's Drugstore for a price of $2,000. The land was sold at its cost; so there was no gain or loss on the transaction.

	Analysis	Rule	Entry
Sale of land on credit	A new asset, Accounts Receivable, was acquired	Increases in assets are recorded by debits	Debit: Accounts Receivable, $2,000
	The asset Land was decreased	Decreases in assets are recorded by credits	Credit: Land, $2,000

Accounts Receivable	
9/10 (d) 2,000	

Land			
9/3	7,000	9/10	(d) 2,000

Transaction (e) On September 14, the Greenhill Real Estate Company purchased office equipment on credit from General Equipment, Inc., in the amount of $1,800.

	Analysis	Rule	Entry
Purchase of an asset on credit	*A new asset, Office Equipment, was acquired*	*Increases in assets are recorded by debits*	*Debit: Office Equipment, $1,800*
	A new liability, Accounts Payable, was incurred	*Increases in liabilities are recorded by credits*	*Credit: Accounts Payable, $1,800*

Office Equipment		Accounts Payable	
9/14 (e) 1,800		9/5 7,000	
		9/14 (e) 1,800	

Transaction (f) On September 20, cash of $500 was received as partial collection of the account receivable from Carter's Drugstore.

	Analysis	Rule	Entry
Collection of an account receivable	*The asset Cash was increased*	*Increases in assets are recorded by debits*	*Debit: Cash, $500*
	The asset Accounts Receivable was decreased	*Decreases in assets are recorded by credits*	*Credit: Accounts Receivable, $500*

Cash			
9/1 20,000	9/3 7,000
9/20 (f) 500	9/5 5,000

Accounts Receivable			
9/10 2,000	9/20 (f) 500

Transaction (g) A cash payment of $1,000 was made on September 30 in partial settlement of the amount owing to General Equipment, Inc.

	Analysis	Rule	Entry
Payment of a liability	The liability Accounts Payable was decreased	Decreases in liabilities are recorded by debits	Debit: Accounts Payable, $1,000
	The asset Cash was decreased	Decreases in assets are recorded by credits	Credit: Cash, $1,000

Cash					Accounts Payable			
9/1	20,000	9/3	7,000	9/30	(g) 1,000	9/5	7,000
9/20	500	9/5	5,000			9/14	1,800
		9/30	(g) 1,000				

Standard form of the ledger account

The standard form of ledger account provides for more information than the T accounts used in preceding illustrations. The only change from the T account to a formal ledger account is the addition of special rulings, as shown by the following illustration:

Standard form of ledger account	Title of Account						Account No.	
	Date	Explanation	Ref	Amount	Date	Explanation	Ref	Amount

Note that each side of the account has identical columns as follows:

Date column   The date of the transaction is listed here.

Explanation column   This column is needed only for unusual items, and in most companies is seldom used.

Ref (Reference) column   The page number of the journal on which the transaction is recorded is listed in this column, thus making it possible to trace ledger entries back to their source. The use of a *journal* is explained later in this chapter.

Amount column   The dollar amount of the journal entry is entered here.

The headings for these columns are usually not printed on ledger paper, although paper with column headings is also available. Since T accounts provide the basic elements of a ledger account, they are used in this text in preference to the standard form of account to achieve simplicity in illustrating accounting principles and procedures.

Sequence and numbering of ledger accounts

Accounts are usually arranged in the ledger in "financial statement order"; that is, assets first, followed by liabilities, owners' equity, revenue, and expenses. The number of accounts needed by a business will depend upon its size, the nature of its operations, and the extent to which management and regulatory agencies want detailed classification of information. An identification number is assigned to each account. A *chart of accounts* is a listing of the account titles and account numbers being used by a given business.

In the following list of accounts, certain numbers have not been assigned; these numbers are held in reserve so that additional accounts can be inserted in the ledger in proper sequence whenever such accounts become necessary. In this illustration, the numbers from 1 to 29 are used exclusively for asset accounts; numbers from 30 to 49 are used for liabilities; numbers in the 50s signify owners' equity accounts; numbers in the 60s represent revenue accounts; and numbers from 70 to 99 designate expense accounts. Revenue and expense accounts are discussed in Chapter 3. The balance sheet accounts with which we are concerned in this chapter are numbered as shown in the following brief chart of accounts.

	Account Title	*Account Number*
System for numbering ledger accounts	*Assets:*	
	Cash	*1*
	Accounts Receivable	*2*
	Land	*20*
	Building	*22*
	Office Equipment	*25*
	Liabilities:	
	Accounts Payable	*30*
	Stockholders' Equity:	
	Capital Stock	*50*

In large businesses with many more accounts, a more elaborate numbering system would be needed. Some companies use a four-digit number for each account; each of the four digits carries special significance as to the classification of the account.

THE JOURNAL

In our description of accounting procedures thus far, emphasis has been placed on the analysis of transactions in terms of debits and credits to ledger accounts. Although transactions could be entered directly in ledger accounts in a very small business, it is much more convenient and efficient in most businesses to record transactions first in a journal and later to transfer the debits and credits to ledger accounts. The *journal,* or ***book of original entry,*** is a chronological record, showing for each transaction the debit and credit changes caused in specific ledger accounts; it may also include a brief written explanation of each transaction. At convenient intervals, the debit and credit entries recorded in the journal are transferred to the accounts in the ledger. The updated ledger accounts, in turn, serve as the basis from which the balance sheet and other financial statements are prepared.

The term *transaction* was explained in Chapter 1, but a concise definition at this point may be a helpful reminder. A transaction is an event causing a dollar change in the assets, liabilities, or owners' equity of a business entity. Common examples are the payment or collection of cash, a purchase or sale on credit, and the payment of dividends to the owners. Note that a transaction has an accounting value and has an influence on financial statements. Events such as the opening of a competing business or the retirement of an employee are not entered in the accounts and are not considered to be transactions.

The unit of organization for the journal is the transaction, whereas the unit of organization for the ledger is the account. By making use of both a journal and a ledger, we can achieve several advantages which are not possible if transactions are recorded directly in ledger accounts:

1 *The journal shows all information about a transaction in one place and also provides an explanation of the transaction.* In a journal entry, the debits and credits for a given transaction are recorded together, but when the transaction is recorded in the ledger, the debits and credits are entered in different accounts. Since a ledger may contain hundreds of accounts, it would be very difficult to locate all the facts about a particular transaction by looking in the ledger. The journal is the record which shows the complete story of a transaction in one entry.

2 *The journal provides a chronological record of all the events in the life of a business.* If we want to look up the facts about a transaction of some months or years back, all we need is the date of the transaction in order to locate it in the journal.

3 *The use of a journal helps to prevent errors.* If transactions were recorded directly in the ledger, it would be very easy to make errors such as omitting the debit or the credit, or entering the debit twice or the credit twice. Such errors are not likely to be made in the journal, since the offsetting debits and credits appear together for each transaction. It is of course possible to forget to transfer a debit or credit from the journal to a ledger account, but such an error can be detected by tracing the entries in the ledger accounts back to the journal.

The general journal: illustration of entries

Many businesses maintain several types of journals. The nature of operations and the volume of transactions in the particular business determine the number and type of journals needed. The simplest type of journal, and the one with which we are concerned in this chapter, is called a *general journal.* It has only two money columns, one for debits and the other for credits; it may be used for all types of transactions.

The process of recording a transaction in a journal is called *journalizing* the transaction. To illustrate the use of the general journal, we shall now journalize the transactions of the Greenhill Real Estate Company which have previously been discussed.

General Journal Page 1

	Date		Account Titles and Explanations	LP	Debit	Credit
September journal entries for Greenhill Real Estate Company	19___ Sept.	1	Cash	1	20,000	
			Capital Stock	50		20,000
			Issued 2,000 shares of capital stock in exchange for cash invested in the business.			
		3	Land	20	7,000	
			Cash	1		7,000
			Purchased land for office site.			
		5	Building	22	12,000	
			Cash	1		5,000
			Accounts Payable	30		7,000
			Purchased building to be moved to our lot. Paid part cash; balance payable within 90 days to X Company.			
		10	Accounts Receivable	2	2,000	
			Land	20		2,000
			Sold the unused part of our lot at cost to Carter's Drugstore. Due within three months.			
		14	Office Equipment.	25	1,800	
			Accounts Payable	30		1,800
			Purchased office equipment on credit from General Equipment, Inc.			
		20	Cash	1	500	
			Accounts Receivable	2		500
			Collected part of receivable from Carter's Drugstore.			
		30	Accounts Payable	30	1,000	
			Cash	1		1,000
			Made partial payment of the liability to General Equipment, Inc.			

Efficient use of a general journal requires two things: (1) ability to analyze the effect of a transaction upon assets, liabilities, and owners' equity and (2) familiarity with the standard form and arrangement of journal entries. Our primary interest is in the analytical phase of journalizing; the procedural steps can be learned quickly by observing the following points in the illustrations of journal entries shown above.

1 The year, month, and day of the first entry on the page are written in the date column. The year and month need not be repeated for subsequent entries until a new page or a new month is begun.

2 The name of the account to be debited is written on the first line of the entry and is customarily placed at the extreme left next to the date column. The amount of the debit is entered on the same line in the left-hand money column.

3 The name of the account to be credited is entered on the line below the debit entry and is indented, that is, placed about 1 inch to the right of the date column. The amount credited is entered on the same line in the right-hand money column.

4 A brief explanation of the transaction is usually begun on the line immediately below the title of the account. The explanation need not be indented.

5 A blank line is usually left after each entry. This spacing causes each journal entry to stand out clearly as a separate unit and makes the general journal easier to read.

6 An entry which includes more than one debit or more than one credit (such as the entry on September 5) is called a *compound journal entry.* Regardless of how many debits or credits are contained in a compound journal entry, all the debits are customarily entered before any credits are listed.

7 The LP (ledger page) column just to the left of the debit money column is left blank at the time of making the journal entry. When the debits and credits are later transferred to ledger accounts, the numbers of the ledger accounts are listed in this column to provide a convenient cross reference with the ledger.

A familiarity with the general journal form of describing transactions is just as essential to the study of accounting as a familiarity with plus and minus signs is to the study of mathematics. The journal entry is a *tool* for *analyzing* and *describing* the impact of various transactions upon a business entity. The ability to describe a transaction in journal entry form requires a complete understanding of the nature of the transaction.

Posting

The process of transferring the debits and credits from the general journal to the proper ledger accounts is called *posting.* Each amount listed in the debit column of the journal is posted by entering it on the debit side of an account in the ledger, and each amount listed in the credit column of the journal is posted to the credit side of a ledger account.

The mechanics of posting may vary somewhat with the preferences of the individual. The following sequence is commonly used:

1 Locate in the ledger the first account named in the journal entry.

2 Enter in the debit column of the ledger account the amount of the debit as shown in the journal.

3 Enter the date of the transaction in the ledger account.

4 Enter in the reference column of the ledger account the number of the journal page from which the entry is being posted.

5 The recording of the debit in the ledger account is now complete; as evidence of this fact, return to the journal and enter in the LP (ledger page) column the number of the ledger account or page to which the debit was posted.

6 Repeat the posting process described in the preceding five steps for the credit side of the journal entry.

ILLUSTRATION OF POSTING To illustrate the posting process, the journal entry for the first transaction of the Greenhill Real Estate Company is repeated at this point, along with the two ledger accounts affected by this entry.

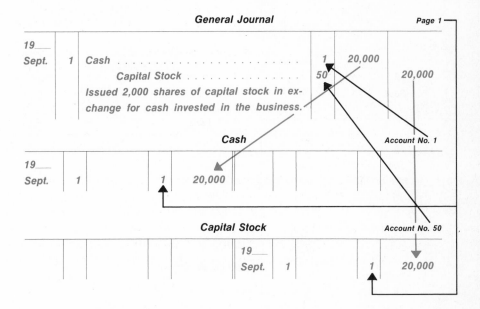

Note that the Ref (Reference) column of each of the two ledger accounts illustrated above contains the number 1, indicating that the posting was made from page 1 of the journal. Entering the journal page number in the ledger account and listing the ledger page in the journal provide a cross reference between these two records. The audit of accounting records always requires looking up some journal entries to obtain more information about the amounts listed in ledger accounts. A cross reference between the ledger and journal is therefore essential to efficient audit of the records. Another advantage gained from entering in the journal the number of the account to which a posting has been made is to provide evidence throughout the posting work as to which items have been posted. Otherwise, any interruption in the posting might leave some doubt as to what had been posted.

Ledger accounts after posting

After all the September transactions have been posted, the ledger of the Greenhill Real Estate Company appears as shown below. The accounts are arranged in the ledger in balance sheet order, that is, assets first, followed by liabilities and stockholders' equity.

Cash　　　　　　　　　　　　　　Account No. 1

Ledger showing September transactions	19___					19___			
	Sept.	1		1	20,000	Sept.	3	1	7,000
		20	7,500	1	500		5	1	5,000
					20,500		30	1	1,000
									13,000

Accounts Receivable　　　　　　　Account No. 2

19___				19___			
Sept.	10	1,500	1	2,000	Sept.	20	1	500

Land　　　　　　　　　　　　　Account No. 20

19___				19___			
Sept.	3	5,000	1	7,000	Sept.	10	1	2,000

Building　　　　　　　　　　　Account No. 22

19___				
Sept.	5		1	12,000

Office Equipment　　　　　　　Account No. 25

19___				
Sept.	14		1	1,800

Accounts Payable　　　　　　　Account No. 30

19___					19___			
Sept.	30		1	1,000	Sept.	5	1	7,000
						14	7,800	1	1,800
								8,800

Capital Stock　　　　　　　　Account No. 50

			19___		
			Sept.	1	1	20,000

Computing balances of ledger accounts

The computation of the balance of the Cash account was illustrated earlier in this chapter, but a concise statement of a commonly used procedure for computing the balance of an account containing several entries may be useful at this point.

1 Add the debits in the account and insert the total in small figures just below the last entry in the debit column.

2 Add the credits in the account and insert the total in small figures just below the last entry in the credit column.

3 Compute the difference between the debit total and the credit total. If the account has a debit balance, enter this amount as a small figure to the left of the last debit entry; if the account has a credit balance, enter this amount to the left of the last credit entry.

THE TRIAL BALANCE

Since equal dollar amounts of debits and credits are entered in the accounts for every transaction recorded, the sum of all the debits in the ledger must be equal to the sum of all the credits. If the computation of account balances has been accurate, it follows that the total of the accounts with debit balances must be equal to the total of the accounts with credit balances.

Before using the account balances to prepare a balance sheet, it is desirable to *prove* that the total of accounts with debit balances is in fact equal to the total of accounts with credit balances. This proof of the equality of debit and credit balances is called a *trial balance.* A trial balance is a two-column schedule listing the names and balances of all the accounts *in the order in which they appear in the ledger;* the debit balances are listed in the left-hand column and the credit balances in the right-hand column. The totals of the two columns should agree. A trial balance taken from the ledger of the Greenhill Real Estate Company appears below:

GREENHILL REAL ESTATE COMPANY
Trial Balance
September 30, 19___

Trial balance at month-end proves ledger is in balance		
Cash	$ 7,500	
Accounts receivable	1,500	
Land	5,000	
Building	12,000	
Office equipment	1,800	
Accounts payable		$ 7,800
Capital stock		20,000
	$27,800	$27,800

Uses and limitations of the trial balance

The trial balance provides proof that the ledger is in balance. The agreement of the debit and credit totals of the trial balance gives assurance that:

1 Equal debits and credits have been recorded for all transactions.

2 The debit or credit balance of each account has been correctly computed.

3 The addition of the account balances in the trial balance has been correctly performed.

Suppose that the debit and credit totals of the trial balance do not agree. This situation indicates that one or more errors have been made. Typical of such errors are: (1) the entering of a debit as a credit, or vice versa; (2) arithmetic mistakes in balancing accounts; (3) clerical errors in copying account balances into the trial balance; (4) listing a debit balance in the credit column of the trial balance, or vice versa; and (5) errors in addition of the trial balance.

The preparation of a trial balance does not prove that transactions have been correctly analyzed and recorded in the proper accounts. If, for example, a receipt of cash were erroneously recorded by debiting the Land account instead of the Cash account, the trial balance would still balance. Also, if a transaction were completely omitted from the ledger, the error would not be disclosed by the trial balance. In brief, the trial balance proves only one aspect of the ledger, and that is the equality of debits and credits entered in the accounting records.

Despite these limitations, the trial balance is a useful device. It not only provides assurance that the ledger is in balance, but it also serves as a convenient steppingstone for the preparation of financial statements. As explained in Chapter 1, the balance sheet is a formal statement showing the financial position of the business, intended for distribution to managers, owners, bankers, and various outsiders. The trial balance, on the other hand, is merely a working paper, useful to the accountant but not intended for distribution to others. The balance sheet and other financial statements can be prepared more conveniently from the trial balance than directly from the ledger, especially if there are a great many ledger accounts.

Locating errors

In the illustrations given thus far, the trial balances have all been in balance. Every accounting student soon discovers in working problems, however, that errors are easily made which prevent trial balances from balancing. The lack of balance may be the result of a single error or a combination of several errors. An error may have been made in adding the trial balance columns or in copying the balances from the ledger accounts. If the preparation of the trial balance has been accurate, then the error may lie in the accounting records, either in the journal or in the ledger accounts. What is the most efficient approach to locating the error or errors? There is no single technique which will give the best results every time, but the following procedures, done in sequence, will often save considerable time and effort in locating errors.

1 Prove the addition of the trial balance columns by adding these columns in the opposite direction from that previously followed.

2 If the error does not lie in addition, next determine the exact amount by which the schedule is out of balance. The amount of the discrepancy is often a clue to the source of the error. If the discrepancy is divisible by 9, this suggests either a *transposition* error or a *slide.* For example, assume that the Cash account has a balance of $2,175, but in copying the balance into the trial balance the figures are *transposed* and written as $2,157. The resulting error is $18, and like all transposition errors is divisible by 9. Another common error is the slide, or incorrect placement of the decimal point, as when $2,175.00 is copied as $21.75. The resulting discrepancy in the trial balance will also be an amount divisible by 9.

To illustrate another method of using the amount of a discrepancy as a clue to locating the error, assume that the Office Equipment account has a *debit* balance of $420 but that it is erroneously listed in the *credit* column of the trial balance. This will cause a discrepancy of two times $420, or $840, in the trial balance totals. Since such errors as recording a debit in a credit column are not uncommon, it is advisable, after determining the discrepancy in the trial balance totals, to scan the columns for an amount equal to exactly one-half of the discrepancy. It is also advisable to look over the transactions for an item of the exact amount of the discrepancy. An error may have been made by recording the debit side of the transaction and forgetting to enter the credit side.

3 Compare the amounts in the trial balance with the balances in the ledger. Make sure that each ledger account balance has been included in the correct column of the trial balance.

4 Recompute the balance of each ledger account.

5 Trace all postings from the journal to the ledger accounts. As this is done, place a check mark in the journal and in the ledger after each figure verified. When the operation is completed, look through the journal and the ledger for unchecked amounts. In tracing postings, be alert not only for errors in amount but for debits entered as credits, or vice versa.

Dollar signs

Dollar signs are not used in journals or ledgers. Some accountants use dollar signs in trial balances; some do not. In this book, dollar signs are used in trial balances. Dollar signs should always be used in the balance sheet, the income statement, and other formal financial reports. In the balance sheet, for example, a dollar sign is placed by the first amount in each column and also by the final amount or total. Many accountants also place a dollar sign by each subtotal or other amount listed below an underlining. In the published financial statements of large corporations, such as those illustrated in the appendix of this book, the use of dollar signs is often limited to the first and last figures in a column.

DEMONSTRATION PROBLEM

a Auto Parks, Inc., was organized on October 1 and carried out several transactions prior to opening for business on November 1. The partially filled in general journal for this organizational period appears below. You are to determine the titles of the accounts to be debited and credited in these journal entries.

General Journal   Page 1

Date		Account Titles and Explanations	LP	Debit	Credit
19___					
Oct.	1			90,000	
					90,000
		Issued 9,000 shares of $10 par value capital stock for cash.			
	2			24,000	
					4,000
					20,000
		Purchased land. Paid part cash and issued note payable for balance.			
	3			3,600	
					3,600
		Purchased a small portable building for cash.			
	4			1,600	
					1,600
		Purchased cash register from Bar & Co. on account.	)		
	24			700	
					700
		Paid part of account payable to Bar & Co.			

b Post the preceding journal entries to the proper ledger accounts. Insert the ledger account number in the LP column of the journal as each item is posted.

Cash   1

Land 21

Building 23

Office Equipment 25

Accounts Payable 43

Notes Payable 45

Capital Stock 50

c Complete the following trial balance as of October 31, 19___.

AUTO PARKS, INC.
Trial Balance
October 31, 19___

Cash . . . . $

Land . . . .

Building . . . .

Office equipment . . . .

Accounts payable . . . . $

Notes payable . . . .

Capital stock . . . .

$ $

SOLUTION TO DEMONSTRATION PROBLEM

a

Date		Account Titles and Explanations	LP	Debit	Credit
19___					
Oct.	1	Cash	1	90,000	
		Capital Stock	50		90,000
		Issued 9,000 shares of $10 par value capital stock for cash.			
	2	Land	21	24,000	
		Cash	1		4,000
		Notes Payable	45		20,000
		Purchased land. Paid part cash and issued note payable for balance.			
	3	Building	23	3,600	
		Cash	1		3,600
		Purchased a small portable building for cash.			
	4	Office Equipment...............	25	1,600	
		Accounts Payable	43		1,600
		Purchased cash register from Bar & Co. on account.			
	24	Accounts Payable	43	700	
		Cash	1		700
		Paid part of account payable to Bar & Co.			

General Journal — Page 1

b To conserve space, the ledger accounts comprising part **b** of the demonstration problem are not shown here. However, the student can readily verify the accuracy of his work on part **b** by referring to the month-end account balances appearing in part **c** below.

c

AUTO PARKS, INC.

Trial Balance

October 31, 19___

Cash	$ 81,700	
Land	24,000	
Building	3,600	
Office equipment..........................	1,600	
Accounts payable		$ 900
Notes payable		20,000
Capital stock		90,000
	$110,900	$110,900

REVIEW QUESTIONS

1 Is it true that favorable events are recorded by credits and unfavorable events by debits? Explain.

2 State briefly the rules of debit and credit as applied to asset, liability, and owners' equity accounts.

3 Explain precisely what is meant by each of the phrases listed below. Whenever appropriate, indicate whether the left or right side of an account is affected and whether an increase or decrease is indicated.
  a A debit of $200 to the Cash account
  b Credit balance
  c Credit side of an account
  d A debit of $600 to Accounts Payable
  e Debit balance
  f A credit of $50 to Accounts Receivable
  g A debit to the Land account

4 What relationship exists between the position of an account on the balance sheet and the rules for recording increases in that account?

5 Certain accounts normally have *debit balances* and other types of accounts normally have *credit balances.* State a rule indicating the position on the balance sheet of each such group of accounts.

6 For each of the following transactions, indicate whether the account in parentheses should be debited or credited, and give the reason for your answer.
  a Purchased a typewriter on credit, promising to make payment in full within 30 days. (Accounts Payable)
  b Purchased land for cash. (Cash)
  c Sold an old, unneeded typewriter on 30-day credit. (Office Equipment)
  d Obtained a loan of $5,000 from a bank. (Cash)
  e Issued 1,000 shares of $25 par value capital stock for cash of $25,000. (Capital Stock)

7 Compare and contrast a *journal* and a *ledger.*

8 What is the primary purpose of journal entries from the point of view of **(a)** a business entity and **(b)** an accounting student?

9 What requirement is imposed by the double-entry system in the recording of any business transaction?

10 During the first week of an accounting course, one student expressed the opinion that a great deal of time could be saved if a business would record transactions directly in ledger accounts rather than entering transactions first in a journal and then posting the debit and credit amounts from the journal to the ledger. Student B agreed with this view but added that such a system should not be called double-entry bookkeeping since each transaction would be entered only once. Student C disagreed with both A and B. He argued that the use of a journal and a ledger was more efficient than entering transactions directly in ledger accounts. Furthermore, he argued that the meaning of double-entry bookkeeping did not refer to the practice of maintaining both a journal and ledger. Evaluate the statements made by all three students.

11 Which step in the recording of transactions requires greater understanding of accounting principles?
  a The entering of transactions in the journal
  b The posting of entries to ledger accounts

12 What purposes are served by the preparation of a trial balance?

13 Criticize the following statement. "Nearly all business enterprises use the double-entry system of accounting. Under this system the number of accounts with debit balances must agree with the number of accounts with credit balances. This equality of accounts causes the ledger to be in balance.''

14 A student beginning the study of accounting prepared a trial balance in which two unusual features appeared. The Buildings account showed a credit balance of $20,000, and the Accounts Payable account a debit balance of $100. Considering each of these two abnormal balances separately, state whether the condition was the result of an error in the records or could have resulted from proper recording of an unusual transaction.

EXERCISES

Ex. 2-1 Enter the following transactions in T accounts drawn on ordinary notebook paper. Label each debit and credit with the letter identifying the transaction. Prepare a trial balance at May 31.

a On May 10, the Cardiff Company was organized and issued 2,000 shares of $10 par value capital stock in exchange for $20,000 cash.

b On May 13, land was acquired for $10,000 cash.

c On May 18, a prefabricated building was purchased from E-Z Built Corporation at a cost of $12,000. A cash payment of $3,000 was made and a note payable was issued for the balance.

d On May 20, office equipment was purchased at a cost of $3,000. A cash down payment of $1,000 was made, and it was agreed that the balance should be paid within 30 days.

e On May 30, $1,000 of the amount due E-Z Built Corporation was paid.

Ex. 2-2 The following accounts show the first six transactions of the Edgemar Corporation. Prepare a journal entry (including written explanation) for each transaction.

Cash				Accounts Payable			
Jan. 1	80,000	Jan. 12	14,000	Jan. 25	200	Jan. 20	1,500
		Feb. 5	1,300	Feb. 5	1,300		

Land				Notes Payable			
Jan. 12	40,000			Feb. 10	10,000	Jan. 12	48,500

Building				Capital Stock, $10 par value			
Jan. 12	22,500					Jan. 1	80,000
						Feb. 10	10,000

Office Equipment			
Jan. 20	1,500	Jan. 25	200

Ex. 2-3 Enter the following transactions in the two-column journal of Blue Water Service Company. Include a brief explanation of the transaction as part of each journal entry. Do not include in the explanation any amounts or account titles since these are shown in the debit-credit portion of the entry.

June 1 Acquired office equipment from Bell Company for $850 cash.

June 3 Collected an account receivable of $2,000 from a customer, William Rinehart.

June 4 Issued a check for $360 in full payment of an account payable to Chemical Supply Company.

June 8 Issued an additional 1,000 shares of $5 par value capital stock in exchange for $5,000 cash.

June 8 Borrowed $7,500 cash from the bank by signing a 90-day note payable.

June 9 Purchased an adjacent vacant lot for use as parking space. The price was $12,000, of which $2,000 was paid in cash; a note payable was issued for the balance.

Ex. 2-4 The trial balance prepared by Field Company at September 30 was not in balance. In searching for the error, an employee discovered that a transaction for the purchase of a typewriter on credit for $610 had been recorded by a **debit** of $610 to the Office Equipment account and a **debit** of $610 to Accounts Payable. The credit column of the incorrect trial balance had a total of $92,600.

In answering each of the following five questions, explain briefly the reasons underlying your answer and state the dollar amount of the error if any.

a Was the Office Equipment account overstated, understated, or correctly stated in the trial balance?

b Was the total of the debit column of the trial balance overstated, understated, or correctly stated?

c Was the Accounts Payable account overstated, understated, or correctly stated in the trial balance?

d Was the total of the credit column of the trial balance overstated, understated or correctly stated?

e How much was the total of the debit column of the trial balance before correction of the error?

Ex. 2-5 Some of the following errors would cause the debit and credit columns of the trial balance to have unequal totals. For each of the four paragraphs, write a statement explaining with reasons whether the error would cause unequal totals in the trial balance. Each paragraph is to be considered independently of the others.

a A $540 payment for a new typewriter was recorded by a debit to Office Equipment of $54 and a credit to Cash of $54.

b A payment of $400 to a creditor was recorded by a debit to Accounts Payable of $400 and a credit to Cash of $40.

c An account receivable in the amount of $800 was collected in full. The collection was recorded by a debit to Cash for $800 and a debit to Capital Stock for $800.

d An account payable was paid by issuing a check for $350. The payment was recorded by debiting Accounts Payable $350 and crediting Accounts Receivable $350.

PROBLEMS

2-1 Information Update, Incorporated, is in the business of providing computerized accounting services to small companies that do not have adequate personnel or equipment to perform this work for themselves. The alphabetical list on page 58 shows the corporation's account balances at June 30, 19___.

Accounts payable	$ 7,410	Notes payable	$79,800
Accounts receivable	2,850	Notes receivable	1,200
Automobiles	6,800	Office building	33,000
Capital stock	50,000	Office supplies	423
Cash	?	Retained earnings	6,270
Computer	58,950	Taxes payable	746
Furniture & fixtures	5,400	U.S. government bonds	
Garage building	4,970	(should follow Cash)	10,000
Land	16,742		

Instructions

a Prepare a trial balance with the above accounts arranged in the usual sequence in which accounts appear in the ledger. (Compute the balance for Cash so that the ledger will be in balance.)

b Prepare a balance sheet at June 30, 19___.

2-2 Mesa Contractors, Incorporated, was started on September 1, 19___, to perform remodeling work on homes and office buildings and to act as general contractor on larger jobs. As of September 30, 19___, the ledger accounts contained entries as follows:

Cash				**Delivery Equipment**			
Sept. 1	40,000	Sept. 2	7,640	Sept. 2	9,400		
30	650	18	1,250				
		28	160				

Accounts Receivable				**Notes Payable**			
Sept. 15	1,300	Sept. 30	650	Sept. 18	1,000	Sept. 2	10,000

Office Supplies				**Accounts Payable**			
Sept. 6	1,500	Sept. 26	20	Sept. 18	250	Sept. 6	1,500
20	180			26	20	20	180
				28	160		

Office Equipment				**Capital Stock, $10 par value**			
Sept. 2	8,240	Sept. 15	1,300			Sept. 1	40,000

Instructions

a Reconstruct the journal entries as they were probably made by the company's accountant, giving a full explanation for each transaction.

b Determine account balances and prepare a trial balance at September 30, 19___.

c Prepare a balance sheet at September 30, 19___.

2-3 Airport Car Rental Co. was organized on January 1. The following account titles and numbers were established for immediate use by the corporation; it was expected that additional accounts would be required before long.

Cash	10	Office equipment	22
Accounts receivable	11	Accounts payable	31
Land	16	Notes payable	32
Building	17	Capital stock	40
Automobiles	20		

The transactions by the corporation during January 19___, including the initial investment by the stockholders, were as follows:

Jan. 1 Issued 35,000 shares of $5 par value capital stock in exchange for $175,000 cash.

Jan. 2 The corporation purchased land for $35,000 and a building on the lot for $24,000. A cash payment of $20,000 was made and a promissory note issued for the balance.

Jan. 4 Purchased 50 new automobiles at $3,500 each from Fleet Motor Company. Paid $50,000 cash, the balance to be paid within 90 days.

Jan. 5 Sold an automobile to one of the stockholders at cost. The stockholder paid $500 in cash and agreed to pay the balance within 30 days.

Jan. 7 One automobile proved to be defective and was returned to Fleet Motor Company. The amount due the creditor was reduced by $3,500.

Jan. 9 Purchased a cash register and office desks at a cost of $2,300 cash.

Jan. 28 Paid $25,000 cash to Fleet Motor Company.

Instructions
a Prepare journal entries for the month of January.
b Post to ledger accounts, and determine their balances.
c Prepare a trial balance at January 31, 19___.

2-4 Channel 35 TV, Inc., was organized in March 19___ to operate as a local educational television station. The account titles and numbers used by Channel 35 TV, Inc., are listed below:

Cash	11	Telecasting equipment	24
Accounts receivable	15	Film library	25
Supplies	19	Notes payable	31
Land	21	Accounts payable	32
Building	22	Capital stock	51
Transmitter	23		

The transactions for March 19___ were as follows:

Mar. 1 A charter was granted to Joseph Blair for the organization of Channel 35 TV, Inc. Blair invested $192,500 cash and received 20,000 shares of stock in exchange.

Mar. 3 Purchased land at a cost of $60,000 from Inland Development Company, making a cash down payment of $20,000 and signing a promissory note for the balance.

Mar. 5 Purchased a transmitter at a cost of $130,000 from AC Mfg. Co., making a cash down payment of $40,000. The balance, in the form of an account payable, was to be paid in monthly installments of $1,500, beginning March 15.

Mar. 6 Erected a telecasting and office building at a cost of $50,000, paying cash.

Mar. 8 Purchased telecasting equipment at a cost of $56,000 from Telequip Corp., paying cash.

Mar. 9 Purchased a film library at a cost of $51,995 from Modern Film Productions, making a down payment of $14,000 cash, with the balance payable in 30 days.

Mar. 12 Sold part of the film library to City College; cost was $10,000, and selling price also was $10,000. City College agreed to pay the full amount in 30 days.

Mar. 15 Paid $1,500 cash to AC Mfg. Co. as the first monthly payment on the account payable created on March 5.

Mar. 25 Bought supplies costing $1,950, paying cash.

Instructions
a Prepare journal entries.
b Post to ledger accounts and determine the balance in each account.
c Prepare a trial balance at March 31, 19___.
d Prepare a balance sheet at March 31, 19___.

2-5 Motocross Cycle Rentals, Inc., was organized on October 1 to rent motorcycles to the public. The clerk who maintained the accounting records of the company did not understand the double-entry system or the proper use of the journal and ledger. The clerk believed that all increases in account balances should be recorded only in the ledger, while all decreases should be recorded only by a written explanation in the journal. He also believed that credit entries should be used to increase all ledger accounts, regardless of whether the accounts were assets, liabilities, or owners' equity. For example, on October 1, the company issued capital stock for cash, which should have been recorded by a debit to Cash and a credit to Capital Stock. Instead, the clerk recorded the increase in the asset cash by crediting the Cash account. (He also credited Capital Stock, which was correct.) During October the clerk made the following entries.

General Journal

Oct. 2 Paid $11,000 cash as part of the purchase price of land and building.

Oct. 6 Sold a part of the land which cost $5,000 to an adjacent business, Community Medical Center, which is expanding its facilities.

Oct. 15 Paid $7,000 cash as part of the purchase price of 25 motorcycles from United Imports.

Oct. 17 Returned two defective motorcycles (cost $680 each) to United Imports, reducing the amount owed on account.

Oct. 27 Community Medical Center paid off $2,100 of the note originating from the sale of land on October 6.

Oct. 31 Paid $8,640 account payable to United Imports.

Ledger

Cash		1		**Motorcycles**		25
Oct. 1	30,000			Oct. 15	17,000	
Oct. 27	2,100					

Notes Receivable		5		**Notes Payable**		30
Oct. 6	5,000			Oct. 2	25,000	

Land		20		**Accounts Payable**		31
Oct. 2	15,000			Oct. 15	10,000	

Building		23		**Capital Stock**		50
Oct. 2	21,000			Oct. 1	30,000	

Instructions
a Prepare proper journal entries for the month of October.
b Post to ledger accounts.
c Prepare a trial balance at October 31.

2-6 John Davis and Tom Marshal have operated as independent real estate agents in Atlanta, Georgia, for many years. Early in 19___, they agree to combine their separate businesses into a corporation. The balance sheets for Davis and Marshal before they combine their businesses follow:

	Davis	Marshal
Cash	$ 1,700	$ 4,300
Accounts receivable	12,300	16,900
Land	35,000	19,000
Buildings	25,000	41,000
Office equipment	8,000	11,500
	$82,000	$92,700
Notes payable	$42,000	$31,500
Accounts payable	10,000	16,200
Owners' capital	30,000	45,000
	$82,000	$92,700

The D & M Realty Corporation was organized on January 20, 19___, issuing 10,000 shares of capital stock with a total par value of $75,000. Asset values stated on the records of each realtor are to be retained by the corporation. Marshal's books will be used to record all transactions of the corporation. Accordingly, assets and liabilities are transferred to the corporation; Marshal's capital account is closed out; and capital stock is issued to Davis and Marshal in proportion to the capital invested (assets less liabilities).

During the remainder of January 19___ the following transactions are completed by the D & M Realty Corporation:

Jan. 21 Collected $4,900 on accounts receivable.
Jan. 23 Paid $5,400 on accounts payable and $4,000 on notes payable.
Jan. 26 Issued an additional 1,000 shares of stock to employees for a total consideration of $7,500 in cash.
Jan. 29 Sold surplus office equipment on account for $2,800. The equipment is carried on the books at $2,800.
Jan. 31 Purchased a vacant lot for $17,500. Paid $1,750 down; balance is due on February 28, 19___.

Instructions
a Prepare journal entries to record the issuance of capital stock to Davis and Marshal on Marshal's books (which are retained by the corporation).
b Prepare journal entries to record the transactions after the corporation is organized.
c Determine account balances after all transactions have been posted to ledger accounts of the corporation and prepare a balance sheet at January 31, 19___. Account numbers need not be assigned to the ledger accounts.

BUSINESS DECISION PROBLEM 2

Robert Steel, a college student with several summers' experience as a guide on canoe camping trips, decided to form a corporation and go into business for himself. He organized River Trails, Inc., on June 1, 19___, investing his personal savings of $2,000 in exchange for 1,000 shares of $2 par value capital stock. Also on June 1, the new corporation borrowed $1,000 from James Steel (father of Robert Steel) by issuing a three-year note payable which stated that no interest would be charged. The following transactions were also carried out by the corporation on June 1.

(1) Bought a number of canoes at a total cost of $4,000; paid $1,000 cash and agreed to pay the balance within 60 days.

(2) Bought camping equipment at a cost of $2,000 payable in 60 days.

(3) Bought supplies for cash, $500.

After the close of the season on September 10, Steel asked another student, Michael Lee, who had taken a course in accounting, to help him determine the financial position of the business.

The only record Steel had maintained was a checkbook with memorandum notes written on the check stubs. From this source Lee discovered that Steel had invested an additional $700 of his savings in the business on July 1 in exchange for another 350 shares of capital stock and also that the accounts payable arising from the purchase of the canoes and camping equipment had been paid in full. A bank statement received from the bank on September 10 showed a balance on deposit of $2,025.

Steel informed Lee that he had deposited in the bank all cash received by the business. He had also paid by check all bills immediately upon receipt; consequently, as of September 10 all bills for the season had been paid. The corporation's bank account had been used for all checks and all deposits. Steel had not intermingled his personal funds with those of the corporation and had received no salary for his personal services in operating the business.

The canoes and camping equipment were all in excellent condition at the end of the season, and Steel planned to resume operations the following summer. In fact he had already accepted reservations from many customers who wished to return. Lee felt that some consideration should be given to the wear and tear on the canoes and equipment but he agreed with Steel that for the present purpose the canoes and equipment should be listed in the balance sheet at the original cost. The supplies remaining on hand had cost $25, and Steel felt that he could obtain a refund for this amount by returning them to the supplier.

Lee suggested that two balance sheets be prepared, one to show the position of the business on June 1 and the other showing the position on September 10. He also recommended to Steel that a complete set of accounting records be established.

Instructions

a Use the information available on June 1 to prepare a balance sheet for River Trails, Inc., at June 1, 19___.

b Prepare a balance sheet for the corporation at September 10. (The September 10 bank statement represents the cash balance of the corporation on that date.)

c By comparing the two balance sheets, explain the sources of the change in total stockholders' equity and state whether you consider the business to be successful. Also comment on the change in the cash position from the beginning to the end of the season. Explain the factors underlying the change.

THREE

MEASURING BUSINESS INCOME

The earning of profits is a major goal of most business concerns. The individuals who organize a corporation and invest in its capital stock do so with the hope and expectation that the business will operate at a profit, thereby increasing their equity ownership. From the standpoint of the individual business firm, profitable operation is essential if the firm is to succeed or even to survive.

Operating profitably causes an increase in total assets; the *source* of these assets is termed *net income,* and represents an increase in the total owners' equity. From the fundamental accounting equation $(A = L + OE)$, we know that any transaction which changes total assets must also change either total liabilities or total owners' equity. For example, borrowing money from a bank increases both total assets and total liabilities. Operating profitably increases both total assets and total owners' equity. Thus, it is often said that profits belong to the stockholders.

The increase in owners' equity resulting from profitable operations is recorded in a balance sheet account entitled *Retained Earnings,* which appears in the stockholders' equity section of the balance sheet. If a business has sufficient cash, a distribution of profits may be made to the stockholders. Distributions of this nature are termed *dividends,* and decrease both total assets and total stockholders' equity. The decrease in stockholders' equity is reflected by a decrease in the Retained Earnings account. Thus, the balance of the Retained Earnings account represents only the earnings which have *not* been distributed as dividends.

Often stockholders prefer to leave profits invested in the business in the hope that the larger total assets will enable the business to earn even greater profits in the future. Leaving in the business the assets generated by profitable operations is termed *retaining* (or reinvesting) the profits. Some of the largest corporations have become large by retaining their profits and using these resources to acquire new plant and equipment, to carry on research leading to new and improved products, and to extend sales operations into new territories. A satisfactory rate of business profits is generally necessary for high employment, an improving standard of living, and a strong and expanding national economy.

Net income

Since the drive for profits underlies the very existence of business organizations, it follows that a most important function of an accounting system is to provide information about the profitability of a business. Before we can measure the profits of a business, we need to establish a sharp, clear meaning for *profits.* Economists define profits as the amount by which an entity becomes *better off* during a period of time. Unfortunately, how much "better off" an entity has become is largely a matter of personal opinion and cannot be measured *objectively* enough to provide a useful definition for accountants.

For this reason, accountants usually look to actual business transactions to provide objective evidence that a business has become better off. For example, if an item which cost a business $60 is sold for $100 cash, we have objective evidence that the business has become $40 better off. Since accountants and economists use the word *profits* in somewhat different senses, accountants prefer to use the alternative term *net income,* and to define this term very carefully. *Net income is the excess of the price of goods sold and services rendered over the cost of goods and services used up during a given time period.* At this point, we shall adopt the technical accounting term *net income* in preference to the less precise term *profits.*

To determine net income, it is necessary to measure for a given time period (1) the price of goods sold and services rendered and (2) the cost of goods and services used up. The technical accounting terms for these items comprising net income are *revenue* and *expenses.* Therefore, we may state that *net income equals revenue minus expenses.* To understand why this is true and how the measurements are made, let us begin with the meaning of revenue.

Revenue

Revenue is the price of goods sold and services rendered during a given time period. When a business renders services to its customers or delivers merchandise to them, it either receives immediate payment in cash or acquires an account receivable which will be collected and thereby become cash within a short time. The revenue for a given period is equal to the inflow of cash and receivables from sales made in that period. For any single transaction, the amount of revenue is a measurement of the asset values received from the customer.

Not all receipts of cash represent revenue; for example, as shown in Chapter 1, a business may obtain cash by borrowing from a bank. This increase in cash is offset by an increase in liabilities in the form of a note payable to the bank. The owners' equity is not changed by the borrowing transaction.

Collection of an account receivable is another example of a cash receipt that does not represent revenue. The act of collection causes an increase in the asset, Cash, and a corresponding decrease in another asset, Accounts Receivable. The amount of total assets remains unchanged, and, of course, there is no change in liabilities or owners' equity.

As another example of the distinction between revenue and cash receipts, let us assume that a business begins operations in March and makes sales of merchandise and/or services to its customers in that month as follows: sales for cash, $25,000; sales on credit (payable in April), $15,000. The revenue for March is $40,000, an amount equal to the cash received or to be received from the month's sales. When the accounts receivable of $15,000 are collected during April, they must not be counted a second time in measuring revenue for April.

Revenue causes an increase in owners' equity. The inflow of cash and receivables from customers increases the total assets of the company; on the other side of the accounting equation, the liabilities do not change, but owners' equity is increased to match the increase in total assets. Thus revenue is the gross increase in owners' equity resulting from business activities. Bear in mind, however, that not every increase in owners' equity comes from revenue. As illustrated in Chapter 1, the owners' equity is also increased by the investment of assets in the business by the owner.

Various terms are used to describe different types of revenue; for example, the revenue earned by a real estate broker may be called *Commissions Earned;* in the professional practice of lawyers, physicians, dentists, and CPAs, the revenue is called *Fees Earned;* a person owning property and leasing it to others has revenue called *Rent Earned;* and businesses selling merchandise rather than services generally use the term *Sales* to describe the revenue earned.

Expenses

Expenses are the cost of the goods and services used up in the process of obtaining revenue. Examples include salaries paid employees, charges for newspaper advertising and for telephone service, and the wearing out (depreciation) of the building and office equipment. All these items are necessary to attract and serve customers and thereby to obtain revenue. Expenses are sometimes referred to as the "cost of doing business," that is, the cost of the various activities necessary to carry on a business.

Expenses cause the owners' equity to decrease. Revenue may be regarded as the positive factor in creating net income, expenses as the negative factor. The relationship between expenses and revenue is a significant one; the expenses of a given month or other period are incurred in order to generate revenue in that same period. The salaries earned by sales employees waiting on customers during July are applicable to July revenue and should be treated as July expenses, even though these salaries may not actually be paid to the employees until sometime in August.

As previously explained, revenue and cash receipts are not one and the same thing; similarly, expenses and cash payments are not identical. Examples of cash payments which are not expenses of the current period include the purchase of an office building for cash, the purchase of merchandise for later sale to customers, the repayment of a bank loan, and the distribution of cash dividends by the business to the stockholders. In deciding whether a given item should be regarded as an expense of the current period, it is often helpful to pose the following questions:

1 Was the alleged "expense" incurred in order to produce revenue of the current period?

2 Does the item in question reduce owners' equity?

Dividends

A dividend is a distribution of assets (usually cash) by a corporation to its stockholders. Although the payment of a dividend reduces the owners' equity in the corporation, a dividend is not an expense. Unlike payments for advertising, rent, and salaries, the payment of dividends does not serve to generate revenue.

Although withdrawals by the owner of an unincorporated business are somewhat similar to dividends paid by a corporation, significant differences exist. Dividends are paid only when the corporation's board of directors takes formal action to declare a dividend, and dividend payments ordinarily cannot be greater than the retained earnings. The dividend is always a specific amount, such as $1 per share.

Since the declaration and payment of a dividend reduces the stockholders' equity, it could be recorded by debiting the Retained Earnings account. A better procedure is to debit an account called *Dividends,* which is then closed into the Retained Earnings account at the end of the year.

Relating revenue and expenses to time periods

A balance sheet shows the financial position of the business at a given date. An income statement, on the other hand, shows the results of operations over *a period of time.* In fact, the concept of income is meaningless unless it is related to a period of time. For example, if a businessman says, "My business produces net income of $5,000," the meaning is not at all clear; it could be made clear, however, by relating the income to a time period, such as "$5,000 a week," "$5,000 a month," or "$5,000 a year."

THE ACCOUNTING PERIOD Every business concern prepares a yearly income statement, and most businesses prepare quarterly and monthly income statements as well. Management needs to know from month to month whether revenue is rising or falling, whether expenses are being held to the level anticipated, and how net income compares with the net income of the preceding month and with the net income of the corresponding month of the preceding year. The term *accounting period* means the span of time covered by an income statement. It may consist of a month, a quarter of a year, a half year, or a year.

Many income statements cover the calendar year ended December 31, but an increasing number of companies are adopting an annual accounting period ending with a month other than December. Generally a business finds it more convenient to end its annual accounting period during a slack season rather than during a time of peak activity. Any 12-month accounting period adopted by a business is called its *fiscal year.* A fiscal year ending at the annual low point of seasonal activity is said to be a *natural business year.* The fiscal year selected by the federal government for its accounting purposes begins on July 1 and ends 12 months later on June 30.

TRANSACTIONS AFFECTING TWO OR MORE ACCOUNTING PERIODS The operation of a business entails an endless stream of transactions, many of which begin in one accounting period but affect several succeeding periods. Fire insurance policies, for example, are commonly issued to cover a period of three years. In this case, the apportionment of the cost of the policy by months is an easy matter. If the policy covers three years (36 months) and costs, for example, $360, the expense each month of maintaining insurance is $10.

Not all transactions can be so precisely divided by accounting periods. The purchase of a building, furniture and fixtures, machinery, a typewriter, or an automobile provides benefits to the business over all the years in which such an asset is used. No one can determine in advance exactly how many years of service will be received from such long-lived assets. Nevertheless, in measuring the net income of a business for a period of one year or less, the accountant must estimate what portion of the cost of the building and similar long-lived assets is applicable to the current year. Since the apportionments for these and many other transactions which overlap two or more accounting periods are in the nature of estimates rather than precise measurements, it follows that income statements should be regarded as *useful approximations* of annual income rather than as absolutely accurate determinations.

If we assume a stable price level, the time period for which the measurement of net income can be most accurate is the entire life span of the business. When a business sells all its assets, pays its debts, and ends its existence, it would then theoretically be possible to determine with precision the net income for the time period from the date of organization to the date of dissolution. Such a theoretically precise measurement of net income would, however, be too late to be of much use to the owners or managers of the business. The practical needs of business enterprise are well served by income statements of reasonable accuracy that tell managers and owners each month, each quarter, and each year the results of business operation.

Rules of debit and credit for revenue and expenses

Our approach to revenue and expenses has stressed the fact that revenue increases the owners' equity and that expenses decrease the owners' equity. The rules of debit and credit for recording revenue and expenses follow this relationship, and therefore the recording of revenue and expenses in ledger accounts requires only a slight extension of the rules of debit and credit presented in Chapter 2. The rule previously stated for recording increases and decreases in owners' equity was as follows:

Increases in owners' equity are recorded by credits.
Decreases in owners' equity are recorded by debits.

This rule is now extended to cover revenue and expense accounts:

Revenue increases owners' equity; therefore revenue is recorded by a credit.
Expenses decrease owners' equity; therefore expenses are recorded by debits.

Ledger accounts for revenue and expenses

During the course of an accounting period, a great many revenue and expense transactions occur in the average business. To classify and summarize these numerous transactions, a separate ledger account is maintained for each major type of revenue and expense. For example, almost every business maintains accounts for Advertising Expense, Telephone Expense, and Salaries Expense. At the end of the period, all the advertising expenses appear as debits in the Advertising Expense account. The debit balance of this account represents the total advertising expense of the period and is listed as one of the expense items in the income statement.

Revenue accounts are usually much less numerous than expense accounts. A small business such as the Greenhill Real Estate Company in our continuing illustration may have only one or two types of revenue, such as commissions earned from arranging sales of real estate and commissions earned from the rental of properties in behalf of clients. In a business of this type, the revenue accounts might be called *Sales Commissions Earned* and *Rental Commissions Earned.*

RECORDING REVENUE AND EXPENSE TRANSACTIONS: ILLUSTRATION The organization of the Greenhill Real Estate Company during September has already been described in Chapters 1 and 2. The illustration is now continued for October, during which month the company earned commissions by selling several residences for its clients. Bear in mind that the company does not own any residential property; it merely acts as a broker or agent for clients wishing to sell their houses. A commission of 6% of the selling price of the house is charged for this service. During October the company not only earned commissions but incurred a number of expenses.

Note that each illustrated transaction which affects an income statement account also affects a balance sheet account. This pattern is consistent with our previous discussion of revenue and expenses. In recording revenue transactions, we shall debit the assets received and credit a revenue account. In recording expense transactions, we shall debit an expense account and credit the asset Cash, or perhaps a liability account if payment is to be made later. The transactions for October were as follows:

Oct. 1 Paid $120 for publication of newspaper advertising describing various houses offered for sale.

	Analysis	Rule	Entry
Advertising expense incurred and paid	The cost of advertising is an expense	Expenses decrease the owners' equity and are recorded by debits	Debit: Advertising Expense, $120
	The asset Cash was decreased	Decreases in assets are recorded by credits	Credit: Cash, $120

Oct. 6 Earned and collected a commission of $2,750 by selling a residence previously listed by a client.

Revenue earned and collected

Analysis	*Rule*	*Entry*
The asset Cash was increased	*Increases in assets are recorded by debits*	*Debit: Cash, $2,750*
Revenue was earned	*Revenue increases the owners' equity and is recorded by a credit*	*Credit: Sales Commissions Earned, $2,750*

Oct. 16 Newspaper advertising was ordered at a price of $90, payment to be made within 30 days.

Advertising expense incurred but not paid

Analysis	*Rule*	*Entry*
The cost of advertising is an expense	*Expenses decrease the owners' equity and are recorded by debits*	*Debit: Advertising Expense, $90*
An account payable, a liability, was incurred	*Increases in liabilities are recorded by credits*	*Credit: Accounts Payable, $90*

Oct. 20 A commission of $1,130 was earned by selling a client's residence. The sales agreement provided that the commission would be paid in 60 days.

Revenue earned, to be collected later

Analysis	*Rule*	*Entry*
An asset in the form of an account receivable was acquired	*Increases in assets are recorded by debits*	*Debit: Accounts Receivable, $1,130*
Revenue was earned	*Revenue increases the owners' equity and is recorded by a credit*	*Credit: Sales Commissions Earned, $1,130*

Oct. 30 Paid salaries of $1,700 to office employees for services rendered during October.

Salaries expense incurred and paid

Analysis	*Rule*	*Entry*
Salaries of employees are an expense	*Expenses decrease the owners' equity and are recorded by debits*	*Debit: Office Salaries Expense, $1,700*
The asset Cash was decreased	*Decreases in assets are recorded by credits*	*Credit: Cash, $1,700*

Oct. 30 A telephone bill for October amounting to $48 was received. Payment was required by November 10.

	Analysis	Rule	Entry
Telephone expense incurred, to be paid later	*The cost of telephone service is an expense*	*Expenses decrease the owners' equity and are recorded by debits*	*Debit: Telephone Expense, $48*
	An account payable, a liability, was incurred	*Increases in liabilities are recorded by credits*	*Credit: Accounts Payable, $48*

Oct. 30 A dividend of 30 cents per share, or a total of $600, was declared and not paid. (As explained earlier on page 66, a dividend is not an expense.)

	Analysis	Rule	Entry
Payment of a dividend	*Payment of a dividend decreases the owners' equity*	*Decreases in owners' equity are recorded by debits*	*Debit: Dividends, $600*
	The asset Cash was decreased	*Decreases in assets are recorded by credits*	*Credit: Cash, $600*

The journal entries to record the October transactions are as follows:

General Journal *Page 2*

	Date		Account Titles and Explanations	LP	Debit	Credit
October journal entries for Greenhill Real Estate Company	*19___*					
	Oct.	*1*	Advertising Expense.	70	120	
			Cash	1		120
			Paid for newspaper advertising.			
		6	Cash	1	2,750	
			Sales Commissions Earned	61		2,750
			Earned and collected commission by selling residence for client.			
		16	Advertising Expense.	70	90	
			Accounts Payable	30		90
			Ordered newspaper advertising; payable in 30 days.			

October journal entries for Greenhill Real Estate Company (continued)	20	Accounts Receivable	2	1,130	
		Sales Commissions Earned	61		1,130
		Earned commission by selling residence for client; commission to be received in 60 days.			
	30	Office Salaries Expense	72	1,700	
		Cash	1		1,700
		Paid office salaries for October.			
	30	Telephone Expense	74	48	
		Accounts Payable	30		48
		To record liability for October telephone service.			
	30	Dividends	51	600	
		Cash	1		600
		Paid dividend to stockholders (2,000 shares at 30 cents per share).			

The column headings at the top of the illustrated journal page *(Date, Account Titles and Explanations, LP, Debit,* and *Credit)* are seldom used in practice. They are included here as an instructional guide but will be omitted from some of the later illustrations of journal entries.

Ledger accounts for Greenhill Real Estate Company: illustration

The ledger of the Greenhill Real Estate Company after the October transactions have been posted is now illustrated. For all accounts with more than one entry, the totals and month-end balances are noted in small handwritten figures. The accounts appear in the ledger in financial statement order as follows:

Balance sheet accounts
  Assets
  Liabilities
  Owners' equity
Income statement accounts
  Revenue
  Expenses

To conserve space in this illustration, several ledger accounts appear on a single page. In actual practice, however, each account occupies a separate page in the ledger.

Cash

Account No. 1

Posting October transactions to ledger accounts

19__					19__				
Sept.	1		1	20,000	Sept.	3		1	7,000
	20	7,500	1	500		5		1	5,000
				20,500		30		1	1,000
Oct.	6	7,830	2	2,750					13,000
				23,250	Oct.	1		2	120
						30		2	1,700
						30		2	600
									15,420

Accounts Receivable

Account No. 2

19__					19__				
Sept.	10	1,500	1	2,000	Sept.	20		1	500
Oct.	20	2,630	2	1,130					
				3,130					

Land

Account No. 20

19__					19__				
Sept.	3	5,000	1	7,000	Sept.	10		1	2,000

Building

Account No. 22

19__									
Sept.	5		1	12,000					

Office Equipment

Account No. 25

19__									
Sept.	14		1	1,800					

Accounts Payable

Account No. 30

19__					19__				
Sept.	30		1	1,000	Sept.	5		1	7,000
						14	7,800	1	1,800
									8,800
					Oct.	16		2	90
						30	7,938	2	48
									8,938

Capital Stock

Account No. 50

					19__				
					Sept.	1		1	20,000

Dividends   Account No. 52

19__									
Oct.	30		2	600					

Sales Commissions Earned   Account No. 61

				19__					
				Oct.	6		2	2,750	
					20		2	1,130	
								3,880	

Advertising Expense   Account No. 70

19__									
Oct.	1		2	120					
	16		2	90					
				210					

Office Salaries Expense   Account No. 72

19__									
Oct.	30		2	1,700					

Telephone Expense   Account No. 74

19__									
Oct.	30		2	48					

Trial balance

The following trial balance was prepared from the preceding ledger accounts.

GREENHILL REAL ESTATE COMPANY
Trial Balance
October 31, 19__

Cash	$ 7,830	
Accounts receivable	2,630	
Land	5,000	
Building	12,000	
Office equipment	1,800	
Accounts payable		$ 7,938
Capital stock		20,000
Dividends	600	
Sales commissions earned		3,880
Advertising expense	210	
Office salaries expense	1,700	
Telephone expense	48	
	$31,818	$31,818

Recording depreciation at the end of the period

This trial balance includes all the October expenses requiring cash payments such as salaries, advertising, and telephone service, but it does not include any depreciation expense. Our definition of expense is **the cost of goods and services used up in the process of obtaining revenue.** Some of the goods used up are purchased in advance and used up gradually over a long period of time. Buildings and office equipment, for example, are used up over a period of years. Each year, a portion of these assets **expires,** and a portion of their total cost should be recognized as **depreciation expense.**

Depreciation expense does not require monthly cash outlays; in effect, it is **paid in advance** when the related asset is originally acquired. Nevertheless, depreciation is an inevitable and continuing expense. Failure to record depreciation would result in understating total expenses of the period and consequently overstating the net income.

BUILDING The office building purchased by the Greenhill Real Estate Company at a cost of $12,000 is estimated to have a useful life of 20 years. The purpose of the $12,000 expenditure was to provide a place in which to carry on the business and thereby to obtain revenue. After 20 years of use the building will be worthless and the original cost of $12,000 will have been entirely consumed. In effect, the company has purchased 20 years of "housing services" at a total cost of $12,000. A portion of this cost expires during each year of use of the building. If we assume that each year's operations should bear an equal share of the total cost (straight-line depreciation), the annual depreciation expense will amount to $\frac{1}{20}$ of $12,000, or $600. On a monthly basis, depreciation expense is $50 ($12,000 cost ÷ 240 months). There are alternative methods of spreading the cost of a depreciable asset over its useful life, some of which will be considered in Chapter 12.

The journal entry to record depreciation of the building during October follows:

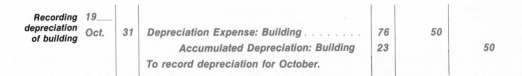

Recording depreciation of building

19—				
Oct.	31	Depreciation Expense: Building 76	50	
		Accumulated Depreciation: Building 23		50
		To record depreciation for October.		

The depreciation expense account will appear in the income statement for October along with the other expenses of salaries, advertising, and telephone expense. The Accumulated Depreciation: Building account will appear in the balance sheet as a deduction from the Building account, as shown by the following illustration of a **partial** balance sheet:

*Showing
accumulated
depreciation
in the
balance
sheet*

GREENHILL REAL ESTATE COMPANY
Partial Balance Sheet
October 31, 19___

Building (at cost) $12,000
Less: Accumulated depreciation 50 $11,950

The end result of crediting the Accumulated Depreciation: Building account is much the same as if the credit had been made to the Building account; that is, the net amount shown on the balance sheet for the building is reduced from $12,000 to $11,950. Although the credit side of a depreciation entry *could* be made directly to the asset account, it is customary and more efficient to record such credits in a separate account entitled Accumulated Depreciation. The original cost of the asset and the total amount of depreciation recorded over the years can more easily be determined from the ledger when separate accounts are maintained for the asset and for the accumulated depreciation.

Accumulated Depreciation: Building is an example of a *contra-asset account,* because it has a credit balance and is offset against an asset account (Building) to produce the proper balance sheet valuation for the asset.

OFFICE EQUIPMENT   Depreciation on the office equipment of the Greenhill Real Estate Company must also be recorded at the end of October. This equipment cost $1,800 and is assumed to have a useful life of 10 years. Monthly depreciation expense on the straight-line basis is, therefore, $15, computed by dividing the cost of $1,800 by the useful life of 120 months. The journal entry is as follows:

19___					
Oct.	31	Depreciation Expense: Office Equipment . .	78	15	
		Accumulated Depreciation: Office			
		Equipment	26		15
		To record depreciation for October.			

No depreciation was recorded on the building and office equipment for September, the month in which these assets were acquired, because regular operations did not begin until October. Generally, depreciation is not recognized until the business begins active operation and the assets are placed in use. Accountants often use the expression "matching costs and benefits" to convey the idea of writing off the cost of an asset to expense during the time periods in which the business enjoys the use of the property.

The journal entry to bring depreciation on the books at the end of the month is called an *adjusting entry.* The adjustment of certain asset accounts and related expense accounts is a necessary step at the end of each accounting period so that the information presented in the financial statements will be as accurate and complete as possible. In the next chapter, adjusting entries will be shown for some other matters in addition to depreciation.

The adjusted trial balance

After all the necessary adjusting entries have been made at the end of the period, an adjusted trial balance is prepared to prove that the ledger is still in balance. The adjusted trial balance illustrated below differs from the trial balance shown on page 74 because it includes accounts for depreciation expense and accumulated depreciation.

GREENHILL REAL ESTATE COMPANY
Adjusted Trial Balance
October 31, 19___

Cash	$ 7,830	
Accounts receivable	2,630	
Land	5,000	
Building	12,000	
Accumulated depreciation: building		$ 50
Office equipment	1,800	
Accumulated depreciation: office equipment		15
Accounts payable		7,938
Capital stock		20,000
Dividends	600	
Sales commissions earned		3,880
Advertising expense	210	
Office salaries expense	1,700	
Telephone expense	48	
Depreciation expense: building	50	
Depreciation expense: office equipment	15	
	$31,883	$31,883

Adjusted trial balance

FINANCIAL STATEMENTS

The income statement

When we measure the net income earned by a business we are measuring its economic performance—its success or failure as a business enterprise. Stockholders, prospective investors, managers, bankers, and other creditors are anxious to see the latest available income statement and thereby to judge how well the company is doing. The October income statement for Greenhill Real Estate Company appears as follows:

GREENHILL REAL ESTATE COMPANY
Income Statement
For the Month Ended October 31, 19___

Income statement for October

Sales commissions earned		$3,880
Expenses:		
Advertising expense	$ 210	
Office salaries expense	1,700	
Telephone expense	48	
Depreciation expense: building	50	
Depreciation expense: office equipment	15	2,023
Net income		$1,857

This income statement shows that the revenue during October exceeded the expenses of the month, thus producing a net income of $1,857. Bear in mind, however, that our measurement of net income is not absolutely accurate or precise, because of the assumptions and estimates involved in the accounting process. We have recorded only those economic events which are evidenced by accounting transactions. Perhaps during October the Greenhill Real Estate Company has developed a strong interest on the part of many clients who are on the verge of buying or selling homes. This accumulation of client interest is an important step toward profitable operation, but is not reflected in the October 31 income statement because it is not subject to objective measurement. Remember also that in determining the amount of depreciation expense we had to estimate the useful life of the building and office equipment. Any error in our estimates is reflected in the net income reported for October. Despite these limitations, the income statement is of vital importance, and indicates that the new business has operated profitably during the first month of its existence.

At this point we are purposely ignoring income taxes on corporations. Corporate income taxes will be introduced in Chapter 7 and considered more fully in Chapter 17.

Alternative titles for the income statement include *earnings statement, statement of operations,* and *profit and loss statement.* However, *income statement* is by far the most popular term for this important financial statement.

Statement of retained earnings

Retained earnings is that portion of the stockholders' equity created by earning and retaining net income. The *statement of retained earnings,* which covers the same time period as the related income statement, shows the sources of increase and decrease in retained earnings for that period.

GREENHILL REAL ESTATE COMPANY
Statement of Retained Earnings
For the Month Ended October 31, 19___

Statement Retained earnings, Oct. 1, 19___	*$ -0-*
of retained Net income for the month	*1,857*
for October Subtotal	*$1,857*
Dividends	*600*
Retained earnings, Oct. 31, 19___	*$1,257*

In this example the company had no retained earnings at the beginning of the period. The statement for the following month would show a beginning balance of $1,257.

The balance sheet

Previous illustrations of balance sheets have been arranged in the *account form,* that is, with the assets on the left side of the page and the liabilities and stockholders' equity on the right side. The balance sheet on page 80 is shown in *report form,* that is, with the liabilities and stockholders' equity sections listed below rather than to the right of the asset section. Both the account form and the report form are widely used.

The relationship between the income statement, the statement of retained earnings, and the balance sheet is shown in the stockholders' equity section of the balance sheet. The stockholders' original capital investment of $20,000 appears unchanged under the caption of Capital Stock. The Retained Earnings account had a zero balance at October 1, but as explained in the retained earnings statement, it was increased by the $1,857 of net income earned during October and decreased by the $600 dividend paid, leaving a balance of $1,257 at October 31.

The amount of the Retained Earnings account at any balance sheet date represents the accumulated earnings of the company since the date of incorporation, minus any losses and minus all dividends distributed to stockholders. One reason for maintaining a distinction between capital stock and retained earnings is that a corporation usually cannot legally pay dividends greater than the amount of retained earnings. The separation of these two elements of ownership

GREENHILL REAL ESTATE COMPANY
Balance Sheet
October 31, 19___

Assets

Cash		$ 7,830
Accounts receivable		2,630
Land		5,000
Building	$12,000	
Less: Accumulated depreciation	50	11,950
Office equipment	$ 1,800	
Less: Accumulated depreciation	15	1,785
Total assets		$29,195

Liabilities & Stockholders' Equity

Liabilities:		
Accounts payable		$ 7,938
Stockholders' equity:		
Capital stock	$20,000	
Retained earnings	1,257	21,257
Total liabilities & stockholders' equity		$29,195

may also be enlightening because it shows how much of the total stockholders' equity resulted from the investment of funds by stockholders and how much was derived from earning and retaining net income.

In the Greenhill Real Estate Company illustration, we have shown the two common ways in which the stockholders' equity may be increased: (1) investment of cash or other assets by the owners and (2) operating the business at a profit. There are also two common ways in which the stockholders' equity may be decreased: (1) payment of dividends and (2) operating the business at a loss.

CLOSING THE ACCOUNTS

The accounts for revenue, expenses, and dividends are *temporary owners' equity accounts* used during the accounting period to classify changes affecting the owners' equity. At the end of the period, we want to transfer the net effect of these various increases and decreases into retained earnings, which is a permanent owners' equity account. We also want to reduce the balances of the temporary owners' equity accounts to zero, so that these accounts will again be ready for use in accumulating information during the next accounting period. These objectives are accomplished by the use of closing entries.

Revenue and expense accounts are closed at the end of each accounting period by transferring their balances to a summary account called *Income Summary.* When the credit balances of the revenue accounts and the debit balances of the expense accounts have been transferred into one summary account, the balance of this Income Summary will be the net income or net loss for the period. If the revenue (credit balances) exceeds the expenses (debit balances), the Income Summary account will have a credit balance representing net income. Conversely, if expenses exceed revenue, the Income Summary will have a debit balance representing net loss. This is consistent with the rule that increases in owners' equity are recorded by credits and decreases are recorded by debits.

	Income Summary	
Revenue *minus* *expenses* *equals net* *income*	*Expenses*	*Revenue*

As previously explained, all debits and credits in the ledger are posted from the journal; therefore, the closing of revenue and expense accounts requires the preparation of journal entries and the posting of these journal entries to ledger accounts. A journal entry made for the purpose of closing a revenue or expense account by transferring its balance to the Income Summary account is called a *closing entry.* This term is also applied to the journal entries (to be explained later) used in closing the Income Summary account and the Dividends account into the Retained Earnings account.

A principal purpose of the year-end process of closing the revenue and expense accounts is to reduce their balances to zero. Since the revenue and expense accounts provide the information for the income statement of *a given accounting period,* it is essential that these accounts have zero balances at the beginning of each new period. The closing of the accounts has the effect of "wiping the slate clean" and preparing the accounts for the recording of revenue and expenses during the succeeding accounting period.

It is common practice to close the accounts only once a year, but for illustration, we shall now demonstrate the closing of the accounts of the Greenhill Real Estate Company at October 31 after one month's operation.

CLOSING ENTRIES FOR REVENUE ACCOUNTS Revenue accounts have credit balances. Closing a revenue account, therefore, means transferring its credit balance to the Income Summary account. This transfer is accomplished by a journal entry debiting the revenue account in an amount equal to its credit balance, with an offsetting credit to the Income Summary account. The only revenue account of the Greenhill Real Estate Company is Sales Commissions Earned, which had a credit balance of $3,880 at October 31. The journal entry necessary to close this account is as follows:

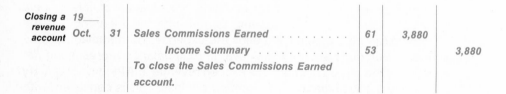

Closing a revenue account

	19___					
Oct.	31	Sales Commissions Earned	61	3,880	
		Income Summary	53		3,880
		To close the Sales Commissions Earned			
		account.			

After this closing entry has been posted, the two accounts affected will appear as shown below. A directional arrow has been added to show how the $3,880 balance of the revenue account is transferred into the Income Summary account.

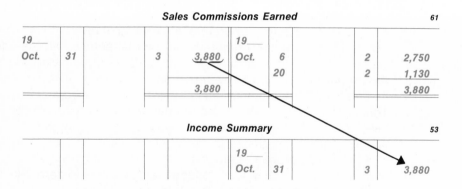

The Sales Commissions Earned account is now closed and has a zero balance. The equal totals on both sides of the account and the ruling of the account (double lines under the totals) show that it has no balance.

CLOSING ENTRIES FOR EXPENSE ACCOUNTS Expense accounts have debit balances. Closing an expense account means transferring its debit balance to the Income Summary account. The journal entry to close an expense account, therefore, consists of a credit to the expense account in an amount equal to its debit balance, with an offsetting debit to the Income Summary account.

There are five expense accounts in the ledger of the Greenhill Real Estate Company. Five separate journal entries could be made to close these five expense accounts, but the use of one *compound journal entry* is an easier, more efficient, timesaving method of closing all five expense accounts.

Closing various expense accounts	*19___* Oct.	31	*Income Summary*	53	*2,023*	
			Advertising Expense...........	70		*210*
			Office Salaries Expense	72		*1,700*
			Telephone Expense	74		*48*
			Depreciation Expense: Building....	76		*50*
			Depreciation Expense:			
			Office Equipment	78		*15*
			To close the expense accounts.			

After this closing entry has been posted, the Income Summary account has a credit balance of $1,857 and all the expense accounts have zero balances, as shown below.

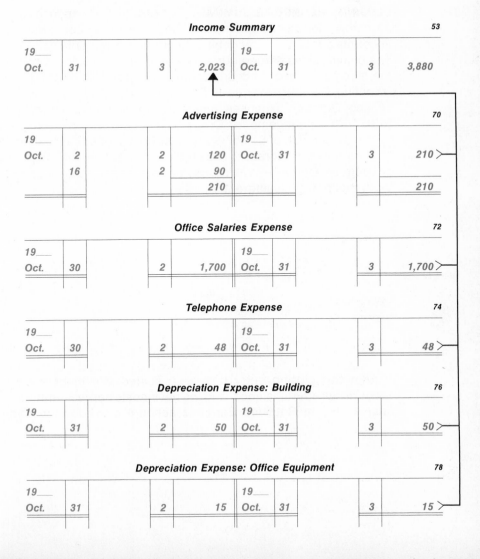

RULING CLOSED ACCOUNTS The ruling of the closed accounts should be studied closely. The ruling process was similar for the Sales Commissions Earned account (page 82) and the Advertising Expense account because both these accounts contained more than one entry on a side. A single ruling was placed on the same line across the debit and credit money columns. The totals were entered just below this single ruling and a double ruling was drawn below the totals. The double ruling was also placed across the date columns and the reference columns in order to establish a clear separation between the transactions of the period just ended and the entries to be made in the following period. All the expense accounts except Advertising Expense contained only one debit entry: In ruling an account with only one debit and one credit, it is not necessary to enter totals; the double lines may be placed just below the debit and credit entries.

CLOSING THE INCOME SUMMARY ACCOUNT The expense accounts have now been closed and the total amount formerly contained in these accounts appears on the debit side of the Income Summary account. The commissions earned during October appear on the credit side of the Income Summary account. Since the credit entry of $3,880 representing October revenue is larger than the debit of $2,023 representing October expenses, the account has a credit balance of $1,857—the net income for October.

   The net income of $1,857 earned during October causes the stockholders' equity to increase. The credit balance of the Income Summary account is, therefore, transferred to the Retained Earnings account by the following closing entry:

Net income earned increases stockholders' equity	*19___*						
	Oct.	*31*	Income Summary	53	1,857		
			Retained Earnings	51			1,857
			To close the Income Summary account for October by transferring the net income to the Retained Earnings account.				

   After this closing entry has been posted, the Income Summary account has a zero balance, and the net income earned during October appears in the Retained Earnings account as shown on page 85.

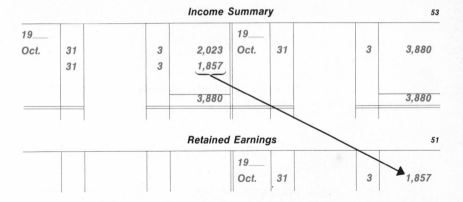

In our illustration the business has operated profitably with revenue in excess of expenses. Not every business is so fortunate; if the expenses of a business are larger than its revenue, the Income Summary account will have a debit balance. In this case, the closing of the Income Summary account would require a debit to the Retained Earnings account and an offsetting credit to the Income Summary account. A debit balance in the Retained Earnings account is referred to as a *deficit;* it would be shown as a deduction from Capital Stock in the balance sheet.

Note that the Income Summary account is used only at the end of the period when the accounts are being closed. The Income Summary account has no entries and no balance except during the process of closing the accounts at the end of the accounting period.

CLOSING THE DIVIDENDS ACCOUNT As explained earlier in this chapter, the payment of dividends to the owners is not considered as an expense of the business and, therefore, is not taken into account in determining the net income for the period. Since dividends do not constitute an expense, the Dividends account is closed not into the Income Summary account but directly to the Retained Earnings account, as shown by the following entry:

Dividends account is closed to Retained Earnings account	19__					
	Oct.	31	Retained Earnings	51	600	
			Dividends	52		600
			To close the Dividends account.			

After this closing entry has been posted, the Dividends account will have a zero balance, and the dividends distributed during October will appear as a deduction or debit entry in the Retained Earnings account, as shown at the top of page 86.

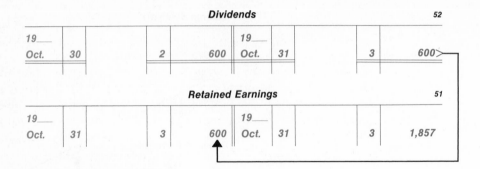

THE CLOSING PROCESS—IN SUMMARY Let us now summarize the process of closing the accounts.

1 Close the various revenue accounts by transferring their balances into the Income Summary account.

2 Close the various expense accounts by transferring their balances into the Income Summary account.

3 Close the Income Summary account by transferring its balance into the Retained Earnings account.

4 Close the Dividends account into the Retained Earnings account.

The closing of the accounts may be illustrated graphically by the use of T accounts as follows:

Diagram showing closing of the accounts

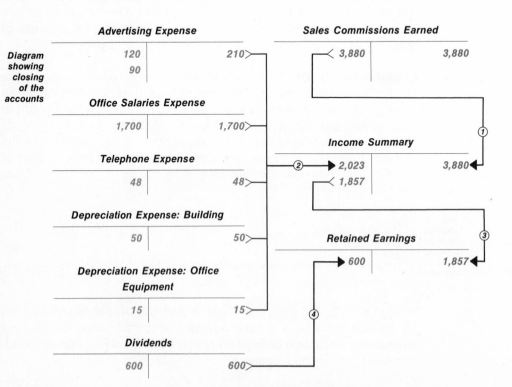

After-closing trial balance

After the revenue and expense accounts have been closed, it is desirable to take an *after-closing trial balance,* which of course will consist solely of balance sheet accounts. There is always the possibility that an error in posting the closing entries may have upset the equality of debits and credits in the ledger. The after-closing trial balance, or *post-closing trial balance,* is prepared from the ledger. It gives assurance that the ledger is in balance and ready for the recording of the transactions of the next accounting period.

GREENHILL REAL ESTATE COMPANY
After-closing Trial Balance
October 31, 19___

Only	Cash	$ 7,830	
balance sheet	Accounts receivable...............................	2,630	
accounts	Land	5,000	
remain open after closing	Building	12,000	
entries are	Accumulated depreciation: building		$ 50
posted	Office equipment....................................	1,800	
	Accumulated depreciation: office equipment...........		15
	Accounts payable		7,938
	Capital stock		20,000
	Retained earnings		1,257
		$29,260	$29,260

Sequence of accounting procedures

The accounting procedures described to this point may be summarized in eight steps, as follows:

1 Journalize transactions Enter all transactions in the journal, thus creating a chronological record of events.

2 Post to ledger accounts Post debits and credits from the journal to the proper ledger accounts, thus creating a record classified by accounts.

3 Prepare a trial balance Prove the equality of debits and credits in the ledger.

4 Prepare end-of-period adjustments Draft adjusting entries in the general journal, and post to ledger accounts.

5 Prepare an adjusted trial balance Prove again the equality of debits and credits in the ledger.

6 Prepare financial statements An income statement is needed to show the results of operation for the period. A statement of retained earnings is needed to show the changes in retained earnings during the period and the closing balance. A balance sheet is needed to show the financial position of the business at the end of the period.

7 Journalize and post the closing entries The closing entries clear the revenue, expense, and dividends accounts, making them ready for recording the events of the next accounting period, and also bring the Retained Earnings account up-to-date.

8 Prepare an after-closing trial balance This step ensures that the ledger remains in balance after posting of the closing entries.

Dividends—declaration and payment

Earlier in this chapter the declaration and the payment of a cash dividend were treated as a single event recorded by one journal entry. A small corporation with only a few stockholders may choose to declare and pay a dividend on the same day. In large corporations with thousands of stockholders and constant transfers of shares, an interval of a month or more will separate the date of declaration from the later date of payment.

Assume for example that on April 1 the board of directors of Universal Corporation declares the regular quarterly dividend of $1 per share on the 1 million shares of outstanding capital stock. The board's resolution specifies that the dividend will be payable on May 10 to stockholders of record on April 25. To be eligible to receive the dividend, an individual must be listed on the corporation's books as a stockholder on April 25, the date of record. Two entries are required: one on April 1 for the declaration of the dividend and one on May 10 for its payment, as shown below.

Dividends declared and . . .	Apr. 1	Dividends 1,000,000	
		Dividends Payable.................	1,000,000
		Declared dividend of $1 per share payable May 10 to stockholders of record April 25.	
. . . Dividends paid	May 10	Dividends Payable 1,000,000	
		Cash	1,000,000
		Paid the dividend declared on April 1.	

The Dividends Payable account is a liability which comes into existence when the dividend is declared and is discharged when the dividend is paid.

Accrual basis of accounting versus cash basis of accounting

A business which recognizes revenue in the period in which it is earned and deducts the expenses incurred in generating this revenue is using the *accrual basis of accounting.* To be meaningful, net income must relate to a specified period of time. Since net income is determined by offsetting expenses against revenue, both the expenses and the revenue used in the calculation must relate to the same time period. This *matching* or offsetting of related revenue and expenses gives a realistic picture of the profit performance of the business each period. The accrual basis is thus essential to income determination, which is a major objective of the whole accounting process.

The alternative to the accrual basis of accounting is the *cash basis*. Under cash basis accounting, revenue is not recorded until received in cash; expenses are assigned to the period in which cash payment is made. Most business concerns use the accrual basis of accounting, but individuals and professionals (such as physicians and lawyers) usually maintain their accounting records on a cash basis.

The cash basis of accounting does not give a good picture of profitability. For example, it ignores uncollected revenue which has been earned and expenses which have been incurred but not paid. Throughout this book we shall be working with the accrual basis of accounting, except for that portion of Chapter 17 dealing with the income tax returns of individuals.

DEMONSTRATION PROBLEM

The trial balance for Key Insurance Company, at November 30, 19___, and data for adjustments are presented below. The business was organized on September 1; the accounts have been closed and financial statements prepared each month.

Cash	$ 3,750	
Accounts receivable	1,210	
Office equipment	4,800	
Accumulated depreciation: office equipment		$ 80
Accounts payable		1,640
Capital stock		6,000
Retained earnings		1,490
Dividends	500	
Commissions earned		4,720
Advertising expense	800	
Salaries expense	2,600	
Rent expense	270	
	$13,930	$13,930

The useful life of the office equipment was estimated at 10 years.

Instructions
a Prepare the adjusting journal entry needed at November 30.
b Prepare an adjusted trial balance.
c For the month ended November 30, prepare an income statement, a statement of retained earnings, and a balance sheet in report form.

SOLUTION TO DEMONSTRATION PROBLEM

a **Adjusting journal entry:**

Depreciation Expense: Office Equipment	40	
Accumulated Depreciation: Office Equipment		40

To record depreciation for November ($4,800 ÷ 120).

b

KEY INSURANCE COMPANY
Adjusted Trial Balance
November 30, 19___

Cash	$ 3,750	
Accounts receivable	1,210	
Office equipment	4,800	
Accumulated depreciation: office equipment		$ 120
Accounts payable		1,640
Capital stock		6,000
Retained earnings		1,490
Dividends	500	
Commissions earned		4,720
Advertising expense	800	
Salaries expense	2,600	
Rent expense	270	
Depreciation expense: office equipment	40	
	$13,970	$13,970

c

KEY INSURANCE COMPANY
Income Statement
For the Month Ended November 30, 19___

Commissions earned		$4,720
Expenses:		
Advertising expense	$ 800	
Salaries expense	2,600	
Rent expense	270	
Depreciation expense: office equipment	40	3,710
Net income		$1,010

KEY INSURANCE COMPANY
Statement of Retained Earnings
For the Month Ended November 30, 19___

Retained earnings, Oct. 31, 19___	$1,490
Net income for the month	1,010
Subtotal	$2,500
Dividends	500
Retained earnings, Nov. 30, 19___	$2,000

KEY INSURANCE COMPANY
Balance Sheet
November 30, 19___

Assets

Cash		$3,750
Accounts receivable		1,210
Office equipment	$4,800	
Less: Accumulated depreciation	120	4,680
Total assets		$9,640

Liabilities & Stockholders' Equity

Liabilities:		
Accounts payable		$1,640
Stockholders' equity:		
Capital stock	$6,000	
Retained earnings	2,000	8,000
Total liabilities & stockholders' equity		$9,640

REVIEW QUESTIONS

1 Explain the effect of operating profitably upon the balance sheet of a business entity.

2 Does the Retained Earnings account represent a supply of cash which could be distributed to stockholders? Explain.

3 Does a well-prepared income statement provide an exact and precise measurement of net income for the period or does it represent merely an approximation of net income? Explain.

4 For each of the following financial statements, indicate whether the statement relates to a single date or to a period of time:
   a Balance sheet
   b Income statement
   c Statement of retained earnings

5 What is the meaning of the term *revenue?* Does the receipt of cash by a business always indicate that revenue has been earned? Explain.

6 What is the meaning of the term *expenses?* Does the payment of cash by a business always indicate that an expense has been incurred? Explain.

7 Explain the rules of debit and credit with respect to transactions recorded in revenue and expense accounts.

8 Supply the appropriate term (debit or credit) to complete the following statements.

    a The Capital Stock account, Retained Earnings account, and revenue accounts are increased by _____ entries.

    b Asset accounts and expense accounts are increased by _____ entries.

    c Liability accounts and owners' equity accounts are decreased by _____ entries.

9 Supply the appropriate term (debit or credit) to complete the following statements.

    a When a business is operating profitably, the journal entry to close the Income Summary account will consist of a _____ to that account and a _____ to Retained Earnings.

    b When a business is operating at a loss, the journal entry to close the Income Summary account will consist of a _____ to that account and a _____ to Retained Earnings.

    c The journal entry to close the Dividends account consists of a _____ to that account and a _____ to Retained Earnings.

10 Jensen Corporation, a firm of real estate brokers, had the following transactions during June. Which of these transactions represented revenue to the firm during the month of June? Explain.

    a Arranged a sale of an apartment building owned by a client, James Robbins. The commission for making the sale was $3,200, but this amount would not be received until July 20.

    b Collected cash of $1,500 from an account receivable. The receivable originated in April from services rendered to a client.

    c Borrowed $4,000 from the National Bank, to be repaid in three months.

    d Collected $150 from a dentist to whom Jensen Corporation rented part of its building. This amount represented rent for the month of June.

    e Issued additional capital stock of $2,000 par value for cash of $2,000.

11 A business had the following transactions, among others, during January. Which of these transactions represented expenses for January? Explain.

    a Paid $600 salary to a salesman for time worked during January.

    b Paid $60 for gasoline purchases for the delivery truck during January.

    c Purchased a typewriter for $300 cash.

    d Paid $2,000 in settlement of a bank loan obtained three months earlier.

    e Paid a dividend of $500.

    f Paid a garage $200 for automobile repair work performed in November.

12 How does depreciation expense differ from other operating expenses?

13 Assume that a business acquires a delivery truck at a cost of $3,600. Estimated life of the truck is four years. State the amount of depreciation expense per year and per month. Give the adjusting entry to record depreciation on the truck at the end of the first month, and explain where the accounts involved would appear in the financial statements.

EXERCISES

Ex. 3-1 Total assets and total liabilities of Mannix Corporation as shown by the balance sheets at the beginning and end of the year were as follows:

	Beginning of Year	End of Year
Assets	$155,000	$200,000
Liabilities	95,000	110,000

Compute the net income or net loss from operations for the year in each of the following independent cases:

a No dividends were declared or paid during the year and no additional capital stock was issued.

b No dividends were declared or paid during the year, but additional capital stock was issued at par in the amount of $25,000.

c Dividends of $10,000 were declared and paid during the year. No change occurred in capital stock.

d Dividends of $3,000 were declared and paid during the year, and additional capital stock was issued at par in the amount of $18,000.

Ex. 3-2 Supply the missing figures in the following independent cases:

a Capital stock (no change during year) .... $ 50,000
  Dividends for the year 6,000
  Retained earnings at beginning of year 24,000
  Net income for the year 17,500
  Total stockholders' equity at end of year .... _____

b Retained earnings at end of year .... $ 83,700
  Dividends for the year 12,400
  Net income for the year 31,200
  Retained earnings at beginning of year .... _____

c Net income for the year .... $_____
  Retained earnings at end of year 47,800
  Retained earnings at beginning of year 42,600
  Dividends for the year 12,400

d Dividends for the year .... $_____
  Retained earnings at end of year 99,700
  Net income for the year 28,500
  Retained earnings at beginning of year 91,200

e Total stockholders' equity at beginning of year .... $ 71,300
  Total stockholders' equity at end of year 88,400
  Amount received from additional capital stock issued during year ... 7,000
  Net income for the year .... _____
  Dividends for the year 7,600

Ex. 3-3 Martin Corporation's income statement showed net income of $25,380 for the month of October. In recording October transactions, however, certain transactions were incorrectly recorded. Study the following list of selected October transactions, and identify any which were incorrectly recorded. Also give the journal entry as it should have been made, and compute the correct amount of net income for October.

a Made an error in computing depreciation on the building for October. Recorded as $25. The correct amount of depreciation was $250.

b Recorded the payment of a $4,000 dividend by debiting Salaries Expense and crediting Cash.

c Earned a commission of $2,500 by selling a residence for a client. Commission to be received in 60 days. Recorded by debiting Commissions Earned and crediting Accounts Receivable.

d A payment of $250 for newspaper advertising was recorded by debiting Advertising Expense and crediting Accounts Receivable.

e Received but did not pay a bill of $285 for October telephone service. Recorded by debiting Telephone Expense and crediting Commissions Earned.

Ex. 3-4 Label each of the following statements as true or false. Explain the reasoning underlying your answer and give an example of a transaction which supports your position.

a Every transaction that affects a balance sheet account also affects an income statement account.

b Every transaction that affects an income statement account also affects a balance sheet account.

c Every transaction that affects an expense account also affects an asset account.

d Every transaction that affects a revenue account also affects another income statement account.

e Every transaction that affects an expense account also affects a revenue account.

Ex. 3-5 A clerk for the Lawn Care Corporation prepared the following closing entries from the ledger accounts for the year of 19___. (a) Identify any errors which the clerk has made and (b) prepare correct closing entries for the business.

Entry 1

Lawn Service Revenue	78,000	
Accumulated Depreciation	8,000	
Retained Earnings	27,000	
Income Summary		113,000

To close accounts with credit balances.

Entry 2

Income Summary	73,000	
Salaries Expense		56,000
Dividends		11,000
Advertising Expense		4,000
Depreciation Expense		2,000

To close accounts with debit balances.

Entry 3

Income Summary	40,000	
Capital Stock		40,000

To close Income Summary account.

PROBLEMS

3-1 During April a portion of the transactions of Valley Motors, an automobile repair shop, were as follows:

(1) On April 1, paid $200 cash for the month's rent.

(2) On April 4, made repairs to the car of C. P. Caron and collected in full the charge of $317 (credit Repair Service Revenue).

(3) On April 6, at request of National Insurance, Inc., made repairs on the car of Ainsley Dart. Sent bill for $416 for services rendered to National Insurance, Inc.

(4) On April 17, placed an advertisement in the **Herald Express** at a cost of $97, payment to be made in 30 days.

(5) On April 21, purchased a hydraulic lift for $4,200 cash.

(6) On April 26, received a check for $416 from National Insurance, Inc.

(7) On April 30, received a bill for $127 from Bell Telephone Company for telephone service during April, payable May 10.

(8) On April 30, declared a cash dividend of $9,000, payable on May 31.

Instructions

a Write an analysis of each transaction and then prepare the necessary journal entry. An example of the type of analysis desired is as follows:

  (1) (a) Rent is an operating expense. Expenses are recorded by debits. Debit Rent Expense, $200.

     (b) The asset Cash was decreased. Decreases in assets are recorded by credits. Credit cash, $200.

b Prepare journal entries to record the transactions.

3-2 Colorado Shuttle Service, Inc., was organized on December 1, 19___ for the purpose of flying skiers among neighboring ski areas and to remote mountain tops. The following transactions were completed during December.

Dec. **1** Issued 5,000 shares of $10 par value capital stock for cash of $50,000.

Dec. **2** Purchased a helicopter for $42,600 and spare parts for $4,000, paying cash.

Dec. **3** Paid $600 cash to rent a building for December.

Dec. 15 Cash receipts from passengers for the first half of December amounted to $3,800.

Dec. 16 Paid $2,475 to employees for services rendered during the first half of December.

Dec. 24 Placed advertising in local newspapers for publication during December. The agreed price of $225 was payable within ten days after the end of the month.

Dec. 28 Paid $780 to United Motors for maintenance and repair service during December.

Dec. 29 Received a gasoline bill from Western Oil Co. amounting to $610 and payable by January 10.

Dec. 31 Paid $2,475 to employees for services rendered during the last half of December.

Dec. 31 Cash receipts from passengers during the last half of December amounted to $4,160.

    The useful life of the helicopter for depreciation purposes was estimated to be 10 years. Depreciation should not be recorded on the spare parts; these are allocated to expense when they are used. The account titles and account numbers used by the company included the following:

Cash	11	*Fees earned*	51
Spare parts	14	*Advertising expense*	61
Helicopter	21	*Depreciation expense: helicopter*	63
Accumulated depreciation:		*Gasoline expense*	65
helicopter	23	*Rent expense*	67
Accounts payable	31	*Repair & maintenance expense*	69
Capital stock	41	*Salaries expense*	71

Instructions

a Prepare journal entries for the operating transactions in December and also for the month-end adjusting entry for depreciation of the helicopter. Number the general journal pages as Page 1 and Page 2.

b Post to ledger accounts.

c Prepare an adjusted trial balance at December 31, 19___.

3-3 Linden Auto Repair was organized on May 1, 19___. The accounts were closed and financial statements prepared each month. An adjusted trial balance as of the succeeding July 31, 19___, is shown below.

LINDEN AUTO REPAIR

Adjusted Trial Balance

July 31, 19___

Cash	$ 1,260	
Accounts receivable	520	
Land	10,500	
Building	18,000	
Accumulated depreciation: building		$ 180
Repair equipment	2,400	
Accumulated depreciation: repair equipment		120
Notes payable		10,000
Accounts payable		300
Capital stock		20,000
Retained earnings		2,000
Dividends	1,500	
Repair service revenue		3,400
Advertising expense	60	
Depreciation expense: building	60	
Depreciation expense: repair equipment	40	
Repair parts expense	260	
Utilities expense	50	
Wages expense	1,350	
	$36,000	$36,000

Instructions

a Prepare the closing entries necessary at July 31, 19___.

b Prepare financial statements (income statement, statement of retained earnings, and a balance sheet in report form).

c What were the estimated lives of the building and equipment as assumed by the company in setting the depreciation rates?

3-4 Image, Incorporated provides public relations services to clients in the entertainment industry. Its offices are rented from a life insurance company on a 10-year lease which expires in three years.

Condensed balance sheet data for the corporation at the end of the last two calendar years are presented at the top of page 97.

	Year 1	Year 2
Cash	$ 20,000	$ 5,000
Receivables from clients	110,000	160,000
Supplies	1,000	1,000
Office equipment..........................	16,500	33,500
Less: Accumulated depreciation	(3,000)	(5,750)
Total assets	$144,500	$193,750
Accounts payable	$ 10,000	$ 10,000
Capital stock	50,000	80,000
Retained earnings	84,500	103,750
Total liabilities & stockholders' equity	$144,500	$193,750

In order to be in a position to carry the expanded amount of receivables from clients and to acquire badly needed office equipment, the owners of Image, Incorporated invested additional cash in the business early in Year 2. At the end of Year 2, the corporation declared and paid a cash dividend. The net income for the corporation for Year 2 follows:

Fees billed to clients		$125,000
Expenses (excluding depreciation)................	$83,000	
Depreciation expense: office equipment	2,750	85,750
Net income		$ 39,250

Instructions
a Prepare a statement of retained earnings for Year 2.
b Prepare closing entries required at the end of Year 2.
c The owners are concerned over the fact that cash decreased by $15,000 during Year 2 despite a profit of $39,250. Prepare a schedule of cash receipts and payments to explain the reasons for the decrease in cash.

3-5 Given below are the balance sheet accounts on June 1, 19___ and the adjusted trial balance as of June 30, 19___ for Coronado Boat Yard, Inc.

	June 1		June 30	
Cash	$15,500		$17,900	
Accounts receivable.............	33,350		28,000	
Supplies on hand	2,650		2,200	
Equipment.....................	17,300		19,000	
Accumulated depreciation: equipment..		$ 3,600		$ 3,800
Payable to suppliers.............		2,150		550
Note payable to bank		16,000		3,500
Capital stock		25,000		25,000
Retained earnings		22,050		22,050
Dividends			8,000	
Revenue				44,000
Operating expenses			23,500	
Depreciation.................			200	
Interest expense			100	
	$68,800	$68,800	$98,900	$98,900

All revenue is recorded in Accounts Receivable.

Instructions

a Prepare the journal entries that were recorded during the month of June. Use one entry for all transactions of a particular type; for example, one entry should be used to summarize all revenue earned during the month. This entry will consist of a debit to Accounts Receivable and a credit to Revenue for $44,000. This entry will account in full for the increase in the balance of the Revenue account during June and in part for the change in Accounts Receivable during the month. In a similar manner, one entry can be prepared to record all cash collections of accounts receivable during June.

b Prepare an after-closing trial balance at June 30, 19____.

3-6 Financial Services, Inc., offers investment counseling and brokerage services to its clients and earns revenue in the form of commissions, dividends on securities owned, and interest on loans made to customers for the purchase of securities. The adjusted trial balance of the corporation was as follows at December 31, 19____.

FINANCIAL SERVICES, INC.

Adjusted Trial Balance

December 31, 19____

Cash	$ 68,400	
Marketable securities	240,500	
Accounts receivable	170,000	
Land	30,000	
Building	80,000	
Accumulated depreciation: building		$ 12,200
Furniture & equipment	120,000	
Accumulated depreciation: furniture & equipment		31,500
Loans payable		230,000
Miscellaneous payables		21,400
Capital stock		250,000
Retained earnings, Jan. 1		191,750
Dividends	10,000	
Commissions earned		183,000
Dividends earned		8,000
Interest earned		11,250
Advertising expense	22,250	
Office expense	42,100	
Interest expense	21,900	
Depreciation expense	18,250	
Salaries and bonuses expense	105,500	
Miscellaneous expense	10,200	
	$939,100	$939,100

Instructions: From the trial balance and supplementary data given, prepare the following at December 31:

a Closing entries

b After-closing trial balance

c Income statement for year 19____

d Balance sheet in report form

e Statement of retained earnings for 19____

3-7 On September 1, 19___, Interstate Moving Company was organized to provide transportation of household furniture. During September the following transactions occurred:

Sept. 1 Cash of $200,000 was received in exchange for 20,000 shares of $10 par value capital stock.

Sept. 2 Purchased land for $50,000 and building for $72,000, paying $42,000 cash and signing an $80,000 mortgage payable bearing interest at 9%.

Sept. 3 Purchased three trucks from Bryan Motors at a cost of $28,800 each. A cash down payment of $40,000 was made, the balance to be paid by November 12.

Sept. 6 Purchased office equipment for cash, $4,800.

Sept. 6 Moved furniture for Mr. and Mrs. John Green from New York to Los Angeles for $3,370. Collected $970 in cash, balance to be paid within 30 days (credit Moving Service Revenue).

Sept. 9 Moved furniture for various clients for $6,470. Collected $3,670 in cash, balance to be paid within 30 days.

Sept. 15 Paid salaries to employees for the first half of the month, $3,020.

Sept. 25 Moved furniture for various clients for a total of $5,400. Cash collected in full.

Sept. 30 Salaries expense for the second half of September amounted to $2,650.

Sept. 30 Received a gasoline bill for the month of September from Midwest Oil Company in the amount of $3,500, to be paid by October 10.

Sept. 30 Received bill of $250 for repair work on trucks during September by Culver Motor Company.

Sept. 30 Paid $1,000 on the mortgage payable, of which $600 represents interest for September.

Sept. 30 Declared a $2,000 cash dividend, payable October 15.

Estimated useful life of the building was 20 years, trucks 4 years, and office equipment 10 years.

Instructions

a Prepare journal entries. (Number journal pages to permit cross reference to ledger.)

b Post to ledger accounts. (Number ledger accounts to permit cross reference to journal.)

c Prepare a trial balance at September 30, 19___.

d Prepare adjusting entries and post to ledger accounts.

e Prepare an adjusted trial balance.

f Prepare an income statement for September, and a balance sheet at September 30, 19___, in report form.

g Prepare closing entries and post to ledger accounts.

h Prepare an after-closing trial balance.

BUSINESS DECISION PROBLEM 3

Carl Mill, owner of a small business called Blue Coral Company, has accepted a salaried position overseas and is trying to interest you in buying his business. He describes the operating results of the business as follows: "The business has been in existence for only 18 months, but the growth trend is very impressive. Just look at these figures."

	Cash Collections from Customers
First six-month period	$12,000
Second six-month period	16,000
Third six-month period	18,000

''I think you'll agree those figures show real growth,'' Mill concluded.

You then asked Mill whether sales were made only for cash or on both a cash and credit basis. He replied as follows:

''At first we sold both for cash and on open account. In the first six months we made total sales of $20,000, and 70% of those sales were made on credit. We had $8,000 of accounts receivable at the end of the first six-month period.

''During the second six-month period we tried to discourage selling on credit because of the extra paper work involved and the time required to follow up on slow-paying customers. Our sales on credit in that second six-month period amounted to $7,000, and our total accounts receivable were down to $6,000 at the end of that period.

''During the third six-month period we made sales only for cash. Although we prefer to operate on a cash basis only, we did very well at collecting receivables. We collected in full from every customer to whom we ever sold on credit, and we don't have a dollar of accounts receivable at this time.''

Instructions

Do you consider Mill's explanation of the ''growth trend'' of cash collections to be a well-founded portrayal of the progress of his business? Explain fully any criticism you may have of Mill's line of reasoning. To facilitate your reaching a decision, it is suggested that you compile data for each of the three six-month periods under review, using the following column headings for the analysis:

Period	(1) Sales on Credit	(2) Collections on Accounts Receivable	(3) Ending Balance of Accounts Receivable	(4) Sales for Cash	(5) Total Cash Collections from Customers	(6) (1) + (4) Total Sales
First 6 mos.						
Second 6 mos.						
Third 6 mos.						

COMPLETION OF THE ACCOUNTING CYCLE

FOUR

To serve the needs of management, investors, bankers, and other groups, financial statements must be as complete and accurate as possible. The balance sheet must contain all the assets and liabilities at the close of business on the last day of the period. The income statement must contain all revenue and expenses applicable to the period covered but must not contain any revenue or expenses relating to the following period. In other words, all transactions affecting the period must be properly recorded before the financial statements are prepared.

Apportioning transactions between accounting periods

Some business transactions are begun and completed within a single accounting period, but many other transactions are begun in one accounting period and concluded in a later period. For example, a building purchased this year may last for 25 years; during each of those 25 years a fair share of the cost of the building should be recognized as expense. The making of *adjusting entries* to record the depreciation expense applicable to a given accounting period was illustrated in the preceding chapter. Let us now consider some other transactions which overlap two or more accounting periods and therefore require adjusting entries.

PRINCIPAL TYPES OF TRANSACTIONS REQUIRING ADJUSTING ENTRIES

The various transactions requiring adjusting entries at the end of the period may be classified into the following four groups:

1 Recorded costs which must be apportioned between two or more accounting periods. Example: the cost of a building.

2 Recorded revenue which must be apportioned between two or more accounting periods. Example: commissions collected in advance for services to be rendered in future periods.

3 Unrecorded expenses. Example: wages earned by employees after the last payday in an accounting period.

4 Unrecorded revenue. Example: commissions earned but not yet collected or billed to customers.

All adjusting entries involve the recognition of either revenue or expense and, therefore, represent a change in owners' equity. Owners' equity, however, cannot change by itself; there must also be a corresponding change in either assets or liabilities. Thus, every adjusting entry must involve both an income statement account (either a revenue or an expense) *and* a balance sheet account (either an asset or a liability).

To demonstrate these various types of adjusting entries, the illustration of the Greenhill Real Estate Company will be continued for November. We shall consider in detail those November transactions relating to adjusting entries. The routine operating transactions during November such as the earning of sales commissions and payment of expenses are not considered individually, but their overall effect is shown in the November 30 trial balance included in the work sheet on page 112.

Recorded costs apportioned between accounting periods

When a business concern makes an expenditure that will benefit more than one period, the amount is usually debited to an asset account. At the end of each period which benefits from the expenditure, an appropriate portion of the cost is transferred from the asset account to an expense account.

Payments in advance are often made for such items as insurance, rent, and office supplies. At the end of the accounting period, a portion of the services or supplies probably will have expired or will have been consumed, but another portion will be unexpired or unused. That portion of the economic benefits from the expenditure which *has expired or has been consumed is an expense of the current period.* However, the *unexpired or unused portion of the economic benefits from the expenditure represents an asset* at the balance sheet date which will not become expense (expired cost) until a later accounting period.

INSURANCE On November 1, the Greenhill Real Estate Company paid $180 for a three-year fire insurance policy covering the building. This expenditure was debited to an asset account by the following journal entry:

Expenditure for insurance recorded as asset	Unexpired Insurance	*180*	
	Cash		*180*
	Purchased three-year fire insurance policy.		

Since this expenditure of $180 will protect the company against fire loss for three years, the cost of protection each year is $\frac{1}{3}$ of $180, or $60. The insurance expense applicable to each month's operations is $\frac{1}{12}$ of the annual expense, or $5. In order that the accounting records for November show insurance expense of $5, the following adjusting entry is required at November 30:

Portion of asset expires (becomes expense)	Insurance Expense	*5*	
	Unexpired Insurance		*5*
	To record insurance expense for November.		

This adjusting entry serves two purposes: (1) it apportions the proper amount of insurance expense to November operations and (2) it reduces the asset account to $175 so that the correct amount of unexpired insurance will appear in the balance sheet at November 30.

OFFICE SUPPLIES On November 2, the Greenhill Real Estate Company purchased a sufficient quantity of stationery and other office supplies to last for several months. The cost of the supplies was $240, and this amount was debited to an asset account by the following journal entry.

Expenditure for office supplies recorded as asset	Inventory of Office Supplies	*240*	
	Cash		*240*
	Purchased office supplies.		

No entries were made during November to record the day-to-day usage of office supplies, but on November 30 a careful count was made of the supplies still on hand. This count showed unused supplies with a cost of $200. It is apparent, therefore, that supplies costing $40 were used during November. An adjusting entry is made on the basis of the November 30 count, debiting an expense account $40 (the cost of supplies consumed during November) and reducing the asset account by $40 to show that only $200 worth of office supplies remained on hand at November 30.

Portion of supplies used represents expense	Office Supplies Expense	*40*	
	Inventory of Office Supplies		*40*
	To record consumption of office supplies in November.		

When payments for insurance, office supplies, and rent are expected to provide economic benefits for more than one accounting period, the advance payment is usually recorded by a debit to an asset account such as Unexpired Insurance or Inventory of Office Supplies, as shown in the preceding examples. However, the advance payment *could* be recorded by debiting an expense account such as Insurance Expense.

At the end of the period, the adjusting entry would then consist of a debit to Unexpired Insurance and a credit to Insurance Expense. This alternative method would lead to the same amounts in the balance sheet and income statement as the method previously illustrated. Under both procedures, we would be treating as an expense of the current period the cost of the economic benefits consumed and carrying forward as an asset the cost of the economic benefits applicable to future periods.

DEPRECIATION OF BUILDING The November 30 journal entry to record depreciation of the building used by the Greenhill Real Estate Company is exactly the same as the October 31 entry explained in Chapter 3.

Cost of building is gradually converted to expense

Depreciation Expense: Building 50
    Accumulated Depreciation: Building 50
To record depreciation for November.

This allocation of depreciation expense to November operations is based on the following facts: The building cost $12,000 and is estimated to have a useful life of 20 years (240 months). Using the straight-line method of depreciation, the portion of the original cost which expires each month is $\frac{1}{240}$ of $12,000, or $50.

The Accumulated Depreciation: Building account now has a credit balance of $100 as a result of the October and November credits of $50 each. The book value of the building is $11,900, that is, the original cost of $12,000 minus the accumulated depreciation of $100. The term *book value* means the net amount at which an asset is shown in the accounting records, as distinguished from its market value. *Carrying value* is an alternative term, with the same meaning as book value.

DEPRECIATION OF OFFICE EQUIPMENT The November 30 adjusting entry to record depreciation of the office equipment is the same as the entry for depreciation a month earlier, as shown in Chapter 3.

Cost of office equipment is gradually converted to expense

Depreciation Expense: Office Equipment 15
    Accumulated Depreciation: Office Equipment 15
To record depreciation for November.

Original cost of the office equipment was $1,800, and the estimated useful life was 10 years (120 months). Depreciation each month under the straight-line method is therefore $\frac{1}{120}$ of $1,800, or $15.

What is the book value of the office equipment at this point? Original cost of $1,800 minus accumulated depreciation of $30 leaves a book value of $1,770.

What would be the effect on the financial statements if the adjusting entries for depreciation of the building and office equipment were omitted at November 30? In the income statement the expenses would be understated by $65 ($50 depreciation of building and $15 depreciation of office equipment), and net income for the month would be overstated by $65. In the balance sheet the assets would be overstated by $65; the owners' equity would be overstated the same amount because of the $65 overstatement of the net income added to retained earnings. If depreciation had not been recorded in either October or November, the overstatement in the balance sheet at November 30 would, of course, amount to $130 with respect both to assets and to owners' equity.

Recorded revenue apportioned between accounting periods

On November 1, James Fortune, a client of the Greenhill Real Estate Company, asked the company to manage a considerable amount of rental properties. The duties consisted of keeping the buildings rented, arranging for repairs, and collecting rents which were to be deposited in Fortune's bank account. It was agreed that $100 a month would be a reasonable fee to the Greenhill Real Estate Company for its services. Since Fortune was leaving the country on an extended trip, he paid the company for six months' service in advance at the time of signing the agreement. The journal entry to record the transaction on November 1 was as follows:

Commission collected but not yet earned

Cash	600	
Unearned Rental Commissions		600
Collected in advance six months' commissions for management of Fortune properties.		

Note that no service had been performed for the customer at the time the $600 was received. As emphasized in Chapter 3, not every receipt of cash represents revenue. In this case the receipt of cash represented an advance payment by the customer which obligated the Greenhill Real Estate Company to render services in the future. Revenue is earned only by the ***rendering of services*** to a customer, or the ***delivering of goods*** to him. A portion of the agreed services ($\frac{1}{6}$, to be exact) will be rendered during November, but it would be unreasonable to regard the entire $600 as revenue in that month. The commission is earned gradually over a period of six months as the Greenhill Real Estate Company performs the required services. The $600 collected in advance is therefore credited to an ***unearned revenue*** account at the time of its receipt. Some accountants prefer the alternative term ***deferred revenue.*** At the end of each month, an amount of $100 will be transferred from unearned revenue to an earned revenue account by means of an adjusting entry. The first in this series of transfers will be made at November 30 as follows:

Entry to recognize earning of a part of commission

Unearned Rental Commissions	100	
Rental Commissions Earned		100
Commission earned from Fortune property management in November.		

The $500 credit balance remaining in the Unearned Rental Commissions account represents an obligation to render $500 worth of services in future months or refund the money; therefore, it belongs on the balance sheet in the liability section. An unearned revenue account differs from other liabilities since it will ordinarily be settled by the rendering of services rather than by making a cash payment, but it is nevertheless a liability. The Rental Commissions Earned account is shown in the income statement as revenue for November.

Unrecorded expenses

Adjusting entries are necessary at the end of each accounting period to record any expenses which have been incurred but not recognized in the accounts. Salaries of employees and interest on borrowed money are common examples of expenses which accumulate day by day but which may not be recorded until the end of the period. These expenses are said to *accrue,* that is, to grow or accumulate.

ACCRUAL OF INTEREST   On November 1, the Greenhill Real Estate Company borrowed the sum of $1,000 from a bank. Banks require every borrower to sign a *promissory note,* that is, a formal, written promise to repay the amount borrowed plus interest at an agreed future date. (Various forms of notes in common use and the accounting problems involved will be discussed more fully in Chapter 10.) The note signed in this case, with certain details omitted, is shown below.

Note payable issued to bank

$1,000   Los Angeles, California   November 1, 19___

Three months .... *after date* ......I...... *promise to pay*

to the order of .... American National Bank ....

————One thousand and no/100———— .... *dollars*

for value received, with interest at .... 6 percent ....

Greenhill Real Estate Company

By ...... John Green ......

President

The note payable is a liability of the Greenhill Real Estate Company, similar to an account payable but different in that a formal written promise to pay is required and interest is charged on the amount borrowed. A Notes Payable account is credited when the note is issued; the Notes Payable account will be debited three months later when the note is paid. Interest accrues throughout the life of the note payable, but it is not payable until the note matures on January 31. To the bank making the loan, the note signed by Greenhill is an asset, a note receivable. The revenue earned by banks consists largely of interest charged borrowers.

The journal entry made on November 1 to record the borrowing of $1,000 from the bank was as follows:

When bank Cash *1,000*
loan is
obtained   Notes Payable *1,000*
Obtained three-month, 6% loan from bank.

On January 31, Greenhill Real Estate Company must pay the bank $1,015, representing repayment of the $1,000 note payable plus $15 interest ($1,000 × 0.06 × $\frac{3}{12}$). The $15 is the total interest expense for the three months. Although no payment will be made until January 31, a portion of the interest expense ($5) is *incurred* each month, as shown below.

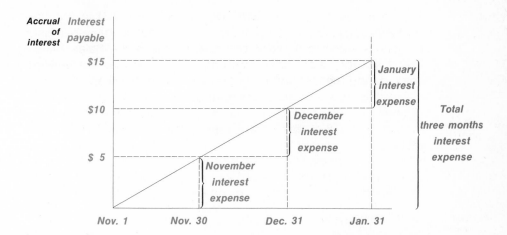

The following adjusting entry is made at November 30 to charge November operations with one month's interest expense and also to record the amount of interest owed to the bank at the end of November.

Interest   Interest Expense 5
expense
incurred in   Interest Payable 5
November   To record interest expense applicable to November.

The debit balance in the Interest Expense account will appear in the November income statement; the credit balances in the Interest Payable and Notes Payable accounts will be shown in the balance sheet as liabilities. These two liability accounts will remain in the accounting records until the maturity date on the loan, at which time a cash payment to the bank will eliminate both the Notes Payable account and the Interest Payable account.

ACCRUAL OF SALARY On November 20, Greenhill hired a part-time salesman whose duties were to work afternoons calling on property owners to secure listings of property for sale or rent. The agreed salary was $75 a week for a five-day week, payable each Friday; payment for the first week was made on Friday, November 24.

Assume that the last day of the accounting period, November 30, fell on Thursday. The salesman had worked four days since being paid the preceding Friday and therefore had earned $60 ($\frac{4}{5} \times$ $75). In order that this $60 of November salary expense be reflected in the accounts before the financial statements are prepared, an adjusting entry is necessary at November 30.

Salaries	*Sales Salaries Expense* *60*	
expense	*Sales Salaries Payable*	*60*
incurred but		
unpaid at	*To record salary expense and related liability to salesman for last four days'*	
November 30	*work in November.*	

The adjusted balance of $135 ($75 + $60 = $135) in the Sales Salaries Expense account will appear as an expense in the November income statement; the credit balance of $60 in the Sales Salaries Payable account is the amount owing to the salesman for work performed during the last four days of November and will appear among the liabilities on the balance sheet at November 30.

The next regular payday for the salesman will be Friday, December 1, which is the first day of the new accounting period. Since the accounts were adjusted and closed on November 30, all the revenue and expense accounts have zero balances at the beginning of business on December 1. The payment of a week's salary to the salesman will be recorded by the following entry on December 1:

Payment of	*Sales Salaries Payable* *60*	
salaries	*Sales Salaries Expense* *15*	
incurred in		
two	*Cash*	*75*
accounting	*Paid weekly salary to salesman, $60 of which was previously recorded as*	
periods	*Sales Salaries Payable.*	

Note that the net result of the November 30 accrual entry has been to split the salesman's weekly salary expense between November and December. Four days of the work week fell in November; so four days' pay, or $60, was recognized as November expense. One day of the work week fell in December; so $15 was recorded as December expense.

No accrual entry is necessary for office salaries in the Greenhill Real Estate Company because the office employees are paid on the last working day of the month.

Unrecorded revenue

The treatment of unrecorded revenue is similar to that of unrecorded expenses. Any revenue which has been earned but not recorded during the accounting period should be recognized in the accounts by means of an adjusting entry, debiting an asset account and crediting a revenue account.

On November 16, the Greenhill Real Estate Company entered into a management agreement with Henry Clayton, the owner of several small buildings. The company agreed to manage the Clayton properties for a commission of $80 a month, payable on the fifteenth of each month. No entry is made in the accounting records at the time of signing the contract, because no services have yet been rendered and no change has occurred in assets or liabilities. The managerial duties were to begin immediately, but the first monthly commission would not be received until December 15. The following adjusting entry is therefore necessary at November 30:

Commissions earned but uncollected	*Rental Commissions Receivable*	*40*
	Rental Commissions Earned	*40*

To record revenue accrued from services rendered Henry Clayton during November.

The debit balance in the Rental Commissions Receivable account will be shown in the balance sheet as an asset. The credit balance of the Rental Commissions Earned account, including earnings from both the Fortune and Clayton contracts, will appear in the November income statement.

The collection of the first monthly commission from Clayton will occur in the next accounting period (December 15, to be exact). Of this $80 cash receipt, half represents collection of the asset account, Rental Commissions Receivable, created at November 30 by the adjusting entry. The other half of the $80 cash receipt represents revenue earned during December; this should be credited to the December revenue account for Rental Commissions Earned. The entry on December 15 appears below:

Collection of commission applicable to two accounting periods	*Cash* *80*	
	Rental Commissions Receivable	*40*
	Rental Commissions Earned	*40*

Collection commission for month ended December 15. One-half of the commission had previously been recorded as Rental Commissions Receivable.

The net result of the November 30 accrual entry has been to divide the revenue from managing the Clayton properties between November and December in accordance with the timing of the services rendered.

Adjusting entries and the accrual basis of accounting

Adjusting entries help make accrual basis accounting work successfully. They bridge the gap between the time of earning revenue and the time of collecting cash. They enable expenses to be recorded in the accounting period in which the benefits from the expenditures are received, even though cash payment is made in an earlier or later period.

THE WORK SHEET

The work necessary at the end of an accounting period includes preparation of a trial balance, journalizing and posting of adjusting entries, preparation of financial statements, and journalizing and posting of closing entries. So many details are involved in these end-of-period procedures that it is easy to make errors. If these errors are recorded in the journal and the ledger accounts, considerable time and effort can be wasted in correcting them. Both the journal and the ledger are formal, permanent records. They may be prepared manually in ink, produced on accounting machines, or created by a computer in a company utilizing electronic data processing equipment. One way of avoiding errors in the permanent accounting records and also of simplifying the work to be done at the end of the period is to use a *work sheet.*

A *work sheet* is a large columnar sheet of paper, especially designed to arrange in a convenient systematic form all the accounting data required at the end of the period. The work sheet is not a part of the permanent accounting records; it is prepared in pencil by the accountant for his own convenience. If an error is made on the work sheet, it may be erased and corrected much more easily than an error in the formal accounting records. Furthermore, the work sheet is so designed as to minimize errors by automatically bringing to light many types of discrepancies which might otherwise be entered in the journal and posted to the ledger accounts.

The work sheet may be thought of as a testing ground on which the ledger accounts are adjusted, balanced, and arranged in the general form of financial statements. The satisfactory completion of a work sheet provides considerable assurance that all the details of the end-of-period accounting procedures have been properly brought together. After this point has been established, the work sheet then serves as the source from which the formal financial statements are prepared and the adjusting and closing entries are made in the general journal.

Preparing the work sheet

A commonly used form of work sheet with the appropriate headings for the Greenhill Real Estate Company is illustrated on page 112. Note that the heading of the work sheet contains six pairs of money columns, each pair consisting of a debit and a credit column. The procedures to be followed in preparing a work sheet will now be illustrated in six simple steps.

1 Enter the ledger account balances in the Trial Balance columns The titles and balances of the ledger accounts at November 30 are copied into the Trial Balance columns of the work sheet, as illustrated on page 112. It would be a duplication of work to prepare a trial balance as a separate schedule and then to copy this information into the work sheet. As soon as the account balances have been listed on the work sheet, these two columns should be added and the totals entered.

2 Enter the adjustments in the Adjustments columns The required adjustments for the Greenhill Real Estate Company have been explained earlier in this chapter; these same adjustments are now entered in the Adjustments columns of the work sheet. (See page 113.) As a cross reference, the debit and credit parts of each adjustment are keyed together by placing a key figure to the left of each amount. For example, the adjustment debiting Insurance Expense and crediting Unexpired Insurance is identified by the key figure *(1)*. The use of the key figures makes it easy to match a debit entry in the Adjustments columns with its related credit. The identifying figures also key the debit and credit entries in the Adjustments columns to the brief explanations which appear at the bottom of the work sheet.

The titles of any accounts debited or credited in the adjusting entries but not listed in the trial balance are written on the work sheet below the trial balance. For example, Insurance Expense does not appear in the trial balance; it is written on the first available line below the trial balance totals. After all the adjustments have been entered in the Adjustments columns, this pair of columns must be totaled. Proving the equality of debit and credit totals tends to prevent arithmetic errors from being carried over into other columns of the work sheet.

3 Enter the account balances as adjusted in the Adjusted Trial Balance columns The work sheet as it appears after completion of the Adjusted Trial Balance columns is illustrated on page 113. Each account balance in the first pair of columns is combined with the adjustment, if any, in the second pair of columns, and the combined amount is entered in the Adjusted Trial Balance columns. This process of combining the items on each line throughout the first four columns of the work sheet requires horizontal addition or subtraction. It is called *cross footing,* in contrast to the addition of items in a vertical column, which is called *footing* the column.

GREENHILL REAL ESTATE COMPANY
Work Sheet
For the Month Ended November 30, 19___

	Trial Balance		Adjustments		Adjusted Trial Balance		Income Statement		Retained Earnings		Balance Sheet	
	Dr	Cr	Dr	Cr	Dr	Cr	Dr	Cr	Dr	Cr	Dr	Cr
Cash	9,600											
Accounts receivable	2,330											
Unexpired insurance	180											
Inventory of office supplies	240											
Land	5,000											
Building	12,000											
Accumulated depreciation: building		50										
Office equipment	1,800											
Accumulated depreciation: office equipment		15										
Notes payable		1,000										
Accounts payable		7,865										
Unearned rental commissions		600										
Capital stock		20,000										
Retained earnings, Nov. 1, 19___		1,257										
Dividends	500											
Sales commissions earned		3,128										
Advertising expense	425											
Office salaries expense	1,700											
Sales salaries expense	75											
Telephone expense	65											
	33,915	33,915										

1. Enter ledger account balances before adjustments in Trial Balance columns on work sheet

GREENHILL REAL ESTATE COMPANY
Work Sheet
For the Month Ended November 30, 19___

	Trial Balance Dr	Trial Balance Cr	Adjustments* Dr	Adjustments* Cr	Adjusted Trial Balance Dr	Adjusted Trial Balance Cr	Income Statement Dr	Income Statement Cr	Retained Earnings Dr	Retained Earnings Cr	Balance Sheet Dr	Balance Sheet Cr
Cash	9,600				9,600							
Accounts receivable	2,330				2,330							
Unexpired insurance	180			(1) 5	175							
Inventory of office supplies	240			(2) 40	200							
Land	5,000				5,000							
Building	12,000				12,000							
Accumulated depreciation: building		50		(3) 50		100						
Office equipment	1,800				1,800							
Accumulated depreciation: office equipment		15		(4) 15		30						
Notes payable		1,000				1,000						
Accounts payable		7,865				7,865						
Unearned rental commissions		600	(5) 100			500						
Capital stock		20,000				20,000						
Retained earnings, Nov. 1, 19___		1,257				1,257						
Dividends	500				500							
Sales commissions earned		3,128				3,128						
Advertising expense	425				425							
Office salaries expense	1,700				1,700							
Sales salaries expense	75		(7) 60		135							
Telephone expense	65				65							
	33,915	33,915										
Insurance expense			(1) 5		5							
Office supplies expense			(2) 40		40							
Depreciation expense: building			(3) 50		50							
Depreciation expense: office equipment			(4) 15		15							
Rental commissions earned				(5) 100 (8) 40		140						
Interest expense			(6) 5		5							
Interest payable				(6) 5		5						
Sales salaries payable				(7) 60		60						
Rental commissions receivable			(8) 40		40							
			315	315	34,085	34,085						

Left margin instructions:

2. Enter required adjustments in Adjustments columns and key them to explanatory footnotes

3. Enter adjusted amounts in Adjusted Trial Balance columns of work sheet

* Adjustments:
(1) Portion of insurance cost which expired during November
(2) Office supplies used
(3) Depreciation of building during November
(4) Depreciation of office equipment during November
(5) Earned ⅙ of commission collected in advance on the Fortune properties
(6) Interest expense accrued during November on note payable
(7) Salesman's salary for last four days of November
(8) Rental commission accrued on Clayton contract in November

For example, the Inventory of Office Supplies account has an unadjusted debit balance of $240 in the Trial Balance columns. This $240 debit amount is combined with the $40 credit appearing on the same line in the Adjustments column; the combination of a $240 debit with a $40 credit produces an adjusted debit amount of $200 in the Adjusted Trial Balance debit column. As another example, consider the Office Supplies Expense account. This account had no balance in the Trial Balance columns but shows a $40 debit in the Adjustments debit column. The combination of a zero starting balance and $40 debit adjustment produces a $40 debit amount in the Adjusted Trial Balance.

Many of the accounts in the trial balance are not affected by the adjustments made at the end of the month; the balances of these accounts (such as Cash, Land, Building, or Notes Payable in the illustrated work sheet) are entered in the Adjusted Trial Balance columns in exactly the same amounts as shown in the Trial Balance columns. After all the accounts have been extended into the Adjusted Trial Balance columns, this pair of columns is totaled to prove that no arithmetic errors have been made up to this point.

4 Extend each amount in the Adjusted Trial Balance columns horizontally across the work sheet into one of the six remaining columns Revenue and expense accounts are extended into the Income Statement columns. The amounts in the Retained Earnings account and the Dividends account are entered in the Retained Earnings columns. Assets and liabilities are entered in the Balance Sheet columns.

The process of extending amounts horizontally across the work sheet should begin with the account at the top of the work sheet, which is usually Cash. The cash figure is extended to the Balance Sheet debit column. Then the accountant goes down the work sheet line by line, extending each account balance to the appropriate column. The work sheet as it appears after completion of this sorting process is illustrated on page 115. Note that each amount in the Adjusted Trial Balance columns is extended to one *and only one* of the six remaining columns.

5 Total the Income Statement columns. The difference of $828 represents the net income and is entered as a balancing figure in the Income Statement debit column. Since net income causes an increase in retained earnings, the $828 figure is also entered in the Retained Earnings credit column. Final totals are now computed for the Income Statement columns The work sheet as it appears after this step is shown on page 116.

As indicated above, the net income or net loss for the period is determined by computing the difference between the two Income Statement columns. In the illustrated work sheet, the credit column total is the larger and the excess of $828 represents net income. Note on the work sheet that the net income of $828 is identified by writing the caption "Net income" in the space provided for account titles.

Let us assume for a moment that the month's operations had pro-

GREENHILL REAL ESTATE COMPANY
Work Sheet
For the Month Ended November 30, 19___

4. Extend each adjusted amount to columns for income statement, retained earnings, or balance sheet

	Trial Balance Dr	Trial Balance Cr	Adjustments* Dr	Adjustments* Cr	Adjusted Trial Balance Dr	Adjusted Trial Balance Cr	Income Statement Dr	Income Statement Cr	Retained Earnings Dr	Retained Earnings Cr	Balance Sheet Dr	Balance Sheet Cr
Cash	9,600				9,600						9,600	
Accounts receivable	2,330				2,330						2,330	
Unexpired insurance	180			(1) 5	175						175	
Inventory of office supplies	240			(2) 40	200						200	
Land	5,000				5,000						5,000	
Building	12,000				12,000						12,000	
Accumulated depreciation: building		50		(3) 50		100						100
Office equipment	1,800				1,800						1,800	
Accumulated depreciation: office equipment		15		(4) 15		30						30
Notes payable		1,000				1,000						1,000
Accounts payable		7,865				7,865						7,865
Unearned rental commissions		600	(5) 100			500						500
Capital stock		20,000				20,000						20,000
Retained earnings, Nov. 1, 19___		1,257				1,257				1,257		
Dividends	500				500				500			
Sales commissions earned		3,128				3,128		3,128				
Advertising expense	425				425		425					
Office salaries expense	1,700				1,700		1,700					
Sales salaries expense	75		(7) 60		135		135					
Telephone expense	65				65		65					
	33,915	33,915										
Insurance expense			(1) 5		5		5					
Office supplies expense			(2) 40		40		40					
Depreciation expense: building			(3) 50		50		50					
Depreciation expense: office equipment			(4) 15		15		15					
Rental commissions earned				(5) 100 / (8) 40		140		140				
Interest expense			(6) 5		5		5					
Interest payable				(6) 5		5						5
Sales salaries payable				(7) 60		60						60
Rental commissions receivable			(8) 40		40						40	
			315	315	34,085	34,085						

* Explanatory notes relating to adjustments are the same as on page 113.

GREENHILL REAL ESTATE COMPANY
Work Sheet
For the Month Ended November 30, 19___

Account	Trial Balance Dr	Trial Balance Cr	Adjustments Dr	Adjustments Cr	Adjusted Trial Balance Dr	Adjusted Trial Balance Cr	Income Statement Dr	Income Statement Cr	Retained Earnings Dr	Retained Earnings Cr	Balance Sheet Dr	Balance Sheet Cr
Cash	9,600				9,600						9,600	
Accounts receivable	2,330				2,330						2,330	
Unexpired insurance	180			(1) 5	175						175	
Inventory of office supplies	240			(2) 40	200						200	
Land	5,000				5,000						5,000	
Building	12,000				12,000						12,000	
Accumulated depreciation: building		50		(3) 50		100						100
Office equipment	1,800				1,800						1,800	
Accumulated depreciation: office equipment		15		(4) 15		30						30
Notes payable		1,000				1,000						1,000
Accounts payable		7,865				7,865						7,865
Unearned rental commissions		600	(5) 100			500						500
Capital stock		20,000				20,000						20,000
Retained earnings, Nov. 1, 19___		1,257				1,257				1,257		
Dividends	500				500				500			
Sales commissions earned		3,128				3,128		3,128				
Advertising expense	425				425		425					
Office salaries expense	1,700				1,700		1,700					
Sales salaries expense	75		(7) 60		135		135					
Telephone expense	65				65		65					
	33,915	33,915										
Insurance expense			(1) 5		5		5					
Office supplies expense			(2) 40		40		40					
Depreciation expense: building			(3) 50		50		50					
Depreciation expense: office equipment			(4) 15		15		15					
Rental commissions earned				(5) 100 / (8) 40		140		140				
Interest expense			(6) 5		5		5					
Interest payable				(6) 5		5						5
Sales salaries payable				(7) 60		60						60
Rental commissions receivable			(8) 40		40						40	
			315	315	34,085	34,085	2,440	3,268				
Net income							828			828		
							3,268	3,268				

Left-margin note: **5. Total Income Statement columns and enter net income as a balancing figure; enter the effect of net income in the Retained Earnings columns**

* Explanatory notes relating to adjustments are the same as on page 113.

GREENHILL REAL ESTATE COMPANY

Work Sheet

For the Month Ended November 30, 19___

6. Complete work sheet by entering new balance of retained earnings in Retained Earnings debit column and Balance Sheet credit column

	Trial Balance		Adjustments*		Adjusted Trial Balance		Income Statement		Retained Earnings		Balance Sheet	
	Dr	Cr	Dr	Cr	Dr	Cr	Dr	Cr	Dr	Cr	Dr	Cr
Cash	9,600				9,600						9,600	
Accounts receivable	2,330				2,330						2,330	
Unexpired insurance	180			(1) 5	175						175	
Inventory of office supplies	240			(2) 40	200						200	
Land	5,000				5,000						5,000	
Building	12,000				12,000						12,000	
Accumulated depreciation: building		50		(3) 50		100						100
Office equipment	1,800				1,800						1,800	
Accumulated depreciation: office equipment		15		(4) 15		30						30
Notes payable		1,000				1,000						1,000
Accounts payable		7,865				7,865						7,865
Unearned rental commissions		600	(5) 100			500						500
Capital stock		20,000				20,000						20,000
Retained earnings, Nov. 1, 19___		1,257				1,257				1,257		
Dividends	500				500				500			
Sales commissions earned		3,128				3,128		3,128				
Advertising expense	425				425		425					
Office salaries expense	1,700				1,700		1,700					
Sales salaries expense	75		(7) 60		135		135					
Telephone expense	65				65		65					
	33,915	33,915										
Insurance expense			(1) 5		5		5					
Office supplies expense			(2) 40		40		40					
Depreciation expense: building			(3) 50		50		50					
Depreciation expense: office equipment			(4) 15		15		15					
Rental commissions earned				(5) 100 / (8) 40		140		140				
Interest expense			(6) 5		5		5					
Interest payable				(6) 5		5						5
Sales salaries payable				(7) 60		60						60
Rental commissions receivable			(8) 40		40						40	
			315	315	34,085	34,085	2,440	3,268				
Net income							828			828		
							3,268	3,268				
Retained earnings, Nov. 30, 19___									1,585			1,585
									2,085	2,085	31,145	31,145

* Explanatory notes relating to adjustments are the same as on page 113.

duced a loss rather than a profit. In that case the Income Statement debit column would exceed the credit column. The excess of the debits (expenses) over the credits (revenue) would have to be entered in the credit column in order to bring the two Income Statement columns into balance. The incurring of a loss would decrease the retained earnings; therefore, the loss would be entered in the Retained Earnings debit column.

6 Compute the amount of retained earnings at the end of the month; enter this amount of $1,585 as a balancing figure in the Retained Earnings debit column and also in the Balance Sheet credit column. Total both pairs of columns The completed work sheet appears on page 117.

The Balance Sheet columns now prove the familiar proposition that assets are equal to the total of liabilities and stockholders' equity. Any lack of agreement in the totals of the Balance Sheet columns would indicate an error in the work sheet.

PREPARING FINANCIAL STATEMENTS FROM THE WORK SHEET Preparing the formal financial statements from the work sheet is an easy step. All the information needed for the income statement, the statement of retained earnings, and the balance sheet has already been sorted and arranged in convenient form in the work sheet.

Income statement The income statement shown below contains the amounts listed in the Income Statement columns of the completed work sheet on page 117.

GREENHILL REAL ESTATE COMPANY
Income Statement
For the Month Ended November 30, 19___

Data taken from Income Statement columns of work sheet	Revenue:		
	Sales commissions earned		$3,128
	Rental commissions earned		140
	Total revenue		$3,268
	Expenses:		
	Advertising	$ 425	
	Office salaries	1,700	
	Sales salaries	135	
	Telephone	65	
	Insurance	5	
	Office supplies	40	
	Depreciation: building	50	
	Depreciation: office equipment	15	
	Interest	5	
	Total expenses		2,440
	Net income		$ 828

As noted in Chapter 3, we are purposely ignoring income taxes on corporations at this stage of our study. Corporate income taxes are introduced in Chapter 7 and considered more fully in Chapter 17.

Statement of retained earnings   The following statement of retained earnings for the month of November shows the amounts listed in the Retained Earnings columns of the work sheet.

GREENHILL REAL ESTATE COMPANY
Statement of Retained Earnings
For the Month Ended November 30, 19___

Data taken Retained earnings, Nov. 1, 19___	$1,257
from Net income for the month (per income statement)	828
Retained *Earnings* Subtotal	$2,085
columns of Dividends	500
work sheet Retained earnings, Nov. 30, 19___	$1,585

Balance sheet   The balance sheet illustrated on page 120 contains the amounts listed in the Balance Sheet columns of the work sheet.

RECORDING ADJUSTING ENTRIES IN THE ACCOUNTING RECORDS   After the financial statements have been prepared from the work sheet at the end of the period, the ledger accounts are adjusted to bring them into agreement with the statements. This is an easy step because the adjustments have already been computed on the work sheet. The amounts appearing in the Adjustments columns of the work sheet and the related explanations at the bottom of the work sheet provide all the necessary information for the adjusting entries, as shown on page 121, which are first entered in the journal and then posted to the ledger accounts.

RECORDING CLOSING ENTRIES   When the financial statements have been prepared from the work sheet, the revenue and expense accounts have served their purpose for the current period and should be closed. These accounts will then have zero balances and will be ready for the recording of revenue and expenses during the next fiscal period.

The journalizing and posting of closing entries were illustrated in Chapter 3. The point to be emphasized now is that the completed work sheet provides in convenient form all the information needed to make the closing entries. The preparation of closing entries from the work sheet may be summarized as follows:

GREENHILL REAL ESTATE COMPANY
Balance Sheet
November 30, 19___

Assets

Cash		$ 9,600
Accounts receivable		2,330
Rental commissions receivable		40
Unexpired insurance		175
Inventory of office supplies		200
Land		5,000
Building	$12,000	
Less: Accumulated depreciation	100	11,900
Office equipment	$ 1,800	
Less: Accumulated depreciation	30	1,770
Total assets		$31,015

Data taken from Balance Sheet columns of work sheet

Liabilities & Stockholders' Equity

Liabilities:		
Notes payable		$ 1,000
Accounts payable		7,865
Sales salaries payable		60
Interest payable		5
Unearned rental commissions		500
Total liabilities		$ 9,430
Stockholders' equity:		
Capital stock	$20,000	
Retained earnings	1,585	21,585
Total liabilities & stockholders' equity		$31,015

1 To close the accounts listed in the Income Statement credit column, debit the revenue accounts and credit Income Summary.

2 To close the accounts listed in the Income Statement debit column, debit Income Summary and credit the expense accounts.

3 To close the Income Summary account, transfer the balancing figure in the Income Statement columns of the work sheet ($828 in the illustration) to the Retained Earnings account. A profit is transferred by debiting Income Summary and crediting the Retained Earnings account; a loss is transferred by debiting the Retained Earnings account and crediting Income Summary.

4 To close the Dividends account, debit the Retained Earnings account and credit the Dividends account.

General Journal   *Page 5*

			Adjusting Entries			

Adjustments on work sheet are entered in general journal

19__					
Nov.	30	Insurance Expense	5		
		Unexpired Insurance		5
		Insurance expense for November.		
	30	Office Supplies Expense	40	
		Inventory of Office Supplies		40
		Office supplies used during November.		
	30	Depreciation Expense: Building	50	
		Accumulated Depreciation:		
		Building		50
		Depreciation for November.		
	30	Depreciation Expense: Office Equipment . .	15	
		Accumulated Depreciation: Office		
		Equipment		15
		Depreciation for November.		
	30	Unearned Rental Commissions	100	
		Rental Commissions Earned		100
		Earned $\frac{1}{6}$ of commission collected in advance for management of the properties owned by James Fortune.		
	30	Interest Expense	5	
		Interest Payable		5
		Interest expense accrued during November on note payable.		
	30	Sales Salaries Expense	60	
		Sales Salaries Payable		60
		To record expense and related liability to salesman for last four days' work in November.		
	30	Rental Commissions Receivable	40	
		Rental Commissions Earned		40
		To record the receivable and related revenue earned for managing properties owned by Henry Clayton.		

The entries to close the revenue and expense accounts, as well as the Dividends account, at November 30 are shown on page 122.

General Journal   Page 6

			Closing Entries			

19___						
Nov.	30	Sales Commissions Earned		3,128		
		Rental Commissions Earned		140		
		Income Summary				3,268
		To close the revenue accounts.				
	30	Income Summary		2,440		
		Advertising Expense.				425
		Office Salaries Expense				1,700
		Sales Salaries Expense.				135
		Telephone Expense				65
		Insurance Expense				5
		Office Supplies Expense				40
		Depreciation Expense: Building				50
		Depreciation Expense: Office Equip-				
		ment				15
		Interest Expense				5
		To close the expense accounts.				
	30	Income Summary		828		
		Retained Earnings				828
		To close the Income Summary account.				
	30	Retained Earnings		500		
		Dividends				500
		To close the Dividends account.				

Sequence of accounting procedures when work sheet is used

In any business which maintains a considerable number of accounts or makes numerous adjusting entries, the use of a work sheet will save much time and labor. Since the work sheet includes a trial balance, adjusting entries in preliminary form, and an adjusted trial balance, the use of the work sheet will modify the sequence of accounting procedures given in Chapter 3 as follows:

1 Record all transactions in the journal as they occur.
2 Post debits and credits from the journal entries to the proper ledger accounts.
3 Prepare the work sheet. (The work sheet includes a trial balance of the ledger and all necessary adjustments.)
4 Prepare financial statements, consisting of an income statement, a statement of retained earnings, and a balance sheet.
5 Using the information shown on the work sheet as a guide, enter the adjusting and closing entries in the journal. Post these entries to ledger accounts.

6 Prepare an after-closing trial balance to prove that the ledger is still in balance.

Note that the first two procedures, consisting of the journalizing and posting of transactions during the period, are the same regardless of whether a work sheet is to be used at the end of the period.

The accounting cycle

The above sequence of accounting procedures constitutes a complete accounting process, which is repeated in the same order in each accounting period. The regular repetition of this standardized set of procedures is often referred to as the *accounting cycle.* The procedures of a complete accounting cycle are illustrated below:

Illustration of the accounting cycle

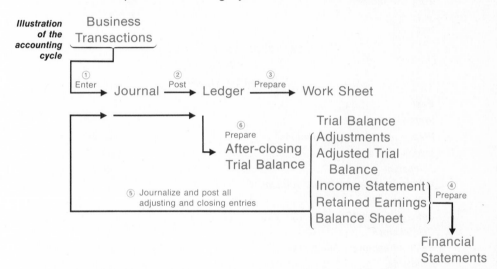

In most business concerns the accounts are closed only once a year; for these companies the accounting cycle is one year in length. For purposes of illustration in a textbook, it is convenient to assume that the entire accounting cycle is performed within the time period of one month. The completion of the accounting cycle is the occasion for closing the revenue and expense accounts and preparing financial statements.

Preparing monthly financial statements without closing the accounts

Many companies which close their accounts only once a year nevertheless prepare *monthly* financial statements for managerial use. These monthly statements are prepared from work sheets, but the adjustments indicated on the work sheets are not entered in the accounting records and no closing entries are made. Under this plan, the time-consuming operation of journalizing and posting adjustments and closing entries is performed only at the end of the fiscal year, but the company has the advantage of monthly financial statements. Monthly and quarterly financial statements are often referred to as *interim statements,* because they are in between the year-end statements. The annual or year-end statements are usually audited by a firm of certified public accountants; interim statements are usually unaudited.

DEMONSTRATION PROBLEM

Reed Geophysical Company adjusts and closes its books at the end of the calendar year. At December 31, 1977, the following trial balance was prepared from the ledger:

REED GEOPHYSICAL COMPANY
Trial Balance
December 31, 1977

Cash	$12,540	
Prepaid office rent	8,400	
Prepaid dues and subscriptions	960	
Inventory of supplies	1,300	
Equipment	20,000	
Accumulated depreciation: equipment		$ 1,200
Notes payable		5,000
Unearned consulting fees		35,650
Capital stock		10,000
Retained earnings, Jan. 1, 1977		12,950
Dividends	7,000	
Consulting fees earned		15,200
Salaries expense	26,900	
Telephone and telegraph expense	550	
Miscellaneous expenses	2,350	
	$80,000	$80,000

Other data
   (1) On January 1, 1977, the Prepaid Office Rent account had a balance of $2,400, representing the prepaid rent for the months from January to June 1977 inclusive. On July 1, 1977, the lease was renewed and office rent for one year at $500 per month was paid in advance.
   (2) Dues and subscriptions expired during the year in the total amount of $710.
   (3) A count of supplies on hand was made at December 31; the cost of the unused supplies was $450.
   (4) The useful life of the equipment has been estimated at 10 years from date of acquisition.
   (5) Accrued interest on notes payable amounted to $100 at year-end. Set up a separate Interest Expense account.

(6) Consulting services valued at $32,550 were rendered during the year for clients who had made payment in advance.

(7) It is the custom of the firm to bill clients only when consulting work is completed or, in the case of prolonged engagement, at six-month intervals. At December 31, engineering services valued at $3,000 had been rendered to clients but not yet billed. No advance payments had been received from these clients.

(8) Salaries earned by staff engineers but not yet paid amounted to $200 at December 31.

Instructions

a Prepare a work sheet for the year ended December 31, 1977.

b Prepare an income statement, a balance sheet, and a statement of retained earnings.

c Prepare adjusting and closing journal entries.

(The Solution to the Demonstration Problem appears on pages 126–129).

REVIEW QUESTIONS

1 May an adjusting entry involve only balance sheet accounts or only income statement accounts? Explain.

2 The Property Management Company manages office buildings and apartment buildings for various owners who wish to be relieved of this responsibility. The revenue earned for this service is credited to Management Fees Earned. On December 1, the company received a check for $1,800 from a client, James Thurston, who was leaving for a six-month stay abroad. This check represented payment in advance for management of Thurston's real estate properties during the six months of his absence. Explain how this transaction would be recorded, the adjustment, if any, to be made at December 31, and the presentation of this matter in the year-end financial statements.

3 At the end of this year, the adjusted trial balance of the Black Company showed the following account balances, among others: Depreciation Expense: Building, $1,610; Building, $32,200; Accumulated Depreciation: Building, $14,490. Assuming that straight-line depreciation has been used, what length of time do these facts suggest that the Black Company has owned the building?

4 The weekly payroll for salesmen of the Ryan Company amounts to $1,250. All salesmen are paid up to date at the close of business each Friday. If December 31 falls on Wednesday, what year-end adjusting entry is needed?

5 The Marvin Company purchased a three-year fire insurance policy on August 1 and debited the entire cost of $540 to Unexpired Insurance. The accounts were not adjusted or closed until the end of the year. Give the adjusting entry at December 31.

6 The net income reported by the Haskell Company for Year 2 was $21,400, and the Retained Earnings account stood at $36,000. However, the company had failed to recognize that interest amounting to $375 had accrued on a note payable to the bank. State the corrected figures for net income and retained earnings. In what other respect was the balance sheet of the company in error?

7 Office supplies on hand in the Melville Company amounted to $642 at the beginning of the year. During the year additional office supplies were purchased at a cost of $1,561 and charged to Inventory of Office Supplies. At the end of the year a physical count showed that supplies on hand amounted to $812. Give the adjusting entry needed at December 31.

SOLUTION TO DEMONSTRATION PROBLEM

REED GEOPHYSICAL COMPANY
Work Sheet
For the Year Ended December 31, 1977

	Trial Balance		Adjustments*		Adjusted Trial Balance		Income Statement		Retained Earnings		Balance Sheet	
	Dr	Cr	Dr	Cr	Dr	Cr	Dr	Cr	Dr	Cr	Dr	Cr
Cash	12,540				12,540						12,540	
Prepaid office rent	8,400			(1) 5,400	3,000						3,000	
Prepaid dues and subscriptions	960			(2) 710	250						250	
Inventory of supplies	1,300			(3) 850	450						450	
Equipment	20,000				20,000						20,000	
Accumulated depreciation: equipment		1,200		(4) 2,000		3,200						3,200
Notes payable		5,000				5,000						5,000
Unearned consulting fees		35,650	(6) 32,550			3,100						3,100
Capital stock		10,000				10,000						10,000
Retained earnings, Jan. 1, 1977		12,950				12,950				12,950		
Dividends	7,000				7,000				7,000			
Consulting fees earned		15,200		(6) 32,550 (7) 3,000		50,750		50,750				
	80,000	80,000										
Salaries expense	26,900		(8) 200		27,100		27,100					
Telephone and telegraph expense	550				550		550					
Miscellaneous expenses	2,350				2,350		2,350					
Rent expense			(1) 5,400		5,400		5,400					
Dues and subscriptions expense			(2) 710		710		710					
Supplies expense			(3) 850		850		850					
Depreciation expense: equipment			(4) 2,000		2,000		2,000					
Interest expense			(5) 100		100		100					
Interest payable				(5) 100		100						100
Consulting fees receivable			(7) 3,000		3,000						3,000	
Salaries payable				(8) 200		200						200
			44,810	44,810	85,300	85,300	39,060	50,750			39,240	17,640
Net income							11,690			11,690		
							50,750	50,750	7,000	24,640		
Retained earnings, Dec. 31, 1977									17,640			17,640
									24,640	24,640	39,240	39,240

a

*Adjustments:
(1) Rent expense for year
(2) Dues and subscriptions expense for year
(3) Drafting supplies used for year
(4) Depreciation expense for year

(5) Accrued interest on notes payable
(6) Consulting services performed for clients who paid in advance
(7) Services rendered but not billed
(8) Salaries earned but not paid

b

REED GEOPHYSICAL COMPANY
Income Statement
For the Year Ended December 31, 1977

Consulting fees earned		$50,750
Expenses:		
Salaries expense	$27,100	
Telephone and telegraph expense	550	
Miscellaneous expenses	2,350	
Rent expense	5,400	
Dues and subscriptions expense	710	
Supplies expense	850	
Depreciation expense: equipment	2,000	
Interest expense	100	
Total expenses		39,060
Net income		$11,690

REED GEOPHYSICAL COMPANY
Balance Sheet
December 31, 1977

Assets

Cash		$12,540
Consulting fees receivable		3,000
Prepaid office rent		3,000
Prepaid dues and subscriptions		250
Inventory of supplies		450
Equipment	$20,000	
Less: Accumulated depreciation	3,200	16,800
Total assets		$36,040

Liabilities & Stockholders' Equity

Liabilities:		
Notes payable		$ 5,000
Interest payable		100
Salaries payable		200
Unearned consulting fees		3,100
Total liabilities		$ 8,400
Stockholders' equity:		
Capital stock	$10,000	
Retained earnings	17,640	27,640
Total liabilities & stockholders' equity		$36,040

REED GEOPHYSICAL COMPANY
Statement of Retained Earnings
For the Year Ended December 31, 1977

Retained earnings, Jan. 1, 1977	$12,950
Net income for year	11,690
Subtotal	$24,640
Dividends	7,000
Retained earnings, Dec. 31, 1977	$17,640

c   *Adjusting Entries*

1977		(1)		
Dec.	31	Rent Expense	5,400	
		Prepaid Office Rent		5,400
		Rent expense for 1977; $2,400 for first six months and $3,000 for last six months.		
		(2)		
	31	Dues and Subscriptions Expense	710	
		Prepaid Dues and Subscriptions . . .		710
		Dues and subscriptions expired during year.		
		(3)		
	31	Supplies Expense	850	
		Inventory of Supplies		850
		Drafting supplies used during year.		
		(4)		
	31	Depreciation Expense: Equipment	2,000	
		Accumulated Depreciation:		
		Equipment		2,000
		Depreciation on equipment for year.		
		(5)		
	31	Interest Expense	100	
		Interest Payable		100
		Accrued interest on notes payable.		
		(6)		
	31	Unearned Consulting Fees	32,550	
		Consulting Fees Earned		32,550
		Consulting services performed for clients who paid in advance.		
		(7)		
	31	Consulting Fees Receivable	3,000	
		Consulting Fees Earned		3,000
		Consulting services rendered but not yet billed.		
		(8)		
	31	Salaries Expense	200	
		Salaries Payable		200
		Salaries earned by employees, but not paid.		

Closing Entries

Dec.	31	Consulting Fees Earned	50,750	
		Income Summary		50,750
		To close revenue account.		
	31	Income Summary	39,060	
		Salaries Expense.		27,100
		Telephone and Telegraph Expense		550
		Miscellaneous Expenses		2,350
		Rent Expense		5,400
		Dues and Subscriptions Expense . .		710
		Supplies Expense		850
		Depreciation Expense: Equipment . .		2,000
		Interest Expense		100
		To close expense accounts.		
	31	Income Summary	11,690	
		Retained Earnings		11,690
		To close Income Summary account.		
	31	Retained Earnings	7,000	
		Dividends		7,000
		To close Dividends account.		

8 The X Company at December 31 recognized the existence of certain unexpired costs which would provide benefits to the company in future periods. Give examples of such unexpired costs and state where they would be shown in the financial statements.

9 In performing the regular end-of-period accounting procedures, does the preparation of the work sheet precede or follow the posting of adjusting entries to ledger accounts? Why?

10 List in order the procedures comprising the accounting cycle when a work sheet is used.

11 Explain why the amount of net income is entered in the Income Statement debit column on a work sheet.

12 Do the totals of the balance sheet ordinarily agree with the totals of the Balance Sheet columns of the work sheet?

13 Is a work sheet ever prepared when there is no intention of closing the accounts? Explain.

EXERCISES

Ex. 4-1 The weekly salaries paid by Edgemar Company to its sales personnel each Friday for a five-day work week amount to $15,000.
a Draft the necessary adjusting entry at year-end, assuming that December 31 falls on Tuesday.
b Also draft the journal entry for the payment by Edgemar Company of a week's salaries to its sales personnel on Friday, January 3, the first payday of the new year.

Ex. 4-2 Field Company adjusts and closes its accounts at the end of the calendar year. Prepare the adjusting entries required at December 31, based on the following information:

  a A six-month bank loan in the amount of $50,000 had been obtained on October 1, at an annual interest rate of 9%. No interest expense has been recorded.

  b A tractor had been rented on December 11 at a daily rate of $40 (including December 11). No rental payment has yet been made. Continued use of the tractor is expected through January.

  c Interest receivable on United States government bonds owned is $690.

  d Accrued wages payable on December 31 are $1,850.

  e On December 31, an agreement was signed to lease a truck for 12 months beginning January 1 at a rate of 15 cents a mile. Estimated usage is 1,200 miles per month.

Ex. 4-3 For each of the following items relating to Bluegrass Racetrack, write first the journal entry (if one is required) to record the external transaction and secondly, the adjusting entry, if any, required on May 31, the end of the fiscal period.

  a On May 1, paid rent for the next four months at $4,500 per month.

  b On May 2, sold season tickets for a total of $120,000. The season includes 60 racing days: 15 in May, 25 in June, and 20 in July.

  c On May 3, an agreement was reached with Snack-Bars, Inc., allowing that company to sell refreshments at the racetrack in return for 10% of the gross receipts from refreshment sales.

  d On May 5, racing forms for the 15 racing days in May and the first 10 racing days in June were printed at a cost of $2,000.

  e On May 31, Snack-Bars, Inc., reported that the gross receipts from refreshment sales in May had been $27,000, and that the 10% owed to Bluegrass Racetrack would be remitted on June 10.

Ex. 4-4 The trial balances of Fisher Insurance Agency, as of September 30, 19____, before and after the posting of adjusting entries, are shown below:

	Before Adjustments		After Adjustments	
	Dr	Cr	Dr	Cr
Cash	$ 6,180		$ 6,180	
Commissions receivable			800	
Inventory of office supplies	600		360	
Office equipment	6,220		6,220	
Accumulated depreciation: office equipment		$ 2,150		$ 2,240
Accounts payable		1,550		1,550
Salaries payable				450
Unearned commissions		400		140
Capital stock		4,500		4,500
Retained earnings		2,500		2,500
Commissions earned		3,900		4,960
Salaries expense	2,000		2,450	
Office supplies expense			240	
Depreciation expense: office equipment . .			90	
	$15,000	$15,000	$16,340	$16,340

Instruction Prepare the adjusting entries in general journal form.

Ex. 4-5 The following amounts are taken from consecutive balance sheets of the Bailey Company:

	Year 1	Year 2
Unexpired insurance	$ –0–	$ 900
Unearned rental revenue	3,000	1,500
Interest payable	100	875
Dividends receivable	450	200

The income statement for Year 2 of the Bailey Company shows the following items:

Insurance expense	$ 700
Rental revenue	18,000
Interest expense	1,000
Dividend revenue	1,200

Instructions Determine the following amounts of cash:
a Paid during Year 2 on insurance policies.
b Received during Year 2 as rental revenue.
c Paid during Year 2 for interest.
d Received during Year 2 as dividends revenue.

PROBLEMS

4-1 Island Water Taxi Service was organized earlier this year to transport tourists to a nearby resort island. The company adjusts and closes its accounts at the end of each month. Selected account balances appearing on the July 31 adjusted trial balance are as follows:

Prepaid rent	$ 2,250	
Unexpired insurance	600	
Water taxi	24,000	
Accumulated depreciation: water taxi		$1,750
Unearned passenger revenue		625

Other data
(1) Four months rent had been prepaid on July 1.
(2) The unexpired insurance is a 36-month fire insurance policy purchased on February 1.
(3) The water taxi is being depreciated over an 8-year estimated useful life, with no residual value.
(4) The unearned passenger revenue represents tickets good for future rides sold to a resort hotel for $5 per ticket on July 1. During July, 175 of the tickets were used.

Instructions
a Determine:
   (1) The monthly rent expense.
   (2) The original cost of the 36-month fire insurance policy.
   (3) The age in months of the water taxi.
   (4) How many $5 tickets for future rides were sold to the resort hotel on July 1.

b Prepare the adjusting entries which were made on July 31.

4-2 Coral Beach Motel maintains its accounting records on the basis of a fiscal year ending September 30. The following information is available as a source for adjusting entries:

(1) Salaries earned by employees but not yet paid amount to $3,620.

(2) As of September 30, the motel has earned $1,680 rental revenue from current guests who will not be billed until they are ready to check out.

(3) On September 16, a suite of rooms was rented to a guest for six months at a monthly rental of $500. The first three months rent was collected in advance and credited to Unearned Rental Revenue.

(4) A one-year bank loan in the amount of $30,000 had been obtained on August 1 at an annual interest rate of 8%. No interest has been paid and no interest expense has been recorded.

(5) Depreciation on the motel for the year ended September 30 was $14,600.

(6) Depreciation on a station wagon owned by the motel was based on a four-year life. The station wagon had been purchased new on July 1 of the current year at a cost of $4,800.

(7) On September 30, Coral Beach Motel entered into an agreement to host the National Building Suppliers Convention in June of next year. The motel expects to earn rental revenue of at least $5,000 from the convention.

Instructions

a From the information given above, draft the adjusting entries (including explanations) required at September 30.

b Assume that all necessary adjusting entries at September 30 have been recorded and that net income for the year is determined to be $100,000. How much net income would have been indicated by the accounting records if the company had failed to make the above adjusting entries? Show computations.

4-3 Plaza Theater began operations on January 1 of the current year. The company's accounting policy is to adjust and close the accounts each month. Before adjustments at March 31, the account balances were as follows:

Cash	$ 3,450	
Unexpired insurance	1,020	
Prepaid film rental	3,700	
Projection equipment	12,600	
Accumulated depreciation: projection equipment		$ 300
Notes payable		6,000
Unearned concessions revenue		1,400
Capital stock		10,000
Retained earnings		1,210
Dividends	1,500	
Admissions revenue		7,470
Salaries expense	3,410	
Building rent expense	700	
	$26,380	$26,380

Other data

(1) A three-year fire insurance policy was purchased on January 2 of the current year for $1,080.

(2) Film rental expense for the month of March amounted to $2,190.

(3) Projection equipment with an estimated useful life of 7 years was purchased on January 1 of the current year.

(4) Interest expense on notes payable amounted to $40 for the month of March.

(5) Paul Bassart, concessionaire, reported that net income from concessions for March amounted to $4,200. Circle Theater's share was 10%, as per agreement. This agreement also provided for semiannual advance payments by Bassart based on estimates of future sales. These advance payments were credited to Unearned Concessions Revenue when received.

(6) Salaries earned by employees but not yet paid amounted to $575.

Instructions

a Prepare adjusting entries.

b Prepare an adjusted trial balance. (*Note:* You may find the use of T accounts helpful in computing the account balances after adjustments.)

c Prepare closing entries.

4-4 Diamond Pools, Inc., was organized on April 1, 1976, and is engaged in the business of building custom swimming pools. All the $50,000 capital stock in the corporation is owned by Bob Diamond and his wife, Ellen, who has been maintaining the accounting records on a somewhat "hit and miss" basis. Early in 1977 Mrs. Diamond prepared the financial statements shown below, which Mr. Diamond presented to the Builders National Bank in support of a $25,000 line of credit.

DIAMOND POOLS, INC.
Balance Sheet
December 31, 1976

Cash	$ 3,250	Accounts payable	$24,450
Receivables	29,800	Capital	52,700
Inventory of building supplies	5,700		
Equipment	38,400		
	$77,150		$77,150

DIAMOND POOLS, INC.
Income Statement
Period: March–December 1976

Contract fees		$84,200
Expenses:		
Building supplies used	$28,000	
Dividends paid	8,500	
Labor	36,300	
Rent	3,600	
Other	5,100	81,500
Net income		$ 2,700

After reviewing the financial statements of Diamond Pools, Inc., the banker instructed Diamond "to restate the financial statements in conformity with generally accepted accounting principles." The banker specifically mentioned the need (1) to record depreciation for nine months, (2) to recognize expenses of 1976 which were not paid as of December 31, 1976, (3) to report the amount of retained earnings on the balance sheet, and (4) to correct the expense total as reported on the income statement.

Mrs. Diamond comes to you for assistance, and with her help, you ascertain the following:

(1) The equipment was acquired on April 1, 1976, and has an estimated useful life of eight years.

(2) Salaries payable on December 31, 1976, are estimated at $4,700.

(3) Building supplies costing $3,400 were erroneously included as an expense on the income statement. These supplies are still in storage and should be reported as an asset.

(4) On December 31, all work was completed on a $3,800 contract; however, the revenue was not recorded until January 4 when a bill was mailed to the customer.

(5) Other expenses reported above as $5,100 consist of oil and gas, $1,100; advertising, $2,200; and office expense, $1,800. (Should be listed separately in the income statement.)

Instructions

a Prepare revised financial statements for Diamond Pools, Inc., including a statement of retained earnings.

b Reconcile the corrected net income with the net income of $2,700 as determined by Mrs. Diamond.

4-5 Shadow Mountain Golf Course began operations on January 1, of the current year, and operates on a site rented from the county. The company's accounting policy is to adjust and close its accounts each month. Before adjustments on August 31, the account balances were as follows:

Cash	$ 7,790	
Unexpired insurance	580	
Prepaid rent	15,000	
Equipment	48,000	
Accumulated depreciation: equipment		$ 3,500
Accounts payable		8,000
Dividends payable		2,000
Unearned greens fees		4,000
Capital stock		50,000
Retained earnings		4,090
Dividends	2,000	
Greens fees earned		12,800
Salaries expense	7,800	
Repairs and maintenance expense	1,920	
Water expense	1,300	
	$84,390	$84,390

Other data

(1) The unexpired insurance represents a three-year fire insurance policy purchased on January 2 for $720.

(2) Monthly rent expense amounted to $5,000.

(3) The equipment was being depreciated over an eight-year life.

(4) On August 10, a local corporation purchased 1,000 special price tickets

for $4,000. Each ticket was good for one round of golf, which normally cost $5. During August, 310 of the tickets were used.

(5) The Elks' Club reserved the entire golf course on the last two days of August and the first day of September for a golf tournament, agreeing to pay greens fees of a flat $1,000 per day at the conclusion of the tournament.

(6) Salaries earned by employees but not paid were $700 at August 31.

Instructions

Based on the trial balance and other data, prepare a work sheet for the month ended August 31, 19___.

4-6 Rapid Transit, Inc., is a bus company in a major metropolitan area. The company adjusts and closes its books each month. At December 31, 19___ the following trial balance was prepared from the ledger.

Cash	$ 66,875	
Prepaid rent	9,000	
Unexpired insurance	10,400	
Inventory of spare parts	28,500	
Buses	405,000	
Accumulated depreciation: buses		$ 77,625
Unearned passenger revenue		30,000
Capital stock, $10 par value		350,000
Retained earnings		57,300
Dividends	6,000	
Passenger revenue		94,900
Fuel expense	12,900	
Repairs & maintenance expense	1,100	
Salaries expense	67,350	
Advertising expense	2,700	
	$609,825	$609,825

Other data

(1) Monthly rent amounted to $1,500.

(2) Insurance expense for December was $2,100.

(3) Maintenance work costing $2,600 was done on the buses by City Garage in late December. No bill has yet been received, and the expense has not been recorded.

(4) Spare parts used in connection with maintenance work during December amounted to $1,850.

(5) The buses are being depreciated over a useful life of 10 years.

(6) Early in December 15,000 special books of bus tickets were sold to the public for $2 per book. Each ticket book contained 10 bus tickets. As of December 31, 45,000 tickets had been used.

(7) Salaries earned by employees but not paid were $1,650 at December 31.

Instructions

a Prepare a work sheet for the month ended December 31, 19___.

b Prepare an income statement, a statement of retained earnings, and a balance sheet (in report form).

c Prepare adjusting and closing entries.

4-7 Given below are the financial statements for Cole Janitor Service, Inc., at the end of its fiscal year July 31, 19___. The accounts are adjusted and closed only once a year. Advance payments from customers are credited to Fees Earned when received. The Unearned Fees account is used only in making year-end adjustments.

COLE JANITOR SERVICE, INC.
Income Statement
For the Year Ended July 31, 19___

Fees earned		$120,000
Expenses:		
Wages expense	$50,140	
Rent expense	4,500	
Insurance expense	1,600	
Janitorial supplies expense	26,560	
Depreciation expense: equipment	6,000	
Interest expense	1,200	
Total expenses		90,000
Net income		$ 30,000

COLE JANITOR SERVICE, INC.
Balance Sheet
July 31, 19___

Assets

Cash		$ 28,925
Fees receivable		30,000
Prepaid rent		375
Unexpired insurance		800
Inventory of janitorial supplies		8,200
Equipment	$88,000	
Less: Accumulated depreciation	36,300	51,700
Total assets		$120,000

Liabilities & Stockholders' Equity

Liabilities:		
Notes payable		$ 40,000
Accounts payable		2,000
Interest payable		200
Wages payable		1,300
Unearned fees		16,900
Total liabilities		$ 60,400
Stockholders' equity:		
Capital stock	$40,000	
Retained earnings	19,600	59,600
Total liabilities & stockholders' equity		$120,000

Selected accounts taken from the unadjusted trial balance on July 31, 19___, follow:

Prepaid rent	*$ 750*
Unexpired insurance	*2,400*
Inventory of janitorial supplies	*6,200*
Accumulated depreciation: equipment	*30,300*
Unearned fees	*12,900*
Fees earned	*94,000*
Wages expense	*48,840*
Interest expense	*1,000*

Dividends of $20,000 were paid in June of the current year.

Instructions
a Prepare the adjusting journal entries that apparently were made by the accountant, and number the adjusting entries.
b Reproduce the complete work sheet as it was prepared by the accountant. (*Suggestion:* Write in all the account titles as a first step, following the usual sequence of assets, liabilities, stockholders' equity, revenue and expenses. Next, fill in the amounts in the last six columns, using figures shown in the financial statements. Then, fill in the adjustments columns using the data developed in part *a* of the solution. Finally, by a "squeezing" process, you can determine the amounts for the adjusted trial balance columns and for the trial balance columns.)

BUSINESS DECISION PROBLEM 4

Emerald Cove Marina rents 50 slips in a large floating dock to owners of pleasure boats in the area. The marina also performs repair services on small craft.

Steve Nuccio, a friend of yours, is convinced that recreational boating will become increasingly popular in the area and he has entered into negotiations to buy Emerald Cove Marina.

Steve does not have quite enough cash to purchase the business at the price the owner has demanded. However, the owner of the marina has suggested that Steve might purchase the marina with what cash he does have, and turn the net income of the business over to the retiring owner until the balance of the purchase price has been paid. A typical month's income for Emerald Cove Marina is determined as follows:

Revenue:		
Slip rentals		*$2,100*
Repairs		*2,650*
Total revenue		*$4,750*
Operating expenses:		
Wages	*$1,600*	
Insurance	*30*	
Depreciation expense: docks	*800*	
Depreciation expense: equipment	*150*	
Other expenses	*200*	*2,780*
Net income		*$1,970*

Steve is concerned about turning the whole net income of the business over to the former owner for the next several months, because he estimates that he and his family will need to keep at least $800 a month to meet their living expenses. In coming to you for advice, Steve explains that all revenue of Emerald Cove Marina is collected when earned and that both wages and "other" expenses are paid when incurred. Steve does not understand, however, when depreciation expense must be paid or why there is any insurance expense when the insurance policies of the business have more than two years to run before new insurance must be purchased.

Instructions
a Advise Steve as to how much cash the business will generate each month. Will this amount of cash enable Steve to withdraw $800 per month to meet his living expenses and pay $1,970 per month to the former owner?
b Explain why insurance expense appears on the income statement of the business if no new policies will be purchased within the next two years.

ACCOUNTING FOR A MERCHANDISING BUSINESS

FIVE

The preceding four chapters have illustrated step by step the complete accounting cycle for a business rendering personal services. In contrast to the service-type business, there are a great many companies whose principal activity is buying and selling merchandise. These **merchandising** companies may be engaged in either the retail or wholesale distribution of goods. The accounting concepts and methods we have studied for a service-type business are also applicable to a merchandising business; however, some additional accounts and techniques are needed in accounting for the purchase and sale of merchandise.

Income statement for a merchandising business

An income statement for a merchandising business consists of three main sections: (1) the revenue section, (2) the cost of goods sold section, and (3) the operating expenses section. This sectional arrangement is illustrated in the income statement for a retail sporting goods store on page 140. We shall assume that the business of the Campus Sports Shop consists of buying sports equipment from manufacturers and selling this merchandise to college students. To keep the illustration reasonably short, we shall use a smaller number of expense accounts than would generally be used in a merchandising business.

ANALYZING THE INCOME STATEMENT How does this income statement compare in form and content with the income statement of the service-type business presented in the preceding chapters? The most important change is the inclusion of the section entitled Cost of Goods

Sold. Note how large the cost of goods sold is in comparison with the other figures on the statement. The cost of the merchandise sold during the month amounts to $6,000, or 60% of the month's net sales of $10,000. Another way of looking at this relationship is to say that for each dollar the store receives by selling goods to customers, the sum of 60 cents represents a recovery of the cost of the merchandise. This leaves a **gross profit** of 40 cents from each net sales dollar, out of which the store must pay its operating expenses. In our illustration the operating expenses for the month were $2,800, that is, 28% of the net sales figure of $10,000. Therefore, the gross profit of 40 cents contained in each dollar of net sales was enough to cover the operating expenses of 28 cents and leave a net income of 12 cents.

CAMPUS SPORTS SHOP
Income Statement
For the Month Ended September 30, 19___

Note distinction between cost of goods sold and operating expenses	Gross sales		$10,070
	Less: Sales returns & allowances		70
	Net sales		$10,000
	Cost of goods sold:		
	Inventory, Sept. 1	$ 4,400	
	Purchases	9,100	
	Cost of goods available for sale	$13,500	
	Less: Inventory, Sept. 30	7,500	
	Cost of goods sold		6,000
	Gross profit on sales		$ 4,000
	Operating expenses:		
	Salaries	$ 2,230	
	Advertising	450	
	Telephone	60	
	Depreciation	40	
	Insurance	20	
	Total operating expenses		2,800
	Net income		$ 1,200

Of course the percentage relationship between net sales and cost of goods sold will vary from one type of business to another; but, in all types of merchandising concerns, the cost of goods sold is one of the largest elements in the income statement. Accountants, investors, bankers, and businessmen in general have the habit of mentally computing percentage relationships when they look at financial statements. Formation of this habit will be helpful throughout the study of accounting, as well as in many business situations.

In analyzing an income statement, it is customary to compare each item in the statement with the amount of net sales. These comparisons are easier to make if we express the data in percentages as well as in dollar amounts. If the figure for net sales is regarded as 100%, then every other item or subtotal on the statement can conveniently be expressed as a percentage of net sales. The cost of goods sold in most types of business will be between 60 and 80% of net sales. Conversely, the **gross profit on sales** (excess of net sales over cost of goods sold) will usually vary between 40 and 20% of net sales. Numerous exceptions may be found to such a sweeping generalization, but it is sufficiently valid to be helpful in visualizing customary relationships on the income statement.

Accounting for sales of merchandise

If merchandising concerns are to succeed or even to survive, they must, of course, sell their goods at prices higher than they pay to the suppliers from whom they buy. The selling prices charged by a retail store must cover three things: (1) the cost of the merchandise to the store; (2) the operating expenses of the business such as advertising, store rent, and salaries of salesmen; and (3) a net income to the business.

When a business sells merchandise to its customers, it either receives immediate payment in cash or acquires an account receivable which will soon become cash. As explained in Chapter 3, the inflow of cash and receivables from sales of the current period is equal to the revenue for that period. The entry to record the sale of merchandise consists of a debit to an asset account and a credit to the Sales account, as shown by the following example:

Journal entry for cash sale

Cash	100	
Sales		100
To record the sale of merchandise for cash.		

If the sale was not a cash transaction but called for payment at a later date, the entry would be:

Journal entry for sale on credit

Accounts Receivable	100	
Sales		100
To record sale of merchandise on account; due in 30 days.		

Revenue from the sale of merchandise is usually considered as earned in the period in which the merchandise is **delivered to the customer,** even though cash is not received for a month or more after the sale. Consequently, the revenue earned in a given accounting period may differ considerably from the cash receipts of that period.

NET SALES Notice that the key figure used in our analysis of the Campus Sports Shop income statement was **net sales.** Most merchandising companies allow customers to obtain a refund by returning merchandise which is found to be unsatisfactory. When customers find that merchandise purchased has minor defects, they may agree to keep such merchandise if an allowance is made on the sales price. Refunds and allowances have the effect of reversing previously recorded sales and reducing the amount of revenue earned by the business. Thus, net sales is the revenue actually earned after giving consideration to sales returns and allowances. The journal entry to record sales returns and allowances is shown below:

Journal entry for returns and sales allowances

Sales Returns and Allowances *70*
  Cash (or Accounts Receivable) *70*
Made refund for merchandise returned by customer.

The use of a Sales Returns and Allowances account rather than recording refunds by direct debits to the Sales account is advisable because the accounting records then show both the total amount of sales and the amount of sales returns. Management is interested in the percentage relationship between goods sold and goods returned as an indication of customer satisfaction with the merchandise.

The amount and trend of sales are watched very closely by management, investors, and others interested in the progress of a company. A rising volume of sales is evidence of growth and suggests the probability of an increase in earnings. A declining trend in sales, on the other hand, is often the first signal of reduced earnings and of financial difficulties ahead. The amount of sales for each year is compared with the sales of the preceding year; the sales of each month may be compared with the sales of the preceding month and also with the corresponding month of the preceding year. These comparisons bring to light significant trends in the volume of sales. The financial pages of newspapers regularly report on the volume and trend of sales for corporations with publicly owned stock.

Inventory of merchandise and cost of goods sold

In the income statement illustrated on page 140, the inventory of merchandise and the cost of goods sold are important new concepts which require careful attention. An inventory of merchandise consists of the goods on hand and available for sale to customers. In the Campus Sports Shop, the inventory consists of golf clubs, tennis rackets, and skiing equipment; in a pet shop the inventory might include puppies, fish, and parakeets. Inventories are acquired through the purchase of merchandise from wholesalers, manufacturers, or other suppliers. A company's inventory is increased by the purchase of merchandise from suppliers and decreased by the sale of merchandise to customers. The cost of the merchandise sold during the month appears in the income statement as a deduction from the sales of the month. The merchandise which is **not sold** during the month constitutes the inventory of merchandise on hand at the end of the accounting period and is included in the balance sheet as an asset. The ending inventory of one accounting period is, of course, the beginning inventory of the following period.

There are two alternative approaches to the determination of inventory and of cost of goods sold, namely, the **periodic inventory system** and the **perpetual inventory system.** Business concerns which sell merchandise of high unit value, such as automobiles or television sets, generally use a perpetual inventory system. This system requires the keeping of records showing the cost of each article in stock. Units added to inventory and units sold are recorded on a daily basis. At the end of the accounting period, the total cost of goods sold is determined by adding the costs recorded from day to day for the units sold.

THE PERIODIC INVENTORY SYSTEM The majority of businesses, however, do not maintain perpetual inventory records; they rely instead upon a periodic inventory (a count of merchandise on hand) to determine the inventory at the end of the accounting period and the cost of goods sold during the period. The periodic inventory system may be concisely summarized as follows:

1 A physical count of merchandise on hand is made at the end of each accounting period.

2 The cost value of this inventory is computed by multiplying the quantity of each item by an appropriate unit cost. A total cost figure for the entire inventory is then determined by adding the costs of all the various types of merchandise.

3 The **cost of goods available for sale** during the period is determined by adding the amount of the inventory at the beginning of the period to the amount of the purchases during the period.

4 The **cost of goods sold** is computed by subtracting the inventory at the end of the period from the cost of goods available for sale. In other words, the difference between the cost of goods available for sale and the amount of goods remaining unsold at the end of the period is presumed to have been sold.

A simple illustration of the above procedures for determining the cost of goods sold follows:

Using the **periodic inventory method** Beginning inventory (determined by count)......................	*$1,000*
Add: Purchases	*1,800*
Cost of goods available for sale	*$2,800*
Less: Ending inventory (determined by count)....................	*1,200*
Cost of goods sold	*$1,600*

The periodic inventory is used throughout most of this book. Because of the importance of the process for determining inventory and cost of goods sold, we shall now consider in more detail the essential steps in using the periodic inventory system.

Taking a physical inventory When the periodic inventory system is in use, there is no day-to-day record of the cost of goods sold. Neither is there any day-to-day record of the amount of goods unsold and still on hand. At the end of the accounting period, however, it is necessary to determine the cost of goods sold during the period and also the amount of unsold goods on hand. The figure for cost of goods sold is used in determining the profit or loss for the period, and the value of the merchandise on hand at the end of the period is included in the balance sheet as an asset.

To determine the cost of the merchandise on hand, a physical inventory is taken. The count of merchandise should be made if possible after the close of business on the last day of the accounting period. It is difficult to make an accurate count during business hours while sales are taking place; consequently, the physical inventory is often taken in the evening or on Sunday. After all goods have been counted, the proper cost price must be assigned to each article. The assignment of a cost price to each item of merchandise in stock is often described as *pricing the inventory.* Inventories of merchandise are usually valued at cost for accounting purposes, although some alternative bases will be discussed in Chapter 11, as well as alternative methods of determining cost.

Computing the cost of goods sold The taking of a physical inventory at the end of the accounting period is a major step toward computing the cost of goods sold during the period. Let us illustrate the computation of cost of goods sold by considering the first year of operation for a new business. We can reasonably assume that there was no beginning inventory of merchandise at the inception of the enterprise. During the first year, the purchases of merchandise totaled $50,000. These purchases constituted the goods available for sale. A physical count of merchandise was made on December 31; the quantities shown as on hand were multiplied by unit cost prices, and a total cost for the inventory was computed as $10,000. If goods costing $50,000 were available for sale during the year and goods costing $10,000 remained unsold at year-end, then the cost of goods sold must have been $40,000, as summarized below:

Computing cost of goods sold in first year	Inventory at beginning of period	$ 0
	Purchases	50,000
	Cost of goods available for sale	$50,000
	Less: Inventory at end of period	10,000
	Cost of goods sold	$40,000

The merchandise on hand at the close of business December 31 of the first year is, of course, still on hand on January 1 of the second year. As previously stated, the *ending* inventory of one year is the *beginning* inventory of the following year. To continue our example, let us assume that in the second year of operation purchases amounted to $75,000 and the inventory of goods on hand at the end of the second year was determined by the taking of a physical inventory that amounted to $25,000. The cost of goods sold during the second year would be computed as follows:

Computing cost of goods sold in second year	*Inventory at beginning of second year*	*$10,000*
	Purchases	*75,000*
	Cost of goods available for sale	*$85,000*
	Less: Inventory at end of second year	*25,000*
	Cost of goods sold	*$60,000*

Dependability of the periodic inventory system In computing the cost of goods sold by the periodic inventory system, we are making a somewhat dangerous assumption that all goods not sold during the year will be on hand at the end of the year.

Referring to the above example, let us assume that, during the second year of operations, shoplifters stole $1,000 worth of merchandise from the store without being detected. The cost of goods available for sale is still $85,000, and the final inventory is still $25,000, but the cost of goods sold is not actually $60,000. The $60,000 difference between goods available for sale and goods in final inventory is composed of two distinct elements: cost of goods sold, $59,000, and cost of goods stolen, $1,000. However, under the periodic inventory system, the loss of goods by theft would not be apparent, and the cost of goods sold would erroneously be shown in the income statement as $60,000. A method of disclosing inventory shortages of this type is explained in Chapter 11.

Accounting for merchandise purchases

The purchase of merchandise for resale to customers is recorded by debiting an account called Purchases. The Purchases account is used *only for merchandise acquired for resale.* Assets acquired for use in the business (such as a delivery truck, a typewriter, or office supplies) are recorded by debiting the appropriate asset account, not the Purchases account. Only merchandise acquired for resale is entered in the Purchases account because this account is used in computing the cost of goods sold. The journal entry to record a purchase of merchandise is illustrated as follows:

Journal entry for purchase of merchandise	*Purchases*	*1,000*
	Accounts Payable (or Cash)	*1,000*
	Purchased merchandise from ABC Supply Co.	

At the end of the accounting period, the balance accumulated in the Purchases account represents the total cost of merchandise purchased during the period. This amount is used in preparing the income statement. The Purchases account has then served its purpose and it is closed to the Income Summary account. Since the Purchases account is closed at the end of each period, it has a zero balance at the beginning of each succeeding period.

TRANSPORTATION-IN The cost of merchandise acquired for resale logically includes any transportation charges necessary to place the goods in the purchaser's place of business.

A separate ledger account is used to accumulate transportation charges on merchandise purchased. The journal entry to record transportation charges on inbound shipments of merchandise is as follows:

Journalizing transportation charges on purchases of merchandise

Transportation-in *169.50*
      Cash (or Accounts Payable) *169.50*
Air freight charges on merchandise purchased from Miller Brothers, Kansas City.

Since transportation charges are part of the **delivered cost** of merchandise purchased, the Transportation-in account is combined with the Purchases account in the income statement to determine the cost of goods available for sale.

Transportation charges on inbound shipments of merchandise must not be confused with transportation charges on outbound shipments of goods to customers. Freight charges and other expenses incurred in making deliveries to customers are regarded as selling expenses; these outlays are debited to a separate account entitled Transportation-out and are not included in the cost of goods sold.

PURCHASE RETURNS AND ALLOWANCES When merchandise purchased from suppliers is found to be unsatisfactory, the goods may be returned to the seller, or a request may be made for an allowance on the price. A return of goods to the supplier is recorded as follows:

Journal entry for return of goods to supplier

Accounts Payable *1,200*
      Purchase Returns and Allowances *1,200*
To charge Marvel Supply Co. for the cost of goods returned.

It is preferable to credit Purchase Returns and Allowances when merchandise is returned to a supplier, rather than crediting the Purchases account directly. The accounts then show both the total amount of purchases and the amount of purchases which required adjustment or return. The percentage relationship between merchandise purchased and merchandise returned is significant, because an excessive number of returns indicates inefficiency in the operation of the purchasing department.

F.O.B. shipping point and F.O.B. destination

The agreement between the buyer and seller of merchandise includes a provision as to which party shall bear the cost of transporting the merchandise. The term *F.O.B. shipping point* means that the seller will place the merchandise "free on board" the railroad cars or other means of transport and that the buyer must pay transportation charges from that point. Many people in negotiating for the purchase of a new automobile have encountered the expression "F.O.B. Detroit," meaning that the buyer must pay the freight charges from the manufacturer's location in Detroit, in addition to the basic price of the car. In most merchandise transactions involving wholesalers or manufacturers, the buyer bears the transportation cost. Sometimes, however, as a matter of convenience, the seller prepays the freight and adds this cost to the amount billed to the buyer.

F.O.B. destination means that the seller agrees to bear the freight cost. If he prepays the truckline or other carrier, the agreed terms have been met and no action is required of the buyer other than to pay the agreed purchase price of the merchandise. If the seller does not prepay the freight, the buyer will pay the carrier and deduct this payment from the amount owed the seller when he makes payment for the merchandise.

Illustration of accounting cycle using periodic inventory system

The October transactions of the Campus Sports Shop will now be used to illustrate the accounting cycle for a business using the periodic inventory system of accounting for merchandise.

RECORDING SALES OF MERCHANDISE Sales of merchandise during October amounted to $10,025. All sales were for cash, and each sales transaction was rung up on a cash register. At the close of each day's business, the total sales for the day were computed by pressing the total key on the cash register. As soon as each day's sales were computed, a journal entry was prepared and posted to the Cash account and the Sales account in the ledger. The daily entering of cash sales in the journal is desirable in order to minimize the opportunity for errors or dishonesty by employees in handling the cash receipts. In Chapter 6 a procedure will be described which provides a daily record of sales and cash receipts yet avoids the making of an excessive number of postings to the Cash and Sales accounts.

RECORDING SALES RETURNS AND ALLOWANCES On October 27 a customer returned unsatisfactory merchandise and was given a refund of $46. Another customer complained on October 28 of a slight defect in an article he had recently purchased and was given a refund of $10, representing half of the original price. The journal entries to record these returns and allowances were as follows:

Oct. 27	Sales Returns and Allowances	46	
	Cash		46
	Made refund for merchandise returned by customer.		
28	Sales Returns and Allowances	10	
	Cash		10
	Allowance to customer for defect in merchandise.		

OTHER OCTOBER TRANSACTIONS Other routine transactions during October included the purchase of merchandise, the return of merchandise to suppliers, payment of charges for transportation-in, payment of accounts payable, and payment of operating expenses, such as salaries, telephone, and advertising. To conserve space in this illustration, these transactions will not be listed individually but are included in the ledger account balances at October 31.

WORK SHEET FOR A MERCHANDISING BUSINESS After the October transactions of the Campus Sports Shop had been posted to ledger accounts, the work sheet illustrated on page 149 was prepared. The first step in the preparation of the work sheet was, of course, the listing of the balances of the ledger accounts in the Trial Balance columns. In studying this work sheet, note that the Inventory account in the Trial Balance debit column still shows a balance of $7,500, the cost of merchandise on hand at the end of September. No entries were made in the Inventory account during October despite the various purchases and sales of merchandise. The significance of the Inventory account in the trial balance is that it shows the amount of merchandise with which the Campus Sports Shop began operations for the month of October.

Omission of Adjusted Trial Balance columns In the work sheet previously illustrated in Chapter 4, page 113, the amounts in the Trial Balance columns were combined with the amounts listed in the Adjustments columns and then extended into the Adjusted Trial Balance columns. When there are only a few adjusting entries, many accountants prefer to omit the Adjusted Trial Balance columns and to extend the trial balance figures (as adjusted by the amounts in the Adjustments columns) directly to the Income Statement, Retained Earnings, or Balance Sheet columns. This procedure is used in the work sheet for the Campus Sports Shop.

Recording the ending inventory on the work sheet The key points to be observed in this work sheet are (1) the method of recording the ending inventory and (2) the method of handling the various accounts making up the costs of goods sold.

CAMPUS SPORTS SHOP
Work Sheet
For the Month Ended October 31, 19___

	Trial Balance		Adjustments*		Income Statement		Retained Earnings		Balance Sheet	
	Dr	Cr	Dr	Cr	Dr	Cr	Dr	Cr	Dr	Cr
Cash	6,569								6,569	
Inventory, Sept. 30, 19___	7,500				7,500					
Unexpired insurance	200			(2) 20					180	
Land	3,000								3,000	
Building	10,000								10,000	
Accumulated depreciation: building		960		(1) 40						1,000
Accounts payable		6,700								6,700
Capital stock		15,000								15,000
Retained earnings, Oct. 1, 19___		4,940						4,940		
Dividends	300						300			
Sales		10,025				10,025				
Sales returns and allowances	56				56					
Purchases	8,100				8,100					
Purchase returns and allowances		600				600				
Transportation-in	200				200					
Advertising expense	250				250					
Salaries expense	2,000				2,000					
Telephone expense	50				50					
	38,225	38,225								
Depreciation expense: building			(1) 40		40					
Insurance expense			(2) 20		20					
			60	60						
Inventory, Oct. 31, 19___						9,000			9,000	
					18,216	19,625				
Net income					1,409			1,409		
					19,625	19,625	300	6,349		
Retained earnings, Oct. 31, 19___							6,049			6,049
							6,349	6,349	28,749	28,749

Note treatment of beginning and ending inventories

* Adjustments
(1) Depreciation of building during October
(2) Insurance premium expired during October

After the close of business on October 31, a physical inventory was taken of all merchandise in the store. The cost of the entire stock of merchandise on hand was determined to be $9,000. This ending inventory, dated October 31, does not appear in the trial balance; it is therefore written on the first available line below the other account titles. The amount of $9,000 is listed in the Income Statement credit column and also in the Balance Sheet debit column. By entering the ending inventory in the Income Statement *credit* column, we are in effect deducting it from the total of the beginning inventory, the purchases, and the transportation-in, all of which are extended from the trial balance to the Income Statement *debit* column.

One of the functions of the Income Statement columns is to bring together all the accounts involved in determining the cost of goods sold. The accounts with debit balances are the beginning inventory, the purchases, and the transportation-in; these accounts total $15,800. Against this total, the two credit items of purchase returns, $600, and ending inventory, $9,000, are offset. The three merchandising accounts with debit balances exceed in total the two with credit balances by an amount of $6,200; this amount is the cost of goods sold and appears in the income statement.

The ending inventory is also entered in the Balance Sheet debit column, because this inventory of merchandise on October 31 will appear as an asset in the balance sheet bearing this date.

Financial statements

The work to be done at the end of the period is much the same for a merchandising business as for a service-type firm. First, the work sheet is completed; then, financial statements are prepared from the data in the work sheet; next, the adjusting and closing entries are entered in the journal and posted to the ledger accounts; and finally, a post-closing trial balance is prepared. This completes the periodic accounting cycle.

The income statement for a merchandising business may be regarded as consisting of three sections: (1) the sales revenue section, (2) the cost of goods sold section, and (3) the operating expense section. This income statement was prepared from the work sheet on page 149. The related statement of retained earnings and balance sheet are not shown since they do not differ significantly from previous illustrations. Note particularly the arrangement of items in the cost of goods sold section of the income statement; this portion of the income statement shows in summary form most of the essential accounting concepts covered in this chapter.

CAMPUS SPORTS SHOP
Income Statement
For the Month Ended October 31, 19___

Sales			$10,025
Less: Sales returns and allowances			56
Net sales			$ 9,969
Cost of goods sold:			
Inventory, Sept. 30		$ 7,500	
Purchases	$8,100		
Less: Purchase returns and allowances	600	7,500	
Transportation-in		200	
Cost of goods available for sale		$15,200	
Less: Inventory, Oct. 31		9,000	
Cost of goods sold			6,200
Gross profit on sales			$ 3,769
Operating expenses:			
Salaries		$ 2,000	
Advertising		250	
Telephone		50	
Depreciation		40	
Insurance		20	
Total operating expenses			2,360
Net income			$ 1,409

Closing entries

The entries used in closing revenue and expense accounts have been explained in preceding chapters. The only new elements in this illustration of closing entries for a trading business are the entries showing the elimination of the beginning inventory and the recording of the ending inventory. The beginning inventory is cleared out of the Inventory account by a debit to Income Summary and a credit to Inventory. A separate entry could be made for this purpose, but we can save time by making one compound entry which will debit the Income Summary account with the balance of the beginning inventory and with the balances of all temporary owners' equity accounts having debit balances. The *temporary owners' equity accounts* are those which appear in the income statement. As the name suggests, the temporary owners' equity accounts are used during the period to accumulate temporarily the increases and decreases in the owners' equity resulting from operation of the business.

Closing	Oct. 31	Income Summary	18,216	
temporary		Inventory (beginning)		7,500
owners'		Purchases		8,100
equity		Sales Returns and Allowances		56
accounts		Transportation-in		200
with debit		Advertising Expense		250
balances		Salaries Expense		2,000
		Telephone Expense		50
		Depreciation Expense		40
		Insurance Expense		20

To close the beginning inventory and the temporary
owners' equity accounts having debit balances.

Note that the above entry closes all the operating expense accounts
as well as the accounts used to accumulate the cost of merchandise
sold and also the Sales Returns and Allowances account. Although
the Sales Returns and Allowances account has a debit balance, it is
not an expense account. In terms of account classification, it belongs
in the revenue group of accounts because it serves as an offset to
the Sales account and appears in the income statement as a deduction
from Sales.

To record the ending inventory after the stocktaking on October 31,
we could make a separate entry debiting Inventory and crediting the
Income Summary account. It is more convenient, however, to combine
this step with the closing of the Sales account and any other temporary
owners' equity accounts having credit balances, as illustrated in the
following closing entry.

Closing	Oct. 31	Inventory (ending)	9,000	
temporary		Sales	10,025	
owners'		Purchase Returns and Allowances	600	
equity		Income Summary		19,625
accounts				
with credit				
balances				

To record the ending inventory and to close all temporary
owners' equity accounts having credit balances.

The remaining closing entries serve to transfer the balance of the
Income Summary account to the Retained Earnings account and to
close the Dividends account, as follows:

Closing	Oct. 31	Income Summary	1,409	
Income		Retained Earnings		1,409
Summary		To close the Income Summary account.		
account and				
Dividends	31	Retained Earnings	300	
account		Dividends		300

To close the Dividends account.

Summary of merchandising transactions and related accounting entries

The transactions regularly encountered in merchandising operations and the related accounting entries are concisely summarized below:

	Transactions during the Period	Related Accounting Entries	
		Debit	*Credit*
Customary journal entries relating to merchandise	Purchase merchandise for resale	Purchases	Cash or Accounts Payable
	Incur transportation charges on merchandise purchased for resale	Transportation-in	Cash or Accounts Payable
	Return unsatisfactory merchandise to supplier, or obtain a reduction from original price	Cash or Accounts Payable	Purchase Returns and Allowances
	Sell merchandise to customers	Cash or Accounts Receivable	Sales
	Permit customers to return merchandise, or grant them a reduction from original price	Sales Returns and Allowances	Cash or Accounts Receivable

Inventory Procedures at End of Period

Transactions during the Period	Debit	Credit
Transfer the balance of the beginning inventory to the Income Summary account	Income Summary	Inventory
Take a physical inventory of merchandise on hand at the end of the period, and price this merchandise at cost	Inventory	Income Summary

Internal control concepts

Our discussion of a merchandising business has emphasized the steps of the accounting cycle, especially the determination of cost of goods sold and the preparation of a work sheet and financial statements. Now we need to round out this discussion by considering methods by which management maintains control over purchases and sales transactions. These methods place particular emphasis upon the subdivision of duties within the company so that no one person or department handles a transaction completely from beginning to end. When duties are divided in this manner, the work of one employee serves to verify that of another and any errors which occur tend to be detected promptly.

SUBDIVISION OF DUTIES STRENGTHENS INTERNAL CONTROL To illustrate the development of internal control through subdivision of duties, let us review the procedures for a sale of merchandise on account by a wholesaler. The sales department of the company is responsible for securing the order from the customer; the credit department must approve the customer's credit before the order is filled; the stock room assembles the goods ordered; the shipping department packs and ships the goods; and the accounting department records the transaction. Each department receives written evidence of the action of the other departments and reviews the documents describing the transaction to see that the actions taken correspond in all details. The shipping department, for instance, does not release the merchandise until after the credit department has approved the customer as a credit risk. The accounting department does not record the sale until it has received documentary evidence that (1) the goods were ordered, (2) the extension of credit was approved, and (3) the merchandise has been shipped to the customer.

Assume for a moment, as a contrast to this procedure, that a single employee were permitted to secure the customer's order, approve the credit terms, get the merchandise from the stock room, deliver the merchandise to the customer, prepare the invoice, enter the transaction in the accounting records, and perhaps even collect the account receivable. If this employee made errors, such as selling to poor credit risks, forgetting to enter the sale in the accounting records, or perhaps delivering more merchandise to the customer than he was charged for, no one would know the difference. By the time such errors came to light, substantial losses would have been incurred.

PREVENTION OF FRAUD If one employee is permitted to handle all aspects of a transaction, the danger of fraud is also increased. Studies of fraud cases suggest that many individuals may be tempted into dishonest acts if given complete control of company property. Most of these persons, however, would not engage in fraud if doing so required collaboration with another employee. Losses through employee dishonesty occur in a variety of ways: merchandise may be stolen; payments by customers may be withheld; suppliers may be overpaid with a view to kickbacks to employees; and lower prices may be allowed to favored customers. The opportunities for fraud are almost endless if all aspects of a sale or purchase transaction are concentrated in the hands of one employee.

Because internal control rests so largely upon the participation of several employees in each transaction, it is apparent that strong internal control is more easily achieved in large organizations than in small ones. In a small business with only one or two office employees, such duties as the issuance of purchase orders, approval of credit, and maintenance of accounting records may necessarily have to be performed by the same employee.

SERIALLY NUMBERED DOCUMENTS—ANOTHER CONTROL DEVICE Another method of achieving internal control, in addition to the subdivision of duties, consists of having the printer include serial numbers on such documents as purchase orders, sales invoices, and checks. The use of serial numbers makes it possible to account for all documents. In other words, if a sales invoice is misplaced or concealed, the break in the sequence of numbers will call attention to the discrepancy.

INTERNAL CONTROL IN PERSPECTIVE A description of internal control solely in terms of the prevention of fraud and the detection of errors represents too narrow a concept of this managerial technique. The building of a strong system of internal control is an accepted means of increasing operational efficiency.

In appraising the merits of various internal control procedures, the question of their cost cannot be ignored. Too elaborate a system of internal control may entail greater operating costs than are justified by the protection gained. For this reason the system of internal control must be tailored to meet the requirements of the individual business. In most organizations, however, proper subdivision of duties and careful design of accounting procedures will provide a basis for adequate internal control and at the same time will contribute to economical operation of the business.

Business papers

Carefully designed business papers and procedures for using them are necessary to ensure that all transactions are properly authorized and recorded. To illustrate this point in a somewhat exaggerated manner, let us assume that every employee in a large department store was authorized to purchase merchandise for the store and that no standard forms or procedures had been provided to keep track of these purchases. The result would undoubtedly be many unwise purchases, confusion as to what had been ordered and received, shortages of some types of merchandise, and an oversupply of other types. The opportunity for fraud by dishonest employees, as well as for accidental errors, would be unlimited under such a haphazard method of operation.

Each step in ordering, receiving, and making payment for merchandise purchases should be controlled and recorded. A similar approach is necessary to establish control over the sales function.

PURCHASE ORDERS A purchase order issued by Zenith Company to Adams Manufacturing Company is illustrated on page 156.

In large companies in which the functions of placing orders, receiv-

PURCHASE ORDER

ZENITH COMPANY

10 Fairway Avenue

San Francisco, California

Order No.

999

Serially numbered order for merchandise

To: Adams Manufacturing Company

19 Union Street

Kansas City, Missouri

Date Nov. 1, 1976

Ship via Jones Truck Co.

Terms: 2/10, n/30

Please enter our order for the following:

Quantity	Description	Price	Amount
15 sets	Model S irons	$60.00	$900.00
50 dozen	X3Y Shur-Par golf balls	7.00	350.00

Zenith Company

By *D. D. McCarthy*

ing merchandise, and making payment are lodged in separate departments, several copies of the purchase order are usually prepared, each on a different color paper. The original is sent to the supplier; this purchase order is his authorization to deliver the merchandise and to submit a bill based on the prices listed. Carbon copies of the purchase order are usually routed to the purchasing department, accounting department, receiving department, and finance department.

The issuance of a purchase order does not call for any debit or credit entries in the accounting records of either the prospective buyer or seller. The company which receives an order does not consider for accounting purposes that a sale has been made until the merchandise is delivered. At that point ownership of the goods changes, and both buyer and seller should make accounting entries to record the transaction.

INVOICES The supplier (vendor) mails an invoice to the purchaser at the time of shipping the merchandise. An invoice contains a description of the goods being sold, the quantities, prices, credit terms, and method of shipment. The illustration on page 157 shows an invoice issued by Adams Manufacturing Company in response to the previously illustrated purchase order from Zenith Company.

From the viewpoint of the seller, an invoice is a *sales invoice;* from the buyer's viewpoint it is a *purchase invoice.* The invoice is the basis

INVOICE

ADAMS MANUFACTURING COMPANY
19 Union Street
Kansas City, Missouri

Invoice is basis for accounting entry

Sold to Zenith Company   **Invoice No.** 777

10 Fairway Avenue   **Invoice date** Nov. 3, 1976

San Francisco, Calif.   **Your Order No.** 999

Shipped to Same   **Date shipped** Nov. 3, 1976

Terms 2/10, n/30   **Shipped by** Jones Truck Co.

Quantity	Description	Price	Amount
15 sets	Model S irons	$60.00	$900.00
50 dozen	X3Y Shur-Par golf balls	7.00	350.00
Total			$1,250.00

for an entry in the accounting records of both the seller and the buyer because it evidences the transfer of ownership of goods. At the time of issuing the invoice, the seller makes an entry debiting Accounts Receivable and crediting Sales. The buyer, however, does not record the invoice as a liability until he has made a careful verification of the transaction, as indicated in the following section.

Verification of invoice by purchaser Upon receipt of an invoice, the purchaser should verify the following aspects of the transaction:

1 The invoice agrees with the purchase order as to prices, quantities, and other provisions.
2 The invoice is arithmetically correct in all extensions of price times quantity and in the addition of amounts.
3 The merchandise covered by the invoice has been received and is in satisfactory condition.

Evidence that the merchandise has been received in good condition must be obtained from the receiving department. It is the function of the receiving department to receive all incoming goods, to inspect them as to quality and condition, and to determine the quantities received by counting, measuring, or weighing. The receiving department should prepare a separate *receiving report* for each shipment received; this report is sent to the accounting department for use in verifying the invoice.

The verification of the invoice in the accounting department is accomplished by comparing the purchase order, the invoice, and the receiving report. Comparison of these documents establishes that the merchandise described in the invoice was actually ordered, has been received in good condition, and was billed at the prices specified in the purchase order.

Debit and credit memoranda

If merchandise purchased on account is unsatisfactory and is to be returned to the supplier (or if a price reduction is agreed upon), a *debit memorandum* may be prepared by the purchasing company and sent to the supplier. The debit memorandum informs the supplier that his account is being debited (reduced) by the buyer and explains the circumstances.

The supplier upon being informed of the return of damaged merchandise (or having agreed to a reduction in price) will issue a *credit memorandum* as evidence that the account receivable from the purchaser is being credited (reduced) by the supplier.

Trade discounts

Many manufacturers and wholesalers publish annual catalogs in which their products are listed at retail prices. Substantial reductions from the *list prices* are offered to dealers. These reductions from list prices (often as much as 30 or 40%) are called *trade discounts.* As market conditions change, the schedule of discounts is revised. This is a more convenient way to revise actual selling prices quickly than by publishing a new catalog.

Trade discounts are not recorded in the accounting records of either the seller or the buyer. A sale of merchandise is recorded at the actual selling price and the trade discount is merely a device for computing the actual sales price. From the viewpoint of the company purchasing goods, the significant price is not the list price but the amount which must be paid, and this amount is recorded as the cost of the merchandise.

For example, if a manufacturer sells goods to a retailer at a list price of $1,000 with a trade discount of 40%, the transaction will be recorded by the manufacturer as a $600 sale and by the retailer as a $600 purchase. Because trade discounts are not recorded in the accounts they should be clearly distinguished from the cash discounts discussed below.

Cash discounts

Manufacturers and wholesalers generally offer a cash discount to encourage their customers to pay invoices. For example, the credit terms may be "2% 10 days, net 30 days"; these terms mean that the authorized credit period is 30 days, but that the customer may deduct 2% of the amount of the invoice if he makes payment within 10 days. On the invoice these terms would appear in the abbreviated form "2/10, n/30"; this expression is read "2, 10, net 30." The selling company regards a cash discount as a *sales discount;* the buyer calls the discount a *purchase discount.*[1]

To illustrate the application of a cash discount, assume that Adams Manufacturing Company sells goods to the Zenith Company and issues a sales invoice for $1,000 dated November 3 and bearing the terms 2/10, n/30. If Zenith Company mails its check in payment on or before November 13, it is entitled to deduct 2% of $1,000, or $20, and settle the obligation for $980. If Zenith Company decides to forego the discount, it may postpone payment for an additional 20 days until December 3 but must then pay $1,000.

REASONS FOR CASH DISCOUNTS By offering cash discounts the seller collects accounts receivable more quickly. There is less danger of accounts receivable becoming uncollectible if they are collected promptly; in other words, the older an account receivable becomes, the greater the risk of nonpayment.

Is it to the advantage of the Zenith Company to settle the $1,000 invoice within the discount period and thereby save $20? The alternative is for Zenith to conserve cash by postponing payment for an additional 20 days. The question may therefore be stated as follows: Does the amount of $20 represent a reasonable charge for the use of $980 for a period of 20 days? Definitely not; this charge is the equivalent of an annual interest rate of about 36%. Although interest rates vary considerably over time, most businesses are able to borrow money from banks at an annual rate of 12% or less. Well-managed businesses, therefore, generally pay all invoices within the discount period even though this policy necessitates borrowing from banks in order to have the necessary cash available.

RECORDING SALES DISCOUNTS Sales of merchandise are generally recorded at the full selling price without regard for the cash discount being offered. The discount is not reflected in the seller's accounting records until payment is received. Continuing our illustration of a sale of merchandise by Adams Manufacturing Company for $1,000 with terms of 2/10, n/30, the entry to record the sale on November 3 is as shown by the following:

Sale *entered at* *full price*	Accounts Receivable	*1,000*
	Sales	*1,000*
	To record sale to Zenith Company, terms 2/10, n/30.	

[1] Some companies issue invoices payable 10 days after the end of the month in which the sale occurs. Such invoices may bear the expression "10 e.o.m."

Assuming that payment is made by the Zenith Company on November 13, the last day of the discount period, the entry by Adams Manufacturing Company to record collection of the receivable is as follows:

Sales discounts recorded at time of collection

Cash	980	
Sales Discounts	20	
Accounts Receivable		1,000

To record collection from Zenith Company of invoice of November 3 less 2% cash discount.

As previously explained, the allowing of a cash discount reduces the amount received from sales. On the income statement, therefore, the sales discounts appear as a deduction from sales, as shown below:

Partial Income Statement

Sales discounts on income statement

Sales		$189,788
Less: Sales returns and allowances	$4,462	
Sales discounts	3,024	7,486
Net sales		$182,302

RECORDING PURCHASE DISCOUNTS On the books of the Zenith Company, the purchase of merchandise on November 3 was recorded at the gross amount of the invoice, as shown by the following entry:

Purchase entered at full price

Purchases	1,000	
Accounts Payable		1,000

To record purchase from Adams Manufacturing Company, terms 2/10, n/30.

When the invoice was paid on November 13, the last day of the discount period, the payment was recorded as follows:

Purchase discount recorded when payment made

Accounts Payable	1,000	
Purchase Discounts		20
Cash		980

To record payment to Adams Manufacturing Company of invoice of November 3, less 2% cash discount.

The effect of the discount was to reduce the cost of the merchandise to the Zenith Company. The credit balance of the Purchase Discounts account should therefore be deducted in the income statement from the debit balance of the Purchases account.

Since the Purchase Discounts account is deducted from Purchases in the income statement, a question naturally arises as to whether the Purchase Discounts account is really necessary. Why not reduce the amount of purchases at the time of taking a discount by crediting Purchases rather than crediting Purchase Discounts? The answer is that management needs to know the amount of discounts taken. The Purchase Discounts account supplies this information. Any decrease in the proportion of purchase discounts to purchases carries the suggestion that the accounts payable department is becoming inefficient. That department has the responsibility of paying all invoices within the discount period, and management should be informed of failure by any department to follow company policies consistently. If management is to direct the business effectively, it needs to receive from the accounting system information indicating the level of performance in every department.

Monthly statements to customers

In addition to sending an invoice to the customer for each separate sales transaction, some concerns send each customer a statement at the end of the month. The statement shows the balance receivable at the beginning of the month, the charges for sales during the month, the credits for payments received or goods returned, and the balance receivable from the customer at the end of the month.

Upon receipt of a monthly statement from a vendor, the customer should make a detailed comparison of the purchases and payments shown on the statement with the corresponding entries in his accounts payable records. Any differences should be promptly investigated. Frequently the balance shown on the statement will differ from the balance of the customer's accounts payable record because shipments of merchandise and letters containing payments are in transit at month-end. These in-transit items will have been recorded by the sender but will not yet appear on the other party's records.

Classified financial statements

The financial statements illustrated up to this point have been rather short and simple because of the limited number of transactions and accounts used in these introductory chapters. Now let us look briefly at a more comprehensive and realistic balance sheet for a merchandising business. A full understanding of all the items on this balance sheet may not be possible until our study of accounting has progressed further, but a bird's-eye view of a fairly complete balance sheet is nevertheless useful at this point.

In the balance sheet of the Fashion Products Company illustrated on page 162, the assets are classified into three groups: (1) current assets, (2) plant and equipment, and (3) other assets. The liabilities are classified into two types: (1) current liabilities and (2) long-term liabilities. This classification of assets and liabilities, subject to minor variations in terminology, is virtually a standard one throughout American business. The inclusion of captions for the balance sheet totals is an optional step.

FASHION PRODUCTS COMPANY
Balance Sheet
December 31, 19___

Assets

Current assets:			
Cash			$ 24,500
U.S. government bonds			10,000
Notes receivable...................................			2,400
Accounts receivable		$26,960	
Less: Allowance for uncollectible accounts		860	26,100
Inventory			35,200
Short-term prepayments			1,200
Total current assets			$ 99,400
Plant and equipment:			
Land		$10,000	
Building	$24,000		
Less: Accumulated depreciation	1,920	22,080	
Store equipment	$ 9,400		
Less: Accumulated depreciation	1,880	7,520	
Delivery equipment	$ 2,800		
Less: Accumulated depreciation	700	2,100	
Total plant and equipment			41,700
Other assets:			
Land (future building site)			16,500
Total assets			$157,600

Liabilities & Stockholders' Equity

Current liabilities:			
Notes payable			$ 11,500
Accounts payable			19,040
Accrued liabilities			1,410
Deferred revenue			1,100
Total current liabilities.......................			$ 33,050
Long-term liabilities:			
Mortgage payable (due in 10 years)............			25,000
Total liabilities...................................			$ 58,050
Stockholders' equity:			
Capital stock		$60,000	
Retained earnings		39,550	99,550
Total liabilities & stockholders' equity			$157,600

Note: A new item introduced in this balance sheet is the Allowance for Uncollectible Accounts of $860, shown as a deduction from Accounts Receivable. This is an estimate of the uncollectible portion of the accounts receivable and serves to reduce the valuation of this asset to the net amount of $26,100 that is considered collectible.

THE PURPOSE OF BALANCE SHEET CLASSIFICATION   The purpose underlying a standard classification of assets and liabilities is to aid management, owners, creditors, and other interested persons in understanding the financial position of the business. The banker, for example, would have a difficult time in reading the balance sheets of all the companies which apply to him for loans, if each of these companies followed its own individual whims as to the sequence and arrangement of accounts comprising its balance sheet. Standard practices as to the order and arrangement of a balance sheet are an important means of saving the time of the reader and of giving him a fuller comprehension of the company's financial position. On the other hand, these standard practices are definitely not iron-clad rules; the form and content of a well-prepared balance sheet today are different in several respects from the balance sheet of 25 years ago. No two businesses are exactly alike and a degree of variation from the conventional type of balance sheet is appropriate for the individual business in devising the most meaningful presentation of its financial position. Standardization of the form and content of financial statements is a desirable goal; but if carried to an extreme, it might prevent the growth of new improved methods and the constructive changes necessary to reflect changes in business practices.

The analysis and interpretation of financial statements is the subject of Chapter 16. At this point our objective is merely to emphasize that classification of the items on a balance sheet aids the reader greatly in appraising the financial position of the business. Some of the major balance sheet classifications are discussed briefly in the following sections.

CURRENT ASSETS   Current assets include cash, government bonds and other marketable securities, receivables, inventories, and short-term prepayments. To qualify for inclusion in the current asset category, an asset must be capable of being converted into cash within a relatively short period without interfering with the normal operation of the business. The period is usually one year, but it may be longer for those businesses having an operating cycle in excess of one year. The sequence in which current assets are listed depends upon their liquidity; the closer an asset is to becoming cash the higher is its liquidity. The total amount of a company's current assets and the relative amount of each type give some indication of the company's short-run, debt-paying ability.

The term *operating cycle* is often used in establishing the limits of the current asset classification. Operating cycle means the average time period between the purchase of merchandise and the conversion of this merchandise back into cash. The series of transactions comprising a complete cycle often runs as follows: (1) purchase of merchandise, (2) sale of the merchandise on credit, (3) collection of the account receivable from the customer. The word *cycle* suggests the circular flow of capital from cash to inventory to receivables to cash again. This cycle of transactions in a merchandising business is portrayed in the following diagram.

The operating cycle repeats continuously

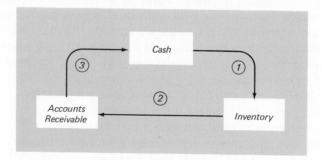

In a business handling fast-moving merchandise (a supermarket, for example) the operating cycle may be completed in a few weeks; for most merchandising businesses the operating cycle requires several months but less than a year.

CURRENT LIABILITIES Liabilities that must be paid within the operating cycle or one year (whichever is longer) are called *current liabilities.* Current liabilities are paid out of current assets, and a comparison of the amount of current assets with the amount of current liabilities is an important step in appraising the ability of a company to pay its debts in the near future.

CURRENT RATIO Many bankers and other users of financial statements believe that for a business to qualify as a good credit risk, the total current assets should be at least twice as large as the total current liabilities. In studying a balance sheet, a banker or other creditor will compute the *current ratio* by dividing total current assets by total current liabilities. In the illustrated balance sheet of Fashion Products Company, the current assets of $99,400 are approximately three times as great as the current liabilities of $33,050; the current ratio is therefore 3 to 1, which would generally be regarded as a strong current position. The current assets could shrink by two-thirds and still be sufficient for payment of the current liabilities. Although a strong current ratio is desirable, an extremely high current ratio (such as 6 to 1 or more) may signify that a company is holding too much of its resources in cash, marketable securities, and other current assets and is not pursuing profit opportunities as aggressively as it might.

WORKING CAPITAL The excess of current assets over current liabilities is called *working capital;* the relative amount of working capital is another indication of short-term financial strength. In the illustrated balance sheet of Fashion Products Company, working capital is $66,350, computed by subtracting the current liabilities of $33,050 from the current assets of $99,400. The importance of solvency (ability to meet debts as they fall due) was emphasized in Chapter 1. Ample working capital permits a company to buy merchandise in large lots, to carry an adequate inventory, and to sell merchandise to customers on favorable credit terms. Many companies have been forced to suspend business because of inadequate working capital, even though total assets were much larger than total liabilities.

CLASSIFICATION IN THE INCOME STATEMENT A new feature to be noted in the illustrated income statement of the Fashion Products Company (page 166) is the division of the operating expenses into the two categories of selling expenses and general and administrative expenses. This classification aids management in controlling expenses by emphasizing that certain expenses are the responsibility of the executive in charge of sales, and that other types of expense relate to the business as a whole. Some expenses, such as depreciation of the building, may be divided between the two classifications according to the portion utilized by each functional division of the business. The item of Uncollectible Accounts Expense listed under the heading of General and Administrative Expenses is an expense of estimated amount. It will be discussed fully in Chapter 10. Income taxes are intentionally ignored in this illustration.

Another feature to note in the income statement of Fashion Products Company is that interest earned on investments is placed after the figure showing income from operations. Other examples of such nonoperating revenue are dividends on shares of stock owned and rent earned by leasing property not presently needed in the operation of the business. Any items of expense not related to selling or administrative functions may also be placed at the bottom of the income statement after the income from operations. Separate group headings of Nonoperating Revenue and Nonoperating Expenses are sometimes used.

CONDENSED INCOME STATEMENT In the published annual reports of most corporations, the income statement is usually greatly condensed because the public is presumably not interested in the details of operations. A condensed income statement usually begins with *net* sales. The details involved in computing the cost of goods are also often omitted and only summary figures are given for selling expenses

FASHION PRODUCTS COMPANY
Income Statement
For the Year Ended December 31, 19___

Gross sales			$310,890
Less: Sales returns and allowances		$ 3,820	
Sales discounts		4,830	8,650
Net sales			$302,240
Cost of goods sold:			
Inventory, Jan. 1, 19___		$ 30,040	
Purchases	$212,400		
Transportation-in	8,300		
Delivered cost of purchases	$220,700		
Less: Purchase returns and allowances $2,400			
Purchase discounts 5,100	7,500		
Net purchases		213,200	
Cost of goods available for sale		$243,240	
Less: Inventory, Dec. 31, 19___		35,200	
Cost of goods sold			208,040
Gross profit on sales			$ 94,200
Operating expenses:			
Selling expenses:			
Sales salaries	$ 38,410		
Advertising	10,190		
Depreciation: building	840		
Depreciation: store equipment	940		
Depreciation: delivery equipment	700		
Insurance	1,100		
Miscellaneous	820		
Total selling expenses		$ 53,000	
General and administrative expenses:			
Office salaries	$ 19,200		
Uncollectible accounts expense	750		
Depreciation: building	120		
Insurance expense	100		
Miscellaneous	930		
Total general and administrative expenses		21,100	
Total operating expenses			74,100
Income from operations			$ 20,100
Interest earned on investments			300
Net income			$ 20,400

and general and administrative expenses. A condensed income statement for Fashion Products Company appears below:

FASHION PRODUCTS COMPANY
Income Statement
For the Year Ended December 31, 19___

Net sales		*$302,240*
Cost of goods sold		*208,040*
Gross profit on sales		*$ 94,200*
Expenses:		
Selling	*$53,000*	
General and administrative	*21,100*	*74,100*
Income from operations		*$ 20,100*
Interest earned on investments		*300*
Net income		*$ 20,400*

A condensed income statement

The statement of retained earnings for Fashion Products Company would not differ significantly from the form shown in previous illustrations.

DEMONSTRATION PROBLEM

The adjusted trial balance of Co-op Supply Company at December 31, 19___, is shown on page 168. An inventory taken on December 31, 19___, amounted to $32,440. The following adjustments have been made to the original trial balance figures:

(1) Depreciation of buildings, $4,100; of delivery equipment, $1,500.

(2) Accrued salaries: office, $845; sales, $950.

(3) Insurance expired, $250.

(4) Store supplies used, $1,000.

CO-OP SUPPLY COMPANY
Adjusted Trial Balance
December 31, 19___

Cash	$ 9,310	
Accounts receivable	10,380	
Inventory, Jan. 1, 19___	28,650	
Inventory of store supplies	270	
Unexpired insurance	360	
Land	89,700	
Buildings	100,000	
Accumulated depreciation: buildings		$ 21,750
Delivery equipment	45,000	
Accumulated depreciation: delivery equipment		16,300
Accounts payable		22,450
Accrued salaries payable		1,795
Capital stock		200,000
Retained earnings, Jan. 1, 19___		85,165
Dividends	40,000	
Sales		171,220
Sales returns & allowances	2,430	
Purchases	138,900	
Purchase returns & allowances		1,820
Sales salaries expense	26,000	
Delivery expense	2,800	
Depreciation expense: delivery equipment	1,500	
Office salaries expense	19,850	
Depreciation expense: buildings	4,100	
Insurance expense	250	
Store supplies used	1,000	
	$520,500	$520,500

Instructions
a Prepare a work sheet at Dec. 31, 19___. You need not use the Adjusted
 Trial Balance columns.
b Prepare an income statement for the year.
c Prepare a classified balance sheet as of Dec. 31, 19___.
d Prepare a statement of retained earnings for the year.
e Prepare closing journal entries.

SOLUTION TO DEMONSTRATION PROBLEM

CO-OP SUPPLY COMPANY
Work Sheet
For the Year Ended December 31, 19___

	Trial Balance		Adjustments*		Income Statement		Retained Earnings		Balance Sheet	
	Dr	Cr	Dr	Cr	Dr	Cr	Dr	Cr	Dr	Cr
Cash	9,310								9,310	
Accounts receivable	10,380								10,380	
Inventory, Jan. 1, 19___	28,650				28,650					
Inventory of store supplies	1,270			(4) 1,000					270	
Unexpired insurance	610			(3) 250					360	
Land	89,700								89,700	
Buildings	100,000								100,000	
Accum. depr.: buildings		17,650		(1) 4,100						21,750
Delivery equipment	45,000								45,000	
Accum. depr.: del. eqpt.		14,800		(1) 1,500						16,300
Accounts payable		22,450								22,450
Accrued salaries payable				(2) 1,795						1,795
Capital stock		200,000								200,000
Retained earnings, Jan. 1, 19___		85,165						85,165		
Dividends	40,000						40,000			
Sales		171,220				171,220				
Sales returns & allowances	2,430				2,430					
Purchases	138,900				138,900					
Purchase returns & allowances		1,820				1,820				
Sales salaries expense	25,050		(2) 950		26,000					
Delivery expense	2,800				2,800					
Depr. expense: del. eqpt.			(1) 1,500		1,500					
Office salaries expense	19,005		(2) 845		19,850					
Depr. expense: buildings			(1) 4,100		4,100					
Insurance expense			(3) 250		250					
Store supplies used			(4) 1,000		1,000					
	513,105	513,105	8,645	8,645	225,480					
Inventory, Dec. 31, 19___						32,440			32,440	
					225,480	205,480	60,000			
Net loss						20,000	20,000			
					225,480	225,480				
Retained earnings, Dec. 31, 19___							25,165	85,165		25,165
							85,165	85,165	287,460	287,460

* Adjustments:
(1) To record depreciation expense for 19___.
(2) To record accrued salaries payable at Dec. 31, 19___.
(3) To record insurance expired.
(4) To record store supplies used.

a

b

CO-OP SUPPLY COMPANY
Income Statement
For the Year Ended December 31, 19___

Sales			$171,220
Less: Sales returns & allowances			2,430
Net sales			$168,790
Cost of goods sold:			
Inventory, Jan. 1, 19___		$ 28,650	
Purchases	$138,900		
Less: Purchase returns & allowances	1,820	137,080	
Cost of goods available for sale		$165,730	
Less: Inventory, Dec. 31, 19___		32,440	
Costs of goods sold			133,290
Gross profit on sales			$ 35,500
Operating expenses:			
Sales salaries expense		$ 26,000	
Delivery expense		2,800	
Depreciation expense: delivery equipment		1,500	
Office salaries expense		19,850	
Depreciation expense: buildings		4,100	
Insurance expense		250	
Supplies expense		1,000	
Total operating expenses			55,500
Net loss			$ 20,000

c

CO-OP SUPPLY COMPANY
Balance Sheet
December 31, 19___

Assets

Current assets:			
Cash			$ 9,310
Accounts receivable			10,380
Inventory			32,440
Inventory of store supplies			270
Unexpired insurance			360
Total current assets			$ 52,760
Plant and equipment:			
Land		$ 89,700	
Buildings	$100,000		
Less: Accumulated depreciation	21,750	78,250	
Delivery equipment	$ 45,000		
Less: Accumulated depreciation	16,300	28,700	
Total plant and equipment			196,650
Total assets			$249,410

Liabilities & Stockholders' Equity

Current liabilities:

Accounts payable		$ 22,450
Accrued salaries payable		1,795
Total current liabilities		$ 24,245

Stockholders' equity:

Capital stock	$200,000	
Retained earnings	25,165	
Total stockholders' equity		225,165
Total liabilities & stockholders' equity		$249,410

---

d

CO-OP SUPPLY COMPANY

Statement of Retained Earnings

For the Year Ended December 31, 19___

Retained earnings, Jan. 1, 19___		$85,165
Less: Net loss	$20,000	
Dividends	40,000	60,000
Retained earnings, Dec. 31, 19___		$25,165

---

e		**Closing Entries**		
19___				
Dec.	31	Income Summary	225,480	
		Inventory, Jan. 1, 19___		28,650
		Sales Returns & Allowances		2,430
		Purchases		138,900
		Sales Salaries Expense		26,000
		Delivery Expense		2,800
		Depreciation Expense: Delivery Equipment		1,500
		Office Salaries Expense		19,850
		Depreciation Expense: Buildings		4,100
		Insurance Expense		250
		Store Supplies Expense		1,000
		To close the beginning inventory account and all temporary owners' equity accounts having debit balances.		
	31	Sales	171,220	
		Inventory, Dec. 31, 19___	32,440	
		Purchase Returns & Allowances	1,820	
		Income Summary		205,480
		To set up the ending inventory and close all temporary owners' equity accounts having credit balances.		

		Closing Entries		
19___				
Dec.	31	Retained Earnings	20,000	
		Income Summary		20,000
		To close the Income Summary account.		
	31	Retained Earnings	40,000	
		Dividends		40,000
		To close the Dividends account.		

REVIEW QUESTIONS

1 During the current year, Bonita Corporation made all sales of merchandise at prices in excess of cost. Will the business necessarily report a net income for the year? Explain.

2 Gable Company during its first year of operation had cost of goods sold of $90,000 and a gross profit equal to 40% of sales. What was the dollar amount of sales for the year?

3 If cost of goods sold amounts to 65% of the sales of a merchandising business and net income amounts to 5% of sales, what percentage of sales is represented by operating expenses? What percentage of gross profit is included in each dollar of sales?

4 Compute the amount of cost of goods sold, given the following account balances: beginning inventory $26,000, purchases $84,000, purchase returns and allowances $4,500, transportation-in $500, and ending inventory $36,000.

5 During the current year, Davis Corporation purchased merchandise costing $200,000. State the cost of goods sold under each of the following alternative assumptions:
a No beginning inventory; ending inventory $38,000
b Beginning inventory $56,000; no ending inventory
c Beginning inventory $54,000; ending inventory $68,000
d Beginning inventory $90,000; ending inventory $71,000

6 Zenith Company uses the periodic inventory system and maintains its accounting records on a calendar-year basis. Does the beginning or the ending inventory figure appear in the trial balance prepared from the ledger on December 31?

7 When the periodic inventory system is in use, how is the amount of inventory determined at the end of the period?

8 State a general principle to be followed in assigning duties among employees if strong internal control is to be achieved.

9 For an invoice dated October 21, what is the last day of the credit period if the credit terms are
a 2/10, n/30?
b 10 e.o.m.?

10 Explain the terms *current asset, current liability, current ratio,* and *working capital.*

11 The Riblet Company has a current ratio of 3 to 1 and working capital of $60,000. What are the amounts of current assets and current liabilities?

12 What advantages do you see in reporting operating expenses in two categories: selling, and general and administrative?

13 Give an example of a nonoperating revenue item and an example of a nonoperating expense item.

14 Define a *condensed income statement* and indicate its advantages and possible shortcomings.

EXERCISES

Ex. 5-1 Income statement data for Reinell Corporation for two years are shown below:

	Year 2	Year 1
Net sales.	$240,000	$180,000
Cost of goods sold	180,000	126,000
Selling expenses	30,000	18,000
General and administrative expenses	12,000	9,000

a The net income decreased from $_____ in Year 1 to $_____ in Year 2.
b The net income as a percentage of net sales was ___% in Year 1 and decreased to ___% of net sales in Year 2.
c The gross profit on sales decreased from 30% in Year 1 to ___% in Year 2.
d Selling expenses increased by $12,000 from Year 1 to Year 2, which represented an increase of ___% from the base of $18,000, while net sales showed an increase of ___% from the base of $180,000.

Ex. 5-2 Use the following information as a basis for computing the amount of total purchases for the period.

Beginning inventory	$ 52,368
Cost of goods sold	156,600
Sales	219,180
Ending inventory	46,200
Transportation-in	2,268
Purchase returns & allowances	2,580

Ex. 5-3 From the following information, compute the amount of the beginning inventory.

Purchases	$78,000
Cost of goods sold	50,280
Purchase discounts	1,320
Purchase returns & allowances	5,520
Transportation-in	2,880
Ending inventory	46,140

Ex. 5-4 Give the journal entry, if any, to be prepared for each of these events:
a Received a telephone order from a customer for $1,800 worth of merchandise.
b Issued a purchase order to Frazee Company for merchandise costing $2,500.

c Received the merchandise ordered from Frazee Company and an invoice for $2,500; credit terms 2/10, n/30.

d Delivered the $1,800 of merchandise ordered in *a* above to the customer and mailed an invoice; credit terms 10 e.o.m.

e Mailed check to Frazee Company in full settlement of amount owed after taking allowable discount.

f Customer returned $400 of goods delivered in *d* above, which were unsatisfactory. A credit memorandum was issued for that amount.

Ex. 5-5 The balance sheet of Ball Company contained the following items, among others:

Cash	$ 86,000
Accounts receivable	30,000
Inventory	124,000
Store equipment (net)	120,000
Other assets	18,000
Mortgage payable (due in 3 years)	30,000
Notes payable (due in 10 days)	72,000
Accounts payable	24,000
Retained earnings	138,000

Instructions

a From the above information compute the amount of current assets and the amount of current liabilities.

b How much working capital does Ball Company have?

c Compute the current ratio.

d Assume that Ball Company pays the notes payable of $72,000 thus reducing cash to $14,000. Compute the amount of working capital and the current ratio after this transaction.

Ex. 5-6 Ryder Company made credit sales during June of $106,000, of which $21,000 was collected in June and the remainder was collected in July. Cash sales in June amounted to $17,000, and an additional $80,000 was received from customers in payment for goods sold to them in May. Sales returns in June amounted to $3,000. Gross profit for the month of June was 40% of net sales, general and administrative expenses were $14,000, and net income was $11,000.

Prepare a condensed income statement for Ryder Company for the month ended June 30. (*Hint:* Selling expenses must be computed. Income taxes are to be ignored.)

Ex. 5-7 Indicate whether each of the following events would increase, decrease, or have no effect upon (1) the current ratio and (2) the working capital of a business with current assets greater than its current liabilities.

Example: An account payable is paid in cash.

(1) Increase current ratio.

(2) No effect on working capital.

a Merchandise is purchased on account.

b An adjusting entry is made to accrue salaries earned by employees but not yet paid.

c An account receivable is collected.

d An adjusting entry is prepared to record depreciation for the period.

e Land is purchased by making a small cash down payment and signing a long-term mortgage payable.

PROBLEMS

5-1 The income statement of Folsom Company contained the following items, among others, for the year ended June 30, 19___.

Sales	$545,250	Ending inventory	$?
Purchases	347,287	Sales returns &	
Transportation-in	3,860	allowances	14,450
Purchase returns &		Beginning inventory	68,600
allowances	1,750	Purchase discounts	605
Sales discounts	4,600	Gross profit on sales	178,908

Instructions
a Compute the amount of net sales.
b Compute the gross profit percentage.
c What percentage of net sales represents the cost of goods sold?
d Prepare a partial income statement utilizing all the accounts listed above, including the determination of the amount of the ending inventory.

5-2 The following is a partial list of the transactions of the Delphi Electronics Company for the month of April:
Apr. 2 Purchased merchandise for cash, $710.
Apr. 5 Sold merchandise to Hunt Industries on open account, $5,200.
Apr. 6 Paid transportation charges on shipment to Hunt Industries, $250.
Apr. 8 Purchased office equipment from ICM Corporation for cash, $5,500.
Apr. 14 Hunt Industries returned for credit $420 of the merchandise purchased on April 5 (no reduction in the transportation charges paid on April 6).
Apr. 19 Sold merchandise for cash, $4,300.
Apr. 22 Refunded $260 to a customer who had made a cash purchase on April 19.
Apr. 26 Purchased merchandise from Marshall & Company on open account, $2,240.
Apr. 27 Paid by check transportation charges on merchandise purchased from Marshall & Company in the amount of $160.
Apr. 29 Returned for credit of $300 merchandise purchased from Marshall & Company (no reduction was allowed with respect to the transportation charges paid April 27).
Apr. 30 Purchased stationery and miscellaneous office supplies on open account, $470.

Instructions
Prepare journal entries for the transactions listed above, assuming that the company uses the periodic inventory system.

5-3 The accounting records of Knox Company are maintained on the basis of a fiscal year ending April 30. After all necessary adjustments had been made at April 30, 19___, the adjusted trial balance appeared as follows:

KNOX COMPANY

Adjusted Trial Balance

April 30, 19___

Cash	$ 19,000	
Accounts receivable	34,000	
Inventory (beginning of fiscal year)	28,900	
Unexpired insurance	700	
Inventory of supplies	1,200	
Furniture and fixtures	20,000	
Accumulated depreciation: furniture and fixtures		$ 1,200
Accounts payable		8,300
Notes payable		7,000
Capital stock		50,000
Retained earnings		35,480
Dividends	30,000	
Sales		293,000
Sales returns and allowances	4,000	
Purchases	191,525	
Purchase returns and allowances		1,545
Transportation-in	10,000	
Salaries and wages expense	45,400	
Rent expense	8,400	
Depreciation expense: furniture and fixtures	1,200	
Supplies expense	1,400	
Insurance expense	800	
	$396,525	$396,525

The inventory on April 30, 19___, as determined by count, amounted to $35,880.

Instructions

a Prepare an income statement for Knox Company for the year ended April 30, 19___.

b Prepare the necessary journal entries to close the accounts on April 30, 19___.

(*Suggestion:* Use four separate closing entries. The first entry may be used to close the beginning inventory and all nominal accounts having debit balances; the second entry to set up the ending inventory and to close nominal accounts having credit balances; the third entry to close the Income Summary account; and the fourth entry to close the Dividends account.)

5-4 The Rio Grande Corporation maintains its accounting records on the basis of a fiscal year ending April 30. After all necessary adjustments had been made at April 30, 1976, the adjusted trial balance prepared by the company's accountant appeared as follows:

RIO GRANDE CORPORATION
Adjusted Trial Balance
April 30, 1976

Cash	$ 27,918	
Accounts receivable	46,224	
Inventory (April 30, 1975)	40,716	
Unexpired insurance	840	
Inventory of supplies	1,392	
Furniture & fixtures	59,640	
Accumulated depreciation: furniture & fixtures		$ 5,070
Accounts payable		15,960
Notes payable		8,400
Capital stock, $1 par value		60,000
Retained earnings, April 30, 1975		37,860
Sales		363,132
Sales returns & allowances	5,124	
Purchases	234,630	
Purchase returns & allowances		1,854
Transportation-in	11,820	
Salaries & wages expense	49,740	
Rent expense	10,080	
Depreciation expense: furniture & fixtures	1,506	
Supplies expense	1,698	
Insurance expense	948	
	$492,276	$492,276

The inventory on April 30, 1976, as determined by count, amounted to $46,500.

Instructions

a Prepare an income statement for Rio Grande Corporation for the year ended April 30, 1976.

b Prepare the necessary entries (in general journal form) to close the accounts at April 30, 1976.

c Assume that the ending inventory of $46,500 was overstated $5,000 as a result of double counting part of the goods on hand at April 30, 1976. Prepare a three-column list of the items in the income statement developed in **a** above which are incorrect as a result of the $5,000 inventory over-statement. List in the second column the reported figures and in the third column the corrected figures.

5-5 On June 30, 19___, the close of the fiscal year for Maverick Corporation, the company's accountant prepared the following trial balance from the ledger.

Cash	$ 24,840	
Accounts receivable	25,218	
Inventory, beginning	44,688	
Unexpired insurance	864	
Inventory of office supplies	606	
Land	36,528	
Buildings	81,600	
Accumulated depreciation: buildings		$ 22,944
Equipment	23,760	
Accumulated depreciation: equipment		13,920
Accounts payable		13,032
Capital stock		120,000
Retained earnings, beginning of year		31,884
Dividends	12,000	
Sales		257,646
Sales returns & allowances	3,948	
Purchases	173,880	
Purchase returns & allowances		2,574
Transportation-in	3,558	
Salaries & wages expense	29,688	
Property taxes expense	822	
	$462,000	$462,000

Other data
(1) The buildings are being depreciated over a 25-year useful life and the equipment over a 12-year useful life.
(2) Accrued salaries payable as of June 30 were $3,360.
(3) Examination of policies showed $540 unexpired insurance on June 30.
(4) Office supplies on hand at June 30 were estimated to amount to $252.
(5) Inventory of merchandise on June 30 was $36,000.

Instructions
a Prepare a work sheet at June 30, 19___. You need not use the Adjusted Trial Balance columns.
b Prepare an income statement for the year.
c Prepare a classified balance sheet as of June 30, 19___.
d Prepare a statement of retained earnings for the year.
e Prepare closing journal entries.

5-6 House of Lights, a lighting fixtures distributor, engaged in the following merchandising transactions during the month of September:
Sept. 1 Purchased merchandise from Morton Co. The list price was $12,500 with a trade discount of 20% and terms of 2/10, n/60.
Sept. 2 Purchased merchandise from Industrial Supply Co. for $5,500; terms 1/10, n/30.
Sept. 5 Sold merchandise to Home Specialties, $6,000; terms 2/10, n/30.

Sept. 6 Returned to Morton Co. damaged merchandise having a cost after trade discount of $1,000.

Sept. 11 Paid Morton Co. for invoice of September 1, less discount and returns.

Sept. 15 Received cash in full settlement of Home Specialties account.

Sept. 22 Sold merchandise to May Co., $20,000; terms 2/10, n/30.

Sept. 25 Purchased from Bright Co. merchandise with list price of $9,000, subject to trade discount of 25% and credit terms of 1/10, n/30.

Sept. 28 Returned for credit part of merchandise received from Bright Co. Cost of the returned goods (after trade discount) was $200.

Sept. 30 Paid Industrial Supply Co. invoice of September 2.

Instructions

a Journalize the above transactions.

b Prepare a partial income statement, showing gross profit on sales. Assume the following inventories: August 31, $20,900; September 30, $26,550.

c Compute the balance of accounts payable.

d Compute the effective annual rate of interest House of Lights would be paying if it failed to take advantage of discount terms on the Morton Co. invoice.

5-7 Lester Hardy had for several years worked as the in-charge accountant for Calloway Company. When he suddenly became ill in late December, his recently employed assistant was called upon to complete the year-end accounting work. The assistant, whose knowledge of accounting was rather limited, prepared the following financial statements. All dollar amounts are correct, although numerous errors exist in the location of accounts in the financial statements.

CALLOWAY COMPANY
Loss Statement
December 31, 19___

Sales	$612,000	
Purchase returns & allowances	4,560	
Purchase discounts	8,838	
Interest earned on investments	1,140	
Increase in inventory	6,156	$632,694
Purchases	$454,380	
Sales returns & allowances	10,776	
Sales discounts	5,568	
Transportation-in	28,482	
Interest expense	2,004	
Uncollectible accounts expense	2,544	
Depreciation expense: building	2,100	
Depreciation expense: store equipment	2,682	
Depreciation expense: delivery equipment	2,208	
Insurance expense	1,920	
Office salaries expense	18,600	
Executive salaries expense	49,200	
Sales salaries expense	73,050	
Miscellaneous selling expense	1,116	
Miscellaneous general expense	1,884	656,514
Net loss for year		$ 23,820

CALLOWAY COMPANY
Balance Sheet
December 31, 19___

Current assets:

Notes receivable	$ 12,000	
Accounts receivable	30,600	
Cash	19,680	
Rent collected in advance	960	
Land	24,000	$ 87,240

Plant and equipment:

Inventory	$ 64,206	
Store equipment	22,920	
Building	57,600	
Delivery equipment	17,400	162,126

Other assets:

Marketable securities held as temporary investments	$ 10,800	
Land held as future building site	15,000	25,800
Total assets		$275,166

Liabilities:

Accounts payable	$ 33,918	
Accrued salaries payable	2,622	
Short-term prepayments	960	
Notes payable	18,000	
First mortgage bonds payable	60,000	
Allowance for uncollectible accounts	1,968	
Accumulated depreciation: building	18,720	
Accumulated depreciation: store equipment	14,400	
Accumulated depreciation: delivery equipment	13,920	
Total liabilities		$164,508

Stockholders' equity:

Capital stock	$120,000	
Less: Deficit	9,342	110,658
Total liabilities & stockholders' equity		$275,166

Instructions

a Prepare in acceptable form an income statement for the year ended December 31, 19___. (Allocate to selling expense 60% of building depreciation and $600 of insurance expense.) The remaining portions of these two expense accounts should be classified under the General and Administrative Expenses heading. The Uncollectible Accounts Expense of $2,544 should also be listed under General and Administrative Expenses.

b Prepare a balance sheet as of December 31, 19___, properly classified. Show the Allowance for Uncollectible Accounts as a deduction from Accounts Receivable in the current asset section of the balance sheet.

c What was the balance in the Retained Earnings account at the beginning of the current year?

BUSINESS DECISION PROBLEM 5

Parker Company and Rhoades Corporation are both merchandising companies applying for nine-month bank loans in order to finance the acquisition of new equipment. Both companies are seeking to borrow the amount of $70,000 and have submitted the following balance sheets with their loan applications:

PARKER COMPANY
Balance Sheet
August 31, 19____

Assets

Current assets:			
Cash			$ 19,000
Accounts receivable			51,000
Inventories			54,000
Short-term prepayments			2,000
Total current assets			$126,000
Plant and equipment:			
Land			$ 50,000
Building	$200,000		
Less: Accumulated depreciation	30,000	170,000	
Store equipment	$ 60,000		
Less: Accumulated depreciation	15,000	45,000	
Total plant and equipment			265,000
Total assets			$391,000

Liabilities & Stockholders' Equity

Current liabilities:			
Accounts payable			$ 45,000
Accrued wages payable			15,000
Total current liabilities			$ 60,000
Long-term liabilities:			
Mortgage payable (due in 13 months)			110,000
Total liabilities			$170,000
Stockholders' equity:			
Capital stock		$100,000	
Retained earnings		121,000	221,000
Total liabilities & stockholders' equity			$391,000

RHOADES CORPORATION
Balance Sheet
August 31, 19___

Assets

Current assets:

Cash	$128,000
U.S. government bonds	70,000
Accounts receivable	201,000
Inventories	189,000
Total current assets	$588,000

Plant & equipment:

Land		$ 60,000
Building and equipment	$410,000	
Less: Accumulated depreciation	60,000	350,000
Total plant & equipment		410,000
Total assets		$998,000

Liabilities & Stockholders' Equity

Current liabilities:

Notes payable		$200,000
Accounts payable		160,000
Miscellaneous accrued liabilities		60,000
Total current liabilities		$420,000
Long-term liabilities:		
Mortgage payable (due in 10 years)		140,000
Total liabilities		$560,000
Stockholders' equity:		
Capital stock	$250,000	
Retained earnings	188,000	438,000
Total liabilities & stockholders' equity		$998,000

Instructions

a Compute the current ratio and amount of working capital for each company as of August 31, 19___.

b Compute the current ratio and amount of working capital that each company would have after obtaining the bank loan and investing the borrowed cash in new equipment (assuming no other transactions affecting current accounts).

c From the viewpoint of a bank loan officer, to which company would you prefer to make a $70,000 nine-month loan? Explain.

SIX

ACCOUNTING SYSTEMS MANUAL AND EDP

In the early chapters of an introductory accounting book, basic accounting principles can most conveniently be discussed in terms of a small business with only a few customers and suppliers. This simplified model of a business has been used in preceding chapters to demonstrate the analysis and recording of the more common types of business transactions.

The recording procedures illustrated thus far call for recording each transaction by an entry in the general journal, and then posting each debit and credit from the general journal to the proper account in the ledger. We must now face the practical problem of streamlining and speeding up this basic accounting system so that the accounting department can keep pace with the rapid flow of transactions in a modern business.

Accounting systems in common use range from manual systems, which use special journals to streamline the journalizing and posting processes, to sophisticated computer systems which maintain accounting records on magnetic tape. The accounting system in use in any given company will be specially tailored to the size and information needs of the business.

MANUAL ACCOUNTING SYSTEMS

In a large business there may be hundreds or even thousands of transactions every day. To handle a large volume of transactions rapidly and efficiently, it is helpful to group the transactions into like classes and to use a specialized journal for each class. This will greatly reduce the amount of detailed recording work and will also permit a division of labor, since each special-purpose journal can be handled by a different employee. The great majority of transactions (perhaps as much as 90 or 95%) usually fall into four types. These four types and the four corresponding special journals are as follows:

Type of Transaction	Name of Special Journal
Sales of merchandise on credit	Sales journal
Purchases of merchandise on credit	Purchases journal
Receipts of cash	Cash receipts journal
Payments of cash	Cash payments journal

In addition to these four special journals, a **general journal** will be used for recording transactions which do not fit into any of the above four types. The general journal is the same book of original entry illustrated in preceding chapters.

Sales journal

Illustrated below is a **sales journal** containing entries for all sales on account made during November by the Seaside Company. Whenever merchandise is sold on credit, several copies of a sales invoice are prepared. The information listed on a sales invoice usually includes the date of the sale, the serial number of the invoice, the customer's name, the amount of the sale, and the credit terms. One copy of the sales invoice is used by the seller as the basis for an entry in the sales journal.

Sales Journal

Page 1

Date		Account Debited	Invoice No.	√	Amount
19__					
Nov.	2	John Adams	301	√	450
	4	Harold Black	302	√	1,000
	5	Robert Cross	303	√	975
	11	H. R. Davis	304	√	620
	18	C. D. Early	305	√	900
	23	John Frost	306	√	400
	29	D. H. Gray	307	√	1,850
					6,195
					(5) (41)

Entries for sales on credit during November

Note that the illustrated sales journal contains special columns for recording each of these aspects of the sales transaction, except the credit terms. If it is the practice of the business to offer different credit terms to different customers, a column may be inserted in the sales journal to show the terms of sale. In this illustration it is assumed that all sales are made on terms of 2/10, n/30; consequently, there is no need to write the credit terms as part of each entry. *Only sales on credit are entered in the sales journal.* When merchandise is sold for cash, the transaction is recorded in a *cash receipts journal,* which is illustrated later in this chapter.

ADVANTAGES OF THE SALES JOURNAL Note that each of the above seven sales transactions is recorded on a single line. Each entry consists of a debit to a customer's account; the offsetting credit to the Sales account is understood without being written, because *all* transactions which are recorded in this special journal include a credit to Sales.

An entry in a sales journal need not include an explanation; if more information about the transaction is desired it can be obtained by referring to the file copy of the sales invoice. The invoice number is listed in the sales journal as part of each entry. The one-line entry in the sales journal requires much less writing than would be required to record a sales transaction in the general journal. Since there may be several hundred or several thousand sales transactions each month, the time saved in recording transactions in this streamlined manner becomes quite important.

Every entry in the sales journal represents a debit to a customer's account. Charges to customers' accounts should be posted daily so that each customer's account will always be up-to-date and available for use in making decisions relating to collections and to the further extension of credit. A check mark ($\checkmark$) is placed in the sales journal opposite each amount posted to a customer's account, to indicate that the posting has been made.

Another advantage of the special journal for sales is the great saving of time in posting credits to the Sales account. Remember that every amount entered in the sales journal represents a credit to Sales. In the illustrated sales journal above, there are seven transactions (and in practice there might be 700). Instead of posting a separate credit to the Sales account for each sales transaction, we can wait until the end of the month and make one posting to the Sales account for the total of the amounts recorded in the sales journal. Much of the efficiency of special journals stems from collecting numerous entries to a specific ledger account in a special column in the journal, and then posting only the column total instead of posting each individual entry.

In the illustrated sales journal for November, the sales on account totaled $6,195. On November 30 this amount is posted as a credit to the Sales account, and the ledger account number for Sales (41) is entered under the total figure in the sales journal to show that the posting operation has been performed. The total sales figure is also posted as a debit to ledger account no. 5, Accounts Receivable. To make clear the reason for this posting to Accounts Receivable, an explanation of the nature of controlling accounts and subsidiary ledgers is necessary.

Controlling accounts and subsidiary ledgers

In preceding chapters all transactions involving accounts receivable from customers have been posted to a single account entitled Accounts Receivable. Under this simplified procedure, however, it is not easy to look up the amount receivable from a given customer. In practice, nearly all businesses which sell goods on credit maintain a separate account receivable with each customer. If there are 4,000 customers this would require a ledger with 4,000 accounts receivable, in addition to the accounts for other assets, and for liabilities, owners' equity, revenue, and expenses. Such a ledger would be cumbersome and unwieldy. Also, the trial balance prepared from such a large ledger would be a very long one. If the trial balance showed the ledger to be out of balance, the task of locating the error or errors would be most difficult. All these factors indicate that it is not desirable to have too many accounts in one ledger. Fortunately, a simple solution is available; this solution is to divide up the ledger into several separate ledgers.

In a business which has a large number of accounts with customers and creditors, it is customary to divide the ledger into three separate ledgers. All the accounts with *customers* are placed in alphabetical order in the *accounts receivable ledger.* All the accounts with *creditors* are arranged alphabetically in the *accounts payable ledger.* Both of these ledgers are known as *subsidiary ledgers* because they support and are controlled by the *general ledger.*

When the numerous individual accounts with customers are placed in a subsidiary ledger, an account entitled Accounts Receivable continues to be maintained in the general ledger. This account shows the total amount due from all customers; in other words, this single *controlling account* in the general ledger takes the place of the numerous customers' accounts which have been removed to form a subsidiary ledger. The general ledger is still in balance because the controlling account, Accounts Receivable, has a balance equal to the total of the customers' accounts contained in the accounts receivable subsidiary ledger. Agreement of the controlling account with the sum of the accounts receivable in the subsidiary ledger also provides assurance of accuracy in the subsidiary ledger.

A controlling account entitled Accounts Payable is also kept in the general ledger in place of the numerous accounts with creditors which have been removed to form the accounts payable subsidiary ledger.

Relationship of subsidiary ledgers to controlling accounts in general ledger
Because the two controlling accounts represent the total amounts receivable from customers and payable to creditors, a trial balance can be prepared from the general ledger alone. The following illustration shows the relationship of the subsidiary ledgers to the controlling accounts in the general ledger:

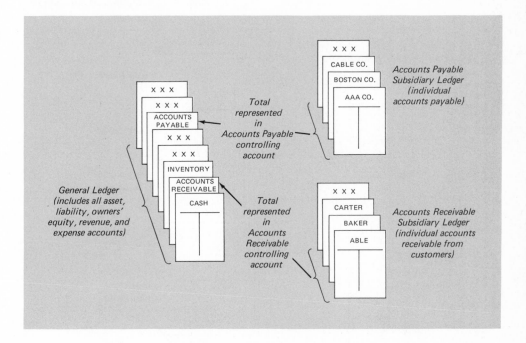

POSTING TO SUBSIDIARY LEDGERS AND TO CONTROLLING ACCOUNTS

To illustrate the posting of subsidiary ledgers and of controlling accounts, let us refer again to the sales journal illustrated on page 184. Each debit to a customer's account is posted currently during the month from the sales journal to the customer's account in the accounts receivable ledger. The accounts in this subsidiary ledger are usually kept in alphabetical order and are not numbered. When a posting is made to a customer's account, a check mark (√) is placed in the sales journal as evidence that the posting has been made to the subsidiary ledger.

At month-end the sales journal is totaled. The total amount of sales for the month, $6,195, is posted as a credit to the Sales account and also as a debit to the controlling account, Accounts Receivable, in the general ledger. The controlling account will, therefore, equal the total of all the customers' accounts in the subsidiary ledger.

The following diagram shows the day-to-day posting of individual entries from the sales journal to the subsidiary ledger. The diagram also shows the month-end posting of the total of the sales journal to the two general ledger accounts affected, Accounts Receivable and Sales. Note that the amount of the monthly debit to the controlling account is equal to the sum of the debits posted to the subsidiary ledger.

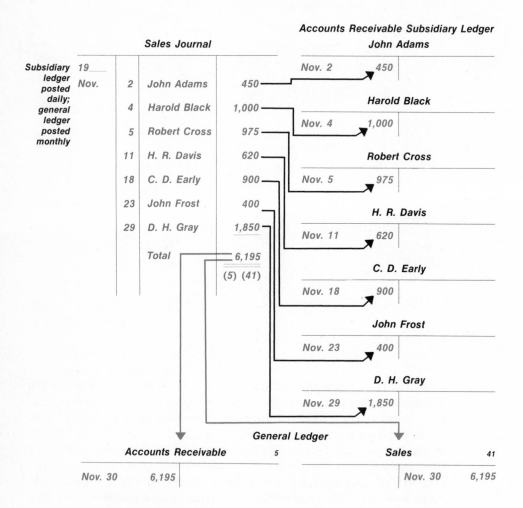

Purchases journal

The handling of purchase transactions when a **purchases journal** is used follows a pattern quite similar to the one described for the sales journal.

Assume that the purchases journal illustrated on page 189 contains all purchases of merchandise on credit during the month by the Seaside Company. The invoice date is shown in a separate column because the cash discount period begins on the invoice date.

The five entries in the purchases journal on page 189 are posted as they occur during the month as credits to the creditors' accounts in the subsidiary ledger for accounts payable. As each posting is completed a check mark (√) is placed in the purchases journal.

Purchases Journal Page 1

Date		Account Credited	Invoice Date	√	Amount
19___			19___		
Nov.	2	Alabama Supply Co.	Nov. 2	√	3,325
	4	Barker & Bright	4	√	700
	10	Canning & Sons	9	√	500
	17	Dennis Co.	15	√	900
	27	Excelsior, Inc.	25	√	1,825
					7,250
					(50) (21)

Entries for purchases on credit during November

At the end of the month the purchases journal is totaled and ruled as shown in the illustration. The total figure, $7,250, is posted to two general ledger accounts as follows:

1 As a debit to the Purchases account
2 As a credit to the Accounts Payable controlling account

The account numbers for Purchases (50) and for Accounts Payable (21) are then placed in parentheses below the column total of the purchases journal to show that the posting has been made.

Under the particular system being described, the only transactions recorded in the purchases journal are **purchases of merchandise on credit.** The term **merchandise** means goods acquired for resale to cus-tomers. If merchandise is purchased for cash rather than on credit, the transaction should be recorded in the **cash payments journal,** as illustrated on pages 194 and 195.

The diagram on page 190 illustrates the day-to-day posting of in-dividual entries from the purchases journal to the accounts with creditors in the subsidiary ledger for accounts payable. The diagram also shows how the column total of the purchases journal is posted at the end of the month to the general ledger accounts, Purchases and Accounts Payable. One objective of this diagram is to emphasize that the amount of the monthly credit to the controlling account is equal to the sum of the credits posted to the subsidiary ledger.

When assets other than merchandise are being acquired, as, for example, a delivery truck or an office desk for use in the business, the journal to be used depends upon whether a cash payment is made. If assets of this type are purchased for cash, the transaction should be entered in the cash payments journal; if the transaction is on credit, the general journal is used. The purchases journal is not used to record

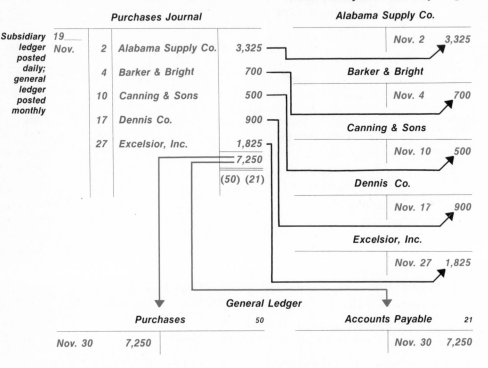

the acquisition of these assets because the total of this journal is posted to the Purchases account and this account (as explained in Chapter 5) is used in determining the cost of goods sold.

Cash receipts journal

All transactions involving the receipt of cash are recorded in the cash receipts journal. One common example is the sale of merchandise for cash. As each cash sale is made, it is rung up on a cash register. At the end of the day the total of the cash sales is computed by striking the total key on the register. This total is entered in the cash receipts journal, which therefore contains one entry for the total cash sales of the day. For other types of cash receipts, such as the collection of accounts receivable from customers, a separate journal entry may be made for each transaction. The cash receipts journal illustrated on pages 192 and 193 contains entries for selected November transactions, all of which include the receipt of cash.

Nov. 1 R. B. Jones organized the Seaside Company by investing $25,000 cash in exchange for 2,500 shares of capital of $10 par value.

    4 Sold merchandise for cash, $300.

    5 Sold merchandise for cash, $400.

8 Collected from John Adams invoice of November 2, $450 less 2% cash discount.

10 Sold portion of land not needed in business for a total price of $7,000, consisting of cash of $1,000 and a note receivable for $6,000. The cost of the land sold was $5,000.

12 Collected from Harold Black invoice of November 4, $1,000 less 2% cash discount.

20 Collected from C. D. Early invoice of November 18, $900 less 2% cash discount.

27 Sold merchandise for cash, $125.

30 Obtained $4,000 loan from bank. Issued a note payable in that amount.

Note that the cash receipts journal shown on pages 192 and 193 has three debit columns and three credit columns. Columns may be created for any account to which numerous entries are made. Thus, we may handle the numerous postings to that account by periodically posting the column total. In this illustration, the following columns were used:

Debits:
  1 Cash. This column is used for every entry, because only those transactions which include the receipt of cash are entered in this special journal.
  2 Sales Discounts. This column is used to accumulate the sales discounts allowed during the month. Only one line of the cash receipts journal is required to record a collection from a customer who takes advantage of a cash discount.
  3 Other Accounts. This third debit column is used for debits to any and all accounts other than cash and sales discounts, and space is provided for writing in the name of the account. For example, the entry of November 10 in the illustrated cash receipts journal shows that cash and a note receivable were obtained when land was sold. The amount of cash received, $1,000, is entered in the Cash debit column, the account title Notes Receivable is written in the Other Accounts debit column and the amount of the debit to this account, $6,000. These two debits are offset by credit entries to Land, $5,000, and to Gain on Sale of Land, $2,000, in the Other Accounts credit column. An Other Accounts column is always necessary on each side of the cash receipts journal to record entries to those accounts not used frequently enough to warrant a special column.

Credits:
  1 Accounts Receivable. This column is used to list the credits to customers' accounts as receivables are collected. The name of the customer is written in the space entitled Account Credited to the left of the Accounts Receivable column.
  2 Sales. The existence of this column will save posting by permitting the accumulation of all sales for cash during the month and the posting of the column total at the end of the month as a credit to the Sales account (41).
  3 Other Accounts. This column is used for credits to any and all accounts other than Accounts Receivable and Sales. In some instances, a transaction may require credits to two accounts. Such cases are handled by using two lines of the special journal, as illustrated by the transaction of November 10, which required credits to both the Land account and to the Gain on Sale of Land account.

Cash Receipts Journal

	Date		Explanations	Debits		Other Accounts		
				Cash	Sales Discounts	Name	LP	Amount
Includes all transactions involving receipt of cash	19 Nov.	1	Investment by owner	25,000				
		4	Cash sales	300				
		5	Cash sales	400				
		8	Invoice Nov. 2, less 2%	441	9			
		10	Sale of land	1,000		Notes Receivable	3	6,000
		12	Invoice Nov. 4, less 2%	980	20			
		20	Invoice Nov. 18, less 2%	882	18			
		27	Cash sales	125				
		30	Obtained bank loan	4,000				
				33,128	47			6,000
				(1)	(43)			(X)

POSTING THE CASH RECEIPTS JOURNAL It is convenient to think of the posting of a cash receipts journal as being divided into two phases. The first phase consists of the daily posting of individual amounts throughout the month; the second phase consists of the posting of column totals at the end of the month.

Posting during the month Daily posting of the Accounts Receivable credits column is desirable. Each amount is posted to an individual customer's account in the accounts receivable subsidiary ledger. A check mark (✓) is placed in the cash receipts journal alongside each item posted to a customer's account to show that the posting operation has been performed. When debits and credits to customers' accounts are posted daily, the current status of each customer's account is available for use in making decisions as to further granting of credit and as a guide to collection efforts on past-due accounts.

The debits and credits in the Other Accounts sections of the cash receipts journal may be posted daily or at convenient intervals during the month. If this portion of the posting work is done on a current basis, less detailed work will be left for the busy period at the end of the month. As the postings of individual items are made, the number of the ledger account debited or credited is entered in the LP column of the cash receipts journal opposite the item posted. Evidence is thus provided in the special journal as to which items have been posted.

Posting column totals at month-end At the end of the month, the cash receipts journal is totaled and ruled as shown above and on page 193.

Page 1

Account Credited	Credits				
	Accounts Receivable			Other Accounts	
	√	Amount	Sales	LP	Amount
Capital Stock, $10 par				30	25,000
			300		
			400		
John Adams	√	450			
Land				11	5,000⎞
Gain on Sale of Land				40	2,000⎠
Harold Black	√	1,000			
C. D. Early	√	900			
			125		
Notes Payable				20	4,000
		2,350	825		36,000
		(5)	(41)		(X)

Before posting any of the column totals, it is first important to prove that **the sum of the debit column totals is equal to the sum of the credit column totals.**

After the totals of the cash receipts journal have been crossfooted, the following column totals are posted:

1 Cash debit column. Posted as a debit to the Cash account.
2 Sales Discounts debit column. Posted as a debit to the Sales Discounts account.
3 Accounts Receivable credit column. Posted as a credit to the controlling account, Accounts Receivable.
4 Sales credit column. Posted as a credit to the Sales account.

As each column total is posted to the appropriate account in the general ledger, the ledger account number is entered in parentheses just below the column total in the special journal. This notation shows that the column total has been posted and also indicates the account to which the posting was made. The totals of the Other Accounts columns in both the debit and credit sections of the special journal are not posted, because the amounts listed in the column affect various general ledger accounts and have already been posted as individual items. The symbol (X) may be placed below the totals of these two columns to indicate that no posting is made.

Cash payments journal

Another widely used special journal is the *cash payments journal,* sometimes called the *cash disbursements journal,* in which all payments of cash are recorded. Among the more common of these transactions are payments of accounts payable to creditors, payment of operating expenses, and cash purchases of merchandise.

The cash payments journal illustrated below and on page 195 contains entries for all November transactions of the Seaside Company which required the payment of cash.

Nov. **1** Paid rent on store building for November, $800.

2 Purchased merchandise for cash, $500.

8 Paid Barker & Bright for invoice of November 4, $700 less 2%.

9 Bought land, $15,000, and building, $35,000, for future use in business. Paid cash of $20,000 and signed a promissory note for the balance of $30,000. (Land and building were acquired in a single transaction.)

17 Paid salesmen's salaries, $600

26 Paid Dennis Co. for invoice of November 17, $900 less 2%.

27 Purchased merchandise for cash, $400.

28 Purchased merchandise for cash, $650.

29 Paid for newspaper advertising, $50.

29 Paid for three-year insurance policy, $720.

Note in the illustrated cash payments journal that the three credit columns are located to the left of the three debit columns; any se-

Cash Payments Journal

				Credits				
						Other Accounts		
	Date	Check No.	Explanations	Cash	Purchase Discounts	Name	LP	Amount
Includes all	19___							
transactions	Nov. 1	101	Paid November rent	800				
involving	2	102	Purchased merchandise	500				
payment of	8	103	Invoice of Nov. 4, less 2%	686	14			
cash	9	104	Bought land and building	20,000		Notes Payable	20	30,000
	17	105	Paid salesmen	600				
	26	106	Invoice of Nov. 17, less 2%	882	18			
	27	107	Purchased merchandise	400				
	28	108	Purchased merchandise	650				
	29	109	Newspaper advertisement	50				
	29	110	Three-year ins. policy	720				
				25,288	32			30,000
				(1)	(52)			(X)

quence of columns is satisfactory in a special journal as long as the column headings clearly distinguish debits from credits. The Cash column is often placed first in both the cash receipts journal and the cash payments journal because it is the column used in every transaction.

Good internal control over cash disbursements requires that all payments be made by check. The checks are serially numbered and as each transaction is entered in the cash payments journal, the check number is listed in a special column provided just to the right of the date column. An unbroken sequence of check numbers in this column gives assurance that every check issued has been recorded in the accounting records.

The use of the six money columns in the illustrated cash payments journal parallels the procedures described for the cash receipts journal.

POSTING THE CASH PAYMENTS JOURNAL The posting of the cash payments journal falls into the same two phases already described for the cash receipts journal. The first phase consists of the daily posting of entries in the Accounts Payable debit column to the individual accounts of creditors in the accounts payable subsidiary ledger. Check marks (√) are entered opposite these items to show that the posting has been made. If a creditor telephones to inquire about any aspect of his account, information on all purchases and payments made to date is readily available in the accounts payable subsidiary ledger.

Page 1

Account Debited	Debits				
	Accounts Payable			Other Accounts	
	√	Amount	Purchases	LP	Amount
Store Rent Expense				54	800
			500		
Barker & Bright	√	700			
Land				11	15,000⎱
Building				12	35,000⎰
Sales Salaries Expense				53	600
Dennis Co.	√	900			
			400		
			650		
Advertising Expense				55	50
Unexpired Insurance				6	720
		1,600	1,550		52,170
		(21)	(50)		(X)

The individual debit and credit entries in the Other Accounts columns of the cash payments journal may be posted daily or at convenient intervals during the month. As the postings of these individual items are made, the page number of the ledger account debited or credited is entered in the LP column of the cash payments journal opposite the item posted.

The second phase of posting the cash payments journal is performed at the end of the month. When all the transactions of the month have been journalized, the six money columns are totaled and ruled. The equality of debits and credits is then proved before posting.

After the totals of the cash payments journal have been proved to be in balance, the totals of the columns for Cash, Purchase Discounts, Accounts Payable, and Purchases are posted to the corresponding accounts in the general ledger. The numbers of the accounts to which these postings are made are listed in parentheses just below the respective column totals in the cash payments journal. The totals of the Other Accounts columns in both the debit and credit section of this special journal are not to be posted, and the symbol (X) may be placed below the totals of these two columns to indicate that no posting is required.

The general journal

When all transactions involving cash or the purchase and sale of merchandise are recorded in special journals, only a few types of transactions remain to be entered in the general journal. Examples include the purchase or sale of plant and equipment on credit, the return of merchandise for credit to a supplier, and the return of merchandise by a customer for credit to his account. The general journal is also used for the recording of adjusting and closing entries at the end of the accounting period.

The following transactions of the Seaside Company during November could not conveniently be handled in any of the four special journals and were therefore entered in the general journal (page 197).

Nov. 25 A customer, John Frost, was permitted to return for credit $50 worth of merchandise that had been sold to him on November 23.

28 The Seaside Company returned to a supplier, Excelsior, Inc., for credit $300 worth of the merchandise purchased on November 27.

29 Purchased for use in the business office equipment costing $1,225. Agreed to make payment within 30 days to XYZ Equipment Co.

Each of the three entries includes a debit or credit to a controlling account (Accounts Receivable or Accounts Payable) and also identifies by name a particular creditor or customer. When a controlling account is debited or credited by a *general journal entry,* the debit or credit must be posted twice: one posting to the controlling account in the general

General Journal
Page 1

Date		Account Titles and Explanations	LP	Dr	Cr
19—					
Nov.	25	Sales Returns and Allowances	42	50	
		Accounts Receivable, John Frost	5/ √		50
		Allowed credit to customer for return of merchandise from sale of Nov. 23.			
	28	Accounts Payable, Excelsior, Inc.	21/ √	300	
		Purchase Returns and Allowances . . .	51		300
		Returned to supplier for credit a portion of merchandise purchased on Nov. 27.			
	29	Office Equipment.	14	1,225	
		Accounts Payable, XYZ Equipment Co.	21/ √		1,225
		Purchased office equipment on 30-day credit.			

Transactions which do not fit any of the four special journals

ledger and another posting to a customer's account or a creditor's account in a subsidiary ledger. This double posting is necessary to keep each controlling account in agreement with the related subsidiary ledger.

For example, in the illustrated entry of November 25 for the return of merchandise by a customer, the credit part of the entry is posted twice:

1 To the Accounts Receivable controlling account in the general ledger; this posting is evidenced by listing the account number (5) in the LP column of the general journal.

2 To the account of John Frost in the subsidiary ledger for accounts receivable; this posting is indicated by the check mark (√) placed in the LP column of the general journal.

Showing the source of postings in ledger accounts

When a general journal and several special journals are in use, the ledger accounts should indicate the journal from which each debit and credit was posted. An identifying symbol is placed opposite each entry in the reference column of the account. The symbols used in this text are as follows:

S1	meaning page 1 of the sales journal
P1	meaning page 1 of the purchases journal
CR1	meaning page 1 of the cash receipts journal
CP1	meaning page 1 of the cash payments journal
J1	meaning page 1 of the general journal

The running balance form of account

The form of account generally used in the subsidiary ledgers for accounts receivable and accounts payable has three money columns: Debit, Credit, and Balance, as illustrated below for an account receivable.

Name of Customer

	19___			Ref	Debit	Credit	Balance
Subsidiary ledger: account receivable	July	1		S1	400		400
		20		S3	200		600
	Aug.	4		CR7		400	200
		15		S6	120		320

The advantage of this three-column form of account is that it shows at a glance the present balance receivable from the customer or payable to a creditor. The current amount of a customer's account, for example, is often needed as a guide to collection activities, or as a basis for granting additional credit. In studying the above illustration note also that the Reference column shows the source of each debit and credit.

The three-column running balance form of account is used by many companies for accounts in the general ledger as well as for subsidiary ledgers.

Accounts appearing in the accounts receivable subsidiary ledger are assumed to have debit balances. If one of these customers' accounts should acquire a credit balance by overpayment or for any other reason, the word *credit* should be written after the amount in the Balance column.

Accounts in the accounts payable subsidiary ledger normally have credit balances. If by reason of payment in advance or accidental overpayment, one of these accounts should acquire a debit balance, the word *debit* should be written after the amount in the Balance column.

Ledger accounts

THE GENERAL LEDGER The general ledger accounts of the Seaside Company illustrated on pages 199–201 indicate the source of postings from the various journals. The subsidiary ledger accounts appear on pages 201–202. To gain a clear understanding of the procedures for posting special journals, the student should trace each entry in the illustrated special journals into the general ledger accounts and also to the subsidiary ledger accounts where appropriate.

Note that the Cash account contains only one debit entry and one credit entry although there were many cash transactions during the month. The one debit, $33,128, represents the total cash received during the month and was posted from the cash receipts journal on November 30. Similarly, the one credit entry of $25,288 was posted on November 30 from the cash payments journal and represents the total of all cash payments made during the month.

Cash   1

General ledger accounts

19—					19—				
Nov.	30		CR1	33,128	Nov.	30		CP1	25,288

Notes Receivable   3

19—									
Nov.	10		CR1	6,000					

Accounts Receivable   5

19—					19—				
Nov.	30		S1	6,195	Nov.	25		J1	50
						30		CR1	2,350

Unexpired Insurance   6

19—									
Nov.	29		CP1	720					

Land   11

19—					19—				
Nov.	9		CP1	15,000	Nov.	10		CR1	5,000

Building   12

19—									
Nov.	9		CP1	35,000					

Office Equipment   14

19—									
Nov.	29		J1	1,225					

Notes Payable   20

					19—				
					Nov.	9		CP1	30,000
						30		CR1	4,000

Accounts Payable 21

| General ledger accounts (continued) | 19__ Nov. | 28 | | J1 | 300 | 19__ Nov. | 29 | | J1 | 1,225 |
| | | 30 | | CP1 | 1,600 | | 30 | | P1 | 7,250 |

Capital Stock, $10 par 30

| | | | | | | 19__ Nov. | 1 | | CR1 | 25,000 |

Gain on Sale of Land 40

| | | | | | | 19__ Nov. | 10 | | CR1 | 2,000 |

Sales 41

| | | | | | | 19__ Nov. | 30 | | CR1 | 825 |
| | | | | | | | 30 | | S1 | 6,195 |

Sales Returns and Allowances 42

| 19__ Nov. | 25 | | J1 | 50 | | | | | | |

Sales Discounts 43

| 19__ Nov. | 30 | | CR1 | 47 | | | | | | |

Purchases 50

| 19__ Nov. | 30 | | CP1 | 1,550 | | | | | | |
| | 30 | | P1 | 7,250 | | | | | | |

Purchase Returns and Allowances 51

| | | | | | | 19__ Nov. | 28 | | J1 | 300 |

Purchase Discounts 52

| | | | | | | 19__ Nov. | 30 | | CP1 | 32 |

Sales Salaries Expense 53

| 19__ Nov. | 17 | | CP1 | 600 | | | | | | |

Store Rent Expense 54

<table>
<tr><td rowspan="2">General ledger accounts (continued)</td><td>19___</td><td></td><td></td><td></td><td></td><td></td><td></td><td></td><td></td><td></td></tr>
<tr><td>Nov.</td><td>1</td><td></td><td>CP1</td><td>800</td><td></td><td></td><td></td><td></td><td></td></tr>
</table>

Advertising Expense 55

19___									
Nov.	29		CP1	50					

ACCOUNTS RECEIVABLE LEDGER The subsidiary ledger for accounts receivable appears as follows after the posting of the various journals has been completed.

John Adams

<table>
<tr><td rowspan="3">Customers' accounts</td><td>19___</td><td></td><td></td><td></td><td></td><td></td></tr>
<tr><td>Nov.</td><td>2</td><td>S1</td><td>450</td><td></td><td>450</td></tr>
<tr><td></td><td>8</td><td>CR1</td><td></td><td>450</td><td>0</td></tr>
</table>

Harold Black

19___					
Nov.	4	S1	1,000		1,000
	12	CR1		1,000	0

Robert Cross

19___					
Nov.	5	S1	975		975

H.R. Davis

19___					
Nov.	11	S1	620		620

C. D. Early

19___					
Nov.	18	S1	900		900
	20	CR1		900	0

John Frost

19___					
Nov.	23	S1	400		400
	25	J1		50	350

D. H. Gray

19___					
Nov.	29	S1	1,850		1,850

ACCOUNTS PAYABLE LEDGER The accounts with creditors in the accounts payable subsidiary ledger are as follows:

Alabama Supply Co.

Creditors' accounts

19____						
Nov.	2		P1		3,325	3,325

Barker & Bright

19____						
Nov.	4		P1		700	700
	8		CP1	700		0

Canning & Sons

19____						
Nov.	10		P1		500	500

Dennis Co.

19____						
Nov.	17		P1		900	900
	26		CP1	900		0

Excelsior, Inc.

19____						
Nov.	27		P1		1,825	1,825
	28		J1	300		1,525

XYZ Equipment Co.

19____						
Nov.	29		J1		1,225	1,225

Proving the ledgers

At the end of each accounting period, proof of the equality of debits and credits in the general ledger is established by preparation of a trial balance, as illustrated in preceding chapters. When controlling accounts and subsidiary ledgers are in use, it is also necessary to prove that each subsidiary ledger is in agreement with its controlling account. This proof is accomplished by preparing a schedule of the balances of accounts in each subsidiary ledger and determining that the totals of these schedules agree with the balances of the corresponding controlling accounts. The trial balance and schedules of accounts receivable and accounts payable for the Seaside Company are shown on page 203.

SEASIDE COMPANY
Trial Balance
November 30, 19___

General ledger trial balance

Cash	$ 7,840	
Notes receivable	6,000	
Accounts receivable (see schedule below)	3,795	
Unexpired insurance	720	
Land	10,000	
Building	35,000	
Office equipment	1,225	
Notes payable		$34,000
Accounts payable (see schedule below)		6,575
Capital stock, $10 par value		25,000
Gain on sale of land		2,000
Sales		7,020
Sales returns and allowances	50	
Sales discounts	47	
Purchases	8,800	
Purchase returns and allowances		300
Purchase discounts		32
Sales salaries expense	600	
Store rent expense	800	
Advertising expense	50	
	$74,927	$74,927

SEASIDE COMPANY
Schedule of Accounts Receivable
November 30, 19___

Subsidiary ledgers in balance with controlling accounts

Robert Cross	$ 975
H. R. David	620
John Frost	350
D. H. Gray	1,850
Total (per general ledger controlling account)	$3,795

SEASIDE COMPANY
Schedule of Accounts Payable
November 30, 19___

Alabama Supply Co.	$3,325
Canning & Sons	500
Excelsior, Inc.	1,525
XYZ Equipment Co.	1,225
Total (per general ledger controlling account)	$6,575

Variations in special journals

The number of columns to be included in each special journal and the number of special journals to be used will depend upon the nature of the particular business and especially upon the volume of the various kinds of transactions. For example, the desirability of including a Sales Discounts column in the cash receipts journal depends upon whether a business offers discounts to its customers for prompt payment and whether the customers frequently take advantage of such discounts.

A retail store may find that customers frequently return merchandise for credit. To record efficiently this large volume of sales returns, the store may establish a sales returns and allowances journal. A purchase returns and allowances journal may also be desirable if returns of goods to suppliers occur frequently.

Special journals should be regarded as laborsaving devices which may be designed with any number of columns appropriate to the needs of the particular business. A business will usually benefit by establishing a special journal for any type of transaction that occurs quite frequently.

Direct posting from invoices

In many business concerns the efficiency of data processing is increased by posting sales invoices directly to the customers' accounts in the accounts receivable ledger rather than copying sales invoices into a sales journal and then posting to accounts in the subsidiary ledger. If the sales invoices are serially numbered, a file or binder of duplicate sales invoices arranged in numerical order may take the place of a formal sales journal. By accounting for each serial number, it is possible to be certain that all sales invoices are included. At the end of the month, the invoices are totaled on an adding machine, and a general journal entry is made debiting the Accounts Receivable controlling account and crediting Sales for the total of the month's sales invoices.

Direct posting may also be used in recording purchase invoices. As soon as purchase invoices have been verified and approved, credits to the creditors' accounts in the accounts payable ledger may be posted directly from the purchase invoices.

The concept of direct posting from invoices to subsidiary ledgers is mentioned here as further evidence that accounting records and procedures can be designed in a variety of ways to meet the individual needs of different business concerns.

MECHANICAL ACCOUNTING SYSTEMS

The processing of accounting data may be performed manually, mechanically, or electronically. The term *data processing* includes the preparation of documents (such as invoices and checks) and the flow of the data contained in these documents through the major accounting steps of recording, classifying, and summarizing. A well-designed system produces an uninterrupted flow of all essential data needed by management for planning and controlling business operations.

Unit record for each transaction

Our discussion has thus far been limited to a manual accounting system. One of the points we have emphasized is that an immediate record should be made of every business transaction. The *medium* used to make this record is usually a document or form, such as an invoice or a check. This concept of a unit record for each transaction is an important one as we consider the alternatives of processing these media by accounting machines, by punched cards, or by a computer. Regardless of whether we use mechanical or electronic equipment, the document representing a single transaction is a basic element of the accounting process.

Use of office equipment in a manual data processing system

Manually kept records are a convenient means of demonstrating accounting principles, and they are also used by a great many small businesses. Strictly defined, a manual system of processing accounting data would call for handwritten journals, ledgers, and financial statements. Even in a small business with some handwritten records, however, the use of office machines and laborsaving devices such as cash registers, adding machines, desk calculators, and multicopy forms has become standard practice.

Simultaneous preparation of documents, journals, and ledgers

Traditionally, each business transaction was recorded, copied, and recopied. A transaction was first evidenced by a document such as a sales invoice, then copied into a journal (book of original entry), and later posted to a ledger. This step-by-step sequence of creating accounting records is time-consuming and leaves room for the introduction of errors at each step. Whenever a figure, an account title, or an account number is copied, the danger of introducing errors exists. This is true regardless of whether the copying is done with pen and ink or by punching a machine keyboard. The copying process is subject to human errors. From this premise it follows that if several accounting records can be created by writing a transaction only once, the recording process will be not only faster but also more accurate.

Accounting machines

The development of accounting machines designed to create several accounting records with a single writing of a transaction has progressed at a fantastic rate. Machines with typewriter keyboards and computing mechanisms were early developments useful in preparing journals, invoices, payrolls, and other records requiring the typing of names and the computation of amounts. *Accounting machines* is a term usually applied to mechanical or electronic equipment capable of performing arithmetic functions and used to produce a variety of accounting records and reports.

Punched cards and tabulating equipment

Punched cards are a widely used medium for recording accounting data. Information such as amounts, names, account numbers, and other details is recorded by punching holes in appropriate columns and rows of a standard-sized card, usually by means of a *key-punch machine.* The information punched on the cards can then be read and processed by a variety of machines, including computers.

Every business receives original documents such as invoices and checks in many shapes and sizes. By punching the information on each such document into a card, we create a document of standard size which machines and computers can use in creating records and reports. For example, once the information on sales invoices has been punched into cards, these cards can be run through machines to produce a schedule of accounts receivable, an analysis of sales by product, by territory, and by each salesman, and a listing of commissions earned by salesmen.

Processing accounting data by means of punched cards may be viewed as three major steps, with specially designed machines for each step. The first step is that of recording data; a machine often used for this purpose is an electrically operated *key punch* with a keyboard similar to that of a typewriter.

The second major step is classifying or sorting the data into related groups or categories. For this step a machine called a *sorter* is used. The sorter reads the information on each punched card and then arranges the cards in a particular order, or sorts a deck of cards into groups based on the relationship of the data punched into the cards.

The third major step is summarizing the data. This step is performed by a *tabulating machine,* which has an *output* of printed information resulting from the classifying and totaling of the data on the cards.

EDP ACCOUNTING SYSTEMS

The term *electronic data processing* (EDP) refers to the processing of data by electronic computers. A computer-based accounting system processes data in basically the same manner as does a manual or mechanical system. Transactions are initially recorded manually on source documents. The data from these source documents are then keypunched into punched cards which can be read by the computer. The computer processes the information and performs such routine tasks as printing journals (called transaction summaries), posting to ledger accounts, determining account balances, and printing financial statements and other reports.

The primary advantage of the computer is its incredible speed. The number of computations made by an electronic computer is measured in millions per second. In one minute, an electronic printer can produce as much printed material as the average clerk typist in a day. Because of this speed, ledger accounts may be kept continually up-to-date and current reports may be quickly prepared at any time to assist executives in making decisions.

Elements of an EDP system

An electronic data processing system includes a computer, also called a *central processing unit* (CPU), and a number of related machines, which are often called *peripheral equipment.* The computer is the heart of the system; it performs the processing function which includes the storage of information, arithmetic computations, and control. The other two major elements are (*1*) *input* devices which prepare and insert information into the computer and (*2*) *output* devices which transfer information out of the computer to the accountant or other user. Both input and output devices perform the function of *translation.* The machines used to feed information into a computer translate the data into computer language; the output devices translate the processed data back into the language of written words, or of punched cards, paper tape, or magnetic tape.

The relationship of the control unit, the arithmetic unit, the storage unit, and the devices for input and output are portrayed in the diagram on page 208.

HARDWARE AND SOFTWARE The machines and related equipment used in an EDP system are called *hardware.* All the other materials utilized in selecting, installing, and operating the system (except the operating personnel) are called *software.* Software includes not only the *computer programs* (the sequence of instructions given to the computer), but also feasibility studies, training materials such as films and

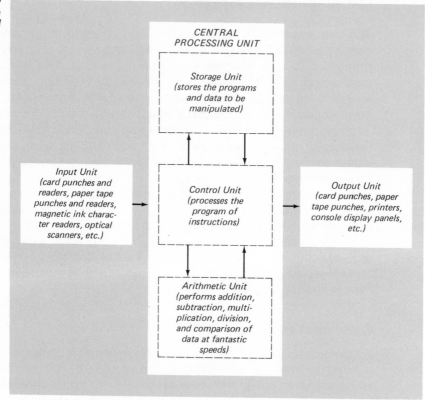

manuals, studies of equipment requirements, and everything about the EDP system other than the hardware.

Input devices

Among the input devices used to transfer instructions and accounting data into a computer are card readers, punched-paper-tape readers, magnetic-tape readers, character readers, and terminals. The card-reading device will either transmit information from punched cards into the memory unit of the computer or convert the information to paper or magnetic tape. Punched cards will be read by the card-reading devices at rates of several hundred or even several thousand per minute.

Punched-paper tape can be created as part of the process of recording transactions on cash registers or adding machines. This type of input medium is inexpensive to create and easy to use, but it does not permit the insertion of additional data or the making of corrections after the tape has been punched. Punched-tape readers deliver the data to the computer at high speeds. Both punched-card readers and paper-tape readers are usually connected directly to the computer and are described as part of the *on-line* (direct access) system. They offer the advantage of compatibility with nonelectronic equipment utilizing punched cards or tape.

Magnetic tape is a far faster means of feeding information into a computer and has the advantage of being easily stored. Corrections are also easily made on magnetic tape. Magnetic-tape reels are, however, more expensive than paper tape.

Character-reading machines are perhaps best known in the banking field. They read the account numbers printed in magnetic ink on checks and deposit tickets and convert these data into codes acceptable to the computer. Another type of character-reading device is the optical scanner, with a photoelectric cell which can read a printed document and convert the characters into computer language. This device makes unnecessary the costly step of translating printed matter into punched-card form.

Terminals are keyboard devices which make it possible to enter limited amounts of data into an EDP system without punching the information into cards or tape as a preliminary step. Terminals are extremely slow in comparison with the operating capacity of the computer because they are manually operated. However, terminals have the advantage of allowing the various departments of a business to enter data directly into the accounting system, without having to send their source documents to an EDP department to be keypunched and read into the computer. Some retail stores use terminals in the sales departments to instantly adjust customers' accounts receivable and record each sale in the accounting records. Terminals are also equipped with a printing device which permits output from the computer to be delivered immediately to the user of the terminal.

Output devices

The *printer* is the most important output device. It interprets the computer code and prints several hundred lines per minute, either at the computer center or at remote locations. The printer might be used to produce payroll checks, customers' statements, and many types of accounting reports.

Card-punching machines and paper-tape-punching machines transfer data from the computer into punch cards and paper tape which later may be used as input data for subsequent analysis or processing.

Processing operations in the computer

The processing operations performed by a computer include storage of information, arithmetic manipulation of data, and control. The computer receives and stores instructions and data; it calls this information from the memory or storage unit as required by the processing routine; it goes through arithmetic operations, makes comparisons of numbers, and takes the action necessary to produce the required output of information.

The term *control* describes the ability of the computer to guide itself through the processing operations utilizing detailed lists of instructions concerning the work to be done.

PROGRAM A *program* is a series of steps planned to carry out a certain process, such as the preparation of a payroll. Each step in the program is a command or instruction to the computer. A program for payroll might be compared with a very detailed written set of instructions given to an inexperienced employee assigned to the payroll function in a manual accounting system. A most important attribute of the computer is its ability to receive and store a set of instructions which controls its behavior.

The preparation of a computer program is a complicated and costly task. A company may employ its own programmers or may rely on outside organizations which specialize in such services.

Differences between mechanical and electronic data processing systems

Mechanical data processing equipment such as electric calculators, mechanical accounting machines, and key-punch machines is extremely slow when compared with electronic equipment. The processing of data in the electronic system is accomplished by electric impulses traveling through electronic circuits. Such equipment functions hundreds of times faster than mechanical devices.

Another point of contrast is that the units of equipment comprising an EDP system are interconnected so that the processing of data is a continuous operation from the point of reading input data to the point of printing the report or other final result. On the other hand, a mechanical data processing system employs separate machines which do not communicate directly with each other. After each machine, such as a key punch, has performed its function, the output media (punched cards or paper tape) must be transported manually to another machine.

Reliability of EDP systems

EDP equipment itself is highly reliable, and the possibility of errors caused by the hardware is very small. However, the use of reliable equipment does not entirely eliminate the possibilities of errors in the accounting records. Errors may still be made in the preparation of source documents. The process of keypunching data into punched cards is comparable to using a typewriter, and making errors is quite possible. Also, the computer program may contain errors which may cause the data to be processed improperly. To reduce the possibility of these types of errors, an EDP system should include both *input controls* and *program controls.*

INPUT CONTROLS Input controls are the precautions taken to insure that the data being entered into the computer are correct. One important input control is the manual preparation of *control totals,* representing the total dollar amount of all source documents sent to the EDP department for processing. The computer will add up the total dollar amount of all data processed and print this total as part of the computer output. The manually prepared control totals may then be compared to the total printed by the computer to ensure that all source documents sent to the EDP department have been processed.

Another input control is the use of a *verifier key punch.* When data are keypunched into punched cards, there is always the possibility of striking the wrong key, causing a keypunching error. A verifier key punch is used to keypunch the source data into the punched cards a second time; any differences between the first and second keypunching cause the machine to signal that an error has been made.

PROGRAM CONTROLS Program controls are error-detecting measures built into the computer program. An example of a program control is a *limit test,* which compares every item of data processed by the computer to a specified dollar limit. In the event an amount exceeds the dollar limit, the computer does not process that item and prints out an *error report.* A limit test is particularly effective in such computer applications as preparing paychecks, when it is known that none of the paychecks should be for more than a specified amount, such as $1,000.

Another example of a program control is an *item count.* The total number of punched cards to be processed by the computer is determined, and that total is entered as part of the input to the computer. The computer then counts the number of cards it processes, and if this number differs from the predetermined total, an error report is printed. This item count ensures that all the punched cards are actually processed by the computer.

Accounting applications of the computer

The use of electronic data processing equipment is possible for virtually every phase of accounting operations. Even the CPA, in conducting an annual audit, may use the computer as an audit tool. For this purpose he may employ specially written computer programs to aid in his work of sampling and analyzing data to determine the fairness of the financial statements.

The most common application of the computer, however, is to process large masses of accounting data relating to routine repetitive operations such as accounts receivable, accounts payable, inventories, payrolls, and posting to ledger accounts.

PAYROLLS In a manual accounting system the preparation of payroll checks is usually separate from the maintenance of records showing pay rates, positions, time worked, payroll deductions, and other personnel data. An EDP system, however, has the capability of maintaining all records relating to payroll as well as turning out the required paychecks. Payroll processing is usually one of the first accounting operations to be placed on the computer.

The payroll procedure consists of determining for each employee gross earnings, making deductions, computing net pay, preparing the payroll check, and maintaining a record of each individual's earnings. In addition, the company needs a payroll summary for each period and usually a distribution of payroll costs by department, by product, or classified by the various productive processes. The payroll function has become increasingly complex and time-consuming in recent years because of the advent of social security taxes, income tax withholding, and other payroll deductions. Each employee must receive not only a payroll check but a statement showing the gross earnings, deductions, and net pay. The company's records must be designed to facilitate filing with the federal and state governments regular payroll reports showing amounts withheld for income taxes, unemployment insurance, and social security. The time and the expense required to prepare payrolls has risen in proportion to the need for more information. The demands by governments, labor unions, credit unions, and other outside agencies have added to the problem.

An EDP payroll system will not only maintain the necessary records, print the checks, and print these reports, but it can also keep management informed of the costs of various functions within the business. For example, data can be produced showing the man-hours and labor costs on each job, labor cost by department for each salesclerk, or the time required by different employees to perform similar work. In other words, much current information can be developed without significant extra expense that will provide management with a detailed breakdown of labor costs. The comparison below and on page 213 illustrates the efficiency of processing payrolls by EDP rather than manually:

	Function	Payroll Prepared Manually	Payroll Prepared by EDP
Payroll may be prepared either manually or by EDP	1 Timekeeping	Employer fills in new set of records each period, making extensions manually.	Employer enters raw data on appropriate forms.

2 Computation of gross pay	Compute gross pay for each employee, perhaps with desk calculator, and enter manually in records.	Performed electronically.
3 Calculation of deductions	For each employee, refer to charts and make computations; enter manually in records.	Performed electronically.
4 Prepare checks, earnings statements, and payroll register	Write by hand or type checks. Proofread and maintain controls.	Performed electronically.
5 Bank reconciliation	Reconcile payroll bank account per books with monthly bank statement.	Performed electronically.
6 Reports to government	Prepare quarterly reports showing for each employee and in total amounts earned, deducted, and paid. Reconcile individual data with controls.	Performed electronically.
7 Managerial control data	Prepare distribution of hours and labor cost by department or by job. Other analyses may be needed.	Performed electronically.

COMPUTER-BASED JOURNALS AND LEDGERS As mentioned earlier in this chapter, computers may also be used to maintain the journals and ledgers and to prepare financial statements. Transactions and end-of-period adjustments must still be analyzed by persons possessing a knowledge of accounting principles. However, after these transactions have been analyzed and prepared in computer input form, the computer can be used to print the journals, post to the ledger accounts, and print the financial statements and other financial reports. The advantage of maintaining accounting records by computer is that the possibility of mathematical errors is greatly reduced, and the speed of the computer permits the records to be kept continuously up-to-date.

Other accounting applications of computers include forecasting the profit possibilities inherent in alternative courses of action, analyzing gross profit margins by department or by product line, and determining future cash requirements long in advance. Recent developments of accounting applications of the computer provide much more information about business operations than was available to management in the past.

Computer service centers and time-sharing

A computer and related hardware are costly to buy or rent. The employment of personnel qualified to operate the equipment is also a major expense, especially for a small business. One way in which a small business can avoid investing large sums yet gain the operating efficiencies of EDP is to turn over its raw data to a bank, an accounting firm, or a computer center that offers EDP services on a fee basis. The small business may either keypunch its data and send the punched cards to the service center for processing or write the data on special forms and let the service center do the keypunching.

Another method of using EDP services without owning a computer is called *time-sharing.* Time-sharing refers to using a large central computer by means of a portable terminal, which is both an input and output device. Through these terminals, hundreds of businesses may make use of the same central computer. The company which owns the central computer sends each of these users a monthly bill, including a fixed monthly charge plus a per-minute charge for the actual time spent using the computer. Since the portable terminals communicate with the central computer using ordinary telephone lines, the terminals may be thousands of miles away from the central computer.

An advantage of time-sharing is the convenience of direct access to the computer through a portable terminal. A disadvantage, however, is that a terminal enters data into the computer using a manual keyboard. This is a relatively slow way of entering large quantities of data into a computer. If large quantities of data must be processed, a computer service center may be less expensive than time-sharing.

Do computers make decisions?

Computers can do only what they have specifically been told to do. Computers cannot make decisions in the sense of exercising judgment. They can choose among alternatives only by following the specific instructions contained in the program. When a computer encounters a situation for which it has not been programmed, it is unable to act. Computer programs must therefore be carefully tested to determine that they provide the computer with adequate instructions for all aspects of the data processing.

Information systems

The automation of an accounting system speeds up the production and transmission of information. The term *integrated data processing* (IDP) describes the current trend of providing attachments for typewriters, accounting machines, cash registers, and other conventional equipment which will, as a by-product, produce perforated tape or cards acceptable to a computer. The typewriter, for example, when equipped with such attachments can be used not only to prepare conventional business documents but simultaneously to provide the same information in a form compatible with input requirements of a computer. The *integration* of processes for recording information in conventional form and concurrently providing input media for an EDP system eliminates the intermediate work of transferring information from invoices, checks, and other documents to the tape or cards acceptable for processing by the computer.

The integration of an accounting system suggests that forms and procedures are not designed for the needs of a single department but rather as part of a complete *information system* for the entire business. To create such an integrated system, the accounting systems specialist tries to coordinate all paper work and procedures in a manner that will provide a rapid and uninterrupted flow of all information needed in the conduct of the business as an entity.

DEMONSTRATION PROBLEM

The Signal Corporation began operations on November 1, 19___. The chart of accounts used by the company included the following accounts, among others:

Cash	*10*	*Purchases*	*60*
Marketable securities	*15*	*Purchase returns & allowances*	*62*
Inventory of office supplies	*18*	*Purchase discounts*	*64*
Notes payable	*30*	*Salaries expense*	*70*
Accounts payable	*32*	*Utilities expense*	*71*

November transactions relating to the purchase of merchandise and to accounts payable are listed below, along with selected other transactions.

Nov. 1 Purchased merchandise from Moss Co. for $3,000. Invoice dated today; terms 2/10, n/30.

Nov. 3 Received shipment of merchandise from Wilmer Co. and invoice dated November 2 for $7,600; terms 2/10, n/30.

Nov. 6 Purchased merchandise from Archer Company at cost of $5,600. Invoice dated November 5; terms 2/10, n/30.

Nov. 9 Purchased marketable securities, $1,200.

Nov. 10 Issued check to Moss Co. in settlement of invoice dated November 1, less discount.

Nov. 12 Received shipment of merchandise from Cory Corporation and their invoice dated November 11 in amount of $7,100; terms net 30 days.

Nov. 14 Issued check to Archer Company in settlement of invoice of November 5.

Nov. 16 Paid cash for office supplies, $110.

Nov. 17 Purchased merchandise for cash, $950.

Nov. 19 Purchased merchandise from Klein Co. for $11,500. Invoice dated November 18; terms 2/10, n/30.

Nov. 21 Purchased merchandise from Belmont Company for $8,400. Invoice dated November 20; terms 1/10, n/30.

Nov. 24 Purchased merchandise for cash, $375.

Nov. 26 Purchased merchandise from Brooker Co. for $6,500. Invoice dated today; terms 1/10, n/30.

Nov. 28 Paid utilities, $150.

Nov. 30 Paid salaries for November, $2,900.

Nov. 30 Paid $2,600 cash to Wilmer Co. and issued 6%, 90-day promissory note for $5,000 in settlement of invoice dated November 2.

Instructions

a Record the transactions in the appropriate journals. Use a single-column purchases journal and a six-column cash payments journal.
b Indicate how postings would be made by placing ledger account numbers and check marks in the appropriate columns of the journals.
c Prepare a schedule of accounts payable at November 30 to prove that the subsidiary ledger is in balance with the controlling account.

SOLUTION TO DEMONSTRATION PROBLEM

a & b   **Purchases Journal**   Page 1

Date		Account Credited		Invoice Date		Amount
19___				19___		
Nov.	1	Moss Co.	(terms 2/10, n/30)	Nov.	1	3,000
	3	Wilmer Co.	(terms 2/10, n/30)		2	7,600
	6	Archer Company	(terms 2/10, n/30)		5	5,600
	12	Cory Corporation	(terms net 30)		11	7,100
	19	Klein Co.	(terms 2/10, n/30)		18	11,500
	21	Belmont Company	(terms 1/10, n/30)		20	8,400
	26	Brooker Co.	(terms 1/10, n/30)		26	6,500
						49,700
						(60)(32)

Cash Payments Journal

				Credits			
						Other Accounts	
Date		Explanation	Cash	Purchase Discounts	Name	LP	Amount
19___							
Nov	9	Bought securities	1,200				
	10	Invoice, Nov. 1,					
		less 2%	2,940	60			
	14	Invoice, Nov. 5,					
		less 2%	5,488	112			
	16	Purchased office					
		supplies	110				
	17	Cash purchases	950				
	24	Cash purchases	375				
	28	Paid utilities	150				
	30	Paid salaries	2,900				
	30	Invoice, Nov. 2, note					
		issued for unpaid					
		balance	2,600		Notes Payable	30	5,000
			16,713	172			5,000
			(10)	(64)			(X)

c

SIGNAL CORPORATION

Schedule of Accounts Payable
November 30, 19___

Belmont Company	$ 8,400
Brooker Co.	6,500
Cory Corporation	7,100
Klein Co.	11,500
Total (*per general ledger controlling account*)	$33,500

REVIEW QUESTIONS

1 What advantages are offered by the use of special journals?

2 Pine Hill General Store makes about 500 sales on account each month, using only a two-column general journal to record these transactions. What would be the extent of the work saved by using a sales journal?

3 When accounts receivable and accounts payable are kept in subsidiary ledgers, will the general ledger continue to be a self-balancing ledger with equal debits and credits? Explain.

4 Explain how, why, and when the cash receipts journal and cash payments journal are crossfooted.

5 During November the sales on credit made by the Hardy Company actually amounted to $41,625, but an error of $1,000 was made in totaling the

Cash Payments Journal (continued)

			Debits		
				Other Accounts	
Account Debited	**√**	**Accounts Payable**	**Purchases**	**LP**	**Amount**
Marketable Securities				15	1,200
Moss Co.	√	3,000			
Archer Company	√	5,600			
Inventory of Office Supplies				18	110
			950		
			375		
Utilities Expense				71	150
Salaries Expense				70	2,900
Wilmer Co.	√	7,600			
		16,200	1,325		4,360
		(32)	(60)		(X)

amount column of the sales journal. When and how will the error be discovered?

6 Considerable repetitious copying work may be entailed in the preparation of a sales invoice, a sales journal, and a receivables ledger. Is this step-by-step sequence with its attendant opportunity for errors a characteristic of all types of accounting systems? Explain.

7 What are the principal advantages of electronic data processing in the accounting department of a company?

8 In which phases or areas of accounting can EDP equipment be used to advantage? Which phases can most conveniently and advantageously be converted to electronic data processing?

9 What avenues are open to a small business interested in gaining the efficiencies of electronic data processing, but which lacks funds for purchase or rental of a computer and also does not have employees familiar with computer operations?

10 Evaluate the following quotation: "The computer will ultimately replace both bookkeepers and accountants and will be able to make many of the decisions now made by top management."

11 Distinguish between *hardware* and *software* as these terms are used in data processing systems.

12 Explain the meaning of the term *computer program.*

13 What are the principal elements of an electronic data processing system?

14 Explain the meaning of the term *input control* and give an example.

15 Explain the meaning of the term *program control* and give an example.

EXERCISES

Ex. 6-1 The Bell Company uses a cash receipts journal, a cash payments journal, a sales journal, a purchases journal, and a general journal.
   a In which of the five journals would you expect to find the smallest number of transactions recorded?
   b At the end of the accounting period, the total of the sales journal should be posted to what account or accounts? As a debit or credit?
   c At the end of the accounting period, the total of the purchases journal should be posted to what account or accounts? As a debit or credit?
   d Name two subsidiary ledgers which would probably be used in conjunction with the journals listed above. Identify the journals from which postings would normally be made to each of the two subsidiary ledgers.
   e In which of the five journals would adjusting and closing entries be made?

Ex. 6-2 Datamatic Company uses a cash receipts journal, a cash payments journal, a sales journal, a purchases journal, and a general journal. Indicate which journal should be used to record each of the following transactions:
   a Purchase of merchandise on account
   b Purchase of delivery truck for cash
   c Return of merchandise by a customer for credit to his account
   d Payment of taxes
   e Adjusting entry to record depreciation
   f Purchase of typewriter on account
   g Sale of merchandise on account
   h Sale of merchandise for cash
   i Refund to a customer who returned merchandise sold him for cash
   j Return of merchandise to a supplier for credit

Ex. 6-3 A check for $4,410 was received from a customer within 10 days from the date of sending him a sales invoice for $4,500, with terms of 2/10, n/30. In recording the receipt of the check, the employee maintaining the cash receipts journal entered $4,410 in the Cash column and $4,500 in the Accounts Receivable column. He made no entry in the Sales Discounts column. What procedure should bring this error to light?

Ex. 6-4 Potter Company maintains a general journal and also four special journals for cash receipts, cash payments, sales, and purchases of merchandise. On January 31, the Accounts Receivable control account in the general ledger had a debit balance of $100,000, and the Accounts Payable control account had a credit balance of $30,000.

During February the sales journal included transactions which totaled $60,000. The purchases journal included transactions totaling $35,000. In the cash receipts journal the Accounts Receivable column showed a credit total for February of $46,000. In the cash payments journal, the Accounts Payable column showed a debit total of $38,000.

a What posting would be made of the total of the $46,000 Accounts Receivable column total in the cash receipts journal at February 28?

b What posting would be made of the $60,000 total of the sales journal at February 28?

c What posting would be made of the $35,000 total of the purchases journal at February 28?

d Based on the above information, state the balances of the Accounts Receivable controlling account and the Accounts Payable controlling account in the general ledger after completion of posting at February 28.

Ex. 6-5 Rager Company maintains its sales journal and accounts receivable subsidiary ledger by EDP. Each day the accounting department prepares a control total of total credit sales and sends the sales invoices to the EDP department. The sales data are keypunched in the EDP department, and the punched cards and a control figure representing the total number of sales transactions (per the invoices) are entered into the computer.

The computer prepares the sales journal, posts to the accounts receivable ledger (maintained on magnetic tape), and performs an item count. Any discrepancy in the item count is printed out on an error report. A copy of the sales journal for each day is sent back to the accounting department for comparison with the daily control totals.

What control procedure will first detect the following independent errors?

a A sales invoice is lost on the way from the accounting department to the EDP department.

b Several punched cards are lost before being processed by the computer.

c A sales invoice for $310 is accidentally keypunched as $3,100.

PROBLEMS

6-1 Yamamoto Company uses a two-column general journal, a one-column sales journal, a one-column purchases journal, a six-column cash receipts journal, and a six-column cash payments journal similar to those illustrated in this chapter. Three ledgers are used: a general ledger, an accounts receivable subsidiary ledger, and an accounts payable subsidiary ledger. The general ledger, as well as the subsidiary ledgers, is in the three-column running balance form. At November 30, the subsidiary ledger for accounts receivable consisted of the following accounts with customers.

A. Ashcroft

Date		Explanation	Ref	Debit	Credit	Balance
19—						
nov.	3		S 4	275		275
	9		S 4	325		600
	27		CR 2		400	200

B. Bradford

Date		Explanation	Ref	Debit	Credit	Balance
19—						
Oct.	31	Balance				1620
nov.	8		CR 1		1000	620
	8		J 1		200	420
	28		CR 2		420	– 0 –

C. Crutchfield

Date		Explanation	Ref	Debit	Credit	Balance
19—						
Oct.	31	Balance				1100
nov.	10		J 1		250	850
	11		S 4	625		1475
	30		CR 2		940	535

D. Dunleer

Date		Explanation	Ref	Debit	Credit	Balance
19—						
nov.	4		S 4	2200		2200
	29		S 4	600		2800
	29		CR 2		2200	600

Instructions Prepare the general ledger controlling account, Accounts Receivable, in a three-column running balance form. Include the beginning balance at October 31, all entries during November, and the running balance of the account. Show the dates and sources (journal and page number) of all items posted to the controlling account.

6-2 The chart of accounts used by the Toole Corporation included the following accounts, among others:

Cash	10	Sales	50
Notes receivable	15	Sales returns & allowances	52

Accounts receivable	17	Sales discounts	54	
Land	20	Purchases	60	
Office equipment	25	Purchase returns & allowances	62	
Notes payable	30	Interest revenue	82	
Accounts payable	32	Gain on sale of land	85	

The sales activity, cash receipts, and certain other transactions for the month of April are presented below:

Apr. 1 Sold merchandise to Logan Company for cash, $1,545.

Apr. 4 Sold merchandise to ExCello Company, $5,300. Invoice No. 618; terms 2/10, n/30.

Apr. 5 Returned $680 of merchandise to a supplier for a cash refund.

Apr. 8 Sold merchandise to Daley Company for $2,700. Invoice No. 619; terms 2/10, n/30.

Apr. 9 Received a check from Brussels Company in payment of a $1,500 invoice, less 2% discount.

Apr. 11 Received $700 from Blue Company in payment of a past-due invoice.

Apr. 13 Received check from ExCello Company in settlement of invoice dated April 4, less discount.

Apr. 16 Sold merchandise to Califax Company, $2,600. Invoice No. 620; terms 2/10, n/30.

Apr. 16 Returned $600 of merchandise to supplier, ABC Corporation, for reduction of account payable.

Apr. 18 Purchased office equipment at a cost of $1,900, signing a 8%, 90-day note payable for the full amount.

Apr. 20 Sold merchandise to Jackson Company for $4,800. Invoice No. 621; terms 2/10, n/30.

Apr. 21 Califax Company returned for credit $400 of merchandise purchased on April 16.

Apr. 23 Borrowed $15,000 cash from a local bank, signing an 8%, six-month note payable.

Apr. 25 Received payment in full from Califax Company in settlement of invoice dated April 16, less return and discount.

Apr. 29 Sold land costing $19,000 for $7,000 cash and a 9%, two-year note receivable for $21,000. (Credit Gain on Sale of Land for $9,000.)

Apr. 30 Collected from Jackson Company amount of invoice dated April 20, less 2% discount.

Apr. 30 Collected $8,120 in full settlement of an $8,000, 9%, 60-day note receivable held since March 1. (No interest revenue has yet been recorded.)

Apr. 30 Received a 60-day, non-interest-bearing note from Daley Company in settlement of invoice dated April 8.

Instructions

Record the above transactions in the appropriate journals. Use a single-column sales journal, a six-column cash receipts journal, and a two-column general journal. Foot and rule the special journals and indicate how postings would be made by placing ledger account numbers and check marks in the appropriate columns of the journals.

6-3 Aztec Corporation began operations on May 1. All May transactions relating to the purchase of merchandise and to accounts payable are listed below, along with selected other transactions.

May 1 Purchased merchandise from Fowler Brothers at cost of $2,600. Invoice dated today; terms 2/10, n/30.

May 4 Purchased merchandise from King Co. for $8,400. Invoice dated May 3; terms 2/10, n/30.

May **5** Returned for credit to Fowler Brothers defective merchandise having a list price of $800.

May **6** Received shipment of merchandise from Lance Company and their invoice dated May 5 in amount of $5,700. Terms net 30 days.

May **8** Purchased merchandise from Davis Company, $6,800. Invoice dated today with terms of 1/10, n/60.

May 10 Purchased merchandise from Ray Company, $8,300. Invoice dated May 9; terms 2/10, n/30.

May 10 Issued check to Fowler Brothers in settlement of balance resulting from purchase of May 1 and purchase return of May 5.

May 11 Issued check to King Co. in payment of May 3 invoice.

May 18 Issued check to Ray Company in settlement of invoice dated May 9.

May 20 Purchased merchandise for cash, $300.

May 21 Bought land, $18,000, and building, $40,000, for expansion of business. Paid cash of $10,000 and signed a promissory note for the balance of $48,000. (Land and building were acquired in a single transaction from R. J. Sheehan.)

May 23 Purchased merchandise for cash, $250.

May 26 Purchased merchandise from Miller Company for $9,000. Invoice dated May 25; terms 2/10, n/30.

May 28 Paid cash for office supplies, $75.

May 29 Purchased merchandise for cash, $525.

May 31 Paid salaries for May, $2,200.

The chart of accounts used by Aztec Corporation included the following accounts, among others.

Cash	10	Accounts payable	30
Inventory of office supplies	18	Purchases	50
Land	20	Purchase returns and allowances	52
Building	22	Purchase discounts	53
Notes payable	28	Salaries	60

Instructions

a Record the transactions in the appropriate journals. Use a single-column purchases journal, a six-column cash payments journal, and a two-column general journal. Foot and rule the special journals. Make all postings to the proper general ledger accounts and to the accounts payable subsidiary ledger.

b Prepare a schedule of accounts payable at May 31 to prove that the subsidiary ledger is in balance with the controlling account for accounts payable.

6-4 Dixieline Company uses multicolumn cash receipts and cash payments journals similar to those illustrated in this chapter. The cash activities for the month of May are presented below:

May **1** Sold additional capital stock in the company for $15,000 cash.

May **1** Purchased U.S. government bonds, $3,000.

May **2** Paid May rent, $1,200.

May **2** Cash sales of merchandise, $4,100.

May **4** Purchased fixtures, $3,500, making a down payment of $500 and issuing a note payable for the balance.

May **9** Received $700 as partial payment of Orr Co. invoice of $2,100 and 60-day, 10% note for the balance.

May 12 Paid Bowker Co. invoice, $3,000 less 2%.

May 13 Sold land costing $2,500 for $2,950.

May 15 Received $1,274 in full settlement of Crosby Company invoice after allowing 2% discount.

May 19 Cash purchase of merchandise, $2,400.

May 20 Paid note due today, $1,700, and accrued interest amounting to $34.
May 21 Sold U.S. government bonds costing $1,000 for $975.
May 23 Paid installment on note payable due today, $480, of which $234 represented interest expense.
May 25 Cash sales of merchandise, $3,015.
May 25 Paid Daly Company invoice, $3,300 less 2%.
May 26 Purchased three-year fire insurance policy, $390.
May 28 Cash purchase of merchandise, $2,150.
May 30 Received payment in full settlement of Jensen Company invoice, $2,600, less 2%.
May 31 Paid monthly salaries, $2,678.

Instructions
Enter the above transactions in a six-column journal for cash receipts and a six-column journal for cash payments. Compute column totals and rule the journals. Determine the equality of debits and credits in column totals.

6-5 Deerborne Company maintains special journals for sales, purchases, cash receipts, and cash payments. All sales and purchases are made on account. During the month of April, all transactions were recorded in the special journals; no entries were made in the general journal. The after-closing trial balance on March 31 and the unadjusted trial balance on April 30 are shown below:

	After-closing Trial Balance, March 31		Trial Balance, April 30	
Cash	$ 35,600		$ 26,800	
Accounts receivable	48,000		52,200	
Inventory	50,400		50,400	
Equipment	70,000		73,600	
Accumulated depreciation: equipment		$ 15,000		$ 15,000
Accounts payable		39,000		26,000
Capital stock		100,000		120,000
Retained earnings		50,000		50,000
Sales				34,000
Purchases			25,000	
Salaries expense			8,000	
Advertising expense			2,000	
Supplies expense			1,500	
Property tax expense			2,500	
Miscellaneous expense			3,000	
	$204,000	$204,000	$245,000	$245,000

Instructions
a Prepare a schedule showing all sources of cash receipts during April.
b Prepare a schedule showing the purpose of all cash payments made during April.
c Prepare one compound journal entry (general journal form) summarizing all April transactions involving the receipt of cash. The entry should include a debit to Cash and credits to other accounts for the amounts indicated in **a**.

d Prepare one compound journal entry (general journal form) summarizing all April transactions involving the payment of cash. The entry should include a credit to Cash and debits to other accounts for amounts indicated in *b.*

6-6 The Neighborhood Store, Inc., began operations on July 1, and established an accounting system using the following accounts:

Cash	10	Sales	50
Marketable securities	13	Sales returns & allowances	52
Notes receivable	14	Sales discounts	54
Accounts receivable	15	Purchases	60
Merchandise inventory	17	Purchase returns & allowances	62
Unexpired insurance	19	Purchase discounts	64
Land	20	Transportation-in	66
Building	21	Rent expense	70
Furniture and fixtures	24	Salaries expense	72
Notes payable	30	Taxes expense	74
Accounts payable	32	Supplies expense	76
Mortgage payable	36	Insurance expense	78
Capital stock	40	Interest earned	80
Retained earnings	42	Interest expense	83
Income summary	45	Loss on sale of securities	84

The transactions for the month of July are listed below and on page 225.

July 1 Sold capital stock for $60,000, and deposited this amount in the bank under the name The Neighborhood Store, Inc.

July 3 Purchased land and building on contract, paying $30,000 cash and signing a mortgage for the remaining balance of $95,000. Estimated value of the land was $55,000.

July 6 Purchased merchandise from Drill Company, $6,100. Invoice dated today; terms 2/10, n/30.

July 7 Sold merchandise to J. V. Thomas, $3,000. Invoice No. 1; terms 2/10, n/60.

July 7 Sold merchandise for cash, $740.

July 7 Paid $270 for a two-year fire insurance policy.

July 10 Paid freight charges of $205 on Drill Company purchase of July 6.

July 12 Sold merchandise to Everett Company, $4,900. Invoice No. 2; terms 2/10, n/60.

July 13 Purchased merchandise for cash, $1,420.

July 15 Received payment in full from J. V. Thomas; Invoice No. 1, less 2% discount.

July 15 Purchased securities for cash, $1,600.

July 16 Issued credit memorandum No. 1 to Everett Company, $400, for goods returned today.

July 16 Paid Drill Company invoice of July 6, less discount.

July 18 Purchased merchandise from Wyatt Corporation, $3,700. Invoice dated today; terms 2/10, n/30.

July 20 A portion of merchandise purchased from Wyatt Corporation was found to be substandard. After discussion with the vendor, a price reduction of $100 was agreed upon and debit memorandum No. 1 was issued in that amount.

July 22 Received payment in full from Everett Company; Invoice No. 2, less returns and discount.

July 23 Purchased merchandise from Drill Company, $4,200. Invoice dated today; terms 2/10, n/60.

July 25 Sold for $1,420 the securities purchased on July 15.

July 27 Sold merchandise for cash, $515.

July 28 Borrowed $3,000 from the bank, issuing a 60-day, 10% note payable as evidence of indebtedness.

July 28 Paid Wyatt Corporation invoice dated July 18, less discount and return of $100.

July 30 Paid first installment on mortgage, $1,100. This payment included interest of $690.

July 30 Purchased merchandise for cash, $920.

July 31 Paid monthly salaries of $2,115.

July 31 Sold merchandise to B. Frank, $2,750. Invoice No. 3; terms 2/10, n/60.

Instructions

Enter the July transactions in the following journals:

Two-column general journal

One-column sales journal

One-column purchases journal

Six-column cash receipts journal

Six-column cash payments journal

Foot and rule all special journals and show how postings would be made by placing ledger account numbers and check marks in the appropriate columns of the journals.

6-7 Sunset Building Supply Co. uses the following accounts in recording transactions:

Cash	10	Dividends	53
Notes receivable	14	Sales	60
Accounts receivable	16	Sales returns and allowances	62
Supplies	17	Sales discounts	64
Unexpired insurance	18	Purchases	70
Equipment	26	Purchase returns and allowances	72
Accumulated depreciation: equip-		Purchase discounts	74
ment	28	Transportation-in	76
Notes payable	30	Salaries expense	80
Accounts payable	32	Supplies expense	84
Dividends payable	34	Insurance expense	86
Mortgage payable	40	Depreciation expense: equipment	88
Capital stock	50	Gain on sale of equipment	90
Retained earnings	52	Interest expense	92

The schedules of accounts receivable and accounts payable for the company at August 31, 19___, are shown below:

Schedule of Accounts Receivable August 31, 19___		Schedule of Accounts Payable August 31, 19___	
Fast Contracting	$4,160	Quality Plaster, Inc.	$6,000
Slowe Paving Co.	1,750		
Total	$5,910		

The September transactions of Sunset Building Supply Co. were as follows:

Sept. 2 Purchased merchandise on account from Quality Plaster, Inc., $5,600. Invoice was dated today with terms of 2/10, n/30.

Sept. 3 Sold merchandise to Fast Contracting, $3,200. Invoice No. 428; terms 2/10, n/30.

Sept. 4 Purchased supplies for cash, $175. (Debit the asset account, Supplies.)

Sept. 5 Sold merchandise for cash, $1,120.

Sept. 7 Paid the Quality Plaster, Inc., invoice for $6,000, representing August purchases. No discount is allowed by Quality Plaster, Inc.

Sept. 10 Purchased merchandise from Axle Company, $6,500. Invoice dated September 9 with terms of 1/10, n/30.

Sept. 10 Collected from Fast Contracting for invoice No. 428 for $3,200, and for August sales of $4,160 on which the discount had lapsed.

Sept. 12 Sold merchandise to Martin Company, $4,350. Invoice No. 429; terms 2/10, n/30.

Sept. 14 Paid freight charges of $410 on goods purchased September 10 from Axle Company.

Sept. 14 Sold equipment for $1,800, receiving cash of $300 and a 30-day, 7% note receivable for the balance. Equipment cost $4,000 and accumulated depreciation was $2,600. (Debit Accumulated Depreciation: Equipment for $2,600 and credit Gain on Sale of Equipment for $400.)

Sept. 15 Issued credit memorandum No. 38 in favor of Martin Company upon return of $200 of merchandise.

Sept. 18 Paid for one-year fire insurance policy, $285.

Sept. 18 Purchased merchandise for cash, $1,525.

Sept. 19 Paid the Axle Company invoice dated September 9, less the 1% discount.

Sept. 20 Sold merchandise on account to Evans Brothers, $2,730; invoice No. 430. Required customer to sign a 30-day, non-interest-bearing note. (Record this sale by a debit to Accounts Receivable, then transfer from Accounts Receivable to Notes Receivable by means of an entry in the general journal.)

Sept. 22 Purchased merchandise for cash, $810.

Sept. 22 Sold merchandise for cash, $935.

Sept. 22 Received payment from Martin Company for invoice No. 429. Customer made deduction for credit memorandum No. 38 issued September 15, and a 2% discount.

Sept. 23 Sold merchandise on account to Tracy Corp., $1,990. Invoice No. 431; terms 2/10, n/30.

Sept. 24 Declared a cash dividend of $7,500 on capital stock, payable October 20, 19___.

Sept. 25 Purchased merchandise from Davis Company, $5,300. Invoice dated September 24 with terms of 2/10, n/60.

Sept. 26 Issued debit memorandum No. 42 to Davis Company in connection with merchandise returned today amounting to $425.

Sept. 27 Purchased equipment having a list price of $12,000. Paid $2,000 down and signed a promissory note for the balance of $10,000.

Sept. 30 Paid monthly salaries of $2,960 for services rendered by employees during September.

Sept. 30 Paid monthly installment on mortgage, $700, of which $204 was interest.

Instructions

a Record the September transactions in the following journals:
    General journal—2 columns
    Sales journal—1 column
    Purchases journal—1 column
    Cash receipts journal—6 columns
    Cash payments journal—6 columns

Foot and rule all special journals and show how postings would be made by placing ledger account numbers and check marks in the appropriate columns of the journals.

b Prepare a schedule of accounts receivable and accounts payable as of September 30, 19___.

BUSINESS DECISION PROBLEM 6

Custom-Look is a mail-order clothing company which sells to the public at discount prices. Recently Custom-Look initiated a new policy allowing a 15-day free trial on all clothes bought from the company. At the end of the 15-day period, the customer may either pay cash for his purchase or return the goods to Custom-Look. The new policy caused such a large boost in sales that, even after considering the many sales returns, the policy appeared quite profitable.

The accounting system of Custom-Look includes a sales journal, purchases journal, cash receipts journal, cash payments journal, and a general journal. As an internal control procedure, an officer of the company reviews and initials every entry in the general journal before the amounts are posted to the ledger accounts. Since the 15-day free trial policy has been in effect, hundreds of entries recording sales returns have been entered in the general journal each week. Each of these entries has been reviewed and initialed by an officer of the firm, and the amounts have been posted to Sales Returns & Allowances and to the Accounts Receivable controlling account in the general ledger, and also to the customer's account in the accounts receivable subsidiary ledger.

Since these sales return entries are so numerous, it has been suggested that a special journal be designed to handle them. This could not only save time in journalizing and posting the entries, but also eliminate the time-consuming individual review of each of these repetitious entries by the officer of the company.

Instructions

a How many amounts are entered in the general journal to record a single sales return transaction? Are these amounts the same?

b Explain why these transactions are suited to the use of a special journal. Explain in detail how many money columns the special journal should have, and what postings would have to be done either at the time of the transaction or at the end of the period.

c Assume that there were 2,000 sales returns during the month. How many postings would have to be made during the month if these transactions were entered in the general journal? How many postings would have to be made if the special journal you designed in *b* were used? (Assume a one-month accounting period.)

d Assume that a general journal entry requires 60 seconds to write and a special journal entry can be written in 20 seconds. Also assume that each posting requires an average of 20 seconds and that the officer of the company averages 25 seconds to review and initial a general journal entry for a sales return. The officer estimates he could review the entire sales return special journal in 10 minutes. How much time (expressed in hours, minutes, and seconds) would be required to journalize, review, and post 2,000 entries in (1) general journal form and (2) special journal form? What is the time savings resulting from using the special journal?

e If the estimated cost of designing a sales returns journal and training employees in its use were $700, would you recommend adopting such a journal? Present a case to support your decision, assuming that the labor cost of operating either system averages $6 per hour.

SEVEN

FORMS OF BUSINESS ORGANIZATION

Three forms of business organization are common to American industry: the single proprietorship, the partnership, and the corporation. When these forms of organization were introduced in Chapter 1, it was emphasized that most accounting principles apply to all three forms and that the main area of difference lies in the accounting for owners' equity. In this chapter we shall describe briefly some accounting processes peculiar to single proprietorships and partnerships, and then move to a discussion of corporations. Our consideration of accounting and reporting problems relating to corporations will be continued in Chapter 8.

SINGLE PROPRIETORSHIPS

Accounting for the owner's equity in a single proprietorship

A balance sheet for a single proprietorship shows the entire ownership equity as a single dollar amount without any effort to distinguish between the amount originally invested by the owner and the later increase or decrease in owner's equity as a result of profitable or unprofitable operations. A corporation must maintain separate accounts for capital stock and retained earnings, because distributions to owners in the form of dividends cannot legally exceed the earnings of the corporation. In an unincorporated business, however, the owner is free to withdraw assets from the business at any time and in any amount.

The accounting records for a single proprietorship do not include accounts for capital stock, retained earnings, or dividends. Instead of these accounts, a *capital* account and a *drawing* account are maintained for the owner.

CAPITAL ACCOUNT (AS, FOR EXAMPLE, JOHN JONES, CAPITAL) The capital account is credited with the amount of the proprietor's original investment in the business and also with any subsequent investments. When the accounts are closed at the end of each accounting period, the Income Summary account is closed into the owner's capital account. Thus the capital account is credited with the net income earned (or debited with the net loss incurred). Withdrawals by the proprietor during the period are debited to a drawing account and later closed to the capital account. The total ownership equity in the business, therefore, appears as a single amount in the balance sheet.

DRAWING ACCOUNT (AS, FOR EXAMPLE, JOHN JONES, DRAWING) A withdrawal of cash or other assets by the owner reduces his ownership equity in the business and could be recorded by debiting his capital account. However, a clearer record is created if a separate drawing account is maintained. The drawing account is debited for any of the following transactions:

1 Withdrawals of cash or other assets. If the proprietor of a clothing store, for example, withdraws merchandise for his personal use, his Drawing account is debited for the cost of the goods withdrawn. The offsetting credit is to the Purchases account (or to Inventory if a perpetual inventory system is maintained).
2 Payment of the proprietor's personal bills out of the business bank account.
3 Collection of an account receivable of the business, with the cash collected being retained personally by the proprietor.

Withdrawals by the proprietor (like dividends to stockholders) are not an expense of the business. Expenses are incurred for the purpose of generating revenue, and a withdrawal of cash or other assets by the proprietor does not have this purpose.

Closing the accounts

The revenue and expense accounts of a single proprietorship are closed into the Income Summary account in the same way as for a corporation. However, the net income or net loss is closed to the proprietor's Capital account rather than to a Retained Earnings account. To complete the closing of the accounts, the balance of the Drawing account is transferred into the proprietor's Capital account.

Financial statements and work sheet for a single proprietorship

The balance sheet of a single proprietorship differs from the balance sheet of a corporation only in the owner's equity section. An illustration of the ownership equity portion of the balance sheet for a proprietorship, a partnership, and a corporation was presented in Chapter 1, page 23.

A statement of owner's equity may be prepared in a form similar to the statement of retained earnings used by a corporation. An illustration follows:

JONES INSURANCE AGENCY
Statement of Owner's Equity
For the Year Ended December 31, 1977

Net income	John Jones, capital, Jan. 1, 1977	$ 80,400
exceeded	Add: Net income for year	30,500
withdrawals		
by owner	Subtotal	$110,900
	Less: Withdrawals	24,000
	John Jones, capital, Dec. 31, 1977	$ 86,900

The income statement for a single proprietorship does not include any salary expense representing managerial services rendered by the owner. One reason for not including among the expenses a salary to the owner-manager is the fact that he would be able to set his own salary at any amount he chose. The use of an unrealistic salary to the proprietor would tend to destroy the significance of the income statement as a device for measuring the earning power of the business. Another reason may be that in the proprietor's own thinking he is not working for a salary when he manages his own business but is investing his time in order to make a profit.

Another distinctive feature of the income statement for a single proprietorship is that income tax is not included. The proprietor reports on his individual tax return the taxable income from his business and from other sources such as personal investments. The rate of tax is determined by the total of his income; consequently, the tax applicable to the income from the business is influenced by factors unrelated to the business enterprise. As explained later in this chapter, the financial statements for a corporation will include income tax expense in the income statement and income taxes payable among the current liabilities in the balance sheet.

The work sheet for a single proprietorship is similar to the work sheet for a corporation, except that a pair of columns for Owner's Capital replaces the pair of columns for Retained Earnings.

PARTNERSHIPS

A *partnership* may be defined as "an association of two or more persons to carry on, as co-owners, a business for profit." In the professions and in businesses which stress the factor of personal service, the partnership form of organization is widely used. The laws of some states may even deny the incorporation privilege to persons engaged in such professions as law and public accounting, because the personal responsibility of the professional practitioner to his client might be lost behind the impersonal corporate entity. However, an increasing number of states are now affording professionals the privilege of incorporating. In the fields of manufacturing, wholesaling, and retail trade, the partnership form is popular, because it affords a convenient means of combining the capital and abilities of two or more persons.

Features of a partnership

Before taking up the accounting problems of partnerships, it will be helpful to point out some of the distinctive characteristics of the partnership form of organization.

EASE OF FORMATION A partnership can be created without any legal formalities. When two or more persons agree to become partners, a partnership is created. The voluntary aspect of a *partnership agreement* means that no one can be forced into a partnership or forced to continue as a partner.

LIMITED LIFE A partnership may be ended at any time by the death or withdrawal of any member of the firm. Other factors which may bring an end to a partnership include the bankruptcy or incapacity of a partner or the completion of the project for which the partnership was formed. The admission of a new partner or the retirement of an existing partner means an end to the old partnership, although the business may be continued by the formation of a new partnership.

MUTUAL AGENCY Each partner generally acts as an agent of the partnership, with authority to enter into contracts. The partnership is bound by the acts of any partner as long as these acts are within the scope of normal operations. The factor of mutual agency suggests the need for exercising great caution in the selection of a partner.

UNLIMITED LIABILITY Each partner in a *general partnership* is personally responsible for the debts of the partnership. The lack of any ceiling on the liability of a general partner may deter a wealthy person from entering a general partnership. In a *limited partnership* one (or more) of the partners has no personal liability for the debts of the partnership.

CO-OWNERSHIP OF PARTNERSHIP PROPERTY AND PROFITS When a partner invests property other than cash in a partnership, he does not retain any personal right to such property. The property becomes jointly owned by all partners. Similarly, each partner has an ownership right in the profits earned by the partnership.

Advantages and disadvantages of a partnership

Perhaps the most important advantage and the principal reason for the formation of most partnerships is the opportunity to bring together sufficient capital to carry on a business. The opportunity to combine special skills, as, for example, the specialized talents of engineers, accountants, or lawyers may also induce individuals to join forces in a partnership. Members of a partnership enjoy more freedom and flexibility of action than do the owners of a corporation; the partners may withdraw funds and make business decisions of all types without the necessity of formal meetings or legalistic procedures. Finally, operating as a partnership may, in certain instances, result in significant income tax advantages.

Offsetting these advantages of a partnership are such serious disadvantages as limited life, unlimited liability, and mutual agency. Furthermore, if a business is to require a very large amount of capital, the partnership is a less effective device for raising the capital than is a corporation.

Partnership accounting

An adequate accounting system and an accurate measurement of net income are needed by every business, but they are especially important in a partnership because the net income is divided among two or more partners. Each partner needs accurate information on net income so that he can make intelligent decisions on such questions as additional investments, expansion of the business, or sale of his ownership interest.

To illustrate the significance to partners of accurate accounting data, consider the following case. Allen and Baker became partners, each investing $50,000. Allen maintained the accounting records and fraudulently contrived to make the financial statements show operating losses although the business was in fact quite profitable. Discouraged by these misleading financial statements, Baker sold his share of the business to Allen for $20,000, when in fact his equity was worth considerably more than his original investment of $50,000.

Partnership accounting requires the maintenance of separate capital and drawing accounts for each partner. The accounting entries in these accounts parallel those discussed earlier in this chapter for a single proprietorship.

The other distinctive feature of partnership accounting is the division of net income or loss among the partners in the proportions specified by the partnership agreement. In the study of partnership accounting, the new concepts lie almost entirely in the owners' equity section; accounting for partnership assets and liabilities follows the same principles as for other forms of business organization.

RECORDING INITIAL INVESTMENTS When a partner invests assets other than cash, a question always arises as to the value of such assets; the valuations assigned to non-cash assets should be their *fair market values* at the date of transfer to the partnership. The valuations assigned must be agreed to by all the partners.

To illustrate the opening entries for a newly formed partnership, assume that on January 1 John Blair and Richard Cross, who operate competing retail stores, decide to form a partnership by consolidating their two businesses. A capital account will be opened for each partner and credited with the agreed valuation of the *net assets* (total assets less total liabilities) he invests. The journal entries to open the accounting records of the partnership of Blair and Cross are as follows:

Formation of partnership	*Cash*	*20,000*	
	Accounts Receivable	*30,000*	
	Inventory	*45,000*	
	Accounts Payable		*10,000*
	John Blair, Capital		*85,000*
	To record the investment by John Blair.		
	Cash	*5,000*	
	Land	*30,000*	
	Building	*50,000*	
	Inventory	*30,000*	
	Accounts Payable		*30,000*
	Richard Cross, Capital		*85,000*
	To record the investment by Richard Cross.		

The values assigned to assets on the books of the new partnership may be quite different from the amounts at which these assets were carried on the records of their previous owners. For example, the land invested by Cross and now valued at $30,000 might have appeared in his records at a cost of $10,000. The building which he invested was valued at $50,000 by the partnership, but it might have cost Cross only $40,000 some years ago and might have been depreciated in his records to a book value of $35,000. Assuming that market values of land and buildings had risen sharply while Cross owned this property, it is no more than fair to recognize the present market value of these assets at the time he transfers them to the partnership and to credit his capital account accordingly. Depreciation of the building will begin anew in the records of the partnership (except for income tax purposes) and will be based on the assigned value of $50,000 at date of acquisition by the partnership.

ADDITIONAL INVESTMENTS BY PARTNERS Any additional investments made by partners after the organization of the partnership will be recorded in the same manner as the initial investments. We shall assume that Blair and Cross made no additional investments during the year.

WITHDRAWALS BY PARTNERS In our example of the Blair and Cross partnership, we might assume that the partners made numerous withdrawals during the year. Partners may make withdrawals at any time; there is no need for a formal "declaration" as in the case of dividends paid by a corporation. The amounts withdrawn need not be the same for all partners. The withdrawals by Blair and Cross are represented by the following summary entry:

Recording
withdrawals
by partners

John Blair, Drawing	*6,000*	
Richard Cross, Drawing	*4,000*	
Cash		*10,000*

To record withdrawals by partners.

CLOSING ENTRIES The revenue and expense accounts of a partnership are closed into the Income Summary account in the same way as for a corporation. However, the net income or net loss shown by the Income Summary account is closed into the partners' Capital accounts rather than to a Retained Earnings account. Finally, the Drawing accounts are closed by transferring their balances into the partners' Capital accounts. The following entries illustrate these procedures:

Dividing the
net income

Income Summary	*30,000*	
John Blair, Capital		*15,000*
Richard Cross, Capital		*15,000*

To transfer net income of $30,000 for the year from the Income Summary account to the partners' Capital accounts. Blair and Cross share net income equally.

Closing the
drawing
accounts

John Blair, Capital	*6,000*	
Richard Cross, Capital	*4,000*	
John Blair, Drawing		*6,000*
Richard Cross, Drawing		*4,000*

To close the Drawing accounts by transferring their debit balances to the respective Capital accounts.

INCOME STATEMENT AND INCOME DISTRIBUTION FOR A PARTNERSHIP
The income statement for a partnership may include a final section to show the division of the net income between the partners, as illustrated at the top of page 235 for the firm of Blair and Cross.

BLAIR AND CROSS
Income Statement
For the Year Ended December 31, 19___

<table>
<tr><td rowspan="4" align="right">**Note**
distribution
of net
income</td><td>Sales . . . .</td><td></td><td>$300,000</td></tr>
<tr><td>Less: Cost of goods sold . . . .</td><td></td><td>130,000</td></tr>
<tr><td>Gross profit on sales . . . .</td><td></td><td>$170,000</td></tr>
<tr><td>Operating expenses:</td><td></td><td></td></tr>
<tr><td></td><td>Selling . . . .</td><td>$100,000</td><td></td></tr>
<tr><td></td><td>General & administrative . . . .</td><td>40,000</td><td>140,000</td></tr>
<tr><td></td><td>Net income . . . .</td><td></td><td>$ 30,000</td></tr>
<tr><td></td><td></td><td></td><td></td></tr>
<tr><td></td><td>Distribution of net income:</td><td></td><td></td></tr>
<tr><td></td><td>To John Blair (50%) . . . .</td><td>$ 15,000</td><td></td></tr>
<tr><td></td><td>To Richard Cross (50%) . . . .</td><td>15,000</td><td>$ 30,000</td></tr>
</table>

STATEMENT OF PARTNERS' CAPITALS The partners will usually want an explanation of the change in their capital accounts from one year-end to the next. A financial statement called a *statement of partners' capitals* is prepared to show this information and is illustrated below for the partnership of Blair and Cross:

BLAIR AND CROSS
Statement of Partners' Capitals
For the Year Ended December 31, 19___

<table>
<tr><td></td><td></td><td>*Blair*</td><td>*Cross*</td><td>*Total*</td></tr>
<tr><td rowspan="5" align="right">*Changes in*
partners'
capitals
during the
year</td><td>Investment, Jan. 1, 19___ . . . .</td><td>$ 85,000</td><td>$ 85,000</td><td>$170,000</td></tr>
<tr><td>Add: net income for the year . . . .</td><td>15,000</td><td>15,000</td><td>30,000</td></tr>
<tr><td>Subtotals . . . .</td><td>$100,000</td><td>$100,000</td><td>$200,000</td></tr>
<tr><td>Less: Withdrawals . . . .</td><td>6,000</td><td>4,000</td><td>10,000</td></tr>
<tr><td>Partners' capitals, Dec. 31, 19___ . . . .</td><td>$ 94,000</td><td>$ 96,000</td><td>$190,000</td></tr>
</table>

The balance sheet for Blair and Cross would show the capital balance for each partner, as well as the total ownership equity of $190,000.

Alternative methods of dividing partnership income

In the preceding illustration, the partners divided net income equally. Partners can, however, share net income in any way they wish. Factors that partners might consider in arriving at an equitable plan to divide net income include (1) the amount of time each partner devotes to the business, (2) the amount of capital invested by each partner, and (3) any other contribution by each partner to the success of the partnership. Net income, for example, may be shared in any agreed ratio such as 4 to 1, in the ratio of average capital invested, or in a fixed ratio after an allowance is made to each partner for salary and interest on capital invested.

Assume that the partnership of Adams and Barnes earned $24,000 (before interest and salary allowances to partners) in Year 1 and that they had agreed to share net income as follows:

1 Salary allowances of $6,000 per year to Adams and $12,000 per year to Barnes. (Partners' salaries are merely a device for sharing net income and are not necessarily withdrawn from the business.)

2 Interest at 6% on average capitals to be allowed to each partner. Average capital balances for Adams and Barnes amounted to $40,000 and $10,000, respectively.

3 Any amount in excess of the foregoing salary and interest allowances to be divided equally.

Pursuant to this agreement, the net income of $24,000 would be divided between Adams and Barnes as follows:

Distribution of Net Income

Income **Net income to be divided**.			*$24,000*
sharing; **Salaries to partners:**			
salaries,			
interest, and **Adams**	*$ 6,000*		
fixed ratio **Barnes**	*12,000*	*$18,000*	
as basis **Interest on average capitals:**			
Adams ($40,000 × 0.06)	*$ 2,400*		
Barnes ($10,000 × 0.06)	*600*	*3,000*	*21,000*
Remaining net income to be divided equally			*$ 3,000*
Adams	*$ 1,500*		
Barnes	*1,500*	*3,000*	

This three-step division of the year's net income of $24,000 has resulted in giving Adams a total of $9,900 and Barnes a total of $14,100. The amounts credited to each partner may be summarized as follows:

	Adams	*Barnes*	*Total*
Income **Salaries**	*$6,000*	*$12,000*	*$18,000*
allocated to **Interest on average capitals**	*2,400*	*600*	*3,000*
each			
partner. . . **Remaining income divided equally**	*1,500*	*1,500*	*3,000*
Totals	*$9,900*	*$14,100*	*$24,000*

The entry to close the Income Summary account will be:

. . .may be Income Summary	24,000	
recorded in Adams, Capital		9,900
a single		
journal Barnes, Capital		14,100

entry To close the Income Summary account by crediting each partner with his authorized salary, with interest on his average capital at 6%, and by dividing the remaining net income equally.

AUTHORIZED SALARIES AND INTEREST IN EXCESS OF NET INCOME In the preceding example the total of the authorized salaries and interest was $21,000 and the net income to be divided was $24,000. Suppose that the net income had been only $15,000; how should the division have been made? If the partnership contract provides for salaries and interest on invested capital, these provisions are to be followed even though the net income for the year is less than the total of the authorized salaries and interest. Thus, a net income of $15,000 would be distributed as follows:

Distribution of Net Income

Net income to be divided			$15,000
Salaries to partners:			
Adams	$ 6,000		
Barnes	12,000	$18,000	
Interest on average capitals:			
Adams ($40,000 × 0.06)	$ 2,400		
Barnes ($10,000 × 0.06)	600	3,000	21,000
Residual loss to be divided equally			$ 6,000
Adams		$ 3,000	
Barnes		3,000	6,000

Authorized salaries and interest may exceed net income

    The result of this distribution of the net income of $15,000 has been to give Adams a total of $5,400 and Barnes a total of $9,600.

    Partnerships are not required to pay income taxes; however, a partnership is required to file an *information tax return* showing the amount of the partnership net income and the share of each partner in the net income. Each partner must include his share of the partnership net income (including interest and salary allowances) on his individual income tax return, regardless of the amount that he actually withdrew from the business. Partnership net income is thus taxable to the partners individually in the year in which it is earned.

Other aspects of partnership accounting

The foregoing discussion of partnership accounting is by no means exhaustive. The admission of a new partner to the partnership, the withdrawal of a partner, and the liquidation of a partnership, for example, may raise some very complex accounting issues. These issues are primarily of interest to advanced accounting students and for that reason are not included in this introductory text.

CORPORATIONS

The corporation has become the dominant form of business organization on the American economic scene, probably because it gathers together large amounts of capital more readily than single proprietorships or partnerships. Because of its efficiency as a device for pooling the savings of many individuals, the corporation is an ideal means of obtaining the capital necessary for large-scale production and its inherent economies. Virtually all large businesses are corporations.

A corporation has been defined as "an artificial being, invisible, intangible, and existing only in contemplation of the law." A corporation is regarded as a legal entity, having a continuous existence apart from that of its owners. By way of contrast, a partnership is a relatively unstable type of organization which is dissolved by the death or retirement of any one of its members, whereas the continuous existence of a corporation is in no way threatened by the death of a stockholder.

Ownership in a corporation is evidenced by transferable shares of stock, and the owners are called *stockholders* or *shareholders.* To administer the affairs of the corporation, the stockholders elect a *board of directors.* The directors in turn select a president and other corporate officers to carry on active management of the business.

Advantages of the corporate form of organization

The corporation offers a number of advantages not available in other forms of organization. Among these advantages are the following:

1 *Greater amounts of capital can be gathered together* Some corporations have a million or more stockholders. The sale of stock is a means of obtaining funds from the general public; both small and large investors find stock ownership a convenient means of participating in ownership of business enterprise.

2 *Limited liability* Creditors of a corporation have a claim against the assets of the corporation only, not against the personal property of the owners of the corporation. Since a stockholder has no personal liability for the debts of the corporation, he can never lose more than the amount of his investment.

3 *Shares of stock in a corporation are readily transferable* The ease of disposing of all or part of one's stockholdings in a publicly owned corporation makes this form of investment particularly attractive.

4 *Continuous existence* A corporation is a separate legal entity with a perpetual existence. The continuous life of the corporation despite changes in ownership is made possible by the issuance of transferable shares of stock.

5 *Centralized authority* The power to make all kinds of operating decisions is lodged in the president of a corporation. He may delegate to others limited authority for various phases of operations, but he retains final authority over the entire business.

6 Professional management The person who owns a few shares of stock in a large corporation usually has neither the time nor the knowledge of the business necessary for intelligent participation in operating problems. Because of this the functions of management and of ownership are sharply separated in the corporate form of organization, and the corporation is free to employ as executives the best managerial talent available.

Disadvantages of the corporate form of organization

Among the disadvantages of the corporation are:

1 Heavy taxation A corporation must pay a high rate of taxation on its income. If part of its net income is distributed to the owners in the form of dividends, the dividends are considered to be personal income to the stockholders and are subject to personal income tax. This practice of first taxing corporate income to the corporation and then dividends to the stockholder is referred to as *double taxation.*

2 Greater regulation Corporations come into existence under the terms of state laws and these same laws may provide for considerable regulation of the corporation's activities. Also, large corporations have gradually come to accept the necessity for extensive public disclosure of their affairs.

3 Separation of ownership and control The separation of the functions of ownership and management may be an advantage in some cases but a disadvantage in others. On the whole, the excellent record of growth and earnings in most large corporations indicates that the separation of ownership and control has benefited rather than injured stockholders. In a few instances, however, a management group has chosen to operate a corporation for the benefit of insiders. The stockholders may find it difficult in such cases to take the concerted action necessary to oust the officers.

The chain of authority in a corporation

As stated earlier, the stockholders elect a board of directors which in turn selects the president and other corporate officers. The rights of stockholders and the function of the board of directors and corporate officers are briefly described below:

RIGHTS OF STOCKHOLDERS The ownership of stock in a corporation usually carries the following basic rights:

1 To vote for directors, and thereby to be represented in the management of the business. The approval of a majority of stockholders may also be required for such important corporate actions as mergers and acquisitions, the selection of auditors, the incurring of long-term debt, and the establishing of stock option plans.

2 To share in profits by receiving dividends declared by the board of directors.

3 To share in the distribution of assets if the corporation is liquidated. When a corporation ends its existence, the creditors of the corporation must first be paid in full; any remaining assets are divided among stockholders in proportion to the number of shares owned.

4 To subscribe for additional shares in the event that the corporation decides to increase the amount of stock outstanding. This *preemptive right* entitles each stockholder to maintain his percentage of ownership in the company by subscribing, in proportion to his present stockholdings, to any additional shares issued. Corporations organized in certain states do not grant preemptive rights to their stockholders. In other cases stockholders sometimes agree to waive their preemptive right in order to grant more flexibility to management in negotiating mergers.

The ownership of stock does not give a stockholder the right to intervene in the management of a corporation or to transact business in its behalf. Although the stockholders as a group own the corporation, they do not personally own the assets of the corporation; neither do they personally owe the debts of the corporation. The stockholders have no direct claim on income earned; income earned by a corporation does not become income to the stockholders unless the board of directors declares a dividend.

Stockholders' meetings are usually held once a year. Each share of stock is entitled to one vote. In large corporations, these annual meetings are usually attended by relatively few persons. Prior to the meeting, the management group will request stockholders who do not plan to attend in person to send in a *proxy* assigning their votes to management. Through this use of the proxy system, management may secure the right to vote 90% or more of the total outstanding shares.

FUNCTIONS OF THE BOARD OF DIRECTORS The primary functions of the board of directors are to manage the corporation and to protect the interests of the stockholders. At this level, management may consist principally of formulating policies and reviewing acts of the officers. Specific duties of the directors include declaring dividends, setting the salaries of officers, authorizing officers to arrange loans from banks, and authorizing important contracts of various kinds.

The extent of active participation in management by the board of directors varies widely from one company to another. In some corporations the officers also serve as directors and a meeting of directors may differ only in form from a conference of operating executives. In other corporations the board may consist of *outside directors* who devote little time to the corporation's affairs.

FUNCTIONS OF CORPORATE OFFICERS Corporate officers usually include a president, one or more vice presidents, a controller, a treasurer, and a secretary. A vice president is often made responsible for the sales function; other vice presidents may be given responsibility for such important functions as personnel, finance, production, and research and development.

The responsibilities of the controller, treasurer, and secretary are most directly related to the accounting phase of business operation. The *controller* is the chief accounting officer. He is responsible for the maintenance of adequate internal control and accounting records and for the preparation of financial statements. Such specialized activities as budgeting, tax planning, and preparation of tax returns are usually placed under his jurisdiction. The *treasurer* is generally responsible for planning and controlling the company's cash position. The *secretary* maintains minutes of the meetings of directors and stockholders and represents the corporation in many contractual and legal matters. Another of his responsibilities is to coordinate the preparation of the *annual report,* which includes the financial statements and other information relating to corporate activities. In small corporations, one officer frequently acts as both secretary and treasurer.

Special records of corporations

When a corporation first issues its stock, the transaction is between the corporation and the investor; once the stock is outstanding, any further stock transactions do not affect the corporation which issued the stock. However, the corporation must be informed of each such stock transaction so that it can update its records of stock ownership by eliminating the name of the former owner and adding the name of the new owner.

For a company with a large number of stockholders, it is not practicable to include in the general ledger an account with each stockholder. Instead, a single controlling account, such as Capital Stock, is carried in the general ledger, and a subsidiary stockholders' ledger with individual stockholders is maintained. (When a great many separate accounts must be maintained, a ledger is usually in the form of punched cards or magnetic tape rather than a book.) In this *stockholders' ledger,* each stockholder's account shows the number of shares which he owns, the certificate numbers, and the dates of acquisition and sale. Entries are made not in dollars but in number of shares.

The large corporation with thousands of stockholders and a steady flow of stock transfers usually turns over the function of maintaining capital stock records to an independent *stock transfer agent* and a *stock registrar.* A bank or trust company serves as stock transfer agent and another bank or trust company acts as the stock registrar. When certificates are to be transferred from one owner to another, the certificates are sent to the transfer agent, who cancels them, makes the necessary entries in the stockholders' ledger, and signs new certificates which are forwarded to the stock registrar. The basic function of the registrar is to prevent any improper issuance of stock certificates.

Another record kept by corporations is the *minutes book,* which consists of a narrative record of all actions taken at official meetings of the corporation's board of directors and of its stockholders. Typical of the actions described in the minutes book are the declaration of dividends by the board of directors, the authorization of important transactions such as mergers, issuance of additional shares of capital stock, and the adoption of pension plans.

Formation of a corporation

To form a corporation, an application is submitted to the corporation commissioner (or other designated official) of the state in which the company is to be incorporated. The approved application contains the *articles of incorporation* and becomes the company *charter.* The incorporators (who have subscribed for capital stock and therefore are now stockholders) hold a meeting to elect *directors* and to pass *bylaws* as a guide to the company's affairs. The directors in turn hold a meeting at which officers of the corporation are appointed. Capital stock certificates are then issued and the formation of the corporation is complete.

ORGANIZATION COSTS   The formation of a corporation is more costly than the organization of a partnership. The necessary costs include the payment of an incorporation fee to the state, the payment of fees to attorneys for their services in drawing up the articles of incorporation, payments to promoters, and a variety of other outlays necessary to bring the corporation into existence. These costs are recorded in an asset account called Organization Costs.

The result of organization costs is the creation of the corporate entity; consequently, the benefits derived from these costs may be regarded as extending over the entire life of the corporation. Since the life of a corporation is indefinite, organization costs may be carried at the full amount until the corporation is liquidated. Because present income tax law permits organization costs to be written off (amortized) as expenses over a period of five years or more, most newly organized companies elect to write off such costs over a five-year period. Accountants have been willing to condone this practice, despite the lack of theoretical support, on the grounds that such costs are relatively immaterial in relation to other assets.

STOCKHOLDERS' EQUITY   The sections of a balance sheet showing assets and liabilities are much the same for a corporation as for a single proprietorship or partnership. The owners' equity section is the principal point of contrast. In a corporation, the term **stockholders' equity** is synonymous with owners' equity. In previous chapters we have seen that corporations use separate owners' equity accounts (Capital Stock and Retained Earnings) to represent (1) the capital invested by the stockholders (paid-in capital) and (2) the capital acquired and retained through profitable operations (earned capital).

Up to this point we have assumed that each of these two categories of stockholders' equity may be represented by a single ledger account. In this chapter we shall see that different classes of capital stock may be issued by a corporation and that capital stock may be issued at a price which differs from its par value. In these situations, additional ledger accounts will be necessary to show the various elements of stockholders' equity received from investors.

The second major type of stockholders' equity is retained earnings. The balance of the Retained Earnings account at any balance sheet date represents the accumulated earnings of the company since the date of incorporation, minus any losses and minus all dividends distributed to stockholders. (Various types of dividends are discussed in Chapter 8.) Alternative names for the Retained Earnings account are Income Retained for Use in the Business, Accumulated Earnings, and Earned Surplus.

For a corporation with $1 million of capital stock and $150,000 of retained earnings, the stockholders' equity section of the balance sheet will appear as follows:

Paid-in capital and earned capital	Stockholders' equity:	
	Capital stock	$1,000,000
	Retained earnings	150,000 $1,150,000

If this same company had been unprofitable and had incurred losses of $80,000 since its organization, the stockholders' equity section of the balance sheet would be as follows:

Paid-in capital reduced by losses	Stockholders' equity:	
	Capital stock	$1,000,000
	Less: Deficit	80,000 $920,000

This second illustration tells us that $80,000 of the original $1 million invested by stockholders has been lost. Note that the capital stock in both illustrations remains at the fixed amount of $1 million, the stockholders' original investment. The accumulated earnings or losses since the organization of the corporation are shown as **retained earnings** or as a **deficit** and are not intermingled with paid-in capital. The term **deficit** indicates a negative amount of retained earnings.

AUTHORIZATION AND ISSUANCE OF CAPITAL STOCK

The articles of incorporation specify the number of shares of capital stock which a corporation is authorized to issue and the par value, if any, per share. The corporation may secure authorization for a larger number of shares than presently needed. In future years, if more capital is needed, the previously authorized shares will be readily available for issue.

Capital stock outstanding

The unit of stock ownership is the *share,* but the corporation may issue stock certificates in denominations of 10 shares, 100 shares, or any other number. The total capital stock outstanding at any given time represents 100% ownership of the corporation. *Outstanding shares* are those in the hands of stockholders. Assume, for example, that the Draper Corporation is organized with authorization to issue 100,000 shares of stock. However, only 50,000 shares are issued, because this amount of stock provides all the capital presently needed. The holders of the 50,000 shares of stock own the corporation in its entirety.

If we assume further that Thomas Draper acquired 5,000 shares of the 50,000 shares outstanding, we may say that he has a 10% ownership interest in the corporation. Suppose that Draper now sells 2,000 shares to Evans. The total number of shares outstanding remains unchanged at 50,000, although Draper's percentage of ownership has declined to 6% and a new stockholder, Evans, has acquired a 4% ownership interest in the corporation. The transfer of 2,000 shares from Draper to Evans had no effect upon the corporation's assets, liabilities, or amount of capital stock outstanding. The only way in which this transfer of stock affects the corporation is that the list of stockholders must be revised to show the number of shares held by each owner.

Par value

In an earlier period of the history of American corporations, all capital stock had par value, but in more recent years state laws have permitted corporations to choose between par value stock and no-par value stock. The corporate charter always states the par value, if any, of the shares to be issued.

Par value may be $1 per share, $5, $100, or any other amount decided upon by the corporation. The par value of the stock is no indication of its market value; the par value merely indicates the amount per share to be entered in the Capital Stock account. The par value of most common stocks is relatively low. Polaroid Corporation common stock, for example, has a par value of $1; General Motors Corporation common stock has a par value of $1\frac{2}{3}$; Avon Products stock has a par value of 50 cents per share. The market value of all these securities is far above their par value.

The chief significance of par value is that it represents the *legal capital* per share, that is, the amount below which stockholders' equity cannot be reduced except by (1) losses from business operations or (2) legal action taken by a majority vote of stockholders. A dividend cannot be declared by a corporation if such action would cause the stockholders' equity to fall below the par value of the outstanding shares. Par value, therefore, may be regarded as a minimum cushion of capital existing for the protection of creditors.

Issuance of par value capital stock

Authorization of a stock issue does not bring an asset into existence, nor does it give the corporation any capital. The obtaining of authorization for a stock issue affords a legal opportunity to obtain assets through the issuance of capital stock. The receipt of an authorization to issue capital stock may be recorded in a memorandum entry in the general journal.

When par value stock is issued, the Capital Stock account is credited with the par value of the shares issued, regardless of whether the issuance price is more or less than par. Assuming that 6,000 shares of an authorized 10,000 shares of $10 par value stock are issued at a price of $10 each, Cash would be debited and Capital Stock would be credited for $60,000. When stock is sold for more than par value, the Capital Stock account is credited with the par value of the shares issued, and a separate account, Paid-in Capital in Excess of Par, is credited for the excess of issuance price over par. If, for example, the issuance price is $15, the entry is as follows:

Stock- *holders'* *investment* *in excess of* *par value*	*Cash*	*90,000*
	Capital Stock, $10 par	*60,000*
	Paid-in Capital in Excess of Par	*30,000*
	Issued 6,000 shares of $10 par value stock at a price of $15 a share.	

The amount received in excess of par value does not represent a profit to the corporation. It is part of the invested capital and it will be added to the capital stock in the balance sheet to show the total paid-in capital. The stockholders' equity section of the balance sheet would be as follows (the existence of $10,000 in retained earnings is assumed in order to present a complete illustration):

Corpora- *tion's* *capital* *classified* *by source*	*Stockholders' equity:*	
	Capital stock, $10 par, authorized 10,000 shares, issued and outstand-	
	ing, 6,000 shares	*$ 60,000*
	Paid-in capital in excess of par	*30,000*
	Total paid-in capital	*$ 90,000*
	Retained earnings	*10,000*
	Total stockholders' equity	*$100,000*

If stock is issued by a corporation for less than par, the account Discount on Capital Stock should be debited for the difference between the issuance price and the par value. The issuance of stock at a discount is seldom encountered, and is illegal in many states.

No-par value stock

An understanding of no-par stock can best be gained by reviewing the reasons why par value was originally required in an earlier period of American corporate history. The use of the par value concept in state laws was intended for the protection of creditors and of public stockholders. In some states stock could not be issued at less than par value; in most states if stock was issued at less than par value the purchaser was contingently liable for the discount below par. Because of these statutes concerning par value, a creditor of a corporation could tell by inspection of the balance sheet the amount which owners had invested permanently in the corporation. This permanent investment of capital (par value times the number of outstanding shares) represented a buffer which protected the creditors of the corporation from the impact of any losses sustained by the corporation. Such protection for creditors was considered necessary because stockholders have no personal liability for the debts of the corporation.

The par value device proved rather ineffective in achieving its avowed objective of protecting creditors and stockholders, and most states later enacted legislation permitting corporations to issue stock without par value. With the advent of no-par stock, state legislatures attempted to continue the protection of corporate creditors by designating all or part of the amount received by the corporation for its no-par shares as *stated capital* not subject to withdrawal.

Assume that a corporation is organized in a state which permits the board of directors to establish a *stated value* on no-par stock, and that the board passed a resolution setting the stated value per share at $5. If a total of 80,000 shares were issued at $12, the journal entry to record the issuance would be:

Note the stated value per share

Cash	960,000	
Capital Stock, $5 stated value		400,000
Paid-in Capital in Excess of Stated Value		560,000

Issued 80,000 shares of no-par value capital stock at $12 each.
Stated value set by directors at $5 per share.

In the absence of a stated value, the entire proceeds on the issuance of no-par stock would be credited to the Capital Stock account and would be viewed as legal capital. However, most companies which issue no-par capital stock do establish a stated value per share.

Stock issued for non-cash assets or services

Corporations generally sell their capital stock for cash and use the cash to buy the various types of assets needed in the business. Sometimes, however, a corporation may issue shares of its capital stock in a direct exchange for land, buildings, or in payment for services rendered by attorneys and promoters.

When a corporation issues capital stock in exchange for services or for assets other than cash, a question arises as to the proper valuation of the property or services received. For example, assume that a corporation issues 1,000 shares of its $1 par value capital stock in exchange for a tract of land. A problem may exist in determining the fair market value of the land and, consequently, in determining the amount of paid-in capital. If there is no direct evidence of the value of the land, we may value it by using indirect evidence as to the alternative amount of cash for which the shares might have been sold. Assume that the company's stock is listed on a stock exchange and is presently selling at $90 a share. The 1,000 shares which the corporation exchanged for the land could have been sold for $90,000 cash, and the cash could have been used to pay for the land. The direct exchange of stock for land may be considered as the equivalent of selling the stock for cash and using the cash to buy the land. It is therefore logical to say that the cost of the land to the company was $90,000, the market value of the stock given in exchange for the land. *Note that the par value of the stock is not any indication of the fair value of the stock or of the land.*

Once the valuation question has been decided, the entry to record the issuance of stock in exchange for land can be made as follows:

How were dollar amounts determined?

Land	90,000	
Capital Stock, $1 par		1,000
Paid-in Capital in Excess of Par		89,000

To record the issuance of 1,000 shares of $1 par value capital stock in exchange for land. Current market value of stock ($90 a share) is used as basis for valuing the land.

Underwriting a stock issue

When a large amount of stock is to be issued, the corporation will probably utilize the services of an investment banking firm, frequently referred to as an *underwriter.* The underwriter guarantees the issuing corporation a specific price for the stock and makes a profit by selling the stock to the investing public at a higher price. For example, an issue of 1,270,000 shares of $1 par value capital stock might be sold to the public at a price of $47 a share, of which $2.35 a share is retained by the underwriter and $44.65 represents the net proceeds to the issuing corporation.[1] The corporation would enter in its records only the net amount received from the underwriter ($44.65) for each share issued. The use of an underwriter assures the corporation that the entire stock issue will be sold without delay, and the entire amount of cash to be raised will be available on a specific date.

Subscriptions to capital stock

Small corporations sometimes sell stock on a subscription plan, in which the investors agree to pay the subscription price at a future date or in installments. When a subscription contract is signed, the accounting entry consists of a debit to Subscriptions Receivable: Capital Stock and a credit to Capital Stock Subscribed. Collections are recorded by debiting Cash and crediting Subscriptions Receivable: Capital Stock. When the entire subscription price has been collected, the stock certificates are issued; this action is recorded by debiting Capital Stock Subscribed and crediting Capital Stock. The following illustration demonstrates this method of accounting for stock subscriptions.

Assume that 10,000 shares of $10 par value capital stock are subscribed at a price of $25. Subscriptions are collected in full at a later date and the stock certificates are then issued.

Subscription price above par value

Subscriptions Receivable: Capital Stock	250,000	
Capital Stock Subscribed		100,000
Paid-in Capital in Excess of Par		150,000
Received subscriptions for 10,000 shares of $10 par value stock at price of $25 a share.		

Certificates issued for fully paid shares

Cash	250,000	
Subscriptions Receivable: Capital Stock		250,000
Collected subscriptions in full for 10,000 shares at $25 each.		
Capital Stock Subscribed	100,000	
Capital Stock, $10 par		100,000
Issued certificates for 10,000 fully paid $10 par value shares.		

From the corporation's point of view, Subscriptions Receivable represents a current asset, which ordinarily will be collected within a short time. If financial statements are prepared between the date of obtaining subscriptions and the date of issuing the stock, the Capital

[1] These figures are taken from a prospectus issued by Levi Strauss & Co. covering the issuance of 1,070,000 shares by the corporation and 200,000 shares by stockholders in an initial public offering. Figures taken from the face of the prospectus follow:

	Price to Public	Underwriting Discounts and Commissions	Proceeds to the Company	Proceeds to Selling Stockholders
Per share	$47.00	$2.35	$44.65	$44.65
Total	$59,690,000	$2,984,500	$47,775,500	$8,930,000

Stock Subscribed account will appear in the stockholders' equity section of the balance sheet.

Preferred and common stock

In order to appeal to as many investors as possible, a corporation may issue more than one kind of stock, just as an automobile manufacturer may make sedans, convertibles, and station wagons in order to appeal to various groups of car buyers. When only one type of stock is issued, it is called **common stock.** Common stock has the four basic rights previously mentioned. Whenever an issue of capital stock restricts these basic rights, the term **preferred stock** (or sometimes Class B Common) is used to describe this second type of stock. A few corporations issue two or more classes of preferred stock, each class having certain distinctive features designed to appeal to a particular type of investor. In summary, we may say that every business corporation has common stock; a good many corporations also issue preferred stock; and some companies have two or more types of preferred stock.

Common stock may be regarded as the basic, residual element of ownership. It carries voting rights and, therefore, is the means of exercising control over the business. Common stock has unlimited possibilities of increase in value. On the other hand, common stocks tend to lose value more rapidly than other types of securities when corporations encounter periods of unprofitable business.

The following stockholders' equity section illustrates the balance sheet presentation for a corporation having both preferred and common stock; note that the item of **retained earnings** is not apportioned between the two groups of stockholders.

Balance sheet presentation of preferred and common stock	

Stockholders' equity:

Preferred stock, 5% cumulative, $100 par, authorized and issued, 100,000 shares	$10,000,000
Common stock, $5 par, authorized and issued, 1 million shares	5,000,000
Retained earnings	3,500,000
Total stockholders' equity	$18,500,000

CHARACTERISTICS OF PREFERRED STOCK Most preferred stocks have the following distinctive features:

1 Preferred as to dividends
2 Preferred as to assets in event of the liquidation of the company
3 Callable at the option of the corporation
4 No voting power

Another very important but less common feature is a clause permitting the **conversion** of preferred stock into common at the option of the holder. Preferred stocks vary widely with respect to the special rights and privileges granted. Careful study of the terms of the individual preferred stock contract is a necessary step in the evaluation of any preferred stock.

Stock preferred as to dividends Stock preferred as to dividends is entitled to receive each year a dividend of specified amount before any dividend is paid on the common stock. The dividend is usually stated as a dollar amount per share. For example, the balance sheet of General Motors Corporation shows two types of preferred stock outstanding, one paying $5.00 a year and the other $3.75 a year, as shown below:

Dividend stated as dollar amount per share

Capital stock:

   Preferred, without par value (authorized 6 million shares):

     $5.00 series; stated value $100 per share, redeemable at $120 per

      share (outstanding 1,835,644 shares) *$183,564,400*

     $3.75 series; stated value $100 per share, redeemable at $101 per

      share (outstanding 1,000,000 shares) *100,000,000*

Some preferred stocks state the dividend preference as a percentage of par value. For example, a $5\frac{1}{2}$% preferred stock with a par value of $100 per share would mean that $5.50 must be paid yearly on each share of preferred stock before any dividends are paid to the common. An example of the percentage method of stating the dividend on a preferred stock is found in the balance sheet of Georgia-Pacific Corporation:

Dividend stated as percentage of par value

Capital stock:

   Preferred, $5\frac{1}{2}$% cumulative, par value $100 per share *$10,000,000*

The holder of a preferred stock has no assurance that he will always receive the indicated dividend. A corporation is obligated to pay dividends to stockholders only when the board of directors declares a dividend. Dividends must be paid on preferred stock before anything is paid to the common stockholders, but if the corporation is not prospering, it may decide not to pay dividends on either preferred or common stock.

Cumulative preferred stock The dividend preference carried by most preferred stocks is a *cumulative* one. If all or any part of the regular dividend on the preferred stock is omitted in a given year, the amount *in arrears* must be paid in a subsequent year before any dividend can be paid on the common stock. Assume that a corporation was organized January 1, Year 1, with 1,000 shares of $4 cumulative preferred stock and 1,000 shares of common stock. Dividends paid in Year 1 were at the rate of $4 per share of preferred stock and $3 per share of common. In Year 2, earnings declined sharply and the only dividend paid was $1 per share on the preferred stock. No dividends were paid in Year 3. What is the status of the preferred stock at December 31, Year 3? Dividends are in arrears in the amount of $7 a share ($3 omitted during Year 2 and $4 omitted in Year 3). On the entire issue of 1,000 shares of preferred stock, the dividends in arrears amount to $7,000.

In Year 4, we shall assume that the company earned large profits and wished to pay dividends on both the preferred and common stocks. Before paying a dividend on the common, the corporation must pay the $7,000 in arrears on the cumulative preferred stock plus the regular $4 a share applicable to the current year. The preferred stock-holders would, therefore, receive a total of $11,000 in dividends in Year 4; the board of directors would then be free to declare dividends on the common stock.

Dividends in arrears *are not listed among the liabilities of a corporation,* because no liability exists until a dividend is declared by the board of directors. Nevertheless, the amount of any dividends in arrears on preferred stock is an important factor to investors and should always be disclosed. This disclosure is usually made by a note accompanying the balance sheet such as the following:

"As of December 31, Year 3, dividends on the $4 cumulative preferred stock were in arrears to the extent of $7 per share and amounted in total to $7,000."

For a *noncumulative preferred stock,* any unpaid or omitted dividend is lost forever. Because of this factor, investors view the noncumulative feature as an unfavorable element, and very few noncumulative preferred stocks are issued.

Participating preferred stock Since participating preferred stocks are very seldom issued, discussion of them will be brief. A participating preferred stock is one which, in addition to the regular specified dividend, is entitled to participate in some manner with the common stock in any additional dividends paid. For example, a $5 participating preferred stock would be entitled to receive $5 a share before the common stock received anything. After $5 a share had been paid to the preferred stockholders, a $5 dividend could be paid on the common stock. If the company desired to pay an additional dividend to the common, say, an extra $3 per share, the preferred stock would also be entitled to receive a specified "extra" dividend of as much as $3 per share.

Stock preferred as to assets Most preferred stocks carry a preference as to assets in the event of liquidation of the corporation. If the business is terminated, the preferred stock is entitled to payment in full of a stated liquidation value plus any dividends in arrears before any payment is made on the common stock.

Callable preferred stock Most preferred stocks are callable at the option of the corporation at a stipulated price, usually slightly above the issuance price. The *call price* or *redemption price* for a $100 par value preferred stock is often $103 or $104 per share.

In the financing of a new or expanding corporation, the organizers usually hold common stock, which assures them control of the company. However, it is often necessary to obtain outside capital. One way of doing this, without the loss of control or any serious reduction in possible future earnings on the common stock, is to issue a callable preferred stock.

It may be argued that the position of the holder of a callable preferred stock is more like that of a creditor than that of an owner. He supplies capital to the company for an agreed rate of return, has no voice in management, and may find his relationship with the company terminated at any time through the calling in of his stock certificate. If a company is so fortunate as to enter upon a period of unusually high earnings, It will probably increase the dividend payments on its common stock, but it will not consider increasing the payments to the preferred stockholders. On the contrary, the corporation may decide that this era of prosperity is a good time to eliminate the preferred stock through exercise of the call provision.

Regardless of the fact that preferred stock lacks many of the traditional aspects of ownership, it is universal practice to include all types of preferred stock in the stockholders' equity section of the balance sheet.

Convertible preferred stock In order to add to the attractiveness of preferred stock as an investment, corporations frequently offer a conversion privilege which entitles the preferred stockholder to exchange his shares for common stock in a stipulated ratio. If the corporation prospers, its common stock will probably rise in market value, and dividends on the common stock will probably be increased. The investor who buys a convertible preferred stock rather than common stock has greater assurance of regular dividends. In addition, through the conversion privilege, he is assured of sharing in any substantial increase in value of the company's common stock.

As an example, assume that the Remington Corporation issued a 5%, $100 par, convertible preferred stock on January 1, at a price of $100 a share. Each share was convertible into four shares of the company's $10 value common stock at any time. The common stock had a market price of $20 a share on January 1, and an annual dividend of 60 cents a share was being paid. The yield on the preferred stock was 5% ($5 ÷ $100); the yield on the common stock was only 3% ($0.60 ÷ $20).

During the next few years, the Remington Corporation's earnings increased, the dividend on the common stock was raised to an annual rate of $1.50, and the market price of the common stock rose to $40 a share. At this point the preferred stock would have a market value of at least $160, since it could be converted at any time into four shares of common stock with a market value of $40 each. In other words, the market value of a convertible preferred stock will tend to move in accordance with the price of the common. When the dividend rate is increased on the common stock, some holders of the preferred stock may convert their holdings into common stock in order to obtain a higher return on their investment.

If the holder of 100 shares of the preferred stock presented these shares for conversion, the Remington Corporation would make the following entry:

Conversion of preferred stock into common stock

5% Convertible Preferred Stock, $100 par	*10,000*	
Common Stock, $10 par		*4,000*
Paid-in Capital in Excess of Par: Common		*6,000*

To record the conversion of 100 shares of $100 par value preferred stock into 400 shares of $10 par value common stock.

The preceding illustration was based on the assumption that the Remington Corporation enjoyed larger earnings after the issuance of its convertible preferred. Let us now make a contrary assumption and say that shortly after issuance of the convertible preferred stock, the company's profits declined and the directors cut the annual dividend on the common stock from 60 to 20 cents a share. A stockholder who acquired common stock at a cost of $20 a share now finds that his dividend income has dropped to a rate of 1% ($0.20 ÷ $20). The dividend on the preferred stock remains at $5 a share.

These two illustrations indicate that the convertible preferred stock has two important advantages from the viewpoint of the investor: It increases in value along with the common stock when the company prospers, and it offers greater assurance of steady dividend income during a period of poor earnings.

Market price of common stock

The preceding sections concerning the issuance of stock at prices above and below par value raise a question as to how the market price of stock is determined. The price which the corporation sets on a **new issue** of stock is based on several factors including (1) an appraisal of the company's expected future earnings, (2) the probable dividend rate per share, (3) the present financial condition of the company, and (4) the current state of the investment market.

After the stock has been issued, the price at which it will be traded among investors will tend to reflect the progress of the company, with primary emphasis being placed on earnings and dividends per share. **Earnings per share** of common stock, for example, is computed by dividing the annual net income available to the common stock by the number of shares of common stock outstanding. At this point in our discussion, the significant fact to emphasize is that market price is not related to par value, and that it tends to reflect current and future earnings and dividends. (Earnings per share is discussed in some detail in Chapter 8.)

Income taxes in corporate financial statements

A corporation is a legal entity subject to corporation income tax; consequently, the ledger of a corporation should include accounts for recording income taxes. No such accounts are needed for a business organized as a single proprietorship or partnership.

Income taxes are computed as a percentage of a corporation's *taxable income.* At year-end, before preparing financial statements, income taxes are recorded by an adjusting entry such as the following:

Recording   Income Taxes 45,650
corporate
income   Income Taxes Payable 45,650
taxes   *To record income taxes for the year.*

The account debited in this entry, Income Taxes, is an expense account and appears in the income statement as follows:

Income   *Income before income taxes* $100,000
taxes in the
income   *Income taxes* . . . . _45,650_
statement   *Net income* . . . . $ 54,350
Earnings per share (50,000 shares outstanding) . . . . _$1.09_

The liability account, Income Taxes Payable, will ordinarily be paid within a few months and should, therefore, appear in the current liability section of the balance sheet. More detailed discussion of corporate income taxes is presented in Chapter 17.

Balance sheet for a corporation illustrated

A fairly complete corporation balance sheet is presented on page 255. In studying this balance sheet, the student should bear in mind that current practice includes many alternatives in the choice of terminology and the arrangement of items in financial statements. Some of these alternatives are illustrated in the Appendix at the end of this book.

DALE CORPORATION
Balance Sheet
December 31, Year 10

Assets

Balance sheet for corporation

Current assets:

Cash			$ 305,600
U. S. government securities, at cost (market value $812,800)			810,000
Accounts receivable (net of allowance for uncollectible accounts)			1,165,200
Subscriptions receivable: preferred stock			50,000
Inventories (lower of fifo, cost or market)			1,300,800
Short-term prepayments			125,900
Total current assets			$3,757,500
Investments: Common stock of Price Corporation			444,900
Plant and equipment:			
Land		$ 500,000	
Buildings	$2,482,100		
Less: Accumulated depreciation	400,000	2,082,100	
Equipment	$1,800,000		
Less: Accumulated depreciation	800,000	1,000,000	3,582,100
Intangibles: Patents and trademarks			110,000
Total assets			$7,894,500

Liabilities & Stockholders' Equity

Current liabilities:

Accounts payable			$1,037,800
Income taxes payable			324,300
Dividends payable			70,000
Interest payable			20,000
Total current liabilities			$1,452,100
Long-term liabilities: Bonds payable, 8%, due Oct. 1, Year 20			1,000,000
Total liabilities			$2,452,100

Stockholders' equity:

Cumulative 5% preferred stock, $100 par, authorized 10,000 shares:			
8,000 shares issued		$ 800,000	
2,000 shares subscribed		200,000	$1,000,000
Common stock, $1 par, authorized			
1,000,000 shares: 600,000 shares issued		600,000	
Paid-in capital in excess of par: common		2,200,000	
Total paid-in capital		$3,800,000	
Retained earnings		1,642,400	
Total stockholders' equity			5,442,400
Total liabilities & stockholders' equity			$7,894,500

DEMONSTRATION PROBLEM

The stockholders' equity section of the Gustafson Corporation's balance sheet at the close of the current year is given below.

GUSTAFSON CORPORATION
Stockholders' Equity
December 31, Current Year

$2.75 preferred stock, $50 par, authorized 50,000 shares:		
Issued	$540,000	
Subscribed	270,000	$ 810,000
Common stock, $5 stated value, authorized 200,000 shares:		
Issued	$510,000	
Subscribed	105,000	615,000
Paid-in capital in excess of par or stated value:		
Preferred stock	$ 81,000	
Common stock...........................	123,000	204,000
Retained earnings (deficit)		(225,000)
Total stockholders' equity		$1,404,000

    Among the assets of the corporation appear the following items: Subscriptions Receivable: Preferred, $135,000; Subscriptions Receivable: Common, $68,250.

Instructions On the basis of this information, answer the following questions, showing any necessary supporting computations.
a How many shares of preferred and common have been issued?
b How many shares of preferred and common have been subscribed?
c What was the average price per share received by the corporation on its preferred stock including preferred stock subscribed?
d What was the average price per share received by the corporation on its common stock including common stock subscribed?
e What is the average amount per share that subscribers of preferred stock have yet to pay on their subscriptions?
f What is the total paid-in capital?
g What is the total legal or stated value of the capital stock?
h What is the average amount per share that common stock subscribers have already paid on their subscriptions? (Assume common was subscribed at $6.)

SOLUTION TO DEMONSTRATION PROBLEM

a Preferred stock issued = 10,800 shares ($540,000 ÷ $50)
    Common stock issued = 102,000 shares ($510,000 ÷ $5)

b Preferred stock subscribed = 5,400 shares ($270,000 ÷ $50)
    Common stock subscribed = 21,000 shares ($105,000 ÷ $5)

c Preferred par value (including shares subscribed) $810,000

  Paid-in capital in excess of par value 81,000

   Total paid in and subscribed.................... $891,000

   Total shares issued and subscribed (10,800 + 5,400) 16,200

   Average per share ($891,000 ÷ 16,200) $55.00

d Common stock stated value (including shares subscribed) $615,000

  Paid-in capital in excess of stated value.................. 123,000

   Total paid in and subscribed.................... $738,000

   Total shares issued and subscribed (102,000 + 21,000)......... 123,000

   Average per share ($738,000 ÷ 123,000) $6.00

e Subscriptions receivable: preferred $135,000

  Shares subscribed 5,400

  Average per share to be paid ($135,000 ÷ 5,400) $25.00

f $1,629,000 (preferred $810,000 + common $615,000 + paid-in capital in excess of par or stated value $204,000)

g $1,425,000 (preferred $810,000 + common $615,000)

h Common stock subscribed (21,000 shares @ $6) $126,000

  Less: Subscriptions receivable: common 68,250

  Amounts already paid in by subscribers .... $ 57,750

  Average paid per share ($57,750 ÷ 21,000) $2.75

REVIEW QUESTIONS

1 Stevens is the proprietor of a small manufacturing business. He is considering the possibility of joining in partnership with Thomas, whom he considers to be thoroughly competent and congenial. Prepare a brief statement outlining the advantages and disadvantages of the potential partnership to Stevens.

2 Vernon has land with a carrying value of $7,500 and a fair value of $20,000, and a building with a carrying value of $60,000 and a fair value of $54,500. The land and building represent Vernon's sole capital contribution to a partnership. What is Vernon's capital balance in the new partnership? Why?

3 State the effect of each of the transactions given below on a partner's capital or drawing accounts:

  a Partner borrows cash from the business and signs a promissory note.

  b Partner collects a partnership account receivable while on vacation and uses the cash for personal purposes.

  c Partner receives in cash the salary allowance provided in the partnership agreement.

  d Partner takes home merchandise (cost $100; selling price $125) for his personal use.

  e Partner has loaned money to the partnership. The principal, together with interest at 8%, is now repaid in cash.

4 Distinguish between corporations and partnerships in terms of the following characteristics:
   a Owners' liability
   b Transferability of ownership interest
   c Continuity of existence
   d Federal taxation on income

5 What are the basic rights of the owner of a share of corporate stock? In what way are these basic rights commonly modified with respect to the owner of a share of preferred stock?

6 Describe three kinds of costs that may be incurred in the process of organizing a corporation. How are such expenditures treated for accounting purposes? Why?

7 Distinguish between **paid-in capital** and **retained earnings** of a corporation. Why is such a distinction useful?

8 Smith owns 200 of the 8,000 shares of common stock issued and outstanding in X Company. The company issued 2,000 additional shares of stock. What is Smith's position with respect to the new issue if he is entitled to preemptive rights?

9 In theory, a corporation may sell its stock for an amount greater or less than par value; in practice, stock is seldom if ever issued for less than par. Explain the significance of par value and why shares are seldom issued for less than par.

10 When stock is issued by a corporation in exchange for assets other than cash, the accountant faces the problem of determining the dollar amount at which to record the transaction. Discuss the factors he should consider and explain their significance.

11 Rosemead Company sold 300,000 shares of no-par common stock through underwriters at $21 per share. The company paid $408,000 in underwriting discounts and commissions, thus receiving only $5,892,000. In addition, the company paid other costs of $82,000 in connection with the underwriting.
   a What benefits did the company receive from the $490,000 of costs and how should these costs be reported in the balance sheet?
   b Is this a steep price to pay for new financing by an established company?

12 State the classification (asset, liability, stockholders' equity, or expense) of each of the following accounts:
   a Subscriptions receivable: common stock
   b Capital stock
   c Retained earnings
   d Common stock subscribed
   e Paid-in capital in excess of par
   f Income taxes

13 Explain the following terms:
   a Stock transfer agent   **d** Minutes book
   b Stockholders' ledger   **e** Stock registrar
   c Underwriter

14 Describe the usual nature of the following features as they apply to a share of preferred stock:
   a Cumulative
   b Participating
   c Convertible
   d Callable

EXERCISES

Ex. 7-1 Clawson Corporation was organized on July 1, 19___. The corporation was authorized to issue 10,000 shares of $100 par value, 8% cumulative preferred stock, and 200,000 shares of no-par common stock with a stated value of $5 per share.

All the preferred stock was issued at par and 160,000 shares of the common stock were sold for $22 per share. Prepare the stockholders' equity section immediately after the issuance of the securities but prior to any operation of the company.

Ex. 7-2 Wolfe Company has outstanding two classes of $100 par value stock: 5,000 shares of 6% cumulative preferred and 25,000 shares of common. The company had a $50,000 deficit at the beginning of the current year, and preferred dividends had not been paid for two years. During the current year, the company earned $250,000. What will be the balance in retained earnings at the end of the current year, if the company pays a dividend of $1.50 per share on the common stock?

Ex. 7-3 Clark and Davis opened a business on January 3 and agree to share net income as follows:

(1) Interest at 8% of beginning capital balance. Clark invested $15,000 in cash, and Davis invested $9,500 in merchandise.

(2) Salary allowances of $8,000 to Clark and $6,000 to Davis.

(3) Any partnership earnings in excess of the amount required to cover the interest and salary allowances to be divided 60% to Clark and 40% to Davis.

The net income for the first year of operation amounted to $25,000 before interest and salary allowances. Show how this $25,000 should be divided between the two partners.

Ex. 7-4 On June 20, Year 1, E and F decide to combine their single proprietorships into a partnership. The partnership will take over all assets and assume all liabilities of E and F. The balance sheets for E and F are shown below:

	E's Business		F's Business	
	Book Value	Fair Value	Book Value	Fair Value
Assets				
Cash	$ 1,500	$ 1,500	$ 8,000	$ 8,000
Accounts receivable	12,000	11,600	30,000	29,000
Inventory	18,000	20,400	40,000	35,000
Equipment (net)	23,000	23,500	62,000	76,200
Total	$54,500	$57,000	$140,000	$148,200
Liabilities & Owners' Capital				
Accounts payable	$19,500	$19,500	$ 38,500	$ 40,000
Accrued wages payable	600	600	1,000	1,000
E, capital.	34,400	36,900		
F, capital			100,500	107,200
Total	$54,500	$57,000	$140,000	$148,200

Accounts receivable of $1,400 are written off as uncollectible. The book value of F's accounts payable was less than fair value because liabilities of $1,500 had not been recorded.

Prepare a *classified* balance sheet in good form for E and F immediately following formation of the partnership.

Ex. 7-5 A portion of the stockholders' equity section for the Mountain Resorts Corporation is shown below:

Stockholders' equity:

Preferred stock, 6% cumulative, $50 par, 40,000 shares authorized and issued	$2,000,000
Preferred stock, 9% noncumulative, $100 par, 8,000 shares authorized and issued	800,000
Common stock, $5 par, 400,000 shares authorized and issued	2,000,000
Total paid-in capital	$4,800,000

Instructions Assume that all the stock was issued on January 1, 19___, and that no dividends were paid during the first two years of operations. During the third year, Mountain Resorts Corporation paid total cash dividends of $516,000.

a Compute the amount of cash dividends paid during the third year to each of the three classes of stock.

b Compute the dividends paid *per share* during the third year for each of the three classes of stock.

Ex. 7-6 Jim Anderson owns 500 shares of convertible preferred stock of Gravity Research, Inc. Each share is convertible into 1.5 shares of common stock. The preferred stock is selling at $80 per share and pays a dividend of $2.50 per year. The common stock is selling for $50 and pays an annual dividend of $2 per share. Anderson wants to convert the preferred stock in order to increase his total dividend income, but an accounting student suggests that he sell his preferred stock and then buy 750 shares of common stock on the open market. Anderson objects to the student's suggestion on the grounds that he would have to pay income taxes at the rate of 25% on the gain from sale of preferred stock, which he had acquired at $68 per share a year ago. Prepare a schedule showing the results under the two alternatives.

Ex. 7-7 The stockholders' equity section of the balance sheet appeared as follows in a recent annual report of Samoa Corporation:

Stockholders' equity:

   Capital stock:

$5.50 dividend cumulative preferred stock; no-par value, 300,000 shares authorized, 180,000 shares outstanding, stated at	$ 18,000,000
Common stock; no-par value, 5,000,000 shares authorized, 4,300,000 shares issued, stated at	32,250,000
Retained earnings	75,800,000
Total stockholders' equity	$126,050,000

Instructions From this information compute answers to the following questions:

a What is the stated value per share of the preferred stock?

b What was the average issuance price of a share of common stock?

c What is the amount of the total legal capital and the amount of the total paid-in capital?

d What is the total amount of the annual dividend requirement on the preferred stock issue?

e Total dividends of $5,200,000 were declared on the preferred and common stock during the year, and the balance in retained earnings at the beginning of the year amounted to $67,800,000. What was the amount of net income for the year?

PROBLEMS

7-1 The account balances of Andrews Company, arranged in alphabetical order, at the end of the current year are as follows:

Accounts payable	$ 32,100
Accounts receivable	67,500
Accrued liabilities	2,400
Accumulated depreciation	15,000
Administrative expenses	76,350
Andrews, capital (beginning of year)	62,000
Andrews, drawing	8,400
Cash	30,850
Equipment	75,000
Farr, capital (beginning of year)	50,000
Farr, drawing	6,000
Inventory (beginning of year)	22,800
Notes payable	8,000
Purchases (including transportation-in)	326,500
Sales	540,800
Selling expenses	93,650
Short-term prepayments	3,250

There were no changes in partners' capital accounts during the year. The inventory at the end of the year was $23,500. The partnership agreement provided that partners are to be allowed 10% interest on invested capital as of the beginning of the year and that the "residual" net income is to be divided equally.

Instructions
a Prepare an income statement for the current year, showing the distribution of net income as illustrated on page 235.
b Prepare a statement of partners' capitals for the current year.
c Prepare a balance sheet at the end of the current year.

7-2 Primrose Corporation has a total stockholders' equity of $4.5 million at January 1, Year 10, represented by 400,000 shares of $5 par value common stock and 6,000 shares of $100 par value $6 convertible preferred stock. The common stock was issued at $7 per share in Year 1 and the preferred stock at $102 per share in Year 5. The balance in retained earnings at January 1, Year 10 is $1,088,000.

The preferred stock is convertible into common at any time on the basis of $16\frac{2}{3}$ shares of common stock for one share of preferred stock. Income before income taxes is expected to be 20% of stockholders' equity during Year 10. The company is subject to income taxes at an average rate of 40%.

Instructions
a Assume that earnings are as forecast for Year 10 and that none of the preferred stock is converted during the year. Compute the estimated amount

of net income for Year 10 that would be applicable to each share of common stock outstanding.

b Assume that the preferred stock had been converted into common stock on March 1, Year 10, and prepare a journal entry to record the conversion. (The balance in the Premium on $6 Convertible Preferred Stock account should be transferred to Paid-in Capital in Excess of Par.)

c Assume that earnings are as forecast for Year 10 and that the preferred stock had been converted into common stock at the beginning of Year 10. Compute the net income for Year 10 applicable to a single share of common stock. If necessary, round off to the nearest cent.

7-3 Swan Corporation was organized on July 1 of Year 1 with the following two types of capital stock:

9% Preferred stock, cumulative, $100 par value, 5,000 shares authorized

Common stock, $2.50 par value, 100,000 shares authorized

On July 1, preferred stock of 100 shares and common stock of 1,000 shares were issued to Frank Swan in payment for his services in organizing the corporation. Market value of these securities on July 1 were $100 per share for the preferred stock and $5 per share for the common stock. Attorneys' fees of $1,200 incurred in connection with the formation of the corporation had been billed to Swan Corporation but not yet paid.

On July 10, Frank Swan transferred to Swan Corporation certain assets (formerly used in another business) and received in exchange 3,000 shares of the 9%, cumulative preferred stock. The current fair value of the assets transferred to Swan Corporation was as follows: notes receivable, $180,000; inventory, $30,000; and equipment, $90,000.

On July 31, common stock consisting of 80,000 shares was sold for cash at $5.50 per share. Also on July 31, Swan Corporation purchased land and a building for $760,000. The total purchase price was allocated $60,000 to the land and $700,000 to the building. Payment for this property consisted of $360,000 in cash and the issuance of an 8% mortgage note payable for $400,000 due in 10 years.

Swan Corporation did not begin regular operations until after July 31, so no revenue from sales was earned during July. On July 31, miscellaneous expenses of $1,250 were paid but were not considered as organization costs. The attorneys' fee of $1,200 mentioned previously remained unpaid. Interest revenue of $750 was recognized as having accrued during July on the notes receivable. The terms of the mortgage note payable provided that interest did not begin to accrue until August 1. (Income taxes are to be ignored.)

Instructions

a Prepare journal entries to record the above transactions in the accounts of Swan Corporation. Include a closing entry to transfer the net income or loss to the Retained Earnings account.

b Prepare a classified balance sheet for Swan Corporation at July 31, Year 1.

7-4 Clark, Drake, and Elvin agreed to incorporate their business on December 31, Year 5. The balance sheet of the partnership at this date is shown on page 263.

Other data The assets and liabilities of the partnership are fairly stated. The partners received a corporate charter on January 2, Year 6, authorizing 100,000 shares of $1 par value common stock and 1,000 shares of $100 par value, $7 cumulative preferred stock for the new corporation, Clark, Inc.

On January 2, Year 6, a new set of accounting records was opened for Clark, Inc. Each partner was issued common stock at an agreed value of $5 per share for one-half of his capital interest and preferred stock valued at par for the remaining half. Organization costs of $3,000 were paid on January 4, and 20% of this amount was amortized during Year 6.

During Year 6 the corporation earned $50,000 before income taxes. Other assets increased by $75,600, organization costs decreased by $600, and accounts payable increased by $25,000 during Year 6 as a result of profitable operations; the only other liability at year-end was income taxes payable. Income taxes were 40% of income before income taxes. Dividends for a full year were paid on the preferred stock outstanding, and dividends of 50 cents per share were paid on common stock outstanding.

CLARK, DRAKE, AND ELVIN
Balance Sheet
December 31, Year 5

Assets		Liabilities & Capital	
Cash	$ 40,000	Accounts payable	$ 45,000
Other assets	180,000	Clark, capital	87,600
		Drake, capital	52,400
		Elvin, capital	35,000
Total assets	$220,000	Total liabilities & capital . . .	$220,000

Instructions
a Prepare the following journal entries:
   (1) Open the accounting records for Clark, Inc., and record payment made for organization costs.
   (2) Record the net changes in assets, liability, and stockholders' equity accounts as a result of profitable operations during Year 6. Include an entry to record income taxes payable and credit Retained Earnings for the net income after income taxes.
   (3) Record the payment of dividends during Year 6. (Debit Retained Earnings.)
b Prepare a balance sheet for Clark, Inc., at December 31, Year 6.

7-5 Mark Corporation was organized early in Year 1 and was authorized to issue 80,000 shares of $5 par value common stock. The stock was issued at $30 per share. The corporation reported a net loss of $60,000 in Year 1 and a net loss of $45,000 in Year 2. In Year 3, net income was $2.20 per share of common stock. No dividends were declared in Years 1 and 2; a dividend of 40 cents per share was declared in Year 3.

Nolan Corporation was organized early in Year 1 and was authorized to issue 100,000 shares of $10 par value common stock and 10,000 shares of $100 par value cumulative preferred stock. All the preferred stock was issued at $102 per share, and 60,000 shares of common stock were issued at $19.50 per share. The preferred stock is callable at $105 per share and is entitled to dividends of $8 per year before any dividends are paid on the common stock. During the first five years of its existence, the Nolan Corporation earned a total of $660,000 and paid annual dividends of 30 cents per share on the common stock.

Instructions Prepare in good form the stockholders' equity section of the balance sheet at December 31, Year 3, for the Mark Corporation and at December 31, Year 5, for the Nolan Corporation. Include a supporting schedule for each company showing your determination of the balance of retained earnings reported in the balance sheet.

7-6 John Riley owned a retail store. Because he needed additional working capital in his business and had an immediate personal need for $12,500 in cash, Riley agreed on July 31, Year 1, to form a partnership with Alan Paley. Riley invested all non-cash assets of his store in the partnership and immediately withdrew (from funds supplied by Paley) $12,500 in cash. Paley invested $42,000 cash in the partnership. The partnership agreement provided for net income to be divided 60% to Riley and 40% to Paley.

Information as to the assets and liabilities of Riley's business on July 31, Year 1, is shown below.

	Per Riley's Records	Agreed Valuation
Accounts receivable	$33,000	$28,400
Inventory	66,400	54,000
Store equipment	12,400 }	9,000
Accumulated depreciation	4,200 }	
7% note payable (dated May 1, Year 1, due Apr. 30, Year 2) .	24,000	24,420
Accounts payable	14,000	14,000

Accounts receivable of $4,600 were identified as definitely uncollectible and should not be recorded in the accounting records of the partnership. Interest of $420 has accrued on the 7% note payable.

The new partnership (to be known as Mod Fashions) will open a new set of accounting records and will assume all present debts of Riley's business.

Instructions
a Prepare the necessary journal entries to record the formation of the Mod Fashions partnership at July 31, Year 1.
b At the end of August, after all adjusting entries, the Income Summary account of Mod Fashions shows a credit balance of $5,000. The partners' regular drawing accounts for August have debit balances as follows: Riley, $2,500; Paley, $2,200. Prepare the journal entries necessary to complete the closing of the partnership accounts for the month of August.
c Prepare a statement of partners' capitals for the month of August.

7-7 Far West Corporation was organized in January of Year 1 and was authorized to issue capital stock as follows:

50,000 shares of 8% cumulative preferred stock with a $50 par value per share

250,000 shares of $1 par value common stock

During January the following transactions were completed:
Jan. 10 Issued 40,000 shares of common stock in exchange for assets with a current fair value as follows:

Inventory	$ 80,000
Equipment	150,000
Building	160,000
Land	60,000

Jan. 12 Issued 20,000 shares of common stock for cash at $11 per share.
Jan. 15 Paid $3,500 for various organization costs.
Jan. 20 Received subscriptions for 10,000 shares of 8% cumulative preferred stock at $50 per share.
Jan. 28 Subscribers for 1,000 shares of 8% cumulative preferred stock paid the full amount of their subscriptions. Stock certificates were issued for the 1,000 shares of preferred stock.

Jan. 31 Purchased merchandise on account, $15,000 (debit Inventory). No revenue was earned and no expenses incurred during January.

Instructions

a Prepare journal entries to record the transactions for January.

b Prepare a classified balance sheet at January 31, Year 1. Show organization costs under Other Assets.

7-8 Each of the cases described below is independent of the others.

Case A Allen Corporation was organized in 1975 and was authorized to issue 200,000 shares of $5 par value common stock. All shares were issued at a price of $8 per share. The corporation reported a net loss of $60,000 for 1975 and a net loss of $140,000 in 1976. In 1977, the net income was $1.80 per share. No dividends were declared during the three-year period.

Case B Bowman Corporation was organized in 1973. The company was authorized to issue 250,000 shares of $10 par value common stock and 20,000 shares of cumulative preferred stock. All the preferred stock was issued at par and 240,000 shares of the common stock were issued at $12. The preferred stock was callable at 105% of its $100 par value and was entitled to dividends of 8% before any dividends were paid on the common stock. During the first five years of its existence, the corporation earned a total of $1,440,000 and paid dividends of 35 cents per share each year on the common stock, in addition to regular dividends on the preferred stock.

Case C Coleman Corporation was organized in 1974, issuing at $22 per share one-half of the 200,000 shares of $20 par common stock authorized. On January 1, 1975, the company sold at par the entire 10,000 authorized shares of $100 par value, 7% cumulative preferred. On January 1, 1976, the company issued 10,000 shares of an authorized 20,000 shares of $6 no-par, cumulative, participating preferred stock for $1,100,000. The $6 preferred stock provided that after common stockholders had received $3 per share in a given year, the $6 preferred stock would participate in additional dividends on a share-for-share basis up to $5 per share. The company suffered losses in 1974 and 1975, reporting a deficit of $300,000 at the end of 1975. During the years 1976 and 1977 combined, the company earned a total of $1,500,000. Dividends of $1 per share were paid on the common stock in 1976 and $4.25 in 1977. Thus in 1977, the $6 preferred stock participated to the extent of $1.25 per share with common stockholders in dividends.

Instructions For each of the independent cases described, prepare in good form the stockholders' equity section of the balance sheet at December 31, 1977. Include a supporting schedule for each case showing your determination of the balance of retained earnings at December 31, 1977.

BUSINESS DECISION PROBLEM 7

City Electric and Metropolitan Power are two utility companies with very stable earnings. City Electric consistently has a net income of approximately $16 million per year, and Metropolitan Power's net income consistently approximates $14 million per year. City Electric has 1,800,000 shares of 6% preferred stock, $50 par value, and 2,650,000 shares of $50 par value common stock outstanding. Metropolitan Power has 800,000 shares of 6% preferred stock, $100 par value, and 1,840,000 shares of $10 par value common stock outstanding. Assume that both companies distribute all net income as dividends every year, and will continue to do so. Neither company plans to issue additional shares of capital stock.

Instructions

a Compute the annual dividend which would be paid on the common stock of each company, assuming that City Electric has a net income of $16 million and Metropolitan Power has a net income of $14 million.

b Which company's common stock would you expect to have the higher *market price per share?* Support your answer with information provided in the problem.

EIGHT

CORPORATIONS EARNINGS AND DIVIDENDS

The most important aspect of corporate financial reporting, in the view of most stockholders, is the determination of periodic net income. Both the market price of common stock and the amount of cash dividends per share depend to a considerable extent on the current level of earnings. The amount of *earnings per share* of common stock for a year, or an *interim* period such as three months, is of particular interest to stockholders and security analysts. Even more important than the absolute amount of earnings per share is the *trend* of such earnings. Are earnings per share in an upward or downward trend? The common stocks of those companies which regularly achieve higher earnings per share year after year become the favorite securities of the investment community. Such stature helps greatly in raising new capital, in attracting and retaining highly competent management, and in many other ways.

REPORTING THE RESULTS OF OPERATIONS

For many years accountants and users of financial statements have grappled with the issues of income measurement. The timing of revenue and expense recognition has received considerable attention, and sharp differences of opinion have existed with respect to the presentation of nonoperating gains and losses in the income statement. Some accountants have taken the position that all gains and losses recognized during an accounting period should be included in the income statement. However, others have argued that only the results of "normal" activities should be included in the income statement and that all nonoperating gains and losses should be entered directly in the Retained Earnings account.

In 1966, the Accounting Principles Board (APB) took the position that net income should include *all items of profit and loss recognized during the period except for certain "prior period adjustments"* (discussed on pages 283 and 284, which should be entered directly in the Retained Earnings account.[1] Separate listing of certain so-called *extraordinary items* was required in the lower section of the income statement as illustrated below for the Ex-Ord Corporation:

EX–ORD CORPORATION
Condensed Income Statement
For Year 1

Revenue	$8,000,000
Less: Costs and expenses (including income taxes)	6,000,000
Income before extraordinary items	$2,000,000
Extraordinary item—loss from earthquake, net of taxes	(400,000)
Net income	$1,600,000
Earnings per share of common stock:	
Income before extraordinary items	$4.00
Extraordinary loss	(0.80)
Net income	$3.20

Abbreviated form of income statement for a corporation

Gains and losses were not considered extraordinary if they were "of a character typical of the customary business activity of the entity"; such gains and losses were to be included in the determination of income *before* extraordinary items. However, the standards first established by the APB for identifying and reporting extraordinary items proved unsatisfactory in practice and were replaced in 1973 by *APB Opinion No. 30.* In this Opinion, the APB established rather rigid guidelines for (1) measuring and reporting the operating results of discontinued segments of a business and (2) identifying and reporting extraordinary items in the income statement.[2]

Discontinued operations of a segment of a business

A *segment of a business* is "a component of a company whose activities represent a major line of business or class of customer."[3] The assets and operating results of a segment of a business should be clearly identifiable from the other assets and results of operations of the company. Several examples of segments of a business are listed below:

1 An electronics division of a highly diversified manufacturing company

---

[1] *APB Opinion No. 9*, "Reporting the Results of Operations," AICPA (New York: 1966), p. 114.
[2] *APB Opinion No. 30*, "Reporting the Results of Operations—Reporting the Effects of Disposal of a Segment of a Business, and Extraordinary, Unusual and Infrequently Occurring Events and Transactions," AICPA (New York: 1973).
[3] *Ibid.*, pp. 560–561.

2 A professional sports team owned by a newspaper publishing company

3 A wholesale milk distributorship owned by a retail food chain

The income statement is probably more useful if the results from the *continuing and ordinary operations* of a business entity are reported separately from the results of unusual transactions or events of material amount. Thus, the operating results of a discontinued segment of a business (including any gain or loss on the disposal of the segment) for the current period should be reported separately in the income statement in arriving at the income *before* extraordinary items. The purpose of such separate disclosure is to enable users of financial statements to make better predictive judgments as to the future earnings performance of the company.

For example, assume that the Childs Company reported a net income of $10 million for Year 10, including $4 million earned on sales of $30 million by an exporting division which was sold near the end of the year. Would the Childs Company be able to earn $10 million in Year 11 without the exporting business? Before answering this question, let us make an alternative assumption, that is, that the exporting division lost $8 million (after income taxes) in Year 10 instead of earning $4 million. What income might the Childs Company be expected to earn in Year 11 without the drain on earnings from the exporting business? The following partial income statement would be helpful to investors contemplating answers to the two questions:

CHILDS COMPANY

Partial Income Statement

For Year 10

	Assuming Exporting Division Earned $4 Million	Assuming Exporting Division Lost $8 Million
Income from continuing operations ..	$ 6,000,000	$18,000,000
Income (or loss) from discontinued operations*	4,000,000	(8,000,000)
Net income	$10,000,000	$10,000,000
Earnings per share of common stock:		
Income from continuing operations .	$1.50	$4.50
Income (or loss) from discontinued operations	1.00	(2.00)
Net income	$2.50	$2.50

Income or loss from discontinued operations in the income statement

*The revenue in Year 10 from the discontinued segment was $30 million.

The income from continuing operations is a logical starting point in forecasting the probable earnings of the Childs Company for Year 11. However, other variables (such as price changes, increase in sales volume, and the acquisition of new lines of business) may cause the income from continuing operations in Year 11 to change materially under either assumption above.

The revenue and expenses shown in an income statement for the year in which a segment of a business is eliminated should consist only of the *revenue and expenses from continuing operations.* The net income or loss from discontinued operations is reported separately in the income statement, and the revenue from the discontinued segment is disclosed in the notes to the financial statements. Any gain or loss on the disposal of a segment should be reported with or near the results of the discontinued operations and *not as an extraordinary item.*

Extraordinary items

From time to time, most businesses will realize gains and incur losses which are not a part of the main activities of the business. Such gains and losses should be reported as extraordinary items *only* when the event or transaction is *unusual in nature and infrequent in occurrence* when considered in relation to the business and economic environment in which the reporting entity operates.

In order to be considered unusual in nature, the underlying event or transaction should be abnormal and clearly unrelated to the ordinary and typical activities of the entity. The scope of operations, lines of business, operating policies, and the environment in which an entity operates should be considered in applying this criterion. The environment of an entity includes such factors as the characteristics of the industry in which it operates, the geographic location of its activities, and the degree of government regulation.

If an event or a transaction is not reasonably expected to take place in the foreseeable future, it is considered to occur infrequently. Past experience of the entity is generally a helpful guide in determining the frequency of an event or transaction.

Thus only *unusual* and *infrequent* events and transactions produce extraordinary gains and losses. However, these qualitative standards are difficult to apply in practice, and differences of opinion still exist as to what is and what is not an extraordinary item. Listed below and on page 271 are some examples of gains or losses which are generally viewed as extraordinary and some which are not.

Extraordinary Items	*Not Extraordinary Items*
1 *Effects of major casualties such as earthquake (if rare in the area)*	1 *Write-down or write-off of receivables, inventories, equipment leased to others, research and development costs, or other intangibles*

2 *Expropriation of assets by foreign governments*

3 *Effects of a prohibition under a newly enacted law or regulation*

2 *Gains or losses on disposal of a segment of a business or from sale or abandonment of plant assets*

3 *Effects of labor strikes or shortages of raw materials*

4 *Changes in estimates of accumulated depreciation, accrued expenses, and profits or losses on long-term construction contracts*

Few extraordinary items currently appear in corporate income statements as a result of the relatively rigid criteria established in *APB Opinion No. 30.* The presentation of extraordinary items in the income statement is illustrated on pages 274, 275, and 286. The effect of a material event or transaction which is considered either unusual in nature or occurs infrequently, but not both, should be included in determining the income before extraordinary items. The nature and effects on net income of each such event or transaction should be disclosed either in the body of the income statement or in notes to the financial statements.

Earnings per share

Perhaps the most widely used of all accounting statistics is *earnings per share* of common stock. To compute earnings per share, the annual net income available to the common stock is divided by the number of shares outstanding. The amount of quarterly and annual earnings per share is used especially in making investment decisions. Since a purchase or sale of common stock is executed on the basis of the market price per share, it is helpful to know the amount of earnings applicable to a single share. Investors use earnings per share in evaluating the past performance of a company and in forming an opinion as to its potential for future performance. By computing the *price-earnings ratio* (the market price of a share of common stock divided by the annual earnings per share), investors can determine whether the market price of the stock appears reasonable or whether it may be unreasonably high or unreasonably low. Because of the wide publicity given to earnings per share data in newspapers and business journals, it is important that these data be computed in a consistent and logical manner.

AVERAGE NUMBER OF SHARES OUTSTANDING The simplest example of computing earnings per share is found when a company has issued common stock only and the number of shares outstanding has not changed during the year. In this situation, the net income for the year divided by the number of shares outstanding at the year-end equals earnings per share.

In many companies, however, the number of shares of stock outstanding is changed one or more times during the year. A **weighted-average** number of shares outstanding during the year must be computed when additional shares **were sold or issued in exchange for assets** during the year. (A different treatment of an increase in the number of shares outstanding resulting from the **conversion** of preferred stock into common shares will be discussed later in this chapter.) The weighted-average number of shares for the year is determined by multiplying the number of shares outstanding by the fraction of the year that said number of shares outstanding remained unchanged. For example, assume that 100,000 shares of common stock were outstanding during the first three months of Year 1 and 140,000 shares during the last nine months. Assume also that the increase in shares outstanding resulted from the sale of 40,000 shares for cash. The weighted-average number of shares outstanding during Year 1 would be 130,000 determined as follows:

100,000 shares × $\frac{1}{4}$ of a year	*25,000*
140,000 shares × $\frac{3}{4}$ of a year	*105,000*
Weighted-average number of common shares outstanding	*130,000*

This procedure gives more meaningful earnings per share data than if the actual number of shares outstanding **at the end** of the year were used in the calculations. The increased significance arises because the proceeds from the sale of the 40,000 shares were available to generate earnings only during the last nine months of the year. These 40,000 shares were outstanding for three-fourths of a year and are, therefore, equivalent to 30,000 shares for a full year. In other words, the weighted-average number of shares outstanding consists of 100,000 shares outstanding during the entire year plus 30,000 full-year equivalent shares sold during the year.[4]

PRIMARY AND FULLY DILUTED EARNINGS PER SHARE The computation of earnings per share is easily done for companies with common stock only, that is, companies not having convertible securities, stock options, or other rights capable of being converted into additional common shares. In companies with such simple capital structures there is no risk of conversion which would increase the number of common shares and probably **dilute** (reduce) earnings per share of common

---

[4]When the number of shares outstanding changes as a result of a stock split or a stock dividend (discussed later in this chapter), the computation of the weighted-average number of shares outstanding should be adjusted retroactively rather than weighted for the period the new shares were outstanding. Earnings per share data for prior years thus will be consistently stated in terms of the current capital structure.

stock. If only one class of stock is outstanding, earnings per share is computed by dividing the net income for the period by the weighted-average number of shares outstanding during the period. When non-convertible preferred stock is outstanding, earnings per share of common stock may be determined as follows:

Earnings per share when preferred stock is outstanding	*Net income*	*$280,000*
	Less: Dividend on preferred stock for current period	*20,000*
	Income available for common stock	*$260,000*
	Weighted-average number of common shares outstanding	*130,000*
	Earnings per share of common stock, $260,000 ÷ 130,000 shares	*$2.00*

Many corporations have **complex capital structures** including various securities convertible into common stock. Some of these convertible securities are considered to be common stock equivalents; others are not. If a significant part of the value of the convertible security at the time it is issued lies in the conversion right rather than in the specified dividend or interest rate, it is considered to be a **common stock equivalent.** Stock options are always treated as common stock equivalents in computing earnings per share. A **dual presentation** is sometimes necessary: **primary earnings per share,** based on the weighted-average number of common shares actually outstanding plus common stock equivalents and **fully diluted earnings per share,** based on the maximum potential number of shares outstanding.[5]

To illustrate, let us assume that a company with a net income of $100,000 for Year 1 has 5,000 shares of $2 convertible preferred stock and 40,000 shares of common stock outstanding. The preferred stock is convertible into two shares of common stock and did not qualify as a common stock equivalent. Primary and fully diluted earnings per share of common stock would be computed as follows:

		Primary	*Fully Diluted*
Primary and fully diluted earnings per share	*Net income*	*$100,000*	*$100,000*
	Less: Dividends on preferred stock, 5,000 × $2	*10,000*	*–0–*
	Earnings available for common stock	*$ 90,000*	*$100,000*
	Number of shares of common stock outstanding:		
	In computing primary earnings per share	*40,000*	
	In computing fully diluted earnings per share, 40,000 + (5,000 × 2)		*50,000*
	Earnings per share of common stock	*$2.25*	*$2.00*

The existence of convertible securities usually poses the threat of diluting (reducing) earnings per common share, but this general rule is subject to exceptions. For example, assume that the dividend rate

[5] *APB Opinion No. 15, "Earnings per Share," AICPA (New York: 1969), p. 221.*

on the preferred stock had been at the annual rate of $6 per share rather than $2 per share as illustrated above. The primary earnings per share would then have been $1.75 (net income of $100,000 less dividends on preferred stock of $30,000 and divided by 40,000 shares of common stock currently outstanding). In this case, only primary earnings per share would be reported in the income statement because earnings per share would be *increased* rather than *diluted* if we assume the conversion of the preferred stock into common shares.

The assumptions and computations for determining primary and fully diluted earnings per share are often quite complex. A detailed discussion of this topic is more appropriately included in the *Intermediate Accounting* volume of this series.

PRESENTATION OF EARNINGS PER SHARE IN THE INCOME STATEMENT
Earnings per share for a company with a complex capital structure which also had extraordinary items is illustrated below:

	Year 2	Year 1
Income before extraordinary items	*$15,090,600*	*$12,640,000*
Extraordinary loss, net of related income tax		
effect	*(2,080,000)*	*(6,100,000)*
Net income	*$13,010,600*	*$ 6,540,000*
Earnings per share of common stock:		
Primary:		
Earnings before extraordinary loss	*$3.77*	*$3.33*
Extraordinary loss	*(0.52)*	*(1.61)*
Net earnings for the year	*$3.25*	*$1.72*
Fully diluted:		
Earnings before extraordinary loss	*$3.51*	*$3.16*
Extraordinary loss	*(0.48)*	*(1.53)*
Net earnings for the year	*$3.03*	*$1.63*

Primary and fully diluted earnings per share in the income statement

Income statement for a corporation illustrated

A comparative income statement which includes losses from discontinued operations and extraordinary losses is illustrated on page 275 for California Industries, Inc. Fully diluted earnings per share are not given because the company has a simple capital structure which does not create a potential for dilution of earnings per common share.

CALIFORNIA INDUSTRIES, INC.
Comparative Income Statement
For Years Ended September 30

	Year 2	Year 1
Net sales.	$81,853,000	$57,167,000
Cost of goods sold	68,649,000	46,114,000
Gross profit on sales	$13,204,000	$11,053,000
Expenses:		
Selling, administrative, and general expenses . . .	$10,072,000	$ 8,493,000
Interest expense	1,504,000	1,325,000
Other expense, net of miscellaneous income	66,000	101,000
Total expenses	$11,642,000	$ 9,919,000
Income (before income taxes) from continuing operations	$ 1,562,000	$ 1,134,000
Federal and state income taxes	658,000	505,000
Income from continuing operations	$ 904,000	$ 629,000
Loss from discontinued operations, net of income tax benefit of $80,000 in Year 2 and $362,000 in Year 1	(94,000)	(342,000)
Income before extraordinary items	$ 810,000	$ 287,000
Extraordinary items: expropriation loss, net of taxes	–0–	(203,000)
Net income	$ 810,000	$ 84,000
Net income (loss) per share of common stock:		
Income from continuing operations	$0.39	$0.27
Loss from discontinued operations	(0.04)	(0.15)
Income before extraordinary items	$0.35	$0.12
Extraordinary items	–0–	(0.08)
Net income	$0.35	$0.04

Income statement with loss from discontinued operations and extraordinary items

Additional examples of income statements are given in the Appendix.

DIVIDENDS

The term *dividend,* when used by itself, is generally understood to mean a distribution of cash by a corporation to its stockholders. Dividends are stated as a specific amount per share as, for example, a dividend of $1 per share. It follows that the amount received by each stockholder is in proportion to the number of shares owned.

Dividends are paid only through action by the board of directors. The board has full discretion to declare a dividend or to refrain from doing so. Once the declaration of a dividend has been announced, the obligation to pay the dividend is a current liability of the corporation and cannot be rescinded.

Dividends are occasionally paid in assets other than cash. When a corporation goes out of existence (particularly a small corporation with only a few stockholders), it may choose to distribute non-cash assets to its owners rather than to convert all assets into cash.

A dividend may also be paid in the form of additional shares of a company's own stock. This type of distribution is called a *stock dividend.*

A *liquidating* dividend occurs when a corporation returns to stockholders all or part of their paid-in capital investment. Liquidating dividends are usually paid only when a corporation is going out of existence or is making a permanent reduction in the size of its operations. Normally dividends are paid as a result of profitable operations, and the recipient of a dividend is entitled to assume that the dividend represents a distribution of income unless he is specifically notified that the dividend is a return of invested capital.

Cash dividends

The prospect of receiving cash dividends is a principal reason for investing in the stocks of corporations. An increase or decrease in the established rate of dividends will usually cause an immediate rise or fall in the market price of the company's stock. Stockholders are keenly interested in prospects for future dividends and as a group are generally strongly in favor of more generous dividend payments. The board of directors, on the other hand, is primarily concerned with the long-run growth and financial strength of the corporation; it may prefer to restrict dividends to a minimum in order to conserve cash for purchase of plant and equipment or for other needs of the company. The so-called "growth companies" generally plow back into the business most of their earnings and pay little or nothing in cash dividends.

The preceding discussion suggests three requirements for the payment of a cash dividend. These are:

1 *Retained earnings.* Since dividends represent a distribution of earnings to stockholders, the theoretical maximum for dividends is the total net income of the company. As a practical matter, most corporations limit dividends to somewhere near 40% of earnings, in the belief that a major portion of the net income must be retained in the business if the company is to grow and to keep pace with its competitors.

2 *An adequate cash position.* The fact that the company reports large earnings does not mean that it has a large amount of cash on hand. Earnings may have been invested in new plant and equipment, or in paying off debts, or in acquiring a larger inventory. There is no necessary relationship between the balance in the Retained Earnings account and the balance in the Cash account. The traditional expression of "paying dividends out of retained earnings" is misleading. Cash dividends can be paid only "out of" cash.

3 *Dividend action by the board of directors.* Even though the company's net income is substantial and its cash position seemingly satisfactory, dividends are not paid automatically. A positive action by the directors is necessary to declare a dividend.

Regular and special dividends

Many corporations establish a regular quarterly or annual dividend rate and pay this same amount for a period of years regardless of the year-to-year changes in earnings. Such a policy gives a higher invest- ment quality to a company's stock. A strong cash position is necessary if a company is to be prepared to make regular dividend payments in the face of irregular earnings.

If earnings increase but the increase is regarded as a temporary condition, the corporation may decide to pay a *special dividend* in addition to the *regular dividend.* The implication of a special dividend is that the company is making no commitments as to a permanent increase in the amount of dividends to be paid. Of course, even a regular dividend may be reduced or discontinued at any time, but well-financed companies which have long-established regular dividend rates are not likely to omit or reduce regular dividend payments except in extreme emergencies.

Dividends on preferred stock

As indicated in Chapter 7, a preferred stock carries a stated annual dividend rate, such as $5 per share, or 5% of par value. Under no circumstances does a corporation pay more than the stated dividend on preferred stock. This policy of not permitting the preferred stock- holder to share in any unusually large earnings suggests that the corporation views the preferred stockholder only as a supplier of capital rather than as a full-fledged owner in the traditional sense of the word.

Dividends on preferred stocks are not paid unless declared by the board of directors. Since most preferred stocks are of the cumulative variety, any omitted dividend must be made up before any payment can be made to the common. Dividends in arrears on preferred stock do not constitute a liability of the corporation but should be disclosed by a footnote to the balance sheet. Separate accounts are used to record the declaration of preferred and common dividends.

Dividend dates

Four significant dates are involved in the distribution of a dividend. These dates are:

1 *Date of declaration.* On the day on which the dividend is declared by the board of directors, a liability to make the payment comes into existence. The journal entries to record the declaration and the later payment of a cash dividend were illustrated on page 88.

2 *Date of record.* The date of record always follows the date of declaration, usually by a period of two or three weeks, and is always stated in the dividend declaration. In order to be eligible to receive the dividend, a person must be listed as the owner of the stock on the date of record.

3 *Ex-dividend date.* The ex-dividend date is significant for investors in companies with stocks traded on the stock exchanges. To permit the compilation of the list of stockholders as of the record date, it is customary for the stock to go "ex-dividend" three business days before the date of record. A stock is said to be selling ex-dividend on the day that it loses the right to receive the latest declared dividend. A person who buys the stock before the ex-dividend date is entitled to receive the dividend; conversely, a stockholder who sells his shares in the period between the date of declaration and the ex-dividend date does not receive the dividend.

4 *Date of payment.* The declaration of a dividend always includes announcement of the date of payment as well as the date of record. Usually the date of payment comes from two to four weeks after the date of record.

Stock dividends

Stock dividend is an important but confusing term which requires close attention. It is confusing because all dividends are distributions to stockholders and "stock dividend" may suggest to some people merely a dividend on capital stock. *A stock dividend is a pro rata distribution of additional shares to a company's stockholders;* in brief, the dividend consists of shares of stock rather than cash. Perhaps a better term for a stock dividend would be a "dividend payable in capital stock," but the expression "stock dividend" is too firmly entrenched to be easily replaced. Most stock dividends consist of common stock distributed to holders of common stock, and our discussion will be limited to this type of stock dividend.

What is the effect of a stock dividend on the company's financial position? Why does a corporation choose to pay a dividend in shares of stock rather than in cash? Would you as an investor prefer to receive a stock dividend or a cash dividend? These questions are closely related, and a careful analysis of the nature of a stock dividend should provide a basis for answering them.

A cash dividend reduces the assets of a corporation and reduces the stockholders' equity by the same amount. A stock dividend, on the other hand, causes no change in assets and no change in the *total* amount of the stockholders' equity. The only effect of a stock dividend on the accounts is to transfer a portion of the retained earnings into the Common Stock and Paid-in Capital from Stock Dividends accounts. In other words, a stock dividend merely "reshuffles" the stockholders' equity accounts, increasing the permanent capital accounts and decreasing the Retained Earnings account. A stockholder who receives a stock dividend will own an increased number of shares, but his total ownership equity in the company will be no larger than before.

An example may make this fundamental point clear. Assume that a corporation with 800 shares of stock is owned equally by James Davis and Frank Miller, each owning 400 shares of stock. The corporation declares a stock dividend of 25% and distributes 200 additional shares (25% of 800 shares), with 100 shares going to each of the two stockholders. Davis and Miller now hold 500 shares apiece, but each still owns one-half of the business. The corporation has not changed; its assets and liabilities and its total stockholders' equity are exactly the same as before the dividend. From the stockholder's viewpoint, the ownership of 500 shares out of a total of 1,000 outstanding shares represents no more than did the ownership of 400 shares out of a total of 800 shares previously outstanding.

Assume that the market price of this stock was $10 per share prior to the stock dividend. Total market value of all the outstanding shares was, therefore, 800 times $10, or $8,000. What would be the market price per share and in total after the additional 200 dividend shares were issued? The 1,000 shares now outstanding should have the same total market value as the previously outstanding 800 shares, because the "pie" has merely been divided into more but smaller pieces. The price per share should have dropped from $10 to $8, and the aggregate market value of outstanding shares would consequently be computed as 1,000 shares times $8, or $8,000. Whether the market price per share will, in actuality, decrease in proportion to the change in number of outstanding shares is another matter, for market prices are subject to many conflicting influences, some as unpredictable as the state of mind of investors.

REASONS FOR DISTRIBUTION OF STOCK DIVIDENDS Many reasons have been given for the popularity of stock dividends; for example:

1 To conserve cash. When the trend of profits is favorable but cash is needed for expansion, a stock dividend may be an appropriate device for "passing along the earnings" to stockholders without weakening the corporation's cash position.[6]

2 To reduce the market price of a corporation's stock to a more convenient trading range by increasing the number of shares outstanding. This objective is usually present in large stock dividends (25 to 100% or more).

3 To avoid income tax on stockholders. For income tax purposes, stock dividends are not considered as income to the recipients; therefore, no income tax is levied.

Some critics of stock dividends argue that a stock dividend is not really a dividend at all. These critics say that a company which cannot afford to pay a cash dividend should declare no dividends, rather than trying to deceive stockholders by increasing the number of outstanding shares. The popularity of stock dividends, according to such critics, is based on a lack of understanding on the part of stockholders.

Regardless of the merit of the arguments for and against stock dividends, most stockholders welcome these distributions. In many

[6] For example, the Standard Oil Company of California, in a letter to its stockholders, gave the following reason for the "payment" of a 5% stock dividend: "Payment of this stock dividend recognizes the continuing increase in your stockholder's equity in the Company's assets, resulting from reinvestment of part of the Company's earnings. Reinvestment of earnings has helped to sustain the Company's long-range program of capital and exploratory expenditures and investments aimed to increase future income and enhance further the value of your shareholding."

cases a small stock dividend has not caused the market price per share to decline appreciably; consequently, the increase in the number of shares in the hands of each stockholder has, regardless of logic, resulted in an increase in the total market value of his holdings.

ENTRIES TO RECORD STOCK DIVIDENDS Assume that a corporation had the following stockholders' equity accounts on December 15, Year 1, just prior to declaring a 10% stock dividend:

Stock-holders' equity before stock dividend

Stockholders' equity:

Common stock, $10 par value, 30,000 shares authorized, 10,000 shares issued and outstanding	$100,000
Paid-in capital in excess of par	50,000
Retained earnings	200,000
Total stockholders' equity	$350,000

Assume also that the closing market price of the stock on December 15, Year 1, was $30 a share. The company declares and distributes a 10% stock dividend, consisting of 1,000 common shares (10% × 10,000 = 1,000). The entry to record the *declaration* of the dividend is as follows:

Stock dividend declared; note use of market price of stock

Year 1

Dec. 15	Retained Earnings	30,000	
	Stock Dividend to Be Distributed		10,000
	Paid-in Capital from Stock Dividends		20,000
	To record declaration of a 10% stock dividend consisting of 1,000 shares of $10 par value common stock. To be distributed on February 9, Year 2, to stockholders of record on January 15, Year 2. Amount of retained earnings transferred to permanent capital is based on market price of $30 a share on December 15, Year 1.		

The entry to record *distribution* of the dividend shares is as follows:

Stock dividend distributed

Year 2

Feb. 9	Stock Dividend to Be Distributed	10,000	
	Common Stock		10,000
	To record distribution of stock dividend of 1,000 shares.		

Note that the amount of retained earnings transferred to permanent capital accounts by the above entries is not the par value of the new shares, but the *market value,* as indicated by the market price prevailing at the date of declaration. The reasoning behind this practice is simple: Since stockholders tend to measure the "worth" of a small stock dividend (say, 20 to 25% or less) in terms of the market value of the additional shares issued, then Retained Earnings should be reduced by this amount.

Large stock dividends (for example, those in excess of 20 to 25%)

should be recorded by transferring only the par or stated value of the dividend shares from the Retained Earnings account to the Common Stock account. Large stock dividends generally have the effect of proportionately reducing the market price of the stock. For example, a 100% stock dividend would reduce the market price by about 50%, because twice as many shares would be outstanding. A 100% stock dividend is very similar to the 2 for 1 stock split discussed on page 282.

To illustrate the accounting for a large stock dividend, let us assume that Randall Company on May 1 declared a 100% stock dividend on the 100,000 shares of $5 par value common stock outstanding. The journal entries to record the declaration and distribution of the stock dividend are shown below:

Declaration and distribution of 100% stock dividend

May 1	*Retained Earnings*	*500,000*	
	Stock Dividend to Be Distributed		*500,000*
	To record 100% stock dividend declared on 100,000 shares of $5 par value common stock outstanding. To be distributed June 1, 19___, to stockholders of record on May 15, 19___ .		
June 1	*Stock Dividend to Be Distributed*	*500,000*	
	Common Stock		*500,000*
	To record distribution of 100,000 shares of $5 par value common stock as a 100% stock dividend.		

The Stock Dividend to Be Distributed account is not a liability, because there is no obligation to distribute cash or any other asset. If a balance sheet is prepared between the date of declaration of a stock dividend and the date of distribution of the shares, this account, as well as Paid-in Capital from Stock Dividends, should be presented in the stockholders' equity section of the balance sheet.

Paid-in capital as a basis for dividends

Among the several sources of paid-in capital in excess of par (or stated value) are: (1) excess of issuance price over the par or stated value of capital stock, (2) excess of proceeds from reissuance of treasury stock over the cost of these shares, (3) purchase and retirement of shares at a cost less than the issuance price, (4) conversion of preferred stock and bonds into common stock, and (5) donations of property to a corporation by local governments seeking to attract new industries.

A separate ledger account may be used for each specific type of paid-in capital in excess of par or stated value. Examples of appropriate ledger account titles are Paid-in Capital in Excess of Par: Common Stock, Paid-in Capital in Excess of Stated Value, Paid-in Capital from Treasury Stock Transactions, Paid-in Capital from Stock Dividends, Paid-in Capital from Conversion of Preferred Stock, and Donated Capital. In a condensed balance sheet, two or more of these ledger accounts may be combined into a single amount and labeled as Additional Paid-in Capital.

Is paid-in capital available for dividends? Although the laws of many states make it legally possible to declare dividends from paid-in capital, this is rarely done. Whenever a corporation does declare a dividend from any source other than retained earnings, it is obligated to disclose to stockholders that the dividend is of a liquidating nature, representing a return of paid-in capital rather than a distribution of earnings. A liquidating dividend does not constitute taxable income to stockholders.

Stock splits

Most large corporations are interested in as wide as possible a distribution of their securities among the investing public. If the market price reaches very high levels as, for example, $150 per share, the corporation may feel that, by splitting the stock 5 for 1 and thereby reducing the price to $30 per share, the number of shareholders may be increased. The bulk of trading in securities occurs in 100-share lots and an extra commission is charged on smaller transactions. Many investors with limited funds prefer to make their investments in 100-share lots of lower-priced stocks. The majority of leading American corporations have split their stock; some have done so several times. Generally the number of shareholders has increased noticeably after the stock has been split.

A stock split consists of increasing the number of outstanding shares and reducing the par or stated value per share in proportion. For example, assume that a corporation has outstanding 1 million shares of $10 par value stock. The market price is $90 per share. The corporation now reduces the par value from $10 to $5 per share and increases the number of shares from 1 million to 2 million. This action would be called a 2 for 1 stock split. A stockholder who formerly owned 100 shares of the $10 par old stock would now own 200 shares of the $5 par new stock. Since the number of outstanding shares has been doubled without any change in the affairs of the corporation, the market price will probably drop from $90 to approximately $45 a share.

A stock split does not change the balance of any ledger account; consequently, the transaction may be recorded merely by a memorandum notation in the general journal and in the Common Stock account. As an alternative, the existing Common Stock account may be debited, with an offsetting credit to a new Common Stock account having a reduced par or stated value.

DISTINCTION BETWEEN STOCK SPLITS AND LARGE STOCK DIVIDENDS
What is the difference between a 2 for 1 stock split and a 100% stock

dividend? Both will double the number of outstanding shares without changing total stockholders' equity, and both will serve to cut the market price of the stock in half. The stock dividend, however, will cause a transfer from the Retained Earnings account to the Common Stock account equal to the par or stated value of the dividend shares, whereas the stock split does not change the dollar balance of any account. After an increase in the number of shares as a result of a stock split or stock dividend, earnings per share are of course computed in terms of the increased number of shares. In presenting five- or ten-year summaries, the earnings per share for earlier years are retroactively revised to reflect the increased number of shares currently outstanding and thus make the trend of earnings per share from year to year a valid comparison.

Retained earnings

Throughout this book the term *retained earnings* is used to describe that portion of stockholders' equity derived from profitable operations. An older term for this part of stockholders' equity is *earned surplus.* Because of the misleading connotations of the word "surplus," a strong trend has developed to use "retained earnings" or "accumulated earnings" in place of "earned surplus" in corporate balance sheets.

Retained earnings is an historical concept, representing the accumulated earnings (including prior period adjustments) minus dividends declared from the date of incorporation to the present. Each year the Income Summary account is closed by transferring the net income or net loss into the Retained Earnings account. If we assume that there are no prior period adjustments, the major sources of entries in the Retained Earnings account will be (1) the periodic transfer of net income (or loss) from the Income Summary account and (2) the debit entries for dividend declarations.

In successful corporations the Retained Earnings account normally has a credit balance; but if total losses should exceed total net income, the Retained Earnings account will have a debit balance. This debit amount is listed in the balance sheet as a *deficit* and is deducted from the total of the paid-in capital, as previously illustrated on page 243.

Prior period adjustments to Retained Earnings account

As previously stated, extraordinary items are included in the income statement, but prior period adjustments are recorded directly in the Retained Earnings account and reported in the statement of retained earnings. Prior period adjustments are relatively rare because they must be material in amount and must also meet the following four criteria:

1 Must be directly related to the activities of a prior period

2 Could not have been measured with reasonable accuracy in the prior period

3 Must not be attributable to an economic event of the current period

4 Must result from decisions and determinations by persons other than management of the reporting corporation, such as a government agency or a court of law

Examples of prior period adjustments include additional income tax assessments for prior years, settlement of litigation based on events of earlier periods, and settlement of rate disputes which affect the income previously reported by public utility companies. To illustrate a prior period adjustment, assume that an additional income tax assessment of $1,950,000 for Year 2 was levied against the Gallero Corporation in Year 4. The assessment would be recorded in Year 4 as follows:

Recording a prior period adjustment

Retained Earnings	*1,950,000*	
Income Tax Assessment Payable		*1,950,000*

To record income tax assessment applicable to Year 2 as a prior period adjustment.

The presentation of this prior period adjustment in the statement of retained earnings for Gallero Corporation is illustrated on page 285.

Appropriations and restrictions of retained earnings

A few corporations transfer a portion of their retained earnings into separate accounts called *appropriations.* The purpose of such appropriations is to indicate to users of financial statements that a portion of retained earnings is not available for the declaration of cash dividends. The limitation on cash dividends may be established voluntarily by the board of directors (perhaps to provide for some contingency) or it may be required by law or contract. An appropriation of retained earnings is recorded by a debit to Retained Earnings and a credit to the appropriation account such as Retained Earnings Appropriated for Contingencies. Appropriation accounts are still a part of total retained earnings as indicated by the following partial stockholders' equity section which appeared in a recent balance sheet of Wm. Wrigley Jr. Company:

Appropriations in the balance sheet

Stockholders' equity:

Capital stock, no par value—authorized and issued—2,000,000 shares	*$ 19,200,000*
Accumulated earnings retained for use in the business	*109,130,000*
Accumulated earnings appropriated for guarantees under employment assurance contracts	*2,000,000*

When the restriction on retained earnings is no longer needed, the appropriation account is eliminated by transferring its balance back to the Retained Earnings account.

Instead of establishing appropriations of retained earnings, most corporations disclose restrictions on the declaration of cash dividends in notes accompanying the financial statements.[7] Two examples of such disclosure are shown below.

Alternative disclosure of restrictions placed on retained earnings

Rockwell International Corporation:
Among other covenants, certain of the long-term debt agreements contain limitations on creation of additional long-term debt and restrictions on payment of dividends and acquisition of treasury stock. Retained earnings . . . not so restricted amounted to approximately $117,000,000.
Ethyl Corporation:
The Corporation's articles of incorporation and note agreements contain restrictions, among others, against the payment of cash dividends. . . . $28,658,000 of retained earnings is free of such restriction under the agreement presently most restrictive.

Since the only purpose of appropriating retained earnings is to inform readers of the financial statements that a portion of the retained earnings is "reserved" for a specific purpose and is not available for declaration of cash dividends, this information can be conveyed more directly, with less danger of misunderstanding, by a note accompanying the financial statements.

Statement of retained earnings

In addition to the balance sheet and the income statement, most corporations include a statement of retained earnings and a statement of changes in financial position in their annual reports to stockholders. (The latter statement will be illustrated in Chapter 15.) The typical format of the statement of retained earnings included in annual reports of publicly owned corporations is illustrated below for the Gallero Corporation:

GALLERO CORPORATION
Statement of Retained Earnings
For Years Ended June 30

Statement of retained earnings shows prior period adjustments, net income, and dividends

	Year 4	Year 3
Retained earnings at beginning of year:		
As originally reported	$15,400,000	$14,850,000
Prior period adjustment—additional income taxes, applicable to Year 2	(1,950,000)	(1,950,000)
As restated	$13,450,000	$12,900,000
Net income	5,500,000	2,350,000
Subtotal	$18,950,000	$15,250,000
Less: Cash dividends on common stock:		
$2.40 per share in Year 4	(2,400,000)	
$1.80 per share in Year 3		(1,800,000)
Retained earnings at end of year	$16,550,000	$13,450,000

[7] According to the 1973 issue of *Accounting Trends & Techniques* published by the AICPA, only four of the 600 annual reports surveyed showed appropriated retained earnings while 425 annual reports referred to restrictions on retained earnings.

The additional income tax applicable to Year 2 was assessed in Year 4 and is shown as a correction to the beginning balance in retained earnings for both years, since both beginning amounts were overstated. The statement of retained earnings thus provides a useful vehicle for the disclosure of prior period adjustments and for the reconciliation of changes in retained earnings resulting from net income (or net loss) and dividends declared.

An alternative presentation of net income and retained earnings is used by some companies. The reconciliation of retained earnings may be shown in the body of a *combined statement of income and retained earnings,* as illustrated below for Lacey Corporation which uses a 52-week fiscal year:

LACEY CORPORATION

Combined Statement of Income and Retained Earnings

(in thousands, except earnings per share)

Combined statement of income and retained earnings

	52 Weeks Ended	
	Oct. 26, Year 2	*Oct. 28, Year 1*
Revenue	$2,832,022	$2,924,449
Cost and expenses	2,805,300	2,872,228
Income before income taxes and extraordinary items	$ 26,722	$ 52,221
Income taxes	(11,289)	(21,281)
Income before extraordinary items	$ 15,433	$ 30,940
Extraordinary loss, net of income tax credit of $43 million	(57,000)	–0–
Net income (loss)	$ (41,567)	$ 30,940
Retained earnings at beginning of year	220,452	202,855
	$ 178,885	$ 233,795
Dividends: $0.90 per share in Year 2 and $1.10 per share in Year 1	(11,016)	(13,343)
Retained earnings at end of year	$ 167,869	$ 220,452
Earnings (loss) per share of common stock:		
Earnings before extraordinary items	$ 1.12	$2.39
Extraordinary loss	(4.66)	–0–
Net income (loss)	$(3.54)	$2.39

The statement for the Lacey Corporation emphasizes the close relationship of operating results and retained earnings. Some readers of financial statements, however, object to the fact that net income (or loss) is "buried" in the body of a combined statement of income and retained earnings rather than being prominently displayed as the final figure before reporting earnings per share.

TREASURY STOCK

Corporations frequently reacquire shares of their own capital stock by purchase in the open market. The effect of reacquiring shares is to reduce the assets of the corporation and to reduce the stockholders' equity by the same amount. One reason for such purchases is to have stock available to reissue to officers and employees under bonus plans. Other reasons may include a desire to increase the reported earnings per share, to support the market price of the stock, and to have shares available for the acquisition of other companies.

Treasury stock may be defined as a corporation's own capital stock which has been issued, fully paid, and reacquired but not canceled. Treasury shares may be held indefinitely or may be issued again at any time. Shares of capital stock held in the treasury are not entitled to receive dividends, vote, or receive cash or other assets upon dissolution of the company.

Recording purchases and reissuance of treasury stock

Purchases of treasury stock should be recorded by debiting the Treasury Stock account with the cost of the stock. For example, if a corporation reacquires 10 shares of its own $100 par stock at a price of $150 per share, the entry is as follows:

Treasury stock recorded at cost

Treasury Stock	1,500	
Cash		1,500
Purchased 10 shares of $100 par treasury stock at $150 per share.		

Treasury stock is customarily recorded *at cost* regardless of whether it is par value stock or no-par stock. When the treasury shares are reissued, the Treasury Stock account is credited for *the cost* of the shares reissued, and Paid-in Capital from Treasury Stock Transactions is debited or credited for the difference between cost and reissuance price.

To illustrate the reissuance of treasury stock at a price above cost, assume that the 10 shares acquired at a cost of $1,500 are reissued for a higher price, $1,800. The entry is:

Reissued at a price above cost

Cash	1,800	
Treasury Stock		1,500
Paid-in Capital from Treasury Stock Transactions		300
Sold 10 shares of treasury stock, which cost $1,500, at a price of $180 each.		

If treasury stock is reissued at a price below cost and a paid-in capital account exists as a result of previous treasury stock transactions, this account may be debited. If there is no paid-in capital as a result of previous treasury stock transactions, the excess of the cost of the treasury shares over reissuance price could be recorded as a debit in any other paid-in capital account or in the Retained Earnings account.

Treasury stock not an asset

Corporations sometimes list treasury stock among the assets on the grounds that the shares could be sold for cash just as readily as shares owned in another corporation. The same argument could be made for treating unissued shares as assets. Treasury shares are basically the same as unissued shares, and an unissued share of stock is definitely not an asset.

When treasury stock is purchased, the corporation is eliminating a part of the stockholders' equity by paying off one or more stockholders. It is, therefore, reasonable to think of the purchase of treasury stock not as the acquisition of an asset, but as the returning of capital to stockholders. For this reason treasury stock should appear in the balance sheet *as a deduction in the stockholders' equity section.*

Conversely, if the treasury shares are later reissued, this is a separate transaction in which the corporation is securing additional invested capital. Assume, for example, that a corporation pays $10 to acquire a share of treasury stock and later reissues this share for $15. Has the corporation made a $5 profit on this transaction with its owners? Definitely not; *there is no profit or loss on treasury stock transactions.* When the treasury share was reissued for $15, the corporation was merely receiving a larger amount of invested capital than was previously withdrawn when a stockholder surrendered the share to the company. A corporation earns profits by selling goods and services to outsiders at a price above cost, not by issuing or reissuing shares of its own stock.

Restriction of retained earnings when treasury stock is acquired

If a corporation is to maintain its paid-in capital intact, it must not pay out to its stockholders any more than it earns. As previously stated in the section dealing with dividends, the amount of dividends to be paid must not exceed the corporation's accumulated earnings, or the corporation will be returning a portion of the stockholders' original investment to them.

The payment of cash dividends and the acquisition of treasury stock have a good deal in common. In both transactions, the corporation is disbursing cash to its stockholders. Of course, the dividend payment is spread out among all the stockholders, whereas the payment to purchase treasury stock may go to only a few stockholders, but this does not alter the fact that the corporation is turning over some of its assets to its owners. The total amount which a corporation may pay to its stockholders without reducing paid-in capital is shown by the balance in the Retained Earnings account. Consequently, it is important that a corporation keep track of the total amount disbursed in payment for treasury stock and make sure that this amount plus any dividends paid does not exceed the company's accumulated earnings. This objective is conveniently accomplished by restricting the availability of retained earnings for dividends to the extent of the cost of treasury stock purchased. The restriction should be disclosed in a note accompanying the financial statements as described on page 290.

BOOK VALUE PER SHARE OF CAPITAL STOCK

Earlier in this chapter, we emphasized that most stockholders are much interested in earnings per share and dividends per share. Another accounting measurement of interest to stockholders is *book value per share of common stock.* In a corporation which has issued common stock only, the book value per share is computed by dividing total stockholders' equity by the number of shares of stock outstanding. Thus book value per share is equal to the *net assets* represented by one share of stock. The term *net assets* means total assets minus total liabilities; in other words, the total net assets are equal to the total stockholders' equity.

Book value is usually computed only for common stock. If a company has both preferred and common stock outstanding, the computation of book value per share of common stock requires two steps. First the redemption value or call price of the entire preferred stock issue and any dividends in arrears are deducted from total stockholders' equity. Secondly, the remaining amount of stockholders' equity is divided by the number of common shares outstanding to determine book value per common share. This procedure reflects the fact that the common stockholders are the residual owners of the corporate entity.

The concept of book value is of vital importance in many contracts. For example, a majority stockholder might obtain an option to purchase the shares of the minority stockholders at book value at a specified future date. Many court cases have hinged on definitions of book value. In Chapter 16 we shall consider book value more fully as a factor in the analysis of financial statements.

Illustration of stockholders' equity section of the balance sheet

The following illustration of a stockholders' equity section of a balance sheet shows a detailed classification by source of the various elements of corporate capital.

Stockholders' equity:

6% preferred stock, $100 par value, 1,000 shares authorized and issued	*$100,000*	
Common stock, no-par, stated value $5 a share, 100,000 shares authorized, 60,000 shares issued (of which 1,000 are held in treasury)	*300,000*	
Common stock dividend to be distributed, 2,950 shares .	*14,750*	
Common stock subscribed, 6,000 shares	*30,000*	*$444,750*
Additional paid-in capital:		
From stock dividends	*$ 50,000*	
From issuance of common stock in excess of stated value	*275,250*	
From treasury stock transactions	*5,000*	*330,250*
Total paid-in capital		*$775,000*
Retained earnings (Note 1)		*162,000*
Total paid-in capital and retained earnings		*$937,000*
Less: Treasury stock, 1,000 shares at cost		*12,000*
Total stockholders' equity		*$925,000*

Note 1: Retained earnings in the amount of $92,000 is not available for declaration of cash dividends because of loan agreements and the purchase of treasury stock.

The published financial statements of leading corporations indicate that there is no one standard arrangement for the various items making up the stockholders' equity section. Variations occur in the selection of titles, in the sequence of items, and in the extent of detailed classification. Many companies, in an effort to avoid excessive detail in the balance sheet, will combine several related ledger accounts into a single balance sheet item. Several examples of published financial statements appear in the Appendix.

DEMONSTRATION PROBLEM

A comparative summary of the stockholders' equity of Sutton Corporation, together with certain additional information, is given on page 291.

	Dec. 31, Year 10		Dec. 31, Year 9	
Stockholders' equity:				
Capital stock, 100,000 shares authorized;				
issued:				
At Dec. 31, Year 10, 70,000 shares, $8				
par value (1,000 held in treasury) . . .	*$560,000*			
At Dec. 31, Year 9, 40,000 shares, $10				
par value			*$ 400,000*	
Stock dividend to be distributed (6,900				
shares)	*55,200*	*$ 615,200*		
Additional paid-in capital:				
From issuance of capital stock in ex-				
cess of par value	*$800,700*		*200,000*	
From stock dividends destributed	*276,000*			
From treasury stock transactions	*8,000*	*1,084,700*		
Total paid-in capital		*$1,699,900*	*$ 600,000*	
Retained earnings		*1,276,800*	*1,500,000*	
Total paid-in capital and retained earnings		*$2,976,700*		
Less: Cost of 1,000 shares held in treasury		*37,000*		
Total stockholders' equity		*$2,939,700*	*$2,100,000*	

Transactions affecting stockholders' equity during Year 10:

Mar. 1 A 5 for 4 stock split proposed by the board of directors was approved by vote of the stockholders.

Mar. 31 Additional shares were distributed to stockholders pursuant to the 5 for 4 split.

Apr. 1 The company purchased 2,000 shares of its capital stock on the open market at $37 per share.

July 1 The company reissued 1,000 shares of treasury stock at $45 per share.

July 1 The net assets of Wizzaro Company were acquired in exchange for 20,000 shares of $8 par value capital stock with a total fair value of $760,700.

Dec. 1 A cash dividend of $1 per share was declared, payable on December 30, to stockholders of record at December 14.

Dec. 22 A 10% stock dividend was declared; the dividend shares to be distributed on January 24, Year 11. The market price of the stock on December 22 was $48 per share.

The net income for the year ended December 31, Year 10, amounted to $177,000, after an extraordinary loss of $35,400 (net of income tax credit of $30,000).

Instructions

a Prepare journal entries to record the transactions relating to stockholders' equity that took place during Year 10.

b Prepare the lower section of the income statement for the year ended December 31, Year 10, beginning with the income before extraordinary items and showing the extraordinary loss and the net income. Also illustrate the presentation of earnings per share in the income statement, assuming that earnings per share is determined on the basis of the weighted-average number of shares outstanding during the year.

c Prepare a statement of retained earnings for the year ended December 31, Year 10.

SOLUTION TO DEMONSTRATION PROBLEM

a
                    General Journal

Mar.	1	Memorandum: Stockholders approved a 5 for 4 stock split. This action increased the number of shares of capital stock outstanding from 40,000 to 50,000 and reduced the par value from $10 to $8 per share.	
	31	Capital Stock, $10 par	400,000
		Capital Stock, $8 par	400,000
		Distributed 10,000 additional shares of stock pursuant to 5 for 4 stock split, and reduced par value.	
April	1	Treasury Stock	74,000
		Cash	74,000
		Acquired 2,000 shares of treasury stock at $37 per share.	
July	1	Cash	45,000
		Treasury Stock	37,000
		Paid-in Capital from Treasury Stock Transactions	8,000
		Sold 1,000 shares of treasury stock at $45 per share.	
	1	Net Assets	760,700
		Capital Stock, $8 par	160,000
		Paid-in Capital in Excess of Par	600,700
		Issued 20,000 shares of previously unissued $8 par value stock (total market value $760,700) in exchange for the net assets of Wizzaro Company.	
Dec.	1	Dividends	69,000
		Dividends Payable	69,000
		To record declaration of cash dividend of $1 per share on 69,000 shares of capital stock outstanding (1,000 shares in treasury are not entitled to receive dividends).	

Note: Entry to record the payment of the cash dividend is not shown here since the action does not affect the stockholders' equity.

Dec.	22	Retained Earnings	331,200
		Stock Dividends to be Distributed	55,200
		Paid-in Capital from Stock Dividends	276,000
		To record declaration of 10% stock dividend consisting of 6,900 shares of $8 par value capital stock to be distributed on Jan. 24, Year 11. Excess of fair market value of stock over par value, $40 ($48 − $8), is credited to Paid-in Capital from Stock Dividends.	
	31	Income Summary	177,000
		Retained Earnings	177,000
		To close Income Summary account.	

Dec. 31	Retained Earnings	69,000	
	Dividends		69,000
	To close Dividends account.		

b

SUTTON CORPORATION
Partial Income Statement
For Year Ended December 31, Year 10

Income before extraordinary items	$212,400
Extraordinary loss, net of income tax credit of $30,000	(35,400)
Net income	$177,000

Earnings per share:*	
Income before extraordinary items	$3.60
Extraordinary loss, net of tax	(0.60)
Net income	$3.00

* On 59,000 weighted-average number of shares of capital stock outstanding during Year 10: determined as follows:

Jan. 1–Mar. 31: (40,000 + 10,000 shares issued pursuant to a 5 for 4 split) × ¼ of year	12,500
Apr. 1–June 30: (50,000 − 2,000 shares of treasury stock) × ¼ of year	12,000
July 1–Dec. 31: (50,000 + 20,000 shares of new stock − 1,000 shares of treasury stock) × ½ of year . .	34,500
Weighted-average number of shares outstanding	59,000

c

SUTTON CORPORATION
Statement of Retained Earnings
For the Year Ended December 31, Year 10

Retained earnings, Jan. 1, Year 10		$1,500,000
Net income		177,000
Subtotal		$1,677,000
Dividends:		
Cash, $1 per share	$ 69,000	
Stock, 10% (to be distributed Jan. 24, Year 11)	331,200	400,200
Retained earnings, Dec. 31, Year 10		$1,276,800

REVIEW QUESTIONS

1 Why is the reporting of the results of operations so important to users of financial statements?

2 Define a **segment of a business** and **extraordinary items** for purposes of reporting the results of operations.

3 Give some examples of **segments of a business** and **extraordinary losses.**

4 Briefly describe how each of the following should be reported in the income statement:
  a Write-off of a large account receivable from a bankrupt customer
  b Large loss from sale of a major segment of a business
  c Large gain from sale of one of many investments in common stock
  d Large write-off of obsolete inventory

     e Large uninsured loss from earthquake
     f Large damages payable as result of unfavorable settlement of a lawsuit applicable to an earlier year

5 How should the effect of a material event or transaction which is either unusual in nature or occurs infrequently, but not both, be disclosed?

6 Briefly define each of the following:
     a Price-earnings ratio
     b Common stock equivalents
     c Primary earnings per share
     d Fully diluted earnings per share

7 Explain the significance of the following dates relating to dividends: date of declaration, date of record, date of payment, ex-dividend date.

8 Distinguish between a *stock split* and a *stock dividend.* Is there any reason for the difference in accounting treatment of these two events?

9 Morrison purchased 200 shares of stock in Z Corporation at the time it was organized. At the end of the first year's operations, the corporation reported earnings (after income taxes) of $4 per share and declared a dividend of $2 per share. Morrison complains that he is entitled to the full distribution of the amount earned on his investment. Is there any reason why a corporation that earns $4 per share may not be able to pay a dividend of this amount? Are there any advantages to Morrison in the retention by the company of one-half of its earnings?

10 If the Retained Earnings account has a debit balance, how is it presented in the balance sheet and what is it called?

11 Favorable settlement of a lawsuit relating to events which occurred several years ago brought the Betty Company a court award during the current year. What special accounting term is used to describe transactions of this type? What four criteria must be met in order for such transactions to be excluded from the income statement? What account should be credited to record receipt of the large cash settlement?

12 What is the purpose of an appropriation of retained earnings? What are the arguments for and against the use of such appropriations?

13 What type of transaction most frequently appears as a deduction in a statement of retained earnings?

14 What is *treasury stock?* Why do corporations purchase their own shares? Is treasury stock an asset? How should it be reported in the balance sheet?

15 In many states, the corporation law requires that retained earnings be restricted for dividend purposes to the extent of the cost of treasury shares. What is the reason for this legal rule?

16 What would be the effect, if any, on book value per share of common stock as a result of each of the following independent events: a corporation (*a*) obtains a bank loan. (*b*) is assessed additional income taxes applicable to prior years, and (*c*) distributes a 5% stock dividend?

EXERCISES

Ex. 8-1 In Year 5, Clemson Company had net sales of $1,500,000, costs and other expenses (including income taxes) of $900,000, a tax refund of $120,000 applicable to Year 3, and an extraordinary loss (net of income tax) of $250,000. Prepare a condensed income statement (including earnings per share) for Year 5, assuming that an average of 100,000 shares of common stock were outstanding during Year 5.

Ex. 8-2 The operations for Replacement Parts, Inc., are summarized below for Year 10:

	From Continuing Operations	From Discontinued Operations
Net sales	$12,000,000	$3,000,000
Costs and expenses (including applicable income tax effects)	8,200,000	3,950,000
Loss on disposal of discontinued segment		850,000

Instructions Assuming that the company had an average of 500,000 shares of a single class of capital stock outstanding during Year 10, prepare a condensed income statement (including earnings per share).

Ex. 8-3 The Grossman Corporation had 3,600,000 shares common stock outstanding at the end of Year 3. In Year 3, the stock was split 3 for 1 on March 1 and 600,000 shares were sold for cash on July 1. During Years 1 and 2, the number of shares outstanding remained unchanged at 1,000,000 shares.

Compute the weighted-average number of shares outstanding for each year that should be used in reporting comparative earnings per share data at the end of Year 3.

Ex. 8-4 Nix Company has 180,000 shares of $10 par common stock and 10,000 shares of $6.60 cumulative preferred stock outstanding at the end of the current year. Each share of preferred stock is convertible into four shares of common stock. The preferred stock did not qualify as a common stock equivalent on the date of issue. Net income for the current year is $660,000. Show how the primary and fully diluted earnings per share should appear in the income statement for the current year.

Ex. 8-5 At the beginning of the current year, the Gordon Corporation had 2 million shares of $10 par value capital stock outstanding. You are to prepare journal entries to record the following transactions during the current year:

Feb. 2 Declared a cash dividend of 10 cents per share.
Mar. 10 Paid the 10-cent cash dividend declared on February 2 to stockholders.
June 14 Declared a 2% stock dividend. Market price of stock was $26 per share.
July 6 Issued 40,000 shares pursuant to the 2% stock dividend.
Dec. 20 Declared a 50% stock dividend. Market price of stock was $40 per share.

Ex. 8-6 Pearson Cotton Co. currently has 40,000 shares of common stock outstanding and no preferred stock. The net assets (stockholders' equity) of the company are $800,000, and the market price of the stock is $48 per share. If the company declares a stock dividend of one share for each five shares held and all parties concerned clearly recognize the nature of the stock dividend, what would you expect the market price per share of the company's common stock to be on the ex-dividend date?

Ex. 8-7 The accountant for Kell Corporation prepared a balance sheet at the end of Year 10 which included the following stockholders' equity accounts:

6% cumulative preferred stock (40,000 shares issued and outstanding) .	$2,000,000
Common stock (60,000 shares outstanding)	546,000
Surplus	1,614,000

The company was authorized to issue 50,000 shares of $50 par value preferred and 100,000 shares of $10 par value common stock. Of the 40,000 shares of preferred issued, 36,000 were issued at par and 4,000 were issued at $53 per share. A total of 66,000 shares of common stock were issued at an average price of $22 per share. Of this total, 6,000 shares have been reacquired by the company at a cost of $114,000, which amount the accountant deducted from the Common Stock account. The preferred stock is callable at any time at $55 per share.

The Surplus account contains the excess of issuance price over par on preferred and common stock and $810,000 of retained earnings.

Prepare in good form the stockholders' equity section for Kell Corporation. Include a full description of each stock issue with respect to par value, call provision, and number of shares authorized, issued, outstanding, and held in treasury.

Ex. 8-8 The following data are taken from the records of the Sears Corporation:

7% cumulative preferred stock, $10 par (liquidation value, $210,000) . . .	$200,000
Common stock, no par, 101,500 shares issued, 1,500 held in treasury . .	940,000
Paid-in capital from treasury stock transactions	11,500
Dividends in arrears on preferred stock, 2 full years	
Deficit	55,000
Organization costs	10,000
Treasury stock, 1,500 shares, at cost	19,500
Total liabilities	423,000

Instructions
a Compute the amount of net assets (stockholders' equity).
b If all assets are sold for 90% of book value, how much would each share of common stock receive as a liquidating dividend?

PROBLEMS

8-1 The balance sheet of Tony's Lumber Company at June 20 of the current year is shown below:

Assets		Liabilities & Stockholders' Equity	
Cash	$ 15,000	Notes payable	$ 10,000
Accounts receivable	55,000	Accounts payable	25,000
Other assets	150,000	Capital stock, $5 par	65,000
		Paid-in capital in excess	
		of par	50,000
		Retained earnings	70,000
	$220,000		$220,000

On June 20 a decision was made to dissolve the business. The transactions listed below were carried out for this purpose.

On June 21 all the accounts receivable were collected, and all the "other assets" were sold for $210,000 cash. A liability for income taxes in the amount of $18,000 was incurred because of the gain on the sale of the "other assets."

On June 21 all liabilities were paid, including the $18,000 liability for income taxes resulting from the sale of the "other assets."

On June 22 all remaining cash was distributed to stockholders. The shareholders surrendered their stock certificates, and all ledger accounts were closed.

Instructions:

a Prepare general journal entries to record the events from June 21 to June 22 inclusive. Assume that the gain (net of income taxes) is credited to Gain on Sale of Other Assets before being closed to Retained Earnings.

b Tony's Lumber Company had paid a total of $325,000 in cash dividends from the date of its organization to June 20 of the current year. Also a 30% stock dividend consisting of 3,000 shares was issued three years ago. You are to compute the total amount of net income earned by Tony's Lumber Company over its entire life (including the gain on sale of "other assets" net of income tax).

8-2 The accountant for Thermal Energy Corporation *improperly* prepared the following income statement for Year 5:

THERMAL ENERGY CORPORATION

Income Statement

For Year 5

Net sales		$ 9,000,000
Sale of treasury stock in Year 5 (cost, $650,000; proceeds,		
$800,000)		150,000
Excess of proceeds over par value of capital stock issued in		
Year 5		960,000
Reduction in appropriation for purchase of treasury stock		650,000
Total revenue		$10,760,000
Less:		
Cost of goods sold	$4,950,000	
Operating expenses	2,040,000	
Loss from earthquake (before tax reduction of		
$180,000)	420,000	
Dividends declared on capital stock	300,000	
Estimated income tax expense, after reduction of		
$180,000 as a result of the loss from earthquake .	670,000	8,380,000
Net income		$ 2,380,000

At the beginning of Year 5, the audited financial statements of the company show unappropriated retained earnings of $3,250,000 and a balance in Retained Earnings Appropriated for Purchase of Treasury Stock account of $1,000,000. The treasury stock transaction is not taxable, and the earthquake loss is fully deductible in computing taxable income. Income tax expense has been properly estimated by a tax advisor. The earthquake loss should be reported in the income statement as an extraordinary item *net of income taxes.*

Instructions

a Prepare a corrected income statement for Year 5. Show data for earnings per share of capital stock in the income statement. Thermal Energy Corporation had a weighted average of 200,000 shares of a single class of capital stock outstanding during the year.

b Prepare a statement of retained earnings for Year 5. (Use three columns as follows: Retained Earnings Appropriated for Purchase of Treasury Stock, Unappropriated, and Total Retained Earnings.)

8-3 The Orinoco Ore Company was organized early in Year 1 and was authorized to issue 100,000 shares of $10 par value common stock and 50,000 shares of $50 par value 7% preferred stock. During Year 1 the company sold 70,000 shares of common stock, at an average price of $30 per share, and issued an additional 10,000 shares of common stock in exchange for patents valued at $320,000. The company earned a net income of $105,000 in Year 1 and paid dividends of 40 cents per share of common stock at the end of Year 1.

On January 1 of Year 2, the company issued 20,000 shares of preferred stock in exchange for land valued at $1,010,000. Quarterly dividends were declared and paid on preferred shares in March, June, and September of Year 2. On December 28 of Year 2, the company declared the fourth quarterly dividend on preferred stock and a 10% stock dividend to be distributed in Year 3 to common stockholders. Net income for Year 2 was $358,000. The market price of common stock at the end of Year 2 was $40 per share.

Instructions Prepare the stockholders' equity section of the balance sheet at
a December 31, Year 1
b December 31, Year 2

8-4 The stockholders' equity of Camm Corporation on January 1 of the current year is as follows:

Stockholders' equity:	
8% cumulative preferred stock, $100 par, 50,000 shares authorized,	
6,000 shares issued	$ 600,000
Common stock, $5 par, 500,000 shares authorized, 192,000 shares	
issued	960,000
Paid-in capital in excess of par:	
Preferred stock	60,000
Common stock	768,000
Total paid-in capital	$2,388,000
Retained earnings	1,560,000
Total stockholders' equity	$3,948,000

The transactions relating to the stockholders' equity accounts during the current year are shown below:

Jan. 27 Paid regular semiannual dividend on preferred stock and $1 per share cash dividend on common stock. Both dividends were declared in December of the prior year and properly recorded at that time.

June 22 Declared semiannual dividend on preferred stock to stockholders of record on July 12, payable on July 26. (Debit Dividends on Preferred Stock.)

July 26 Paid preferred dividend declared on June 22.

Oct. 10 Declared a 5% stock dividend on common stock to stockholders of record on October 24, to be distributed November 15; market price, $14 a share.

Nov. 15 Distributed 5% stock dividend declared on October 10.

Nov. 30 Sold 18,400 shares of common stock for $16 per share.

Dec. 23 Declared regular semiannual dividend on preferred stock and a dividend of $1 per share on common stock of record at January 12, payable on January 26.

Dec. 31 Net income for the current year amounted to $420,000. (Debit Income Summary and credit Retained Earnings.)

Dec. 31 Closed dividend accounts to Retained Earnings account.

Instructions

a Prepare in general journal form the entries necessary to record these transactions.

b Comment on whether Camm Corporation increased or decreased the total amount of cash dividends *declared* on the common stock during the current year in comparison with the dividends declared in the past year.

c Prepare a balance sheet for Camm Corporation at the end of the current year, assuming that total assets amount to $6 million. (Hint: Prepare the stockholders' equity section of the balance sheet and "plug" the amount of other liabilities after computing the amount of dividends payable.)

8-5 Goodman Corporation was organized early in Year 5. The company uses a perpetual inventory system whereby the Cost of Goods Sold account is debited for the cost of merchandise sold during the accounting period. The trial balance at the end of Year 5 is shown below:

GOODMAN CORPORATION
Trial Balance
December 31, Year 5

Cash	$ 27,120	
Accounts receivable	58,000	
Inventory of merchandise	59,100	
Inventory of office supplies	3,500	
Unexpired insurance	2,400	
Equipment	150,000	
Organization costs	4,000	
Accounts payable		$ 33,000
Long-term notes payable		80,000
Capital stock, $5 par		135,000
Treasury stock, 750 shares	3,000	
Sales		350,000
Sales discounts	4,500	
Sales returns and allowances	5,500	
Cost of goods sold	210,000	
Wages expense	28,600	
Rent expense	24,000	
Advertising expense	5,400	
Other operating expenses	12,880	
	$598,000	$598,000

Data for adjustments and corrections

(1) Accrued wages at the end of Year 5 amount to $900.

(2) Office supplies on hand amount to $1,200 and unexpired insurance amounts to $1,000 at the end of Year 5. (Debit Other Operating Expenses.)

(3) Depreciation expense for Year 5 is determined to be $12,800. (Debit Depreciation Expense.)

(4) Organization costs are to be amortized over a 5-year period by charges to Other Operating Expenses.

(5) Accrued interest on notes payable is $2,100. The notes were issued in connection with the purchase of equipment.

(6) The company issued 20,000 shares of capital stock, the entire proceeds were incorrectly recorded in the Capital Stock account.

(7) During the year 1,500 shares of capital stock were acquired for $10,000; subsequently, one-half of these shares were reissued for $7,000, and the proceeds were incorrectly credited to the Treasury Stock account.

(8) A cash dividend of 50 cents per share was declared on December 20, Year 5. No entry was made to record the declaration of the dividend.

(9) Income tax expense is estimated at $12,100 for Year 5.

Instructions

a Prepare a work sheet with columns for Trial Balance, Adjustments and Corrections, Income Statement, Retained Earnings, and Balance Sheet.

b Prepare a balance sheet at December 31, Year 5.

c Prepare a schedule of cash receipts and payments for Year 5 in order to arrive at the ending cash balance of $27,120.

8-6 The accounts listed alphabetically below appear in the general ledger of the Alaska Development Corporation at December 31, 1975, after the accounts have been closed.

Accounts payable	$ 52,000
Accounts receivable (net)	75,030
Accrued miscellaneous liabilities	13,230
Accumulated depreciation: buildings	180,000
Accumulated depreciation: equipment	159,600
Buildings	610,000
Cash	35,530
Common stock, no par, $5 stated value	320,000
Dividends payable	15,000
Equipment	526,300
Income taxes payable	34,000
Inventories	145,000
Land (held for future plant site)	10,000
Land (used in operations)	50,000
Long-term notes payable, due July 1, 1987	250,000
Notes receivable	51,050
Patents	20,000
8% preferred stock, $100 par	200,000
Paid-in capital from treasury stock transactions	13,000
Paid-in capital in excess of stated value: common	32,000
Paid-in capital in excess of par: preferred	10,000
Retained earnings, Dec. 31	319,580
Short-term prepayments	6,500
Trademarks	9,000
Treasury stock (10,000 shares of common stock, at cost)	60,000

The company was authorized to issue 20,000 shares of 8%, $100 par value preferred stock and 100,000 shares of no-par common stock, stated value $5.

Instructions Prepare the December 31, 1975, balance sheet in a form suitable for publication. (Use the illustrated balance sheet on page 255 as a guide.)

8-7 The stockholders' equity of Elmer Corporation at December 31, Year 5, includes the following accounts:

Stockholders' equity:

6% cumulative preferred stock, $10 par; 200,000 shares authorized,	
100,000 shares issued and outstanding	*$1,000,000*
Common stock, no par, $1 stated value; 1,000,000 shares authorized,	
500,000 shares issued and outstanding	*500,000*
Paid-in capital in excess of stated value: common	*4,075,000*
Retained earnings (deficit)	*(50,000)*
Total stockholders' equity	*$5,525,000*

The income statement for Year 5, as prepared by the company's treasurer, is shown below:

ELMER CORPORATION

Income Statement

For Year 5

Sales (net)		*$4,780,000*
Cost of goods sold		*3,560,000*
Gross profit on sales		*$1,220,000*
Operating expenses		*1,165,600*
Income before extraordinary items		*$ 54,400*
Extraordinary items:		
Loss from discontinued operations	*$(360,000)*	
Damages collected on contract dispute (applicable to		
Year 3)	*180,000*	
Flood loss	*(40,000)*	*(220,000)*
Net loss		*$ (165,600)*

The company did not declare any dividends in Year 5. An audit at the end of Year 5 disclosed the following: On July 1, Year 5, the company purchased equipment for $66,000 which was debited to an operating expense account by mistake. The equipment has an estimated service life of 10 years and an estimated salvage value of $6,000. On March 1, Year 5, the company paid a three-year insurance premium in the amount of $3,600, which was debited to an expense account.

Instructions

a Prepare the necessary journal entries at December 31 to correct the errors discovered in the audit. Record depreciation expense for one-half year on the equipment acquired July 1. Any adjustments of revenue or expense for Year 5 should be made through the Income Summary account.

b Prepare a corrected income statement for Year 5, showing extraordinary items and earnings per share.

c Prepare a corrected statement of retained earnings for Year 5 (Deficit of $50,000 at December 31, combined with the reported net loss of $165,600 indicates a balance of $115,600 in the Retained Earnings account at January 1, Year 5.)

BUSINESS DECISION PROBLEM 8

Near the end of the current year, the board of directors of the Irish Tea Corporation is presented with the following statement of stockholders' equity:

Capital stock (60,000 shares issued)	*$1,200,000*
Paid-in capital in excess of par	*720,000*
Retained earnings	*960,000*
Total stockholders' equity	*$2,880,000*

Irish Tea Corporation has paid dividends of $3.60 per share in each of the last five years. After careful consideration of the company's cash needs, the board of directors declared a stock dividend of 12,000 shares. Shortly after the stock dividend had been distributed and before the end of the year, the company declared a cash dividend of $3 per share.

Don Rollinson owned 5,000 shares of Irish Tea Corporation's stock which he acquired several years ago. The market price of this stock before any dividend action in the current year was $60 per share.

Instructions Based on the information given above, answer each of the following questions, showing all relevant computations.

a What is Rollinson's share (in dollars) of the net assets as reported in the balance sheet of the Irish Tea Corporation before the stock dividend action? What is his share after the stock dividend action? Explain why there is or is not any change as a result of the 20% stock dividend.

b What are the probable reasons why the market value of Rollinson's stock differs from the amount of net assets per share shown in the accounting records?

c How does the amount of cash dividends that Rollinson received in the current year compare with dividends received in prior years.

d On the day the stock went ex-dividend (with respect to the 20% stock dividend), its quoted market price fell from $60 to $50 per share. Did this represent a loss to Rollinson? Explain.

e If the Irish Tea Corporation had announced that it would continue its regular cash dividend of $3.60 per share on the increased number of shares outstanding after the 20% stock dividend, would you expect the market price of the stock to react in any way different from the change described in *d?* Why?

CASH AND MARKETABLE SECURITIES

NINE

CASH

Accountants use the word *cash* to include coin, paper money, checks, money orders, and money on deposit with banks. However, cash does not include postage stamps, IOU's, or postdated checks.

In deciding whether a particular item comes within the classification of cash, the following rule is a useful one: Any medium of exchange which a bank will accept for deposit and immediate credit to the depositor's account is included in cash. As an example, personal checks and money orders are accepted by banks for deposit and are considered as cash. Postage stamps and postdated checks are not acceptable for deposit at a bank and are not included in the accountant's definition of cash.

Balance sheet presentation of cash

Cash is a current asset. In fact, cash is the most current and most liquid of all assets. In judging whether other types of assets qualify for inclusion in the current assets section of the balance sheet, we consider the length of time required for the asset to be converted into cash.

Some bank accounts are restricted as to their use, so that they are not available for disbursement to meet normal operating needs of the business. An example is a bond sinking fund, consisting of cash being accumulated by a corporation for the specific purpose of paying bonded indebtedness at a future date. Such restricted bank deposits are not regarded as current assets because they are not available for use in paying current liabilities.

The banker, credit manager, or investor who studies a balance sheet critically will always be interested in the total amount of cash as compared with other balance sheet items, such as accounts payable. These outside users of a company's financial statements are not interested, however, in such details as the number of separate bank accounts, or in the distinction between the cash on hand and cash in banks. A business that carries checking accounts with several banks will maintain a separate ledger account for each bank account. On the balance sheet, however, the entire amount of cash on hand and cash on deposit with the several banks will be shown as a single amount. One objective in preparing financial statements is to keep them short, concise, and easy to read.

Management responsibilities relating to cash

Efficient management of cash includes measures that will:

1 Prevent losses from fraud or theft
2 Provide accurate accounting for cash receipts, cash payments, and cash balances
3 Maintain a sufficient amount of cash at all times to make necessary payments, plus a reasonable balance for emergencies
4 Prevent unnecessarily large amounts of cash from being held idle in bank accounts which produce no revenue

Internal control over cash is sometimes regarded merely as a means of preventing fraud or theft. A good system of internal control, however, will also aid in achieving management's other objectives of accurate accounting and the maintenance of adequate but not excessive cash balances.

Basic requirements for internal control over cash

Cash is more susceptible to theft than any other asset. Furthermore, a large portion of the total transactions of a business involve the receipt or disbursement of cash. For both these reasons, internal control over cash is of great importance to management and also to the employees of a business. If a cash shortage arises in a business in which internal controls are weak or nonexistent, every employee is under suspicion. Perhaps no one employee can be proved guilty of the theft, but neither can any employee prove his innocence.

On the other hand, if internal controls over cash are adequate, theft without detection is virtually impossible except through the collusion of two or more employees. To achieve internal control over cash or any other group of assets requires first of all that the custody of assets be clearly separated from the recording of transactions. Secondly, the recording function should be subdivided among employees, so that the work of one person is verified by that of another. This subdivision of duties discourages fraud, because collusion among employees would be necessary to conceal an irregularity. Internal control is more easily achieved in large companies than in small ones because extensive subdivision of duties is more feasible in the larger business.

The major steps in establishing internal control over cash include the following:

1 Separate the function of handling cash from the maintenance of accounting records. The cashier should not maintain the accounting records and should not have access to the records. Accounting personnel should not have access to cash.

2 Separate the function of receiving cash from that of disbursing cash. The same person should not handle cash receipts and also make cash disbursements.

3 Require that all cash receipts be deposited daily in the bank and that all cash payments be made by check. Keep cash on hand under lock.

The application of these principles in building an adequate system of internal control over cash can best be illustrated by considering separately the topics of cash receipts and cash disbursements.

Cash receipts

Cash receipts consist of two major types: cash received over the counter at the time of a sale and cash received through the mail as collections on accounts receivable.

USE OF CASH REGISTERS Cash received over the counter at the time of a sale should be rung up on a cash register, so located that the customer will see the amount recorded. If store operations can be so arranged that two employees must participate in each sales transaction, stronger internal control will be achieved than when one employee is permitted to handle a transaction in its entirety. In some stores this objective is accomplished by employing a central cashier who rings on a cash register the sales made by all clerks.

At the end of the day, the store manager or other supervisor should compare the cash register tape, showing the total sales for the day, with the total cash collected.

USE OF PRENUMBERED SALES TICKETS Internal control may be further strengthened by writing out a prenumbered sales ticket in duplicate at the time of each sale. The original is given to the customer and the carbon copy retained. At the end of the day an employee computes a total sales figure from these duplicate tickets and also makes sure that no tickets are missing from the series. The total amount of sales as computed from the duplicate sales tickets is then compared with the total sales recorded on the cash register.

CASH RECEIVED THROUGH THE MAIL The procedures for handling checks and currency received through the mail are also based on the internal control principle that two or more employees should participate in every transaction.

The employee who opens the mail should prepare a list of the amounts received. In order that this list shall represent the total receipts of the day, the totals recorded on the cash registers may be included in the list. One copy of the list is forwarded with the cash to the cashier, who will deposit the cash in the bank. Another copy of the list is sent to the accounting department which will record the cash collections.

The total cash receipts recorded each day in the accounting records should agree with the amount of the cashier's deposit and also with the list of total cash receipts for the day.

CASH OVER AND SHORT In handling over-the-counter cash receipts, a few errors in change making will inevitably occur. These errors will cause a cash shortage or overage at the end of the day, when the cash is counted and compared with the reading on the cash register.

For example, assume that the total cash sales for the day as recorded by the cash register amount to $500, but that the cash in the drawer when counted amounts to only $490. The following entry would be made to record the day's sales and the cash shortage of $10.

Recording cash shortage

Cash	*490*
Cash Over and Short	*10*
Sales	*500*

To record the day's receipts and a cash shortage.

The account entitled Cash Over and Short is debited with shortages and credited with overages. If the cash shortages during an entire accounting period are in excess of the cash overages, the Cash Over and Short account will have a debit balance and will be shown as a miscellaneous expense in the income statement. On the other hand, if the overages exceed the shortages, the Cash Over and Short account will show a credit balance at the end of the period and should be treated as an item of miscellaneous revenue.

Cash disbursements

An adequate system of internal control requires that each day's cash receipts be deposited intact in the bank and that all disbursements be made by check. Checks should be prenumbered. Any spoiled checks should be marked "Void" and filed in sequence so that all numbers in the series can be accounted for.

The official designated to sign checks should not be given authority to approve invoices for payment or to make entries in the accounting records. When a check is presented to an official for signature, it should be accompanied by the approved invoice and voucher showing that the transaction has been fully verified and that payment is justified. When the check is signed, the supporting invoices and vouchers should be perforated or stamped "Paid" to eliminate any possibility of their later being presented in support of another check. If these rules are followed, it is almost impossible for a fraudulent cash disbursement to be concealed without the collusion of two or more persons.

BANK CHECKING ACCOUNTS

Opening a bank account

When a depositor first opens a bank account, he must sign his name on a signature card, exactly as he will sign checks. The signature card is kept on file by the bank, so that any check bearing a signature not familiar to bank employees may be compared with the depositor's signature card. When a corporation opens a bank account, the board of directors will pass a resolution designating the officers or employees authorized to sign checks. A copy of this resolution is given to the bank.

Making deposits

The depositor fills out a *deposit ticket* (usually in duplicate) for each deposit. The deposit ticket includes a listing of each check deposited and the code number of the bank on which it is drawn. Space is also provided for listing the amounts of coin and currency deposited.

The bank statement

Each month the bank will provide the depositor with a statement of his account, accompanied by the checks paid and charged to his account during the month. The bank statement illustrated on page 308 shows the balance on deposit at the beginning of the month, the deposits, the checks paid, any other debits and credits during the month, and the new balance at the end of the month.

UNCOLLECTED CHECKS Certain items in the bank statement of The Parkview Company shown on page 308 warrant explanation. On July 12 The Parkview Company received a check for $50.25 from J. B. Ball, and the check was included in the bank deposit made on that day. The Ball check was returned to Western National Bank by the bank on which it was drawn marked NSF (Not Sufficient Funds), indicating that Mr. Ball did not have a sufficient balance in his account to cover the check. Western National Bank therefore charged the NSF check against The Parkview Company's account as shown by the July 18 item of $50.25. (The symbol M alongside this entry stands for Miscellaneous Entry.)

STATEMENT OF ACCOUNT WITH

WESTERN NATIONAL BANK

PERIOD ENDING
July 31, 1976

ACCOUNT NO.
7 00532

The Parkview Company
19101 Parkview Road
Los Angeles, Calif. 90018

FOLD HERE

CHECKS—LISTED IN ORDER OF PAYMENT—READ ACROSS				DEPOSITS	DATE	NEW BALANCE
				300 00	7-1-76	5329 30
100 00				250 00	7-2-76	5479 30
415 20	10 00				7-3-76	5054 10
25 00	90 00	36 50		185 10	7-5-76	5087 70
				60 00	7-7-76	5147 70
96 00	400 00				7-10-76	4651 70
500 00				147 20	7-12-76	4298 90
425 00					7-15-76	3873 90
50 25M				200 00	7-18-76	4023 65
85 00				101 19	7-21-76	4039 84
150 27				83 25	7-24-76	3972 82
95 75				500 00M	7-28-76	4377 07
5 00S				628 10	7-31-76	5000 17

SUMMARY OF ACTIVITY

BALANCE FORWARD	DEBITS		CREDITS		SERVICE CHARGE		NEW BALANCE
	NUMBER	AMOUNT	NUMBER	AMOUNT	ITEMS	AMOUNT	
5 029 30	14	2 478 97	10	2 454 84	1	5 00	5 000 17

Please examine this statement at once. If no error is reported in ten days the account will be considered correct. All items are credited subject to final payment.

EXPLANATION OF SYMBOLS

S SERVICE CHARGE   M MISCELLANEOUS ENTRY

Upon receipt of the NSF check returned by the bank, The Parkview Company should remove this item from the cash classification by a journal entry debiting an account receivable from J. B. Ball and crediting Cash. The NSF check is thus regarded as a receivable until it is collected directly from J. B. Ball and redeposited or is determined to be worthless.

BANK SERVICE CHARGES Under the date of July 31 on the illustrated bank statement is a debit for $5 accompanied by the symbol S. This symbol means Service Charge, a charge made by the bank to cover the expense of handling the account. The amount of the service charge is based upon such considerations as the average balance of the account and the number of checks and deposits. (Most banks would probably not make a service charge on The Parkview Company's account because the balance is substantial and the activity is low. However, a service charge is shown here for the purpose of illustrating its use.) When the bank sends the monthly statement and paid checks to the depositor, it will include debit memoranda for service charges and any other charges not represented by checks.

MISCELLANEOUS CHARGES Other charges which may appear on the bank statement include rental fees for safe deposit boxes, charges for printing checks, collection charges on notes left with the bank for collection, and interest charges on borrowing from the bank.

Reconciling the bank account

The balance shown on the monthly statement received from the bank will usually not agree with the balance of cash shown by the depositor's records. Certain transactions recorded by the depositor will not yet have been recorded by the bank. The most common examples are:

1 Outstanding checks. These are checks issued and recorded by the depositor but not yet presented to the bank for payment.
2 Deposits in transit. Deposits mailed to the bank are usually not entered on the bank's records until a day or two later than the entry on the depositor's records.

Similarly, some transactions may appear on the bank statement which have not yet been recorded by the depositor. Examples of these transactions include:

1 Service charges
2 Charges for NSF checks
3 Miscellaneous bank charges and credits

In some cases the bank reconciliation will be complete after such items as outstanding checks, deposits in transit, and miscellaneous bank charges and credits have been taken into account. Other cases may require the correction of errors by the bank or by the depositor to complete the reconciliation. When a company maintains accounts in several banks, one possible type of error is to record a check drawn on one bank as a payment from another bank account. Similar errors may occur in recording deposits.

Procedures for preparing a bank reconciliation

The term *reconciliation* means determining those items which make up the difference between the balance appearing on the bank statement and the balance of cash according to the depositor's records. By listing and studying these discrepancies, it is possible to determine the correct figure for cash to appear on the balance sheet. Specific steps to be taken in preparing a bank reconciliation are:

1 Compare the deposits listed on the bank statement with the deposits shown in the company's records. Place check marks in the company's cash records and on the bank statement beside the items which agree. Any unchecked items in the company's record of deposits will be deposits not yet recorded by the bank, and should be added to the balance reported by the bank. Determine that any deposits in transit listed in last month's bank reconciliation are included in the current month's bank statement.

2 Arrange the paid checks in numerical order and compare each check with the corresponding entry in the cash payments journal. (In the case of personal bank accounts for which the only record maintained is the checkbook, compare each paid check with the check stub.) Place a check mark in the depositor's cash payments journal opposite each entry for which a paid check has been returned by the bank. The unchecked entries should be listed in the bank reconciliation as outstanding checks to be deducted from the balance reported by the bank. Determine whether the checks listed as outstanding in the bank reconciliation for the preceding month have been returned by the bank this month. If not, such checks should be listed as outstanding in the current reconciliation.

3 Deduct from the balance per the depositor's records any debit memoranda issued by the bank which have not been recorded by the depositor. In the illustrated bank reconciliation on page 311, examples are the NSF check for $50.25 and the $5 service charge.

4 Add to the balance per the depositor's records any credit memoranda issued by the bank which have not been recorded by the depositor. An example in the illustrated bank reconciliation on page 311 is the credit of $500 collected by the bank in behalf of The Parkview Company.

5 Prepare a bank reconciliation, reflecting the preceding steps, similar to the illustration on page 311.

6 Make journal entries for any items on the bank statement which have not yet been recorded in the depositor's accounts.

ILLUSTRATION The July bank statement prepared by the bank for The Parkview Company was illustrated on page 308. This statement shows a balance of cash on deposit at July 31 of $5,000.17. We shall assume that The Parkview Company's records at July 31 show a cash balance of $4,175.57. Our purpose in preparing the bank reconciliation is to identify the items that make up this difference and to determine the correct cash balance.

Assume that the specific steps to be taken in preparing a bank reconciliation have been carried out and that the following reconciling items have been discovered:

1 A deposit of $310.90 mailed to the bank on July 31 does not appear on the bank statement.

2 A credit memorandum issued by the bank on July 28 in the amount of $500 was returned with the July bank statement and appears in the Deposits column of that statement. This credit represents the proceeds of a note receivable left with the bank by The Parkview Company for the purpose of collection. The collection of the note has not yet been recorded by The Parkview Company.

3 Four checks issued in July or prior months have not yet been paid by the bank. These checks are:

Check No.	Date	Amount
801	June 15	$100.00
888	July 25	10.25
890	July 27	402.50
891	July 30	205.00

4 A debit memorandum issued by the bank on July 31 for a $5 service charge was enclosed with the July bank statement.

5 Check No. 875 was issued July 20 in the amount of $85 but was erroneously listed on the check stub and in the cash payments journal as $58. The check, in payment of telephone service, was paid by the bank, returned with the July bank statement, and correctly listed on the bank statement as an $85 charge to the account.

6 No entry has as yet been made in The Parkview Company's accounts to reflect the bank's action on July 18 of charging against the company's account the NSF check for $50.25 drawn by J. B. Ball.

The July 31 bank reconciliation for The Parkview Company follows:

THE PARKVIEW COMPANY
Bank Reconciliation
July 31, 1976

Bank statement and depositor's records must be reconciled

Balance per depositor's records July 31			$4,175.57
Add: Note receivable collected for us by bank			500.00
			$4,675.57
Less: Service charge		$ 5.00	
NSF check of J. B. Ball		50.25	
Error on check stub No. 875 ($85 to $58)		27.00	82.25
Adjusted balance			$4,593.32
Balance per bank statement, July 31			$5,000.17
Add: Deposit of July 31 not recorded by bank			310.90
			$5,311.07
Less: Outstanding checks			
No. 801		$100.00	
No. 888		10.25	
No. 890		402.50	
No. 891		205.00	717.75
Adjusted balance (as above)			$4,593.32

The adjusted balance of $4,593.32 is the amount of cash owned by The Parkview Company and is, therefore, the amount which should appear as cash on the July 31 balance sheet.

Note that the adjusted balance of cash differs from both the bank statement and the depositor's records. This difference is explained by the fact that neither set of records is up to date as of July 31, and also by the existence of an error on The Parkview Company's records.

ADJUSTING THE RECORDS AFTER THE RECONCILIATION The balance per the company's records should be brought up-to-date as soon as the bank reconciliation is completed. This is done by making journal entries to record each of the items shown as adjustments to the balance per the depositor's records on the bank reconciliation. In our illustration, entries are necessary to record:

1 The note receivable collected by the bank. Debit Cash $500; credit Notes Receivable $500.
2 The service charge by the bank. Debit Miscellaneous Expense $5; credit Cash $5.
3 The NSF check of J. B. Ball. Debit Accounts Receivable, J. B. Ball $50.25; credit Cash $50.25.
4 The error in recording the $85 check for telephone service as a $58 item. Debit Telephone Expense $27; credit Cash $27.

Petty cash

As previously emphasized, adequate internal control over cash requires that all receipts be deposited in the bank and all disbursements be made by check. However, every business finds it convenient to have a small amount of cash on hand with which to make some very small expenditures. Examples include payments for postage stamps, collect telegrams, and taxi fares. Internal control over these small cash payments can best be achieved through a petty cash fund.

ESTABLISHING THE PETTY CASH FUND To create a petty cash fund, also called an *imprest fund,* a check is written for a round amount such as $50 or $100, which will cover the small expenditures to be paid in cash for a period of two or three weeks. This check is cashed and the money kept on hand in a petty cash box or drawer in the office.

The entry for the issuance of the check is:

Creating the petty cash fund

Petty Cash	100	
Cash		100

To establish a petty cash fund.

MAKING DISBURSEMENTS FROM THE PETTY CASH FUND As cash payments are made out of the petty cash box, the custodian of the fund is required to fill out a *petty cash voucher* for each expenditure. A petty cash voucher shows the amount paid, the purpose of the expenditure, the date, and the signature of the person receiving the money. A petty cash voucher should be prepared for every payment made from the fund. The petty cash box should, therefore, always contain cash and/ or vouchers totaling the exact amount of the fund.

The petty cash custodian should be informed that occasional surprise counts of the fund will be made and that he is personally responsible for the fund being intact at all times. Careless handling of petty cash has often been a first step toward large defalcations; consequently, misuse of petty cash funds should not be tolerated.

REPLENISHING THE PETTY CASH FUND Assume that a petty cash fund of $100 was established on June 1 and that payments totaling $89.75 were made from the fund during the next two weeks. Since the $100 originally placed in the fund is nearly exhausted, it is necessary that the fund be replenished. A check is drawn payable to Petty Cash for the exact amount of the expenditures, $89.75. This check is cashed and the money placed in the petty cash box. The vouchers totaling that amount are perforated to prevent their reuse and filed in support of the replenishment check. The journal entry to record the issuance of the check will debit the expense accounts indicated by inspection of the vouchers, as follows:

Replenishment of petty cash fund	*Postage Expense*	*60.60*	
	Telephone & Telegraph Expense	*4.80*	
	Freight-in	*6.00*	
	Gasoline Expense	*5.25*	
	Miscellaneous Expense	*13.10*	
	Cash		*89.75*
	To replenish the petty cash fund.		

In studying the procedures for operation of a petty cash fund, emphasis should be placed on the fact that the Petty Cash account *is debited only when the fund is first established. Expense accounts will be debited each time the fund is replenished.* Ordinarily, there will be no further entries in the petty cash fund after it is established, unless the fund is discontinued or a decision is made to change the size of the fund from the original $100 amount.

The petty cash fund is usually replenished at the end of an accounting period, even though the fund is not running low, so that all vouchers in the fund are charged to expense accounts before these accounts are closed and financial statements prepared. If, through oversight, the petty cash fund were not replenished at the end of the period, expenditures from petty cash could still be reflected in the income statement for the period in which these expenditures occurred, by an entry debiting the expense accounts and crediting Petty Cash. The result would be an unintentional reduction in the Petty Cash fund, which would presumably be restored in the following period.

INVESTMENTS IN MARKETABLE SECURITIES

In Chapters 7 and 8, the issuance of securities and such related transactions as the payment of dividends and interest have been considered primarily from the viewpoint of the issuing corporation. Now we shall consider these transactions from the viewpoint of the investor.

Reasons for investing in marketable securities

The term *marketable securities* refers primarily to U.S. government bonds and the bonds and stocks of large corporations. Investments in these types of securities are almost as liquid as cash itself. In fact, investments in marketable securities are often called "secondary cash resources." If cash is needed for any operating purpose, these securities may quickly be converted into cash; in the meantime, investments in marketable securities are preferable to cash because of the interest or dividend revenue which they produce. Most companies watch their cash balances very carefully and invest any cash not needed for current operations in high-grade marketable securities.

A special tax incentive exists for corporations to invest in the capital stocks of other corporations; 85% of most dividend revenue earned by a corporation is not subject to federal income tax.[1] The reason for this exclusion is to limit the *double taxation* of these corporate earnings. Dividends are a distribution of earnings on which income tax has already been paid; if the recipient were to pay income tax on the full amount of dividends received, these earnings would be taxed twice.

Marketable securities as current assets

To be considered a marketable security, an investment must meet the test of being *readily marketable.* This means that (1) the securities *can be converted into cash at any time without interfering with the normal operations of the business* and (2) there must be a *ready market for the security at quoted market prices.* The ability to sell securities without interfering with normal business operations implies that the securities are *not* being held for purposes of controlling the issuing company or fostering other operating relationships. A ready market exists when the security is listed on an organized *securities exchange,* or is actively traded in the *over-the-counter* market.

From the viewpoint of creditors, assets which can easily be converted into cash are important considerations in evaluating a company's debt-paying ability. A principal purpose of the balance sheet classification of current assets and current liabilities is to aid in portraying short-run debt-paying ability. Therefore, investments in marketable securities are current assets and deserve to be listed immedi-

[1] The taxation of dividend revenue to corporations and individuals is discussed in Chapter 17.

ately after cash because they are more liquid than accounts receivable or inventory. The following excerpt from a recent balance sheet of Eastman Kodak Company illustrates a typical balance sheet presentation of marketable securities:

Current assets:

Cash *$150,531,000*

Marketable securities at cost (approximates market value) *885,259,000*

To a loan officer in a bank, when reviewing an application for a loan, there is no more impressive or reassuring asset on the balance sheet of a prospective borrower than a large amount of high-quality marketable securities.

Some accounting writers have attempted to distinguish between "temporary" and "permanent" investments in marketable securities with the objective of excluding the latter type from current assets. In the opinion of the authors, such a distinction cannot be made consistently in practice and, furthermore, is quite unnecessary. In measuring debt-paying ability, the important consideration is whether these securities **can be** converted quickly into cash, not whether they **will be** converted during the current period. Investments in marketable securities should be classified as current assets regardless of the maturity dates of the securities and regardless of how long the securities have been held or of how long the company expects to hold them.

In summary, if security investments are limited to securities of unquestioned marketability (and are not owned for the purpose of bolstering business relations with the issuing corporation), these stocks and bonds may be converted into cash at any time without interfering with normal operations. An expressed **intention** by management as to near-term sale of the securities is **not** a requisite for classification as a current asset.

INVESTMENTS FOR PURPOSE OF CONTROL Some corporations buy stocks of other corporations in sufficient quantity so that a degree of control may be exercised over the issuing corporation. Sometimes a substantial investment in stock of a customer company may be helpful in maintaining good business relations. Investments of this type cannot be sold without disturbing established policies; therefore, such investments should not be classified as current assets. On the balance sheet, they should be listed below the current asset section under a heading such as Investments.

Securities exchanges

The capital stocks and bonds of most large corporations are listed on organized securities exchanges, such as the **New York Stock Exchange.** Among the investors in these securities are mutual funds, universities, banks, insurance companies, industrial corporations, and individuals. An investor may either buy or sell these listed securities through any brokerage house which is a member of the exchange. The broker represents the investor and negotiates with other exchange members to either buy or sell the securities on behalf of his customer. The price at which the broker negotiates the transaction represents the current market value of the security and is publicly quoted for reference by other investors. The stocks and bonds of many smaller companies are not listed on an organized securities exchange, but brokerage firms also arrange for the purchase and sale of these unlisted or over-the-counter securities.

At the time of issuance of stocks or bonds, the transaction is between the investor and the issuing corporation (or its underwriting agent). The great daily volume of security transactions, however, consists of the sale of stocks and bonds by investors to other investors. Virtually all these security transactions are made through a stockbroker acting as intermediary.

LISTED CORPORATIONS REPORT TO A MILLION OWNERS When a corporation invites the public to purchase its stocks and bonds, it accepts an obligation to keep the public informed on its financial condition and the profitability of operations. This obligation of disclosure includes public distribution of financial statements. The Securities and Exchange Commission is a government agency responsible for seeing that corporations make adequate disclosure of their affairs so that investors have a basis for intelligent investment decisions. The flow of corporate accounting data distributed through newspapers and financial advisory services to millions of investors is a vital force in the functioning of our economy; in fact, the successful working of a profit-motivated economy rests upon the quality and dependability of the accounting information being reported.

LISTED CORPORATIONS ARE AUDITED BY CERTIFIED PUBLIC ACCOUNTANTS Corporations with securities listed on organized stock exchanges are required to have regular audits of their accounts by independent public accountants. The financial statements distributed each year to stockholders are accompanied by a report by a firm of certified public accountants indicating that an audit has been made and expressing an opinion as to the fairness of the company's financial statements. It is the independent status of the auditing firm that enables investors to place confidence in audited financial statements.

Valuation of marketable securities

VALUATION AT COST Investments in securities have traditionally been carried at cost, and no gain or loss recognized until the securities were sold. One of the basic concepts in accounting is that gains shall not be recognized until they are *realized,* and the usual test of realization is the sale of the asset in question. In current practice the market value of marketable securities is often disclosed in a parenthetical note on the balance sheet.

VALUATION AT THE LOWER OF COST OR MARKET The valuation of investment securities at cost is generally accepted, but accounting theory also treats as acceptable the lower-of-cost-or-market method. The objective of this method of valuation is to give effect to market declines without recognizing market increases, and the result is a more conservative valuation of investments in the balance sheet.

One argument against market price as a valuation basis is that in a rising market the writing up of the Investments account would involve the recording of an unrealized profit. However, accountants often recognize losses on the basis of objective evidence, even though the amount of the loss has not been established through sale of the property. Consequently, when the current value of marketable securities declines *significantly* below cost, some accountants would favor writing down the Investment account and recognizing a loss. The write-down of an investment to a market value below cost is an end-of-period adjusting entry, and should be based upon the market price at the date of the balance sheet.

For example, assume an investment in common stock is acquired early in the year at a cost of $58,000, but at year-end the quoted market value is $42,000. Valuation at the lower of cost or market would be accomplished by the following entry:

Write-down uses end-of-period market value	*Loss from Decline in Market Value of Securities* *16,000*	
	Investment in Marketable Securities	*16,000*
	To write down investment in common stock to lower of cost or market.	

The lower-of-cost-or-market concept has two alternative interpretations. It may be applied by (1) taking the lower of cost or market for each security owned or (2) comparing the cost of the total holdings of securities with the market value of the securities as a group. Application of the lower-of-cost-or-market rule to each security individually will produce the lowest possible valuation for security investments, as shown by the following example:

		Cost	Present Market Value	Lower of Cost or Market
Lower of cost or market: alternative methods	*Adams Corporation stock*	*$10,000*	*$ 9,000*	*$ 9,000*
	King Corporation stock	*15,000*	*17,000*	*15,000*
	Totals	*$25,000*	*$26,000*	*$24,000*

If the lower-of-cost-or-market rule is applied to these two securities individually, the amount to appear in the balance sheet for marketable securities would be $24,000, which is the present *market value* of the Adams stock plus the *cost* of the King stock. In other words, the decrease in value of the Adams stock would be recognized but the increase in value of the King stock would be ignored. The alternative application of the lower-of-cost-or-market rule would be made as follows: The cost of the two securities together amounted to $25,000; the present market value of the two stocks is $26,000; the lower of these two totals is the amount to be used in the balance sheet and would be labeled as follows in the current assets section:

Marketable securities, at cost (market value, $26,000) **$25,000**

Once the carrying value of an investment in securities has been written down to reflect a decline in market price, it is not considered acceptable to restore the amount written off even though the market price afterward recovers to as much as or more than the original cost. To do so would be regarded as recording an unrealized profit. When the security is sold, the gain or loss to be recorded is the difference between the sale price and the adjusted carrying value of the security in the accounts.

In terms of the usefulness of the balance sheet to creditors and other readers, it seems probable that the lower-of-cost-or-market rule should be applied to the securities holdings as a group rather than on an individual basis. Assume, for example, that a company owned a dozen securities and 11 of them advanced strongly in price during the year while the price of the twelfth security declined below its cost. If the lower-of-cost-or-market rule were applied on an individual basis, the company's balance sheet at the end of the year would show a reduction in the carrying value of securities and the income statement would show a loss from decline in market value of securities. Such reporting seems to have no justification other than conservatism, and *conservatism is surely not a virtue when it results in misleading financial statements.*

VALUATION AT MARKET An increasing number of accountants argue that investments in marketable securities *should* be valued in the balance sheet at *current market price* regardless of whether this price is above or below cost. Although it is *not* present practice to value security investments at market value (except for certain types of investment companies), there appear to be at least four strong arguments in favor of using market prices:

1 Market value is a better indicator of the current debt-paying ability represented by the securities than is their original cost.

2 Market values may be objectively determined from market price quotations.

3 The market price may be realized at any time without interfering with the normal operations of the business.

4 Changes in market price may constitute a major portion of the economic benefit resulting from investments in common stock.

If the carrying value of an investment in marketable securities is to be adjusted for changes in market prices, there must also be a corresponding change in owners' equity, as illustrated below:

Revaluation of assets causes a change in owners' equity

Assets = Liabilities + Owners' Equity

Write-up of = No effect + Increase
  investment

Write-down of = No effect + Decrease
  investment

Advocates of using current market values on the balance sheet have proposed two alternative methods of recording the related change in owners' equity: The first method is to revalue the Investment account and recognize a corresponding gain or loss, which would appear in the income statement. The journal entries to revalue the Investment account to current market prices using this method would be as follows:

Gain or loss appears in income statement

Investment in Marketable Securities . . . . *xxx*
    Gain from Increase in Market Value of Securities . . . .   *xxx*
To write up investment to current market value and recognize gain.

or

Loss from Decline in Market Value of Securities . . . .   *xxx*
    Investment in Marketable Securities . . . .   *xxx*
To write down investment to current market value and recognize loss.

The argument for including the gain or loss in the determination of net income is that the change in market value represents a change in the economic well-being of the investing company which has occurred during the period.

The second method is to record the change in owners' equity in a special owners' equity account, which is not included in the income statement. The journal entries to apply this method are illustrated below:

Unrealized gain or loss is not included in net income

Investment in Marketable Securities . . . .   *xxxx*
    Unrealized Gains and Losses on Marketable Securities . . . . .   *xxxx*
To write up investment to current market value and record an unrealized gain.

or

Unrealized Gains and Losses on Marketable Securities . . . .   *xxxx*
    Investment in Marketable Securities . . . .   *xxxx*
To write down investment to current market value and record an unrealized loss.

The word **unrealized** in the above account title emphasizes that the gain or loss should not be included in the determination of net income. The Unrealized Gains and Losses on Marketable Securities account would appear in the balance sheet as a special element of owners' equity. When the securities are eventually sold, the related unrealized gain or loss would become realized. At this time, the amount previously considered unrealized would be transferred from Unrealized Gains and Losses on Marketable Securities to an income statement account entitled Gain (or Loss) on Sale of Marketable Securities. This treatment will cause the timing of income recognized on the income statement to be exactly the same as if the securities were being valued at cost rather than at current market prices on the balance sheet.

At this point it is important to stress that the valuation of marketable securities at current market prices is **not** in accordance with current accounting practice. The lack of agreement as to whether such re-valuations should be recognized in measuring net income is one reason why market values are not presently used as the primary basis for valuation of investments in marketable securities.

Another argument against the use of current market values is that these values may change quickly; values used when the financial statements are prepared may no longer be representative of the current values at some later date when a decision maker is evaluating those financial statements. Nevertheless, the possible use of current values in the valuation of marketable securities is receiving serious consideration by the accounting profession, and may be an area of forthcoming change in generally accepted accounting principles.

DISCLOSING THE BASIS OF VALUATION IN THE BALANCE SHEET Because of the variety of methods possible for valuation of investments in securities, the balance sheet should contain a notation as to the valuation method being used. It is also important that the method selected be used consistently from year to year. To illustrate the balance sheet presentation of marketable securities under different valuation methods, the following excerpts are taken from published financial statements of leading corporations:

Reporting marketable securities in the balance sheet

General Motors Corporation:

United States and other government securities and time deposits—

at cost, which approximates market $2,160,446,064

International Business Machines Corporation:

Marketable securities, at lower of cost or market . . . . : $3,154,518,917

Exxon Corporation:

Marketable securities, at cost, which approximates market $2,525,429,000

In all these examples, marketable securities appeared immediately after Cash in the current asset group.

EFFECT OF INCOME TAX REGULATIONS UPON SECURITY VALUATION

For tax purposes, no gain or loss is recognized on an investment in securities until the time of sale. Many businesses which invest in securities prefer to follow this policy for general accounting purposes as well and therefore carry their security investments at cost, unless there is a substantial and apparently permanent decrease in the market value of securities owned.

Determining the cost of investments in stocks and bonds

The par value or face value of the security is not used in recording an investment; only the cost is entered in the Investments account. Cost includes any commission paid to a broker.

The principal distinction between the recording of an investment in bonds and an investment in stocks is that interest on bonds accrues from day to day. The interest accrued since the last semiannual interest payment date is paid for by the purchaser and should be recorded separately from the cost of the bond itself. Dividends on stock, however, do not accrue and the entire purchase price paid by the investor in stocks is recorded in the Investments account.

QUOTED MARKET PRICES The market price of stocks is quoted in terms of dollars per share. Bond prices, however, are quoted as a percentage of their par or *maturity* value, which is usually $1,000. The maturity value is the amount the issuing company must pay to redeem the bond at the date it matures (becomes due). A bond quoted at 96 would therefore have a market price of $960 (96% of $1,000).

As a bond nears its maturity date, the market price of the bond approaches its maturity value. At the maturity date the market price of the bond should be exactly equal to its maturity value, and the issuing corporation will redeem the bond for that amount.

PURCHASE OF BONDS BETWEEN INTEREST DATES When bonds are purchased between interest dates, the purchaser pays the quoted market price for the bond *plus* the interest accrued since the last interest payment date. By this arrangement the new owner becomes entitled to receive in full the next semiannual interest payment. An account called Accrued Bond Interest Receivable should be debited for the amount of interest purchased. For example, assume the purchase of a 9%, $1,000 bond at a price of 100 (100% of maturity value) and two months' accrued interest of $15. The entry is as follows:

Separate account for accrued bond interest purchased	Investment in Bonds	1,000
	Accrued Bond Interest Receivable	15
	Cash	1,015
	Purchased 9% bond of XYZ Co. at 100 and accrued interest.	

Four months later at the next semiannual interest payment date, the investor will receive an interest check for $45, which will be recorded as follows:

Note portion	Cash	45	
of interest		
check	Accrued Bond Interest Receivable		15
earned	Bond Interest Earned		30
	Received semiannual interest on XYZ Co. bond.		

This $30 credit to Bond Interest Earned represents the amount actually earned during the four months the bond was owned.

ENTRIES TO RECORD BOND INTEREST EARNED EACH PERIOD If the investor in bonds is to determine bond interest earned each year on an accrual basis, an adjusting entry will be necessary at the balance sheet date for any interest earned but not yet received. The following series of entries illustrates the accounting for bond interest earned by a company on a calendar-year basis of accounting. The investment consists of $100,000 face value of 9% bonds (purchased at par) with interest dates of February 28 and August 31.

	Year 1		
Allocating	Dec. 31	Accrued Bond Interest Receivable	3,000	
bond		Bond Interest Earned		3,000
interest		*To accrue four months' interest earned (Sept. 1–Dec. 31) on*	
earned by		*$100,000 face value of 9% bonds.*	
years			
	Year 2		
	Feb. 28	Cash	4,500	
		Accrued Bond Interest Receivable		3,000
		Bond Interest Earned		1,500
		Received semiannual bond interest.	
	Aug. 31	Cash	4,500	
		Bond Interest Earned		4,500
		Received semiannual bond interest.	
	Dec. 31	Accrued Bond Interest Receivable	3,000	
		Bond Interest Earned		3,000
		To accrue four months' interest earned (Sept. 1–Dec. 31) on	
		$100,000 face value of 9% bonds.	

INCOME ON INVESTMENTS IN STOCKS Cash dividends are seldom recorded as income until received. The entry upon receipt of a dividend check consists of a debit to Cash and a credit to Dividends Earned.

Dividends in the form of additional shares of stock *are not income* to the stockholder, and only a *memorandum entry* needs to be made to record the increase in number of shares owned. The *cost basis per share* is decreased, however, because of the larger number of shares comprising the investment after distribution of a stock dividend. As an example, assume that an investor paid $72 a share for 100 shares of stock, a total cost of $7,200. Later he received 20 additional shares as a stock dividend. His cost per share is thereby reduced to $60 a share, computed by dividing his total cost of $7,200 by the 120 shares owned after the 20% stock dividend.

Gains and losses from sale of investments in securities

Since the market prices of securities are continually fluctuating, sale of an investment in marketable securities is likely to result in either a gain or a loss. The sale of an investment in stocks is recorded by debiting Cash for the amount received and crediting the Investment account for the carrying value of the stocks sold. Any difference between the proceeds of sale and the carrying value of the investment is recorded by a debit to Loss on Sale of Marketable Securities or by a credit to Gain on Sale of Marketable Securities.

At the date of sale of an investment in bonds, any interest accrued since the last interest payment date should be recorded. For example, assume that 10 bonds of the Elk Corporation carried in the records of an investor at $9,600 are sold at a price of 94 and accrued interest of $90. The commission on the sale is $50. The following entry should be made:

Investment *Cash*	*9,440*	
in bonds *Loss on Sale of Marketable Securities*	*250*	
sold at a		
loss *Investment in Bonds*		*9,600*
Bond Interest Earned		*90*

Sold 10 bonds of Elk Corporation at 94 and accrued interest of $90
less broker's commission of $50.

Gains and losses on the sale of marketable securities, as well as interest earned and dividends earned, are all nonoperating types of income. These items should be shown separately in the income statement after the determination of income from operations.

DEMONSTRATION PROBLEM

The information listed below is available in reconciling the bank statement for the Glendale Company on November 30, 19___.

(1) The ledger account for Cash showed a balance at November 30 of $7,766.64, including a $100 petty cash fund. Petty cash should be transferred to a separate account. The bank statement at November 30 indicated a balance of $9,734.70.

(2) The November 30 cash receipts of $5,846.20 had been mailed to the bank on that date and did not appear among the deposits on the November bank statement. The receipts include a check for $4,000 from a brokerage house for the sale of 150 shares of stock of the Axe Co. which cost $6,270. Neither the proceeds on the sale of stock nor the collections on accounts

receivable ($1,846.20) has been recorded in the accounts of the Glendale Company.

(3) Included with the November bank statement was an NSF check for $220 signed by a customer James Ruddock. This amount had been charged against the bank account on November 30.

(4) Of the checks issued in November, the following were not included among the paid checks returned by the bank:

Check No.	Amount	Check No.	Amount
924	$136.25	944	$ 95.00
940	105.00	945	716.15
941	11.46	946	60.00
943	826.70		

(5) A service charge for $340 by the bank had been made in error against the Glendale Company's account.

(6) A non-interest-bearing note receivable for $690 owned by the Glendale Company had been left with the bank for collection. On November 30 the company received a memorandum from the bank indicating that the note had been collected and credited to the company's account after deduction of a $5 collection charge. No entry has been made by the company to record collection of the note.

(7) A debit memorandum for $7.50 was enclosed with the paid checks at November 30. This charge covered the printing of checkbooks bearing the Glendale Company's name and address.

Instructions

a Prepare a bank reconciliation at November 30, 19___.

b Prepare journal entries required as of November 30, 19___, to bring the company's records up to date.

SOLUTION TO DEMONSTRATION PROBLEM

a

GLENDALE COMPANY
Bank Reconciliation
November 30, 19___

Balance per depositor's records, Nov. 30		$ 7,766.64
Add: Proceeds on sale of stock	$4,000.00	
Collection on accounts receivable	1,846.20	
Note receivable collected by bank, $690, less col-		
lection charge, $5	685.00	6,531.20
		$14,297.84
Less: Petty cash fund reported separately	$ 100.00	
NSF check, James Ruddock	220.00	
Charge by bank for printing checks	7.50	327.50
Adjusted balance		$13,970.34
Balance per bank statement, Nov. 30		$ 9,734.70
Add: Deposit of Nov. 30 not recorded by bank	$5,846.20	
Service charge made by bank in error	340.00	6,186.20
		$15,920.90
Less: Outstanding checks on Nov. 30:		
No. 924	$ 136.25	
No. 940	105.00	
No. 941	11.46	
No. 943	826.70	
No. 944	95.00	
No. 945	716.15	
No. 946	60.00	1,950.56
Adjusted balance (as above)		$13,970.34

b   **General Journal**

19___			
Nov. 30	Cash	6,531.20	
	Loss on Sale of Marketable Securities	2,270.00	
	Miscellaneous Expense	5.00	
	Investment in Marketable Securities		6,270.00
	Notes Receivable		690.00
	Accounts Receivable		1,846.20
	To record increase in Cash account as indicated		
	by bank reconciliation.		

Nov. 30	Petty Cash	100.00	
	Miscellaneous Expense	7.50	
	Accounts Receivable, James Ruddock	220.00	
	Cash		327.50

To record cash disbursements as indicated by bank reconciliation and to record petty cash in a separate account.

REVIEW QUESTIONS

1 Name three internal control practices relating to cash which would be practicable even in a small business having little opportunity for division of duties.

2 Mention some principles to be observed by a business in establishing strong internal control over cash receipts.

3 Explain how internal control over cash transactions is strengthened by compliance with the following rule: "Deposit each day's cash receipts intact in the bank, and make all disbursements by check."

4 Classify each of the numbered reconciling items listed below under one of the following headings: (*a*) an addition to the balance per depositor's records; (*b*) a deduction from the balance per depositor's records; (*c*) an addition to the balance per bank statement; (*d*) a deduction from the balance per bank statement.
  (*1*) Deposits in transit
  (*2*) Outstanding checks
  (*3*) Customer's check deposited but returned by bank marked NSF.
  (*4*) Bank service charges
  (*5*) Collection by bank of note receivable left with bank for collection in behalf of depositor

5 In the reconciliation of a bank account, what reconciling items necessitate a journal entry on the depositor's records?

6 Pico Stationery Shop has for years maintained a petty cash fund of $100, which is replenished twice a month.
  a How many debit entries would you expect to find in the Petty Cash account each year?
  b When would expenditures from the petty cash fund be entered in the ledger accounts?

7 A check for $455 issued in payment of an account payable was erroneously listed in the cash payments journal as $545. The error was discovered early in the following month when the paid check was returned by the bank. What corrective action is needed?

8 In bidding for some surplus property offered at auction by a government agency, the Argus Company on December 28 drew a check for $3,000 and mailed it with the bid. The government agency on January 3 rejected the bid and returned the check. Should the $3,000 be included as cash in the December 31 balance sheet, which was prepared by the Argus Company on January 5 after the check had been returned? Explain.

9 To what extent should the maturity date or the intention of management as to the holding period of an investment in marketable securities influence its classification on the balance sheet?

10 What are the criteria for determining whether an investment is *readily marketable*?

11 Explain the two alternative interpretations of the lower-of-cost-or-market concept. Which interpretation do you favor?

12 Writing down securities to market value when market is below cost, but refusing to recognize an increase in valuation when market is above cost is an inconsistent procedure. What arguments may be given *in favor* of this treatment?

13 "To substitute market value for cost as a basis for valuing marketable securities would represent a departure from traditional accounting practice." Discuss the case for and against using market value consistently as the basis of valuation in accounting for marketable securities.

14 Explain the two alternative means by which an investment in marketable securities might be revalued to current market prices. Which of these methods do you favor? Explain.

15 Should stock dividends received be considered revenue? Explain.

EXERCISES

Ex. 9-1 The Cash account in the ledger of Major Company showed a balance of $9,200 at September 30. The bank statement, however, showed a balance of $11,600 at the same date. If the only reconciling items consisted of an $800 deposit in transit, a bank service charge of $4, and 30 outstanding checks, what was the total amount of the outstanding checks?

Ex. 9-2 Small Company received a bank statement showing a balance of $7,500 on deposit at the end of the month. Among the reconciling items were outstanding checks totaling $1,450, bank service charges of $6, a deposit in transit of $1,100, and a memorandum showing that a $600 note receivable owned by Small Company and left with the bank for collection had been collected and credited to the company's account.
a What is the adjusted amount of cash which should appear on the Small Company's balance sheet?
b What was the balance per the depositor's records before making adjusting entries for any of the reconciling items?

Ex. 9-3 The following information relates to the Garner Company's September 30 cash balance:
(*1*) As of September 30, cash per books was $5,770; per bank statement, $4,697.
(*2*) Cash receipts of $1,451 on September 30 were not deposited until October 1.
(*3*) Among the paid checks returned by the bank was a stolen check for $630 paid in error by the bank after Garner Company had issued a "stop payment" order to the bank.
(*4*) The following memoranda accompanied the bank statement:
(*a*) A debit memo for service charges for the month of September, $3.
(*b*) A debit memo attached to a $200 check of Joseph Voss, marked NSF.
(*5*) The following checks had been issued but were not included in the canceled checks returned by the bank: No. 921 for $326, No. 924 for $724, and No. 925 for $161.

Instructions
a Prepare a bank reconciliation as of September 30.
b Prepare the necessary adjusting journal entries.

Ex. 9-4 On March 31 the petty cash drawer of the Mondo Company includes the following:

Cash on hand	$ 99.41
Expense vouchers:	
Flowers for funeral of deceased customer	20.40
Box of cigars for purchasing agent of the James Corporation	7.09
Office supplies expense	23.10
Salary advance to employee	50.00
Total	$200.00

Instructions Prepare the journal entry required at the end of the month to replenish the petty cash fund.

Ex. 9-5 At year-end Allied Corporation prepared the following schedule of its investments in marketable securities:

	Cost	Current Market Value
Bayonne Company stock	$21,000	$34,000
Magna Company stock	17,000	21,000
Superior Oil Company stock	32,000	28,000
	$70,000	$83,000

Prepare journal entries necessary to adjust Allied Corporation's Investment in Marketable Securities account at year-end under each of the following independent assumptions:

a The lower-of-cost-or-market rule is applied to each security individually.
b The lower-of-cost-or-market rule is applied by comparing the total cost of all marketable securities to the combined market value.
c The investment account is adjusted to current market value, but no gain or loss is recognized in the income statement.

Ex. 9-6 Vickers Company acquired $10,000 par value 9% bonds of Dunbar Co. on March 31, 19___, for a total cost of $10,125, including interest accrued since January 1, 19___. Interest is paid by Dunbar Co. on June 30 and December 31 of each year. On July 31, 19___, Vickers Company sold the bonds and interest accrued since July 1 for a total price of $10,105.
Prepare all entries required on the records of Vickers Company during 19___, relating to the investment in Dunbar Co. bonds.

PROBLEMS

9-1 James Aarons, a trusted employee of the Rimforest Company, found himself in personal financial difficulties and carried out the following plan to steal $1,000 from the company and to conceal his fraud.
Aarons removed $1,000 in currency from the cash register. This amount represented the bulk of the cash received in over-the-counter sales during the three business days since the last bank deposit. Aarons then removed a $1,000 check from the day's incoming mail; this check had been mailed by a customer, Keith Parker, in full payment of his account. Aarons made no entry in the cash receipts journal for the $1,000 collection from Parker, but deposited the check in Rimforest Company's bank account in place of the $1,000 of cash receipts he had stolen. In order to keep Parker from protesting when his month-end statement reached him, Aarons made a general journal entry debiting Sales Returns and Allowances and crediting Accounts Receivable, Keith Parker. Aarons posted this entry to the two general ledger accounts

affected and also to Parker's account in the subsidiary ledger for accounts receivable.

Instructions
a Did these actions by Aarons cause the general ledger to be out of balance or the subsidiary ledger to disagree with the controlling account? Explain.
a What weaknesses in internal control apparently exist in the Rimforest Company? Indicate the corrective actions needed.

9-2 Information necessary for the preparation of a bank reconciliation and related journal entries for the Core Company at March 31 is listed below.
(1) The balance per records of the Core Company is $16,604.02.
(2) The bank statement shows a balance of $20,638.29 as of March 31.
(3) Accompanying the bank statement was a check of Dale Tegard for $186.00, which was marked NSF by the bank.
(4) Checks outstanding as of March 31 were as follows: No. 84 for $1,841.02; No. 88 for $1,323.00; No. 89 for $16.26.
(5) Also accompanying the bank statement was a debit memorandum for $44.80 for safe deposit box rent; the bank had erroneously charged this item to the account of the Core Company.
(6) On March 29, the bank collected a non-interest-bearing note for Core Company. The note was for $2,963; the bank charged a collection fee of $8.40.
(7) A deposit of $2,008.50 was in transit; it had been mailed to the bank on March 31.
(8) In recording a $160 check received on account from a customer, Ross Company, the accountant for the Core Company erroneously listed the collection in the cash receipts journal as $16. The check appeared correctly among the deposits on the March bank statement.
(9) The bank service charge for March amounted to $5.31; a debit memo in this amount was returned with the bank statement.

Instructions
a Prepare a bank reconciliation at March 31.
b Prepare the necessary journal entries.

9-3 Standard Top Company reports the following information concerning cash balances and cash transactions for the month of September.
(1) Cash balance per bank statement as of September 30 was $8,793.25.
(2) Two debit memoranda accompanied the bank statement: one for $4 was for service charges for the month; the other for $64.60 was attached to an NSF check from James Muche.
(3) The paid checks returned with the September bank statement disclosed two errors in the cash records. Check No. 832 for $456.30 had been erroneously recorded as $465.30 in the cash disbursements journal, and check No. 851 for $77.44 had been recorded as $44.77. Check No. 832 was issued in payment for a store display counter; check No. 851 was for telephone expense.
(4) A collection charge for $126.00 (not applicable to Standard Top Company) was erroneously deducted from the account by the bank.
(5) Cash receipts of September 30 amounting to $585.25 were mailed to the bank too late to be included in the September bank statement.
(6) Checks outstanding as of September 30 were as follows: No. 860 for $151.93, No. 867 for $82.46, and No. 869 for $123.61.
(7) The Cash account showed the following entries during September:

Cash *111*

Sept.	*1*	*Balance*		*6,341.82*	*Sept.*	*30*		*CD7*	*11,514.63*
	30		*CR5*	*14,411.58*					

Instructions

a Prepare a bank reconciliation at September 30.

b Prepare the necessary adjusting entries in general journal form.

9-4 Paige Company had not established adequate internal control over its cash transactions. John Keane served as cashier and also performed accounting work. He handled cash receipts, made small disbursements from the cash receipts, maintained accounting records, and prepared the monthly reconciliations of the bank account. At November 30, the statement received from the bank showed a balance of $18,400. The outstanding checks were as follows: No. 5312 for $446.38; No. 5389 for $572.16; No. 5410 for $81.46; No. 6133 for $186.04; No. 6137 for $418.57; and No. 6138 for $161.49. The balance of cash as shown by the Paige Company records was $20,986.47, which included the cash on hand. The bank statement for November showed a credit of $300 arising from the collection of a note left with the bank; the company's records did not include an entry to record this collection.

Recognizing the weakness existing in internal control over cash transactions, Keane removed all the cash on hand in excess of $3,252.57, and then prepared the following reconciliation in an attempt to conceal his theft.

Balance per books, Nov. 30		$20,986.47
Add: Outstanding checks:		
No. 6133	$186.04	
No. 6137	418.57	
No. 6138	161.49	666.10
		$21,652.57
Less: Cash on hand		3,252.57
Balance per bank statement, Nov. 30		$18,400.00
Less: Unrecorded credit		300.00
True cash, Nov. 30		$18,100.00

Instructions

a Determine how much the cashier took and explain how he attempted to conceal his theft. Prepare a correct bank reconciliation.

b Suggest some specific internal control procedures for the Paige Company.

9-5 Mark Krasner purchased 500 shares of Mason Company common stock at $36 per share plus brokerage fees of $200 on March 31. The company had declared a cash dividend of 50 cents per share on March 20, payable on April 15 to stockholders of record on April 6. On June 30 the company declared a 20% stock dividend. On December 15 the shares were split 2 for 1. On December 20 the company declared a cash dividend of 25 cents per share to stockholders of record on December 30, payable on January 10. On December 31, Krasner sold 300 shares of the stock at $21 per share, net of commission.

Instructions Prepare journal entries to account for this investment on Krasner's accounting records. Since Krasner keeps accrual records, an entry to Dividends Receivable should be made on December 30.

9-6 The portfolio of marketable securities of the Bengal Corporation on January 1, of the current year, consisted of the following three securities:

$100,000 par value Bay Resorts Corp. $7\frac{1}{2}$% bonds due Dec. 31, 1988. Interest is payable on June 30 and Dec. 31 of each year $97,600

$50,000 par value Copper Products Co. 9% bonds due Apr. 30. 1990, Interest is payable on Apr. 30 and Oct. 31 of each year *52,720*

1,200 shares of no-par $4.50 cumulative preferred stock of Donner-Pass, Inc. *96,000*

Transactions relating to investments that were completed during the first six months of the current year follow:

Jan. 10 Acquired 500 shares of Rhodes Co. common stock at 66. Brokerage commissions paid amounted to $180.

Jan. 21 Received quarterly dividend of $1.12½ per share on 1,200 shares of Donner-Pass, Inc., preferred stock.

Mar. 5 Sold 200 shares of Donner-Pass, Inc., preferred stock at 84½, less commissions and transfer taxes amounting to $105.

Apr. 1 Received additional 1,000 shares of Rhodes Co. common stock as a result of a 3 for 1 split.

Apr. 20 Received quarterly dividend of $1.12½ per share on 1,000 shares of Donner-Pass, Inc., preferred stock.

Apr. 30 Received semiannual interest on Copper Products Co. 9% bonds. Accrued interest of $750 had been recorded on December 31, of last year in the Accrued Bond Interest Receivable account.

May 1 Sold entire holdings of Copper Products Co. 9% bonds at 102½ net of commissions.

June 4 Received a cash dividend of 70 cents per share on Rhodes Co. common stock.

June 30 Received semiannual interest on Bay Resorts Corp. 7½% bonds.

Instructions

a Prepare journal entries to record the foregoing transactions.

b Prepare a schedule of the portfolio of investment securities for the Bengal Corporation as of June 30. Show the name of the security, the number of shares (or par value), and the cost basis for financial reporting purposes.

9-7 John Sands, a wealthy investor, held the portfolio of investments shown below throughout the current year:

1,000 shares of Ling Corporation common stock; cost $98 per share, market value at December 31, $160,000. Received dividends of $3.10 per share on March 1, 10% stock dividend on June 1, and $2.50 per share on December 1 of current year.

$20,000 in 6% Clark County school bonds, maturing eight years from the date of purchase. Purchased for $18,440, market value on December 31, 94½. Received two regular semiannual interest payments during the current year.

$50,000 in 8% Ross Corporation bonds, due four years and two months from date of purchase. Purchased for $51,500; market value at end of current year, 101¾. Received two regular semiannual interest payments during current year.

800 shares of Silmar Corporation $4.50 convertible preferred stock, no par value. Purchased for $90,000, current market value at end of year, 130½. Received regular dividends on March 1 and September 1 of current year.

Instructions

a Prepare a schedule showing the amount earned during the current year on each of these investments and the amount earned stated as a percentage of cost and of market value at the end of the year (round to the nearest tenth of a percent). This schedule may be in columnar form with the following column headings:

Name of Security	Original Cost	End-of-year Market Value	Earnings This Year	Rate Earned on Cost, %	Rate Earned on Market Value, %

b In a friendly discussion with a business associate, Sands commented on his average rate earned for the year on the total cost of his investment. His friend retorted that the rate earned on market value was a better measure of earning performance. Discuss the merits of the rate earned on cost and the rate earned on market value as measures of investment success.

BUSINESS DECISION PROBLEM 9

Don Landry inherited a highly successful business, Gateway Corporation, shortly after his twenty-second birthday and took over the active management of the business. A portion of the company's business consisted of over-the-counter sales for cash, but most sales were on credit and were shipped by truck. Landry had no knowledge of internal control practices and relied implicitly upon the bookkeeper-cashier, T. A. Baylis, in all matters relating to cash and accounting records. Baylis had been with the company for many years. He maintained the accounting records and prepared all financial statements with the help of two assistants, made bank deposits, signed checks, and prepared bank reconciliations.

The monthly income statements submitted to Landry by Baylis showed a very satisfactory rate of net income; however, the amount of cash in the bank declined steadily during the first 18 months after Landry took over the business. To meet the company's weakening cash position, a bank loan was obtained and a few months later when the cash position again grew critical, the loan was increased.

On April 1, two years after Landry assumed the management of the company, Baylis suddenly left town, leaving no forwarding address. Landry was immediately deluged with claims of creditors who stated their accounts were several months past due and that Baylis had promised all debts would be paid by April 1. The bank telephoned to notify Landry that the company's account was overdrawn and that a number of checks had just been presented for payment.

In an effort to get together some cash to meet this emergency, Landry called on two of the largest customers of the company, to whom substantial sales on account had recently been made, and asked if they could pay their accounts at once. Both customers informed him that their accounts were paid in full. They produced paid checks to substantiate these statements and explained that Baylis had offered them reduced prices on merchandise if they would pay within 24 hours after delivery.

To keep the business from insolvency, Landry agreed to sell at a bargain price a half interest in the company. The sale was made to Brown, who had had considerable experience in the industry. One condition for the sale was that Brown should become the general manager of the business. The cash investment by Brown for his half interest was sufficient for the company to meet the demands on it and continue operations.

Immediately after Brown entered the business, he launched an investigation of Baylis's activities. During the course of this investigation the following irregularities were disclosed:

(1) During the last few months of Baylis's employment with the company, bank deposits were much smaller than the cash receipts. Baylis had abstracted most of the receipts and substituted for them a number of worthless checks

bearing fictitious signatures. These checks had been accumulated in an envelope marked "Cash Receipts—For Deposit Only."

(2) Numerous legitimate sales of merchandise on account had been charged to fictitious customers. When the actual customer later made payment for the goods, Baylis abstracted the check or cash and made no entry. The account receivable with the fictitious customer remained in the accounting records.

(3) When checks were received from customers in payment of their accounts, Baylis had frequently recorded the transaction by debiting an expense account and crediting Accounts Receivable. In such cases Baylis had removed from the cash receipts an equivalent amount of currency, thus substituting the check for the currency and causing the bank deposit to agree with the recorded cash receipts.

(4) More than $3,000 a month had been stolen from petty cash. Fraudulent petty cash vouchers, mostly charged to the Purchases account, had been created to conceal these thefts and to support the checks cashed to replenish the petty cash fund.

(5) For many sales made over the counter, Baylis had recorded lesser amounts on the cash register or had not rung up any amount. He had abstracted the funds received but not recorded.

(6) To produce income statements that showed profitable operations, Baylis had recorded many fictitious sales. The recorded accounts receivable included many from nonexistent customers.

(7) In preparing bank reconciliations, Baylis had omitted many outstanding checks, thus concealing the fact that the cash in the bank was less than the amount shown by the ledger.

(8) Inventory had been recorded at inflated amounts in order to increase reported profits from the business.

Instructions

a For each of the numbered paragraphs, describe one or more internal control procedures you would recommend to prevent the occurrence of such fraud.

b Apart from specific internal controls over cash and other accounts, what general precaution could Landry have taken to assure himself that the accounting records were properly maintained and the company's financial statements complete and dependable? Explain fully.

TEN

RECEIVABLES AND PAYABLES

One of the key factors underlying the growth of the American economy has been the trend toward selling all types of goods and services on credit. The automobile industry has long been the classic example of the use of retail credit to achieve the efficiencies of large-scale output. Today, however, in nearly every field of retail trade it appears that sales and profits can be increased by granting customers the privilege of making payment a month or more after the date of sale. The sales of manufacturers and wholesalers are made on credit to an even greater extent than in retail trade.

ACCOUNTS RECEIVABLE

The credit department

No business concern wants to sell on credit to a customer who will prove unable or unwilling to pay his account. Consequently, most business organizations include a credit department which must reach a decision on the credit worthiness of each prospective customer. The credit department investigates the debt-paying ability and credit record of each new customer and determines the maximum amount of credit to be extended.

If the prospective customer is a business entity as, for example, a retail store, the financial statements of the store will be obtained and analyzed to determine its financial condition and the trend of operating results. The credit department will always prefer to rely upon financial statements which have been audited by certified public accountants.

Regardless of whether the prospective customer is a business concern or an individual consumer, the investigation by the credit department will probably include the obtaining of a credit report from a local credit agency or from a national credit-rating institution such as Dun & Bradstreet, Inc. A credit agency compiles credit data on individuals and business concerns, and distributes this information to its clients. Most business concerns that make numerous sales on credit find it worthwhile to subscribe to the services of one or more credit agencies.

Uncollectible accounts

A business that sells its goods or services on credit will inevitably find that some of its accounts receivable are uncollectible. Regardless of how thoroughly the credit department investigates prospective customers, some uncollectible accounts will arise as a result of errors in judgment or because of unanticipated developments. As a matter of fact, a limited amount of uncollectible accounts is evidence of a sound credit policy. If the credit department should become too cautious in rating customers, it might avoid all credit losses, but in so doing, lose profitable business by rejecting many acceptable accounts.

Reflecting uncollectible accounts in the financial statements

One of the most fundamental principles of accounting is that *revenue must be matched with the expenses incurred in securing that revenue.*

Uncollectible accounts expense is caused by selling goods on credit to customers who fail to pay their bills; such expenses, therefore, are incurred *in the year in which the sales are made,* even though the accounts are not determined to be uncollectible until the following year. An account receivable which originates from a sale on credit in Year 1, and is determined to be uncollectible sometime during Year 2 represents an expense of Year 1. Unless each year's uncollectible accounts expense is *estimated* and reflected in the year-end balance sheet and income statement, both of these financial statements will be seriously deficient.

To illustrate, let us assume that Arlington Corporation began business on January 1, Year 1, and made most of its sales on credit throughout the year. At December 31, Year 1, accounts receivable amounted to $200,000. On this date the management reviewed the status of the accounts receivable, giving particular study to accounts which were past due. This review indicated that the collectible portion of the $200,000 of accounts receivable amounted to approximately $190,000. In other words, management estimated that uncollectible accounts expense for the first year of operations amounted to $10,000. The following adjusting entry should be made at December 31, Year 1:

Provision for uncollectible accounts

Uncollectible Accounts Expense *10,000*	
Allowance for Uncollectible Accounts	*10,000*
To record the estimated uncollectible account expense for Year 1.	

The Uncollectible Accounts Expense account created by the debit part of this entry is closed into the Income Summary account in the same manner as any other expense account. The Allowance for Uncollectible Accounts which was credited in the above journal entry will appear in the balance sheet as a deduction from the face amount of the accounts receivable. It serves to reduce the accounts receivable

to their *net realizable value* in the balance sheet, as shown by the
following illustration:

ARLINGTON CORPORATION
Partial Balance Sheet
December 31, Year 1

Assets

Current assets:		
Cash		$ 75,000
Accounts receivable	$200,000	
Less: Allowance for uncollectible accounts	10,000	190,000
Inventory		100,000
Total current assets		$365,000

How much is the estimated net realizable value of the accounts receivable?

The allowance for uncollectible accounts

There is no way of telling in advance which accounts receivable will
be collected and which ones will prove to be worthless. It is therefore
not possible to credit the account of any particular customer to reflect
our overall estimate of the year's credit losses. Neither is it desirable
to credit the Accounts Receivable controlling account in the general
ledger. If the Accounts Receivable controlling account were to be credited with the estimated amount of expense from uncollectible accounts,
this controlling account would no longer be in balance with the total
of the numerous customers' accounts in the subsidiary ledger. The
only practicable alternative, therefore, is to credit a separate account
called Allowance for Uncollectible Accounts with the amount estimated
to be uncollectible. The credit balance of the Allowance for Uncollectible Accounts is shown on the balance sheet as a deduction from the
total amount of accounts receivable. The resulting net figure is the
estimated net realizable value of the accounts receivable.

In the preceding chapters accounts have repeatedly been classified
into five groups: (1) assets, (2) liabilities, (3) owners' equity, (4) revenue,
and (5) expenses. In which of these five groups of accounts does the
Allowance for Uncollectible Accounts belong? The answer is indicated
by the position of the Allowance for Uncollectible Accounts on the
balance sheet. It appears among the assets and is used to reduce an
asset (Accounts Receivable) from a gross value to a net realizable
value. From the standpoint of account classification, the Allowance
for Uncollectible Accounts is, therefore, included in the asset category.

The Allowance for Uncollectible Accounts is sometimes described
as a *contra* account, an *offset* account, an *asset reduction* account, a
negative asset account, and most frequently of all, a *valuation* account.
All these terms are derived from the fact that the Allowance for Uncollectible Accounts is an account with a credit balance, which is offset

against an asset account to produce the proper balance sheet value for an asset.

Alternative titles for the Allowance for Uncollectible Accounts are Allowance for Bad Debts, Allowance for Doubtful Accounts, or Reserve for Bad Debts. Bad Debts Expense is also commonly used as an alternative title for Uncollectible Accounts Expense.

Estimating uncollectible accounts expense

Before the accounts are closed and financial statements are prepared at the end of the accounting period, an estimate of uncollectible accounts expense must be made. This estimate will usually be based upon past experience, perhaps modified in accordance with current business conditions.

Since the allowance for uncollectible accounts is necessarily an estimate and not a precise calculation, the factor of personal judgment may play a considerable part in determining the size of this valuation account. There is a fairly wide range of reasonableness within which the amount may be set. Most businessmen intend that the allowance shall be adequate to cover probable losses. The term *adequate,* when used in this context, suggests an amount somewhat larger than the minimum probable amount.

CONSERVATISM AS A FACTOR IN VALUING ACCOUNTS RECEIVABLE The larger the allowance established for uncollectible accounts, the lower the net valuation of accounts receivable will be. Some accountants and some businessmen tend to favor the most conservative valuation of assets that logically can be supported. Conservatism in the preparation of a balance sheet implies a tendency to state assets at their minimum values rather than to establish values in a purely objective manner. From a theoretical point of view, the doctrine of balance sheet conservatism is difficult to support, but from the viewpoint of bankers and others who use financial statements as a basis for granting loans, conservatism in valuing assets has long been regarded as a desirable policy.

Assume that the balance sheet of Company A presents optimistic, exaggerated values for the assets owned. Assume also that this "unconservative" balance sheet is submitted to a banker in support of an application for a loan. The banker studies the balance sheet and makes a loan to Company A in reliance upon the values listed. Later the banker finds it impossible to collect the loan and also finds that the assets upon which he had based the loan were greatly overstated in the balance sheet. The banker will undoubtedly consider the overly optimistic character of the balance sheet as partially responsible for his loss. Experiences of this type have led bankers as a group to stress the desirability of conservatism in the valuation of assets.

In considering the argument for balance sheet conservatism, it is important to recognize that the income statement is also affected by the estimates made of uncollectible accounts expense. The act of providing a relatively large allowance for uncollectible accounts involves a correspondingly heavy charge to expense. Setting asset values at a minimum in the balance sheet has the related effect of stating the current year's net income at a minimum amount.

Two methods of estimating uncollectible accounts expense

The provision for uncollectible accounts is an estimate of expense to be sustained. Two alternative approaches are widely used in making the annual estimate for uncollectible accounts. One method consists of adjusting the valuation account to a new balance equal to the estimated uncollectible portion of the existing accounts receivable. This method is referred to as the *balance sheet* approach and rests on an *aging of the accounts receivable.* The adjusting entry takes into consideration the existing balance in the Allowance for Uncollectible Accounts.

The alternative method requires an adjusting entry computed as a percentage of the year's net sales. This method may be regarded as the *income statement* approach to estimating uncollectible accounts. This *percentage of sales* method emphasizes the expense side of the adjustment and leaves out of consideration any existing balance in the valuation account. If any substantial balance should accumulate in the allowance account, however, a change in the percentage figure being applied to sales might be appropriate. These two methods are explained below.

AGING THE ACCOUNTS RECEIVABLE A past-due account is always viewed with some suspicion. The fact that an account is past due suggests that the customer is either unable or unwilling to pay. The analysis of accounts by age is known as *aging the accounts,* as illustrated by the schedule at the top of page 339.

This analysis of accounts receivable gives management a useful picture of the status of collections and the probabilities of credit losses. Almost half of the total accounts receivable are past due. The question "How long past due?" is pertinent, and is answered by the bottom line of the aging analysis. About 29% of the total receivables are past due from 1 to 30 days; another 12% are past due from 31 to 60 days; about 3% are past due from 61 to 90 days; and 5% of the total receivables consist of accounts past due more than three months. If an analysis of this type is prepared at the end of each month, management will be continuously informed of the trend of collections and can take appropriate action to ease or tighten credit policy. Moreover, a yardstick is available to measure the effectiveness of the persons responsible for collection activities.

Analysis of Accounts Receivable by Age
December 31, 19___

	Customer	Total	Not Yet Due	1–30 Days Past Due	31–60 Days Past Due	61–90 Days Past Due	Over 90 Days Past Due
If you were	A. B. Adams	$ 500	$ 500				
credit	B. L. Baker	150			$ 150		
man-							
ager . . .?	R. D. Carl	800	800				
	H. V. Davis	900				$ 800	$ 100
	R. M. Evans	400	400				
	Others	32,250	16,300	$10,000	4,200	200	1,550
	Totals	$35,000	$18,000	$10,000	$4,350	$1,000	$1,650
	Percentage	100	51	29	12	3	5

The further past due an account receivable becomes, the greater the likelihood that it will not be collected in full. In recognition of this principle, the analysis of receivables by age groups can be used as a steppingstone in determining a reasonable amount to add to the Allowance for Uncollectible Accounts. To make this determination it is desirable to estimate the percentage of probable expense for each age group of accounts receivable. This percentage, when applied to the dollar amount in each age group, gives a probable expense for each group. By adding together the probable expense for all the age groups, the required balance in the Allowance for Uncollectible Accounts is determined. The following schedule lists the group totals from the preceding illustration and shows how the total probable expense from uncollectible accounts is computed.

Accounts Receivable by Age Groups

	Amount	% Considered Uncollectible	Allowance for Uncollectible Accounts
Estimate of Not yet due	$18,000	1	$ 180
probable 1–30 days past due	10,000	3	300
uncollect-			
ible 31–60 days past due	4,350	10	435
accounts 61–90 days past due	1,000	20	200
expense Over 90 days past due	1,650	50	825
Totals	$35,000		$1,940

This summary indicates that an allowance for uncollectible accounts of $1,940 is required. Before making the adjusting entry, it is necessary to *consider the existing balance* in the allowance account. If the Allowance for Uncollectible Accounts presently has a credit balance of, say, $500, the adjusting entry should be for $1,440 in order to bring the account up to the required balance of $1,940. This entry is as follows:

Increasing allowance for uncollect- ible accounts

Uncollectible Accounts Expense	*1,440*	
Allowance for Uncollectible Accounts		*1,440*

To increase the valuation account to the estimated probable expense of $1,940, computed as follows:

Present credit balance of valuation account	$ 500
Current provision for uncollectible accounts	1,440
New credit balance in valuation account	$1,940

On the other hand, if the Allowance for Uncollectible Accounts contained a *debit* balance of $500 before adjustment, the adjusting entry would be made in the amount of $2,440 ($1,940 + $500) in order to create the desired credit balance of $1,940.

ESTIMATING UNCOLLECTIBLE ACCOUNTS AS A PERCENTAGE OF NET SALES An alternative approach to providing for uncollectible accounts preferred by some companies consists of computing the charge to uncollectible accounts expense as a percentage of the net sales for the year. The question to be answered is not "How large a valuation allowance is needed to show our receivables at realizable value?" Instead, the question is stated as "How much uncollectible accounts *expense* is associated with this year's volume of sales?"

As an example, assume that for several years the expense of un-collectible accounts for Clark Company has averaged 1% of net sales (sales minus returns and allowances and sales discounts). At the end of the current year, before adjusting entries, the following account balances appear in the ledger:

	Debit	**Credit**
Sales		$1,260,000
Sales returns and allowances	$40,000	
Sales discounts	20,000	
Allowance for uncollectible accounts		1,500

The net sales of the current year amount to $1,200,000; 1% of this amount is $12,000. The existing balance in the Allowance for Un-collectible Accounts *should be ignored in computing the amount of the adjusting entry,* because the percentage of net sales method stresses the relationship between uncollectible accounts expense and net sales rather than the valuation of receivables at the balance sheet date. The entry is:

Provision for uncollect- ible accounts based on percentage of net sales

Uncollectible Accounts Expense	*12,000*	
Allowance for Uncollectible Accounts		*12,000*

To record uncollectible accounts expense of 1% of the year's net sales (.01 × $1,200,000).

If a business makes both cash sales and credit sales, it may be desirable to exclude the cash sales from consideration and to compute the percentage relationship of uncollectible accounts expense to credit sales only.

The percentage of credit sales approach has the advantage of being much easier to apply than the aging of accounts receivable method. The aging of receivables, however, tends to give a more reliable estimate of uncollectible accounts because of the consideration given to the age and collectibility of the specific accounts receivable at the balance sheet date. Many companies use the income statement approach for preparing interim financial statements and internal reports but use the balance sheet method for preparing annual financial statements.

Writing off an uncollectible account receivable

Whenever an account receivable from a customer is determined to be uncollectible, it no longer qualifies as an asset and should immediately be written off. To write off an account receivable is to reduce the balance of the customer's account to zero. The journal entry to accomplish this consists of a debit to the Allowance for Uncollectible Accounts and an offsetting credit to the Accounts Receivable controlling account in the general ledger (and to the customer's account in the subsidiary ledger).

Referring again to the example of the Arlington Corporation as shown on pages 335 and 336, the ledger accounts were as follows after the adjusting entry for estimated uncollectible accounts had been made on December 31, Year 1.

Accounts receivable	$200,000
Less: Allowance for uncollectible accounts	10,000

Next let us assume that on January 27, Year 2, a customer by the name of William Benton became bankrupt and the account receivable from him in the amount of $1,000 was determined to be worthless. The following entry should be made by the Arlington Corporation:

Writing off an uncollect-ible account

Allowance for Uncollectible Accounts	1,000	
Accounts Receivable, William Benton		1,000
To write off the receivable from William Benton as uncollectible.		

The important thing to note in this entry is that the debit is made to the Allowance for Uncollectible Accounts and *not* to the Uncollectible Accounts Expense account. The estimated expense is charged to the Uncollectible Accounts Expense account at the end of each accounting period. When a particular account receivable is later ascertained to be worthless and is written off, this action does not represent an additional expense but merely confirms our previous estimate of the expense. If the Uncollectible Accounts Expense account were first charged with estimated credit losses and then later charged with proved credit losses, we would be guilty of double counting of un-collectible accounts expense.

After the entry writing off William Benton's account has been posted, the Accounts Receivable controlling account and the Allowance for Uncollectible Accounts appear as follows:

Accounts Receivable

Year 1		Year 2	
Dec. 31	200,000	Jan. 27 (Benton write-off)	1,000

Both accounts reduced by write-off of worthless receivable

Allowance for Uncollectible Accounts

Year 2		Year 1	
Jan. 27 (Benton write-off)	1,000	Dec. 31	10,000

Note that the *net* amount of the accounts receivable was unchanged by writing off William Benton's account against the Allowance for Uncollectible Accounts.

Net value of receivables unchanged by write-off

Before the Write-off		After the Write-off	
Accounts receivable	$200,000	Accounts receivable	$199,000
Less: Allowance for un-		Less: Allowance for un-	
collectible accounts	10,000	collectible accounts	9,000
Net value of receivables . . .	$190,000	Net value of receivables . . .	$190,000

The fact that writing off an uncollectible receivable against the Allowance for Uncollectible Accounts does not change the net carrying value of accounts receivable shows that no expense is entered in the accounting records when an account is written off. This example bears out the point stressed earlier in the chapter: Credit losses belong in the period in which the sale is made, not in a later period in which the account is discovered to be uncollectible.

WRITE-OFFS SELDOM AGREE WITH PREVIOUS ESTIMATES The total amount of accounts receivable written off in a given year will seldom, if ever, be exactly equal to the estimated amount previously credited to the Allowance for Uncollectible Accounts.

If the amounts written off as uncollectible turn out to be less than the estimated amount, the Allowance for Uncollectible Accounts will continue to show a credit balance. If the amounts written off as un-collectible are greater than the estimated amount, the Allowance for Uncollectible Accounts will acquire a debit balance, which will be eliminated by the adjustment at the end of the period.

Recovery of an account previously written off

Occasionally an account which has been written off as worthless will later be collected in full or in part. Such collections are often referred to as *recoveries* of bad debts. Collection of an account previously written off is evidence that the write-off was an error; the write-off entry should therefore be reversed.

Let us assume, for example, that a past-due account receivable in the amount of $400 from J. B. Barker was written off by the following entry:

Barker account considered uncollectible

Allowance for Uncollectible Accounts	400	
Accounts Receivable, J. B. Barker		400
To write off the receivable from J. B. Barker as uncollectible.		

At some later date Barker pays his account in full. The entry to restore Barker's account will be:

Barker account reinstated

Accounts Receivable, J. B. Barker	400	
Allowance for Uncollectible Accounts		400
To reverse the entry writing off J. B. Barker's account.		

A separate entry will be made in the cash receipts journal to record the collection from Barker. This entry consists of a debit to Cash and a credit to Accounts Receivable.

Direct charge-off method of recognizing uncollectible accounts expense

Instead of making adjusting entries to record uncollectible accounts expense on the basis of estimates, some companies merely charge uncollectible accounts to expense at the time such receivables are determined to be uncollectible. This method makes no attempt to match revenue and related expenses. Uncollectible accounts expense is recorded in the period in which the individual accounts are determined to be worthless rather than in the period in which the sales were made.

When the direct charge-off method is in use, the accounts receivable will be listed in the balance sheet at their gross amount, and no valuation allowance will be used. The receivables, therefore, are not stated at their probable net realizable value.

In the determination of taxable income under present federal income tax regulations, both the direct charge-off method and the allowance method of estimating uncollectible accounts expense are acceptable. From the standpoint of accounting theory, the allowance method is much the better, for it enables expenses to be matched with related revenue and thus aids in making a logical measurement of net income.

Credit card sales

Many retailing businesses avoid the risk of uncollectible accounts by making credit sales to customers who use well-known credit cards, such as American Express, BankAmericard, or Master Charge. When a customer makes a purchase using one of these credit cards the retailer acquires an account receivable from the credit card company, rather than from the customer. The credit card company promptly pays the retailer and redeems the sales invoice. At the end of each month, the credit card company bills the credit card holder for all the invoices it has redeemed during the month. If the credit card holder fails to pay the amount owed, it is the credit card company which sustains the loss.

By making credit sales through credit card companies, retailers receive cash more quickly from credit sales and avoid uncollectible accounts expense. Also, the retailers avoid the expense of investigating customers' credit, maintaining subsidiary ledgers for accounts receivable, and making collections from customers. Credit card companies, however, do not redeem sales invoices at the full sales price. The agreement between the credit card company and the retailer allows the credit card company a substantial discount (usually between 3% and 7% of the amount of the sales invoice).

When a retailer makes sales to credit card customers, he may record the receivables from the credit card company at the net amount and debit an expense account for the amount of the credit card fee. These two debits will offset the credit to the Sales account for the retail price of the goods or services. To illustrate this procedure, assume Bradshaw Camera Shop sells a camera for $200 to a customer who uses a Quick Charge credit card. The entry would be:

Receivable is from the credit card company

Accounts Receivable, Quick Charge	190	
Credit Card Discount Expense	10	
Sales		200

To record a sale to a customer using a Quick Charge credit card and the discount expense of 5% charged by Quick Charge.

Bradshaw Camera Shop may then mail the sales invoice to Quick Charge and receive an immediate cash payment of $190. The expense account, Credit Card Discount Expense, should be included among the selling expenses on the income statement of Bradshaw Camera Shop.

An alternative accounting procedure leading to the same end result is to record the receivable from the credit card company at the full amount of the sale ($200 in the above example). When payment of $190 is received from the credit card company, the collection would be recorded by debiting Cash for $190 and debiting Credit Card Discount Expense for $10, offset by a credit to Accounts Receivable, Quick Charge for $200.

Analysis of accounts receivable

What dollar amount of accounts receivable would be reasonable for a business making annual credit sales of $1,200,000? Comparison of the average amount of accounts receivable with the sales made on credit during the period indicates how long it takes to convert receivables into cash. For example, if annual credit sales of $1,200,000 are made at a uniform rate throughout the year and the accounts receivable at year-end amount to $200,000, we can see at a glance that the receivables represent one-sixth of the year's sales, or about 60 days of uncollected sales. Management naturally wants to make efficient use of the available capital in the business, and therefore is interested in a rapid "turnover" of accounts receivable. If the credit terms offered by the business in the above example were, say, 30 days net, the existence of receivables equal to 60 days' sales would warrant investigation. The analysis of receivables is considered more fully in Chapter 16.

Receivables from installment sales

The importance of *installment sales* is emphasized by a recent annual report of Sears, Roebuck and Co., which shows over $4 billion of "customer installment accounts receivable." Nearly all the company's receivables call for collection in periodic installments.

An installment sale may or may not require a down payment; substantial interest charges are usually added to the "cash selling price" of the product in determining the total dollar amount to be collected in the series of installment payments. The seller usually has the right to repossess the merchandise if installments are not collected according to the terms of the installment contract. Repossessed merchandise is recorded at its current value rather than at its original cost or at the uncollected portion of the installment receivable.

Although the collection period for an installment sale often runs as long as 24 to 36 months, such installment receivables are regarded as current assets, if they correspond to customary terms of the industry.

Installment basis accounting for income tax purposes

Current provisions of the federal income tax law permit a dealer in personal property to spread the profit from installment sales over the years in which collections are received. The result is to defer the recognition of taxable income and the payment of income tax.

Assume, for example, that Cross Company sells an article for $3,000 which cost $1,800. No down payment is received, but the buyer promises to make 30 monthly payments of $100 each. The gross profit on the sale is 40% of the $3,000 total price or $1,200; therefore 40% of each installment collected is regarded for tax purposes as profit realized. If three $100 monthly collections were received in the year in which the sale occurred, the profit reported for tax purposes would be only $120 (that is, 40% × $300). In following years the same 40% rate would be applied to all collections under the contract.

The installment basis of measuring income is acceptable for income tax purposes but not for financial statements. The Accounting Principles Board of the AICPA in **Opinion No. 10** reaffirmed that "revenues should ordinarily be accounted for at the time a transaction is completed, with appropriate provision for uncollectible accounts."[1] Thus in our example of a $3,000 sale on a 30-month installment plan, proper accounting (for all purposes other than income tax returns) would require a $3,000 debit to Accounts Receivable and a $3,000 credit to Sales. The entire gross profit of $1,200 would be regarded as earned in the year of the sale.

The basic accounting principle of matching revenues with related expenses will usually best be accomplished by recognizing the entire gross profit in the period of sale, and by charges to expense to establish an adequate allowance for uncollectible installment accounts. There are a number of other more complex issues relating to installment sales; these are covered in **Modern Advanced Accounting** of this Series.

NOTES RECEIVABLE

Definition of a promissory note

A **promissory note** is an unconditional promise in writing to pay on demand or at a future date a definite sum of money.

The person who signs the note and thereby promises to pay is called the **maker** of the note. The person to whom payment is to be made is called the **payee** of the note. In the illustration below G. L. Smith is the maker of the note and A. B. Davis is the payee.

Simplified form of promissory note

$1,000   Los Angeles, California   July 10, 19--

One month .... after date .... I .... promise to pay

to the order of .... A. B. Davis

------One thousand and no/100------- dollars

payable at .... First National Bank of Los Angeles

for value received, with interest at 6%

G. L. Smith

[1]*APB Opinion No. 10*, "Ominbus Opinion–1966," AICPA (New York: 1967), p. 149.

From the viewpoint of the maker, G. L. Smith, the illustrated note is a liability and is recorded by crediting the Notes Payable account. However, from the viewpoint of the payee, A. B. Davis, this same note is an asset and is recorded by debiting the Notes Receivable account. The maker of a note expects to pay cash at the maturity date; the payee expects to receive cash at that date.

Nature of interest

Interest is a charge made for the use of money. To the borrower (maker of a note) interest is an expense; to the lender (payee of a note) interest is revenue.

COMPUTING INTEREST A formula used in computing interest is as follows:

Principal × rate of interest × time = interest

Interest rates are usually stated on an *annual basis.* For example, the interest on a $1,000, one-year, 6% note is computed as follows:

$1,000 × 0.06 × 1 = $60

If the term of the note were only four months instead of a year, the interest charge would be $20, computed as follows:

$1,000 × 0.06 × $\frac{4}{12}$ = $20

If the term of the note is expressed in days, the exact number of days must be used in computing the interest. As a matter of convenience, however, it is customary to assume that a year contains 360 days. Suppose, for example, that a 75-day, 6% note for $1,000 is drawn on June 10. The interest charge would be computed as follows:

$1,000 × 0.06 × $\frac{75}{360}$ = $12.50

The principal of the note ($1,000) plus the interest ($12.50) equals $1,012.50, and this amount (the maturity value) will be payable on August 24. The computation of days to maturity is as follows:

Days remaining in June (30 − 10)	20
Days in July	31
Days in August to maturity date	24
Total days called for by note	75

SIXTY-DAY, 6% METHOD FOR COMPUTING INTEREST A considerable saving of time is often possible by using the 60-day, 6% method of computing interest. If the interest rate is 6% a year, the interest for 60 days on any amount of money may be determined merely by *moving the decimal point two places to the left.* For example,

The interest at 6% for 60 days on $1,111.00 is $11.11
The interest at 6% for 60 days on $9,876.43 is $98.76

The reasoning underlying the 60-day, 6% shortcut may be summarized as follows:

Since interest on $1.00 for one year is $0.06
And 60 days is $\frac{1}{6}$ of a year
Interest on $1.00 for 60 days is $0.01 ($\frac{1}{6}$ of $0.06)

If the interest on $1.00 at 6% for 60 days can be computed by moving the decimal point two places to the left, then the interest on any amount at 6% for 60 days can be computed in the same manner.

The 60-day, 6% method can be used for time periods other than 60 days. The time of the note can be stated as a fraction or a multiple of 60 days and the interest quickly computed. For example, assuming an annual interest rate of 6%, what is the interest on $8,844 for 15 days?

Interest for 60 days on $8,844 is $88.44
Interest for 15 days on $8,844 is $\frac{1}{4}$ of $88.44, or $22.11

The 60-day, 6% method can also be applied when the interest rate is higher or lower than 6%. If the interest rate is something other than 6%, the interest is first computed at 6%, and an adjustment is then made for the difference between 6% and the actual rate. For example, what is the interest at 8% on $963 for 60 days?

Interest at 6% on $963 for 60 days is $ 9.63
Interest at 2% on $963 for 60 days is   3.21 ($\frac{1}{3}$ × $9.63)
Interest at 8% on $963 for 60 days is $12.84

Accounting for notes receivable

In some lines of business, notes receivable are seldom encountered; in other fields they occur frequently and may constitute an important part of total assets. Business concerns that sell high-priced durable goods such as automobiles and farm machinery often accept notes receivable from their customers. Many companies obtain notes receivable in settlement of past-due accounts.

All notes receivable are usually posted to a single account in the general ledger. A subsidiary ledger is not essential because the notes themselves, when filed by due dates, are the equivalent of a subsidiary ledger and provide any necessary information as to maturity, interest rates, collateral pledged, and other details. The amount debited to Notes Receivable is always the face amount of the note, regardless of whether or not the note bears interest. When an interest-bearing note is collected, the amount of cash received will be larger than the face amount of the note. The interest collected is credited to an Interest Earned account, and only the face amount of the note is credited to the Notes Receivable account.

ILLUSTRATIVE ENTRIES Assume that a 9%, 90-day note receivable is acquired from a customer, Marvin White, in settlement of an existing account receivable of $2,000. The entry for acquisition of the note is as follows:

Note
received to
replace
account
receivable

Notes Receivable	*2,000*	
Accounts Receivable, Marvin White		*2,000*
Accepted 9%, 90-day note in settlement of account receivable.		

The entry 90 days later to record collection of the note will be:

Collection
of principal
and interest

Cash	*2,045*	
Notes Receivable		*2,000*
Interest Earned		*45*
Collected 9%, 90-day note from Marvin White.		

When a note is received from a customer at the time of making a sale of merchandise, two entries should be made as follows:

Sale may be
run through
accounts
receivable
when note
is received
from
customer

Accounts Receivable, F. H. Russ . . . . : . .	*1,500*	
Sales		*1,500*
To record sale of merchandise.		
Notes Receivable	*1,500*	
Accounts Receivable, F. H. Russ		*1,500*
To record acquisition of note from customer.		

When this procedure is employed, the customer's account in the subsidiary ledger for accounts receivable provides a complete record of all transactions with him, regardless of the fact that some sales may have been made on open account and others may have involved a note receivable. Having a complete history of all transactions with a customer on a single ledger card may be helpful in reaching decisions as to collection efforts or further extensions of credit.

WHEN THE MAKER OF A NOTE DEFAULTS A note receivable which cannot be collected at maturity is said to have been *dishonored* by the maker. Failure by the maker to pay interest or principal of a note at the due date is also known as *defaulting* on the note. Immediately after the dishonor or default of a note, an entry should be made by the holder to transfer the amount due from the Notes Receivable account to an account receivable from the debtor.

Assuming that a 60-day, 9% note receivable from Robert Jones is not collected at maturity, the following entry would be made:

Default of	Accounts Receivable, Robert Jones	*1,015*	
note	Notes Receivable		*1,000*
receivable	Interest Earned		*15*

To record dishonor by Robert Jones of a 9%, 60-day note.

The interest earned on the note is recorded as a credit to Interest Earned and is also included in the account receivable from the maker. The interest receivable on a defaulted note is just as valid a claim against the maker as is the principal of the note; if the principal is collectible, then presumably the interest too can be collected.

By transferring past-due notes receivable into Accounts Receivable, two things are accomplished. First, the Notes Receivable account is limited to current notes not yet matured and is, therefore, regarded as a highly liquid type of asset. Secondly, the accounts receivable subsidiary ledger card will show that a note has been dishonored and will present a complete picture of all transactions with the customer.

RENEWAL OF A NOTE RECEIVABLE Sometimes the two parties to a note agree that the note shall be renewed rather than paid at the maturity date. If the old note does not bear interest, the entry could be made as follows:

Renewal of	Notes Receivable	*1,000*	
note should	Notes Receivable		*1,000*
be recorded			

A 60-day, non-interest-bearing note from Ray Bell renewed today with
new 60-day, 9% note.

The renewal of a note is an important transaction requiring managerial attention; a general journal entry is needed to record the action taken by management and to provide a permanent record of the transaction. If journal entries were not made to record the renewal of notes, confusion might arise as to whether some of the notes included in the balance of the Notes Receivable account were current or dishonored.

ADJUSTMENTS FOR INTEREST AT END OF PERIOD Notes receivable acquired in one accounting period often do not mature until a following period. Interest is being earned throughout the life of the note, and this revenue should be apportioned between the two accounting periods on a time basis. At the end of the accounting period, interest earned to date on notes receivable should be accrued by an adjusting entry debiting the asset account, Accrued Interest Receivable, and crediting the revenue account, Interest Earned. When the note matures and the interest is received in the following period, the entry to be made consists of a debit to Cash, a credit to Accrued Interest Receivable for the amount of the accrual, and a credit to Interest Earned for the remainder of the interest collected.

Discounting notes receivable

Many companies which obtain notes receivable from their customers prefer to sell the notes to a bank for cash rather than to hold them until maturity. Selling a note receivable to a bank or finance company is often called *discounting* a note receivable. The holder of the note signs his name on the back of the note (as in endorsing a check) and delivers the note to the bank. The bank expects to collect the *maturity value* (principal plus interest) from the maker of the note at the maturity date, but if the maker fails to pay, the bank can demand payment from the endorser.

The amount of cash received from discounting a note receivable is called the *proceeds* or *cash proceeds.* The term *carrying value* means the face amount of the note plus any accrued interest which has been recorded. Usually the cash proceeds will be less than the carrying value of the note; the difference is recorded by a debit to Interest Expense. If the cash proceeds were greater than the carrying value, the excess received would be credited to Interest Earned.

For example, assume that we own a note receivable for $10,000 on which we have recorded $100 of accrued interest receivable. We now discount the note receivable at the bank and receive cash of $10,020. The entry would be as follows:

Discounting a note receivable

Cash	*10,020*	
Interest Expense	*80*	
Notes Receivable		*10,000*
Accrued Interest Receivable		*100*

To record discounting of a note receivable.

When a businessman endorses a note and turns it over to a bank for cash, he is promising to pay the note if the maker fails to do so. The endorser is therefore contingently liable to the bank. A *contingent liability* may be regarded as a potential liability which either will develop into a full-fledged liability or will be eliminated entirely by a subsequent event. The subsequent event in the case of a discounted note receivable is the payment (or dishonoring) of the note by the maker. If the maker pays, the contingent liability of the endorser is thereby ended. If the maker fails to pay, the contingent liability of the endorser becomes a real liability. In either case the period of contingent liability ends at the maturity date of the note.

Classification of receivables in the balance sheet

Accounts receivable from customers will ordinarily be collected within the operating cycle; they are therefore listed among the current assets on the balance sheet. Receivables may also arise from miscellaneous transactions other than the sale of goods and services. These miscellaneous receivables, such as advances to officers and employees and claims against insurance companies for losses sustained, should be listed separately on the balance sheet and should not be combined with trade accounts receivable. If an account receivable from an officer or employee originates as a favor to the officer or employee, efforts at collection may await the convenience of the debtor. Consequently, it is customary to exclude receivables of this type from the current asset category.

Notes receivable usually appear among the current assets; however, if the maturity date of a note is more than a year distant and beyond the operating cycle of the business, it should be listed as noncurrent under a heading such as Investments. Any accrued interest receivable at the balance sheet date is a current asset but may be combined on the balance sheet with other accrued items such as accrued rents receivable or royalties receivable.

Contingent liabilities should be reflected in the balance sheet, because they have a considerable bearing on the credit rating of the person or firm contingently liable. A business concern with large contingent liabilities may encounter greater difficulties in obtaining bank loans than would otherwise be the case. The contingent liability arising from the discounting of notes receivable is usually disclosed by a *footnote* to the balance sheet. The following footnote is typical: "Note: At December 31, 19___, the company was contingently liable for notes receivable discounted in the amount of $250,000."

CURRENT LIABILITIES

Current liabilities are obligations that must be paid within the operating cycle or one year (whichever is longer). Comparison of the amount of current liabilities with the amount of current assets is one means of appraising the financial position of a business. In other words, a comparison of the amount of current liabilities with the amount of current assets available for paying these debts helps us in judging a company's short-run debt-paying ability.

In accounting for current liabilities, we are especially interested in making certain that all such obligations are included in the balance sheet. Fraud may be concealed by deliberate understatement of a liability. The omission or understatement of a liability will usually be accompanied by an overstatement of owners' equity or else by an understatement of assets. Depending on the nature of the error, the net income of the business may also be overstated.

Among the more common current liabilities are notes payable, accounts payable, and accrued or estimated liabilities, such as wages, interest, and taxes. An *estimated* liability is an obligation known to exist but for which the dollar amount is uncertain. In this chapter we shall consider the accounting problems relating to notes payable; the liabilities arising from payrolls will be considered in Chapter 13.

NOTES PAYABLE

Notes payable are issued whenever bank loans are obtained. Other transactions which may give rise to notes payable include the purchase of real estate or costly equipment, the purchase of merchandise, and the substitution of a note for a past-due account payable.

Notes payable issued to banks

Assume that John Caldwell, the sole proprietor of a retail business, applies to his bank for a 90-day, unsecured loan of $10,000. In support of the loan application Caldwell submits a balance sheet and income statement.

After studying the financial statements, reading the auditor's report, and making inquiries about Caldwell's credit rating, the bank indicates its willingness to lend the $10,000 requested, at an interest rate of 8%. The note which Caldwell signs will read as shown below, if we omit some of the minor details.

Interest stated separately

Los Angeles, California   June 15, 19—

.... Ninety days .... after date I promise to pay to Security National Bank the sum of .... $10,000 .... with interest at the rate of 8% per annum.

John Caldwell

The journal entry in Caldwell's accounts to record this borrowing from the bank is:

Face amount of note

Cash	10,000	
Notes Payable		10,000

Borrowed $10,000 for 90 days at annual rate of 8%.

No interest expense is recorded at the time of issuing the note. When the note is paid on September 13, the entry to be made is:

Payment of principal and interest

Notes Payable	10,000	
Interest Expense	200	
Cash		10,200

Paid bank at maturity date of loan.

ALTERNATIVE FORM OF NOTES FOR BANK LOANS Instead of stating the interest separately as in the preceding illustration, the note payable to the bank could have been so drawn as to include the interest charge in the *face amount* of the note, as shown below:

Interest included in face amount of note

Los Angeles, California   June 15, 19—

On .... September 13, 19— .... the undersigned promises to pay to

Security National Bank or order the sum of $10,200

John Caldwell

When the note is drawn in this manner the entry in Caldwell's accounts is:

Notes payable credited for face amount of note

Cash	10,000	
Discount on Notes Payable	200	
Notes Payable		10,200
Borrowed $10,000 for 90 days at annual rate of 8%.		

Notice that the amount borrowed ($10,000) was less than the face amount of the note ($10,200). The borrower's liability at this time is only $10,000; the other $200 of the face amount of the note represents *future interest expense.* As this interest expense is incurred over the life of the note, the borrower's liability will grow to $10,200, just as in the previous illustration.

The entry to record borrowing $10,000 from the bank might have been recorded by crediting Notes Payable for only $10,000 and gradually recording a liability for Accrued Interest Payable. However, standard practice is to credit the Notes Payable account for the face amount of the note. It is then necessary to debit a *contra-liability* account for the amount of the future interest expense. This contra-liability account, called *Discount on Notes Payable,* is listed in the balance sheet as a deduction from the Notes Payable account. The result is $10,200 minus $200, or a net liability of $10,000.

On September 13, the maturity date of the note, Caldwell will hand the bank $10,200 in payment of the note. At this time the $200 interest charge no longer represents future interest expense. Therefore, the balance of the Discount on Notes Payable account is transferred to Interest Expense. The journal entries to record the payment of the note would be:

Payment of	Interest Expense	200	
note and			
interest	Discount on Notes Payable		200
expense	To record interest expense on matured note.		

	Notes Payable	10,200	
	Cash		10,200
	Paid bank at maturity date of loan.		

Adjustments for interest at end of period

When a note is issued in one accounting period and matures in a later period, the interest expense must be apportioned. Adjusting entries for interest-bearing notes were illustrated in Chapter 4.

A different type of adjustment is necessary at the end of the period for notes payable to banks in which the interest has been included in the face amount of the note. The portion of the interest expense which has been incurred must be removed from the Discount on Notes Payable account, and recognized as interest expense. For example, assume that Baker Company borrows $20,000 from its bank on November 1 on a 6%, six-month note with interest of $600 included in the face of the note. The entry for the borrowing on November 1 would be:

Interest	Cash	20,000	
included in			
face of note	Discount on Notes Payable	600	
and . . .	Notes Payable		20,600
	Issued to bank a 6%, six-month note payable with interest included		
	in face amount of note.		

At December 31, the adjusting entry required is:

. . . related	Interest Expense	200	
adjusting			
entry	Discount on Notes Payable		200
	To record interest expense incurred to end of year on 6%, six-month note		
	dated Nov. 1.		

On May 1, when the six-month note matures and the Baker Company pays the bank, the entry is as follows:

Two-thirds	Notes Payable	20,600	
of interest	Interest Expense	400	
applicable			
to second	Cash		20,600
year	Discount on Notes Payable		400
	To record payment to bank of 6%, six-month note dated Nov. 1, with		
	interest included in face amount of note.		

Remember, Discount on Notes Payable should be classified as a contra-liability account and deducted from the face value of notes payable in the current liability section of the balance sheet. This treatment results in showing as a liability at statement date the principal of the debt plus the interest accrued to that date.

Prepaid interest

Discount on notes payable is sometimes called *prepaid interest* and classified as a current asset, a practice which has little theoretical justification. To prepay interest on a loan has the effect of reducing the amount of money borrowed and increasing the effective rate of interest. Assume that on July 1 you borrow $1,000 from a bank for a period of $1\frac{1}{2}$ years at an annual interest rate of 8%. Assume also that you pay the bank the full 18 months' interest of $120 ($1,000 × 8% × 1.5) at the date of borrowing the $1,000. Under this procedure you have increased your cash position by only $880. A more realistic view of the transaction is to say you have incurred a liability of $880 which will increase to $1,000 during the next year and one-half.

Current income tax regulations recognize the concept of prepaid interest. A taxpayer on the cash basis (and this includes most individuals) may deduct interest when it is paid, even though paid in advance. Thus, in the example of borrowing $1,000 and concurrently paying $1\frac{1}{2}$ years' interest in advance, you could deduct the entire interest charge of $120 for income tax purposes in the year paid. At present, however, tax regulations do not permit the deduction of prepaid interest for more than one year beyond the year in which the payment occurs.

Imputed interest on notes payable and notes receivable

Notes are often issued in connection with the acquisition of plant assets. If a realistic interest rate is not specified in the note, a portion of the face value of the note must be assumed to represent a charge for interest. Recognizing the economic reality that a portion of such a note represents an interest charge is termed *imputing* the interest. If the buyer fails to impute interest in a note payable which has an interest charge included in the face amount, the result will be to overstate the cost of the asset acquired and the amount of the related liability. It is equally important for the seller to impute interest in a note receivable containing an element of interest in the face amount. This interest charge represents *future interest revenue* to the holder of the note, and *is not part of the sale price of the asset.* If the seller fails to impute interest, the current sales revenue and notes receivable will both be overstated.

For example, assume that on July 1 Tru-Tool Company sells a large metal lathe to Everts Company for $15,000. In payment for the lathe, Everts Company issues a one-year note payable with a face amount of $16,200. The additional $1,200 included in the face amount of the note represents an interest charge of 8%. Tru-Tool Company should record the sale as follows:

Interest is not included in sales revenue

Accounts Receivable, Everts Company	15,000	
Sales		15,000
To record sale of lathe.		

Notes Receivable	16,200	
Discount on Notes Receivable		1,200
Accounts Receivable, Everts Company		15,000

Obtained note receivable from Everts Company with one-year interest charge included in face amount of note.

Notice that the sale is recorded at the price of the lathe, *not* at the face amount of the note receivable. The future interest revenue included in the face amount of the note is credited to Discount on Notes Receivable. As this revenue is earned, the balance of the Discount on Notes Receivable account will be transferred to Interest Earned. At December 31, the adjusting entry to recognize interest earned through year-end will be:

Interest revenue recognized when earned

Discount on Notes Receivable	600	
Interest Earned		600

To record interest earned through end of year on Everts Company 8% note dated July 1.

On June 30, of the following year, when the note receivable is collected from Everts Company, the entry required will be:

Collection of note receivable

Cash	16,200	
Discount on Notes Receivable	600	
Notes Receivable		16,200
Interest Earned		600

To record collection of Everts Company note.

Discount on Notes Receivable is a contra-asset account which is deducted from the face amount of notes receivable on the balance sheet. Had Tru-Tool Company failed to impute interest on the Everts Company note, the financial statements for the year ended December 31 would contain the following errors: (1) sales revenue would be overstated by $1,200, (2) interest revenue would be understated by $600, and (3) notes receivable would be overstated by $600.

Failure to impute adequate interest on long-term notes receivable has occasionally resulted in large overstatements of sales revenue, especially by real estate development companies. In recognition of this problem, the Accounting Principles Board issued *Opinion No. 21* which requires imputing interest on long-term notes receivable (and also notes payable) which do not bear adequate stated rates of interest.[2]

DEMONSTRATION PROBLEM

General Contractors Supply Co. is short of cash and regularly discounts the notes receivable obtained from customers. Banks apply a discount rate to the maturity value of the notes which varies depending on the quality of the note

---

[2] *APB Opinion No. 21,* "Interest on Receivables and Payables," AICPA (New York: 1971).

and the level of interest rates. The company makes some sales on 30-day open account, but any customer who does not pay in full within 30 days is asked to substitute an interest-bearing note for the past-due account. Some customers are required to sign promissory notes at the time of sale.

The company uses the allowance method in accounting for uncollectible accounts.

A partial list of transactions for the six months ended December 31, 19___, is given below.

July 1 Sale of merchandise to P. Linn on account, $1,545. It was agreed that Linn would submit a 60-day, 8% note upon receipt of the merchandise, and should deduct any freight he paid on the goods.

July 3 Received from Linn a letter stating that he had paid $45 freight on the shipment of July 1. He enclosed a 60-day, 8% note dated July 3 for $1,500.

July 18 Sold merchandise on account, $2,200, to Baxter Company; terms 2/10, n/30.

July 27 Discounted Linn note at bank and received $1,508 in cash.

July 28 Baxter Company paid account in full.

Aug. 8 Sold merchandise to E. Jones on account, $1,200; terms 2/10, n/30.

Sept. 1 Received notice from the bank that Linn had defaulted on his note due today. The bank charged the company's account for $1,520, the maturity value of the note.

Sept. 7 Received a 60-day note receivable from E. Jones in settlement of $1,200 open account. The note was drawn to include 60 days interest computed at 8% per annum on the face amount.

Sept. 10 It was ascertained that an account receivable from K. L. Treff amounting to $120 cannot be collected and was written off.

Oct. 15 An account receivable of $300 from Allen Blaine had been written off in June; full payment was unexpectedly received from Blaine.

Oct. 25 Received cash from P. Linn in full settlement of his account due today, including interest of 8% on $1,520 from September 1, maturity date of defaulted note.

Nov. 6 E. Jones paid his note due today.

Dec. 31 As a result of substantial write-offs, the Allowance for Uncollectible Accounts has a *debit* balance of $200. Aging of the accounts receivable (which amount to $80,000) indicates that a credit balance of $1,200 in the Allowance for Uncollectible Accounts is required.

Instructions

Prepare general journal entries to record the transactions and adjustments listed above.

SOLUTION TO DEMONSTRATION PROBLEM

General Journal

19___

July	1 Accounts Receivable, P. Linn	1,545.00	
	Sales		1,545.00
	Sale of merchandise on account.		
	3 Notes Receivable	1,500.00	
	Freight-out Expense	45.00	
	Accounts Receivable, P. Linn		1,545.00
	To record credit to P. Linn for freight paid by him and receipt of 60-day, 8% note for balance of account owed.		

July 18 Accounts Receivable, Baxter Company 2,200.00
        Sales 2,200.00
    Sale of merchandise on account, terms 2/10, n/30.

  27 Cash 1,508.00
        Interest Earned 8.00
        Notes Receivable 1,500.00
    Discounted note from P. Linn at bank.

  28 Cash 2,156.00
    Sales Discounts 44.00
        Accounts Receivable, Baxter Company 2,200.00
    Received payment from Baxter Company within discount period.

Aug. 8 Accounts Receivable, E. Jones 1,200.00
        Sales 1,200.00
    Sale of merchandise on account, terms 2/10, n/30.

Sept. 1 Accounts Receivable, P. Linn 1,520.00
        Cash 1,520.00
    To record payment to bank on dishonored note, and to charge this amount to maker of note.

  7 Notes Receivable 1,216.00
        Discount on Notes Receivable 16.00
        Accounts Receivable, E. Jones 1,200.00
    Received 60-day note with interest included in face amount in settlement of open account.

  10 Allowance for Uncollectible Accounts 120.00
        Accounts Receivable, K. L. Treff 120.00
    Wrote off uncollectible account from K. L. Treff.

Oct. 15 Accounts Receivable, Allen Blaine 300.00
        Allowance for Uncollectible Accounts 300.00
    To reverse the entry writing off Blaine's account.

  15 Cash 300.00
        Accounts Receivable, Allen Blaine 300.00
    To record collection of Blaine's account which was written off in June.

  25 Cash 1,538.24
        Accounts Receivable, P. Linn 1,520.00
        Interest Earned 18.24
    Collected Linn account in full plus interest @ 8% for 54 days as follows: $1,520 \times 8\% \times \frac{54}{360}$, or $18.24.

Nov. 6 Cash 1,216.00
    Discount on Notes Receivable 16.00
        Notes Receivable 1,216.00
        Interest Earned 16.00
    Received payment on note from E. Jones dated Sept. 7.

Dec. 31 Uncollectible Accounts Expense *1,400.00*

    Allowance for Uncollectible Accounts *1,400.00*

  To provide for estimated uncollectibles as follows:

   Balance required *$1,200*

   Present balance (debit) *200*

   Required increase in allowance *$1,400*

REVIEW QUESTIONS

1 In making the annual adjusting entry for uncollectible accounts, a company may utilize a *balance sheet approach* to make the estimate or it may use an *income statement approach.* Explain these two alternative approaches.

2 At the end of its first year in business, Baxter Laboratories had accounts receivable totaling $148,500. After careful analysis of the individual accounts, the credit manager estimated that $146,100 would ultimately be collected. Give the journal entry required to reflect this estimate in the accounting records.

3 In February of its second year of operations, Baxter Laboratories (Question 2 above) learned of the failure of a customer, Sterling Corporation, which owed Baxter $800. Nothing could be collected. Give the journal entry to recognize the uncollectibility of the receivable from Sterling Corporation.

4 What is the *direct charge-off method* of handling credit losses as opposed to the *allowance method?* What is its principal shortcoming?

5 Morgan Corporation has decided to write off the account receivable from Brill Company because the latter has entered bankruptcy. What general ledger accounts should be debited and credited, assuming that the allowance method is in use? What general ledger accounts should be debited and credited if the direct charge-off method is in use?

6 Magnum Corporation had accounts receivable of $100,000 and an Allowance for Uncollectible Accounts of $3,500 just prior to writing off as worthless an account receivable from Standard Company in the amount of $1,000. State the net realizable value of the accounts receivable before and after the write-off of this receivable from Standard Company.

7 Describe a procedure by which management could be informed each month of the status of collections and the overall quality of the accounts receivable on hand.

8 What are the advantages to a retailer of making credit sales only to customers who use nationally recognized credit cards?

9 Alta Mine Co. is a restaurant that had always made cash sales only until a new policy was adopted to honor several nationally known credit cards. Sales did not increase, but many of Alta Mine Co.'s regular customers began charging dinner bills on the credit cards. Has the new policy been beneficial to Alta Mine Co.? Explain.

10 Determine the maturity date of the following notes:
 a A three-month note dated March 10
 b A 30-day note dated August 15
 c A 90-day note dated July 2

11 X Company acquires a 6%, 60-day note receivable from a customer, Robert Waters, in settlement of an existing account receivable of $4,000. Give the journal entry to record acquisition of the note and the journal entry to record its collection at maturity.

12 Jonas Company issues a 90 day, 6% note payable to replace an account payable to Smith Supply Company in the amount of $8,000. Draft the journal entries (in general journal form) to record the issuance of the note payable and the payment of the note at the maturity date.

13 Distinguish between
  a Current and long-term liabilities
  b Estimated and contingent liabilities

14 Howard Benson applied to the City Bank for a loan of $20,000 for a period of three months. The loan was granted at an annual interest rate of $7\frac{1}{2}$%. Show how the note would be drawn if
  a Interest is stated separately in the note.
  b Interest is included in the face amount of the note.

15 With reference to Question 14 above, give the journal entry required on the books of Howard Benson for issuance of each of the two types of notes.

16 Rager Products sold merchandise to Baron Company in exchange for a one-year note receivable. The note was made out in the face amount of $13,189, including a 9% interest charge. Compute the amount of sales revenue to be recognized by Rager Products.

EXERCISES

Ex. 10-1 The unadjusted trial balance for the Filtron Corporation at the end of the current year includes the following accounts:

	Debit	Credit
Accounts receivable.	$120,000	
Allowance for uncollectible accounts		$ 910
Sales (25% represent cash sales)		480,000

Compute the uncollectible accounts expense for the current year, assuming that uncollectible accounts expense is determined as follows:
a 1% of total sales.
b $1\frac{1}{2}$% of credit sales.
c Allowance for uncollectible accounts is increased to equal 3% of gross accounts receivable.

Ex. 10-2 Standard Paint, Inc., reported the following balances on its balance sheet at the close of last year:

Notes receivable from customers	$10,000
Accrued interest on notes receivable	200
Accounts receivable.	42,000
Less: Allowance for uncollectible accounts	(1,000)

Record the following in journal entry form during the current year:
a Accounts receivable of $960 are written off as uncollectible.
b A customer's note for $275 on which interest of $15 has been accrued in the accounts is deemed uncollectible, and both balances are written off against the Allowance for Uncollectible Accounts.
c An account receivable for $130 previously written off is collected.
d Aging of accounts receivable at the end of the current year indicates a need for a $1,500 allowance to cover possible failure to collect accounts currently outstanding.

Ex. 10-3 The Southern Textile Corp. has been in business for three years and has charged off accounts receivable as they proved to be uncollectible. At the end of 1978, management decides to adopt the allowance method of accounting for uncollectible accounts and asks you to help them determine the proper balance in the Allowance for Uncollectible Accounts. The following information is available for your consideration:

| Year | Sales | Accounts Written Off | Year of Origin of Accounts Written Off | | | Net Income |
			1976	1977	1978	
1976	$300,000	$2,400	$2,400			$20,000
1977	500,000	5,200	1,200	$4,000		40,000
1978	880,000	9,000		3,600	$5,400	50,000

Accounts receivable at the end of 1978 amount to $160,000, all from 1978 sales.

a Based on the average experience for 1976 and 1977, compute the amount of the *total* uncollectible accounts that can reasonably be anticipated on the sales for 1978.

b Since $5,400 of accounts receivable originating in 1978 have already been written off, compute the amount of the allowance that should be established at the end of 1978 to cover estimated uncollectible accounts.

c In comparison with the actual write-off of receivables originating in 1976 and 1977 and in comparison with the estimated uncollectibles for 1978, the use of the direct charge-off method caused the income before taxes to be overstated in each of the three years. Compute the amount of the overstatement for each year and in total. Show computations.

Ex. 10-4 Use the 60-day, 6% method to compute interest on the following notes:
a $2,167 at 6% for 60 days
b $3,946 at 6% for 90 days
c $7,124 at 6% for 30 days
d $8,415 at 4% for 60 days
e $12,636 at 7% for 120 days
f $4,626 at 5% for 90 days

Ex. 10-5 On November 1, Bayard Corporation borrowed $25,000 from a local bank, agreeing to repay that amount plus 9% interest (per annum) in six months. Show the presentation of the bank loan on Bayard Corporation's December 31 balance sheet, assuming the company signed a note as follows:
a For $25,000, interest payable at maturity
b With the interest charge included in the face amount of the note

Ex. 10-6 Mac Motors sold two trucks to DeNault Trucking, Inc., on April 1, Year 1, at a sales price of $34,000. DeNault Trucking, Inc., paid $10,000 cash and signed an 18-month note payable for a face amount of $26,880. Prepare all journal entries for Mac Motors relating to the sale and the note for the year ended September 30, Year 1.

PROBLEMS

10-1 The balance sheet of Dawson Company at December 31 of last year showed $252,000 in accounts receivable and a credit balance of $13,000 in the allowance for uncollectible accounts. The following summary shows the totals of certain types of transactions occurring during January of the current year.

(1) Sales on account	*$180,000*
(2) Sales returns & allowances	*3,400*
(3) Cash payments by customers (no cash discounts)	*177,000*
(4) Account receivable from Rex Wiley written off as worthless following	
the failure of his business	*3,800*

At January 31, after a careful aging and analysis of all customers' accounts, the company decided that the allowance for uncollectible accounts should be adjusted to the amount of $14,600 in order to reflect accounts receivable at net realizable value in the January 31 balance sheet.

Instructions
a Give the appropriate entry in general journal form for each of the four numbered items above and the adjusting entry at January 31 to provide for uncollectible accounts.
b Show the amounts of accounts receivable and the allowance for uncollectible accounts as they would appear in the balance sheet at January 31.
c Assume that six months after the receivable from Rex Wiley had been written off as worthless, he won $100,000 in a lottery and immediately paid the $3,800 owed to Dawson Company. Give the general journal entry or entries to reflect this collection in Dawson Company's accounts.

10-2 The balance sheet of the Lyon Company at December 31, 1976, included accounts receivable of $761,280 and an allowance for uncollectible accounts of $19,440. The company's sales volume in 1977 reached a new high of $5,124,000 and cash collections from customers amounted to $4,957,536. Among these collections was the recovery in full of a $9,360 receivable from James Cowart, a customer whose account had been written off as worthless late in 1976. During 1977 it was necessary to write off as uncollectible customers' accounts totaling $20,196.

On December 1, 1977, the Lyon Company sold for $432,000 a tract of land acquired as a building site several years earlier at a cost of $288,000. The land was now considered unsuitable as a building site. Terms of sale were $120,000 cash and a 6%, six-month note for $312,000. The buyer was a large corporation and the note was regarded as fully collectible. Income taxes applicable to the sale of the land may be ignored.

At December 31, 1977, the accounts receivable included $120,348 of past-due accounts. After careful study of all past-due accounts, the management estimated that the probable loss contained therein was 10%, and that in addition, 2% of the current accounts receivable ($796,560) might prove uncollectible.

Instructions
a Prepare journal entries, in general journal form, for all 1977 transactions relating to accounts and notes receivable. All sales are on credit.
b Prepare the necessary adjusting entries at December 31, 1977.
c What amount should appear in the income statement for 1977 as uncollectible accounts expense?
d Prepare a partial balance sheet at December 31, 1977, showing the accounts indicated above.

10-3 The following information concerning the receivables of the James Corporation appeared in the accounts on January 1, 1977:

Accounts receivable:

C. L. Laurence	$ 1,815
E. D. Nemson	2,870
C. A. Shively	6,200
Total	$10,885

Notes receivable:

A. P. Marra, 8%, 45-day note, dated Dec. 6, 1976	$5,000
C. M. Hines, 7%, 90-day note, dated Dec. 31, 1976	3,000
Total	$8,000

Installment contracts receivable:

M. Moyers (monthly payment $150)	$2,475

Unearned interest on installment contracts:

Applicable to M. Moyers contract	$ 210

During the month of January, 1977, the following additional transactions took place:

Jan. 3 Received a 60-day, 8% note from C. L. Laurence in full settlement of his account.

Jan. 14 E. D. Nemson paid $870 on his account and gave a 30-day, 8% note to cover the balance.

Jan. 20 A. P. Marra wrote that he would be unable to pay his note due today. He included a check to cover the interest due and a new 30-day, 7% note renewing the old note. No accrued interest has been recorded.

Jan. 27 Discounted the C. L. Laurence note at the bank. The proceeds on the note amounted to $1,820.

Jan. 31 Received the monthly payment on the M. Moyers contract. The payment of $150 includes $15 of interest revenue which was originally recorded as unearned interest.

Instructions

a Prepare journal entries (in general journal form) for January, including an adjusting entry relating to accrued interest at January 31. (Hint: Three notes require adjustment.)

b Show how the accounts relating to notes receivable, accounts receivable, installment contracts receivable, and accrued interest receivable would appear in the balance sheet as of January 31. Show the actual balances.

10-4 Haines Corporation engaged in the following transactions involving promissory notes during the fiscal year ended October 31.

June 6 Borrowed $8,000 from E. J. Davis, issuing to him a 45-day, 7% note payable.

July 13 Purchased office equipment from Blane Company. This invoice amount was $16,000 and the Blane Company agreed to accept as full payment an 8%, three-month note for the invoiced amount.

July 21 Paid the Davis note plus accrued interest.

Sept. 1 Borrowed $168,000 from Security Bank at an interest rate of 9% per annum; signed a 90-day note with interest included in the face amount of the note.

Oct. 1 Purchased merchandise in the amount of $1,800 from Camp Co. Gave in settlement a 90-day note bearing interest at 8%.

Oct. **13** The $16,000 note payable to Blane Company matured today. Paid the interest accrued and issued a new 45-day, $9\frac{1}{2}$% note to replace the maturing note.

Instructions
a Prepare general journal entries to record the above transactions.
b Prepare the adjusting entries needed at October 31, prior to closing the accounts.

10-5 The transactions listed below represent a small portion of the business transacted by the firm of Ross and Morris, a partnership, during the three months ended December 31.

Oct. **2** Purchased fixtures from Axel Company for $10,800, paying $1,800 as a cash down payment and signing a one-year, 8% note payable for the balance. The interest charges of $720 were included in the face amount of the note and were recorded as Discount on Notes Payable.

Oct. **20** Gave $4,000 cash and a 90-day, $7\frac{1}{2}$% note to Lees Company in settlement of open account due today in the amount of $12,000.

Oct. **27** Purchased factory machinery from ELB Company for $17,400, giving a 60-day, 6% note in settlement thereof.

Oct. **31** Borrowed $72,000 from Manufacturers Bank, giving a 90-day note as evidence of indebtedness. Interest at 8% per annum was included in the face of the note.

Nov. **23** Purchased merchandise on account from Herman Buckle, $44,000.

Nov. **26** Issued a 60-day note bearing interest at 9% in settlement of the Buckle account.

Dec. **26** Paid the 60-day, 6% note due to ELB Company.

Instructions
a Prepare journal entries (in general journal form) to record the listed transactions for the three months ended December 31.
b Prepare an adjusting entry for accrued interest at December 31. (Hint: Four notes must be considered. The computation of interest on each can be shown as part of the explanation of the adjusting entry.)
c Prepare a partial balance sheet as of December 31 reflecting the above transactions. Show Notes Payable to Bank (minus the discount) as one item and Notes Payable: Other (minus the discount) as a separate liability.

10-6 Selected transactions of the Discount Carpet Center relating to receivables and payables for the month of October are shown below:

Oct. **1** Sold merchandise to G. Blair for $1,500. Blair issued a 90-day, 8% note for the amount of the purchase.

Oct. **4** Received a 30-day, 8% note from Thomas Crowne for $4,200 in settlement of open account.

Oct. **11** Issued a 60-day, $7\frac{1}{2}$% note payable to Prescott Company for $5,040 in settlement of open account.

Oct. **16** Borrowed $12,000 from United States Bank and signed a six-month, 9% note payable which included the interest in the face amount.

Oct. **17** Discounted the Thomas Crowne note. The proceeds from the bank amounted to $4,212.

Oct. **21** Sold merchandise to Howard Wright. As payment, Wright issued a 60-day note for a face amount of $6,318, which included an interest charge of $468.

Oct. **24** Received payment from W. Harned of a $3,000, 60-day, 9% note dated August 25. Accrued interest receivable of $27 had been recorded in prior months.

Oct. **26** A long overdue account receivable from J. Bartlett in the amount of $720 was written off as uncollectible against the allowance for uncollectible accounts.

Oct. 28 Full payment of a $290 account receivable was unexpectedly received from J. Kievits. This account had been written off as uncollectible several months ago.

Oct. 31 Sales to HandyCharge credit card customers in October amounted to $9,500 (record the receivable at the full amount).

Oct. 31 Collected cash from HandyCharge for October credit card sales, less 6% discount charged by HandyCharge.

Oct. 31 An aging of accounts receivable on October 31 indicates the allowance for uncollectible accounts should be increased to $1,950. On September 30, the balance in the allowance account had been $1,830. No entries other than those described above have been made in the allowance account during October.

Instructions

a Prepare in general journal form the entries necessary to record the above transactions.

b Prepare any adjusting entries needed at October 31. (Hint: Four notes require adjusting entries.)

c Draft the appropriate footnote to the financial statements to disclose the contingent liability relating to the discounted note receivable.

BUSINESS DECISION PROBLEM 10

Fidelity Systems and House of Sound are two companies engaged in selling stereo equipment to the public. Both companies sell equipment at a price 50% greater than cost. Customers may pay cash, purchase on open 30-day accounts, or make installment payments over a 36-month period. The installment receivables include a three-year interest charge, which amounts to 30% of the sales price, in the face amount of the contract. Condensed income statements prepared by the companies for their first year of operations are shown below:

	Fidelity Systems	House of Sound
Sales	$129,000	$96,000
Cost of goods sold	70,000	64,000
Gross profit on sales	$ 59,000	$32,000
Operating expenses	21,000	20,000
Operating income	$ 38,000	$12,000
Interest earned	–0–	3,600
Net income	$ 38,000	$15,600

House of Sound imputes interest on its installment receivables and recognizes the interest earned during the year as interest revenue. Fidelity Systems records the face amount of installment receivables as sales revenue at the time of the sale. The interest charges included in Fidelity Systems' installment receivables originating in the first year amount to $24,000, of which $19,700 is unearned at the end of the first year.

House of Sound provides for uncollectible accounts by the allowance method. The company recognized uncollectible accounts expense of $3,700 during the year, which was adequate. Fidelity Systems uses the direct charge-off method to recognize uncollectible accounts expense. During the year, $700 of accounts were written-off as uncollectible, but no entry was made for $12,400 of accounts estimated to be uncollectible at year-end.

Instructions
a Prepare a condensed income statement for Fidelity Systems for the year, using the same methods of accounting for installment sales and uncollectible accounts as were used by House of Sound.
b Compare the income statement you have prepared in part *a* to the one originally prepared by Fidelity Systems. Which income statement do you believe better reflects the results of the company's operations during the year? Explain.
c What do you believe to be the key factor responsible for making one of these companies more profitable than the other? What corrective action would you recommend be taken by the less profitable company to improve future performance?

ELEVEN

INVENTORIES

Some basic questions relating to inventory

In earlier sections of this book the procedures for recording inventory at the end of the accounting period have been illustrated. The use of the inventory figure in both the balance sheet and the income statement has been demonstrated, and particular emphasis has been placed on the procedure for computing the cost of goods sold by deducting the ending inventory from the cost of goods available for sale during the period.

In all the previous illustrations, the dollar amount of the ending inventory has been given with only a brief explanation as to how this amount was determined. The valuation of inventory, as for most other types of assets, has been stated to be at cost, but the concept of cost as applied to inventories of merchandise has not been explored or defined.

In this chapter we shall consider some of the fundamental questions involved in accounting for inventories. Among the questions to be considered are these:

1 What goods are to be included in inventory?
2 How are the physical quantities in the ending inventory determined?
3 What is the cost of the ending inventory?
4 What are the arguments for and against each of several alternative methods of inventory valuation?

Inventory defined

One of the largest assets in a retail store or in a wholesale business is the inventory of merchandise, and the sale of this merchandise at prices in excess of cost is the major source of revenue. The inventory of a merchandising concern consists of all goods owned and held for sale in the regular course of business. Merchandise held for sale will normally be converted into cash within less than a year's time and is therefore regarded as a current asset. In the balance sheet, inventory is listed immediately after accounts receivable, because it is just one step further removed from conversion into cash than are the accounts receivable.

In manufacturing businesses there are three major types of inventories: *raw materials, goods in process of manufacture,* and *finished goods.*

All three classes of inventories are included in the current asset section of the balance sheet.

The term *inventory* has been defined to mean "the aggregate of those items of tangible personal property which (1) are held for sale in the ordinary course of business, (2) are in process of production for such sale, or (3) are to be currently consumed in the production of goods or services to be available for sale." [1]

Inventory valuation and the measurement of income

In measuring the gross profit on sales for an accounting period, we subtract the *cost of goods sold* from the total *sales* of the period. The figure for sales is easily accumulated from the daily record of sales transactions, but in many businesses no day-to-day record is maintained showing the cost of goods sold.[2] The figure representing the cost of goods sold during an entire accounting period is computed at the end of the period by separating the cost of goods available for sale into two elements:

1 The cost of the goods sold
2 The cost of the goods not sold, which therefore comprise the ending inventory

This idea, with which you are already quite familiar, may be concisely stated in the form of an equation as follows:

Finding cost of goods sold

$$\text{Cost of Goods Available for Sale} - \text{Ending Inventory} = \text{Cost of Goods Sold}$$

Determining the amount of the ending inventory is the key step in establishing the cost of goods sold. In separating the *cost of goods available for sale* into its components of *goods sold* and *goods not sold,* we are just as much interested in establishing the proper amount for cost of goods sold as in determining a proper figure for inventory. Throughout this chapter you should bear in mind that the procedures for determining the amount of the ending inventory are also the means for determining the cost of goods sold. The valuation of inventory and the determination of the cost of goods sold are in effect the two sides of a single coin.

The American Institute of Certified Public Accountants has summarized this relationship between inventory valuation and the measurement of income in the following words: "A major objective of accounting for inventories is the proper determination of income through

---

[1] AICPA, *Accounting Research and Terminology Bulletins,* Final Edition (New York: 1961), p. 28.
[2] As explained in Chap. 5, a company that maintains perpetual inventory records will have a day-to-day record of the cost of goods sold and of goods in inventory. Our present discussion, however, is based on the assumption that the periodic system of inventory is being used.

the process of matching appropriate costs against revenues." [3] The expression "matching costs against revenues" means determining what portion of the cost of goods available for sale should be deducted from the revenue of the current period and what portion should be carried forward (as inventory) to be matched against the revenue of the following period.

Importance of an accurate valuation of inventory

The most important current assets in the balance sheets of most companies are cash, accounts receivable, and inventory. Of these three, the inventory is usually much the largest. Because of the relatively large size of this asset, an error in the valuation of inventory may cause a material misstatement of financial position. An error of 20% in valuing the inventory may have as much effect on the financial statements as would the complete omission of the asset cash.

An error in inventory will of course lead to other erroneous figures in the balance sheet, such as the total current assets, total assets, owners' equity, and the total of liabilities and owners' equity. The error will also affect key figures in the income statement, such as the cost of goods sold, the gross profit on sales, and the net income for the period. Finally, it is important to recognize that the ending inventory of one year is also the beginning inventory of the following year. Consequently, the income statement of the second year will also be in error by the full amount of the original error in inventory valuation.

ILLUSTRATION OF THE EFFECTS OF AN ERROR IN VALUING INVENTORY Assume that on December 31, 1976, the inventory of the Hillside Company is actually $100,000 but, through an accidental error, it is recorded as $90,000. The effects of this $10,000 error on the income statement for the year 1976 are indicated in the first illustration on page 371 showing two income statements side by side. The left-hand set of figures shows the inventory of December 31, 1976, at the proper value of $100,000 and represents a correct income statement for the year 1976. The right-hand set of figures represents an incorrect income statement, because the ending inventory is erroneously listed as $90,000. Note the differences between the two income statements with respect to net income, gross profit on sales, and cost of goods sold. Income taxes have purposely been omitted in this illustration.

---

[3] AICPA, *op. cit.*, p. 28.

HILLSIDE COMPANY
Income Statement
For the Year Ended December 31, 1976

		With Correct Ending Inventory		With Incorrect Ending Inventory
Sales		$240,000		$240,000
Cost of goods sold:				
Beginning inventory, Dec. 31, 1975	$ 75,000		$ 75,000	
Purchases (net)	210,000		210,000	
Cost of goods available for sale	$285,000		$285,000	
Less: Ending inventory, Dec. 31, 1976	100,000		90,000	
Cost of goods sold		185,000		195,000
Gross profit on sales		$ 55,000		$ 45,000
Operating expenses		30,000		30,000
Net income		$ 25,000		$ 15,000

Effect of error in inventory

This illustration shows that an understatement of $10,000 in the ending inventory for the year 1976 caused an understatement of $10,000 in the net income for 1976. Next, consider the effect of this error on the income statement of the following year. The ending inventory of 1976 is, of course, the beginning inventory of 1977. The preceding illustration is now continued to show side by side a correct statement and an incorrect statement for 1977. The ending inventory of $120,000 for the year 1977 is the same in both statements and is to be considered correct. Note that the $10,000 error in the beginning inventory of the right-hand statement causes an error in the cost of goods sold, in gross profit, and in net income for the year 1977.

HILLSIDE COMPANY
Income Statement
For the Year Ended December 31, 1977

		With Correct Beginning Inventory		With Incorrect Beginning Inventory
Sales		$265,000		$265,000
Cost of goods sold:				
Beginning inventory, Dec. 31, 1976	$100,000		$ 90,000	
Purchases (net)	230,000		230,000	
Cost of goods available for sale	$330,000		$320,000	
Less: Ending inventory, Dec. 31, 1977	120,000		120,000	
Cost of goods sold		210,000		200,000
Gross profit on sales		$ 55,000		$ 65,000
Operating expenses		33,000		33,000
Net income		$ 22,000		$ 32,000

Effect on succeeding year

COUNTERBALANCING ERRORS The illustrated income statements for the years 1976 and 1977 show that an understatement of the ending inventory in 1976 caused an understatement of net income in that year and an offsetting overstatement of net income for 1977. Over a period of two years the effects of an inventory error on net income will *counterbalance,* and the total net income for the two years together is the same as if the error had not occurred. Since the error in reported net income for the first year is exactly offset by the error in reported net income for the second year, it might be argued that an inventory error has no serious consequences. Such an argument is not sound, for it disregards the fact that accurate yearly figures for net income are a primary objective of the accounting process. Moreover, many actions by management and many decisions by creditors and owners are based upon *trends* indicated in the financial statements for two or more years. Note that the inventory error has made the 1977 net income appear to be more than twice as large as the 1976 net income, when in fact less net income was earned in 1977 than in 1976. Anyone relying on the erroneous financial statements would be greatly misled as to the trend of Hillside Company's earnings.

To produce dependable financial statements, inventory must be accurately determined at the end of each accounting period. The counterbalancing effect of the inventory error by the Hillside Company is illustrated below:

		With Inventory at Dec. 31, 1976, Understated	
	With Inventory Correctly Stated	*Reported Net Income Will Be*	*Reported Net Income Will Be Overstated (Understated)*
Net income for 1976	$25,000	$15,000	($10,000)
Net income for 1977	22,000	32,000	10,000
Total net income for two years	$47,000	$47,000	$ –0–

Counterbalancing effect on net income

RELATION OF INVENTORY ERRORS TO NET INCOME The effects of errors in inventory upon net income may be summarized as follows:

1 When the *ending* inventory is understated, the net income for the period will be understated.

2 When the *ending* inventory is overstated, the net income for the period will be overstated.

3 When the *beginning* inventory is understated, the net income for the period will be overstated.

4 When the *beginning* inventory is overstated, the net income for the period will be understated.

Taking a physical inventory

At the end of each accounting period up-to-date balances for most of the assets will be shown in the ledger accounts. For inventory, however, the balance in the ledger account represents the **beginning** inventory, because no entry has been made in the Inventory account since the end of the preceding period. All purchases of merchandise during the present period have been recorded in the Purchases account. The ending inventory does not appear anywhere in the ledger accounts; it must be determined by a physical count of merchandise.

Establishing a balance sheet valuation for the ending inventory requires two steps: (1) determining the quantity of each kind of merchandise on hand and (2) determining the cost of the items comprising the inventory. The first step is called **taking the inventory;** the second is called **pricing the inventory.** Taking inventory, or more precisely, taking a physical inventory, means making a systematic count of all merchandise on hand.

In most merchandising businesses the taking of a physical inventory is a year-end event. In some lines of business an inventory may be taken at the close of each month. It is common practice to take inventory after regular business hours or on Sunday. By taking the inventory while business operations are suspended, a more accurate count is possible than if goods were being sold or received while the count is in process.

PLANNING THE PHYSICAL INVENTORY Unless the taking of a physical inventory is carefully planned and supervised, serious errors are apt to occur which will invalidate the results of the count. To prevent such errors as the double counting of items, the omission of goods from the count, and other quantitative errors, it is desirable to plan the inventory so that the work of one person serves as a check on the accuracy of another.

There are various methods of counting merchandise. One of the simplest procedures is carried out by the use of two-man teams. One member of the team counts and calls the description and quantity of each item. The other person lists the descriptions and quantities on an inventory sheet. (In some situations, a tape recorder is useful in recording quantities counted.) When all goods have been counted and listed, the items on the inventory sheet are priced at cost, and the unit prices are multiplied by the quantities to determine the valuation of the inventory.

To assure the accuracy of the recorded counts, a representative number of items should be recounted by supervisors. Some businesses make a practice of counting all merchandise a second time and comparing the quantities established by the different teams. The initials of the persons making both the first and the second counts should be placed on an inventory tag attached to each lot of merchandise counted. Once it is known that all merchandise has been tagged and that the counts are accurate, the tags are gathered and sent to the accounting office for completion of the inventory.

INCLUDING ALL GOODS OWNED All goods to which the company has title should be included in the inventory, regardless of their location. Title to merchandise ordinarily passes from seller to buyer at the time the goods are delivered. No question arises as to the ownership of merchandise on the shelves, in stock rooms, or in warehouses. A question of ownership does arise, however, for merchandise en route from suppliers but not yet received on the last day of the year. A similar question of ownership concerns goods in the process of shipment to customers at year-end.

Goods in transit Do goods in transit belong in the inventory of the seller or of the buyer? If the seller makes delivery of the merchandise in his own trucks, the merchandise remains his property while in transit. If the goods are shipped by rail, air, or other public carrier, the question of ownership of the goods while in transit depends upon whether the public carrier is acting as the agent of the seller or of the buyer. If the terms of the shipment are *F.O.B.* (free on board) *shipping point,* title passes at the point of shipment and the goods are the property of the buyer while in transit. If the terms of the shipment are *F.O.B. destination,* title does not pass until the shipment reaches the destination, and the goods belong to the seller while in transit. In deciding whether goods in transit at year-end should be included in inventory, it is therefore necessary to refer to the terms of the agreements with vendors (suppliers) and customers.

At the end of the year a company may have received numerous orders from customers, for which goods have been segregated and packed but not yet shipped. These goods should generally be included in inventory. An exception to this rule is found occasionally when the goods have been prepared for shipment but are being held for later delivery at the request of the customer.

Passage of title to merchandise The debit to the customer's account and the offsetting credit to the Sales account should be made **when title to the goods passes to the customer.** It would obviously be improper to set up an account receivable and at the same time to include the goods in question in inventory. Great care is necessary at year-end to ensure that all last-minute shipments to customers are recorded as sales of the current year and, on the other hand, that no customer's order is recorded as a sale until the date when the goods are shipped. Sometimes, in an effort to meet sales quotas, companies have recorded sales on the last day of the accounting period, when in fact the merchandise was not shipped until early in the next period. Such practices lead to an overstatement of the year's earnings and are not in accordance with generally accepted principles of accounting.

Merchandise in inventory is valued at *cost,* whereas accounts receivable are stated at the *sales price* of the merchandise sold. Consequently, the recording of a sale prior to delivery of the goods results in an unjustified increase in the total assets of the company. The increase will equal the difference between the cost and the selling price of the goods in question. The amount of the increase will also be reflected in the income statement, where it will show up as additional gross profit. An unscrupulous company, which wanted to make its financial statements present a more favorable picture than actually existed, might do so by treating year-end orders from customers as sales even though the goods were not yet shipped.

Pricing the inventory

One of the most interesting and widely discussed problems in accounting is the pricing of inventory. Even those businessmen who have little knowledge of accounting are usually interested in the various methods of pricing inventory, because inventory valuation has a direct effect upon reported net income. Federal income taxes are based on income, and the choice of inventory method may have a considerable effect upon the amount of income taxes payable. Federal income tax authorities are therefore much interested in the problem of inventory valuation and have taken a definite position on the acceptability of various alternative methods of pricing inventory.

In approaching our study of inventory valuation, however, it is important that we do not overemphasize the income tax aspects of the problem. It is true that in selected cases one method of inventory valuation may lead to a substantially lower income tax liability than would another method, but there are other important considerations in pricing inventory apart from the objective of minimizing the current income tax burden.

Proper valuation of inventory is one part of a larger undertaking, that is, to measure net income accurately and to provide all those persons interested in the financial position and operating results of a business with accounting data which are dependable and of maximum usefulness as a basis for business decisions.

The most significant basis of accounting for inventories is cost.[4] An understanding of the meaning of the term *cost* as applied to inventories is a first essential in appreciating the complexity of the overall problem of inventory valuation.

---

[4] Special situations in which inventory is carried at a basis other than cost are discussed in Chap. 14.

Cost basis of inventory valuation

"The primary basis of accounting for inventory is cost, which has been defined generally as the price paid or consideration given to acquire an asset. As applied to inventories, cost means in principle the sum of the applicable expenditures and charges directly or indirectly incurred in bringing an article to its existing condition and location." [5]

TRANSPORTATION-IN AS AN ELEMENT OF COST The starting point in determining the cost of an article of merchandise is the price paid, as shown by the vendor's invoice. To this acquisition cost should be added the cost of transportation incurred in bringing the merchandise to the location where it is to be offered for sale.

At the end of the year when a physical inventory is taken, the cost of each kind of merchandise is multiplied by the quantity on hand to determine the dollar amount of the ending inventory. The price paid for an article may readily be found by referring to the invoice from the supplier, but often there is no convenient method of determining how much transportation cost may have been incurred on specific types of merchandise. This is particularly true when certain shipments have included various kinds of merchandise and the freight charge was for the shipment as a whole. For reasons of convenience and economy, therefore, a merchandising business may choose to determine inventory cost at year-end by listing each item in stock at the purchase invoice price, and then adding to the inventory as a whole a reasonable proportion of the transportation charges incurred on inbound shipments during the year.

In many lines of business it is customary to price the year-end inventory without giving any consideration to transportation charges. This practice may be justified by the factors of convenience and economy, even though it is not theoretically sound. If freight charges are not material in amount, it may be advisable in terms of operating convenience to treat the entire amount as part of the cost of goods sold during the year. Accounting textbooks stress theoretical concepts of cost and of income determination; the student of accounting should be aware, however, that in many business situations an approximation of cost will serve the purpose at hand. In other words, the extra work involved in computing more precise cost data must be weighed against the benefits to be obtained.

OTHER COSTS RELATING TO ACQUISITION OF MERCHANDISE If transportation-in is part of the cost of merchandise purchased, what about the other incidental payments relating to the acquisition of merchandise, such as the salary of the purchasing agent, insurance of goods in transit, cost of receiving and inspecting the merchandise, etc.?

[5] AICPA, *op. cit.,* p. 28.

Although in theory these incidental costs should be identified and apportioned among the various items of merchandise purchased, the expense of computing cost of merchandise on such a precise basis would usually outweigh the benefits to be derived. The costs of operating the purchasing department and the receiving department are customarily treated as expense of the period in which incurred, rather than being carried forward to another period by inclusion in the balance sheet amount for inventory.

PURCHASE DISCOUNTS AS A FACTOR IN INVENTORY VALUATION When a merchant purchases goods he often has the opportunity of saving 1 to 2% of the invoiced amount by making payment within a specified period, usually 10 days. Since purchase discounts are shown as a deduction from purchases in the income statement, they should logically be deducted from the invoice price of the items comprising the year-end inventory. Often, however, it is impracticable to compute the precise amount of discount applicable to each item in inventory. One reasonable alternative is to deduct from the invoice cost of the ending inventory an amount representing the estimated purchase discounts applicable to these goods. If purchase discounts are not significant in amount, they may be ignored for the purpose of inventory pricing.

Inventory valuation methods

The prices of many kinds of merchandise are subject to frequent change. When identical lots of merchandise are purchased at various dates during the year, each lot may be acquired at a different cost price.

To illustrate the several alternative methods in common use for determining which purchase prices apply to the units remaining in inventory at the end of the year, assume the data shown below.

	Number of Units	Cost per Unit	Total Cost
Beginning inventory	10	$ 8	$ 80
First purchase (Mar. 1)	5	9	45
Second purchase (July 1)	5	10	50
Third purchase (Oct. 1)	5	12	60
Fourth purchase (Dec. 1)	5	13	65
Available for sale	30		$300
Units sold	18		
Units in ending inventory	12		

This schedule shows that 18 units were sold during the year and that 12 units are on hand at year-end to make up the ending inventory. In order to establish a dollar amount for cost of goods sold and for the ending inventory, we must **make an assumption** as to which units were sold and which units remain on hand at the end of the year. There are several acceptable assumptions on this point; four of the most common will be considered. Each assumption made as to the cost of the units in the ending inventory leads to a different method of pricing inventory and to different amounts in the financial statements. The four assumptions (and inventory valuation methods) to be considered are known as: (1) specific identification, (2) average cost, (3) first-in, first-out, and (4) last-in, first-out.

Although each of these four methods will produce a different answer as to the cost of goods sold and the cost of the ending inventory, the valuation of inventory in each case is said to be at "cost." In other words, *these methods represent alternative definitions of inventory cost.*

SPECIFIC IDENTIFICATION METHOD If the units in the ending inventory can be identified as coming from specific purchases, they *may* be priced at the amounts listed on the purchase invoices. Continuing the example already presented, if the ending inventory of 12 units can be identified as, say, five units from the purchase of March 1, four units from the purchase of July 1, and three units from the purchase of December 1, the cost of the ending inventory may be computed as follows:

Specific *Five units from the purchase of Mar. 1 @ $9*	*$ 45*
identification *method* *Four units from the purchase of July 1 @ $10*	*40*
and . . . *Three units from the purchase of Dec. 1 @ $13*	*39*
Ending inventory (specific identification)	*$124*

The cost of goods sold during the period is determined by subtracting the ending inventory from the cost of goods available for sale.

. . . cost of *Cost of goods available for sale*	*$300*
goods sold *computation* *Less: Ending inventory*	*124*
Cost of goods sold	*$176*

A business may prefer not to use the specific identification method even though the cost of each unit sold could be identified with a specific purchase. The flow of cost factors may be more significant than the flow of specific physical units in measuring the net income of the period.

As a simple example, assume that a coal dealer purchased 100 tons of coal at $60 a ton and a short time later made a second purchase of 100 tons of the same grade coal at $80 a ton. The two purchases are in separate piles and it is a matter of indifference as to which pile is used in making sales to customers. Assume that the dealer makes a retail sale of one ton of coal at a price of $100. In measuring the gross profit on the sale, which cost figure should be used, $60 or $80? To insist that the cost depended on which of the two identical piles of coal was used in filling the delivery truck is an argument of questionable logic.

A situation in which the specific identification method is more likely to give meaningful results is in the purchase and sale of such high-priced articles as boats, automobiles, and jewelry.

AVERAGE-COST METHOD Average cost is computed by dividing the total cost of goods available for sale by the number of units available for sale. This computation gives a **weighted-average unit cost,** which is then applied to the units in the ending inventory.

Average-cost method and . . . Cost of goods available for sale	*$300*
Number of units available for sale	*30*
Average unit cost ($300 ÷ 30)	*$ 10*
Ending inventory (at average cost, 12 units @ $10)	*$120*

Note that this method, when compared with the actual invoice price method, leads to a different amount for cost of goods sold as well as a different amount for the ending inventory.

. . . cost of goods sold computation Cost of goods available for sale	*$300*
Less: Ending inventory	*120*
Cost of goods sold	*$180*

When the average-cost method is used, the cost figure determined for the ending inventory is influenced by all the various prices paid during the year. The price paid early in the year may carry as much weight in pricing the ending inventory as a price paid at the end of the year. A common criticism of the average-cost method of pricing inventory is that it attaches no more significance to current prices than to prices which prevailed several months earlier.

FIRST-IN, FIRST-OUT METHOD The first-in, first-out method, which is often referred to as **fifo,** is based on the **assumption** that the first merchandise acquired is the first merchandise sold. In other words, each sale is made out of the oldest goods in stock; the ending inventory therefore consists of the most recently acquired goods. The fifo method of determining inventory cost may be adopted by any business, regardless of whether or not the physical flow of merchandise actually corresponds to this assumption of selling the oldest units in stock. Using the same data as in the preceding illustrations, the 12 units in the ending inventory would be regarded as consisting of the most recently acquired goods, as follows:

First-in, first-out method and . . . Five units from the Dec. 1 purchase @ $13	*$ 65*
Five units from the Oct. 1 purchase @ $12	*60*
Two units from the July 1 purchase @ $10	*20*
Ending inventory, 12 units (at fifo cost)	*$145*

During a period of rising prices the first-in, first-out method will result in a larger amount being assigned as the cost of the ending inventory than would be assigned under the average-cost method. When a relatively large amount is allocated as cost of the ending inventory, a relatively small amount will remain as cost of goods sold, as indicated by the following calculation:

. . . cost of goods sold computation

Cost of goods available for sale	$300
Less: Ending inventory	145
Cost of goods sold	$155

It may be argued in support of the first-in, first-out method that the inventory valuation reflects recent costs and is therefore a realistic value in the light of conditions prevailing at the balance sheet date.

LAST-IN, FIRST-OUT METHOD The title of this method of pricing suggests that the most recently acquired goods are sold first, and that the ending inventory consists of "old" merchandise acquired in the earliest purchases. Such an assumption is, of course, not in accord with the actual physical movement of goods in most businesses, but there is nevertheless a strong logical argument to support this method. As merchandise is sold, more goods must be purchased to replenish the stock on hand. Since the making of a sale necessitates a replacement purchase of goods, the cost of replacement should be offset against the sales price to determine the gross profit realized.

The supporters of last-in, first-out, or *lifo,* as it is commonly known, contend that the accurate determination of income requires that primary emphasis be placed on the *matching of current costs of merchandise against current sales prices,* regardless of which physical units of merchandise are being delivered to customers. Keeping in mind the point that the *flow of costs* may be more significant than the *physical movement* of merchandise, we can say that, under the lifo method, the cost of goods sold consists of the cost of the most recently acquired goods, and the ending inventory consists of the cost of the oldest goods which were available for sale during the period.

Using the same data as in the preceding illustrations, the 12 units in the ending inventory would be priced as if they were the oldest goods available for sale during the period, as follows:

Last-in, first-out method and . . .

Ten units from the beginning inventory @ $8	$80
Two units from the purchase of Mar. 1 @ $9	18
Ending inventory, 12 units (at lifo cost)	$98

Note that the lifo cost of the ending inventory ($98) is very much lower than the fifo cost ($145) of ending inventory in the preceding example. Since a relatively small part of the cost of goods available for sale is assigned to ending inventory, it follows that a relatively large portion must have been assigned to cost of goods sold, as shown by the following computation:

... cost of
goods sold
computation

Cost of goods available for sale *$300*

Less: Ending inventory *98*

    Cost of goods sold *$202*

COMPARISON OF THE ALTERNATIVE METHODS OF PRICING INVENTORY

We have now illustrated four common methods of pricing inventory at cost; the specific identification method, the average-cost method, the first-in, first-out method, and the last-in, first-out method. By way of contrasting the results obtained from the four methods illustrated, especially during a period of rapid price increases, let us summarize the amounts computed for ending inventory, cost of goods sold, and gross profit on sales under each of the four methods. Assume that sales for the period amounted to $275.

	Specific Identification Method	*Average-cost Method*	*First-in, First-out Method*	*Last-in, First-out Method*
Sales	*$275*	*$275*	*$275*	*$275*
Cost of goods sold:				
Beginning inventory	*$ 80*	*$ 80*	*$ 80*	*$ 80*
Purchases	*220*	*220*	*220*	*220*
Cost of goods available for sale	*$300*	*$300*	*$300*	*$300*
Less: Ending inventory	*124*	*120*	*145*	*98*
Cost of goods sold	*$176*	*$180*	*$155*	*$202*
Gross profit on sales	*$ 99*	*$ 95*	*$120*	*$ 73*

Four methods of determining inventory cost compared

This comparison of the four methods makes it apparent that during periods of **rising prices,** the use of lifo will result in lower profits being reported than would be the case under the other methods of inventory valuation. This is because lifo causes the most current (and therefore the highest) costs to be included in the cost of goods sold. Perhaps for this reason many businesses have adopted lifo. Current income tax regulations permit virtually any business to use the last-in, first-out method in determining taxable income.

During a period of **declining prices,** the use of lifo will cause the reporting of relatively large profits as compared with fifo, which will hold reported profits to a minimum. Obviously, the choice of inventory method becomes of greatest significance during prolonged periods of drastic changes in price levels.

WHICH METHOD OF INVENTORY VALUATION IS BEST?

All four of the inventory methods described are regarded as acceptable accounting practices and all four are acceptable in the determination of taxable income. No one method of inventory valuation can be considered as the "correct" or the "best" method. In the selection of a method, consideration should be given to the probable effect upon the balance sheet, upon the income statement, upon the amount of taxable income, and upon such business decisions as the establishment of selling prices for goods.

The specific identification method has the advantage of portraying the actual physical flow of merchandise. However, this method permits manipulation of income by selecting which items to deliver in filling a sales order. Also, the specific identification method may lead to faulty pricing decisions by implying that identical items of merchandise have different economic values.

Identical items will have the same accounting values only under the average-cost method. Assume for example that a hardware store sells a given size nail for 65 cents per pound. The hardware store buys the nails in 100-pound quantities at different times at prices ranging from 40 to 50 cents per pound. Several hundred pounds of nails are always on hand, stored in a large bin. The average-cost method properly recognizes that when a customer buys a pound of nails it is not necessary to know exactly which nails the customer happened to select from the bin in order to measure the gross profit on the sale.

A shortcoming in the average-cost method is that changes in current replacement costs of inventory are concealed because these costs are averaged with older costs. As a result of this averaging, the reported gross profit may not reflect current market conditions. This problem is illustrated in the following section of this chapter.

When prices are changing drastically, the most significant cost data to use as a guide to sales policies are probably the current replacement costs of the goods being sold. The lifo method of inventory valuation comes closer than any of the other methods described to measuring net income in the light of current selling prices and current replacement costs.

On the other hand, the use of lifo during a period of rising prices is apt to produce a balance sheet figure for inventory which is far below the current replacement cost of the goods on hand. The fifo method of inventory valuation will lead to a balance sheet valuation of inventory more in line with current replacement costs.[6]

Some companies which adopted lifo more than 30 years ago now show a balance sheet figure for inventory which is less than half the present replacement cost of the goods in stock. An inventory valuation method which gives significant figures for the income statement may thus produce misleading amounts for the balance sheet, whereas a method which produces a realistic figure for inventory on the balance sheet may provide less realistic data for the income statement.

[6] First-in, first-out (fifo) is the most frequently used method, according to a study of 600 corporations. Last-in, first-out (lifo) has been declining in use and is now used less frequently than the average-cost method. AICPA, *Accounting Trends & Techniques, 27th ed.* (New York: 1973), p. 98.

The search for the "best" method of inventory valuation is rendered difficult because the inventory figure is used in both the balance sheet and the income statement, and these two statements are intended for different purposes. In the income statement the function of the inventory figure is to permit a matching of costs and revenue. In the balance sheet the inventory and the other current assets are regarded as a measure of the company's ability to meet its current debts. For this purpose a valuation of inventory in line with current replacement cost would appear to be most significant.

The high rates of income tax in recent years have stimulated the interest of businessmen in the choice of inventory methods. No one can predict with certainty the course of future prices or income tax rates. Impressive numbers of businesses, however, have reacted to the experience of rising prices, large profits, and high income taxes by adopting lifo as a means of minimizing reported net income and required income tax payments.

Inventory profits

Many accountants believe that the use of fifo or of average cost during a period of inflation results in the reporting of fictitious profits and consequently in the payment of excessive income taxes. A portion of the reported profits are considered to be fictitious because under both the fifo and average-cost methods, the gross profit is computed by subtracting old inventory costs rather than current replacement costs from sales revenue. These old costs are relatively low, resulting in a high reported gross profit. However, the company must pay the higher current cost in order to replenish its inventory.

To illustrate this concept, assume that TV Sales Shop has an inventory of 20 television sets which were acquired at an average cost of $270. During the current month, 10 television sets are sold for cash at a sales price of $350 each. Using the average-cost method to value inventory, the company will report the following gross profit for the month:

Sales (10 × $350)	*$3,500*
Cost of goods sold (10 × $270)	*2,700*
Gross profit on sales	*$ 800*

However, TV Sales Shop must replace its inventory of television sets to continue in business. Because of inflation, TV Sales Shop can no longer buy 10 television sets for $2,700. Let us assume that the current replacement cost of television sets is $325 each; TV Sales Shop must pay $3,250 to replenish its inventory. Thus, TV Sales Shop is able to keep only $250 ($3,500 − $3,250) of the reported $800 gross profit; the remaining $550 has to be reinvested in inventory because of the increasing cost of television sets. This $550 would be considered a fictitious profit, or an *inventory profit,* by many accountants and busi-nessmen.

In periods of rapid inflation, a significant portion of the reported net income of companies using fifo or average cost may actually be inventory profits. The net income of companies using lifo will include much less inventory profit because lifo causes more current costs to be included in the cost of goods sold.

The lower-of-cost-or-market rule

Although cost is the primary basis for valuation of inventories, circum-stances may arise under which inventory may properly be valued at less than its cost. If the *utility* of the inventory has fallen below cost by reason of physical deterioration, obsolescence, or decline in the price level, a loss has occurred. This loss may appropriately be recog-nized as a loss of the current period by reducing the accounting value of the inventory from cost to a lower level designated as market. The word *market* as used in this context means *current replacement cost.* For a merchandising concern, market is the amount which the concern would have to pay at the present time for the goods in question, purchased in the customary quantities through the usual sources of supply and including transportation-in. To avoid misunderstanding, the rule might better read "lower of cost or replacement cost."

In the early days of accounting when the principal users of financial statements were creditors and attention was concentrated upon the balance sheet, conservatism was a dominant consideration in asset valuation. The lower-of-cost-or-market rule was then considered justi-fiable because it tended to produce a "safe" or minimum value for inventory. The rule was widely applied for a time without regard for the possibility that, although replacement costs had declined, there might be no corresponding and immediate decline in selling prices.

As the significance of the income statement has increased, consid-erable dissatisfaction with the lower-of-cost-or-market rule has devel-oped. If ending inventory is written down from cost to a lower market figure but the merchandise is sold during the next period at the usual selling prices, the effect of the write-down will have been to reflect a fictitious loss in the first period and an exaggerated profit in the second period. Arbitrary application of the lower-of-cost-or-market rule ignores the historical fact that selling prices do not always drop when replacement prices decline. Even if selling prices do follow replacement prices downward, they may not decline by a proportionate amount.

Because of these objections, the lower-of-cost-or-market rule has undergone some modification. If the inventory can probably be sold at prices which will yield a *normal profit,* the inventory should be carried at cost even though current replacement cost is lower. Assume, for example, that merchandise is purchased for $1,000 with the intention of reselling it to customers for $1,500. The replacement cost then declines from $1,000 to $800, but it is believed that the merchandise can still be sold to customers for $1,450. In other words, the normal anticipated profit has shrunk by $50. The carrying value of the inventory could then be written down from $1,000 to $950. There is no justification for reducing the inventory to the replacement cost of $800 under these circumstances.

Another qualification of the lower-of-cost-or-market rule is that inventory should never be carried at an amount greater than *net realizable value,* which may be defined as prospective selling price minus anticipated selling expenses. Assume, for example, that because of unstable market conditions, it is believed that goods acquired at a cost of $500 and having a current replacement cost of $450 will probably have to be sold for no more than $520 and that the selling expenses involved will amount to $120. The inventory should then be reduced to a carrying value (net realizable value) of $400, which is less than current replacement cost.

APPLICATION OF THE LOWER–OF–COST–OR–MARKET RULE The lower of cost or market for an inventory is most commonly computed by determining the cost and the market figures for each item in inventory and using the lower of the two amounts in every case. If, for example, item A cost $100 and market is $90, the item should be priced at $90. If item B cost $200 and market is $225, this item should be priced at $200. The total cost of the two items is $300 and total market is $315, but the total inventory value determined by applying the lower-of-cost-or-market rule to each item in inventory is only $290. This application of the lower-of-cost-or-market rule is illustrated by the tabulation shown below.

Application of Lower-of-Cost-or-Market Rule, Item-by-Item Method

			Unit Price		Lower of Cost or Market
Item		**Quantity**	**Cost**	**Market**	
Pricing inventory at lower of cost or market	A	10	$100	$ 90	$ 900
	B	8	200	225	1,600
	C	50	50	60	2,500
	D	80	90	70	5,600
Total (total cost is $12,300 and total market value is $11,300)					$10,600

If the lower-of-cost-or-market rule is applied item by item, the carrying value of the above inventory would be $10,600. However, an alternative and less rigorous version of the lower-of-cost-or-market rule calls for applying it to the total of the entire inventory rather than to the individual items. If the above inventory is to be valued by applying the lower-of-cost-or-market rule to the total of the inventory, the balance sheet amount for inventory is determined merely by comparing the total cost of $12,300 with the total replacement cost of $11,300 and using the lower of the two figures. Still another alternative method of using the lower-of-cost-or-market concept is to apply it to categories of the inventory rather than item by item. These alternative methods of applying the lower-of-cost-or-market rule are appropriate when no loss of income is anticipated, because the decline in replacement costs of certain goods is fully offset by higher replacement costs for other items.

Gross profit method of estimating inventories

The taking of a physical inventory is a time-consuming and costly job in many lines of business; consequently, a physical inventory may be taken only once a year. Monthly financial statements are needed, however, for intelligent administration of the business, and the preparation of monthly statements requires a determination of the amount of inventory at the end of each month. In many cases this dilemma may be solved satisfactorily by estimating the inventory each month by using the *gross profit method.*

The gross profit method of estimating the inventory is based on the assumption that the rate of gross profit remains approximately the same from year to year. This assumption is a realistic one in many fields of business. The first step in using the gross profit method is to obtain from the ledger the figures for beginning inventory, net purchases, and net sales. Cost of goods sold is then computed by reducing the net sales figure by the usual gross profit rate. The difference between the cost of goods available for sale and the estimated cost of goods sold represents the estimated ending inventory.

To illustrate, let us assume that the beginning inventory is $25,000, the net purchases of the period $70,000, and the net sales $100,000. The gross profit rate is assumed to have approximated 40% of net sales for the past several years. This information is now assembled in the customary form of an income statement as follows:

Gross profit method . . .

Net sales		$100,000	(100%)
Cost of goods sold:			
Beginning inventory	$25,000		
Net purchases	70,000		
Cost of goods available for sale	$95,000		
Less: Ending inventory	?		
Cost of goods sold		60,000	(60%)
Gross profit on sales (40% × $100,000)		$ 40,000	(40%)

Customarily, in preparing an income statement, the ending inventory is deducted from the cost of goods available for sale to determine the cost of goods sold. In this case our calculation to determine the ending inventory consists of deducting the estimated cost of goods sold from the cost of goods available for sale.

. . . to	*Cost of goods available for sale*	*$95,000*
estimate ending	*Less: Cost of goods sold (60% of $100,000)*	*60,000*
inventory	*Ending inventory (estimate)*	*$35,000*

The gross profit method of estimating inventory has several uses apart from the preparation of monthly financial statements. This calculation may be used after the taking of a physical inventory to confirm the overall reasonableness of the amount determined by the counting and pricing process. In the event of a fire which destroys the inventory, the approximate cost of goods on hand at the date of the fire may also be computed by the gross profit method.

The retail method of inventory valuation

The retail method of estimating an ending inventory is somewhat similar to the gross profit method. It is widely used by chain stores, department stores, and other types of retail business. Goods on sale in retail stores are marked at the retail prices; it is therefore more convenient to take inventory at current retail prices than to look up invoices to find the unit cost of each item in stock. After first determining the value of the inventory at retail price, the next step is to convert the inventory to cost price by applying the ratio prevailing between cost and selling price during the current period. This method of approximating an inventory may also be carried out by using data from the accounts without taking any physical count of the goods on hand. The underlying basis for the retail method of inventory valuation is the percentage of markup for the current period, whereas the gross profit method of estimating inventory rests on the rate of gross profit experienced in preceding periods.

When the retail method of inventory is to be used, it is necessary to maintain records of the beginning inventory and of all purchases during the period in terms of selling price as well as at cost. Goods available for sale during the period can then be stated both at cost and at selling price. By deducting the sales for the period from the sales value of the goods available for sale, the ending inventory at selling price may be determined without the need for a physical count. The ending inventory at selling price is then converted to a cost basis by using the percentage of cost to selling price for the current period.

In practice, the application of this method may be complicated because the originally established sales prices are modified by frequent price markups and markdowns. These frequent changes in retail price present some difficulties in determining the cost percentage to use in reducing the inventory from selling price to cost. The following illustration shows the calculation of inventory by the retail method, without going into the complications which would arise from markups and markdowns in the original retail selling price.

	Cost Price	Selling Price
Beginning inventory	*$20,000*	*$30,000*
Net purchases during the month	*11,950*	*15,000*
Cost of goods available for sale	*$31,950*	*$45,000*
Less: Net sales for the month		*20,000*
Ending inventory at selling price		*$25,000*
Cost percentage ($31,950 ÷ $45,000) = 71%		
Ending inventory at cost (71% × $25,000)	*$17,750*	

Used by many department stores

Consistency in the valuation of inventory

A business has considerable latitude in selecting a method of inventory valuation best suited to its needs; once a method has been selected, however, that method should be followed consistently from year to year. A change from one inventory method to another will ordinarily cause reported income to vary considerably in the year in which the change occurs. Frequent switching of methods would therefore make the income statements quite undependable as a means of portraying operating results.

The need for consistency in the valuation of inventory does not mean that a business should *never* make a change in inventory method. However, when a change is made, the approval of tax authorities must be obtained, and full disclosure of the nature of the change and of its effect upon the year's net income should be included in the financial statements or in a footnote to the statements. Even when the same method of inventory pricing is being followed consistently, the financial statements should include a disclosure of the pricing method in use.[7]

Comparability among companies

Because several different inventory valuation methods are in common use, the financial statements of different companies may not be directly comparable. In recognition of this problem, *Accounting Research Study No. 13* recommends that all companies which do not use the fifo valuation method prepare a *pro forma footnote* to the financial statements showing what inventory and net income *would have been* if fifo had been in use.[8] With this supplementary information, users of financial statements could better compare the financial statements of vari-

---

[7] *APB Opinion No. 22*, "Disclosure of Accounting Policies," AICPA (New York: 1972), p. 436.
[8] Horace G. Barden, *Accounting Research Study No. 13*, "The Accounting Basis of Inventories," AICPA (New York: 1973), p. 151.

ous companies regardless of which inventory valuation method each company uses. In the opinion of the authors, such disclosure would increase the comparability and usefulness of financial statements.

Perpetual inventory system

Many businesses, especially those handling products of high unit cost, prefer to use a perpetual inventory system which provides a continuous running record of the inventory. Under the perpetual inventory system, a purchase of merchandise is debited to the Inventory account rather than to a Purchases account. A sale of merchandise requires two entries: (1) a debit to Cash or Accounts Receivable and a credit to Sales for an amount equal to the sales price of the merchandise and (2) a debit to a Cost of Goods Sold account and a credit to the Inventory account for an amount equal to the cost of the merchandise sold. The balance in the Cost of Goods Sold account at any time during the accounting period shows the total cost of the merchandise sold to date and the Inventory account shows the cost of merchandise on hand.

The use of a perpetual inventory system does not eliminate the need for taking a physical inventory. When the physical count indicates a disagreement with the book record (perhaps because of theft of goods or from accounting errors), the Inventory account and the Cost of Goods Sold account are adjusted to agree with the results of the physical count.

Inventories for a manufacturing business

A typical manufacturing firm buys raw materials and converts them into a finished product. The raw materials purchased by an aircraft manufacturer, for example, include sheet aluminum, steel, paint, and a variety of electronic gear and control instruments. The completed airplanes assembled from these components are the *finished goods* of the aircraft manufacturer. The terms *raw materials* and *finished goods,* as used in accounting, are defined from the viewpoint of each manufacturing firm. Sheet aluminum, for example, is a raw material from the viewpoint of an aircraft company, but it is a finished product of an aluminum company.

In converting raw materials into finished goods, the manufacturer employs factory labor, uses machinery, and incurs many other manufacturing costs, such as heat, light, and power, machinery repairs, and supervisory salaries. These production costs are added to the cost of raw materials to determine the cost of the finished goods manufactured during any given period. The accounting records of a manufacturing firm must be expanded to include ledger accounts for these various types of factory costs. Financial statements must also be changed to reflect the costs of manufacturing and several new classes of inventories. At any given moment, a manufacturer will have on hand a stock of raw materials, finished goods awaiting shipment and sale, and partially completed products in various stages of manufacture. Inventories of each of these three classes of items must be taken at the end of each accounting period in order to measure the cost of goods that have been completed and the cost of goods sold during the period.

In place of the single inventory account found on the balance sheet of a retail or wholesale business, a manufacturing concern has three separate inventory accounts, all of which are current assets.

1 *Raw materials inventory.* This account represents the unused portion of the raw materials purchased. As a matter of convenience, factory supplies on hand (oil, grease, sweeping compounds) acquired for use in maintaining and servicing the factory building and machinery are often merged with raw materials.

2 *Goods in process inventory.* This inventory consists of the partially completed goods on hand in the factory at year-end. The cost of these partially manufactured goods is determined by estimating the costs of the raw materials, direct labor, and factory overhead associated with these units.

3 *Finished goods inventory.* This account shows the cost of finished goods on hand and awaiting sale to customers as of the end of the year. The cost of these finished units is composed of the factory costs of raw material, direct labor, and factory overhead.

COMPARISON OF INCOME STATEMENTS FOR MANUFACTURING AND MERCHANDISING COMPANIES The treatment of sales, selling expenses, general administrative expenses, and income taxes is the same on the income statement of a manufacturing company as for a merchandising company. The only difference in the two partial income statements shown on page 391 lies in the cost of goods sold section. In the income statement of the manufacturing company, Cost of Finished Goods Manufactured replaces the item labeled Purchases in the income statement of the merchandising company.

STATEMENT OF COST OF FINISHED GOODS MANUFACTURED The principal new item in the illustrated income statement for a manufacturing company is the item: "Cost of finished goods manufactured . . . $600,000." This amount was determined from the Statement of Cost of Finished Goods Manufactured, a statement prepared to accompany and support the income statement. This statement is illustrated in condensed form on page 391.

Observe that the final amount of $600,000 on the statement of cost of finished goods manufactured (page 391) is carried forward to the income statement and is used in determining the cost of goods sold, as illustrated in the income statement for the manufacturing company.

MERCHANDISING COMPANY
Partial Income Statement
For the Current Year

Sales		$1,000,000
Cost of goods sold:		
Beginning inventory of merchandise	$300,000	
➤ Purchases.............................	600,000	
Cost of goods available for sale	$900,000	
Less: Ending inventory of merchandise	250,000	
Cost of goods sold......................		650,000
Gross profit on sales		$ 350,000

MANUFACTURING COMPANY
Partial Income Statement
For the Current Year

Sales		$1,000,000
Cost of goods sold:		
Beginning inventory of finished goods	$300,000	
➤ Cost of finished goods manufactured (Exhibit A)	600,000	
Cost of goods available for sale	$900,000	
Less: Ending inventory of finished goods	250,000	
Cost of goods sold......................		650,000
Gross profit on sales		$ 350,000

MANUFACTURING COMPANY   Exhibit A
Statement of Cost of Finished Goods Manufactured
For the Current Year

Goods in process inventory, beginning of year			$ 70,000
Raw materials used:			
Beginning raw materials inventory.................		$50,000	
Purchases of raw materials	$100,000		
Less: Purchase returns and allowances	3,000	97,000	
Transportation-in		5,000	
Cost of raw materials available for use............		$152,000	
Less: Ending raw materials inventory.............		42,000	
Cost of raw materials used		$110,000	
Direct labor		230,000	
Factory overhead (detail omitted)..................		250,000	
Total manufacturing costs			590,000
Total cost of goods in process during the year			$660,000
Less: Goods in process inventory, end of year			60,000
Cost of finished goods manufactured			$600,000

**PREPARING A STATEMENT OF COST OF FINISHED GOODS MANUFAC-
TURED** The following steps briefly describe the preparation of a statement of cost of finished goods manufactured:

1 The starting point of the statement is the cost of goods in process at the
beginning of the period. These items represent *partially* completed goods.

2 To complete the goods in process and to manufacture more goods a
company incurs *manufacturing costs,* consisting of *raw materials used, direct
labor,* and *factory overhead.*

3 The sum of the cost of goods in process at the beginning of the period
plus the total manufacturing costs represents the *total cost of goods in process
during the period.* However, not all the goods in process during the period
are finished and available for sale at year-end.

4 To determine the *cost of finished goods manufactured* during the period, it is
necessary to subtract the cost of goods still in process at the end of the
period from the total cost of goods in process during the period.

The accounting procedures for a manufacturing business are discussed thoroughly in courses on cost accounting.

DEMONSTRATION PROBLEM

The operating results (ignoring income taxes) achieved by Bond Company
for the years ended December 31, 1976 and 1977, are summarized as follows:

	1977	*1976*
Net sales	*$760,000*	*$710,000*
Cost of goods sold:		
Beginning inventory	*$253,040*	*$240,000*
Net purchases	*426,960*	*409,326*
Cost of goods available for sale	*$680,000*	*$649,326*
Ending inventory	*260,000*	*253,040*
Cost of goods sold	*$420,000*	*$396,286*
Gross profit on sales	*$340,000*	*$313,714*
Expenses	*180,000*	*143,714*
Net income	*$160,000*	*$170,000*

The balance sheets of the company showed retained earnings as follows:
December 31, 1975, $300,000; December 31, 1976, $370,000; and December
31, 1977, $410,000.

Other data
In December, 1977, Jim Klein, accountant for the Bond Company, decided
to make a careful review of the documents and procedures which had been
used in taking the physical inventory at December 31, 1976. Klein felt that
this review might disclose errors which still required correction or, at least,
should be given consideration to assure maximum accuracy in the taking of
the next annual physical inventory. Klein's investigation disclosed three questionable items which are described on page 393. No adjustment or correction
of any kind was made for these possible errors prior to preparing the 1977
income statement.

(1) Merchandise costing $9,840, which had been received on December 31, 1976, had been included in the inventory taken on that date, although the purchase was not recorded until January 4, when the vendor's invoice arrived. The invoice was then recorded in the purchases journal as a January transaction.

(2) Merchandise shipped to a customer on December 31, 1976, F.O.B. shipping point, was included in the physical inventory taken that day. The cost of the merchandise was $2,600 and the sales price was $3,600. Because of the press of year-end work, the sales invoice was not prepared until January 6, 1977. On that date the sale was recorded as a January transaction by entry in the sales journal, and the sales invoice was mailed to the customer.

(3) An error of $2,000 had been made in footing one of the inventory sheets at December 31, 1976. This clerical error had caused the inventory total to be overstated.

Instructions

a Prepare corrected income statements for the years ended December 31, 1976 and 1977. It may be helpful to set up T accounts for Sales, 1976 and Sales, 1977; Purchases, 1976 and Purchases, 1977; and Inventory, December 31, 1976. Corrections may then be entered in these accounts. Ignore income taxes.

b Compute corrected amounts for retained earnings at December 31, 1976 and 1977.

c Prepare any correcting journal entries that you consider should have been made at December 12, 1977, the date these items came to Klein's attention. Any items relating to the net income for 1976 may be entered in an account entitled Correction in Net Income for 1976.

d Assume that the $9,840 worth of merchandise described in item (1) had not been included in inventory on December 31, 1976. Would this handling of the transaction have caused an error in the cost of goods sold for 1976?

SOLUTION TO DEMONSTRATION PROBLEM

a

BOND COMPANY

Income Statement

For the Years Ended December 31, 1976 and 1977

	1977	1976
Net sales ($3,600 represents sales of 1976, not 1977)	$756,400	$713,600
Cost of goods sold:		
Beginning inventory	$248,440 (2)	$240,000
Net purchases	417,120 (3)	419,166 (1)
Cost of goods available for sale	$665,560	$659,166
Ending inventory	260,000	248,440 (2)
Cost of goods sold	$405,560	$410,726
Gross profit on sales	$350,840	$302,874
Expenses	180,000	143,714
Net income	$170,840	$159,160

(1) $409,326 + $9,840 = $419,166
(2) $253,040 − $2,600 − $2,000 = $248,440
(3) $426,960 − $9,840 = $417,120

b Retained earnings, Dec. 31, 1975 . . . . $300,000

  Add: Corrected net income for 1976 159,160

  Less: Dividends for 1976 (see note below) . . . . (100,000)

  Retained earnings as corrected, Dec. 31, 1976 . . . . $359,160

  Add: Corrected net income for 1977 170,840

  Less: Dividends for 1977 ($370,000 + $160,000 − $410,000) . . . . (120,000)

  Retained earnings as corrected, Dec. 31, 1977 . . . . $410,000

Note: The amount of dividends declared in 1976 is determined as follows: Retained earnings on December 31, 1975, $300,000 plus net income for 1976 as reported, $170,000, less retained earnings at the end of 1976, $370,000. The difference, $100,000, represents dividends declared. Similar calculations for 1977 indicate dividends declared of $120,000.

The errors counterbalanced between the years 1976 and 1977; therefore, the amount of retained earnings reported at Dec. 31, 1977, $410,000, was correct.

c

Correcting Journal Entry

1977

Dec. 12 Sales 3,600

    Correction in Net Income for 1976 10,840

        Purchases 9,840

        Inventory, Jan. 1, 1977 ($2,600 + $2,000) 4,600

    To correct errors in cutoff of sales and purchases at

    Dec. 31, 1976, and to correct clerical error in compiling

    physical inventory on that date.

d No. If the $9,840 worth of merchandise described in item (*1*) had not been included in inventory on December 31, 1976, the error of not including the goods in inventory would have offset the error of failing to record the purchase, with no net effect on cost of goods sold for 1976. However, the current ratio and other balance sheet relationships would have been slightly distorted through understatement of $9,840, both in inventory and in accounts payable.

REVIEW QUESTIONS

1 Through an error in counting of merchandise at December 31, 1976, the Trophy Company overstated the amount of goods on hand by $8,000. Assuming that the error was not discovered, what was the effect upon net income for 1976? Upon the owners' equity at December 31, 1976? Upon the net income for 1977? Upon the owners' equity at December 31, 1977?

2 Is the establishment of an appropriate valuation for the merchandise inventory at the end of the year more important in producing a dependable income statement, or in producing a dependable balance sheet?

3 Explain the meaning of the term **physical inventory.**

4 Near the end of December, Hadley Company received a large order from a major customer. The work of packing the goods for shipment was begun at once but could not be completed before the close of business on December 31. Since a written order from the customer was on hand and the goods were nearly all packed and ready for shipment, Hadley felt that this merchandise should not be included in the physical inventory taken on December 31. Do you agree? What is probably the reason behind Hadley's opinion?

5 During a prolonged period of rising prices, will the fifo or lifo method of inventory valuation result in higher reported profits?

6 Throughout several years of strongly rising prices, Company A used the lifo method of inventory valuation and Company B used the fifo method. In which company would the balance sheet figure for inventory be closer to current replacement cost of the merchandise on hand? Why?

7 Why do some accountants consider a portion of the income reported by businesses during a period of rising prices to be "fictitious profits"?

8 Explain the usefulness of the *gross profit method* of estimating inventories.

9 A store using the *retail inventory method* takes its physical inventory by applying current retail prices as marked on the merchandise to the quantities counted. Does this procedure indicate that the inventory will appear in the financial statements at retail selling price? Explain.

10 Estimate the ending inventory by the gross profit method, given the following data: beginning inventory $40,000, net purchases $100,000, net sales $106,667, average gross profit rate 25% of net sales.

11 One of the items in the inventory of Grayline Stores is marked for sale at $125. The purchase invoice shows the item cost $95, but a newly issued price list from the manufacturer shows the present replacement cost to be $90. What inventory valuation should be assigned this item if Grayline Stores follows the lower-of-cost-or-market rule?

12 You are making a detailed analysis of the financial statements and accounting records of two companies in the same industry, Adams Corporation and Bar Corporation. Price levels have been rising steadily for several years. In the course of your investigation, you observe that the inventory value shown on the Adams Corporation balance sheet is quite close to the current replacement cost of the merchandise on hand. However, for Bar Corporation, the carrying value of the inventory is far below current replacement cost. What method of inventory valuation is probably used by Adams Corporation? By Bar Corporation? If we assume that the two companies are identical except for the inventory valuation method used, which company has probably been reporting higher net income in recent years?

13 Explain the meaning of the term *market* as used in the expression "lower of cost or market."

14 Summarize the difference between the *periodic system* and the *perpetual system* of accounting for inventory. Which system would usually cost more to maintain? Which system would be most practicable for a restaurant, a retail drugstore, a new car dealer?

15 What are the three basic types of *manufacturing costs?*

16 Distinguish between *total manufacturing costs* and the *cost of finished goods manufactured.*

EXERCISES

Ex. 11-1 Typon Company has prepared the following condensed income statements for the last two years.

	Year 2	Year 1
Sales	$157,200	$144,000
Cost of goods sold	91,200	115,200
Gross profit on sales	$ 66,000	$ 28,800
Operating expenses	24,000	24,000
Net income	$ 42,000	$ 4,800

The inventory at the end of Year 1 was understated by $14,400, but the error was not discovered until after the accounts had been closed and financial statements prepared at the end of Year 2. The balance sheets for the two years showed owners' equity of $61,200 at the end of Year 1 and $84,400 at the end of Year 2.

Compute the correct net income figure for Year 1 and Year 2 and the gross profit percentage for each year based on corrected data. What correction, if any, should be made in owners' equity at the end of Year 1 and at the end of Year 2?

Ex. 11-2 The beginning inventory balance of item Y on July 1 and the purchases of this item during July were as follows:

July 1 Beginning inventory	360 units @ $1.00	$ 360
July 7 Purchase	1,440 units @ $1.10	1,584
July 14 Purchase	720 units @ $1.15	828
July 22 Purchase	720 units @ $1.20	864
July 28 Purchase	360 units @ $1.25	450
Totals	3,600	$4,086

At July 31 the ending inventory consisted of 600 units. Determine the cost of the ending inventory, based on each of the following methods of inventory valuation:
a Weighted-average cost
b First-in, first-out
c Last-in, first-out

Ex. 11-3 Milo Company has compiled the following information concerning items in its inventory at December 31:

		Unit Price	
Item	Quantity	Cost (fifo)	Market
A	120	$ 96	$ 98
B	72	180	168
C	96	48	57
D	84	240	241

Determine the total inventory value to appear on Milo Company's balance sheet under the lower-of-cost-or-market rule, assuming (*a*) that the rule is applied to inventory as a whole and (*b*) that the rule is applied on an item-by-item basis.

Ex. 11-4 When John Ryan arrived at his store on the morning of May 29, he found empty shelves and display racks; thieves had broken in during the night and stolen the entire inventory. Ryan's accounting records showed that he had $36,000 inventory on May 1 (at cost). From May 1 to May 29, he had made net sales of $144,000 and net purchases of $113,400. The gross profit during the past several years had consistently averaged 30% of net sales. Ryan wishes to file an insurance claim for the theft loss. What is the estimated cost of his inventory at the time of the theft? Show computations.

Ex. 11-5 Forrest Dress Shop wishes to determine the approximate month-end inventory using data from the accounting records without taking a physical count of merchandise on hand. From the following information, estimate the cost of the September 30 inventory by the retail method of inventory valuation.

	Cost Price	Selling Price
Inventory of merchandise, Aug. 31	$198,600	$300,000
Purchases (net) during September	127,800	180,000
Sales (net) during September		206,400

Ex. 11-6 The records of the Draco Mfg. Co. include the following information:

	July 1	July 31
Raw materials inventory	$18,000	$21,000
Goods in process inventory	8,000	9,500
Finished goods inventory, July 1 (2,000 units)	34,000	-0-
Purchases of raw materials in July		56,000
Direct labor cost for July		80,000
Factory overhead costs for July		48,500

During July 10,000 units were produced and 9,000 units were sold.

Instructions
a Prepare a statement of cost of finished goods manufactured for July.
b Compute the cost of producing a single unit during July.
c Compute the cost of goods sold during July, assuming that the first-in, first-out method of inventory costing is used.

PROBLEMS

11-1 Circle Company, a family-owned corporation, is being offered for sale, and the owners are emphasizing the rising trend of the gross profit percentage as a very favorable factor. The income statements prepared by the company for a three-year period included the following information:

	Year 3	Year 2	Year 1
Net sales	$240,000	$150,000	$120,000
Cost of goods sold	160,800	102,000	84,000
Gross profit on sales	$ 79,200	$ 48,000	$ 36,000
Gross profit percentage	33%	32%	30%

Assume that you are retained by a prospective purchaser of the business to make an investigation of the fairness and reliability of the Circle Company's accounting records and financial statements. You find everything in order except for the following: (1) The inventory was understated by $3,000 at the end of Year 1, and (2) it was overstated by $9,600 at the end of Year 3. The company uses the periodic inventory system, and these errors had not been brought to light prior to your investigation.

Instructions

a Prepare a revised three-year schedule along the lines of the one illustrated above.

b Comment on the trend of gross profit percentages before and after the revision.

11-2 Merriam Corporation is a wholesaling company which deals in a single product of relatively low cost. The volume of sales in 1977 was $700,000, at a unit price of $7. The inventory at January 1, 1977, amounted to 17,400 units valued at cost of $52,200; purchases for the year were as follows: 24,600 units @ $3.10; 39,600 units @ $3.25; 27,600 units @ $3.40, and 10,800 units @ $3.50.

Instructions

a Compute the December 31, 1977, inventory using

  (1) The weighted-average method (Compute average unit cost to the nearest cent.)

  (2) The first-in, first-out method

  (3) The last-in, first-out method

b Prepare income statement data for each of the above three methods of pricing inventory. The income statements are to be carried only to the determination of gross profit on sales.

c Which of the three methods of pricing inventory would be most advantageous from an income tax standpoint during a period of rising prices? Comment on the relationship of the inventory value under the method you recommend as compared with the current replacement cost of the inventory.

11-3 Bacon Company reported the following operating results for the years 1976 and 1977:

	1977	*1976*
Net sales	*$420,000*	*$396,000*
Cost of goods sold:		
Beginning inventory	*$151,824*	*$144,000*
Net purchases	*256,176*	*245,596*
Cost of goods available for sale	*$408,000*	*$389,596*
Ending inventory	*156,000*	*151,824*
Cost of goods sold	*$252,000*	*$237,772*
Gross profit on sales	*$168,000*	*$158,228*
Expenses	*60,000*	*54,000*
Net income	*$108,000*	*$104,228*

The owners' equity as shown in the company's balance sheets was as follows: December 31, 1975, $120,000; December 31, 1976, $224,228; and December 31, 1977, $332,228.

Early in 1978, Tom Wake, accountant for the Bacon Company, made a review of the documents and procedures used in taking the physical inventory at December 31, 1976 and 1977. His investigation disclosed the two questionable items listed below:

(1) Merchandise shipped to a customer on December 31, 1976, F.O.B. shipping point, was included in the physical inventory taken that date. The cost of the merchandise was $1,740 and the sales price was $2,160. Because of the press of year-end work, the sales invoice was not prepared

until January 6, 1977. On that date the sale was recorded as a January transaction by entry in the sales journal, and the sales invoice was mailed to the customer.

(2) Merchandise costing $4,104, which had been received on December 31, 1976, had been included in the inventory taken on that date, although the purchase was not recorded until January 8 when the vendor's invoice arrived. The invoice was then recorded in the purchases journal.

Instructions

a Prepare corrected income statements for the years ended December 31, 1976 and 1977. (You may find it helpful to set up T accounts for Sales, 1976 and Sales, 1977; Purchases, 1976 and Purchases, 1977; and Inventory, December 31, 1976.)

b Compute corrected amounts for owners' equity at December 31, 1976 and 1977.

11-4 The entire inventory of Mitty Company was destroyed by fire on May 15, 1977, and an estimate of the inventory value must be prepared in order to file an insurance claim. The following income statement for the year 1976 is available to aid you in estimating the amount of inventory at the date of the fire.

MITTY COMPANY

Income Statement

For the Year Ended December 31, 1976

Net sales		$492,000
Cost of goods sold:		
Inventory, Jan. 1	$ 96,000	
Purchases	444,000	
Cost of goods available for sale	$540,000	
Less: Inventory, Dec. 31	156,000	384,000
Gross profit on sales		$108,000
Expenses		48,000
Net income		$ 60,000

Other data Included in the purchases figure shown in the income statement was $15,000 of office equipment which the Mitty Company had acquired late in December for its own use from a competing concern which was quitting business. The accountant of the Mitty Company had not understood the nature of this transaction and had recorded it by debiting the Purchases account. The office equipment, however, was not included in the inventory at December 31, 1976.

Records salvaged from the fire revealed the merchandise transactions from December 31, 1976, to the date of the fire to be: sales, $204,000; sales returns and allowances, $1,800; transportation-in, $1,200; purchases, $130,800; purchase returns and allowances, $2,400.

Instructions

a Prepare a report directed to the insurance adjuster summarizing your findings. Include an estimate of the inventory cost as of the date of the fire and a computation of the applicable gross profit rate, after making any required corrections to the 1976 income statement.

b Explain how the gross profit method of estimating inventories may be used other than in case of a fire loss.

c Is the rate of gross profit customarily computed as a percentage of the cost of merchandise or as a percentage of sales? Show how the gross profit rate in this problem would vary if based on cost of goods sold rather than on sales.

11-5 Acme Incorporated, a retail store, carries a wide range of merchandise consisting mostly of articles of low unit price. The selling price of each item is plainly marked on the merchandise. At each year-end, the company has taken a physical count of goods on hand and has priced these goods at cost by looking up individual purchase invoices to determine the unit cost of each item in stock. The store manager is anxious to find a more economical method of assigning dollar values to the year-end inventory. He explains that it takes much more time to price the inventory than to count the merchandise on hand.

By analyzing the accounting records you are able to determine that the net sales of the current year, 1977, amounted to $780,000. During the year, net purchases of merchandise totaled $600,000; the retail selling price of this merchandise was $840,000. At the end of 1977, a physical inventory showed goods on hand priced to sell at $180,000. This represented a considerable increase over the inventory of a year earlier. At December 31, 1976, the inventory on hand had appeared in the balance sheet at cost of $72,000, although it had a retail value of $120,000.

Instructions

a Outline a plan whereby the inventory can be computed without the necessity of looking up individual purchase invoices. List step by step the procedures to be followed. Ignore the possibility of markups and markdowns in the original retail price of merchandise.

b Compute the cost of the inventory at December 31, 1977, using the method described in **a.**

c Explain how the adoption of the inventory method you have described would facilitate the preparation of monthly financial statements.

11-6 The following information was taken from the books of Texatron Manufacturing Company for the month of August, 19___.

	Aug. 31	Aug. 1
Inventories:		
Raw materials	$ 47,200	$ 60,600
Goods in process	38,000	43,400
Finished goods	654,200	543,400

	Month of August
Purchases of raw materials	$458,400
Transportation-in on raw materials	55,600
Factory overhead	163,200
Direct labor	217,600
Selling expenses	77,200
Raw material purchase discounts	4,600
Raw material purchase returns	4,800
General expenses	153,600
Income taxes	40,000

Instructions

a Prepare a statement of cost of finished goods manufactured for the month of August.

b Prepare a schedule showing the cost of goods sold for the month of August.

BUSINESS DECISION PROBLEM 11

You are the sales manager of Continental Motors, an automobile dealership specializing in European imports. Among the automobiles on Continental Motors' showroom are two Italian sports cars, which are identical in every respect except for color; one is red and the other white. The red car had been ordered last February, at a cost of $4,200 American dollars. The white car had been ordered early last March, but because of a revaluation of the Italian lira relative to the dollar, the white car had cost only $3,900 American dollars. Both cars arrived in the United States on the same boat and had just been delivered to your showroom. Since the cars were identical except for color and both colors were equally popular, you had listed both cars at the same suggested retail price, $6,000.

Smiley Jones, one of your best salesmen, comes into your office with a proposal. He has a customer in the showroom who wants to buy the red car for $6,000. However, when Smiley pulled the inventory card on the red car to see what options were included, he happened to notice the inventory card of the white car. Continental Motors, like most automobile dealerships, uses the specific identification method to value inventory. Consequently, Smiley noticed that the red car had cost $4,200, while the white one had cost Continental Motors only $3,900. This gave Smiley the idea for the following proposal.

"If I sell the red car for $6,000, Continental Motors makes a gross profit of $1,800. But if you'll let me discount that white car $100, I think I can get my customer to buy that one instead. If I sell the white car for $5,900, the gross profit will be $2,000; so Continental Motors is $200 better off than if I sell the red car for $6,000. Since I came up with this plan, I feel I should get part of the benefit; Continental Motors should split that extra $200 with me. That way, I'll get an extra $100 commission, and the company still makes $100 more than if I sell the red car."

Instructions
a Prepare a schedule which shows the total revenue, cost of goods sold, and gross profit to Continental Motors if **both** cars are sold for $6,000 each.
b Prepare a schedule showing the revenue, cost of goods sold, and gross profit to Continental Motors if both cars are sold but Smiley's plan is adopted and the white car is sold for $5,900. Assume the red car is still sold for $6,000. To simplify comparison of this schedule to the one prepared in part *a,* include the extra $100 commission to Smiley in the cost of goods sold of the part *b* schedule.
c Write out your decision whether or not to accept Smiley's proposal, and explain to Smiley why the proposal either would or would not be to the advantage of Continental Motors: (*Hint:* Refer in your explanation to the schedules prepared in parts *a* and *b*.)

TWELVE

PLANT AND EQUIPMENT DEPRECIATION NATURAL RESOURCES AND INTANGIBLES

PLANT AND EQUIPMENT

The term *plant and equipment* is used to describe long-lived assets acquired for use in the operation of the business and not intended for resale to customers. Among the more common examples are land, buildings, machinery, furniture and fixtures, office equipment, and automobiles. A delivery truck in the showroom of an automobile dealer is inventory; when this same truck is sold to a drugstore for use in making deliveries to customers, it becomes a unit of plant and equipment.

The term *fixed assets* has long been used in accounting literature to describe all types of plant and equipment. This term, however, has virtually disappeared from the published financial statements of large corporations. *Plant and equipment* appears to be a more descriptive term. Another alternative title used on many corporation balance sheets is *property, plant, and equipment.*

Plant and equipment represent bundles of services to be received

It is convenient to think of a plant asset as a bundle of services to be received by the owner over a period of years. Ownership of a delivery truck, for example, may provide about 100,000 miles of transportation. The cost of the delivery truck is customarily entered in a plant and equipment account entitled Delivery Truck, which in essence represents payment in advance for several years of transportation service. Similarly, a building may be regarded as payment in advance for several years' supply of housing services. As the years go by, these services are utilized by the business and the cost of the plant asset is gradually transferred into depreciation expense.

An awareness of the similarity between plant assets and prepaid expenses is essential to an understanding of the accounting process by which the cost of plant assets is allocated to the years in which the benefits of ownership are received.

Major categories of plant and equipment

Plant and equipment items are often classified into one of the following groups:

1 Tangible plant assets. The term *tangible* denotes physical substance, as exemplified by land, a building, or a machine. This category may be subdivided into two distinct classifications:
   a Plant property subject to depreciation; included are plant assets of limited useful life such as buildings and office equipment.
   b Land. The only plant asset not subject to depreciation is land, which has an unlimited term of existence.
2 Intangible assets. Examples are patents, copyrights, trademarks, franchises, organization costs, leaseholds, and goodwill. Current assets such as accounts receivable or prepaid rent are not included in the intangible classification, even though they are lacking in physical substance. The term *intangible assets* is used to describe noncurrent assets which are lacking in physical substance.

Natural resources

Natural resources are subject to depletion rather than to depreciation. Examples are mines, oil and gas wells, and tracts of timber. The term *depletion* means the exhaustion of a natural resource through mining, pumping, cutting, or otherwise using up the deposit or growth.

Accounting problems relating to plant and equipment

Some major accounting problems relating to plant and equipment are indicated by the following questions:

1 How is the cost of plant and equipment determined?
2 How should the costs of plant and equipment be allocated against revenue?
3 How should expenditures for repairs and maintenance be treated?
4 How should disposals of plant assets be recorded?

We are presently concerned with answering the first of these questions; an understanding of how the cost of plant and equipment is determined will be helpful in subsequent study of depreciation.

DETERMINING THE COST OF PLANT AND EQUIPMENT The cost of plant and equipment includes all expenditures reasonable and necessary in acquiring the asset and placing it in a position and condition for use in the operations of the business. Only *reasonable* and *necessary* expenditures should be included. For example, if the company's truck driver receives a traffic ticket while hauling a new machine to the plant, the traffic fine is *not* part of the cost of the new machine. If the machine is dropped and damaged while being unloaded, the expense of repairing the damage should *not* be added to the cost of the machine.

Cost is most easily determined when an asset is purchased for cash. The cost of the asset is then equal to the cash outlay necessary in acquiring the asset plus any expenditures for freight, insurance while in transit, installation, trial runs, and any other costs necessary to make the asset ready for use. If plant assets are purchased on the installment plan or by issuance of notes payable, the interest element or carrying charge should be recorded as interest expense and not as part of the cost of the plant assets.

This principle of including in the cost of a plant asset all the incidental charges necessary to put the asset in use is illustrated by the following example. A factory in Minneapolis orders a machine from a San Francisco tool manufacturer at a list price of $10,000, with terms of 2/10, n/30. A sales tax of 6% must be paid, also freight charges of $1,250. Transportation from the railroad station to the factory costs $150, and installation labor amounts to $400. The cost of the machine to be entered in the Machinery account is computed as follows:

Items	*List price of machine*	*$10,000*
included in	*Less: Cash discount (2% × $10,000)*	*200*
cost of		
machine	*Net cash price*	*$ 9,800*
	Sales tax (6% × $9,800)	*588*
	Freight	*1,250*
	Transportation from railroad station to factory	*150*
	Installation labor	*400*
	Cost of machine	*$12,188*

Why should all the incidental charges relating to the acquisition of a machine be included in its cost? Why not treat these incidental charges as expenses of the period in which the machine is acquired?

The answer is to be found in the basic accounting principle of *matching costs and revenue.* The benefits of owning the machine will be received over a span of years, 10 years, for example. During those 10 years the operation of the machine will contribute to revenue. Consequently, the total costs of the machine should be recorded in the accounts as an asset and allocated against the revenue of the 10 years. All costs incurred in acquiring the machine are costs of the services to be received from using the machine.

Land When land is purchased, various incidental costs are generally incurred, in addition to the purchase price. These additional costs may include commissions to real estate brokers, escrow fees, legal fees for examining and insuring the title, delinquent taxes paid by the purchaser, and fees for surveying, draining, clearing, grading, and landscaping the property. All these expenditures are part of the cost of the land. Special assessments for local improvements, such as the paving of a street or the installation of sewers, may also be charged to the Land account, for the reason that a more or less permanent value is being added to the land.

Separate ledger accounts are necessary for land and buildings, because buildings are subject to depreciation and land is not. The treatment of land as a nondepreciable asset is based on the premise that land used as a building site has an unlimited life. When land and building are purchased for a lump sum, the purchase price must be apportioned between the land and the building. An appraisal may be necessary for this purpose. Assume, for example, that land and a building are purchased for a bargain price of $100,000. The apportionment of this cost on the basis of an appraisal may be made as follows:

		Value per Appraisal	Percentage of Total	Apportionment of Cost
Apportion-	Land	$ 48,000	40%	$ 40,000
ing cost	Building	72,000	60%	60,000
between				
land and	Total	$120,000	100%	$100,000
building				

Sometimes a tract of land purchased as a building site has on it an old building which is not suitable for the buyer's use. The Land account should be charged with the entire purchase price plus any costs incurred in tearing down or removing the building. Proceeds received from sale of the materials salvaged from the old building are recorded as a credit in the Land account.

Land acquired as a future building site should be reported under Investments or Other Assets, rather than as part of Plant and Equipment, since it is not currently used in operations.

Land improvements Improvements to real estate such as driveways, fences, parking lots, and sprinkler systems have a limited life and are therefore subject to depreciation. For this reason they should be recorded not in the Land account but in a separate account entitled Land Improvements. On the other hand, any improvements such as grading or leveling, which will last indefinitely and are not to be depreciated are entered in the Land account.

Buildings Old buildings are sometimes purchased with the intention of repairing them prior to placing them in use. Repairs made under these circumstances are charged to the Buildings account. After the building has been placed in use, **ordinary repairs** are considered as maintenance expense when incurred.

When a building is constructed by the business itself, rather than being purchased, cost includes the materials and labor used plus an equitable portion of overhead or other indirect costs, such as executive salaries. Any other outlays specifically relating to the construction such as architectural fees, insurance during the construction period, and building permits should also be included in the cost of the building. A building or machine constructed by a company for its own use should be recorded in the accounts at cost, not at the price which might have been paid to outsiders if the asset had been acquired through purchase.

Leasehold improvements When buildings or other improvements are constructed on leased property by the lessee, the costs should be recorded in a Leasehold Improvements account, and written off as expense during the remaining life of the lease or of the estimated useful life of the building, whichever is shorter. This procedure is usually followed even though the lessee has an option to renew the lease, because there is no assurance in advance that conditions will warrant the exercise of the renewal clause.

DEPRECIATION

Allocating the cost of plant and equipment

Plant assets, with the exception of land, are of use to a company for only a limited number of years, and the cost of each plant asset is allocated as an expense of the years in which it is used. Accountants use the term **depreciation** to describe this gradual conversion of the cost of a plant asset into expense.

Depreciation, as the term is used in accounting, does not mean the physical deterioration of an asset. Neither does depreciation mean the decrease in market value of a plant asset over a period of time. **Depreciation means the allocation of the cost of a plant asset to the periods in which services are received from the asset.**

When a delivery truck is purchased, its cost is first recorded as an asset. This cost becomes expense over a period of years through the accounting process of depreciation. When gasoline is purchased for the truck, the price paid for each tankful is immediately recorded as expense. In theory, both outlays (for the truck and for a tank of gas) represent the acquisition of assets, but since it is reasonable to assume that a tankful of gasoline will be consumed in the accounting period in which it is purchased, we record the outlay for gasoline as an expense immediately. It is important to recognize, however, that both the outlay for the truck and the payment for the gasoline become expense in the period or periods in which each renders services.

A separate Depreciation Expense account and a separate Accumulated Depreciation account are generally maintained for each group of depreciable assets such as factory buildings, delivery equipment, and office equipment so that a proper allocation of depreciation expense can be made between functional areas of activity such as sales and manufacturing. Depreciation on manufacturing facilities is not necessarily an expense of the period in which it is recorded; the depreciation charge is first embodied in the inventory of finished goods manufactured, and the cost of this inventory is later deducted from revenue as an expense of the period when the goods are sold.

Because of the non-cash nature of depreciation expense and because the dollar amount is materially affected by the depreciation method selected, it is generally desirable that the total amount of depreciation be disclosed in the income statement.

Depreciation not a process of valuation

Accounting records and financial statements do not purport to show the constantly fluctuating market values of plant and equipment. Occasionally the market value of a building may rise substantially over a period of years because of a change in the price level, or for other reasons. Depreciation is continued, however, regardless of the increase in market value. The accountant recognizes that the building will render useful services for only a limited number of years, and that its full cost must be allocated as expense of those years regardless of fluctuations in market value.

The *book value* or *carrying value* of a plant asset is its cost minus the related accumulated depreciation. Plant assets are shown in the balance sheet at their book values, representing the portion of their cost which will be allocated to expense in future periods. Accumulated depreciation represents the portion of the assets' cost which has already been recognized as expense.

Causes of depreciation

There are two major causes of depreciation, physical deterioration and obsolescence.

PHYSICAL DETERIORATION Physical deterioration of a plant asset results from use, and also from exposure to sun, wind, and other climatic factors. When a plant asset has been carefully maintained, it is not uncommon for the owner to claim that the asset is as "good as new." Such statements are not literally true. Although a good repair policy may greatly lengthen the useful life of a machine, every machine eventually reaches the point at which it must be discarded. In brief, the making of repairs does not lessen the need for recognition of depreciation.

OBSOLESCENCE The term *obsolescence* means the process of becoming out of date or obsolete. An airplane, for example, may become obsolete even though it is in excellent physical condition; it becomes obsolete because better planes of superior design and performance have become available. Obsolescence relates to the capacity of a plant asset to render services to a particular company for a particular purpose.

The usefulness of plant assets may also be reduced because the rapid growth of a company renders such assets inadequate. Inadequacy of a plant asset may necessitate replacement with a larger unit even though the asset is in good physical condition and is not obsolete. Obsolescence and inadequacy are often closely associated; both relate to the opportunity for economical and efficient use of an asset rather than to its physical condition. Obsolescence is probably a more significant factor than physical deterioration in putting an end to the usefulness of most depreciable assets. Current accounting practice, however, does not usually attempt to separate the effects of physical deterioration and obsolescence.

Methods of computing depreciation

A business need not use the same method of depreciation for all its various assets. Management also has the option of using different methods of depreciation in the accounting records and financial statements than are employed in the determination of taxable income. The most widely used methods (straight-line, units-of-output, fixed-percentage-on-declining-balance, and sum-of-the-years'-digits) are explained and illustrated in the following sections.

STRAIGHT–LINE METHOD The simplest and most widely used method of computing depreciation is the straight-line method. This method was described in Chapter 3 and has been used repeatedly in problems throughout this book. Under the straight-line method, an equal portion of the cost of the asset is allocated to each period of use; consequently, this method is most appropriate when usage of an asset is fairly uniform from year to year.

In theory, the computation of the periodic charge for depreciation is made by deducting the estimated *residual* or *salvage value* from the cost of the asset and dividing the remaining *depreciable cost* by the years of estimated useful life, as shown in the following example:

Computing depreciation by straight-line method

Cost of the depreciable asset	$5,200
Less: Estimated residual value (amount to be realized by sale of asset when it is retired from use)	400
Total amount to be depreciated (depreciable cost)	$4,800
Estimated useful life	4 years
Depreciation expense each year ($4,800 ÷ 4)	$1,200

The following schedule summarizes the accumulation of depreciation over the useful life of the asset. The amount to be depreciated is $4,800 (cost of $5,200 minus estimated residual value of $400).

Depreciation Schedule: Straight-Line Method

Year	Computation	Depreciation Expense	Accumulated Depreciation	Book Value
				$5,200
First	($\frac{1}{4}$ × $4,800)	$1,200	$1,200	4,000
Second	($\frac{1}{4}$ × $4,800)	1,200	2,400	2,800
Third	($\frac{1}{4}$ × $4,800)	1,200	3,600	1,600
Fourth	($\frac{1}{4}$ × $4,800)	1,200	4,800	400
		$4,800		

Constant annual depreciation expense

In practice, the possibility of residual value is often ignored and the annual depreciation charge computed by dividing the total cost of the asset by the number of years of estimated useful life. This practice is justified in many cases in which residual value is not material and is difficult to estimate accurately. Under this approach the yearly depreciation expense in the above example would be $5,200 ÷ 4, or $1,300.

UNITS–OF–OUTPUT METHOD A more equitable allocation of the cost of some plant assets can be obtained by dividing the cost (minus salvage value, if significant) by the estimated units of output rather than by the estimated years of useful life. A truck line or bus company, for example, might compute depreciation on its vehicles by a mileage basis. If a truck with a depreciable cost of $10,000 has a useful life of 200,000 miles, the depreciation rate per mile of operation is 5 cents ($10,000 ÷ 200,000). At the end of each year, the amount of depreciation to be recorded would be determined by multiplying the 5-cent rate by the number of miles the truck had operated during the year. This method is suitable only when the total units of output of the asset over its entire useful life can be estimated with reasonable accuracy.

ACCELERATED DEPRECIATION METHODS The term *accelerated depreciation* means recognition of relatively large amounts of depreciation in the early years of use and reduced amounts in the later years. Many types of plant and equipment are most efficient when new and therefore provide more and better services in the early years of useful life. If we assume that the benefits derived from owning an asset are greatest in the early years when the asset is relatively new, then the amount of the asset's cost which we allocate as depreciation expense should be greatest in these same years. This is consistent with the basic accounting concept of matching costs with related revenue.

One reason for adoption of accelerated methods of depreciation is that the increasingly rapid pace of invention of new products is making obsolescence a factor of greater significance than physical deterioration. When an industry is in a period of rapid technological change, plant and equipment may have to be replaced within shorter periods than would be necessary in a less dynamic economy. Businesses may, therefore, reason that the acquisition of a new plant facility is justified only if most of the cost can be recovered within a comparatively short period of years. Also significant is the pleasing prospect of reducing the current year's income tax burden by recognizing a relatively large amount of depreciation expense.

Another argument for allocating a comparatively large share of the cost of a depreciable asset to the early years of use is that repair expenses tend to increase as assets grow older. The combined expense of depreciation and repairs may be more uniform from year to year under an accelerated method of depreciation than when straight-line depreciation is followed. Whether a uniform total amount of depreciation expense plus repairs expense from year to year is realistic accounting, however, depends upon whether the benefits received from owning the asset are relatively constant from year to year.

Fixed-percentage-on-declining-balance method For income tax purposes one of the acceptable methods of "rapid write-off" of certain depreciable assets consists of doubling the normal rate of depreciation and applying this doubled rate each year to the undepreciated cost (book value) of the asset.

Assume, for example, that an automobile is acquired for business use at a cost of $4,000. Estimated useful life is four years; therefore, the depreciation rate under the straight-line method would be 25%. To depreciate the automobile by the fixed-percentage-on-declining-balance method, we double the straight-line rate of 25% and apply the doubled rate of 50% to the book value. Depreciation expense in the first year would then amount to $2,000. In the second year the depreciation expense would drop to $1,000, computed at 50% of the remaining book value of $2,000. In the third year depreciation would be $500, and in the fourth year only $250. The following table shows the allocation of cost under this method of depreciation:

Depreciation Schedule: Fixed-Percentage-on-Declining-Balance Method

	Year	Computation	Depreciation Expense	Accumulated Depreciation	Book Value
					$4,000
Accelerated depreciation: fixed-percentage-on-declining-balance	First	(50% × $4,000)	$2,000	$2,000	2,000
	Second	(50% × $2,000)	1,000	3,000	1,000
	Third	(50% × $1,000)	500	3,500	500
	Fourth	(50% × $500)	250	3,750	250

If the automobile is continued in use beyond the estimated life of four years, depreciation will be continued at the 50% rate on the book value. In the fifth year, for example, the depreciation expense will be $125 (50% × $250), and in the sixth year $62.50 (50% × $125). When the fixed-percentage-on-declining-balance-method is used, the cost of a depreciable asset will never be entirely written off as long as the asset continues in use. Perhaps because of the existence of this undepreciated balance of original cost, the tax regulations do not require any deduction from original cost for residual value when this method of depreciation is used.

Sum-of-the-years'-digits method This is another method of allocating a large portion of the cost of an asset to the early years of its use. The depreciation rate to be used is a fraction, of which the numerator is the remaining years of useful life (as of the beginning of the year) and the denominator is the sum of the years of useful life. Consider again the example of an automobile costing $4,000 and having an estimated life of four years, but in this instance assume an estimated residual value of $400. (Present income tax regulations require that residual value be taken into account when either the straight-line method or the sum-of-the-years'-digits method of depreciation is used.) Since the automobile has an estimated life of four years, the denominator of the fraction will be 10, computed as follows (1 + 2 + 3 + 4 = 10). For the first year, the depreciation will be $\frac{4}{10}$ × $3,600, or $1,440. For the second year, the depreciation will be $\frac{3}{10}$ × $3,600, or $1,080; in the third year $\frac{2}{10}$ × $3,600, or $720; and in the fourth year, $\frac{1}{10}$ × $3,600, or $360. In tabular form this depreciation program will appear as follows:

Depreciation Schedule: Sum-of-the-years'-digits Method

	Year	Computation	Depreciation Expense	Accumulated Depreciation	Book Value
					$4,000
Accelerated depreciation: sum-of-the-years'-digits	First	($\frac{4}{10}$ × $3,600)	$1,440	$1,440	2,560
	Second	($\frac{3}{10}$ × $3,600)	1,080	2,520	1,480
	Third	($\frac{2}{10}$ × $3,600)	720	3,240	760
	Fourth	($\frac{1}{10}$ × $3,600)	360	3,600	400

DEPRECIATION FOR FRACTIONAL PERIODS In the case of depreciable assets acquired sometime during the year, it is customary to figure depreciation to the nearest month. For example, if an asset is acquired on July 12, depreciation would be computed from July 1; if the asset had been acquired on July 18 (or any other date in the latter half of July), depreciation would be recorded for only five months (August through December) for the current calendar year.

Some businesses prefer to begin depreciation on the first of the month following the acquisition of a depreciable asset. This method, or any one of many similar variations, is acceptable so long as it is followed consistently.

Revision of depreciation rates

Depreciation rates are based on estimates of the useful life of assets. These estimates of useful life are seldom precisely correct and sometimes are grossly in error. Consequently, the annual depreciation expense based on the estimated useful life may be either excessive or inadequate. What action should be taken when, after a few years of using a plant asset, it is decided that the asset is actually going to last for a considerably longer or shorter period than was originally estimated? When either of these situations arises, a revised estimate of useful life should be made and the periodic depreciation expense decreased or increased accordingly.

The procedure for correcting the depreciation program may be stated in a very few words: *Spread the remaining undepreciated cost of the asset over the years of remaining useful life.* The annual depreciation expense is increased or decreased sufficiently so that the depreciation program will be completed in accordance with the revised estimate of remaining useful life. The following data illustrate a revision which increases the estimate of useful life and thereby decreases the annual depreciation expense.

Data prior to revision of depreciation rate Cost of asset	$10,000
Estimated useful life (no residual value)	10 years
Annual depreciation expense (prior to revision)	$ 1,000
Accumulated depreciation at end of six years ($1,000 × 6)	$ 6,000

At the beginning of the seventh year, it is decided that the asset will last for eight more years. The revised estimate of useful life is, therefore, a total of 14 years. The depreciation expense to be recognized for the seventh year and for each of the remaining years is $500, computed as follows:

Revision of depreciation program Undepreciated cost at end of sixth year ($10,000 − $6,000)	$4,000
Revised estimate of remaining years of useful life	8 years
Revised amount of annual depreciation expense ($4,000 ÷ 8)	$ 500

The method described above for the revision of a depreciation program is generally used and is acceptable in the determination of taxable income. The Accounting Principles Board of the AICPA also supports this approach for financial reporting purposes.[1]

Depreciation and income taxes

Different methods of depreciation may be used for the purpose of preparing financial statements and the purpose of preparing income tax returns.[2] The vast majority of businesses use straight-line depreciation in their financial statements, possibly motivated in part by a desire to report higher earnings per share of stock. For income tax purposes, however, most businesses use an accelerated depreciation method.[3]

Accelerated methods of depreciation became quite popular some years ago when the federal government approved their use for income tax purposes. By offering businessmen the opportunity of writing off as depreciation expense a large portion of the cost of a new asset during its early years of use, the government has provided a powerful incentive for investment in new productive facilities. Since an increased charge for depreciation expense will reduce taxable income, the businessman may feel that by purchasing new assets and writing off a large part of the cost in the early years of use, he is in effect paying for the new assets with dollars that otherwise would have been used to pay income taxes.

In theory, the ideal depreciation policy is one that allocates the cost of a depreciable asset to the several periods of its use in proportion to the services received each period. Accelerated methods of depreciation sometimes fail to allocate the cost of an asset in proportion to the flow of services from the property and therefore prevent the determination of annual net income on a realistic basis. If annual net income figures are misleading, stockholders, creditors, management, and others who use financial statements as a basis for business decisions may be seriously injured. For income tax purposes, however, accelerated methods of depreciation may be effective in encouraging businessmen to invest in new productive facilities and thereby to raise the level of business activity.

Depreciation and inflation

The valuation of plant and equipment on a cost basis and the computation of depreciation in terms of cost work very well during periods

[1] *APB Opinion No. 20,* "Accounting Changes," AICPA (New York: 1971), par. 31–33. The Board considers changes in estimated useful life of assets as "prospective" rather than retroactive. Such changes, therefore, do not require a correction in retained earnings for past errors in recording depreciation.

[2] When different depreciation methods are used for financial reporting purposes and tax purposes, interperiod tax allocation procedures are necessary. These procedures are described in Chap. 17.

[3] AICPA, *Accounting Trends & Techniques,* 27th ed. (New York: 1973), p. 231.

of stable price levels. However, the substantial rise in the price level in recent years has led many businessmen to suggest that a more realistic measurement of net income could be achieved by basing depreciation on the estimated replacement cost of plant assets rather than on the original cost of the assets presently in use. An alternative proposal is to adjust each year's depreciation expense by a price index measuring changes in the purchasing power of the dollar. This price-level adjustment would cause depreciation expense to be stated in *current dollars,* as are such expenses as wages and taxes.

As a specific illustration, assume that a manufacturing company purchased machinery in 1962 at a cost of $100,000. Estimated useful life was 15 years and straight-line depreciation was used. Throughout this 15-year period the price level rose sharply. By 1977 the machinery purchased in 1962 was fully depreciated; it was scrapped and replaced by new machinery in 1977. Although the new machines were not significantly different from the old, they cost $300,000, or three times as much as the depreciation expense which had been recorded during the life of the old machinery. Many businessmen would argue that the depreciation expense for the 15 years was in reality $300,000, because this was the outlay required for new machinery if the company was merely to "stay even" in its productive facilities. It is also argued that reported profits will be overstated during a period of rising prices if depreciation is based on the lower plant costs of some years ago. An overstatement of profits causes higher income taxes and perhaps larger demands for wage increases than are justified by the company's financial position and earnings.

As yet there has been no general acceptance of the suggestion for basing depreciation on replacement cost. Replacement cost is difficult to determine on any objective basis. Who can say how much it will cost to buy a new machine 15 years from now? The proposal to use a general price index to adjust each year's depreciation expense appears more promising; it is discussed and illustrated in Chapter 14.

Depreciation and the problem of asset replacement

Many readers of financial statements who have not studied accounting mistakenly believe that accumulated depreciation accounts (depreciation reserves) represent funds accumulated for the purpose of buying new equipment when the present equipment wears out. Perhaps the best way to combat such mistaken notions is to emphasize that a credit balance in an accumulated depreciation account represents the expired cost of assets acquired in the past. The amounts credited to the accumulated depreciation account could, as an alternative, have been credited directly to the plant and equipment account. An accumulated depreciation account has a *credit* balance; it does not represent an asset; and it cannot be used in any way to pay for new equipment. To buy a new plant asset requires cash; the total amount of cash owned by a company is shown by the asset account for cash.

Capital expenditures and revenue expenditures

The term *expenditure* means making a payment or incurring an obligation to make a future payment for an asset or service received. The acquisition of an asset (such as an automobile) or of a service (such as repairs to the automobile) may be for cash or on credit. In either situation the transaction is properly referred to as an expenditure.

Expenditures for the purchase or expansion of plant assets are called *capital expenditures* and are recorded in asset accounts. Expenditures for repairs, maintenance, fuel, and other items necessary to the ownership and use of plant and equipment are called *revenue expenditures* and are recorded by debits to expense accounts. The charge to an expense account is based on the assumption that the benefits from the expenditure will be used up in the current period, and the payment should therefore be deducted from the revenue of the current period in determining the net income. In brief, *any expenditure that will benefit several accounting periods is considered a capital expenditure; any expenditure that will benefit only the current accounting period is referred to as a revenue expenditure.*

Careful distinction between capital and revenue expenditures is important in the determination of net income. If the cost of constructing a new building, for example, is recorded as ordinary repairs expense (a revenue expenditure), the net income of the current period will be understated. The net income of future periods will be overstated because of the absence of depreciation expense applicable to the unrecorded asset.

Extraordinary repairs

The term *extraordinary repairs* has a specific meaning in accounting terminology; it means a reconditioning or major overhaul that will extend the useful life of a plant asset beyond the original estimate. For example, a new automobile may be depreciated on the basis of an estimated useful life of four years. Assume that after three years of use, a decision is made to rebuild the engine in the automobile and thereby to extend its overall useful life from the original estimate of four years to a total of six years.

An extraordinary repair of this type may be recorded by debiting the Accumulated Depreciation account. This entry is sometimes explained by the argument that the extraordinary repair cancels out some of the depreciation previously recorded. The effect of this reduction (debit entry) in the Accumulated Depreciation account is to *increase* the book value of the asset by the cost of the extraordinary repair.

Since an extraordinary repair causes an increase in the carrying value of the asset and has no immediate direct effect upon net income, it may be regarded as a form of capital expenditure.

Disposal of plant and equipment

When depreciable assets are disposed of at any date other than the end of the year, an entry should be made to record depreciation for the fraction of the year ending with the date of disposal. In the following illustrations of the disposal of items of plant and equipment, it is assumed that any necessary entries for fractional-period depreciation have been recorded.

As units of plant and equipment wear out or become obsolete, they must be scrapped, sold, or traded in on new equipment. Upon the disposal or retirement of a depreciable asset, the cost of the property is removed from the asset account, and the accumulated depreciation is removed from the related valuation account. Assume, for example, that office equipment purchased 10 years ago at a cost of $500 has been fully depreciated and is no longer useful. The entry to record the scrapping of the worthless equipment is as follows:

Scrapping fully depreciated asset

Accumulated Depreciation: Office Equipment *500*
    Office Equipment *500*
To remove from the accounts the cost and the accumulated depreciation on fully depreciated office equipment now being scrapped. No salvage value.

Once an asset has been fully depreciated, no more depreciation should be recorded on it, even though the property is in good condition and is continued in use. The objective of depreciation is to spread the **cost** of an asset over the periods of its usefulness; in no case can depreciation expense be greater than the amount paid for the asset. When a fully depreciated asset is continued in use beyond the original estimate of useful life, the asset account and the Accumulated Depreciation account should remain in the accounting records without further entries until the asset is retired.

GAINS AND LOSSES ON DISPOSAL OF PLANT AND EQUIPMENT Since the residual value and useful life of plant assets are only estimates, it is not uncommon for plant assets to be sold at a price which differs from their book value at the date of disposal. When plant assets are sold, any gain or loss on the disposal is computed by comparing the book value with the amount received from the sale. A sales price in excess of the book value produces a gain; a sales price below the book value produces a loss. These gains or losses, if material in amount, should be shown separately in the income statement in computing the income from operations; however, such gains and losses are not considered as extraordinary items.

Disposal at a price above book value Assume that a machine which cost $10,000 and has a book value of $2,000 is sold for $3,000. The journal entry to record this disposal is as follows:

Gain on disposal of plant asset

Cash	*3,000*	
Accumulated Depreciation: Machinery	*8,000*	
Machinery		*10,000*
Gain on Disposal of Plant Assets		*1,000*

To record sale of machinery at a price above book value.

Disposal at a price below book value Now assume that the same machine is sold for $500. The journal entry in this case would be as follows:

Loss on disposal of plant asset

Cash	*500*	
Accumulated Depreciation: Machinery	*8,000*	
Loss on Disposal of Plant Assets	*1,500*	
Machinery		*10,000*

To record sale of machinery at a price below book value.

The disposal of a depreciable asset at a price equal to book value would result in neither a gain nor a loss. The entry for such a transaction would consist of a debit to Cash for the amount received, a debit to Accumulated Depreciation for the balance accumulated, and a credit to the asset account for the original cost.

Trading in used assets on new

Certain types of depreciable assets, such as automobiles and office equipment, are customarily traded in on new assets of the same kind. The trade-in allowance granted by the dealer may differ materially from the book value of the old asset. If the dealer grants a trade-in allowance in excess of the book value of the asset being traded in, there is the suggestion of a profit being realized on the exchange. The evidence of a gain is not conclusive, however, because the list price of the new asset may purposely have been set higher than a realistic cash price to permit the offering of inflated trade-in allowances.

For the purpose of determining taxable income, no gain or loss is recognized when a depreciable asset is traded in on another similar asset. The tax regulations provide that the cost of the new asset shall be the sum of the book value of the old asset traded in plus the additional amount paid or to be paid in acquiring the new asset. The Accounting Principles Board of the AICPA also supported this approach for financial reporting purposes.[4]

[4] *APB Opinion No. 29,* "Accounting for Nonmonetary Transactions," AICPA (New York: 1973), par. 21.

To illustrate the handling of an exchange transaction in this manner, assume that a delivery truck is acquired at a cost of $4,000. The truck is depreciated on the straight-line basis with the assumption of a five-year life and no salvage value. After four years of use, the truck is traded in on a new model having a list price of $5,000. The truck dealer grants a trade-in allowance of $1,200 for the old truck; the additional amount to be paid to acquire the new truck is, therefore, $3,800 ($5,000 list price minus $1,200 trade-in allowance). The *cost basis* of the new truck is computed as follows:

Trade-in: cost of new equipment	Cost of old truck	$4,000
	Less: Accumulated depreciation ($800 × 4)	3,200
	Book value of old truck	$ 800
	Add: Cash payment for new truck (list price, $5,000 − $1,200 trade-in	
	allowance)	3,800
	Cost basis of new truck	$4,600

The trade-in allowance and the list price of the new truck are not recorded in the accounts; their only function lies in determining the amount which the purchaser must pay in addition to turning in the old truck. The journal entry for this exchange transaction is as follows:

Entry for trade-in	Delivery Truck (new)	4,600	
	Accumulated Depreciation: Delivery Truck (old)	3,200	
	Delivery Truck (old)		4,000
	Cash		3,800

To remove from the accounts the cost of old truck and accumulated depreciation thereon, and to record new truck at cost equal to book value of old truck traded in plus cash paid.

An alternative method of recording trade-ins (not currently acceptable for financial reporting or income tax purposes but having some theoretical support) calls for recognizing a gain or loss on the exchange in an amount equal to the difference between the book value of the old asset and its estimated fair market value at the time of the trade-in. The validity of this alternative method rests upon the assumption that the trade-in allowance represents the fair market value of the old asset being traded in. If we make that assumption for the preceding example of the trading in of a truck, the journal entry would be as follows:

Trade-in: alternative method	Delivery Truck (new)	5,000	
	Accumulated Depreciation: Delivery Truck (old)	3,200	
	Delivery Truck (old)		4,000
	Cash		3,800
	Gain on Disposal of Plant Assets		400

To remove from the accounts the cost of the old truck and accumulated depreciation thereon, and to record the new truck at its list price.

NATURAL RESOURCES

Accounting for natural resources

Mining properties, oil and gas wells, and tracts of standing timber are leading examples of natural resources or "wasting assets." The distinguishing characteristics of these assets are that they are physically consumed and converted into inventory. In a theoretical sense, a coal mine might even be regarded as an "underground inventory of coal"; however, such an inventory is certainly not a current asset. In the balance sheet, mining property and other natural resources are usually listed as a separate group of tangible assets.

Natural resources should be recorded in the accounts at cost. As the resource is removed through the process of mining, cutting, or pumping, the asset account must be proportionately reduced. The carrying value (book value) of a coal mine, for example, is reduced by a small amount for each ton of coal mined. The original cost of the mine is thus gradually transferred out of the asset account and becomes part of the cost of the coal mined and sold.

DEPLETION The term *depletion* is used to describe the pro rata allocation of cost of a natural resource to the units removed. Depletion is computed by dividing the cost of the natural resource by the estimated available number of units, such as barrels of oil or tons of coal. The depletion charge per unit is then multiplied by the number of units actually removed during the year to determine the total depletion charge for that period.

To illustrate the computation of depletion expense, assume that the sum of $500,000 is paid for a coal mine believed to contain 1 million tons of coal. The depletion charge per unit is $500,000 ÷ 1,000,000, or 50 cents a ton. If we assume that 200,000 tons of coal were mined and sold during the first year of operation, the depletion charge for the year would be 50 cents × 200,000, or $100,000. The journal entry necessary at the end of the year to record depletion of the mine would be as follows:

Recording depletion	*Depletion Expense*	*100,000*
	Accumulated Depletion: Coal Mine	*100,000*
	To record depletion expense for the year; 200,000 tons mined @ 50 cents per ton.	

In reporting natural resources in the balance sheet, accumulated depletion should be deducted from the cost of the property. A recent balance sheet of Anaconda Company, for example, reports its natural resources as follows:

Natural resources in the balance sheet	*Mines and mining claims, water rights and lands, less accumulated depletion of $149,874,000*	*$138,410,000*
	Timberlands and phosphate and gravel deposits, less accumulated depletion of $5,602,000	*2,111,000*

Depletion expense in a mining business might be compared with the Purchases account in the ledger of a retail store. The Purchases account represents part of the cost to the store of the goods available for sale; the Depletion Expense account in a mining company represents a part of the cost of the coal or other product available for sale. To the extent that coal produced during the year is not sold but is carried forward as inventory for sale in the following year, *the depletion charge will also be carried forward as part of the inventory value.* In other words, depletion is recorded in the year in which extraction of the product occurs but becomes a deduction from revenue in the period in which the product is sold. Of course, the cost of the inventory of coal or other extracted product on hand at the end of the year includes not only the depletion charge but also the labor cost and other expenditures incurred in bringing the coal to the surface.

PERCENTAGE DEPLETION VERSUS COST DEPLETION Depletion for income tax purposes has been widely publicized in the news media. For the determination of taxable income, the Internal Revenue Code permits a deduction for depletion expense equal to a specified percentage of the revenue from production. Consequently, *percentage depletion* can exceed the cost of the natural resource, which could never happen when depletion is based on cost. Currently, the percentage depletion rate for oil and gas wells is 22% of the revenue from the property during the year, subject to certain exceptions. The percentage depletion rate may be changed by Congress at any time.

Percentage depletion is used *only for income tax purposes, not for financial statements.* The topic is mentioned here because nearly everyone is exposed to political arguments over the merits of percentage depletion. Percentage depletion is a special tax advantage granted to oil, gas, and other natural resource companies. The purpose of this favorable tax treatment is to encourage the risk-taking inherent in the search for and development of natural resources. Also, without this tax advantage these companies would probably have to increase the price of their products to offset the increase in their income tax expense.

DEVELOPMENT COSTS The cost of a natural resource may include not only the purchase price of the property, but also expenditures for recording fees, surveying, and a variety of exploratory and developmental activities.

Some exploratory and developmental expenditures will prove to be unproductive; these expenditures should be recognized as losses or expenses of the current period and not carried forward as assets. The dividing line between productive and nonproductive expenditures for exploration and development is not always easy to draw. The drilling of a dry hole in a new oil field might be regarded as a loss, or, on the other hand, as an integral step in an overall successful development of the field.

There is a noticeable trend for companies engaged in the extraction of natural resources to plan for continuity of existence, rather than to end their operations with the exhaustion of a single property. These companies maintain their productive capacity by carrying on a continuous program of exploration and development of new areas. Since outlays for exploration and development thus become normal and continuous, these expenditures are commonly charged to expense in the year in which the exploration or development is performed. Such practices have been condoned by accountants more on the grounds of expediency and conservation than on theoretical considerations.

DEPRECIATION OF BUILDINGS AND EQUIPMENT CLOSELY RELATED TO NATURAL RESOURCES Assume that a building costing $20,500 and having a normal useful life of 20 years is erected at the site of a mine estimated to contain 100,000 tons of ore. Once the mine is exhausted, the building will have only residual value, say, $500. Production of ore is being carried on at a rate which will probably exhaust the mine within four to six years. During the first year after construction of the building, ore is mined in the amount of 25,000 tons. How much depreciation should be recognized on the building?

In this situation, depreciation of the building should be based on the life of the mine, and computed in the same manner as depletion. Cost, $20,500, minus residual value, $500, times 25,000/100,000 equals $5,000 depreciation for the first year. The formula may be concisely stated as

$$\text{Depreciation per Year} = (\text{Cost} - \text{Residual Value}) \times \frac{\text{Units Produced}}{\text{Estimated Total Units}}$$

INTANGIBLE ASSETS

Characteristics

As the word *intangible* suggests, assets in this classification have no physical substance. Leading examples are goodwill, leaseholds, copyrights, franchises, licenses, and trademarks. Intangible assets are classified on the balance sheet as a subgroup of plant assets. However, not all assets which lack physical substance are regarded as intangible assets; an account receivable, for example, or a short-term prepayment, is of nonphysical nature but is classified as a current asset and is not regarded as an intangible. In brief, intangible assets are noncurrent and nonphysical.

The basis of valuation for intangible assets is cost. In some companies, certain intangible assets such as trademarks may be of great importance but may have been acquired without the incurring of any cost. An intangible asset should appear on the balance sheet *only* if a cost of acquisition or development has been incurred.

However, accounting for an intangible asset is rendered somewhat difficult because the lack of physical substance makes evidence of its existence more elusive, may make its value more debatable, and may make the length of its useful life more questionable. These characteristics of intangible assets suggest that realizable value may be undeterminable or even nonexistent. Perhaps because of the lack of clear support for precise valuation of intangibles, many companies choose to carry their intangible assets on the balance sheet at a nominal valuation of $1; Jantzen Inc., and the Polaroid Corporation are prominent examples.

There is little doubt, however, that in some companies the intangible assets, such as goodwill or trademarks, may be vitally important to profitable operations. The carrying of intangible assets on the balance sheet is justified only when there is good evidence that future earnings will be derived from these assets.

Operating expenses versus intangible assets

Many types of expenditures offer at least a half promise of yielding benefits in subsequent years, but the evidence is so nebulous and the period of usefulness so hard to define that it is expedient to treat these expenditures as expense when incurred. Another reason for charging these outlays to expense is the practical difficulty of separating them from the recurring expenses of current operations.

Examples are the expenditures for intensive advertising campaigns to introduce new products, and the expense of training employees to work with new types of machinery or office equipment. There is little doubt that some benefits from these outlays continue beyond the current period, but because of the indeterminable duration of the benefits, it is almost universal practice to treat expenditures of this nature as expense of the current period. Although the dividing line between expenditures to be expensed and those to be charged to intangible asset accounts is admittedly somewhat arbitrary, the establishment of a universal rule has the merit of narrowing the range of acceptable accounting alternatives and thereby contributing to more comparability in financial statements.

For income tax purposes, a business has an option to deduct its outlays for research and similar expenditures as current expense or to capitalize them for later amortization.

Amortization

The term *amortization* is used to describe the systematic write-off to expense of the cost of an intangible asset over the periods of its economic usefulness. The usual accounting entry for amortization consists of a debit to an expense account and a credit to the intangible asset account. There is no theoretical objection to crediting an accumulated amortization account rather than the intangible asset account, but this method is seldom encountered in practice.

For many years some accountants argued that certain intangibles, such as trademarks, had **unlimited** useful lives and therefore should not be amortized. However, the Accounting Principles Board concluded that "the value of intangible assets at any one date eventually disappears," and ruled that **all** intangible assets must be amortized over their useful lives.[5]

Although it is difficult to estimate the useful life of an intangible such as goodwill, it is highly probable that such an asset will not contribute to future earnings on a permanent basis. The cost of the intangible asset should, therefore, be deducted from revenue during the years in which it may be expected to aid in producing revenue.[6] The Accounting Principles Board has ruled, however, that the period of amortization should not exceed 40 years.[7] The straight-line method of amortization is generally used for intangible assets.

ARBITRARY WRITE–OFF OF INTANGIBLES   Arbitrary, lump-sum write-off of intangibles (leaving a nominal balance of $1 in the accounts) is a practice sometimes found in companies which have not adopted a systematic amortization program. Arguments for this practice emphasize the element of conservatism, the practical difficulty of estimating an appropriate period for amortization, and the absence of any realizable value for intangibles. Accountants generally agree that whenever any event occurs which indicates that an intangible has lost all value, immediate write-off of the entire cost is warranted regardless of whether an amortization program has previously been followed.

On the other hand, arbitrary write-offs of valuable, revenue-producing intangible assets are no more in accordance with accounting theory than would be the arbitrary write-off of land or buildings.

Goodwill

Businessmen and lawyers used the term **goodwill** in a variety of meanings before it became a part of accounting terminology. One of the more common meanings of goodwill in a nonaccounting sense concerns the benefits derived from a favorable reputation among customers. To accountants, however, goodwill has a very specific meaning not necessarily limited to customer relationships. It means the **present value of future earnings in excess of the earnings normally realized in the industry.** Above-average earnings may arise not only from favorable

[5] APB Opinion No. 17, "Intangible Assets," AICPA (New York: 1970), par. 27.
[6] Present tax regulations do not permit the amortization of goodwill in computing taxable income.
[7] APB Opinion No. 17, op. cit., par. 29.

customer relations but also from such factors as location, monopoly, manufacturing efficiency, and superior management.

The existence of the intangible asset of goodwill is indicated when an entire business is sold for a price in excess of the fair market value of the other assets. The willingness of the purchaser of a going business to pay a price greater than the sum of the values of the tangible assets indicates that he is paying for intangible assets as well. If the business does not include such specific intangibles as patents or franchises, the extra amount paid is presumably for goodwill. Superior earnings in past years are of significance to a prospective purchaser of a going business only to the extent that he believes such earnings may continue after he acquires the business. If the prospective purchaser believes that, by purchasing a particular company with a record of superior earnings in the past, he will earn these above-average earnings in the future, he may reasonably be expected to pay a premium price for the business. The premium which he pays represents the cost of purchased goodwill and may properly be recorded in the accounting records of the new owner in a Goodwill account.

Assume that two businesses in the same line of trade are for sale and that the normal rate of earnings on capital invested in this industry is 10% a year. The relative earning power of the two companies during the past five years is indicated by the following schedule.

	Company X	Company Y
Net assets other than goodwill	*$1,000,000*	*$1,000,000*
Normal rate of earnings on invested capital	*10%*	*10%*
Average net income for past five years	*$ 100,000*	*$ 140,000*
Net income computed at normal rate (10%) on net assets other than goodwill	*100,000*	*100,000*
Annual earnings in excess of average for the industry	*$ –0–*	*$ 40,000*

Measuring superior earning power

A prospective investor would be willing to pay more for Company Y than for Company X because Company Y has a record of superior earnings which will presumably continue for some time in the future. Company Y has goodwill; Company X does not. Very few concerns are able to maintain above-average earnings for more than a few years. Consequently, the purchaser of a business will usually limit his payment for goodwill to not more than four or five times the excess annual earnings.

ESTIMATING THE AMOUNT OF GOODWILL Goodwill is to be recorded in the accounts only when paid for; this situation usually occurs only when a going business is purchased in its entirety. When ownership of a business changes hands, any amount paid for goodwill rests on the assumption that earnings in excess of normal will continue under the new ownership. The following are methods of estimating a value for goodwill:

1 Arbitrary agreement between buyer and seller of the business may be reached on the amount of goodwill. For example, it might be agreed that the fair market value of the net tangible assets is $1,000,000 and that the total purchase price for the business will be $1,100,000, thus providing a $100,000 payment for goodwill. (We are assuming in this example that the business has no identifiable intangible assets such as patents.) The term *net tangible assets* may require explanation. *Net assets* means assets minus liabilities; *net tangible assets* therefore means all assets (except the intangibles) minus liabilities. Another way of computing the amount of net tangible assets is merely to deduct the intangible assets from the owners' equity.

2 Goodwill may be determined as a multiple of the average net income of past years. For example, assume that a business has earned an average annual net income of $25,000 during the past five years. The business is sold for the book value of the net tangible assets, plus two years' average net income. The payment for goodwill is, therefore, $50,000. This method may be criticized because it ignores completely the concept of *excess earnings* as a basis for estimating goodwill.

3 Goodwill may be determined as a multiple of the amount by which the average annual earnings exceed normal earnings. To illustrate, assume the following data:

Average investment in the business	*$100,000*
Average annual earnings (rate of 14%)	*$ 14,000*
Normal earnings for this industry (rate of 10%)	*10,000*
Average earnings in excess of normal	*$ 4,000*
Multiple of excess annual earnings	*4*
Goodwill	*$ 16,000*

Goodwill as multiple of excess earnings

The multiple applied to the excess annual earnings may vary widely from perhaps 1 to 10, depending on the nature of the industry and the reliance placed on the earnings projections. This method is more in accord with the concept of goodwill as earning power in *excess* of normal, whereas method 2 relates goodwill to the *total* earnings.

4 Goodwill may be determined as the capitalized value of excess earning power, using a capitalization rate considered normal in the industry. Assume that the normal rate of earnings in a given line of business is 10% and that a particular company presents the following picture:

Average investment in the business	*$100,000*
Average annual earnings (rate of 14%)	*$ 14,000*
Normal earnings for this industry (rate of 10%)	*10,000*
Average earnings in excess of normal	*$ 4,000*
Goodwill, computed by capitalizing average excess earnings at 10% ($4,000 ÷ .10)	*$ 40,000*

Goodwill based on capitalization of excess earnings

In estimating the amount of goodwill, the buyer and seller may agree to capitalize excess earnings at a rate either higher or lower than the normal earnings rate in the industry.

Patents

A patent is an exclusive right granted by the federal government for manufacture, use, and sale of a particular product. Patents, like other intangible assets, should be recorded in the accounts at cost. Since patents may be acquired by purchase or may be obtained directly from the government by the inventor, the cost may consist of the purchase price or of the expenditures for research and development leading to the application for the patent. In addition, cost may include legal fees for obtaining the patent and for infringement suits. Companies which carry on extensive research and development programs on a permanent basis often treat the costs of such work as expense when incurred, on the grounds that constant research is necessary merely to maintain a competitive position in the industry.

Patents are granted for a period of 17 years, and the period of amortization must not exceed that period. However, if the patent is likely to lose its usefulness in less than 17 years, amortization should be based on the shorter period of estimated useful life. Assume that a patent is purchased from the inventor at a cost of $30,000, after five years of the legal life have expired. The remaining *legal* life is, therefore, 12 years, but if the estimated *useful* life is only five years, amortization should be based on this shorter period. The entry to be made to record the annual amortization expense would be:

Entry for amortization of patent	Amortization Expense: Patents	6,000
	Patents	6,000

To amortize cost of patent on a straight-line basis and estimated useful life of five years.

Copyrights

A copyright is an exclusive right granted to protect the production and sale of literary or artistic materials for a period of 28 years. The cost of obtaining a copyright is minor and therefore is chargeable to expense when paid. Only when a copyright is purchased will the expenditure be material enough to warrant capitalization and spreading over the useful life. The revenue from copyrights is usually limited to only a few years, and the purchase cost should, of course, be amortized over the years in which the revenue is expected.

Trademarks

A permanent exclusive right to the use of a trademark, brand name, or commercial symbol may be obtained by registering it. Because of the unlimited legal life, a trademark may be carried without amortization at the original cost. If the use of the trademark is abandoned or if its contribution to earnings becomes doubtful, immediate write-off of the cost is called for. The outlay for securing a trademark is often not material, and it is common practice to treat such outlays as expense when incurred.

Other intangibles and deferred charges

Many other types of intangible assets are found in the published balance sheets of large corporations. Some examples are oil exploration costs, formulas, processes, designs, research and development costs, franchises, name lists, and film rights.[8]

Intangibles, particularly those with limited lives, are sometimes classified as "deferred charges" in the balance sheet. A *deferred charge* is an expenditure which is expected to yield benefits for several accounting periods and which should be amortized over its estimated useful life. Included in this category are such items as bond issuance costs, plant rearrangement and moving costs, start-up costs, and organization costs. The distinction between intangibles and deferred charges is not an important one; both represent "bundles of services" in the form of long-term prepayments awaiting allocation to those accounting periods in which the services will be consumed.

DEMONSTRATION PROBLEM

After several years of managerial experience in the retailing of sporting goods, Arthur Barr decided to buy an established business in this field. He is now attempting to make a choice among three similar companies which are available for purchase. All three companies have been in business for exactly five years. The balance sheets presented by the three companies are summarized as follows:

Assets	*Company A*	*Company B*	*Company C*
Cash	$ 45,000	$ 18,000	$ 25,000
Accounts receivable	95,000	119,000	85,000
Inventories	212,500	140,000	180,000
Plant and equipment (net)	90,000	120,000	100,000
Intangible assets	7,500	3,000	
Total assets	$450,000	$400,000	$390,000

Liabilities & Stockholders' Equity			
Current liabilities	$208,000	$185,000	$200,000
Capital stock	150,000	100,000	25,000
Retained earnings	92,000	115,000	165,000
Total liabilities & stockholders' equity . .	$450,000	$400,000	$390,000

[8] In a recent survey of the financial statements of 600 leading corporations, 364 carried one or more types of intangible assets on their balance sheets. AICPA, *Accounting Trends & Techniques, op. cit.,* p. 138.

The average net income of the three companies during the past five years had been as follows: Company A, $35,600; Company B, $29,300; Company C, $38,200.

With the permission of the owners of the three companies, Barr arranged for a certified public accountant to examine the accounting records of the companies. This investigation disclosed the following information:

Accounts receivable In Company A, no provision for uncollectible accounts had been made at any time, and no accounts receivable had been written off. Numerous past-due receivables were on the books, and the estimated uncollectible items which had accumulated during the past five years amounted to $6,000. In both Company B and Company C, the receivables appeared to be carried at net realizable value.

Inventories Company B had adopted the first-in, first-out method of inventory valuation when first organized but had changed to the last-in, first-out method after one year. As a result of this change in method of accounting for inventories, the present balance sheet figure for inventories was approximately $13,500 less than replacement cost. The other two companies had used the first-in, first-out method continuously, and their present inventories were approximately equal to replacement cost.

Plant and equipment Each of the companies owns a building, acquired at the beginning of Year 1 at a cost of $52,500, which had an estimated useful life of 20 years with no residual value. Company A had taken no depreciation on its building; Company B had used straight-line depreciation at 5% annually, and Company C had depreciated its building by using the sum-of-the-years'-digits method. All plant assets other than buildings had been depreciated on a straight-line basis by the three companies. Barr believed that the book value of the plant assets of all three companies would approximate fair market value if depreciation were uniformly computed on a straight-line basis.

In addition to the foregoing, the following items relate to plant and equipment: A fully depreciated machine for which Company A paid $3,500 is no longer in use but has not been formally retired. Company B sold an asset in Year 4 and recorded the transaction by a debit to Cash and a credit to Machinery for $4,000. The cost of the machine was $10,000 and the book value was $5,400. No depreciation was recorded on this machine in Year 5. Installation costs on another machine amounting to $2,400 were charged to expense by Company C at the beginning of Year 3. The machine is being depreciated on a straight-line basis over a five-year life.

Intangible assets The $7,500 reported as an intangible asset by Company A represents the cost of a patent acquired two years ago. The patent has not been amortized, although its useful life will probably not extend beyond four more years. The $3,000 item in the balance sheet of Company B is the cost of a nonrecurring advertising campaign conducted during the first year of operation.

Current liabilities The following accrued liabilities have not been recorded by Companies A and C:

	Company A	Company C
End of Year 4	$600	$360
End of Year 5	420	800

Barr is willing to pay for net assets (excluding cash but including the patent) at book value, plus an amount for goodwill equal to three times the average annual net income for the past five years in excess of 10% on current stock-holders' equity, as adjusted (excluding goodwill). Cash will not be included in the transfer of assets.

Instructions

a Prepare a revised summary of balance sheet data after correcting all errors made by the companies. In addition to correcting errors, make the necessary changes to apply straight-line depreciation and first-in, first-out inventory methods in all three companies.

b Determine revised amounts for average net income of the three companies after taking into consideration the correction of errors and changes in accounting methods called for in **a** above.

c Determine the price which Barr should offer for each of the three companies. Compute all amounts to the nearest dollar.

SOLUTION TO DEMONSTRATION PROBLEM

a

Assets	*Company A*	*Company B*	*Company C*
Cash	$ 45,000	$ 18,000	$ 25,000
Accounts receivable (net)	89,000	119,000	85,000
Inventories	212,500	153,500	180,000
Plant and equipment (net)	76,875 *(1)*	118,600 *(2)*	110,335 *(3)*
Intangible assets	5,000 *(4)*		
Total assets	$428,375	$409,100	$400,335

Liabilities & Stockholders' Equity			
Current liabilities	$208,420	$185,000	$200,800
Capital stock	150,000	100,000	25,000
Retained earnings	69,955	124,100	174,535
Total liabilities & stockholders' equity .	$428,375	$409,100	$400,335

(1) $90,000, less depreciation at 5% per year for five years on building costing $52,500, or $13,125. Plant and equipment = $90,000 − $13,125, or $76,875

(2) $120,000, less loss of $1,400 not recognized in Year 4 = $118,600

(3) $100,000 + 40% of $2,400 (undepreciated portion of installation costs) + $9,375, which is determined as follows:

Depreciation recorded last five years, $\frac{90}{210} \times$ $52,500	$22,500
Depreciation for five years using straight-line method, see *(1)*	13,125
Increase in book value of plant and equipment	$ 9,375

Plant and equipment = $100,000 + $960 + $9,375, or $110,335

(4) $7,500 less amortization to date, $2,500 ($7,500 × $\frac{2}{6}$) = $5,000

b *Revised amounts of average net income:*

	Company A	Company B	Company C
Total net income for last five years (before corrections average net income × 5).	$178,000	$146,500	$191,000
Corrections:			
Estimated uncollectible accounts . .	(6,000)		
Inventory understated		13,500	
Depreciation restated—see part a . .	(13,125)		9,375
Loss on disposal of plant asset . . .		(1,400)	
Installation costs, $2,400, less depreciation of 60% to date			960
Intangible assets amortized	(2,500	(3,000)	
Accrued liabilities at end of Year 5 (understatement of net income at end of Year 4 counterbalanced in Year 5)	(420)		(800)
Revised total net income for five years	$155,955	$155,600	$200,535
Average net income (divide by 5) . . .	$ 31,191	$ 31,120	$ 40,107

C *Price to be offered for each company:*

	Company A	Company B	Company C
Average net income **b**	$ 31,191	$ 31,120	$ 40,107
Less: 10% of adjusted stockholders' equity **a**	21,996	22,410	19,954
Average superior earnings	$ 9,195	$ 8,710	$ 20,153
Multiplied by three years	×3	×3	×3
Estimated amount of goodwill	$ 27,585	$ 26,130	$ 60,459
Add: Net tangible assets, excluding cash	174,955	206,100	174,535
Price to be offered	$202,540	$232,230	$234,994

REVIEW QUESTIONS

1 The following expenditures were incurred in connection with a large new machine acquired by a metals manufacturing company. Identify those which should be included in the cost of the asset. (*a*) Freight charges, (*b*) sales tax on the machine, (*c*) payment to a passing motorist whose car was damaged by the equipment used in unloading the machine, (*d*) wages of employees for time spent in installing and testing the machine before it was placed in service, (*e*) wages of employees assigned to lubrication and minor adjustments of machine one year after it was placed in service.

2 Which of the following statements best describes the nature of depreciation?

    a Regular reduction of asset value to correspond to changes in market value as the asset ages *b* A process of correlating the carrying value of an asset with its gradual decline in physical efficiency

c Allocation of cost in a manner that will ensure that plant and equipment items are not carried on the balance sheet at amounts in excess of net realizable value

d Allocation of the cost of a plant asset to the periods in which services are received from the asset

3 Should depreciation continue to be recorded on a building when ample evidence exists that the current market value is greater than original cost and that the rising trend of market values is continuing? Explain.

4 A factory machine acquired at a cost of $93,600 was to be depreciated by the sum-of-the-years'-digits method over an estimated life of eight years. Residual salvage value was estimated to be $1,600. State the amount of depreciation during the first year and during the eighth year.

5 Identify the following expenditures as capital expenditures or revenue expenditures:

a Purchased new spark plugs at a cost of $9.20 for two-year-old delivery truck.

b Installed an escalator at a cost of $3,800 in a three-story building which had previously been used for some years without elevators or escalators.

c Purchased an electric pencil sharpener at a cost of $3.95.

d Immediately after acquiring new delivery truck at a cost of $5,800, paid $75 to have the name of the store and other advertising material painted on the truck.

e Painted delivery truck at a cost of $82 after two years of use.

6 What is an *extraordinary repair* and how is it recorded in the accounts?

7 Company A's balance sheet shows accumulated depreciation on machinery and equipment of $100,000 and Company B shows accumulated depreciation of $50,000. Both companies are considering the acquisition of new equipment costing $60,000. From the information given, can you determine which company is in a better position to purchase the new equipment for cash? Explain.

8 After four years of using a machine acquired at a cost of $15,000, Kral Construction Company determined that the original estimated life of 10 years had been too short and that a total useful life of 12 years was a more reasonable estimate. Explain briefly the method that should be used to revise the depreciation program, assuming that straight-line depreciation has been used.

9 Explain what is meant by the following quotation: "In periods of rising prices companies do not recognize adequate depreciation expense, and reported corporate profits are substantially overstated."

10 LoveMatch Company traded in its old computer on a new model. If the trade-in allowance for the old computer is greater than its book value, would LoveMatch Company recognize a gain on the exchange? Explain.

11 Lead Hill Corporation recognizes $1 of depletion for each ton of ore mined. During the current year the company mined 600,000 tons but sold only 500,000 tons, as it was attempting to build up inventories in anticipation of a possible strike by employees. How much depletion should be deducted from revenue of the current year?

12 Define *intangible asset.* Would an account receivable arising from a sale of merchandise under terms of 2/10, n/30 qualify as an intangible asset under your definition?

13 Under what circumstances should *goodwill* be recorded in the accounts?

14 In reviewing the financial statements of Digital Products Co. with a view to investing in the company's stock, you notice that net tangible assets total $1 million, that goodwill is listed at $100,000, and that average earnings for the past five years have been $20,000 a year. How would these relationships influence your thinking about the company?

15 Over what period of time should the cost of various types of intangible assets be amortized by regular charges against revenue? (Your answer should be in the form of a principle or guideline rather than a specific number of years.) What method of amortization is generally used?

EXERCISES

Ex. 12-1 Machinery with a useful life of five years was acquired by Gulf Converters at a cost of $61,300. The estimated residual salvage value was $1,300. You are to compute the annual depreciation charges applicable to the machinery under each of the following methods of depreciation:
a Straight-line
b Sum-of-the-years'-digits
c Double-declining-balance

Ex. 12-2 A truck with a book value of $1,000 is traded in on a new truck with a list price of $10,000. The trade-in allowance on the old truck is $1,500.
a How much cash must be paid for the new truck?
b What is the cost basis of the new truck for income tax purposes?
c How much depreciation should be recorded on the new truck for the first year of use, assuming a four-year life, a residual value of $1,100, and the use of straight-line depreciation?

Ex. 12-3 The general manager of Catalog Printers attended an auction of used machinery. He was the successful bidder on a lot consisting of three machines for which he paid $14,100. Freight charges of $900 were incurred to have the three machines delivered to Catalog Printers plant. In anticipation of this auction the company had borrowed $15,000 in order to be able to make cash bids for the equipment being auctioned. The interest charge on the borrowing amounted to $500.

The estimated fair market values of the machines and the costs of installations and trial runs necessary to prepare them for regular operations were as follows:

	Machine No. 1	Machine No. 2	Machine No. 3
Fair market value	$7,000	$9,000	$4,000
Installation costs	400	800	300
Costs of trial runs	100	150	None

Determine the cost of each machine for accounting purposes, assuming that the auction and delivery cost is apportioned to the three machines on the basis of relative market value.

Ex. 12-4 River Farms, Inc., acquired a tractor at a cost of $6,600. The estimated useful life was five years and the estimated salvage value $600. The company used straight-line depreciation on all its depreciable assets. Prepare the journal entry to record the later sale or other disposition of the tractor by River Farms, Inc., under each of the following alternative assumptions:
a The tractor was sold for cash of $3,500 after two years' use.
b After three years the tractor was traded in on another tractor with a list price of $8,000. Trade-in allowance was $3,600. The trade-in was recorded in a manner acceptable for income tax purposes.

c The tractor was scrapped after four years' use. Since scrap dealers were unwilling to pay anything for the tractor, it was given to a scrap dealer for his services in removing it.

Ex. 12-5 During the past several years the net sales of Lincoln Company have averaged $900,000 annually and net income has averaged 6% of net sales. At the present time the company is being offered for sale. Its accounting records show net assets (total assets minus all liabilities) to be $300,000.

An investor negotiating to buy the company offers to pay an amount equal to the book value for the net assets and to assume all liabilities. In addition, he is willing to pay for goodwill an amount equal to net earnings in excess of 15% on net assets, capitalized at a rate of 25%.

On the basis of this agreement, what price should the investor offer for the Lincoln Company?

Ex. 12-6 Early in 1977 Silver Knife Mining began mining operations. At the end of the year its accountant prepared the following summary of mining costs:

Labor	*$2,040,000*
Materials	*210,000*
Miscellaneous	*270,400*

These costs do not include any charges for depletion or depreciation. Data relating to assets used in mining the ore follow:

Cost of mine (estimated deposit, 10 million tons; residual value of the mine estimated at $360,000)	*$1,800,000*
Buildings (estimated life, 15 years; no residual value)	*150,000*
Equipment (useful life, six years regardless of number of tons mined; residual value $30,000)	*270,000*

During the year 900,000 tons (9%) of ore were mined, of which 700,000 tons were sold. It is estimated that it will take at least 15 years to extract the ore.

Determine the cost that should be assigned to the inventory of unsold ore at the end of 1977.

PROBLEMS

12-1 Blue Ridge Company, a small, newly organized corporation, has purchased equipment at a cost of $91,600. The estimated life of these assets is five years and the residual value $1,600. The company is considering whether to use straight-line depreciation, the sum-of-the-years'-digits method, or the double-declining-balance method. Consideration is also being given to the possibility of using one method for the preparation of income tax returns and another method for financial reporting to stockholders.

The president of Blue Ridge Company informs you that he wants to keep income taxes at a minimum during the coming year (Year 1), but to report the largest possible earnings per share in the company's first annual report to its stockholders.

Instructions

a Compute the annual depreciation expense throughout the five-year life of the equipment under each of the three methods under consideration. (Use a work sheet with three money columns headed respectively Straight-line, Sum-of-the-years'-digits, and Double-declining-balance. Also show the total depreciation under each method and show in footnotes how the calculations were made.)

b Advise the president of Blue Ridge Company which method of depreciation should be used for income tax purposes and which method for the company's financial statements in order to achieve his stated objectives of holding income taxes to a minimum in Year 1 while showing the maximum earnings per share in the company's financial statements.

12-2 The accounting records of Snow-Machines Company are adjusted and closed at the end of each calendar year. Straight-line depreciation is used on all the company's depreciable assets. On January 2, 1974, the company purchased machinery for cash at a cost of $119,400. Useful life was estimated to be 10 years and residual value $5,400.

After almost three years of using the machinery, the company decided in December 1976 that, in view of technological changes in the industry, the total estimated useful life of the machinery should be revised from 10 years to 6 years and that the residual scrap value estimate should be lowered from $5,400 to $3,600. The revised estimate of useful life was made prior to recording depreciation for the year ended December 31, 1976.

On June 30, 1978, the company decided to lease new, more efficient machinery, and the machinery described above was sold for $20,550 cash.

Instructions Prepare journal entries in chronological order for the above events beginning with the purchase of the machinery on January 2, 1974. Show separately the depreciation for each year from 1974 to 1978, inclusive. Conclude with the journal entry recording the disposal of the machinery. Closing entries are not required.

12-3 The Oregon Corporation has had numerous changes in accounting personnel in recent years with the result that different methods of depreciation have been adopted for similar items of plant and equipment acquired at different dates. Information appears below for four machines for which different methods of depreciation have been in use.

Machine	Date Acquired	Cost	Estimated Useful Life, Years	Estimated Residual Value	Method of Depreciation
A	Jan. 1, 1976	$ 90,000	6	None	Fixed-percentage-on-declining-balance
B	June 30, 1976	100,000	8	10%	Straight-line
C	Jan. 1, 1977	85,000	10	$2,500	Sum-of-the-years'-digits
D	Jan. 1, 1978	60,000	12	None	Fixed-percentage-on-declining-balance

Instructions

a Compute the amount of accumulated depreciation, if any, on each machine at December 31, 1977. For machines A and D, assume that the depreciation rate was double the rate which would be applicable under the straight-line method.

b Prepare a depreciation schedule for use in the computation of the 1978 depreciation expense. Use the following column headings:

Machine	Method of Depre- ciation	Date Acquired	Cost	Estimated Residual Value	Amount to Be Depre- diated	Useful Life, Years	Accum- ulated Depre- ciation, Dec. 31, 1977	Depre- ciation Expense, 1978

c Prepare a journal entry to record the depreciation expense for 1978.

12-4 Oak Harbor Company purchased a new machine on July 1, 1977, at the advertised price of $42,000. The terms of payment were 2/10, n/30 and payment was made immediately, including a 6% state sales tax on $41,160. On July 3, the machine was delivered; Oak Harbor Company paid freight charges of $765.40 and assigned its own employees to the task of installation. The labor costs for installing the machine amounted to $605. During the process of installation, carelessness by a workman caused damage to an adjacent machine, with resulting repairs of $350.

On November 10, 1977, after more than four months of satisfactory operations, the machine was thoroughly inspected, cleaned, and oiled at a cost of $440.

The useful life of the machine was estimated to be 10 years and the residual value to be zero. The policy of the Oak Harbor Company is to use straight-line depreciation and to begin depreciation as of the first of the month in which a plant asset is acquired. During 1977 and 1978, however, numerous changes in the company's accounting personnel were responsible for a number of errors and deviations from accounting policies.

At December 31, 1978, unaudited financial statements of the Oak Harbor Company showed the machine to be carried at a cost of $41,160 and the accumulated depreciation as $6,174. Net income reported for 1977 was $98,400 and for 1978 it was $115,700.

Instructions

a Prepare journal entries for all the above transactions from July 1 to December 31, 1977. Include the year-end entry for depreciation and the related closing entry.

b Compute the correct balances for the Machinery account and for the Accumulated Depreciation: Machinery account at December 31, 1978.

c Compute revised figures for net income for 1977 and 1978. Disregard income taxes.

12-5 On January 1, 1977, Northern Company, an established concern, borrowed $5.4 million from the Bank of Tundra, issuing a note payable in five years with interest at 8% payable annually, on December 31. Also on January 1, the company purchased for $2.88 million a Northwest Yukon oil field estimated to contain at least 7.2 million barrels of crude oil. Movable oil-field equipment having an estimated useful life of five years and no residual value was acquired at a cost of $93,600 on January 1.

During January the company spent $450,000 in developing the oil field and several shallow wells were brought into production. The established accounting policy of the company was to treat drilling and development costs of this type as expense of the period in which the work was done.

Construction of a pipeline was completed on May 1, 1977, at a cost of $864,000. Although this pipeline was physically capable of being used for 10 years or more, its economic usefulness was limited to the productive life of the wells; therefore, the depreciation method employed was based on the estimated number of barrels of crude oil to be produced.

Operating costs incurred during 1977 (other than depreciation and depletion) amounted to $576,000; 828,000 barrels of oil were produced and sold.

In January, 1978, additional drilling costs were incurred in the amount of $360,000, and the estimated total capacity of the oil field was raised from the original 7.2 million barrels to 9,324,000 barrels, including the 828,000 barrels of oil produced to date.

Cash operating costs for 1978 amounted to $1,260,000, including the $360,000 of drilling cost mentioned above. Oil production during 1978 totaled 2.88 million barrels, of which all but 288,000 barrels were sold during the year.

Instructions Prepare journal entries to record the transactions of 1977 and 1978, including the setting up of the inventory at December 31, 1978. The inventory valuation should include an appropriate portion of the operating costs of the year, including depreciation and depletion. (Debit Inventory of Oil and credit respective expense accounts for costs allocable to ending inventory.)

12-6 The Anacapa Company is considering purchase of the assets, exclusive of cash, of Santa Cruz Co., a single proprietorship owned by Ken May. Santa Cruz Co. has been a going business for six years and has reported an average net income of $30,000 (excluding income taxes) during this period.

The purchase plan, dated January 2, 1977, calls for a cash payment of $120,000 and a $7\frac{1}{2}$% note payable, due January 2, 1979, with interest payable annually, as payment for the assets, including goodwill but excluding the cash of $15,000, after any necessary adjustments have been made. The Anacapa Company has agreed to assume all the liabilities of Santa Cruz Co. The goodwill is to be determined as four times the average excess earnings over a normal rate of return of $12\frac{1}{2}$% (excluding income taxes) on the present *net tangible assets* (capital less patent and goodwill).

The balance sheet for Santa Cruz Co. on December 31, 1976, follows:

Assets

Cash			$ 15,000
Other current assets			72,000
Plant and equipment:			
Land		$ 42,000	
Buildings	$146,400		
Less: Accumulated depreciation	37,800	108,600	
Machinery	$114,000		
Less: Accumulated depreciation	77,400	36,600	
Equipment	$ 72,000		
Less: Accumulated depreciation	40,200	31,800	219,000
Patent			63,000
Goodwill			12,000
Total assets			$381,000

Liabilities & Owner's Equity

Current liabilities		$ 61,500
Long-term liabilities:		
Mortgage note payable, $6\frac{1}{2}$%		110,100
Ken May, capital		209,400
Total liabilities & owner's equity		$381,000

The goodwill was recorded in the accounts three years ago when May decided that the increasing profitability of his business should be recognized. The patent appears at original cost; it was acquired by purchase six years ago from a competitor who had recorded amortization for two years on the basis of its legal life. The patent is considered to be very valuable to the business and should have a useful life equal to its legal life (15 years from date May acquired it).

Instructions

a Prepare any adjusting entries needed in the accounts of Santa Cruz Co. as a preliminary step toward carrying out the sale agreement.

b Determine the amount to be paid by Anacapa Company for goodwill after considering the effects of the entries in a.

c Prepare the entry or entries in the accounts of Santa Cruz Co. to record the sale to Anacapa Company.

d Prepare the entry or entries on Anacapa Company's books to record the purchase of assets (including the goodwill as determined above) and the assumption of liabilities of the Santa Cruz Co. The Anacapa Company records the assets acquired net of accumulated depreciation.

12-7 Hemet Motors on January 1, 1977, purchased a tract of land as a site for construction of a new plant. Two old buildings in poor condition were already standing on the newly acquired site, but Hemet Motors had no intention of using them. The old buildings were torn down and construction of a new plant was begun at once. All expenditures relating to the new plant were charged to a single account entitled Land and Buildings.

Construction of the new plant was completed on November 30, 1977, and regular production operations were begun in the new facilities on December 1, 1977. The balance in the Land and Buildings account at the end of the year was $1,092,000, determined as shown on page 438.

Land and Buildings

Debit entries:

Cost of land and old buildings purchased as site for construction of new plant (appraised value of old buildings, $48,000)	$ 203,400
Legal fees involved in securing title to property	360
Cost of demolishing old buildings	15,240
Surveying and grading costs	16,800
Contract price of new plant building, $558,000, paid for by delivery to contractor of $576,000 par value of United States government bonds, which had cost the Hemet Motors $588,000 and had a market value at date of delivery to contractor of $558,000	588,000
Salary paid R. Jones, plant engineer, assigned to supervise construction of new plant (Jan. 1 to Nov. 30)	14,400
Paving of plant parking lot	8,400
Cost of machinery badly damaged by fire while awaiting installation in new building. Sold as scrap. Not insured	48,000
Machinery for new plant, including units to replace those damaged by fire	144,000
Cost of installing machinery in new plant	7,200
Landscaping of grounds	4,800
Office equipment	28,800
Rent for December on old plant. Vacated on Nov. 30; lease expired Dec. 12	2,400
Retaining walls and fences	16,800
Payment to architect for plans and for services during construction	22,800
Insurance on new building during construction	2,400
Repairs to building damaged by earthquake on Dec. 20 (not insured)	4,200
Total debits	$1,128,000

Credit entries:

Proceeds from sale of materials from old buildings demolished	$12,000	
Proceeds from sale of machinery damaged by fire	24,000	
Total credits		36,000
Balance, Dec. 31, 1977		$1,092,000

Information for use in computing depreciation follows:

Asset	Useful Life, Years	Residual Value, %
Building	20	10
Land improvements	20	–0–
Machinery	15	10
Office equipment	10	10

Instructions

a Reclassify the items in the Land and Buildings account to the proper ledger accounts. This reclassification may conveniently be made on an analytical working paper with the following column headings:

				Other Accounts	
Entries to Account	Land and Buildings	Land	Building	Title	Amount

b Prepare a depreciation schedule showing the fractional-year depreciation for 1977 (straight-line method) for each type of depreciable asset.

Asset	Date of Completion	Cost	Residual Value (10%)	Amount to Be Depreciated	Useful Life, Months	Depreciation Expense for 1977 (1 mo.)

BUSINESS DECISION PROBLEM 12

Samuel Slater is interested in buying a manufacturing business and has located two similar companies being offered for sale. Both companies began operations three years ago, each with invested capital of $300,000. A considerable part of the assets in each company is represented by a building with an original cost of $100,000 and an estimated life of 40 years, and by machinery with an original cost of $100,000 and an estimated life of 20 years. Residual value is negligible.

Alpha Company uses straight-line depreciation and Beta Company uses fixed-percentage-on-declining-balance depreciation (double the straight-line rate). In all other respects the accounting policies of the two companies are quite similar. Neither company has borrowed from banks or incurred any indebtedness other than normal trade payables. The nature of products and other characteristics of operations are much the same for the two companies.

Audited financial statements for the three years show net income as follows:

Year	Alpha Company	Beta Company
1	$21,000	$20,000
2	23,100	22,100
3	25,400	24,300

Slater asks your advice as to which company he should buy. They are offered for sale at approximately the same price, and he is inclined to choose Alpha Company because of its consistently higher earnings. On the other hand, he is impressed with the fact that Beta Company has more cash and a stronger working capital position. The audited financial statements show that withdrawals by the two owners have been approximately equal during the three-year life of the two companies.

Instructions
a Compute the depreciation recorded by each company in the first three years. Round off depreciation expense for each year to the nearest dollar.
b Write a memorandum to Slater advising him as to which company in your judgment represents the more promising purchase. Give specific reasons to support your recommendation.

THIRTEEN

BONDS PAYABLE LEASES AND OTHER LIABILITIES

One of the most important functions of management is providing the funds required to operate the business. Several alternatives are generally available in meeting the temporary and the more permanent cash and working capital needs of a business. Management evaluates the cost and availability of each form of financing and selects the type most advantageous to the company and to its stockholders.

Inventories needed to meet seasonal peaks of activity may be obtained on account from trade creditors. Accounts payable, however, seldom constitute a sufficient source. Cash needed for seasonal peaks of activity may be obtained through borrowing from banks. For example, a six-month bank loan might be arranged in order to buy merchandise for the peak selling season. The sale of the merchandise would provide cash with which to repay the bank loan.

If funds are needed for long-term purposes such as the construction of a new factory building, the borrowing may take the form of long-term mortgage notes or bonds. This will allow time for the increased earnings from the new plant facilities to be used in retiring the debt. A small business in need of permanent financing will often issue a long-term note secured by a mortgage on its plant assets; a large corporation in need of permanent financing will probably consider the issuance of bonds or additional shares of capital stock.

BONDS PAYABLE

A corporation may obtain money for a long-term purpose, such as construction of a new plant, by issuing long-term mortgage notes or bonds payable. Usually the amount of money needed is greater than any single lender can supply. In this case the corporation may sell bonds to the investing public, thus splitting the loan into a great many units, usually of $1,000 each. An example of corporation bonds is the 8% sinking fund debentures of The Singer Company due January 15, 1999, by which The Singer Company borrowed $100 million.

Characteristics of a bond

A bondholder is a creditor of the corporation; a stockholder is an owner. From the viewpoint of the issuing corporation, bonds payable constitute a long-term liability. Throughout the life of this liability the corporation makes semiannual payments of interest to the bondholder for the use of his money. These interest payments constitute an expense to the corporation and are deducted from revenue in arriving at net income.

Formal approval of the board of directors and of the stockholders is usually required before bonds can be issued. The contract between the corporation and the *trustee* (usually a bank) representing the bondholders may place some limitation on the payment of dividends to stockholders during the life of the bonds. For example, dividends may be permitted only when working capital is above specified amounts.

Of course, in the event that the corporation encounters financial difficulties and is unable to make the required payments of interest or principal, the bondholders may foreclose on the pledged assets, but this is a slow and complicated procedure which bondholders look upon only as a last-ditch alternative. When investing in a bond, the bondholder hopes and expects to receive all payments promptly without the need for taking any legal action.

Not all bonds are secured by the pledge of specific assets. An unsecured bond is called a *debenture bond;* its value rests upon the general credit of the corporation. A debenture bond issued by a very large and strong corporation may have a higher investment rating than a secured bond issued by a corporation in less satisfactory financial condition.

Some bonds have a single fixed maturity date for the entire issue. Other bond issues, called *serial bonds,* provide for varying maturity dates to lessen the problem of accumulating cash for payment. For example, serial bonds in the amount of $10 million issued in 1975 might call for $1 million of bonds to mature in 1985, and an additional $1 million to become due in each of the succeeding nine years. Almost all bonds are *callable,* which means that the corporation has the right to pay off the bonds in advance of the scheduled maturity date. The call price is usually somewhat higher than the face value of the bonds.

As an additional attraction to investors, corporations sometimes include a conversion privilege in the bond indenture. A *convertible bond* is one which may be exchanged for common stock at the option of the bondholder. The advantages to the investor of the conversion feature in the event of increased earnings for the company were described in Chapter 7 with regard to convertible preferred stock.

REGISTERED BONDS AND COUPON BONDS Most corporation bonds issued in recent years have been *registered* bonds; that is, the name of the owner is registered with the issuing corporation. Payment of interest is made by semiannual checks mailed to the registered owner. *Coupon* bonds were more popular some years ago and many are still outstanding. Coupon bonds have interest coupons attached; each six months during the life of the bond one of these coupons becomes due. The bondholder detaches the coupon and deposits it with his bank for collection.

TRANSFERABILITY OF BONDS Corporation bonds, like capital stocks, are traded daily on organized security exchanges. The holder of a 25-year bond need not wait 25 years to convert his investment into cash. By placing a telephone call to a broker, he may sell his bond within a matter of minutes at the going market price. This quality of liquidity is one of the most attractive features of an investment in corporation bonds.

QUOTATIONS FOR BONDS Corporate bond prices are quoted at a given amount per $100 of face value. For example, assume that a bond of $1,000 face amount (par value) is quoted at 106. The total price for the bond is 10 times 106, or $1,060. Market quotations for corporate bonds use an eighth of a dollar as the minimum variation. The following line from the financial page of a daily newspaper summarizes the previous day's trading in the bonds of Sears, Roebuck and Co.

	Bonds	Sales	High	Low	Close	Net Change
What is the market value of this bond?	Sears R 4¾s 83	66	80	79⅛	79½	−1

This line of condensed information indicates that 66 of Sears, Roebuck and Co.'s 4¾%, $1,000 bonds maturing in 1983 were traded. The highest price is reported as 80, or $800 for a bond of $1,000 face value. The lowest price was 79⅛, or $791.25 for a $1,000 bond. The closing price (last sale of the day) was 79½, or $795. This was one point below the closing price of the previous day, a decrease of $10 in the price of a $1,000 bond.

Effect of bond financing on holders of capital stock

Interest payments on bonds payable are deductible as an expense in determining the income subject to corporation income tax, but dividends paid on capital stock are not. High tax rates on corporate earnings thus encourage the use of bonds to obtain long-term capital.

Assume that a growing and profitable corporation with 100,000 shares of capital stock outstanding is in need of $10 million cash to finance a new plant. The management is considering whether to issue an additional 100,000 shares of stock or to issue 8% bonds. Assume also that after acquisition of the new plant, the annual earnings of the corporation, before deducting interest expense or income taxes, will amount to $2 million. From the viewpoint of the stockholders, which financing plan is preferable? The following schedule shows the earnings per share of capital stock under the two alternative methods of financing:

	If Capital Stock Is Issued	If 8% Bonds Are Issued
Which financing plan is better? Annual earnings before bond interest and income taxes	$2,000,000	$2,000,000
Less: Interest on bonds (8% of $10,000,000)		800,000
Earnings before income taxes	$2,000,000	$1,200,000
Less: Income taxes (assume 50% rate)	1,000,000	600,000
Net income	$1,000,000	$ 600,000
Number of shares of capital stock outstanding	200,000	100,000
Earnings per share of capital stock	$5.00	$6.00

Financing through issuance of additional capital stock rather than issuance of bonds saves $400,000 (after taxes) but results in *lower earnings per share* because of the *dilution* caused by doubling the number of shares outstanding.

The use of borrowed capital by business firms is referred to as *trading on the equity;* this concept is discussed further in Chapter 16.

Management planning of the bond issue

A corporation wishing to borrow money by issuing bonds faces months of preliminary work. Decisions must be made on such points as the amount to be borrowed, the interest rate to be offered, the conversion privilege, if any, the maturity date, and the property to be pledged, if any.

In forecasting the company's cash position for future periods, consideration must be given to the new requirement of semiannual bond interest payments as well as to the long-range problem of accumulating the cash required to pay the bonds at maturity. If the borrowed funds are to be invested in new plant facilities, will this expansion produce an increase in the cash inflow sufficient to meet the interest payments? If the bond issue includes a call provision, the company may plan to call in bonds in small amounts each year as cash becomes available. Perhaps the bond issue should be of the convertible variety; this feature might attract investors even though the interest rate were set at a relatively low level. In addition, if the bonds are convertible, the company may not have to accumulate cash for repayment of the entire issue. Effective long-range planning of the company's financial needs will greatly reduce the cost of securing capital and will leave the door open to issuing additional securities in the future on advantageous terms.

AUTHORIZATION OF A BOND ISSUE After the board of directors has decided upon the details of a bond issue, the proposal is presented to stockholders for their approval. Once this approval has been gained, the *deed of trust* is drawn and the bonds are printed. If the company's present financial requirements are for less than the amount of bonds authorized, only a portion of the bonds may be issued at this time.

No formal entry in the accounts is required for the act of authorization; however, a memorandum notation may be made in the Bonds Payable ledger account indicating the total amount of bonds authorized. The total authorized amount of a bond issue should be disclosed in the balance sheet.

THE ROLE OF THE UNDERWRITER IN MARKETING A BOND ISSUE An investment banker or underwriter is usually employed to market a bond issue, just as in the case of capital stock. The corporation turns the entire bond issue over to the underwriter at a specified price (say, 98); the underwriter sells the bonds to the public at a slightly higher price (say, 100). By this arrangement the corporation is assured of receiving the entire proceeds on a specified date. The calculation of the bond discount or bond premium is based on the net amount which the issuing corporation receives from the underwriter, not on the price paid by investors for the bonds.

RECORDING THE ISSUANCE OF BONDS To illustrate the entries for issuance of bonds, assume that Wells Corporation was authorized on June 1, 1976, to issue $1 million of 20-year, 9% bonds. All the bonds in the issue bear the June 1, 1976, date, and interest is computed from this date. Eighty percent of the bonds were issued on June 1 at par value, and the following entry was made:

Issuance of bonds at par value	*Cash*	*800,000*
	9% Bonds Payable	*800,000*
	To record issuance of 9%, 20-year bonds at par.	

The balance sheet should disclose all significant features of each bond issue, including exact title, interest rate, maturity date, and amounts authorized and issued. Thus, in our example, the fact that only 80% of the authorized bonds have been issued is significant; issuance of the remaining 20% would materially change the ratio of total debt to stockholders' equity and also the relationship between bond interest expense and the company's earnings.

RECORDING THE ISSUANCE OF BONDS BETWEEN INTEREST DATES The semiannual interest dates (such as January 15 and July 15, or April 1 and October 1) are printed on the bond certificates. However, bonds are often issued between the specified interest dates. The investor is then required to pay the interest accrued to date of issuance in addition to the stated price of the bond. This practice enables the corporation to pay a full six month's interest on all bonds outstanding at the semiannual interest payment date. The accrued interest collected from an investor purchasing a bond between interest payment dates is thus returned to him on the next interest payment date. To illustrate, let us modify our previous example for Wells Corporation and assume that the $800,000 face value of 9% bonds were issued at par and accrued interest, *two months after the interest date printed on the bonds.* The entry will be:

Bonds	*Cash*	*812,000*	
issued	*9% Bonds Payable*		*800,000*
between			
interest	*Bond Interest Payable*		*12,000*
dates	*Issued $800,000 face value of 9%, 20-year bonds at 100 plus*		
	accrued interest for two months.		

Four months later on the regular semiannual interest payment date, a full six months' interest ($45 per each $1,000 bond) will be paid to all bondholders, regardless of when they purchased their bonds. The entry for the semiannual interest payment is illustrated below:

What is the	*Bond Interest Payable*	*12,000*	
net interest	*Bond Interest Expense*	*24,000*	
expense?	*Cash*		*36,000*
	Paid semiannual interest on $800,000 face value of 9% bonds.		

Now consider these interest transactions from the standpoint of the investor. He paid for two months' accrued interest at the time of purchasing the bonds, and he received a check for six months' interest after holding the bonds for only four months. He has, therefore, been reimbursed properly for the use of his money for four months.

Bond discount

A corporation wishing to borrow money by issuing bonds must pay the going market rate of interest. On any given date, the going market rate of interest is in reality a whole schedule of rates corresponding to the financial strength of different borrowers. Since market rates of interest are constantly fluctuating, it must be expected that the *contract rate* of interest printed on the bonds will seldom agree with the *market rate* of interest at the date the bonds are issued.

If the interest rate carried by an issue of bonds is lower than the market rate for bonds of this grade, the bonds can be sold only at a discount. For example, assume that a corporation issues $1 million face value of 7%, 10-year bonds. Each bond will pay the holder $70 interest (7% × $1,000) each year, consisting of two semiannual payments of $35 each. If the market rate of interest were exactly 7%, the bonds would sell at par, but if the market rate of interest is above 7%, no one will be willing to pay $1,000 for a bond which will return only $70 a year. The price at which the bonds can be sold will, therefore, be less than par. Assuming that the best price obtainable is 98 ($980 for each $1,000 bond), the issuance of the bonds will be recorded by the following entry:

Issuing bonds at discount	*Cash*	*980,000*	
	Discount on Bonds Payable	*20,000*	
	Bonds Payable		*1,000,000*
	Issued $1,000,000 face value of 7%, 10-year bonds at 98.		

BOND DISCOUNT AS PART OF THE COST OF BORROWING Whenever bonds are issued at a discount, *the total interest cost over the life of the bonds is equal to the amount of the discount plus the regular cash interest payments.*

For the $1 million bond issue in our example, the total interest cost over the life of the bonds is $720,000, of which $700,000 represents 20 semiannual cash payments of interest and $20,000 represents the discount on the issue. On a yearly basis, total interest expense is $72,000, consisting of $70,000 paid in cash and $2,000 of the bond discount. This analysis is illustrated by the following tabulation of the total amounts of cash received and paid out by the corporation over the life of the bond issue.

Cash received and paid over life of bond issue	*Cash to be paid by the borrowing corporation:*	
	Face value of bonds at maturity	*$1,000,000*
	Interest ($70,000 a year for 10 years)..................	*700,000*
	Total cash to be paid	*$1,700,000*
	Cash received:	
	From issuance of bonds at a discount	*980,000*
	Excess of cash to be paid over cash received (total bond interest expense)	*$ 720,000*
	Yearly bond interest expense ($720,000 ÷ 10)..............	*$ 72,000*

In our example the Discount on Bonds Payable account has an initial debit balance of $20,000; each year one-tenth of this amount, or $2,000, will be amortized to Bond Interest Expense. Amortizing bond discount means transferring a portion of the discount to Bond Interest Expense each accounting period during the life of the bonds. Assuming that the interest payment dates are June 30 and December 31, the entries to be made each six months to record bond interest expense are as follows:

Payment of bond interest and amortization of discount	Bond Interest Expense	35,000	
	Cash		35,000

Paid semiannual interest on $1,000,000 of 7%, 10-year bonds.

	Bond Interest Expense	1,000	
	Discount on Bonds Payable		1,000

Amortized $\frac{1}{20}$ of discount on 10-year bond issue.

The above entries serve to charge Bond Interest Expense with $36,000 each six months, or a total of $72,000 a year. Bond interest expense will be uniform throughout the 10-year life of the bond issue, and the Discount on Bonds Payable account will be completely written off by the end of the tenth year. As an alternative, some companies choose to record amortization of bond discount or premium only at the end of the year rather than at each interest-payment date.

Bond premium

Bonds will sell above par if the contract rate of interest specified on the bonds is higher than the current market rate for bonds of this grade. Let us now change our basic illustration by assuming that the $1 million issue of 7%, 10-year bonds is sold at a price of 102 ($1,020 for each $1,000 bond). The entry is shown below:

Issuing bonds at premium	Cash	1,020,000	
	Bonds Payable		1,000,000
	Premium on Bonds Payable		20,000

Issued $1,000,000 face value of 7%, 10-year bonds at price of 102.

The amount received from issuance of the bonds is $20,000 greater than the amount which must be repaid at maturity. This $20,000 premium is not a gain but is to be offset against the periodic interest payments in determining the net cost of borrowing. Whenever bonds are issued at a premium, *the total interest cost over the life of the bonds is equal to the regular cash interest payments minus the amount of the premium.* In our example, the total interest cost over the life of the bonds is computed as $700,000 of cash interest payments minus $20,000 of premium amortized, or a net borrowing cost of $680,000. The annual interest expense will be $68,000, consisting of $70,000 paid in cash less an offsetting $2,000 transferred from the Premium on Bonds Payable account to the credit side of the Bond Interest Expense account. The semiannual entries on June 30 and December 31 to record the payment of bond interest and amortization of bond premium are as follows:

Payment of bond interest and amortization of bond premium	Bond Interest Expense	35,000	
	Cash		35,000

Paid semiannual interest on $1,000,000 of 7%, 10-year bonds.

Premium on Bonds Payable *1,000*
      Bond Interest Expense *1,000*
Amortized $\frac{1}{20}$ of premium on 10-year bond issue.

Year-end adjustments for bond interest expense

In the preceding illustration, it was assumed that one of the semiannual dates for payment of bond interest coincided with the end of the company's accounting year. In most cases, however, the semiannual interest payment dates will fall during an accounting period rather than on the last day of the year.

For purposes of illustration, assume that $1 million of 8%, 10-year bonds are issued at a price of 97 on October 1, Year 1. Interest payment dates are April 1 and October 1. The total discount to be amortized amounts to $30,000, or $1,500 in each six-month interest period. The company keeps its accounts on a calendar-year basis; consequently, the adjusting entries shown below will be necessary at December 31 for the accrued interest and the amortization of discount applicable to the three-month period since the bonds were issued.

Adjusting bond interest expense at year-end

Bond Interest Expense *20,000*
      Bond Interest Payable *20,000*
To record interest accrued on bonds for three-month period from Oct. 1 to Dec. 31 ($1,000,000 × .08 × $\frac{3}{12}$).

Bond Interest Expense *750*
      Discount on Bonds Payable *750*
To record amortization of bond discount for three-month period from Oct. 1 to Dec. 31 ($30,000 × $\frac{3}{120}$ = $750).

The effect of these year-end adjusting entries is to make the Bond Interest Expense account show the proper interest expense ($20,750) for the three months that the bonds were outstanding (October 1 to December 31) during Year 1. The Bond Interest Expense account will be closed to the Income Summary account; the Bond Interest Payable account will remain in the accounting records as a liability until the next regular interest payment date (April 1, Year 2), at which time $20,000 of the interest payment will be charged to Bond Interest Payable and the other $20,000 to Bond Interest Expense.

If the above bonds had been issued at a premium, similar entries would be made at the end of the period for any accrued interest and for amortization of premium for the fractional period from October 1 to December 31.

Bond discount and premium in the balance sheet

In the preceding example an 8%, 10-year bond issue of $1 million was issued for $970,000, and bond discount of $30,000 was recorded. One year later, on October 1, Year 2, the bond discount would have been amortized to the extent of $3,000 and the *net liability* would have risen accordingly in the balance sheet as illustrated below:

Bond discount in the balance sheet

Long-term liabilities:

8% bonds payable, due Oct. 1, Year 11	*$1,000,000*	
Less: Discount on bonds payable	*27,000*	*$973,000*

At the maturity of the bond issue 10 years after issuance, the corporation must pay $1 million, but at the time of issuing bonds, the "present value" of this debt is $970,000. As the bond discount is amortized, the *net amount* of the liability shown on each succeeding balance sheet will be $3,000 greater than for the preceding year. At the maturity date of the bonds, the valuation account, Discount on Bonds Payable, will have been reduced to zero and the liability will have risen to $1 million.

Parallel reasoning applies to bond premium, which is logically shown in the balance sheet as an addition to bonds payable. As the premium is amortized, the net amount of the liability is reduced year by year, until, at the maturity date of the bonds, the premium will have been completely eliminated and the liability will stand at the face amount of the bond issue.

Retirement of bonds payable

Bonds are sometimes retired before the scheduled maturity date. Most bond issues contain a call provision, permitting the corporation to redeem the bonds by paying a specified price, usually a few points above par. Even without a call provision, the corporation may retire its bonds before maturity by purchasing them in the open market. If the bonds can be purchased by the issuing corporation at less than their carrying value, a gain is realized on the retirement of the debt. If the bonds are reacquired by the issuing corporation at a price in excess of their carrying value, a loss must be recognized. *Carrying value* is equal to the face value of the bonds plus any unamortized premium or minus any unamortized discount.

For example, assume that the Briggs Corporation has outstanding a $1 million bond issue and there is unamortized premium on the books in the amount of $20,000. The bonds are callable at 105 and the company exercises the call provision on 100 of the bonds, or 10% of the issue. The entry would be as follows:

Bonds called at price above carrying value

Bonds Payable	*100,000*	
Premium on Bonds Payable	*2,000*	
Loss on Retirement of Bonds	*3,000*	
Cash		*105,000*

To record retirement of $100,000 face value of bonds called at 105.

The carrying value of each of the 100 called bonds was $1,020, whereas the call price was $1,050. For each bond called the company incurred a loss of $30, a total loss of $3,000. Note that when 10% of the total issue was called, 10% of the unamortized premium was written off.

By the maturity date of the bonds, the discount or premium will have been completely amortized and the accounting entry to retire the bonds (assuming that interest is paid separately) will consist of a debit to Bonds Payable and a credit to Cash.

One year before the maturity date, the bonds payable may be reclassified from long-term debt to a current liability in the balance sheet if payment is to be made from current assets rather than from a bond sinking fund.

Conversion of bonds payable into common stock

Convertible bonds represent a popular form of financing, particularly during periods when common stock prices are rising. The conversion feature gives the bondholder a potential opportunity to profit from a rise in the market price of the issuing company's common stock despite the fact that he still maintains the status of a creditor. Because of this potential gain, convertible bonds generally carry lower interest rates than nonconvertible bonds.

The conversion ratio is typically set at a price above the current market price of the common stock. For example, if the current market price of the common stock with a par value of $10 per share is $42 per share, the conversion price might be set at $50 per share, thus enabling a holder of a $1,000 par value convertible bond to exchange his bond for 20 shares of common stock.[1] Let us assume that $5 million of such bonds are issued at par, and that some time later when the common stock has risen in price to $60 per share, the holders of 100 bonds decide to convert their bonds into common stock. The conversion transaction would be recorded as follows:

Conversion of bonds into common stock

Convertible Bonds Payable	100,000	
Common Stock, $10 par		20,000
Paid-in Capital in Excess of Par		80,000

To record the conversion of 100 bonds into 2,000 shares of common stock.

No gain or loss is recognized by the issuing corporation upon conversion of bonds; the book value of the bonds is simply assigned to the common stock issued in exchange. If the bonds had been issued at a price above or below par, the unamortized premium or discount relating to the bonds should be written off at the time of conversion in order to assign the carrying value of the bonds to the common stock.

---

[1] $1,000 ÷ $50 conversion price = 20 shares of common stock.

Bond sinking fund

To make a bond issue attractive to investors, corporations may agree to create a sinking fund, exclusively for use in paying the bonds at maturity. A bond sinking fund is created by setting aside a specified amount of cash at regular intervals. The cash is usually deposited with a trustee, who invests it and adds the earnings to the amount of the sinking fund. The periodic deposits of cash plus the earnings on the sinking fund investments should cause the fund to approximately equal the amount of the bond issue by the maturity date. When the bond issue approaches maturity, the trustee sells all the securities in the fund and uses the cash proceeds to pay the holders of the bonds. Any excess cash remaining in the fund will be returned to the corporation by the trustee.

A bond sinking fund is not included in current assets because it is not available for payment of current liabilities. The cash and securities comprising the fund are usually shown as a single amount under Investments, placed just below the current asset section. Interest earned on sinking fund securities constitutes revenue to the corporation.

Mortgages payable

Mortgages are usually payable in equal monthly installments. A portion of each payment represents interest on the unpaid balance of the loan and the remainder of the payment reduces the amount of the unpaid balance (principal). This process is illustrated by the following schedule of payments for a three-month period on a 6.6% mortgage note with an unpaid balance of $100,000 at September 11 of the current year.

	Monthly Payment	Interest for One Month at 6.6% on Unpaid Balance	Reduction in Principal	Unpaid Principal Balance
Monthly *payments* *on a* *mortgage* *note* Sept. 11				$100,000.00
Oct. 11	$1,000.00	$550.00	$450.00	99,550.00
Nov. 11	1,000.00	547.53	452.47	99,097.53
Dec. 11	1,000.00	545.04	454.96	98,642.57

On December 31 of the current year, the portion of the unpaid principal balance of $98,642.57, due within one year, should be classified as a current liability and the remainder as a long-term liability. In addition, the accrued interest for 20 days amounting to $361.69 ($98,642.57 $\times$ 6.6% $\times$ $\frac{20}{360}$) would be included under current liabilities.

LEASES

Most business assets may be purchased or leased. A *lease* is a contract in which the *lessor* gives the *lessee* the right to use an asset in return for periodic rental payments. Accounting for the many forms of lease transactions and the disclosure of lease obligations by lessees are among the most important issues facing accountants today.

Lease obligations

When the lessor gives the lessee the right to use the leased property but retains the usual risks and rewards of ownership, the periodic rentals are recorded as revenue by the lessor and as rental expense by the lessee. Such a contract is known as an *operating lease* and does not require the recognition of a liability in the records of the lessee, other than for any accrued monthly rentals.

When the objectives of the lease contract are to provide financing to the lessee for the eventual purchase of the property and to transfer the usual risks and rewards of ownership to the lessee, the contract is referred to as a *financing lease.* Some financing leases are essentially equivalent to a sale of an asset by the lessor and a purchase of an asset by the lessee. A lease which is equivalent to a sale and purchase should be recorded as an installment sale by the lessor and as a purchase by the lessee. The asset and related liability should be recorded by the lessee at an amount equal to the present value of the future rental payments. The present value is determined by discounting the rental payments at a fair rate of interest. The lessee should depreciate the asset over its estimated useful life rather than over the period of the lease.

Other financing leases are considered to give the lessee a *property right* in the leased asset but are not treated as installment sales and purchases for accounting purposes. Many accountants are of the opinion that such leases call for the recognition (generally referred to as *capitalization*) of both an asset and a liability by the lessee. Proponents of this position argue that a financing lease which is not equivalent to a purchase represents an acquisition of significant property rights by the lessee in exchange for an obligation to make future rental payments. Failure to record these property rights and related obligations, they point out, has the effect of understating both assets and liabilities in the balance sheet. Although the capitalization by lessees of financing leases which are not considered to be equivalent to installment purchases is not currently required, it is probably safe to conclude that continual pressure from security analysts and the Securities and Exchange Commission will result in significant changes in the accounting practices for leases by lessees.

Opinion No. 31 issued by the Accounting Principles Board required the following disclosures relating to leases in notes accompanying the financial statements of the lessee:

1 Total rental expense for each fiscal year (or period)
2 Minimum rental commitments under all noncancelable leases for each of the five succeeding fiscal years, each of the next three five-year periods, and the remainder as a single amount

3 Additional information such as the basis of calculating rental payments, terms of renewal or purchase options, restrictions on dividend payments or on incurring additional debt, and any other information necessary to assess the effect of lease commitments upon the financial position and results of operations[2]

OTHER LIABILITIES

Pension plans

A *pension plan* is a contract between a company and its employees under which the company agrees to pay retirement benefits to eligible employees. An employer company generally provides for the payment of retirement benefits by making payments at regular intervals to an insurance company or some other outside agency. Pension obligations currently accruing are recorded by the employer company as a debit to Pension Expense and as a credit to Cash (or Liability under Pension Plan). When employees retire, the retirement benefits are paid by the insurance company. This type of arrangement is known as a *funded pension plan* and does not create a long-term pension liability in the balance sheet of the employer company.

When a company does not engage an outside agent to administer the pension plan, the entry to record the pension obligation currently accruing calls for a debit to Pension Expense and a credit to Liability under Pension Plan. Payments to retired employees would be recorded by debits to Liability under Pension Plan and credits to Cash. In the balance sheet, the portion of the *unfunded* pension liability expected to be paid currently would be shown as a current liability; the balance of the pension liability would be shown as long-term debt. Occasionally, a company-administered pension fund may be established to accumulate resources for payment of retirement benefits.

Among the more important accounting and reporting problems relating to pension plans are: (1) determining the proper accounting period which should be charged for the pension benefits accruing to employees, (2) measuring the amount of pension expense in the determination of periodic net income, and (3) presenting the significant pension plan information in the financial statements and the accompanying notes. A discussion of these issues is appropriate in advanced accounting courses.[3]

Payroll accounting

Labor costs and related payroll taxes constitute a large and constantly increasing portion of the total costs of operating most business orga-

---

[2] *APB Opinion No. 31,* "Disclosure of Lease Commitments by Lessees," AICPA (New York: 1973), pp. 576–577.
[3] Accounting principles for pension plans are discussed in detail in *Intermediate Accounting* of this series and in *APB Opinion No. 8,* "Accounting for the Cost of Pension Plans," AICPA (New York: 1966).

nizations. In the commercial airlines, for example, labor costs represent over 50% of total operating expenses.

The task of accounting for payroll costs would be an important one simply because of the large amounts involved; however, it is further complicated by the many federal and state laws which require employers to maintain certain specific information in their payroll records not only for the business as a whole but also for each individual employee. Regular reports of total wages and amounts withheld must be filed with government agencies, accompanied by payments of the amounts withheld from employees and payroll taxes levied on the employer.

A distinction must be drawn between *employees* and *independent contractors.* Public accountants, architects, attorneys, and other persons who render services to a business for a fee but are not controlled or directed by the client are not employees but independent contractors, and the amounts paid to them are not subject to payroll taxes.

Deductions from earnings of employees

The take-home pay of most employees is considerably less than the gross earnings. Major factors explaining this difference between the amount earned and the amount received are social security tax, federal income tax withheld, and other deductions discussed below.

SOCIAL SECURITY TAX (FICA) Under the terms of the Social Security Act, qualified workers in covered industries who retire after reaching a specified age receive monthly retirement payments and Medicare benefits. Benefits are also provided for the family of a worker who dies before or after reaching this retirement age. Funds for the operation of this program are obtained through a tax levied under the Federal Insurance Contributions Act, often referred to as FICA tax, or simply as *social security tax.*

Employers are required by the Federal Insurance Contributions Act to withhold a portion of each employee's earnings as a contribution to the social security program. A tax at the same rate is levied against the employer. For illustrative purposes, we shall assume the rate of tax to be 6% on both the employee and the employer of the first $13,200 of wages paid to each employee in each calendar year. The rate and taxable earnings have been increased many times in recent years and probably will continue to be changed in future years.[4] However, these changes do not affect the accounting principles or procedures involved. Consequently, our assumption of a 6% rate and a $13,200 ceiling on the amount of earnings subject to tax is a convenient one, regardless of frequent changes in the rate and the amount of earnings subject to the tax.

[4] In 1974 the rate was 5.85% on the first $13,200 earned by each employee.

INCOME TAX WITHHOLDING The pay-as-you-go system of federal income tax requires employers to withhold a portion of the earnings of their employees. The amount withheld depends upon the amount of the earnings and upon the number of *exemptions* allowed the employee. The employee is entitled to one exemption for himself, and an additional exemption for each person qualifying as a dependent. (More extensive consideration of exemptions and other aspects of federal income taxes is found in Chapter 17.) The government provides withholding tax tables which indicate the amount to withhold for any amount of earnings and any number of exemptions.

The graduated system of withholding is designed to make the amount of tax withheld closely approximate the rates used in computing the individual's tax liability at the end of the year. Since persons in higher income brackets are subject to higher rates of taxation, the withholding rates are correspondingly higher for them.

States and cities which levy income taxes may also require the employer to withhold the tax from employees' earnings; the accounting for such withholdings would be similar to the procedures used for federal income taxes withheld.

OTHER DEDUCTIONS FROM EMPLOYEES' EARNINGS Programs of unemployment compensation insurance are found in every state, but they are generally financed by taxes on employers rather than on employees. In a few states unemployment insurance tax is levied on employees and such tax is withheld by employers from employees' earnings.

In addition to the compulsory deductions for taxes, many other deductions are voluntarily authorized by employees. Union dues and insurance premiums have already been mentioned as examples of payroll deductions. Others include charitable contributions, supplementary retirement programs and pension plans, and repayments of salary advances or other loans.

EMPLOYER'S RESPONSIBILITY FOR AMOUNTS WITHHELD When an employer withholds a portion of an employee's earnings for any reason, he must maintain accounting records which will enable him to file required reports and make designated payments of the amounts withheld. From the employer's viewpoint, most amounts withheld from employees' earnings represent current liabilities. In other words, the employer must pay to the government or some other agency the amounts which he withholds from the employee's earnings.

Payroll records and procedures

Although payroll records and procedures vary greatly according to the number of employees and the extent of automation in processing payroll data, there are fundamental steps common to payroll work in most organizations. One of these steps taken at the end of each pay period is the preparation of a *payroll sheet* showing the names, earnings, and the net amount payable to each employee. When the computation of the payroll sheet has been completed, the next step is to distribute the payroll costs to various expense accounts and to record the expenses and the related liabilities in the ledger. A general journal entry, such as shown below, may be made to bring into the accounts the data summarized on the payroll sheet.

Sales Salaries Expense	*1,200*	
Office Salaries Expense	*800*	
FICA Tax Payable (6% of $2,000)		*120*
Liability for Income Tax Withheld		*320*
Liability for Group Insurance Withheld		*10*
Accrued Payroll		*1,550*

Recording periodic payroll

To record the payroll for the period Jan. 1–Jan. 15.

The two debits to expense accounts indicate that the business has incurred a total salary expense of $2,000; however, only $1,550 of this amount will be paid to the employees on payday. Payment can be made in cash or by check. The payment will be recorded by a debit to Accrued Payroll and a credit to Cash. The remaining $450 (consisting of deductions for taxes and insurance premiums withheld) is lodged in liability accounts. Payment of these liabilities will be made at various later dates.

An earnings record must be maintained for each employee showing gross earnings, withholdings, and other information required by government agencies and by management.

WITHHOLDING STATEMENT By January 31 each year, employers are required to furnish every employee with a *withholding statement (Form W-2).* This form shows the gross earnings for the preceding calendar year, and the amounts withheld for FICA tax and income tax. The employer sends one copy of this form to the Director of Internal Revenue (possibly one copy to the state) and also gives two copies to the employee. When the employee files his federal income tax return, he must attach a copy of the withholding statement.

Payroll taxes on the employer

The discussion of payroll taxes up to this point has dealt with taxes levied on the employee and withheld from his pay. From the viewpoint of the employer, such taxes are significant because he must account for and remit the amounts withheld to the appropriate government agencies. Payroll taxes are also levied on the *employer;* these taxes are expenses of the business and are recorded by debits to expense accounts, just as in the case of property taxes or license fees for doing business.

SOCIAL SECURITY (FICA) TAX The employer is taxed to help finance the social security program. The tax is figured at the same rate and on the same amount of earnings used to compute FICA tax on employees. (In all problems and illustrations in this book, the tax is assumed to be 6% on the first $13,200 of gross earnings by each employee in each calendar year.)

FEDERAL UNEMPLOYMENT INSURANCE TAX Unemployment insurance is a separate element of the national social security program designed to offer temporary relief to unemployed persons. The federal unemployment tax is levied on employers only and is not deducted from the wages of employees. The tax (assumed for our purposes to be 3.2%) applies to approximately the same classes of employment as the FICA tax. The federal unemployment tax currently applies to the first $4,200 of wages paid to each employee during the calendar year. The federal law provides that the employer may take a credit against his federal tax (not in excess of 2.7% of the wages) for amounts paid by him into state unemployment funds. As a result, an employer may be subject to a *federal* tax of only 0.5% on wages up to $4,200 per employee.

STATE UNEMPLOYMENT COMPENSATION TAX All the states participate in the federal-state unemployment insurance program. Although the state laws vary somewhat as to types of covered employment, the usual rate of tax is 2.7% of the first $4,200 of earnings by each employee during a calendar year. Most states have a *merit-rating plan* which causes changes in the tax rate for employers reflecting their record of stability of employment.

ACCOUNTING ENTRY FOR EMPLOYER'S PAYROLL TAXES The entry to record the employer's payroll taxes is usually made at the same time the payroll is recorded. For the payroll illustrated on page 456, the entry for all three of the payroll taxes on the employer is as follows:

Payroll	Payroll Taxes Expense	*184*
taxes on	FICA Tax Payable (6% of $2,000)	*120*
employer	State Unemployment Tax Payable (2.7% of $2,000)	*54*
	Federal Unemployment Tax Payable (0.5% of $2,000)	*10*
	To record payroll taxes on employer for period ended January 15.	

Thus the total payroll expense for the employer is $2,184 which consists of wages of $2,000 and payroll taxes of $184.

ACCRUAL OF PAYROLL TAXES AT YEAR–END The payroll taxes levied against an employer become a legal liability when wages are actually paid, rather than at the time the services by employees are rendered. If the wages earned in a given accounting period are paid in the same period, the payroll tax expense is clearly applicable to that period. However, at year-end, most businesses make an adjusting entry to accrue wages earned by employees but not payable until the following period. Should the related payroll taxes on the employer also be accrued? Logically, both wages and taxes on such wages are an expense of the period in which the wages are earned and should therefore be accrued. However, as a practical matter, many businesses do not accrue payroll taxes because legally the liability does not come into being until the following year when the wages are paid. In determining income subject to federal income tax, the legal concept prevails, and payroll taxes cannot be deducted until the period in which paid.

PRESENTATION OF PAYROLL TAXES IN THE FINANCIAL STATEMENTS
The payroll taxes levied on the employer and the taxes withheld from employees are current liabilities of the business until payment to the government is made. The following accounts are, therefore, classified in the balance sheet as current liabilities: FICA Tax Payable, Federal Unemployment Tax Payable, State Unemployment Tax Payable, and Liability for Income Tax Withheld. In many localities, additional liabilities may exist because of state and city income taxes.

Payroll Taxes Expense appears in the income statement: it may be apportioned between selling expenses and general expenses on the basis of the amount of payroll originating in each functional division. Thus, payroll taxes on salaries of salesmen are classified as a selling expense, and payroll taxes on office salaries are classified as a general expense.

PAYMENT OF PAYROLL TAXES A business must use the calendar year in accounting for payroll taxes, even though it uses a fiscal year for its financial statements and its income tax returns. Four times a year, the employer is required to report to the government the amounts withheld from employees' pay for income tax and FICA tax. The FICA tax on the employer is also reported on the same tax form. These reports are made during the month following the close of each quarter of the year. If the amounts withheld from employees plus payroll taxes on the employer are significant in amount, they must be deposited at frequent intervals with a Federal Reserve bank or a designated commercial bank.

The employer must file his federal unemployment tax return by January 31 of each year for the preceding calendar year. Most states require employers to file tax returns and to make payment of the state unemployment compensation tax on a quarterly basis.

Other current liabilities

In addition to the current liabilities discussed in this chapter, a wide variety of short-term obligations may be found in the balance sheet of a typical business unit. Some of these, such as accounts payable, dividends payable, and deferred revenue were discussed in earlier chapters. Other examples of current liabilities include advances from customers, corporation income taxes payable, liabilities for services received by the business before the end of the period but not billed until the following period, and *estimated liabilities.*

As stated earlier, an estimated liability is one known to exist, but for which the dollar amount is uncertain. A common example is that of a company which issues coupons redeemable in merchandise. The company's experience may show that only a portion of the coupons will ever be redeemed. The liability represented by the outstanding coupons must be estimated at the balance sheet date by use of a percentage based on prior experience as to the portion of outstanding coupons which will eventually be presented for redemption.

A distinction should be made between an estimated liability and a *contingent liability.* A contingent liability may or may not become an actual liability, depending on the outcome of some future event, such as a pending lawsuit or possible additional income tax assessments. Contingent liabilities should be fully disclosed in the balance sheet or in the notes accompanying the financial statements.

DEMONSTRATION PROBLEM

The balance sheet for the Colorado Corporation on December 31, Year 6, included the following liabilities:

Current liabilities:		
Notes payable, due June 30, Year 7	$ 100,000	
Less: Discount on notes payable	3,750	$ 96,250
Accounts payable		141,000
Income taxes payable, due March 15, Year 7		85,000
Accrued liabilities relating to payroll:		
FICA tax payable	$ 1,500	
Liability for income tax withheld	4,200	
State unemployment tax payable	360	
Federal unemployment tax payable	1,400	7,460
Total current liabilities		$ 329,710
Long-term liabilities:		
8% bonds payable, due Jan. 1, Year 15	$5,000,000	
Less: Discount on bonds payable	72,000	4,928,000
Total liabilities		$5,257,710

During January of Year 7, the corporation completed the following transactions relating to liabilities:

(1) Borrowed $50,000 from City Bank on January 11, Year 7, and issued a 6½%, 6-month promissory note for $50,000 to the bank.

(2) Cash disbursements during January include payments to merchandise creditors, $128,000, and to liquidate the accrued liabilities relating to payroll, $7,460.

(3) Purchases of merchandise on account during January amounted to $112,500. The company uses a periodic inventory system.

(4) The payroll for January is summarized below:

Wages Expense	FICA Tax Withheld	Income Tax Withheld	Take-home Pay	Payroll Taxes on Employer
$65,000	$3,900	$5,050	$56,050	$5,980

Payroll taxes on the employer consist of FICA tax, 6%; state unemployment tax, 2.7%; federal unemployment tax, 0.5%. Employees were paid on January 31; however, none of the taxes relating to the January payroll has been remitted to governmental agencies.

(5) On January 1, Year 7, the 8% bonds were called at a price of 102 and new 6%, 20-year bonds were issued on January 10 as follows:

6% bonds—$10,000,000 @ 101½	$10,150,000
Add: Interest from Jan. 1 to Jan. 10 (nine days)	15,000
Proceeds on issuance of bonds	$10,165,000

The face value of the 6% bonds ($10,000,000), the premium on bonds payable ($150,000), and the bond interest payable ($15,000) should be recorded in three separate liability accounts. The 6% bonds mature on January 1, Year 27, and call for the payment of interest at January 1 and July 1 of each year.

(6) The corporation has 250,000 shares of $10 par value capital stock outstanding. On January 5, Year 7, a cash dividend of 30 cents a share was declared, payable on February 10, Year 7, to holders of record on January 28, Year 7.

Instructions

a Prepare the journal entries to record the foregoing transactions.

b Prepare the adjusting entries required to bring the accounts up to date at January 31, Year 7. Assume that the premium on bonds payable is amortized for one month as an adjustment to Bond Interest Expense. Compute accrued interest on bonds payable to nearest dollar.

c Prepare the liabilities section of the balance sheet at January 31, Year 7.

SOLUTION TO DEMONSTRATION PROBLEM

a (1) Cash 50,000
        Notes Payable 50,000
        Borrowed $50,000 from City Bank on Jan. 11,
        Year 7. Issued a 6-month, 6½% note payable.

(2) Accounts Payable	**128,000**	
FICA Tax Payable	1,500	
Liability for Income Tax Withheld	4,200	
State Unemployment Tax Payable	360	
Federal Unemployment Tax Payable	1,400	
Cash		135,460

To record cash disbursements during January in
payment for current liabilities.

(3) Purchases	**112,500**	
Accounts Payable		112,500

To record purchase of merchandise on account
during January.

(4) Wages Expense	**65,000**	
FICA Tax Payable		3,900
Liability for Income Tax Withheld		5,050
Accrued Payroll		56,050

To record payroll for January.

Accrued Payroll	56,050	
Cash		56,050

To record payment of wages for January.

Payroll Taxes Expense	5,980	
FICA Tax Payable		3,900
State Unemployment Tax Payable		1,755
Federal Unemployment Tax Payable		325

To record payroll taxes on employer for January.

(5) 8% Bonds Payable	**5,000,000**	
Loss on Retirement of Bonds	172,000	
Discount on Bonds Payable		72,000
Cash		5,100,000

To record retirement of bonds at 102 on Jan. 1,
Year 7.

Cash	10,165,000	
6% Bonds Payable		10,000,000
Premium on Bonds Payable		150,000
Bond Interest Payable		15,000

To record issuance of bonds on Jan. 10, Year 7
at $101\frac{1}{2}$ plus accrued interest for nine days.

(6) Dividends	**75,000**	
Dividends Payable		75,000

To record declaration of a cash dividend of 30
cents a share on 250,000 shares of capital stock.
The dividend is payable on Feb. 10, Year 7, to holders of record on Jan. 28, Year 7.

b Adjusting entries:

Interest Expense	625	
Discount on Notes Payable		625

To record January interest on $100,000 note payable maturing June 30, Year 7: $3,750 × $\frac{1}{6}$, or $625.

Interest Expense	181	
Interest Payable		181

To record accrued interest on $50,000, $6\frac{1}{2}$% note from Jan. 11 to Jan. 31: $50,000 × $\frac{20}{360}$ × $6\frac{1}{2}$% or $181.

Bond Interest Expense	34,375	
Premium on Bonds Payable ($150,000 × $\frac{1}{240}$)	625	
Bond Interest Payable		35,000

To record accrued interest and amortization of premium on bonds payable for January, $50,000 ($10,000,000 × 6% for one month, less $15,000 recorded on Jan. 10 when bonds were issued.)

c Liabilities section of the balance sheet at Jan. 31, Year 7:

Current liabilities:

Notes payable	$ 150,000	
Less: Discount on notes payable	3,125	$ 146,875
Accounts payable		125,500
Income taxes payable, due March 15, Year 7		85,000
Dividends payable		75,000
Accrued liabilities:		
Liability for income tax withheld and payroll		
taxes*	$ 14,930	
Interest on notes and bonds payable	50,181	65,111
Total current liabilities		$ 497,486

Long-term liabilities:

6% bonds payable, due Jan. 1, Year 27	$10,000,000	
Add: Premium on bonds payable	149,375	10,149,375
Total liabilities		$10,646,861

*$5,050 + $3,900 + $5,980 = $14,930

REVIEW QUESTIONS

1 Distinguish between the two terms in each of the following pairs:
   a Long-term notes; bonds
   b Mortgage bonds; debenture bonds
   c Fixed-maturity bonds; serial bonds
   d Coupon bonds; registered bonds
   e Operating lease; financing lease

2 Discuss the advantages and disadvantages of a *call provision* in a bond contract from the viewpoint of (*a*) the bondholder and (*b*) the issuing corporation.

3 What are *convertible bonds?* Discuss the advantages and disadvantages of convertible bonds from the standpoint of the investor and the issuing corporation.

4 Computer Systems Corporation has stockholders' equity of $10 million and no long-term debt. The company has just issued $2 million in 20-year, 8% bonds. It is proposed that a voluntary policy be established of depositing $100,000 in a sinking fund each year to enable the company to retire the bonds at maturity. Evaluate the merits of this proposal.

5 The following quotation appeared in a leading business periodical: "In the bond market high interest rates mean low prices. Bonds pay out a fixed percentage of their face value, usually $1,000; a 5% bond, for instance, will pay $50 a year. In order for its yield to rise to $6\frac{1}{4}$%, its price would have to drop to $800." Give a critical evaluation of this quotation.

6 The annual report of Seagull, Inc., contained the following note accompanying the financial statements: "The loan agreements . . . contain provisions as to working capital requirements and payment of cash dividends. At June 30, retained earnings of approximately $13.4 million were available for payment of cash dividends." What is the meaning of this note, and why is it considered necessary to attach such a note to financial statements? (The total retained earnings of Seagull, Inc., at this date amounted to $77.5 million; working capital amounted to $100 million; and total liabilities amounted to $142 million.)

7 What are three important accounting and reporting problems relating to pension plans?

8 Name the federal taxes that most employers are required to withhold from employees. What account or accounts would be credited with the amounts withheld?

9 Distinguish between an *employee* and an *independent contractor.* Why is this distinction important with respect to payroll accounting?

10 Explain which of the following taxes relating to an employee's wages are borne by the employee and which by the employer:
   a FICA tax
   b Federal unemployment tax
   c State unemployment tax
   d Federal income tax

11 What purposes are served by maintaining a detailed earnings record for each employee?

12 Are the payroll taxes levied against employers considered a legal liability and a deductible expense for income tax purposes in the period the wages are earned by the employees or in the period the wages are paid?

EXERCISES

Ex. 13-1 Companies W and X have the same amount of operating income. Determine the amount earned per share of common stock for each company and explain the source of any difference in the earnings per share for each company.

	Company W	Company X
8% debenture bonds	$1,000,000	$ 500,000
Common stock, $10 par value	500,000	1,000,000
Retained earnings	250,000	250,000
Operating income, before bond interest expense and		
income taxes (assume a 40% income tax rate)	300,000	300,000

Ex. 13-2 The following liability appears on the balance sheet of the Sunrise Company on December 31, Year 1:

Long-term liabilities:

Bonds payable, 6%, due December 31, Year 15	$1,000,000	
Premium on bonds payable	42,000	$1,042,000

On January 1, Year 2, 20% of the bonds are retired at 98. Interest was paid on December 31, Year 1.

a Record the retirement of $200,000 of bonds on January 1, Year 2.

b Record the interest payment for the six months ending December 31, Year 2, and the amortization of the premium on December 31, Year 2, assuming that amortization is recorded only at the end of each year.

Ex. 13-3 Determine the average annual interest cost of the following bond issues:

	Company Y	Company Z
Face amount of bonds	$1,000,000	$4,000,000
Contract interest rate	5%	4%
Price received for bonds on issue date	103	96
Length of time from issue date to maturity	10 years	10 years

Ex. 13-4 Crest Company issued $100,000 par value 6% bonds on July 1, Year 5, at 97½. Interest is due on June 30 and December 31 of each year, and the fiscal year ends on December 31. The bonds mature on June 30, Year 15. Prepare the following journal entries:

a July 1, Year 5, to record the issuance of the bonds.

b December 31, Year 5, to pay interest and amortize the bond discount.

c June 30, Year 15, to pay interest, amortize the bond discount, and retire the bonds at maturity.

Ex. 13-5 Gary Handler earned a salary of $20,000 from Livingston Corporation during the current year. FICA tax is 6% of wages up to $13,200 a year. Federal unemployment tax was 3.2% of wages up to $4,200 a year, but a credit against this FUTA tax was allowed for payment to the state of 2.7% of wages up to $4,200 a year. Federal income tax of $4,150 was withheld from Handler's paychecks during the year.

a Prepare in general journal form a compound entry summarizing the payroll transactions for employee Handler for the full year. (In drafting this entry, record payroll taxes on the employer in separate expense accounts and ignore any payments of payroll and payroll taxes during the year.)

b What is the total yearly cost (including taxes) to Livingston Corporation of having Handler on the payroll at an annual salary of $20,000?

Ex. 13-6 During the current year, the payroll of Poxon Company may be summarized as follows:

Gross earnings of employees	*$100,000*
Employee earnings not subject to FICA tax	*20,000*
Employee earnings not subject to unemployment taxes	*70,000*

Assuming that the payroll is subject to FICA tax rate of 6%, a 2.7% state unemployment tax rate, and a federal unemployment tax rate of 0.5%, compute the amount of the Poxon Company's payroll taxes expense for the year, showing separately the amount of each of the three taxes. (Note: Taxes on employees are not involved in this exercise.)

PROBLEMS

13-1 North Company issued $10 million of 7%, 10-year bonds on January 1, Year 1. Interest is payable semiannually on June 30 and December 31. The bonds were sold to an underwriting group at 105.

South Company issued $10 million of 6%, 10-year bonds on January 1, Year 1. Interest is payable semiannually on June 30 and December 31. The bonds were sold to an underwriting group at 95.

Instructions
a Prepare journal entries, omitting explanations, to record all transactions relating to the bond issues of these two companies during Year 1. Assume that bond premium and bond discount are amortized at each interest payment date.
b Explain why the bond interest expense per year is the same for the two companies, despite the difference in the terms of the two bond contracts.

13-2 Solar Energy, Inc., issued, on September 1, Year 1, $3 million in 9% debenture bonds. Interest is payable semiannually on March 1 and September 1, and the bonds mature on September 1, Year 11. The company's fiscal year ends at December 31.

Instructions Make the necessary adjusting entries at December 31, Year 1, and the journal entry to record the payment of bond interest on March 1, Year 2, under each of the following assumptions:
a The bonds were issued at 96.
b The bonds were issued at 102.
c Compute the net bond liability at December 31, Year 1, under assumptions in *a* and *b* above.

13-3 The items shown below appear in the balance sheet of the Purdy Corporation at December 31, Year 6:

Current liabilities:		
Bond interest payable (for three months from Oct. 1		
to Dec. 31)		*$ 200,000*
Long-term debt:		
Bonds payable, 8%, due Apr. 1, Year 17	*$10,000,000*	
Less: Discount on bonds payable	*196,800*	*9,803,200*

The bonds are callable on any interest date. On October 1, Year 7, the Purdy Corporation called $2 million of the bonds at 103.

Instructions

a Prepare journal entries to record the semiannual interest payment on April 1, Year 7. Discount was amortized to December 31, Year 6, and is amortized at each interest payment date. Base the amortization on the 123-month period from December 31, Year 6 to April 1, Year 17.

b Prepare journal entries to record the amortization of bond discount and payment of bond interest at October 1, Year 7, and also to record the calling of $2 million of the bonds at this date.

c Prepare a journal entry to record the accrual of interest at December 31, Year 7. Include the amortization of bond discount to the year-end.

13-4 The following information is taken from the trial balances for Nakazawa Imports, Inc.

	Adjusted December 31		Unadjusted December 31
	Year 1	Year 2	Year 3
6% Bonds payable, due Oct. 1, Year 11 . . .	$1,000,000	$1,000,000	$800,000
Discount on bonds payable	23,400	21,000	19,200
Bond interest expense (including amortization of discount)	10,400	62,400	46,800
Bond interest payable	15,000	15,000	
Gain on retirement of bonds			10,000

The bonds were issued on November 1, Year 1, with one month's accrued interest. On October 1 of Year 3, $200,000 of bonds were retired at a price of 95. No discount on bonds payable was written off at the time of the retirement, thus resulting in a recorded gain of $10,000 on the retirement. **The company adjusts its books at the end of every calendar quarter.** (Note the $2,400 decrease in Discount on Bonds Payable during the 12 months between the first two trial balances.)

Instructions

a Prepare the entry that was made to record the issuance of bonds on November 1, Year 1. (First, compute the discount at date of issuance.)

b Prepare a correcting entry required to measure properly the gain on retirement of bonds. (Compute the carrying value of the bonds retired.)

c Prepare the adjusting entry required at the end of Year 3 to record the accrued interest and to amortize the discount for the period October 1 to December 31.

d What will be the adjusted bond interest expense for Year 4 if $800,000 of bonds remain outstanding? Why does it differ from the bond interest expense in Year 2 and Year 3?

13-5 Tallman & Co. has had an excellent record of maintaining a stable labor force. The state in which the company operates has a merit-rating plan which permits an employer to pay a reduced state unemployment tax rate if his employees have collected little or no unemployment insurance. Tallman & Co. qualifies under the merit-rating plan for a rate of 1.2% rather than the usual 2.7% of gross earnings.

The employees' earnings records so far in the current year are as follows:

Employee	Cumulative Earnings	Employee	Cumulative Earnings
Barr, A. B.	$ 6,744	Hall, J. T.	$ 3,050
Dane, L. M.	13,956	Kay, M. M.	14,050
Fox, R. A.	850	Land, L. T.	1,300
Garr, E. F.	5,056	Neal, J. C.	4,500

The FICA tax is assumed to be 6% on the first $13,200 of gross earnings. The rate of federal unemployment tax is assumed to be 3.2% of the first $4,200 of gross earnings, but with credit to the employer for a maximum of 2.7% of gross earnings for state unemployment tax.

Instructions

a Prepare a schedule showing for employees the cumulative earnings, the earnings subject to unemployment tax, and the earnings subject to FICA tax.

b Compute the total payroll taxes deducted from the earnings of employees as a group.

c Compute the total payroll taxes expense for Tallman & Co., and the percentage of the total payroll represented by payroll taxes expense. (Round off to the nearest tenth of a percent.)

13-6 Custom Design Corporation has five employees; two are employed on a monthly salary, and three are paid an hourly rate with provision for time and one-half for overtime. The basic data for the May 31 payroll are given below:

| | Hours | | | Com- pensation to April 30 | Gross Pay for May | Federal Income Tax Withheld |
Employee	Regular	OT	Pay Rate			
Allen	160	15	$ 8.00/hr	$ 6,000	$1,460	$ 275
Benson	160		7.00/hr	4,000	1,120	230
Cramer	160	10	4.00/hr	2,850	700	100
Dodson	Salary		1,440.00/mo	5,760	1,440	300
Eller	Salary		3,000.00/mo	12,000	3,000	505
Totals					$7,720	$1,410

Compensation of Dodson and Eller is recorded in Administrative Salaries; the balance of the earnings is chargeable to Shop Wages. Payroll taxes apply as follows: FICA tax, 6% up to a maximum of $13,200; state unemployment tax, 2.7% up to a maximum of $4,200; federal unemployment tax, 0.5% up to a maximum of $4,200. Custom Design Corporation has group insurance and a retirement plan under which each employee contributes 5% of his gross pay, with the company matching this contribution. Both employees' and employer's contributions are deposited with the Reliable Insurance Company at the end of each month.

Instructions

a Prepare a payroll record for May using the following columns:

| | | Amount Subject to | | Federal Income Tax Withheld | FICA Tax Withheld | Retire- ment Deduc- tion | Net Pay Due |
Employee	Gross Pay	Unemploy- ment Taxes	FICA Tax				

b Explain how the gross pay for Cramer was computed for the month of May.

c Explain why the federal income tax withheld for Allen is less than that withheld for Dodson despite the fact that Allen received a higher gross compensation.

d Prepare in general journal form the entry to record the payroll for the month of May.

e Prepare in general journal form the entry to record the employer's payroll taxes and insurance plan contributions for the month of May. Record payroll taxes expense in a single account.

f Prepare a journal entry to record the payment of accrued payroll and the insurance plan contributions (both the employer's and the employees' portions).

BUSINESS DECISION PROBLEM 13

Diversified Products Company reported the balances given below at the end of the current year:

Total assets	$7,400,000
Current liabilities	1,800,000
Long-term liabilities	200,000
Stockholders' equity:	
Capital stock, $10 par value	2,000,000
Paid-in capital in excess of par	1,500,000
Retained earnings	1,900,000

The company is planning an expansion of its plant facilities, and a study shows that $6 million of new funds will be required to finance the expansion. Two proposals are under consideration:

   Stock Financing   Issue 100,000 shares of capital stock at a price of $60 per share.

   Bond Financing   Borrow $6 million on a 20-year bond issue, with interest at 7%.

The assets and liabilities of Diversified Products Company have remained relatively constant over the past five years, and during this period the earnings *after* income taxes have averaged 10% of the stockholders' equity as reported at the end of the current year. The company expects that its earnings *before* income taxes will increase by an amount equal to 12% of the new investment in plant facilities.

Past and future income taxes for the company may be estimated at 40% of income before income taxes.

Instructions

a Prove that the company's average income before income taxes during the past five years was $900,000.

b Prepare a schedule showing the expected earnings per share of capital stock during the first year of operations following the completion of the $6 million expansion, under each of the two proposed means of financing.

c Evaluate the two proposed means of financing from the viewpoint of a major stockholder of Diversified Products Company.

ACCOUNTING PRINCIPLES

FOURTEEN

The basic objective of accounting

The basic objective of accounting is to provide useful information for making economic decisions. Investors, managers, economists, bankers, labor leaders, and government administrators all rely upon financial statements and other accounting reports in making the economic decisions which shape our economy. In determining the proper content of financial statements and other accounting reports, it is necessary to consider the *information needs* of the users of these statements and reports.

THE NEEDS OF MANAGEMENT Managers are interested in having information that will aid them in making business decisions. This phase of accounting is primarily concerned with generating reports and summaries for internal use by management and is known as *management accounting.*

In management accounting, theory is not a major issue, since any information that aids in making rational choices among alternative courses of action is relevant and useful. One measurement method may be used for one managerial purpose and another for a different purpose. Accounting measurements of past operating results and current financial position are useful to management, but it is not necessary that all internal information be developed in accordance with any particular set of accounting principles.

THE NEEDS OF STOCKHOLDERS AND CREDITORS While management accounting provides information for internal purposes, *financial accounting* deals primarily with reporting of financial information to outsiders. Measurement of periodic net income and financial position and the reporting of the results to stockholders and creditors are the key objectives of financial accounting.

In reporting to stockholders and creditors, different considerations come into play. Corporate managers, even in small companies, have always been accountable to the owners who employ them. But the responsibility for managing a large corporation carries with it a great deal of economic and social power and requires a more extensive accountability. In most large corporations, stock ownership is widely scattered. The owner of even several thousand of the nearly 300 million shares of General Motors common stock can scarcely expect to exert much influence on managerial policy. As stockholder power has diminished, managerial power and responsibility have broadened.

Modern corporate managers are accountable not only to stockholders and creditors but also to employees, customers, potential investors, and the public at large. Financial statements are the primary means by which management reports on its accountability. Such statements are used to evaluate management's performance, to measure borrowing power, to guide investment decisions, and to support arguments on taxes, prices and other public policy issues.

In this book we are primarily concerned with the reporting of financial information to outsiders. We shall therefore concentrate on the accounting principles and reporting standards relating to general-purpose financial statements, rather than special-purpose accounting reports to management.

THE NEED FOR ACCOUNTING PRINCIPLES   It is vital to the functioning of our economy that financial statements be widely used and clearly understood. Users of these statements must have confidence in the reliability of the accounting information. Also, it is important for financial statements to be prepared in a manner which permits them to be compared fairly with prior years' statements and with financial statements of other companies. In short, we need *standards of disclosure* and a well-defined body of accounting principles to guide corporate managers in preparing financial statements which will achieve the objectives of *understandability, reliability,* and *comparability.*

Generally accepted accounting principles

The principles which constitute the "ground rules" for financial reporting are termed *generally accepted accounting principles.* The financial statements of all publicly owned corporations are prepared in conformity with generally accepted accounting principles. To assure outsiders that financial statements have been prepared in accordance with these principles, the financial statements of publicly owned corporations are audited by independent certified public accountants.

Accounting principles are occasionally termed *standards, assumptions, postulates, and concepts.* The various terms used to describe accounting principles indicate the many efforts which have been made to develop a satisfactory framework of accounting theory.[1] These

---

[1] See, for example, *Accounting Research Study No. 1,* "The Basic Postulates of Accounting," AICPA (New York. 1961); *Accounting Research Study No. 3,"* A Tentative Set of Broad Accounting Principles for Business Enterprises," AICPA (New York: 1962); and *Objectives of Financial Statements,* AICPA (New York: 1973).

efforts are still in process, since accounting theory must continually change with changes in the business environment and changes in the needs of financial statement users. Accounting principles are not rooted in laws of nature, as are the laws of the physical sciences. *Accounting principles are developed in relation to what we consider to be the most important objectives of financial reporting.*

For example, in recent years accountants as well as business executives have recognized that the cost to society of maintaining an economic activity, such as a manufacturing plant, includes the pollution of air and water and other damage to the environment. Research is currently being undertaken to develop accounting principles for the identification and measurement of these "social costs."

Authoritative support for accounting principles

To qualify as "generally accepted," an accounting principle must usually receive "substantial authoritative support." The most influential authoritative groups in this country have been: (1) the American Institute of Certified Public Accountants (AICPA), the professional association of licensed CPAs; (2) the American Accounting Association (AAA), an academic organization composed primarily of accounting professors; and (3) the Securities and Exchange Commission (SEC), an agency of the federal government established to administer laws and regulations relating to the publication of financial information by corporations whose stock is publicly owned.[2]

ACCOUNTING PRINCIPLES BOARD (APB) The AICPA has long been concerned with stating and defining accounting principles because its members face the problem of making decisions every day about generally accepted principles in their professional work. Some years ago, the AICPA established an Accounting Principles Board, composed of practitioners, educators, and industry representatives. This Board was authorized to issue *Opinions* which would improve financial reporting and narrow areas of differences and inconsistencies in accounting practices and which would be regarded as expressions of generally accepted accounting principles. At the same time, the AICPA expanded its research efforts and sponsored a series of Accounting Research Studies to aid the APB in its work. The Accounting Principles Board issued 31 formal *Opinions* on specific accounting problems, and also issued broad *Statements* designed to improve the quality of financial reporting. For example, *Statement No. 4,* "Basic Concepts and Accounting Principles Underlying Financial Statements of Business En-

[2] Other professional organizations which have influenced the development of accounting principles are the National Association of Accountants and the Financial Executives Institute. In addition to the SEC, the following government regulatory agencies influence financial reporting of business units falling under their jurisdiction: Federal Power Commission, Interstate Commerce Commission, Civil Aeronautics Board, and Federal Communications Commission.

terprises," was issued in 1970, with the objective of advancing the written expression of financial accounting principles.

In 1973, the AICPA replaced the Accounting Principles Board with the Financial Accounting Standards Board. However, the *Opinions* and *Statements* of the APB remain in effect.

FINANCIAL ACCOUNTING STANDARDS BOARD (FASB) The FASB was established by the AICPA as an independent body to assume the responsibilities of the former Accounting Principles Board. The FASB consists of seven full-time, well-paid members, including representatives from public accounting, industry, and accounting education. The Accounting Principles Board had consisted of 21 part-time, unpaid members, primarily from public accounting.

Lending support to the FASB are an advisory council and a large research staff. The FASB is authorized to issue *Statements of Financial Accounting Standards,* which represent expressions of generally accepted accounting principles.

AMERICAN ACCOUNTING ASSOCIATION (AAA) The AAA has sponsored a number of research studies and monographs in which individual authors and Association committees attempt to summarize accounting principles. These statements have no doubt had considerable influence on the thinking of accounting theorists and practitioners. However, the AAA lacks the power of the AICPA to impose its collective view on accounting practice; it therefore exercises its influence through the prestige of its authors and the persuasiveness of their views.

SECURITIES AND EXCHANGE COMMISSION (SEC) The SEC has considerable opportunity to exercise its authority since it may reject corporate financial statements that do not, in the opinion of the Commission, meet acceptable standards. The views of the Commission on various accounting issues are published in the SEC's *Accounting Series Releases.*

In addition to the foregoing, "substantial authoritative support" may include accounting practices commonly found in certain industries and in the literature of accounting, including books, journal articles, and expert testimony offered in court.

The accounting environment

The principles of accounting are to a considerable extent shaped by the environment in which the accounting process is employed. Accounting is concerned with economic activity, that is, the ownership and exchange of goods and services. Accounting systems developed in response to the need for information about business activity as an aid both to management and outsiders in making rational economic decisions. Since money is a common denominator in which the value of goods and services is measured, the accounting process is implemented in terms of a monetary unit. Most goods and services produced in our economy are distributed through exchange rather than being directly consumed by producers. It is logical, therefore, to base accounting measurements on exchange (market) prices generated by *past, present,* and *future* transactions and events.

For example, when the accountant reports the original cost of a plant site acquired some years ago, he is reflecting a past exchange. When he states inventory at market under the lower-of-cost-or-market rule, he is using a present exchange price (market value) as the basis for his measurement. When he records a liability for income taxes, he is measuring the present effect of a future cash outflow to the government.

Since present decisions can affect only current and future outcomes, current and future exchange prices are in general more relevant for decision making than past exchange prices. We live in a world of uncertainty, however, and estimates of future, and even current, exchange prices are often subject to wide margins of error. Where to draw the line of acceptability in the trade-off between *reliability* and *relevance* is one of the crucial issues in accounting theory. The need for reliable and verifiable data is an important constraint, particularly with respect to information reported to outsiders. This factor has led the accountant to rely heavily on past exchange prices as the basis for his measurements.

In the remaining sections of this chapter we shall summarize briefly the major principles that govern the accounting process and comment on some areas of controversy. We have noted the need for accepted principles to foster confidence in the published financial statements of large publicly owned corporations. Most accounting principles are equally applicable to profit-making organizations of any size or form.

The accounting entity principle

One of the basic principles of accounting is that information is compiled for a clearly defined accounting entity. Most economic activity is carried on through entities. An individual person is an accounting entity. So is a business enterprise, whether conducted as a single proprietorship, partnership, or corporation. The estate of a deceased person is an accounting entity, as are all nonprofit clubs and organizations. The basic accounting equation, Assets = Liabilities + Owners' Equity, reflects the *accounting entity principle* since the elements of the equation relate to the particular entity whose economic activity is being metered in financial statements.

We should distinguish between accounting and legal entities. In some cases the two coincide. For example, corporations, estates, trusts, and governmental agencies are both accounting and legal entities. In other cases, accounting entities differ from legal entities. For example, the *proprietorship* is an *accounting* entity, as indicated by the fact that only the assets and liabilities of the business unit are included in its financial statements. The proprietorship is not a legal entity; the *proprietor* is a *legal* entity. He is legally liable both for his personal obligations and for those incurred in his business. For accounting purposes, the proprietor as an individual and his business enterprise are separate entities. Furthermore, a proprietor may own several businesses, each of which is treated as a separate entity for accounting purposes.

CONSOLIDATED ACCOUNTING ENTITIES A single accounting entity may also include more than one legal entity. Several corporations, for example, may be combined to form a single accounting entity. Since corporations are usually granted the power to hold title to any form of property, one corporation may own shares of stock in another. When one corporation controls another corporation through the ownership of a majority of its capital stock, the controlling corporation is called a *parent* company, and the company whose stock is owned is called a *subsidiary* company. Because both the parent and subsidiary companies are legal entities, separate financial statements may be prepared for each company. However, it may also be useful to prepare financial statements which view the *affiliated* companies (the parent company and its subsidiaries) as if they were a single unified business. Such statements are called *consolidated financial statements.*

In a *consolidated balance sheet,* the assets and liabilities of the affiliated companies are combined and reported as though only a single entity existed. Similarly, in a *consolidated income statement,* the revenue and expenses of the affiliated companies are combined, on the assumption that the results of operations for a single economic entity are being measured.

There are a number of economic, financial, legal, and tax advantages which encourage businessmen to operate through subsidiaries rather than through a single business entity. As a result corporate affiliations are common in the United States. A majority of the companies with shares listed on the New York Stock Exchange or the American Stock Exchange have one or more subsidiaries and include consolidated financial statements in their annual reports. (See the titles of the financial statements in the Appendix of this book.) The preparation of consolidated financial statements is a complex topic which is covered in *Modern Advanced Accounting* of this Series.

The choice of an accounting entity is somewhat flexible and is based on informational needs. As a general rule, we can say that any legal or economic unit which controls economic resources and is accountable for these resources is an accounting entity.

The going-concern principle

An underlying assumption in accounting is that an accounting entity will continue in operation for an indefinite period of time sufficient to carry out its existing commitments. This assumption is sometimes called the *going-concern principle.* Since most accounting entities have indefinite lives, the assumption of continuity is in accord with experience in our economic system. In general, the going-concern principle justifies ignoring immediate liquidating values in presenting assets and liabilities in the balance sheet.

For example, suppose that a company has just purchased a five-year insurance policy for $5,000. If we assume that the business will continue in operation for five years or more, we will consider the $5,000 payment for the insurance as an asset whose services (freedom from risk) will be enjoyed by the business over a five-year period. On the other hand, if we assume that the business is likely to terminate in the near future, the insurance policy should be recorded at its cancellation value—the amount of cash which can be obtained from the insurance company as a refund on immediate cancellation of the policy, which may be, say, $4,800.

In summary, the going-concern principle may be dropped when it is not in accord with the facts. Accountants are sometimes asked to prepare a statement of financial position for an enterprise that is about to liquidate. In this case the assumption of continuity is no longer valid and the accountant drops the going-concern principle and reports assets at their current liquidating value and liabilities at the amount required to settle the debts immediately.

The time period principle

We assume an indefinite life for most accounting entities. But accountants are asked to measure operating progress and changes in economic position at relatively short time intervals during this indefinite life. Users of financial statements want periodic measurements for decision-making purposes. The selection of a *fiscal period,* such as a quarter of a year or a full year, facilitates periodic reporting by business units.

Dividing the life of an enterprise into time segments and measuring changes in financial position periodically is a difficult process. A precise measurement of net income and financial position can be made only when a business has been liquidated and its resources have been fully converted into cash. At any time prior to liquidation, the worth of some assets and the amount of some liabilities are matters of speculation. Thus periodic measures of net income and financial position are at best only informed estimates.

Periodic measurements of net income are generally *tentative.* This fact should be clearly understood by those who rely on periodic accounting information. The need for periodic measurements creates many of accounting's most serious problems. For example, the attempt to measure net income over short time periods requires the selection of inventory flow assumptions and depreciation methods. The end-of-period adjustments discussed in Chapter 4 stem directly from the need to update accounting information to a particular point in time.

The monetary principle

The monetary principle means that money is used as the basic measuring unit for financial reporting. Money is the common denominator in which accounting measurements are made and summarized. The dollar, or any other monetary unit, represents a unit of value; that is, it reflects the ability to command goods and services. Implicit in the use of money as a measuring unit is the *assumption that the dollar is a stable unit of value,* just as the mile is a stable unit of distance, and an acre is a stable unit of area.

Having accepted money as his measuring unit, the accountant freely combines dollar measures of economic transactions that occur at various times during the life of an accounting entity. He combines, for example, a $5,000 cost of equipment purchased in 1965 and the $10,000 cost of similar equipment purchased in 1975 and reports the total as a $15,000 investment in equipment.

Unlike the mile and the acre, which are stable units of distance and area, the dollar *is not a stable unit of value.* The prices of goods and services in our economy change over time. When the *general price level* (a phrase used to describe the average of all prices) increases, the value of money (that is, its ability to command goods and services) decreases.

Despite the steady erosion in the purchasing power of the dollar in the United States during the last 40 years, accountants continue to assume that the value of the dollar is stable. This somewhat unrealistic assumption is one of the reasons why financial statements are viewed by some users as misleading. Restatement of accounting information for the changing value of the dollar and the preparation of supplementary statements in terms of constant dollars have received much attention in recent years. Such *common dollar statements* will be discussed in a subsequent section of this chapter.

The objectivity principle

A basic principle of accounting is that changes in the valuations assigned to assets and liabilities, and their resultant effect on net income and owners' equity, should not be recognized until they can be measured objectively in terms of an *exchange price (cost).*

The term *objective* refers to measurements that are unbiased and subject to verification by independent experts. For example, the price established in an arm's-length transaction is an objective measure of exchange value at the time of the transaction. It is not surprising, therefore, that exchange prices established in business transactions constitute much of the raw material from which accounting information is generated.

If a measurement is objective, 10 competent investigators who make the same measurement will come up with substantially identical results. It is probably true, however, that 10 competent accountants who set out independently to measure the net income of a given business would not arrive at an identical result. In the light of the objectivity principle, why is this so? The variation would probably arise because of the existence of alternative accounting measurement methods, rather than the lack of objectivity in any given measurement method. To illustrate, in measuring the cost of goods sold one accountant might use the lifo method, and another the weighted average method for valuing inventory. These choices could produce significant variations in net income.

The accountant relies on various kinds of evidence to support his financial measurements, but he seeks always the most objective evidence he can get. Invoices, contracts, canceled checks, and physical counts of inventory are examples of objective evidence used by accountants.

Despite the goal of objectivity, it is not possible to insulate accounting information from opinion and personal judgment. The cost of a depreciable asset can be objectively determined but not the periodic depreciation expense. To measure the cost of the asset services that have been used up during a given period requires estimates of the residual value and service life of the asset and judgment as to the depreciation method that should be used.

Objectivity in accounting has its roots in the quest for reliability. The accountant wants to make his economic measurements reliable and, at the same time, as relevant to decision makers as possible. The accountant is constantly faced with the necessity of compromising between what users of financial information would like to know and what it is possible to measure with a reasonable degree of reliability.

Asset valuation: the cost principle

Both the balance sheet and the income statement are extensively affected by the cost principle. Assets are initially recorded in the accounts at cost, and no adjustment is made to this valuation in later periods, except to allocate a portion of the original cost to expense as the assets expire. At the time an asset is originally acquired, cost represents the "fair market value" of the goods or services exchanged, as evidenced by an arm's-length transaction. With the passage of time, however, the fair market value of such assets as land and buildings may vary greatly from their historical cost. These later changes in fair market value are generally ignored in the accounts, and the assets continue to be valued in the balance sheet at historical cost (less the portion of that cost which has been allocated to expense).

Some accountants believe that current market values, or *fair values,* should be used as the basis for asset valuation rather than historical cost. These accountants argue that current values would result in a more meaningful balance sheet. Also, they claim that current values should be allocated to expense to represent fairly the cost to the entity of the goods or services consumed in the effort to generate revenue.

The cost principle is derived from the principle of objectivity. Those who support present measurement principles argue that it is important that users have confidence in financial statements, and this confidence can best be maintained if the accountant recognizes changes in assets and liabilities only on the basis of objective evidence. Objective evidence generally exists to support cost, but fair value is usually a far less objective measurement.

Measuring revenue: the realization principle

When should revenue be recognized? Under the assumptions of accrual accounting, revenue should be recognized "when it is earned." However, the "earning" of revenue is an *economic process* and does not actually take place at a single point in time.

Some revenue, such as interest earned, is directly related to time periods. For this type of revenue, it is easy to determine how much revenue has been earned by computing how much of the earning process is complete. However, the earning process for sales revenue relates to *economic activity* rather than to a specific period of time. In a manufacturing business, for example, the earning process involves (1) acquisition of raw materials, (2) production of finished goods, (3) sale of the finished goods, and (4) collection of cash from credit customers.

In the manufacturing example, there is little objective evidence to indicate how much revenue has been earned during the first two stages of the earning process. Accountants therefore usually do not recognize revenue until the revenue has been *realized.* Revenue is realized (1) when the earning process is essentially complete and (2) when objective evidence exists as to the amount of revenue earned.

In most cases, the realization principle indicates that revenue should be recognized *at the time of the sale of goods or the rendering of services.* Recognizing revenue at this point is logical because the firm has essentially completed the earning process and the realized value of the goods or services sold can be objectively measured in terms of the price billed to customers. At any time prior to sale, the ultimate realizable value of the goods or services sold can only be estimated. After the sale, the only step that remains is to collect from the customer, and this is usually a relatively certain event.

Under certain special circumstances, accountants may deviate from the realization principle. In Chapter 3, we described a complete *cash basis* of income measurement whereby revenue is considered realized only when cash is collected from customers and expenses are recorded only when cash is actually paid out. Lawyers, accountants, and doctors, for example, generally use the cash basis of accounting in computing their taxable income. In computing realized revenue on the cash basis, receivables from clients or customers are ignored; only the actual cash collections are recorded as revenue.

THE INSTALLMENT METHOD Companies selling goods on the installment plan sometimes use the *installment method* of accounting. This method would be considered appropriate when collections extend over relatively long periods of time and there is a strong possibility that full collection will not be made. As customers make installment payments, the seller recognizes the gross profit on sales in proportion to the cash collected. If the gross profit on installment sales is 30%, then out of every dollar collected on installment accounts receivable, the sum of 30 cents represents *realized gross profit.* For example, assume that a retailer sells a television set in Year 1 for $400 which cost him $280, or 70% of sales price. The collections and the profit earned would be recognized over a three-year period as follows:

	Year	Cash Collected	—	Cost Recovery, 70%	=	Profit Earned, 30%
Installment method illustrated	1	$150		$105		$ 45
	2	200		140		60
	3	50		35		15
	Totals	$400		$280		$120

This method of profit recognition exists largely because it is allowed for income tax purposes; it postpones the payment of income taxes until cash is collected from customers. From an accounting viewpoint, there is little theoretical justification for delaying the recognition of profit beyond the point of sale, because few if any cases exist where the realizable value of the receivable cannot be measured at that time through the establishment of an adequate allowance for uncollectible accounts.

LONG–TERM CONSTRUCTION CONTRACTS There are some circumstances in which the accountant finds it appropriate to recognize revenue as realized *during production* or when production is completed. An example arises in the case of *long-term construction contracts,* such as the building of a dam over a three-year period. In this case the revenue (contract price) is known when the construction job is begun, and it would be unreasonable to assume that the entire revenue is realized in the accounting period in which the project is completed. The accountant therefore estimates the portion of the dam completed during each accounting period, and recognizes revenue and profits in proportion to the work completed. This is known as the *percentage-of-completion method* of accounting for long-term contracts.

Assume, for example, that the costs to be incurred over a three-year period on a $500,000 contract are estimated at $400,000. Using the percentage-of-completion method of accounting, the profits on the contract would be recognized over the three-year period as follows:

	Year	Actual Cost Incurred	Actual Cost as Percentage of Estimated Total Cost	Portion of Contract Price Realized	Profit Considered Realized
Profit recognized as work progresses	1	$ 60,000	15	$ 75,000	$15,000
	2	200,000	50	250,000	50,000
	3	145,200	*	175,000 *balance*	29,800 *balance*
	Totals	$405,200		$500,000	$94,800

*Balance required to complete the contract.

The portion of the contract price realized in Years 1 and 2 is determined by taking the percentage of estimated total cost incurred in each year and applying it to the contract price of $500,000. Because 15% ($60,000/$400,000) of the total estimated cost was incurred in Year 1, 15% of the total estimated profit of $100,000 ($500,000 − $400,000) was considered realized; in Year 2, 50% ($200,000/$400,000) of the cost was incurred, and therefore 50% of the estimated profit was considered realized. In Year 3, however, the total actual cost is known and the profit on the contract is determined to be $94,800 ($500,000 − $405,200). Since profits of $65,000 ($15,000 + $50,000) were previously recognized in Years 1 and 2, the rest of the profit, $29,800, must be recognized in Year 3. If at the end of any accounting period it appears that a loss will be incurred on a contract in progress, *the loss should be recognized at once.*

If it is difficult to estimate the degree of contract completion or if there are extreme uncertainties involved in measuring the ultimate profit on a contract in progress, profit may be recognized when the *production is completed.* This approach is often referred to as the *completed-contract method* and is supported by many accountants because it is conservative, requires little subjective judgment, and is advantageous for income tax purposes. If the completed-contract method of accounting for long-term construction contracts had been used in the preceding example, no profit would have been recognized in Years 1 and 2; the entire profit of $94,800 would be recorded in Year 3 when the contract was completed and actual costs known.

Measuring expenses: the matching principle

Revenue, the gross increase in net assets resulting from the production or sale of goods and services, is offset by expenses incurred in bringing the firm's output to the point of sale. Examples of expenses relating to revenue are the cost of merchandise sold, the expiration of asset services, and out-of-pocket expenditures for operating costs. The measurement of expenses occurs in two stages: (1) measuring the *cost* of goods and services that are consumed or expire in generating revenue and (2) determining when the goods and services acquired have contributed to revenue and their cost thus *becomes an expense.* The second aspect of the measurement process is often referred to as *matching costs and revenue* and is fundamental to the *accrual method* of accounting.

Costs are associated with revenue (and thus become expenses) in two major ways:

1 IN RELATION TO THE PRODUCT SOLD OR SERVICE RENDERED If a good or service can be related to the product or service which consti- tutes the output of the enterprise, its cost becomes an expense when the product is sold or the service rendered to customers. The cost of goods sold in a merchandising firm is a good example of this type of expense. Similarly, a commission paid to a real estate salesperson by a real estate brokerage office is an expense directly related to the revenue generated by the salesperson.

2 IN RELATION TO THE TIME PERIOD DURING WHICH REVENUE IS EARNED Some costs incurred by businesses cannot be directly related to the product or service output of the firm. Expired fire insurance, property taxes, depreciation on a building, the salary of the president of the company—all are examples of costs incurred in generating revenue which cannot be related to specific transactions. The ac- countant refers to this class of costs as *period costs,* and charges them to expense by associating them with the period of time during which they are incurred and presumably contribute to revenue, rather than by associating them with specific revenue-producing transactions.

Recognition of gains and losses

The same principles applied in recognizing revenue are applicable to the measurement of gains and losses on assets other than inventories. In general, an increase in the value of a productive asset, such as a machine or a building, is not recognized until the asset in question is sold, in which case the amount of the gain is objectively determin- able.

If a productive asset increases in value while it is in service, the accountant ordinarily does not record this gain because it has not been realized. "Not realized" means that the gain in value has not been substantiated by a transaction in which an exchange price has been established.

Accountants are not so insistent on following the rules of *realization* in measuring losses. We have seen in Chapter 11, for example, that the lower-of-cost-or-market valuation of inventories results in the recognition of losses in inventory investment prior to the sale of the goods in question. Recognizing losses when inventories appear to be worth less than their cost but refusing to recognize gains when inventories appear to be worth more than their cost is logically inconsistent. This inconsistency is justified by an accounting presumption that assets should not be reported in the balance sheet in excess of the amount which can be expected to be recovered through revenue.

The consistency principle

The principle of *consistency* implies that a particular accounting method, once adopted, will not be changed from period to period. This assumption is important because it enables users of financial statements to interpret intelligently the changes in financial position and the amount of net income.

As a practical matter, management (with approval from its accountants) can change an accounting method when in its judgment a different method would better serve the needs of users of financial statements. It would hardly be a virtue to employ an improper accounting method consistently year after year. When a significant change in accounting occurs, however, the independent public accountant is obliged to report both the fact that a change in method has been made and the dollar effect of the change. In published financial statements, this disclosure is incorporated in the CPA's opinion. A typical disclosure might be as follows: "During the current year the company changed from the declining balance method of computing depreciation to the straight-line method. This change in method had the effect of increasing net income by $210,000."

If income statements for previous years are included alongside the current statement for comparison purposes, the statements for the preceding years should be presented as previously reported. The cumulative effect of retroactive application of the new accounting principle on the owners' equity at the beginning of the period in which the change is made should be included in the net income of that period.[3]

Consistency applies to a single accounting entity and increases the comparability of financial statements from period to period. Different companies, even those in the same industry, may follow different

---

[3] For a full discussion of this subject, see "Accounting Changes," *Opinion No. 20* issued by the Accounting Principles Board of the AICPA (New York: 1971).

accounting methods. For this reason, it
accounting methods used by companies whe
are being compared.

The disclosure principle

One of the most important principles of financial reporting is to make certain that all *material* and *relevant facts* concerning financial position and the results of operations *are communicated to users.* This can be accomplished either in the financial statements or in the notes accompanying the statements. Such disclosure should make the statements more useful and less subject to misinterpretation.

Naturally, there are practical limits to the amount of disclosure that can be made in financial statements or the accompanying notes. As a minimum, the following information should generally be disclosed:

1 Terms of major borrowing arrangements and existence of large contingent liabilities
2 Contractual provisions relating to leasing arrangements, employee pension and bonus plans, and major proposed asset acquisitions
3 Accounting methods used in preparing the financial statements
4 Changes in accounting methods made during the latest period
5 Other significant events affecting financial position, including major new contracts for sale of goods or services, labor strikes, shortages of raw materials, and pending legislation which may significantly affect operations

Supplementary disclosure through footnotes, however, should not take the place of sound accounting practices in preparing financial statements. The primary information made available to readers of financial statements is derived from the accounting records, but it is not necessarily limited to such information. The key point to keep in mind is that the supplementary information should be *relevant to the user.* Even significant events which occur *after* the end of the accounting period but before the financial statements are released should be disclosed.

Materiality

The term *materiality* refers to the *relative importance* of an item or event. Disclosure of relevant information is closely related to the concept of materiality; what is material is likely to be relevant. For practical reasons, accountants are primarily concerned with significant information and are not overly concerned with those items which have little effect on financial statements. For example, should the cost of a pencil sharpener, a wastepaper basket, or a stapler be set up as assets and depreciated over their useful lives? Even though more than one period will benefit from the use of these assets, the concept of materiality permits the immediate recognition of the cost of these items as an expense on grounds that it would be too expensive to undertake depreciation accounting for such low-cost assets and that the results would not differ significantly.

We must recognize that the materiality of an item is a relative thing; what is material for one business unit may not be material for another. Materiality of an item may depend not only on its *amount* but also on its *nature.* In summary, we can state the following rule: *An item is material if there is a reasonable expectation that knowledge of it would influence the decisions of prudent users of financial statements.*

Conservatism as a guide in resolving uncertainties

We have previously referred to the use of *conservatism* in connection with the measurement of net income and the reporting of accounts receivable and inventories in the balance sheet. Although the concept of conservatism may not qualify as an accounting principle, it has long been a powerful influence upon asset valuation and income determination. Conservatism is most useful when matters of judgment or estimates are involved. Ideally, the accountant should base his estimates on sound logic and select those acceptable accounting methods which neither overstate nor understate the facts. When some doubt exists in the accountant's mind, however, he traditionally leans in the direction of caution and selects the accounting option which produces a lower net income for the current period and a less favorable financial position. Conservatism, however, may be viewed as a double-edged sword. If an asset is prematurely recognized as an expense in Year 1, for example, the balance sheet and net income for Year 1 will be conservatively stated but the net income for Year 2 will be overstated.

An example of conservatism is the traditional practice of pricing inventory at the lower of cost or market (replacement cost). Decreases in the market value of the inventory are recognized as a part of the cost of goods sold in the current period, but increases in market value of inventory are ignored. A judicious application of conservatism to the accounting process should produce more useful information; in contrast, the excessive use of conservatism or failure to apply conservatism may produce misleading information and result in losses to creditors and stockholders.

Opinion on financial statements rendered by independent CPAs

After independent certified public accountants have audited the financial statements and accounting records of a business, they attest to the reasonableness of the financial statements by issuing an *audit opinion* (sometimes called a *certificate*). This opinion is published as part of the company's annual report to stockholders. Because of its importance, the wording of the audit opinion has been carefully considered and a standard form has been developed. Considering the extensive investigation that precedes it, the audit opinion is surprisingly short. It usually consists of two brief paragraphs, unless the CPAs comment on unusual features of the financial picture. The first paragraph describes the *scope* of the auditors' examination; the second states their *opinion* of the financial statements. A report of independent accountants might read as follows:

Typical audit opinion

We have examined the balance sheet of the Reed Company as of September 30, 19___, and the related statements of income, retained earnings, and changes in financial position for the year then ended. Our examination was made in accordance with generally accepted auditing standards, and accordingly included such tests of the accounting records and such other auditing procedures as we considered necessary in the circumstances.

In our opinion, the above financial statements present fairly the financial position of the Reed Company at September 30, 19___, and the results of its operations and the changes in its financial position for the year then ended, in conformity with generally accepted accounting principles applied on a basis consistent with that of the preceding year.

Observe that CPAs *do not guarantee* the accuracy of the financial statements. The financial statements are issued by management of the business: the CPAs render a professional opinion as to the "fairness" of the presentation. The important point to keep in mind is that the *primary responsibility for the accuracy of the financial statements rests with the management* of the business entity issuing the statements.

The phrase "in conformity with generally accepted accounting principles" in the second paragraph of the audit opinion is particularly relevant to our discussion in this chapter. *An authoritative and exhaustive list of generally accepted accounting principles does not exist.* Yet the widespread reliance upon this phrase implies that there is general consensus as to what these accounting principles are.

THE SEARCH FOR BETTER FINANCIAL REPORTING

Accounting is a man-made information system. It is an imperfect system, and constant efforts are being made to improve the precision and relevance of accounting measurements and the usefulness of the end products of the accounting process—financial statements. Because economic conditions are full of uncertainty and business transactions are often complex, the end products of the accounting process must be accepted for what they are—tentative in nature and subject to certain limitations. Accordingly, we should not expect financial statements to attain a higher level of certainty than the business transactions which they summarize.

While accounting may never become a precise science, no one can argue that further improvements are not possible in measuring and communicating financial information. Should accountants, for example, continue to adhere to the assumption that the monetary unit is stable and that historical costs are the most relevant measures of "value" for financial reporting purposes? In the remaining pages of this chapter, we shall examine the implications of this important question.

Financial statements adjusted for changes in the value of the dollar

As stated earlier, the general price level[4] in the United States has been going up for many years, yet accountants continue to assume that the value of the dollar is stable. What effect do material changes in general price levels, and thus changes in the value of money, have on accounting measurements? By combining transactions measured in dollars of varying years, the accountant in effect ignores changes in the size of his measuring unit. For example, suppose that a company purchased land early in Year 1 for $50,000 and sold this land for $100,000 late in Year 10. If prices roughly doubled during that 10-year period and the value of money was cut in half, we might say that the company was no better off as a result of these two transactions; the $100,000 received for the land in Year 10 represented approximately the same command over goods and services as $50,000 did when invested in the land in Year 1. In terms of the *dollar* as a measuring unit, however, the accountant would recognize a gain of $50,000 ($100,000 − $50,000) at the time the land was sold in Year 10. Thus, by comparing the Year 1 and Year 10 transactions in dollar terms to measure gains and losses, *the accountant assumes that a firm is as well off when it has recovered its original dollar investment, and that it is better off whenever it recovers more than the original number of dollars invested in any given asset.*

The assumption that the dollar is a stable measuring unit can hardly be defended on factual grounds. The issue is not whether money is a stable measuring unit; we know it is not. The question is whether financial statements prepared using historical dollars as the measuring unit are more useful than financial statements prepared on some other basis. Years ago methods were devised for making accounting measurements and presenting financial statements in terms of current dollars rather than historical dollars. Such statements have come to be known as *common dollar financial statements* or *price-level financial*

[4] The general price level is the weighted average of the prices of goods and services within the economy. Generally, it is measured by an index with a base year assigned a value of 100. The reciprocal of the price index represents the purchasing power of the dollar. Thus, if Year 1 = 100 and Year 5 = 125, prices have risen 25% and purchasing power has decreased by 20% [100 − (100 ÷ 125)]. The most common measures of the general price level are the consumer price index, the wholesale price index, and the Gross National Product Implicit Price Deflator. The GNP Deflator is the most comprehensive index and is widely accepted as the best measure of the general price level.

statements, because all historical dollar amounts are restated in terms of the current value of the dollar.

An extended discussion of the procedures used to prepare common dollar statements is beyond the scope of this book, but the process may be visualized through a brief discussion of a simplified example.

Illustration of common dollar financial statements

Assume that Flation Company began business on January 1, Year 1, when the general price level index stood at 100. During the year, the price level rose at a uniform rate. The average price level during the year was 125, and at December 31 the price level was 150. During the year, Flation Company sold $25,000 of its beginning inventory for $50,000 cash and paid $20,000 of its current liabilities. We shall assume that the sales and debt repayment were Flation Company's only transactions during the year, and that these transactions occurred uniformly throughout the year. Flation Company's equipment is being depreciated over four years. Comparative historical dollar balance sheets at the beginning and end of the year are shown below:

FLATION COMPANY

Comparative Balance Sheets

At Beginning and End of Year 1

	December 31	*January 1*
Assets:		
Cash	$50,000	$ 20,000
Inventory	15,000	40,000
Equipment (net of accumulated depreciation)	30,000	40,000
Total assets	$95,000	$100,000
Liabilities & stockholders' equity:		
Current liabilities	$10,000	$ 30,000
Capital stock	70,000	70,000
Retained earnings	15,000	–0–
Total liabilities & stockholders' equity	$95,000	$100,000

Preparing a common dollar balance sheet

The basic feature of a common dollar balance sheet is that all amounts are stated in terms of current dollars. The conversion of Flation Company's December 31 balance sheet from historical dollars to common dollars is illustrated on page 488.

FLATION COMPANY
Conversion to Common Dollar Balance Sheet
December 31, Year 1

	Historical Dollars	Conversion Ratio	Common Dollars
Assets:			
Cash	$50,000		$ 50,000
Inventory	15,000	× 150/100	22,500
Equipment (net of accumulated deprecia-tion)	30,000	× 150/100	45,000
Total assets	$95,000		$117,500
Liabilities & stockholders' equity:			
Current liabilities	$10,000		$ 10,000
Capital stock	70,000	× 150/100	105,000
Retained earnings	15,000	*	2,500
Total liabilities & stockholders' equity	$95,000		$117,500

*See common dollar income statement on p. 489.

In a common dollar balance sheet, the assets, liabilities, and stock-holders' equity are **restated in the number of current dollars equivalent in purchasing power to the historical dollar amounts.** To restate a historical dollar amount in terms of current dollars, we multiply the historical amount by the **ratio of the current price level to the historical price level.** For example, assume land was purchased for $10,000 when the price level stood at 100. If the price level is now 170, we may find the number of current dollars equivalent to the purchasing power originally in-vested in the land by multiplying the $10,000 historical cost by **170/100.** The result, $17,000, represents the number of current dollars equiva-lent in purchasing power to the 10,000 historical dollars.

An explanation of the differences between the historical dollar balances and the common dollar balances will make clear the nature of the conversion process.

MONETARY ITEMS First note that the balances of two items, cash and current liabilities, are exactly the same in both the historical dollar and common dollar balance sheets. The reason for this is that cash, claims to cash, and obligations to pay cash represent monetary resources and obligations which are **fixed in terms of dollars.** If we have $50,000 cash and the price level rises, we still have $50,000 even though these dollars will now buy fewer goods and services. Similarly, if we owe $10,000 and the price level rises, we still owe $10,000 even though the debt may be paid using less valuable dollars.

Assets representing claims to a fixed number of dollars and liabilities to pay a fixed number of dollars are called *monetary items.* The dollar amounts of monetary items should not be restated in preparing a common dollar balance sheet.

NONMONETARY ITEMS Nonmonetary items include all items in the balance sheet which *are not* claims or obligations of fixed-dollar amount. The historical dollar amount of nonmonetary items *must be restated in terms of current dollars.*

In our example, the inventory and equipment were acquired when the general price level was 100. Since the general price level is now 150, the cost of these assets would be restated in current dollars by multiplying the historical cost by the conversion ratio *150/100.* Capital stock is also a nonmonetary item. To determine the number of current dollars equivalent in purchasing power to the original investment made by stockholders when the general price level was 100, we would again multiply by the conversion ratio of *150/100.*

The restated balance of the retained earnings will be derived from the common dollar income statement.

Preparing a common dollar income statement

The conversion of Flation Company's conventional income statement to common dollars is illustrated below:

FLATION COMPANY
Conversion to Common Dollar Income Statement
For the Year Ended December 31, Year 1

	Historical Dollars	Conversion Ratio	Common Dollars
Sales	$50,000	× 150/125	$60,000
Cost of goods sold	25,000	× 150/100	37,500
Gross profit on sales	$25,000		$22,500
Depreciation expense	10,000	× 150/100	15,000
Net income (in historical dollars)	$15,000		
Operating income (in purchasing power)			$ 7,500
Less: Loss in purchasing power from holding monetary assets during rising price levels (Schedule A)*			(16,000)
Add: Gain in purchasing power from owing money during rising price levels (Schedule A)*			11,000
Net income (in purchasing power)			$ 2,500

*See p. 491.

RESTATING SALES Notice that the conversion ratio used to restate sales revenue in current dollars is *150/125* rather than 150/100. The reason for this is that the dollars representing the sales revenue were received uniformly throughout the year. Thus, *on the average,* these dollars were received when the price level was 125 (average price level during the year).

RESTATING THE COST OF GOODS SOLD The cost of goods sold in our example came entirely from the beginning inventory, which had been acquired when the price level was 100. To determine the number of current dollars equivalent to the historical cost of goods sold, we must multiply the historical amount by the conversion ratio of *150/100.* If the cost of goods sold had not come entirely from beginning inventory the restatement of the cost of goods sold would be more complex.

RESTATING DEPRECIATION EXPENSE Depreciation expense represents the allocation of the historical cost of the equipment against revenue. Since the equipment was acquired when the price level stood at 100, the conversion ratio of *150/100* should be used to restate the depreciation expense in terms of current dollars. Since depreciable assets are long-lived, the price level prevailing when the assets were acquired may be substantially different from the current price level. In such cases, the amount of depreciation expense recognized becomes one of the most significant differences between historical dollar and common dollar financial statements.

Gains and losses in purchasing power

The common dollar income statement introduces a new consideration in the determination of net income: gains and losses in purchasing power from holding monetary items. Holding monetary assets during a period of rising prices results in a loss of purchasing power because the value of money is falling. In contrast, owing money during a period of rising prices gives rise to a gain in purchasing power because debts may be repaid using dollars of less purchasing power than those originally borrowed. Purchasing power gains and losses may be computed by the type of analysis illustrated on page 491.

The analysis of cash transactions is begun by restating the beginning cash balance, the cash receipts throughout the year, and the cash payments throughout the year in terms of current dollars. From this analysis, we see that Flation Company started with $30,000 of purchasing power (stated in current dollars), received another $60,000 of purchasing power, and paid out $24,000 of purchasing power. This implies that $66,000 of purchasing power should still be on hand, if there had been no loss. However, the actual cash on hand amounts to only $50,000. Thus, Flation Company has lost $16,000 in *purchasing*

FLATION COMPANY   **Schedule A**
Analysis of Cash Transactions for Year 1

	Historical Dollars	Conversion Ratio	Common Dollars
Beginning cash balance, Jan. 1	$20,000	× 150/100*	$30,000
Cash received from sales	50,000	× 150/125†	60,000
Cash payments on liabilities	(20,000)	× 150/125†	(24,000)
Ending cash balance, Dec. 31	$50,000		

Implied purchasing power on hand, in current dollars	$66,000
Less: Actual cash on hand, Dec. 31	50,000
Loss in purchasing power from holding cash during rising price levels . .	$16,000

Analysis of Current Liability Transactions for Year 1

Beginning balance of current liabilities, Jan. 1 . .	$30,000	× 150/100*	$45,000
Payments made on liabilities	(20,000)	× 150/125†	(24,000)
Ending balance of current liabilities, Dec. 31 . . .	$10,000		

Implied purchasing power owed, in current dollars	$21,000
Less: Actual amount owed, Dec. 31	10,000
Gain in purchasing power from owing money during rising price levels . . .	$11,000

*Historical amount recorded when price level was 100.
†Historical amount recorded at average price level of 125.

power by holding cash while the value of money declined. Flation Company *has not actually lost any cash;* the cash on hand has lost $16,000 of its purchasing power.

Similar reasoning is used in the analysis of current liabilities. Flation Company started out owing $45,000 in terms of the purchasing power of current dollars. The company repaid $24,000 of purchasing power during the year, implying that it still owed $21,000 if the original purchasing power were to be repaid. However, current liabilities are a monetary item, and Flation Company must only pay the fixed dollar amount of $10,000 to eliminate the debts. Thus, Flation Company will have to repay $11,000 less *purchasing power* than it originally borrowed, resulting in a gain in purchasing power.

Interpreting the common dollar income statement

The basic difference between historical dollar and common dollar financial statements is the unit of measure. Historical dollar statements use the dollar as a basic unit of measure. The unit of measure in common dollar financial statements is the *purchasing power of the current dollar.*

A conventional income statement shows how many dollars were added to stockholders' equity from the operation of the business. Identifying a dollar increase in stockholders' equity as "income" implies that the stockholders are better off when they recover more than the original number of dollars they invested. No attention is given to the fact that a greater number of dollars may still have less purchasing power than was originally invested.

A common dollar income statement measures changes in the purchasing power represented by stockholders' equity. An increase in the purchasing power of stockholders' equity means that the amount currently invested in the business commands more goods and services than the amount originally invested. Our conventional income statement shows us that Flation Company increased stockholders' equity by $15,000 during the year, but our common dollar income statement shows us that the purchasing power of stockholders' equity increased by only $2,500.

COMMON DOLLAR STATEMENTS IN PRACTICE Common dollar financial statements are *not* generally accepted as primary reports to stockholders. A few companies have published some version of common dollar financial statements in supplementary schedules included in their annual reports.[5]

The conversion of accounting data into common dollars is not widely used in the United States because thus far the business community is apparently not convinced of the increased usefulness of this information.

The effort required to make accounting measurements in common dollar terms and to prepare financial statements on this basis is considerable. In an age of electronic computers, however, this additional data processing effort is not a practical barrier to the preparation of common dollar statements.

Fair-value accounting distinguished from common dollar accounting

We have used the expression *common dollar accounting* to describe financial statements in which historical costs were adjusted to reflect changes in the general price level. Common dollar accounting *does not abandon historical cost* as the basis of measurement but simply expresses cost in terms of the current value of money. Also, common dollar accounting does not mean that current fair values or replacement values are used in the preparation of financial statements. For example, a tract of land which cost $100,000 many years ago would

[5] See Accounting Research Study No. 6, *Reporting the Financial Effects of Price-Level Changes,* AICPA (New York: 1963), pp. 169–219. See also Accounting Principles Board Statement No. 3, *Financial Statements Restated for General Price-Level Changes,* AICPA (New York: 1969).

be stated at $150,000 in common dollars if the general price level had risen by 50%. However, the current fair value of the land might be $400,000 because land prices might have risen much more than the general price level.

If accountants were to use current fair values in financial statements, the unit of measurement would be current dollars since current fair values are stated in these terms. But the use of current fair values in preparing financial statements *would be a departure from the historical cost concept,* and would require that accountants develop reliable techniques for measuring the current cost of replacing various types of assets.

Some accountants have recommended that supplementary financial statements using current fair values of assets be prepared and submitted along with conventional statements. Accountants for the most part are not in favor of this, because such estimates of current values lack the objectivity desired by most users of financial statements. When assets show a significant increase in value, it is difficult to argue that historical costs continue to provide investors with useful information, even though the estimates of current fair values are subject to some lack of precision and objectivity. In dealing with this problem, accountants are faced with a fundamental issue: Can the usefulness of financial statements be improved by providing more relevant information while sacrificing some objectivity? Accountants continue to seek a satisfactory answer to this question.

DEMONSTRATION PROBLEM

The information below relates to the operations of The Hobby Shop, Inc., during the current year:

Sales (net of returns and allowances)	*$400,000*
Cost of goods purchased for resale (net)	*270,000*
Inventory at Jan. 1 (at sales price)	*50,000*
Inventory at Dec. 31 (at sales price), replacement cost $58,000	*100,000*
Cash payments for operating expenses, including prepayments	*80,000*
Estimated profit on sales orders for goods not yet delivered to customers	*12,100*
Depreciation expense based on actual cost	*10,000*
Depreciation expense based on current fair value	*15,000*
Increase in short-term prepayments during the year	*300*
Estimated uncollectible accounts receivable at end of year	*1,100*
Increase in accrued liabilities during the year	*1,500*
Increase in goodwill (value of the business) during the year	*25,000*
Net purchasing power gain resulting from increase in general price level during the year	*4,200*

The gross profit on sales is constant on all items normally included in inventory.

Instructions

a Prepare a schedule computing the relationship between the sales value and the cost of the merchandise handled by The Hobby Shop, Inc., during the current year.

b Prepare an income statement for the current year in accordance with generally accepted accounting principles. Ending inventory is to be valued at the lower of cost or market. Indicate the proper disposition of any item not used in preparing the income statement. Ignore income taxes.

SOLUTION TO DEMONSTRATION PROBLEM

a
Computation of cost percentage:

Sales, net	$400,000
Add: Ending inventory, at sales price	100,000
Goods available for sale, at sales price.	$500,000
Less: Beginning inventory, at sales price	50,000
Purchases, at sales price	$450,000
Cost percentage ($270,000 ÷ $450,000)	60%

b
THE HOBBY SHOP, INC.
Income Statement
For the Current Year

Sales, net		$400,000
Cost of goods sold:		
Inventory, Jan. 1 (60% × $50,000)	$ 30,000	
Purchases, net	270,000	
Cost of goods available for sale	$300,000	
Less: Inventory at Dec. 31, at lower of cost or market		
(cost = 60% × $100,000, or $60,000)	58,000	
Cost of goods sold		242,000
Gross profit on sales		$158,000
Operating expenses (see below)		92,300
Net income		$ 65,700

Operating expenses:	
Cash payments	$ 80,000
Depreciation (on actual cost)	10,000
Increase in accrued liabilities during the year	1,500
Uncollectible accounts expense	1,100
Subtotal	$ 92,600
Less: Increase in short-term prepayments during the year .	300
Operating expenses on accrual basis	$ 92,300

The estimated profit on sales orders for goods not yet delivered to customers, $12,100, is not realized and should not appear in the income statement. The sales have not been completed.

Depreciation expense based on current fair value, $15,000, does not appear in the conventional income statement prepared on the basis of historical costs.

The increase in the value of goodwill, $25,000, is not realized and therefore does not appear in the income statement.

The net purchasing power gain resulting from increase in the general price level during the year, $4,200, would appear in common dollar statements but not in historical cost financial statements prepared in accordance with generally accepted accounting principles.

REVIEW QUESTIONS

1 What is the basic objective of accounting?

2 What is the primary informational need of managers? How do the needs of creditors and owners differ from those of management?

3 Accounting measurements are based on past, present, and future exchange transactions. Give an example of accounting measurement based on each kind of transaction.

4 Explain what is meant by the expression "trade-off between *reliability* and *relevance*" in connection with the preparation of financial statements.

5 Barker Company has at the end of the current period an inventory of merchandise which cost $500,000. It would cost $600,000 to replace this inventory, and it is estimated that the goods will probably be sold for a total of $700,000. If the firm were to terminate operations immediately, the inventory could probably be sold for $480,000. Discuss the relative reliability and relevance of each of these dollar measurements of the ending inventory.

6 Why is it necessary for accountants to assume the existence of a clearly defined accounting entity?

7 What are *consolidated financial statements?*

8 If the going-concern assumption were dropped, there would be no point in having current asset and current liability classifications in the balance sheet. Explain.

9 "The matching of costs and revenue is the natural extension of the fiscal period principle." Evaluate this statement.

10 Define *objectivity, consistency, materiality,* and *conservatism.*

11 Is the assumption that the dollar is a stable unit of measure realistic? What alternative procedure would you suggest?

12 a Why is it important that any change in accounting methods from one period to the next be disclosed?

b Does the concept of consistency mean that all companies in a given industry follow similar accounting methods?

13 Briefly define the principle of *disclosure.* List five examples of information that should be disclosed in financial statements or in notes accompanying the statements.

14 In the phrase "generally accepted accounting principles," what determines general acceptability? Name four authoritative bodies that have exercised influence over the development of accounting principles.

15 List four stages of the productive process which might become the accountant's basis for recognizing changes in the value of a firm's output. Which stage is most commonly used as a basis for revenue recognition? Why?

16 The CPA's standard audit opinion consists of two major paragraphs. Describe the essential content of each paragraph.

17 Define *monetary assets* and indicate whether a gain or loss results from the holding of such assets during a period of rising prices.

18 Why is it advantageous to be in debt during an inflationary period?

19 Evaluate the following statement: "During a period of rising prices, the conventional income statement overstates net income because the amount of depreciation recorded is less than the value of the service potential of assets consumed."

20 In presenting financial information to their stockholders and the public, it is not generally acceptable practice for corporations to report in *common dollar* terms, although such statements are occasionally presented in addition to regular financial statements as supplementary information. Why has the use of common dollars in financial reporting not gained general acceptance?

21 Publicly owned corporations are required to include in their annual report a description of the accounting principles followed in the preparation of their financial statements. What advantages do you see in this practice?

EXERCISES

Ex. 14-1 For each situation described below, indicate the principle (or principles) of accounting that is violated, if any. You may choose among the following principles: Conservatism, consistency, disclosure, entity, going concern, matching, materiality, objectivity.

Situations
a The assets of a partnership are combined with the separate assets of the partners in preparing a balance sheet.
b The estimated salvage value of equipment is reported in the balance sheet; book value exceeds salvage value.
c The cost of merchandise purchased is recognized as expense before it is sold in order to report a less favorable financial position.
d Plans to dispose of a major segment of the business are not communicated to readers of the financial statements.
e A portion of the cost of a major television promotional campaign in the month of May is deferred and arbitrarily allocated to revenue over a five-year period.
f The method of depreciation is changed every two years and the change is disclosed in financial statements.

Ex. 14-2 The J. D. Rogers Corporation recognizes the profit on a long-term construction project as work progresses. From the information given below, compute the profit that should be recognized each year, assuming that the original cost estimate on the contract was $600,000 and that the contract price is $750,000:

Year	Costs Incurred	Profit Considered Realized
1	$120,000	$?
2	300,000	?
3	176,190	?
Totals	$596,190	$153,810

Ex. 14-3 On September 15, Year 1, Robert Hamilton sold a piece of property which cost him $48,000 for $80,000, net of commissions and other selling expenses. The terms of sale were as follows: Down payment, $8,000; balance, $3,000 on the fifteenth day of each month for 24 months, starting October 15, Year 1. Compute the gross profit to be recognized by Hamilton in Year 1, Year 2, and Year 3 *(a)* on the *accrual basis* of accounting and *(b)* on the *installment basis* of accounting.

Ex. 14-4 Three companies started business with $100,000 at the beginning of the current year when the general price index stood at 125. The First Company invested the money in a note receivable due in four years; the Second Company invested its cash in land; and the Third Company purchased a building for $400,000, assuming a liability for the unpaid balance of $300,000. The price level stood at 140 at the end of the year. Compute the purchasing power gain or loss for each company during the year.

Ex. 14-5 In Year 1, the New Company was started with a total capitalization of $5 million in order to acquire land for long-term investment. At this time, the general price index was 100. In Year 5, the general price index stands at 140 but the price of all land in the area in which the New Company invested has doubled in value. Rental receipts for grazing and farming during the five-year period were sufficient to pay all carrying charges on the land.
a What is the purchasing power gain or loss for the New Company during the five-year period?
b What would be the "economic" (common dollar) gain or loss if the land were sold at its present fair value?

Ex. 14-6 The following information relating to the latest fiscal year is available for Bartel's Hardware Store, a single proprietorship:

	Balance, Jan. 1	Cash Receipts or (Payments)	Balance, Dec. 31
Accounts receivable—sale of merchandise	$17,000	$180,000	$25,500
Accounts payable	9,750	(88,200)	11,200
Prepaid supplies	1,360	(4,900)	750
Merchandise inventories	21,000		23,600
Accrued wages payable	2,500	(39,000)	6,000

Compute the net income for the year:
a On a *cash basis,* showing only cash receipts and disbursements.
b On an *accrual basis,* as required by generally accepted accounting principles.

PROBLEMS

14-1 In each of the situations described below, the question is whether generally accepted accounting principles have been violated. In each case state the accounting principle or concept, if any, that has been violated and explain briefly the nature of the violation. If you believe the treatment *is in accord with generally accepted accounting principles,* state this as your position and briefly defend it.
a Merchandise inventory which cost $2 million is reported in the balance sheet at $3 million, the expected sales price less estimated direct selling expenses.
b New Mining Company reports net income for the current year of $1,300,010. In the audit report the auditors stated: "We certify that the results of operations shown in the income statement are a true and accurate portrayal of the company's operations for the current year."

c The Mundie Company has purchased a computer for $1.5 million. The company expects to use the computer for five years, at which time it will acquire a larger and faster computer. The new computer is expected to cost $3.5 million. During the current year the company debited $700,000 to the Depreciation Expense account to "provide for one-fifth of the estimated cost of the new computer."

d John Lucky operates a mine as a single proprietorship. During the current year, geologists and engineers revised upward the estimated value of ore deposits on his property. Lucky instructed his accountant to record goodwill of $2 million, the estimated value of unmined ore in excess of previous estimates. The offsetting credit was made to John Lucky, Capital.

e The Rex Oil Company reported on its balance sheet the total of all wages, supplies, depreciation on equipment, and other costs related to the drilling of a producing oil well as an intangible asset, and then amortized this asset as oil was produced from the well.

14-2 Cameo Company sells its products on open account due 90 days after the date of sale. The company pays a commission of 10% of selling price to its saleswomen as soon as the customers pay their accounts.

During the first three years of operations, the company reported sales on a cash basis; that is, it did not record the sale until the cash was collected. Commissions to saleswomen were recorded only when cash was collected from customers. Net income figures computed on this basis were:

Year 1	$ 50,000
Year 2	75,000
Year 3	112,500

An accountant, called in at the end of Year 3 to review the store's accounting system, suggested that a better picture of earnings would be obtained if both sales and commissions were recorded on the accrual basis. After analyzing the company's records, he reported that accounts receivable at the end of each year were as follows:

Year 1	$37,500
Year 2	60,000
Year 3	27,500

Sales commissions should be accrued at the rate of 10% of accounts receivable.

Instructions

a On the basis of this information, prepare a schedule showing the amount of net income Cameo Company would have reported in each of the three years if it had followed accrual accounting for its sales and sales commissions.

b Comment on the differences in net income under the two methods and the significance of the trend in the net income figures as revised.

14-3 Roadbuilders, Inc., began business early in Year 1 with $15 million in cash. The company was the successful bidder on the construction of a section of highway. The bid price of the construction was $20 million. The construction will begin in Year 1 and will take two years to complete; the deadline for completion is near the end of Year 2.

The contract calls for payments of $4 million per year to Roadbuilders, Inc., at the end of Year 1 and at the end of each of the next four years. The company expects that construction costs will total $15 million, of which $6 million will be incurred in Year 1 and $9 million in Year 2.

The controller of the company recognizes that there are a number of ways he might account for this contract. He might recognize income at the time the contract is completed (sales method), near the end of Year 2. Alternatively, he might recognize income during construction (production method), in proportion to the percentage of the total cost incurred in each of Years 1 and 2. Finally, he might recognize income in proportion to the percentage of the total contract price collected in installment receipts during the five-year period (installment method).

Instructions

a Assuming that the timing and cost of construction are exactly according to plan and that this contract is the sole activity of Roadbuilders, Inc., during the five-year period beginning with Year 1, prepare a comparative five-year statement (in millions of dollars) showing the amount of annual net income that would be reported each year and the balance in retained earnings at the end of each year under each of the accounting methods considered by the controller. (Ignore income taxes.)

b Prepare comparative balance sheets (in millions of dollars) for Roadbuilders, Inc., as of the end of Year 1 and Year 2, under each of the three accounting methods.

14-4 James B. Stowe had substantial income from many sources. He instructed his accountant to prepare the income statement for his business, the Stowe Construction & Sales Company, on the most conservative basis possible in order to minimize his income taxes. Following his instructions, the accountant prepared the following income statement:

STOWE CONSTRUCTION & SALES COMPANY
Income Statement
First Year of Operations

Revenue:		
Sales—regular		$126,000
Collections on installment sales		180,000
Construction work completed		54,000
Total revenue		$360,000
Costs and expenses:		
Cost of goods sold—regular	$100,800	
Cost of goods sold—installment basis, 80% of collec-		
tions	144,000	
Cost of construction work completed	43,800	
Operating expenses	72,000	
Interest expense	29,400	
Total costs and expenses		390,000
Loss for first year of operations		$(30,000)

Stowe was pleased to know that he will be able to reduce his other taxable income as a result of the loss from his business. He was, however, concerned because his banker refused to lend him $60,000 for use in his business because, as the banker put it, "You've lost too much money in your first year of operations and I have a policy against lending money to unprofitable businesses." At this point, Stowe comes to you for advice and gives you additional information relating to the items appearing in the income statement. After reviewing this information, you suggest that the following changes be made:

(1) Installment sales amounted to $390,000, the cost of the goods was $312,000, or 80% of sales. The accountant reported only the cash collections as revenue and deducted a proportional amount as the cost of the goods sold on the installment basis. You recommend that the entire income on installment sales be included in the income statement.

(2) The revenue and cost of construction work include three contracts started and completed in the first year. In addition, the following data relate to the six contracts started in the first year which will be completed in the following year.

Total contract price	$648,000
Total estimated cost of contracts	540,000
Actual costs incurred in first year	180,000

You suggest that profit on these contracts be recognized on the percentage-of-completion basis.

(3) The ending inventory of goods to be sold on the regular basis was valued on the lifo basis at $30,600, this inventory on a fifo basis would have been $33,600. You propose that the first-in, first-out method be used in preparing the income statement to be resubmitted to the banker.

(4) Included in operating expense is depreciation of $9,600, computed by using an accelerated method. You recommend the use of the straight-line depreciation method, which would result in depreciation of only $7,200.

(5) Also included in operating expenses is $18,000 of expenditures which are applicable to future periods. You suggest that these items be deferred and reported in the balance sheet as assets.

Instructions

a Prepare a revised income statement for Stowe Construction & Sales Company, giving effect to the changes in accounting you suggested to Stowe. (Ignore income taxes.) Certain key figures to appear in the revised income statement should be computed in supporting schedules. Reference to these supporting schedules should appear in the revised income statement. The appropriate supporting schedules are indicated in *b* below. (The first item of revenue, Sales—regular, means sales made on 30-day open account as opposed to sales on the installment plan.)

b Prepare the following separate schedules to support the revised income statement:

(1) A schedule showing the revenue from construction work measured on the percentage-of-completion basis

(2) A schedule showing the cost of goods sold—regular (30-day open account sales)

(3) A schedule showing the cost of construction work

(4) A schedule showing operating expenses

14-5 Mayhew Corporation invested $300,000 cash, which was not needed for current operations, in a time deposit at the beginning of Year 1. The cash remained in the time deposit throughout the year; and since the company has ample cash on hand to meet future requirements, the board of directors is considering leaving the $300,000 invested in the time deposit (with extension of the maturity date, as appropriate) for an indefinite period of time.

An index of the general price level stood at 150 at the beginning of Year 1 and at 200 at the end of Year 1. In a presentation to the board of directors, the controller of the company wishes to demonstrate the loss of purchasing power that has resulted from holding this investment during a period of inflation. He is uncertain whether to measure the purchasing power loss in terms of end-of-year dollars, beginning-of-year dollars, or base-year dollars. The controller's assistant has made the following comparative calculations:

	End-of-year Dollars (Index = 200)	Beginning-of-year Dollars (Index = 150)	Base-year Dollars (Index = 100)
Balance of time deposit at beginning of Year 1	$400,000 (D)	$300,000	$200,000 (A)
Balance of time deposit at the end of Year 1	300,000	225,000 (C)	150,000 (B)
Loss of purchasing power . .	$100,000	$ 75,000	$ 50,000

Instructions

a Explain how the figures labeled *(A), (B), (C), (D),* in the assistant's schedule were computed, and why.

b Which measuring unit would you suggest that the controller use in making his presentation to the board of directors? Explain your reasoning.

c On a common dollar balance sheet prepared at the end of Year 1, at what figure would the time deposit be reported? Why? What would be the amount of purchasing power loss reported on common dollar financial statements, relating to the ownership of this time deposit?

d If, instead of a time deposit, the $300,000 were a note payable by the Mayhew Corporation, due two years after the beginning of Year 1, how would this affect the assistant's analysis of the effect of the decline in the purchasing power of money during the period?

14-6 Gemini Corporation was organized at the beginning of Year 1. The opening balance sheet is shown below:

GEMINI CORPORATION

Balance Sheet

Beginning of Year 1

Cash	$100,000	Accounts payable	$150,000
Inventories	350,000	Capital stock	300,000
		Total liabilities &	
Total assets	$450,000	stockholders' equity	$450,000

At the beginning of Year 1, the general price index stood at 100; during Year 1 the average price level was 120, and at year-end the price level was 140. During Year 1, Gemini Corporation sold $200,000 of its inventory for $300,000 cash, paid $120,000 cash on accounts payable, and paid cash operating expenses of $72,000. These transactions occurred at a uniform rate throughout the year. The company was involved in no other transactions during Year 1.

Instructions

a Prepare an analysis of cash transactions in terms of historical dollars and common (end-of-year) dollars.

b Prepare an analysis of accounts payable transactions in terms of historical dollars and common (end-of-year) dollars.

c Prepare a comparative income statement for Year 1 in historical and common (end-of-year) dollars.

d Prepare a comparative balance sheet as of the end of Year 1 in historical and common (end-of-year) dollars.

e Write a brief statement comparing the results as shown in the financial statements prepared in historical and common (end-of-year) dollars.

BUSINESS DECISION PROBLEM 14

For many years, Hanson Company used the lifo method of inventory valuation and the declining balance method of depreciation in measuring the net income of its mail order business. In addition, the company charged off all costs of catalogs as incurred. In Year 10, the company changed its inventory pricing method to fifo, adopted the straight-line method of depreciation, and decided to charge off catalog costs only as catalogs are distributed to potential customers.

The following information for the last three years is taken from the company's accounting records:

	Year 10	Year 9	Year 8
Sales (net).	$500,000	$400,000	$350,000
Purchases (net)	300,000	220,000	200,000
Ending inventory—fifo	50,000	45,000	40,000
Ending inventory—lifo	30,000	28,000	25,000
Depreciation—declining balance method	27,500	30,000	35,000
Depreciation—straight-line method	20,000	20,000	20,000
Operating expenses other than depreciation	120,500	93,000	80,000
Catalog costs included in operating expenses but			
considered applicable to future revenue	18,500	8,000	5,000
Net income as computed by Hanson Company . .	100,000	60,000	37,000

At the end of Year 10, Hanson Company prepared the following comparative income statement and presented it to a banker in connection with an application for a substantial, long-term loan:

HANSON COMPANY
Comparative Income Statement
For Years Ended December 31

	Year 10	Year 9
Sales (net).	$500,000	$400,000
Cost of goods sold*	278,000	217,000
Gross profit on sales	$222,000	$183,000
Operating expenses	122,000	123,000
Net income	$100,000	$ 60,000

*Based on lifo inventory method in Year 9; inventory at end of Year 10 was valued on fifo basis.

The loan officer for the Plaza National Bank, where Hanson Company has applied for the loan, asks you to help him decide whether to lend the money to Hanson Company.

Instructions
a Prepare a detailed explanation of the way Hanson Company computed the income statement for Year 10, and briefly evaluate its approach.
b Determine whether Hanson Company's net income has, in fact, increased in Year 10, and recommend whether the comparative income statement for Years 9 and 10 should be prepared (*1*) on the same accounting basis as in prior years or (*2*) on the revised accounting basis. You should prepare a comparative income statement both ways and indicate which approach is more appropriate.

FIFTEEN

STATEMENT OF CHANGES IN FINANCIAL POSITION
CASH FLOWS

The heartbeat of any profit-making enterprise is reflected in the pulsing rhythm of its operating cycle. The business obtains capital from various sources and invests it in revenue-producing assets. These investments are in turn converted into goods and services which are sold to customers. When customers pay their accounts, the company again has resources to apply against its debts and begin the operating cycle anew.

The balance sheet portrays the overall financial position of the business at any given time in this recurring cycle of investment, recovery of investment, and reinvestment. The income statement shows the growth in the amount of resources as a result of operations. In a sense, the fate of any given business investment is read in the income statement, since it tells whether revenue is larger or smaller during any period than the cost of the resources used up in generating this revenue. In this chapter we introduce a third major financial statement, the **statement of changes in financial position**[1] and a related summary of cash movements, the **cash flow statement.**

[1] In *Opinion No. 19,* "Reporting Changes in Financial Position," issued in 1971, the Accounting Principles Board of the AICPA concluded (p. 373) that "information concerning the financing and investing activities of a business enterprise and the changes in its financial position for a period is essential for financial statement users, particularly owners and creditors, in making economic decisions. When financial statements purporting to present both financial position (balance sheet) and results of operations (statement of income and retained earnings) are issued, a statement summarizing changes in financial position should also be presented as a basic financial statement for each period for which an income statement is presented."

STATEMENT OF CHANGES IN FINANCIAL POSITION

A statement of changes in financial position shows the sources and uses of working capital during an accounting period. It also reports the financing and investing activities not directly affecting working capital. For example, the issuance of capital stock or bonds in exchange for equipment is both a financing and an investing transaction which does not affect working capital. However, the statement of changes in financial position should include such a transaction as both a source and use of working capital in order to give the reader a complete picture of the inflow and outflow of all financial resources during an accounting period.

In published annual reports of corporations, the funds flow statement has often been labeled as a *statement of sources and uses of working capital, a statement of source and application of funds,* or simply a *funds statement.* In 1971, the Accounting Principles Board recommended the title *statement of changes in financial position.* A statement of changes in financial position is useful to management, creditors, investors, and financial analysts because it can help answer questions such as: What use was made of net income? Why have current assets declined even though net income has increased? How was new construction of plant and equipment financed? What became of the proceeds from a stock (or bond) issue? How much long-term debt or preferred stock was converted into common stock?

Working capital viewed as a fund of liquid resources

In ordinary usage, the term *funds* usually means cash. Businessmen and financial analysts, however, think of "funds" in a broader sense. Short-term credit is often used as a substitute for cash; notes and accounts payable as well as various accrued liabilities are used to meet the short-term financing needs of a business. Current assets are constantly being converted into cash, which is then used to pay current liabilities. The net amount of short-term liquid resources available to a business firm at any given time, therefore, is represented by its working capital—the difference between current assets and current liabilities. This explains why it is natural to think of working capital as a "fund" of liquid resources on hand at any given time.

If the amount of working capital increased during a given fiscal period, this means that more working capital was generated than was used for various business purposes; if a decrease in working capital occurred the reverse is true. One of the key purposes of the statement of changes in financial position is to explain fully the increase or decrease in working capital during a fiscal period. This is done by showing where working capital originated and how it was used.

Sources and uses of working capital

Any transaction that increases the amount of working capital is a *source of working capital.* For example, the sale of merchandise for an amount greater than its cost is a source of working capital, because the increase in cash or receivables is greater than the decrease in inventories.

Any transaction that decreases working capital is a *use of working capital.* For example, either incurring a current liability to acquire a noncurrent asset or paying expenses in cash represents a decrease in working capital.

On the other hand, any transaction that changes current assets or current liabilities but does not result in a change in working capital is not a source or use of liquid funds (working capital). For example, the collection of an account receivable (which increases cash and decreases an account receivable by an equal amount) is not a source of working capital. Similarly, the payment of an account payable (which decreases cash and decreases an account payable by an equal amount) does not change the amount of working capital.

The principal sources and uses of working capital are listed below:

Sources of working capital:

Operations (revenue minus expenses that require the use of funds)
Sale of noncurrent assets
Borrowing by issuance of long-term notes or bonds
Issuing additional shares of capital stock

Uses of working capital:

Declaration of cash dividends
Repayment of long-term debt
Purchase of noncurrent assets
Repurchase of outstanding shares of capital stock

The relationship between working capital and other balance sheet accounts is illustrated in the diagram on page 507.

The shaded area in the diagram represents working capital, that is, current assets less current liabilities. The arrows flowing into the shaded area represent sources of working capital; the arrows flowing out of the shaded area represent uses of working capital. You may find it useful to refer to this diagram as you study the effect of transactions on working capital in the discussion and illustrations which follow.

Simple illustration

Let us begin with a very simple set of facts. Suppose that John Claire started a business as a single proprietorship on April 30 by investing $30,000 cash; he rented a building on May 1 and completed the transactions shown on page 507 during the month of May.

ANY COMPANY
Balance Sheet
End of Year 1

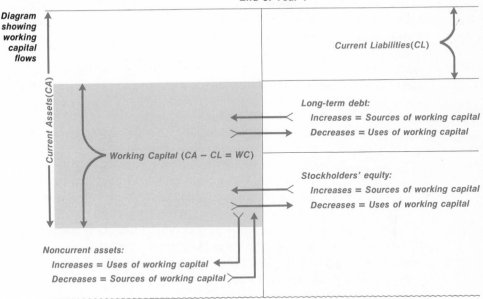

Diagram showing working capital flows

(1) Invested an additional $10,000 cash in the business.

(2) Purchased merchandise costing $40,000 on credit and sold three-fourths of this, also on credit, for $58,000.

(3) Collected $45,000 on receivables; paid $32,000 on accounts payable.

(4) Paid $15,500 cash for operating expenses.

(5) Purchased land for the construction of a store. Gave $15,000 cash and a six-month note for $12,000 in payment for the land.

(6) Withdrew $2,000 from the business for personal use.

Claire's financial statements at the end of May are shown below and on page 508.

JOHN CLAIRE
Income Statement
For Month of May

Sales		$58,000
Cost of goods sold:		
Purchases	$40,000	
Less: Ending inventory (one-fourth of purchases)	10,000	30,000
Gross profit on sales		$28,000
Operating expenses		15,500
Net income for month of May		$12,500

Statements covering one month's operations of single proprietorship

JOHN CLAIRE
Comparative Balance Sheet

Assets	May 31	May 1
Cash	$20,500	$30,000
Accounts receivable	13,000	
Inventory	10,000	
Land	27,000	
Total assets	$70,500	$30,000

Liabilities & Owner's Equity		
Note payable	$12,000	
Accounts payable	8,000	
John Claire, capital	50,500	$30,000
Total liabilities & owner's equity	$70,500	$30,000

The working capital amounted to $30,000 (consisting entirely of cash) on May 1 but was only $23,500 ($43,500 − $20,000) on May 31, a decrease of $6,500. In analyzing the six transactions completed during the month of May, we see that working capital was increased and decreased as follows:

JOHN CLAIRE
Effect of Transactions on Working Capital
For Month of May

Land and the owner's capital accounts were increased as a result of these transactions

Increases:		
Additional investment by owner		$10,000
Sale of merchandise for more than cost ($58,000 − $30,000)		28,000
Total increases in working capital		$38,000
Decreases:		
Payment of operating expenses	$15,500	
Payment of cash for purchase of land	15,000	
Issuance of current note payable for purchase of land	12,000	
Withdrawal by owner	2,000	44,500
Decrease in working capital during May		$ 6,500

A complete list of transactions for a fiscal period may not be readily available, and even if it were, analysis of such a list would be a laborious process. In practice, the statement of changes in financial position is generally prepared in summary form by analyzing the changes that occurred in the noncurrent accounts during a fiscal period. An analysis of the comparative balance sheet for John Claire indicates that the

Land account increased by $27,000 (a use of working capital) and that Claire's capital account increased by $20,500 as a result of (1) additional investment of $10,000 (a source of working capital), (2) net income of $12,500 (a source of working capital), and (3) a withdrawal of $2,000 (a use of working capital). We can therefore prepare the following statement of changes in financial position, including the composition of working capital, for the month of May:

JOHN CLAIRE
Statement of Changes in Financial Position
For Month of May

A simple statement of changes in financial position

Sources of working capital:		
Operations (net income)		$12,500
Additional investment by owner		10,000
Total sources of working capital		$22,500
Uses of working capital:		
Purchase of land	$27,000	
Withdrawal by owner	2,000	
Total uses of working capital		29,000
Decrease in working capital		$ 6,500

	End of May	Beginning of May	Increase or (Decrease) in Working Capital
Composition of working capital:			
Current assets:			
Cash	$20,500	$30,000	$(9,500)
Accounts receivable	13,000	–0–	13,000
Inventory	10,000	–0–	10,000
Total current assets	$43,500	$30,000	
Current liabilities:			
Note payable	$12,000	$ –0–	(12,000)
Accounts payable	8,000	–0–	(8,000)
Total current liabilities	$20,000	$ –0–	
Working capital	$23,500	$30,000	
Decrease in working capital			$ (6,500)

The differences between net income, net cash flow, and the change in working capital should be carefully noted in the foregoing example. Although John Claire's net income for May was $12,500, his cash account *decreased* by $9,500 and his working capital *decreased* by $6,500.

Effect of transactions on working capital

In preparing a statement of changes in financial position, it is convenient to view all business transactions as falling into three categories:

1 Transactions which affect *only current asset or current liability accounts* but which do not change the amount of working capital. These transactions produce changes in working capital accounts but are not a factor in explaining any change in the amount of working capital. For example, the purchase of merchandise increases inventory and accounts payable but has no effect on working capital; it may therefore be ignored in preparing a statement of changes in financial position.

2 Transactions which affect a *current asset or current liability account and a non-working capital account.* These transactions bring about either an increase or a decrease in the amount of working capital. The issuance of long-term bonds, for example, increases current assets and increases bonds payable, a non-working capital account; therefore, the issuance of bonds payable is a source of working capital. Similarly, when the bonds approach maturity they are transferred to the current liability classification in the balance sheet. This causes a reduction (a use) of working capital. If changes in non-working capital accounts are analyzed, these events are brought to light, and their effect on working capital will be reported in the statement of changes in financial position.

3 Transactions which affect *only noncurrent accounts* and therefore have no direct effect on the amount of working capital. The entry to record depreciation and the entry to record a stock dividend are examples of such transactions. Other transactions in this category, such as the issuance of capital stock in exchange for plant assets, are called *exchange transactions* and are viewed as both a source and use of working capital, but do not change the amount of working capital.

EXCHANGE TRANSACTIONS Suppose that a building worth $105,000 is acquired in exchange for 10,000 shares of $5 par value capital stock. The entry to record this purchase would be:

An exchange transaction	*Building*	*105,000*
	Capital Stock	*50,000*
	Paid-in Capital in Excess of Par	*55,000*

Exchange of 10,000 shares of $5 par value capital stock for building worth $105,000.

It is quite clear that this exchange transaction did not increase or decrease any current asset or current liability account and for that reason had no *direct* effect on working capital. An *exchange transaction* of this type, however, may be viewed as consisting of two transactions: (1) the issuance of capital stock for $105,000, and (2) the use of the proceeds to purchase a building for $105,000. Instead of ignoring an *exchange transaction* of this type in analyzing the flow of working capital, it is possible for us to view the exchange as both a source of working capital (issuance of capital stock) and a use of working capital (purchase of the building). This treatment is more informative for purposes of the statement of changes in financial position because it shows more completely the movement of the company's *financial resources* during the year.

Similarly, the conversion of bonds payable or preferred stock into common stock results only in changes in noncurrent accounts but should be reported as both a source and a use of working capital. On the other hand, the distribution of a stock dividend or the retirement of a fully depreciated asset are not exchange transactions and are not reported in the statement of changes in financial position.

EFFECT OF DEPRECIATION ON WORKING CAPITAL PROVIDED BY OPER-ATIONS Some expenses, such as depreciation, deferred income tax expense (which will not be paid within one year), amortization of intangibles, and amortization of discount on bonds payable, reduce net income but have no immediate effect on the amount of working capital provided by normal operations. Such expenses *should be added back to net income in measuring the increase in working capital as a result of normal operations.*

To illustrate the reason for this, assume the following: Pedro Rey starts a delivery service on January 2, with a truck that cost $10,000; he has no other assets or liabilities at this time. He does business on a cash basis and during the year collects $12,500 in revenue and pays out $4,500 in expenses, thus showing an $8,000 increase in cash, which is his only working capital account. Rey then records depreciation expense of $3,000 on the truck, resulting in a net income of $5,000 for the year. The recording of depreciation expense did not change any current account for Pedro Rey, and his increase in working capital remains at $8,000. Thus, in order to measure this increase in working capital from operations, we can either take the income figure *before depreciation expense,* $8,000, or take the net income of $5,000 and add back depreciation expense of $3,000.

Obviously, the depreciation expense itself is not a source of working capital. The net income figure, however, understates the amount of working capital provided by operations. The *depreciation expense recorded during the period is therefore shown as an addition to net income in measuring the working capital actually provided by operations.*

We have seen that some expenses do not reduce working capital. Similarly, some items in the income statement increase net income without increasing working capital and should be deducted from net income in arriving at the liquid resources provided by operations. An example of such an item is the amortization of premium on bonds payable, which causes annual interest expense to be less than the cash payments of interest to bondholders.[2]

Extraordinary and nonoperating gains and losses, if material in amount, should be eliminated from net income in order to show the working capital generated from recurring activities (operations). For example, if land costing $100,000 is sold at a net gain of $50,000, the net proceeds received on the sale, $150,000, should be reported as

[2] The treatment of this item in the working paper and in the statement of changes in financial position is illustrated in the Demonstration Problem on pages 524–527.

"working capital provided through sale of land," and the nonoperating gain should be deducted from net income. As a separate example, assume that the same land is sold for $70,000; then the nonoperating loss of $30,000 should be added to net income in arriving at the income from operations, and the working capital provided through sale of land should be reported at $70,000. The foregoing discussion relating to the measurement of working capital provided by operations can be summarized as follows:

Computation of Working Capital Provided by Operations

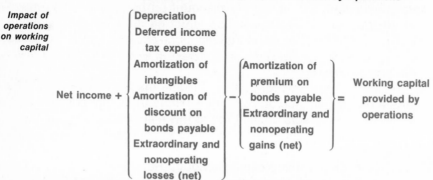

Impact of operations on working capital

Preparation of more complex statement of changes in financial position illustrated

To illustrate the points just discussed, we shall prepare a statement of changes in financial position for the Allison Corporation from the comparative balance sheet and the condensed income statement shown below and on page 513. Note that the balance sheet is not classified, except for current assets and current liabilities.

ALLISON CORPORATION
Comparative Balance Sheet
At December 31

Can you give the reasons for the increase of $57,500 in working capital?

Assets	Year 4	Year 3
Current assets:		
Cash	$ 15,000	$ 35,000
Accounts receivable (net)	105,000	85,000
Inventory	200,000	120,000
Short-term prepayments	25,000	12,000
Total current assets	$345,000	$252,000
Land	140,000	50,000
Equipment	290,000	230,000
Less: Accumulated depreciation	(107,500)	(80,000)
Total assets	$667,500	$452,000

Liabilities & Stockholders' Equity

Current liabilities:		
Notes payable to merchandise creditors	$ 60,000	$ 40,000
Accounts payable	85,000	50,000
Accrued liabilities	22,500	42,000
Total current liabilities	$167,500	$132,000
Notes payable, due Jan. 1, Year 17	15,000	10,000
Bonds payable, due June 30, Year 20	160,000	100,000
Capital stock, $5 par	215,000	110,000
Paid-in capital in excess of par	50,000	30,000
Retained earnings	60,000	70,000
Total liabilities & stockholders' equity	$667,500	$452,000

ALLISON CORPORATION
Condensed Income Statement
For Year Ended December 31, Year 4

Sales (net)		$900,000
Cost of goods sold		↘ 585,000
Gross profit on sales		$315,000
Operating expenses and income taxes	$255,000	
Gain on sale of land	(20,000)	235,000
Net income		$ 80,000

A summary of the transactions completed by the Allison Corporation which resulted in changes in *noncurrent accounts* during Year 4 follows:

1 Changes in noncurrent assets:
  a Land costing $10,000 was sold for $30,000. Another parcel of land was acquired in exchange for bonds payable of $100,000.
  b Equipment was purchased for $60,000; the invoice was paid within ten days.
  c Depreciation of $27,500 was recorded.

2 Changes in noncurrent liabilities:
  a An additional $5,000 was borrowed on long-term notes due in Year 17.
  b Bonds payable of $40,000 were retired at a price equal to par value and additional bonds of $100,000 were issued in exchange for land.

3 Changes in stockholders' equity accounts:
  a A 50% stock dividend was declared in January, requiring a transfer of $55,000 from the Retained Earnings account to the Capital Stock account.
  b In February, 10,000 shares of $5 par value stock were sold at $7 per share, thus increasing Capital Stock by $50,000 and Paid-in Capital in Excess of Par by $20,000.
  c In addition to the $55,000 reduction in retained earnings as a result of the 50% stock dividend, cash dividends of $35,000 were declared.
  d The net income for the year, $80,000 (including the nonoperating gain of $20,000), was transferred to the Retained Earnings account.

From the comparative balance sheets, the income statement, and the summary of the transactions during the year which changed non-current accounts, we can prepare a statement of changes in financial position by completing the following three steps:

Follow these steps

1 Compute the change in working capital during the period.

2 Prepare a working paper for analysis of changes in noncurrent accounts.

3 Prepare the statement of changes in financial position.

COMPUTATION OF INCREASE IN WORKING CAPITAL DURING THE PERIOD The first step in preparing a statement of changes in financial position is to determine the net increase or decrease in working capital during the period covered by the statement.

The working capital of the Allison Corporation increased by $57,500 during Year 4, determined as follows:

ALLISON CORPORATION

Computation of Increase in Working Capital during Year 4

	Dec. 31, Year 4	Dec. 31, Year 3
Current assets	$345,000	$252,000
Less: Current liabilities	167,500	132,000
Working capital	$177,500	$120,000
Increase in working capital during Year 4		57,500
	$177,500	$177,500

Sources of working capital exceed uses by $57,500

The purpose of the statement of changes in financial position is to explain the reasons for the change in working capital. This is accomplished by listing the specific sources and uses of working capital during the period. Since the working capital for the Allison Corporation increased by $57,500, the sources of working capital during Year 4 exceeded the uses by this amount. But before a statement of changes in financial position can be prepared, it is generally useful to analyze the changes in noncurrent accounts which took place during the year by preparing a working paper.

PREPARATION OF WORKING PAPER FOR ANALYSIS OF CHANGES IN NONCURRENT ACCOUNTS A working paper showing the analysis of changes in noncurrent accounts for the Allison Corporation is illustrated on page 515. The amount of working capital and the balances in noncurrent accounts at the beginning of the period are listed in the first column of the working paper. Transactions for the period (in summary form) are then recorded in the next pair of columns. Here the impact of each transaction on noncurrent accounts is recorded as a debit or a credit and the effect on working capital (funds) is listed

ALLISON CORPORATION
Working Paper for Statement of Changes in Financial Position
For Year Ended December 31, Year 4

Debits	Account Balances, Jan. 1, Year 4	Analysis of Transactions for Year 4 Debit	Analysis of Transactions for Year 4 Credit	Account Balances, Dec. 31, Year 4
Working capital	120,000	(x) 57,500		177,500
Land	50,000	(4) 100,000	(3) 10,000	140,000
Equipment	230,000	(7) 60,000		290,000
Total	400,000			607,500
Credits				
Accumulated depreciation	80,000		(2) 27,500	107,500
Notes payable, due Jan. 1, Year 17	10,000		(6) 5,000	15,000
Bonds payable, due June 30, Year 20	100,000	(8) 40,000	(4) 100,000	160,000
Capital stock, $5 par	110,000		(5) 50,000 (10) 55,000	215,000
Paid-in capital in excess of par	30,000		(5) 20,000	50,000
Retained earnings	70,000	(9) 35,000 (10) 55,000	(1) 80,000	60,000
Total	400,000	347,500	347,500	607,500
Sources of working capital:				
Operations—net income		(1) 80,000		(From
Add: Depreciation		(2) 27,500		operations,
Less: Gain on sale of land			(3) 20,000	$87,500)
Sale of land		(3) 30,000		
Issuance of bonds payable		(4) 100,000		
Sale of capital stock		(5) 70,000		
Borrowed on notes payable, due Jan. 1, Year 17		(6) 5,000		
Uses of working capital:				
Purchase of land in exchange for bonds payable			(4) 100,000	
Purchase of equipment			(7) 60,000	
Retirement of bonds payable			(8) 40,000	
Cash dividends declared			(9) 35,000	
Total sources and uses of working capital		312,500	255,000	
Increase in working capital during Year 4			(x) 57,500	
		312,500	312,500	

Explanation of transactions for Year 4:
(1) Net income $80,000 (including a gain of $20,000 on sale of land) is transferred to Retained Earnings. This is a tentative source of working capital to be adjusted in (2) and (3) below.
(2) Depreciation for the year, $27,500, is added to net income in arriving at the working capital provided by operations because it did not reduce a current asset or increase a current liability.
(3) Sale of land for $30,000; the gain of $20,000 is deducted from net income in order that entire proceeds can be reported separately as a source of working capital.
(4) Issuance of $100,000 of bonds payable in exchange for land.
(5) Sale of capital stock, providing working capital of $70,000.
(6) Working capital was provided by borrowing $5,000 on long-term notes.
(7) Working capital was reduced through purchase of equipment, $60,000.
(8) Working capital of $40,000 was used to retire bonds payable.
(9) Cash dividends declared, $35,000; this is a use of working capital.
(10) Board of directors declared a 50% stock dividend; this transaction had no effect on working capital.
(x) Balancing figure—increase in working capital during Year 4.

either as a *source* of working capital or as a *use* of working capital in the lower section of the working paper.

Explanation of transactions in working paper By studying the changes in the noncurrent accounts during Year 4, we are able to find the specific reasons for the $57,500 increase in working capital. As previously stated, only changes in the noncurrent accounts represent sources and uses of working capital. The analyses of the transactions completed by the Allison Corporation during Year 4 are explained below:

(1) The net income of $80,000 is closed to the Retained Earnings account and is shown under "sources of working capital: operations." Net income represents an increase in stockholders' equity and is one of the major sources of working capital for most businesses. Net income, however, is only a tentative measure of the increase in working capital from operations because not all revenue and expense items represent sources and uses of working capital (depreciation, for example). Furthermore, any extraordinary and nonoperating items are eliminated from net income because the transactions giving rise to such items are reported separately if they generate or use working capital.

(2) Since depreciation expense does not reduce a current asset or increase a current liability, it has no effect on working capital. Therefore, the depreciation expense of $27,500 for the year is shown as an increase to net income in the working paper and is credited to Accumulated Depreciation. The net income, $80,000, plus depreciation expense, $27,500, or a total of $107,500, represents a *tentative* increase in working capital as a result of profitable operations. This $107,500 figure is viewed as tentative because it will be reduced in adjustment (3) by the amount of the gain on the sale of land ($20,000) which was included in the net income of $80,000; this gain will be included in the $30,000 source of working capital on the sale of land.

(3) The sale of land is recorded as a source of working capital of $30,000 because cash was generated when the land was sold. The cost of the land, $10,000, is credited to the Land account and the gain, $20,000, is shown as a reduction to the net income in order that the net proceeds on the sale of the land ($30,000) can be listed as a source of working capital. This adjustment gives us net "working capital provided by operations," $87,500, consisting of income *before the gain on the sale of land,* $60,000, plus depreciation, $27,500.

(4) The issuance of $100,000 par value bonds in exchange for land is recorded in the top portion of the working paper and also as a *source* and *use* of working capital in the lower portion of the working paper. This is an example of an *exchange transaction* described earlier in the chapter.

(5) The sale of capital stock in February for $70,000 is recorded in the working paper as a source of working capital (debit entry); the credits are made to Capital Stock, $50,000 (10,000 shares with a $5 par value), and to Paid-in Capital in Excess of Par, $20,000. This transaction results in an increase to stockholders' equity, and such an increase is a source of working capital.

(6) An increase in a long-term debt as a result of borrowing is a source of liquid assets (cash). Therefore, the borrowing of $5,000 on long-term notes payable is recorded in the working paper as a source of working capital (debit entry) and a credit to Notes Payable, due January 1, Year 17.

(7) Equipment was purchased for $60,000, causing a reduction in working capital. This is recorded in the working paper as a debit to Equipment and a credit to Purchase of Equipment.

(8) A reduction in long-term debt represents a use of liquid assets (cash). During Year 4, the Allison Corporation retired $40,000 of bonds payable at par. This is recorded in the working paper as a debit to Bonds Payable and a credit to Retirement of Bonds Payable. If a retirement of bonds payable results in a material loss or gain, the loss or gain would be reported in the income statement and would be eliminated from net income in the same manner as the gain on sale of land in transaction *(3)* above.

(9) Cash dividends declared on capital stock outstanding reduce both working capital and stockholders' equity and should be listed on a statement of changes in financial position as a use of working capital. The required working paper entry is a debit to Retained Earnings and a credit to Cash Dividends Declared for $35,000. A cash dividend need not be paid in order to represent a reduction in working capital. The *declaration* of the cash dividend establishes a current liability and thus reduces working capital. The actual payment of the cash dividend has no effect on working capital because the payment merely reduces a current liability (Dividends Payable) and a current asset (Cash) by the same amount; *a transaction which changes only current accounts cannot be a source or use of working capital.*

(10) The declaration of a stock dividend is merely a transfer from retained earnings to paid-in capital; a stock dividend has no effect on working capital because no working capital account is changed. The working paper entry to recognize the 50% stock dividend distributed by the Allison Corporation in January is a debit to Retained Earnings for $55,000 and a credit to Capital Stock for the same amount.

(x) After all changes in noncurrent accounts are analyzed in the working paper, the gross sources, $312,500, and uses, $255,000, of working capital are totaled. At this point, the increase in working capital during the year, $57,500, should be entered as a debit to Working Capital on the first line of the second column in the working paper and also as a balancing figure on the next to the last line of the third column in the working paper. The account balances at December 31, Year 4, can now be determined and totals obtained for the debits and credits in the top portion of the working paper. If the totals agree, we know that our analysis is correct, at least so far as the mechanics are concerned.

PREPARATION OF STATEMENT OF CHANGES IN FINANCIAL POSITION

The foregoing working paper analysis explained all changes in noncurrent accounts that took place during Year 4. In making this analysis, we listed the sources and uses of working capital in the lower section of the working paper on page 515. The increase of $57,500 in working capital has been confirmed and a statement of changes in financial position, including the composition of working capital, can now be prepared as shown on page 518.

We can see that the $87,500 of working capital provided by operations exceeds the income before the gain on the sale of land because depreciation expense was added to net income; another $205,000 of working capital came from nonoperating sources (sale of land, sale of additional capital stock, and long-term borrowing). Working capital

ALLISON CORPORATION
Statement of Changes in Financial Position
For Year Ended December 31, Year 4

Sources of working capital:

Operations:

Income before gain on sale of land	$ 60,000
Add: Expense not requiring the use of current funds—depreciation	27,500
Total working capital provided by operations	$ 87,500
Sale of land	30,000
Issuance of bonds payable	100,000
Sale of capital stock	70,000
Borrowed on long-term notes payable, due Jan. 1, Year 17	5,000
Total sources of working capital	$292,500

Uses of working capital:

Purchase of land in exchange for bonds payable	$100,000	
Purchase of equipment	60,000	
Retirement of bonds payable	40,000	
Declaration of cash dividends	35,000	
Total uses of working capital		235,000
Increase in working capital		$ 57,500

	End of Year 4	End of Year 3	Increase or (Decrease) in Working Capital
Composition of working capital:			
Current assets:			
Cash	$ 15,000	$ 35,000	$(20,000)
Accounts receivable (net)	105,000	85,000	20,000
Inventory	200,000	120,000	80,000
Short-term prepayments	25,000	12,000	13,000
Total current assets	$345,000	$252,000	
Current liabilities:			
Notes payable to merchandise creditors . .	$ 60,000	$ 40,000	(20,000)
Accounts payable	85,000	50,000	(35,000)
Accrued liabilities	22,500	42,000	19,500
Total current liabilities	$167,500	$132,000	
Working capital	$177,500	$120,000	
Increase in working capital			$ 57,500

totaling $235,000 was used to purchase land and equipment, retire bonds payable, and declare cash dividends. These sources and uses resulted in a net increase of $57,500 in working capital. The statement of changes in financial position thus provides a concise view of the way in which the Allison Corporation generated and used its working capital during the year.

Investors and creditors find the statement of changes in financial position helpful not only in evaluating the past performance of a company but also in projecting its future movements of working capital and in evaluating probable *liquidity* (the ability to pay debts as they become payable).

Statements of changes in financial position for Carnation Company and for Johnson & Johnson appear in the Appendix of this book.

CASH FLOW ANALYSIS

While the statement of changes in financial position reports the inflow and outflow of liquid resources (working capital) during an accounting period, management is often more concerned with having enough cash to meet its operating needs and to pay maturing liabilities. Cash is the most liquid asset, and the efficient use of cash is one of the most important tasks of management. A *cash flow statement* is often prepared in order to give a full and complete picture of cash receipts and disbursements for an accounting period. Such a cash flow statement may also be useful in preparing a cash budget.

A few years ago such terms as *cash earnings* or *cash generated per share* appeared in financial magazines and annual reports of some corporations. The cash earnings referred to in these reports were usually computed by adding back to net income such expenses as depreciation and amortization of intangibles, which do not reduce working capital. The term *cash earnings* used in this context was ambiguous, and the implication that the resulting figure reflected the cash flow from operations was erroneous. Both the public accounting profession and the Securities and Exchange Commission took action to discourage publication of such computations. In order to understand why publication of "cash earnings per share" may be misleading, it is important to understand the relation between net income and cash flows from operations.

Income statements, as we have shown in prior chapters, are prepared on an accrual basis. Accrual accounting was developed to overcome the limitations of cash movements as indicators of business performance. Cash outlays simply represent investments which may or may not prove sound. Cash receipts represent disinvestment and, taken by themselves, tell nothing about whether the inflow is beneficial or not. The accountant's measurement of net income is designed to tell something about the fate of a company's overall investment and disinvestment activities during a given period of time. Granting its imperfections, the income statement is still the best means we have for reporting operating performance of business enterprises.

However, there are occasions when one may wish to reverse the accrual process and determine the amount of cash generated by operations. Reports of past cash flow may reveal a good deal about the financial problems and policies of a company. Forecasts of cash flows and cash budgets are useful managerial planning tools. The measurement of past and future cash flows from all sources, including operations, provides valuable information. But cash flow data are in no way a substitute for an income statement nor is the "cash earnings" figure in any sense a better indication of a company's operating performance.

Cash flow from operations

Suppose we wished to convert a company's income statement into a report of its cash flow from operations. How should we go about adjusting the data on the income statement to convert it into cash flow information?

To answer this question, we must consider the relationship between accrual basis income statement amounts and cash movements within the firm. For illustrative purposes, consider the income statement of the Allison Corporation for Year 4, which was presented earlier in this chapter.

ALLISON CORPORATION
Condensed Income Statement
For Year Ended December 31, Year 4

Condensed income statement: accrual basis	Sales (net)		$900,000
	Cost of goods sold		585,000
	Gross profit on sales		$315,000
	Operating expenses and income taxes	$255,000	
	Gain on sale of land	(20,000)	235,000
	Net income		$ 80,000

From the statement of changes in financial position presented on page 518, we already know that cash was received from the sale of land ($30,000), from the sale of capital stock ($70,000), and from borrowing on long-term notes ($5,000). We also know that cash was paid to acquire equipment ($60,000), to retire bonds payable ($40,000), and to pay cash dividends ($35,000). The remaining cash movements must consist of cash receipts from customers and cash payments for purchases and expenses, including income taxes.

CASH RECEIPTS FROM CUSTOMERS Sales on account are an important factor in most companies. The relationship between the amount of cash collected from customers and the net sales reported in the income statement depends on the change in accounts receivable between the beginning and end of any period. The relationship may be stated as follows:

Converting sales to cash basis

$$\text{Net sales} \begin{cases} - \text{increase in accounts receivable} \\ \text{or} \\ + \text{decrease in accounts receivable} \end{cases} = \begin{array}{l} \text{cash receipts from} \\ \text{customers} \end{array}$$

In the Allison Corporation example, a glance at the comparative balance sheet on page 512 tells us that net accounts receivable increased from $85,000 to $105,000 during Year 4, an increase of $20,000. Therefore, the cash receipts from customers during Year 4 can be determined as follows:

Net sales on cash basis	*Net sales*	*$900,000*
	Less: Increase in net accounts receivable during the year	*20,000*
	Cash receipts from customers	*$880,000*

CASH PAYMENTS FOR PURCHASES The relationship between the cost of goods sold for a period and the cash payments for the purchase of merchandise depends both on the change in inventory and the change in notes and accounts payable to merchandise creditors during the period. The relationship may be stated, in two stages, as follows:

Converting cost of goods sold to cash basis

$$\text{Cost of goods sold} \begin{cases} - \text{decrease in inventory} \\ \text{or} \\ + \text{increase in inventory} \end{cases} = \text{net purchases}$$

$$\text{net purchases} \begin{cases} - \text{increase in notes and accounts payable} \\ \text{or} \\ + \text{decrease in notes and accounts payable} \end{cases} = \begin{array}{l} \text{cash payments} \\ \text{for purchases} \end{array}$$

Again referring to the Allison Corporation example, we can see that the company increased its inventory by $80,000 and that notes and accounts payable to merchandise creditors increased by $55,000 during the year. The cash payments for purchases during Year 4 would be computed as follows:

Cost of goods sold on cash basis	*Cost of goods sold*	*$585,000*
	Add: Increase in inventory	*80,000*
	Net purchases (accrual basis)	*$665,000*
	Less: Increase in notes and accounts payable to creditors	*55,000*
	Cash payments for purchases	*$610,000*

The result of this computation makes sense. If a company is increasing its inventory, it will be buying more merchandise than it sells during the period; furthermore, if the company is increasing its notes and accounts payable to merchandise creditors, it is not paying for all its current purchases.

CASH PAYMENTS FOR EXPENSES Expenses in the income statement arise from three major sources: cash expenditures, the write-off of prepayments, and incurring obligations for accrued expenses. The relationship between operating expenses and cash payments, therefore, depends on changes in asset accounts representing the prepayment of expenses, and on changes in accrued liability accounts. These relationships may be stated as follows:

Converting an expense on accrual basis to cash basis

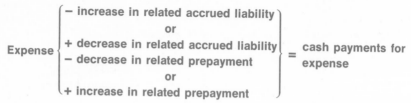

$$\text{Expense} \begin{cases} - \text{ increase in related accrued liability} \\ \quad\quad\quad\quad \text{or} \\ + \text{ decrease in related accrued liability} \\ - \text{ decrease in related prepayment} \\ \quad\quad\quad\quad \text{or} \\ + \text{ increase in related prepayment} \end{cases} = \begin{array}{l} \text{cash payments for} \\ \text{expense} \end{array}$$

In the case of a non-cash expense such as depreciation, the decrease in the book value of a depreciable asset is exactly equal to the expense recorded, and the resultant cash payment is zero.

Using the information for the Allison Corporation, we can summarize the relationship between the operating expenses and income taxes reported in the income statement and cash payments for these expenses during Year 4 as follows:

Expenses on cash basis

Total operating expenses and income taxes in the income statement . . .	$255,000
Add: Decrease in accrued liabilities	19,500
Increase in short-term prepayments	13,000
Less: Depreciation, a non-cash expense	(27,500)
Cash payments for operating expenses and income taxes	$260,000

CASH EARNINGS The conversion of the income statement of the Allison Corporation from an accrual to a cash basis is summarized on page 523. Note that this schedule incorporates the adjustments discussed in the preceding paragraphs.

The cash flow from operations for the Allison Corporation, $10,000, is lower than the amount of income before the gain on the sale of land, $60,000, during Year 4. This difference is caused by a series of variations between revenue and expense transactions on the accrual basis and the related cash inflows and outflows during the year.

In the past, some financial analysts added back depreciation to net income and referred to the total as "cash flow from operations." In our example, such an approach would lead to the figure of $107,500,

ALLISON CORPORATION
Conversion of Income Statement from Accrual to Cash Basis
For Year Ended December 31, Year 4

	Income Statement (Accrual Basis)	Add (Deduct)	Cash Basis
Net sales	$900,000		
Less: Increase in accounts receivable		$(20,000)	$880,000
Cost of goods sold	585,000		
Add: Increase in inventory		80,000	
Less: Increase in notes and accounts payable to merchandise creditors		(55,000)	610,000
Gross profit on sales	$315,000		$270,000
Operating expenses and income taxes	255,000		
Add: Decrease in accrued liabilities		$ 19,500	
Increase in short-term prepayments		13,000	
Less: Depreciation expense		(27,500)	260,000
Income before gain on sale of land (accrual basis)	$ 60,000		
Cash flow from operations			$ 10,000

How much is "cash flow" for Year 4?

that is, $80,000 net income plus depreciation of $27,500. However, the actual cash flow from operations for the Allison Corporation is only $10,000, and not $107,500. It would be misleading to say that the *cash earnings* of the Allison Corporation for Year 4 were $2.50 per share of capital stock ($107,500 divided by 43,000 shares of capital stock outstanding at year-end), and to suggest that this is a better measure of the company's performance than the *earnings per share* figure of $1.86 (net income, including the gain on sale of land, $80,000, divided by 43,000 shares of capital stock outstanding at year-end). In *Opinion No. 19,* the Accounting Principles Board made the following recommendation:

> The amount of working capital or cash provided from operations is not a substitute for or an improvement upon properly determined net income as a measure of results of operations and the consequent effect on financial position. . . . The Board strongly recommends that isolated statistics of working capital or cash provided from operations, especially per-share amounts, not be presented in annual reports to shareholders.[3]

CASH FLOW STATEMENT The cash flow from operations computed above for the Allison Corporation does not tell the complete story of cash movements during the period. Let us now combine the $10,000 cash flow from operations with the information relating to cash receipts and payments gleaned from the comparative balance sheet by way of the statement of changes in financial position. The result will be

[3] *APB Opinion No. 19,* op. cit., p. 377.

a statement that explains in full the $20,000 decrease in the cash balance during Year 4. Such a cash flow statement for the Allison Corporation is shown below:

ALLISON CORPORATION
Cash Flow Statement
For Year Ended December 31, Year 4

Complete summary of cash movements for Year 4	*Cash payments:*		
	Purchase of equipment		$ 60,000
	Retirement of bonds payable		40,000
	Payment of cash dividends		35,000
	Total cash payments		$135,000
	Cash receipts:		
	Cash generated from operations (see schedule on page 523)	$10,000	
	Sale of land	30,000	
	Sale of capital stock	70,000	
	Borrowing on long-term notes	5,000	
	Total cash receipts		115,000
	Decrease in cash during the year		$ 20,000

The Allison Corporation example was sufficiently simple that we could develop cash flow information from a direct inspection of the income statement and comparative balance sheets. In more complex situations, the accountant will usually use a working paper to convert the income statement from an accrual to a cash basis and to develop cash flow information in a systematic fashion. Familiarity with these working paper procedures is not necessary in order to be able to understand and interpret cash flow information; therefore, discussion of this process is reserved for the *Intermediate Accounting* volume in this series.

DEMONSTRATION PROBLEM

The comparative financial data for W & C, Inc., for the last two years are shown below and on page 525.

	December 31	
Debits	**Year 2**	**Year 1**
Cash	$ 39,220	$ 15,800
Receivables (net of allowance for uncollectible accounts)	41,400	24,000
Inventories, lower of cost or market	27,600	36,800
Short-term prepayments	4,180	4,400
Land	9,000	19,000
Buildings	270,000	250,000
Equipment	478,600	450,000
Total debits	$870,000	$800,000

Credits	Year 2	Year 1
Accumulated depreciation: buildings	$ 95,000	$ 77,000
Accumulated depreciation: equipment...............	153,000	120,000
Accounts payable	59,200	30,000
Accrued liabilities	20,000	10,000
Bonds payable	90,000	90,000
Premium on bonds payable	2,800	3,000
Preferred stock ($100 par).......................	70,000	100,000
Common stock ($25 par).......................	260,000	250,000
Paid-in capital in excess of par.................	45,000	40,000
Retained earnings	75,000	80,000
Total credits	$870,000	$800,000

Other data

(1) During Year 2, the board of directors of the company authorized a transfer of $15,000 from retained earnings to reflect a 4% stock dividend on the common stock.

(2) Cash dividends of $6,000 were paid on the preferred stock, and cash dividends of $50,000 were paid on the common stock.

(3) During Year 2, 300 shares of preferred stock were retired at par value.

(4) The only entries recorded in the Retained Earnings account were for dividends and to close the Income Summary account, which had a credit balance of $66,000 after the loss on the sale of the land.

(5) There were no sales or retirements of buildings and equipment during the year; land was sold for $8,000, resulting in a loss of $2,000.

Instructions

a Compute the change in working capital during Year 2. You may use totals for current assets and current liabilities.

b Prepare a working paper for a statement of changes in financial position for Year 2.

c Prepare a statement of changes in financial position for Year 2, without showing the composition of working capital.

d Prepare a cash flow statement, with a supporting schedule converting the net income from the accrual basis to the cash basis.

SOLUTION TO DEMONSTRATION PROBLEM

a Computation of decrease in working capital:

	As of December 31	
	Year 2	Year 1
Current assets	$112,400	$81,000
Less: Current liabilities.....................	79,200	40,000
Working capital	$ 33,200	$41,000
Decrease in working capital during Year 2	7,800	
	$ 41,000	$41,000

b

W & C, Inc.
Working Paper for Statement of Changes in Financial Position
For Year 2

Debits	Account Balances Dec. 31, Year 1	Analysis of Transactions for Year 2		Account Balances Dec. 31, Year 2
		Debit	Credit	
Working capital	41,000		(x) 7,800	33,200
Land	19,000		(5) 10,000	9,000
Buildings	250,000	(6) 20,000		270,000
Equipment	450,000	(7) 28,600		478,600
Total	760,000			790,800
Credits				
Accumulated depreciation: buildings . .	77,000		(2) 18,000	95,000
Accumulated depreciation: equipment . .	120,000		(2) 33,000	153,000
Bonds payable	90,000			90,000
Premium on bonds payable	3,000	(8) 200		2,800
Preferred stock, $100 par	100,000	(9) 30,000		70,000
Common stock, $25 par	250,000		(3) 10,000	260,000
Paid-in capital in excess of par	40,000		(3) 5,000	45,000
Retained earnings	80,000	(3) 15,000	(1) 66,000 ⎫	75,000
		(4) 56,000	⎬	
Total	760,000	149,800	149,800	790,800
Sources of working capital:				
Operations—net income		(1) 66,000	⎫	
Add: Depreciation		(2) 51,000	⎪	
Loss on sale of land		(5) 2,000	⎪	(From
Less: Amortization of premium			⎬	operations,
on bonds payable			(8) 200 ⎪	$118,800)
Sale of land		(5) 8,000	⎭	
Uses of working capital:				
Payment of cash dividends			(4) 56,000	
Purchase of buildings			(6) 20,000	
Purchase of equipment			(7) 28,600	
Retirement of preferred stock			(9) 30,000	
Total sources and uses of working capital		127,000	134,800	
Decrease in working capital		(x) 7,800		
		134,800	134,800	

Explanation of transactions for Year 2:

(1) Net income, $66,000, including a loss of $2,000 on sale of land, transferred to Retained Earnings.
(2) Depreciation for the year, $51,000 (buildings, $18,000, and equipment, $33,000) is added to net income because it is an expense which did not reduce working capital.
(3) Entry to record 4% stock dividend; no effect on working capital.
(4) Cash dividends declared, $56,000 (preferred stock, $6,000, and common, $50,000).
(5) To record sale of land for $8,000; the loss of $2,000 is added to net income because the loss reduced net income but had no effect on working capital.
(6) To record working capital used for purchase of buildings.
(7) To record working capital used for purchase of equipment.
(8) To record amortization of premium on bonds payable; the amortization increased net income but had no effect on working capital.
(9) To record working capital applied to retirement of preferred stock.
(x) Balancing figure—decrease in working capital during Year 2.

c

W & C, INC.
Statement of Changes in Financial Position
For Year 2

Sources of working capital:
Operations:

Income before loss on sale of land		$ 68,000
Add: Expense not requiring the use of working capital— depreciation	$51,000	
Less: Increase in net income which did not provide working capital— amortization of premium on bonds payable	200	50,800
Total working capital provided by operations		$118,800
Sale of land		8,000
Total sources of working capital		$126,800

Uses of working capital:

Payment of cash dividends	$ 56,000	
Purchase of buildings	20,000	
Purchase of equipment	28,600	
Retirement of preferred stock	30,000	
Total uses of working capital		134,600
Decrease in working capital		$ 7,800

d

W & C, INC.
Cash Flow Statement
For Year 2

Cash receipts:

Cash generated from operations (see Schedule A below)		$150,020
Sale of land		8,000
Total cash receipts		$158,020

Cash payments:

Payment of cash dividends	$56,000	
Purchase of buildings	20,000	
Purchase of equipment	28,600	
Retirement of preferred stock	30,000	
Total cash payments		134,600
Increase in cash during the year		$ 23,420

Schedule A—Cash generated from operations:

Working capital provided by operations—part c		$118,800
Add: Decrease in inventories	$ 9,200	
Decrease in short-term prepayments	220	
Increase in accounts payable	29,200	
Increase in accrued liabilities	10,000	48,620
Less: Increase in receivables		(17,400)
Cash generated from operations		$150,020

REVIEW QUESTIONS

1 Why is working capital viewed as a "fund of liquid resources"?

2 What are the primary ways in which a firm generates working capital and the primary ways in which a firm uses working capital?

3 What information can a reader gain from a statement of changes in financial position that is not apparent from reading an income statement?

4 In preparing a statement of changes in financial position, business transactions may be classified into three categories. List these categories and indicate which category results in changes in working capital.

5 Give examples of expenses, other than depreciation expense, which reduce net income but which do not result in the use of working capital during the period.

6 Give an example of an increase in net income which does not result in an increase in working capital during the period.

7 The following quotation appeared in a report issued by a major investment banking firm: "Depreciation, depletion, and amortization charges, etc., which supply the funds for the new facilities that sustain the competitive competence of our leading companies, are increasing at a faster rate than is net income." Evaluate this quotation.

8 Although extraordinary and nonoperating gains and losses may be included in net income in measuring the working capital generated by operations, can you give a reason for excluding such gains and losses from net income? Use the following facts to illustrate your point: Net income including gain on sale of land, $100,000; sale of land, with a book value of $70,000, for $150,000.

9 What is the major difference between the statement of changes in financial position and a cash flow statement?

10 Criticize the following statement: "Although earnings fell from $3.40 per share in the previous year to $2.50 per share in the current year, cash earnings increased from $4.00 to $4.80 per share, a 20% increase that testifies to the continuing strength in the company's profitability."

11 The president of a small corporation was puzzled by the following statement made by his accountant: "Our cash flow, net income plus depreciation, amounted to $85,000 last year but our cash generated from operations was only $10,000 because of the increases in our inventory and receivables and the decrease in our accounts payable." Explain what the accountant meant.

12 An outside member of the board of directors of a small corporation made the following comment after studying the comparative financial statements for the past two years: "I have trouble understanding why our cash has increased steadily during the past two years, yet our profits have been negligible; we have paid no dividends; and inventories, receivables, payables, cost of plant and equipment, long-term debt, and capital stock have remained essentially unchanged." Write a brief statement to the director explaining how this situation might occur.

EXERCISES

Ex. 15-1 Indicate the amount of the increase or decrease (if any) in working capital as a result of each of the following events:

a Purchase and retirement of bonds payable, $1,000,000, at 96. The unamortized premium on bonds payable at the time of the retirement was $50,000.
b Declaration of a 25% stock dividend on $600,000 of par value capital stock outstanding.
c Purchase of equipment costing $400,000 for $100,000 cash and $75,000 (plus interest) payable every six months over the next two years.
d A $40,000 write-down of inventory to a market value below cost.

Ex. 15-2 The Samuelson Company reports a net loss of $20,000 on its income statement. In arriving at this figure, the following items among others were included:

Amortization of patents	$ 4,000
Amortization of premium on bonds payable	2,500
Gain on sale of land	10,000
Depreciation expense	12,500
Uninsured fire damage to building	22,100

What was the working capital increase or decrease as a result of *operations?*

Ex. 15-3 The information below is taken from comparative financial statements for the Mulvey Corporation:

	Year 10	Year 9
Net income (there were no extraordinary items)	$60,000	$37,000
Depreciation expense	42,500	31,800
Inventory at end of year	15,000	28,000
Accounts receivable at end of year	9,000	12,000
Accounts payable at end of year	8,000	6,000
Cash dividends declared in December of each year payable Jan. 15 of following year	22,500	15,000

From the data above, determine the following:
a The working capital provided by operations in Year 10.
b The cash generated by operations in Year 10.
c Working capital used for dividends in Year 10.

Ex. 15-4 The data below are taken from the records of the Ferraro Company:

	End of Year	Beginning of Year
Accounts receivable	$ 20,200	$10,200
Inventories	32,000	40,000
Short-term prepayments	2,300	1,500
Accounts payable (merchandise creditors)	28,000	25,000
Miscellaneous current liabilities (accrued expenses)	1,000	1,200
Net sales	300,000	
Cost of goods sold	180,000	
Operating expenses (includes depreciation of $10,000) . . .	80,000	

From the foregoing information, compute the following:
a Cash collected from customers during the year.
b Cash paid to merchandise creditors during the year.
c Cash paid for operating expenses during the year.

Ex. 15-5 A summary of the comparative financial position for the Miklos Corporation for the current year follows:

	End of Current Year	Beginning of Current Year
Working capital.	$ 77,500	$ 90,000
Investment in stock of Rio Company	82,500	75,000
Land	80,000	50,000
Buildings	120,000	100,000
Less: Accumulated depreciation	(50,000)	(45,000)
	$310,000	$270,000
Notes payable, due in 5 years	$ 30,000	$ -0-
Capital stock, no par value	200,000	200,000
Retained earnings	80,000	70,000
	$310,000	$270,000

The net income was $25,000 and included unrealized net income of $7,500 on the investment in stock of Rio Company (the investment account was debited). Depreciation expense for the current year was $5,000. A cash dividend was declared at the end of the current year.

Prepare a statement of changes in financial position for the current year without using a working paper.

Ex. 15-6 Briefly explain how each of the following situations should be reported in the statement of changes in financial position.

a Depreciation of $100,000 was recorded in Year 1; however, $25,000 of this amount is included in the ending inventory of finished goods.

b In July of Year 1, the 10,000 shares of $50 par value capital stock were split 3 for 1 and in November of Year 1, a 10% stock dividend was distributed.

c Cash of $10,000 and capital stock with a market value of $90,000 were used to acquire land worth $100,000.

PROBLEMS

15-1 Below is given a list of business transactions and adjustments. For each item you are to indicate the effect first on working capital, and second on cash. In each case the possible effects are an increase, a decrease, or no change.

(1) Purchase of patent, giving 200 shares of the company's common stock in exchange

(2) Sale of long-term investment at a loss

(3) Payment of the current year's income tax liability, which was previously recorded in the accounting records

(4) Exchange of convertible bonds for the company's common stock

(5) An uncollectible account receivable written off against the Allowance for Uncollectible Accounts

(6) Machinery sold for cash in excess of its carrying value

(7) Warehouse destroyed by fire; one-half of its carrying value covered by insurance and recorded as a receivable from the insurance company

(8) Amortization of discount on bonds payable

(9) Premium paid for a three-year insurance policy

(10) Declaration of a cash dividend

(11) Payment of previously declared cash dividend on common stock

(12) Declaration of a 20% stock dividend on common stock

(13) Payment of an account payable

(14) Depreciation recorded for the period

Instructions

a List the numbers 1 to 14 on your answer sheet, and set up two columns headed "working capital effect" and "cash effect." For each transaction, write the words *increase, decrease,* or *no change* in the appropriate column to indicate the effect of the transaction on working capital and cash.

b Are any of the transactions listed above considered "exchange transactions" which would be listed as both a source and use of working capital in a statement of changes in financial position? Explain.

15-2 Given below are the changes in account balances for Cornwell Corporation during Year 6:

**Change during
Year 6**

	Debit	Credit
Current assets	$ 80,000	
Plant and equipment	100,000	
Accumulated depreciation		$ 35,000
Land for future plant expansion	30,000	
Current liabilities.	20,000	
Capital stock, $10 par		90,000
Paid-in capital in excess of par.		50,000
Retained earnings		55,000
	$230,000	$230,000

During Year 6 the company issued 9,000 shares of capital stock. Part of the proceeds were applied to the purchase of equipment and to acquire land for future plant expansion. There were no retirements of plant and equipment items in Year 6. Cash dividends of $60,000 were declared during Year 6.

Instructions Prepare a statement of changes in financial position for Year 6, without using a working paper.

15-3 A condensed balance sheet at January 1, Year 10, and the statement of changes in financial position for Year 10 for Tom Loo Company are given below and on page 532.

TOM LOO COMPANY
Balance Sheet
January 1, Year 10

Assets

Current assets	$ 43,000
Land	20,000
Equipment	48,000
Less: Accumulated depreciation	(15,000)
Patents (net of accumulated amortization)	5,000
Total assets.	$101,000

Liabilities & Stockholders' Equity

Current liabilities.	$ 18,000
Capital stock, no-par value	47,000
Retained earnings	36,000
Total liabilities & stockholders' equity	$101,000

TOM LOO COMPANY
Statement of Changes in Financial Position
For Year 10

Working capital, Jan. 1, Year 10		$25,000
Sources of working capital:		
Operations:		
Net income	$24,000	
Add: Depreciation expense	10,000	
Amortization of patents	1,000	
Less: Gain on disposal of equipment	(4,000)	
Working capital provided by operations		31,000
Issuance of capital stock		11,000
Disposal of equipment		7,000
Subtotal		$74,000
Uses of working capital:		
Dividends paid	$ 8,000	
Purchase of land	14,000	
Purchase of equipment	31,000	53,000
Working capital, Dec. 31, Year 10		$21,000

Accumulated depreciation on the equipment sold in Year 10 was $6,000 and total assets at December 31, Year 10, were $139,000.

Instructions Using the information above, prepare a condensed balance sheet at December 31, Year 10. Supporting schedules should be in good form.

15-4 The account balances for San Miguel Company at the end of Year 2 and Year 1 are shown below:

Assets	Year 2	Year 1
Cash	$ 45,000	$ 40,000
Accounts receivable	55,000	35,000
Inventory	95,000	150,000
Long-term investments	15,000	
Equipment	390,000	225,000
Accumulated depreciation	(80,000)	(60,000)
Land	80,000	35,000
Total assets	$600,000	$425,000

Liabilities & Stockholders' Equity	Year 2	Year 1
Accounts payable . . . . : .	$ 45,000	$ 20,000
Notes payable (current)	4,000	30,000
Bonds payable, due in Year 20	115,000	80,000
Premium on bonds payable	1,800	1,900
Capital stock, $1 par	200,000	150,000
Paid-in capital in excess of par	80,000	50,000
Retained earnings	154,200	93,100
Total liabilities & stockholders' equity	$600,000	$425,000

Net income for Year 2 amounted to $85,000. Cash dividends of $23,900 were paid during Year 2. Additional purchases of investments, equipment, and land were completed during Year 2, financed in part through the sale of bonds at par and 50,000 shares of capital stock. Equipment costing $25,000 was sold at a price equal to its carrying value of $15,000.

Instructions
a Prepare a schedule to determine the increase or decrease in working capital during Year 2.
b Prepare a working paper for a statement of changes in financial position for Year 2. See the solution to the demonstration problem on page 527 for proper handling of the premium on bonds payable.
c Prepare a statement of changes in financial position for Year 2.

15-5 The following balance sheet data for Year 5 were obtained from the records of Ferris Company:

	Dec. 31	Jan. 1
Current assets	$298,700	$202,500
Plant and equipment (net)	334,000	319,000
Goodwill (amortized over 10 years)	8,500	10,000
Current liabilities	150,000	81,500
Bonds payable, 7%	200,000	–0–
Discount on bonds payable	3,800	–0–
Preferred stock, $10 par	–0–	200,000
Common stock, no par	190,000	150,000
Retained earnings	105,000	100,000

Additional data
(1) The statement of retained earnings for Year 5 follows:

Beginning balance		$100,000
Add: Net income, including gain on disposal of land		80,000
Subtotal		$180,000
Less: Amount paid to retire preferred stock in excess of		
carrying (book) value	$10,000	
Stock dividend on common stock	40,000	
Cash dividends	25,000	75,000
Ending balance		$105,000

(2) Ten-year bonds of $200,000 were issued on July 1 at 98; the proceeds were used to retire the preferred stock at 105.
(3) Land having a cost of $60,000 was exchanged at an agreed value of $100,000 for new equipment costing $120,000; the balance of $20,000 was paid in cash.
(4) Depreciation for the year was $45,000.

Instructions
a Prepare a working paper for a statement of changes in financial position.
b Prepare a statement of changes in financial position. Report working capital provided f om operations in a single amount as determined in the working paper.

15-6 The following information is presented to you by Fred Simiar, owner of Simiar's Tobacco Shop:

Balance Sheet

Assets	Year 2	Year 1
Cash	$ 10,000	$ 40,000
Marketable securities	15,000	20,000
Accounts receivable (net)	100,000	35,000
Inventory	80,000	60,000
Equipment (net of accumulated depreciation)	35,000	45,000
Total assets	$240,000	$200,000

Liabilities & Owner's Capital

	Year 2	Year 1
Accounts payable	$ 37,000	$ 40,000
Accrued liabilities	8,000	2,500
Note payable to bank (due early in Year 2)		12,500
Fred Simiar, capital	195,000	145,000
Total liabilities & owner's capital	$240,000	$200,000

Income Statement for Year 2

Sales (net)		$400,000
Cost of goods sold		300,000
Gross profit on sales		$100,000
Operating expenses (including $10,000 depreciation)	$60,000	
Loss on sale of marketable securities	500	60,500
Net income		$ 39,500
Drawings by owner		22,500
Increase in owner's capital as a result of operations		$ 17,000

Simiar is concerned over the decrease in his cash position during Year 2, particularly in view of the fact that he invested an additional $33,000 in the business and had a net income of $39,500 during the year. He asks you to prepare a statement which will explain the decrease in the Cash account. You point out that while cash decreased by $30,000, the working capital increased by $60,000. You conclude that a statement of cash receipts and cash disbursements, showing cash collected from customers, cash paid to merchandise creditors, cash paid for operating expenses, etc., would give him the information he needs.

Instructions

a Prepare a schedule showing the conversion of the income statement from an accrual to a cash basis, thus determining the net cash outflow from operations.

b Prepare a cash flow statement which explains the decrease of $30,000 in cash during Year 2.

c Prepare a statement of changes in financial position without using a working paper.

15-7 When the controller of Sunray Corporation presented the following condensed comparative financial statements to the board of directors at the close of Year 2, the reaction of the board members was very favorable.

SUNRAY CORPORATION
Comparative Income Statements
(in thousands of dollars)

	Year 2	Year 1
Net sales	$ 985	$700
Cost of goods sold	610	480
Gross profit on sales	$ 375	$220
Operating expenses, including depreciation	(190)	(160)
Income taxes	(80)	(25)
Net income	$ 105	$ 35

SUNRAY CORPORATION
Comparative Financial Position
As of December 31
(in thousands of dollars)

Current assets	$ 370	$365
Less: Current liabilities	190	225
Working capital	$ 180	$140
Plant and equipment (net)	995	680
Total assets minus current liabilities	$1,175	$820
Financed by following sources of long-term capital:		
Long-term liabilities	$ 250	$-0-
Capital stock ($50 par value)	500	500
Retained earnings	425	320
Total sources of long-term capital	$1,175	$820

Noting that net income rose from $3.50 per share of capital stock to $10.50 per share, one member of the board proposed that a substantial cash dividend be paid. "Our working capital is up by $40,000; we should be able to make a distribution to stockholders," he commented. To which the controller replied that the company's cash position was precarious and pointed out that at the end of Year 2, a cash balance of only $5,000 was on hand, a decline from $145,000 at the end of Year 1. He also reminded the board that the company bought $400,000 of new equipment during Year 2. When a board member asked for an explanation of the increase of $40,000 in working capital, the controller presented the following schedule (in thousands of dollars):

		Effect on Working Capital
Increase in working capital:		
Accounts receivable increased by		$ 83
Inventories increased by		45
Short-term prepayments increased by		17
Accounts payable were reduced by		52
Accrued liabilities were reduced by		28
Total increases in working capital		$225
Decreases in working capital:		
Cash decreased by	$140	
Income tax liability increased by	45	185
Increase in working capital during Year 2		$ 40

After examining this schedule, the board member shook his head and said, "I still don't understand how our cash position can be so tight in the face of a tripling of net income and a substantial increase in working capital!"

Instructions

a Prepare a statement converting Sunray Corporation's income statement to a cash basis, determining the cash generated by operations during Year 2.

b From the information in *a* and an inspection of the comparative balance sheet, prepare a cash flow statement for Year 2, explaining the $140,000 decrease in the cash balance.

c Prepare a statement accounting for the increase in working capital (statement of changes in financial position) for Sunray Corporation in a more acceptable form.

d Write a brief note of explanation to the board member.

15-8 The account balances given on page 537 in alphabetical order are taken from the ledger of Oriental Exports, Inc.

The analysis of the Retained Earnings account for the fiscal year ended June 30, Year 2, is given below:

Balance, June 30, Year 1	$ 99,900
Net income	49,500
Dividends declared	(20,000)
Balance, June 30, Year 2	$129,400

Additional information available for the fiscal year follows:

(1) Land was sold at no gain or loss.

(2) Owners of $30,000 of the convertible bonds exchanged their bonds for 400 shares of common stock.

(3) Fully depreciated equipment costing $8,000 was abandoned and written off.

(4) Other changes in noncurrent accounts resulted from the usual transactions affecting these accounts.

(5) The notes payable represent bank loans. The balance payable at June 30, Year 1, was paid in December, Year 1, and a new loan was negotiated early in Year 2.

	June 30, Year 2		June 30, Year 1	
	Debit	Credit	Debit	Credit
Accounts payable		$ 43,500		$ 24,500
Accounts receivable	$ 78,500		$ 48,000	
Accrued current liabilities		18,600		28,400
Accumulated depreciation: buildings . .		52,100		45,700
Accumulated depreciation: equipment. .		48,600		31,900
Allowance for uncollectible accounts . .		5,000		4,600
Buildings.	186,700		156,300	
Cash	48,400		30,200	
Common stock, $50 par		220,000		200,000
Convertible bonds payable		20,000		50,000
Equipment	190,500		198,500	
Inventories	58,400		49,400	
Land	21,000		30,000	
Notes payable (short-term)		22,500		15,000
Paid-in capital in excess of par		30,000		20,000
Retained earnings		129,400		99,900
Short-term prepayments	6,200		7,600	
Totals	$589,700	$589,700	$520,000	$520,000

Instructions

a Compute the change in working capital for the fiscal year ended June 30, Year 2.

b Prepare a working paper for a statement of changes in financial position for the fiscal year ended June 30, Year 2. You need not prepare a formal statement of changes in financial position.

c Prepare a schedule converting the net income of $49,500 to a cash basis, and prepare a cash flow statement explaining the $18,200 increase in cash.

BUSINESS DECISION PROBLEM 15

Forecast Data Corporation has working capital of $2,050,000 at the beginning of Year 10. Restrictions contained in bank loans require that working capital not fall below $2,000,000. The following projected information is available for Year 10:

(1) Budgeted net income (including nonoperating items) is $2,500,000. In addition to the nonoperating items described below, the following items were included in estimating net income: Depreciation, $700,000; amortization of premium on bonds payable, $50,000; uncollectible accounts expense, $60,000; and income taxes, $2,100,000.

(2) Cash dividends of $1,500,000 have been paid in recent years. The company would like to maintain dividends at this level.

(3) Sale of plant assets with a carrying value of $400,000 is expected to bring $500,000 net of income taxes.

(4) Additional plant assets costing $5,000,000 will be acquired. Payment will be as follows: 20% cash, 20% short-term note, and 60% through issuance of capital stock.

(5) Long-term investment will be sold at cost, $100,000.
(6) Bonds payable in the amount of $500,000, bearing interest at 11%, will be redeemed at 105 approximately 10 years prior to maturity in order to eliminate the high interest expense of $55,000 per year. The elimination of this interest and the gain or loss on the retirement of bonds payable were taken into account in estimating net income for Year 10. These bonds had been issued at par.

Instructions

a Consider all the information given above and prepare a projected statement of changes in financial position (without showing the composition of working capital) in order to determine the estimated increase or decrease in working capital for Year 10. Some of the information given may be irrelevant.

b Does it appear likely that the past dividend policy can be maintained in Year 10? What factors other than working capital position should be considered in determining the level of cash dividends declared by the board of directors?

SIXTEEN

ANALYSIS OF FINANCIAL STATEMENTS

Financial statements are the instrument panel of a business enterprise. They constitute a report on managerial performance, attesting to managerial success or failure and flashing warning signals of impending difficulties. In reading a complex instrument panel, one must understand the gauges to make sense out of the information they convey. Similarly, one must understand the inner workings of the accounting system and the significance of various financial relationships to interpret the information appearing in financial statements. To an astute reader, a set of financial statements tells a great deal about a business enterprise.

The financial affairs of any business are of interest to a number of different groups: management, creditors, investors, union officials, and government agencies. Each of these groups has somewhat different needs, and accordingly each tends to concentrate on particular aspects of a company's financial picture.

Sources of financial information

For the most part, the discussion in this chapter will be limited to the kind of analysis that can be made by "outsiders" who do not have access to internal accounting records. Investors must rely to a considerable extent on financial statements in published annual and quarterly reports. In recent years, the Securities and Exchange Commission (SEC) and financial analysts have exerted considerable pressure on corporations to include more information in their annual and quarterly reports. In the case of large publicly owned corporations, certain statements that must be filed with public agencies, such as the 10K report filed with the SEC, are available to the public. Financial information for many corporations is also published by Moody's Investors Service, Standard & Poor's Corporation, and stock brokerage firms.

Bankers are usually able to secure more detailed information by requesting it as a condition for granting a loan. Trade creditors may obtain financial information for businesses of almost any size from credit-rating agencies such as Dun & Bradstreet, Inc.

Tools of analysis

Financial statements cannot be interpreted mérely by reference to a few key figures. The significance of individual figures lies in their relationship to other quantities, or the amount and direction of change since a previous date. Analysis is largely a matter of establishing significant relationships and pointing up changes and trends. There are three widely used analytical techniques: (1) dollar and percentage changes, (2) component percentages, and (3) ratios.

DOLLAR AND PERCENTAGE CHANGES The change in financial data over time is best exhibited in statements showing data for a series of years in adjacent columns. Such statements are called *comparative financial statements.* A condensed comparative balance sheet is shown below:

RITTER CORPORATION
Comparative Balance Sheet
December 31
(in thousands of dollars)

Assets	Year 3	Year 2	Year 1
Current assets	$180	$150	$120
Plant and equipment (net)	450	300	345
Total assets	$630	$450	$465
Liabilities & Stockholders' Equity			
Current liabilities	$ 60	$ 80	$120
Long-term liabilities	200	100	
Capital stock	300	300	300
Retained earnings (deficit)	70	(30)	45
Total liabilities & stockholders' equity	$630	$450	$465

Condensed three-year balance sheet

The usefulness of comparative financial statements covering two or more years is well recognized. Published annual reports often contain comparative financial statements covering a period as long as 10 years. By observing the change in various items period by period, the analyst may gain valuable clues as to growth in working capital and in sales and earnings, along with other important trends affecting the business.

The dollar amount of any change is the difference between the amount for a *base* year and for a *comparison* year. The percentage change is computed by dividing the amount of the change between years by the amount for the base year. This is illustrated in the tabulation below, using data from the comparative balance sheet for Ritter Corporation on page 540.

				Increase or (Decrease)			
	In Thousands			Year 3 over Year 2		Year 2 over Year 1	
	Year 3	Year 2	Year 1	Amount	%	Amount	%
Current assets	$180	$150	$120	$30	20%	$30	25%
Current liabilities	$ 60	$ 80	$120	($20)	(25%)	($40)	(33.3%)

Dollar and percentage changes

Although current assets increased $30,000 in both Year 2 and Year 3, the percentage of change differs because of the shift in the base year from Year 1 to Year 2.

The dollar amount of change in a financial statement item from one year to the next is significant, but expressing this change as a percentage adds valuable perspective. For example, assume that a comparative income statement shows that sales increased by $100,000 this year. If sales for the prior year were $1,000,000, the increase this year is a very impressive 10%. However, if sales for the prior year were $10,000,000, this year's increase of $100,000 represents a very modest improvement of only 1%.

COMPONENT PERCENTAGES The phrase "a piece of pie" is subject to varying interpretations until it is known whether the piece represents, say, one-sixth or one-half of the total pie. The percentage relationship between any particular financial item and a significant total that includes this item is known as a *component percentage;* this is often a useful means of showing relationships or the relative importance of the item in question. Thus if inventories are 50% of total current assets, they are a far more significant factor in the current position of a company than if they are only 10% of total current assets.

One application of component percentages is to express each asset group on the balance sheet as a percentage of total assets. This shows quickly the relative importance of current and noncurrent assets, and the relative amount of financing obtained from short-term creditors, long-term creditors, and stockholders.

Another application is to express all items in an income statement as a percentage of net sales. Such a statement is sometimes called a *common size* income statement. A highly condensed income statement showing both dollar amounts and component percentages is illustrated on page 542.

PACIFIC COMPANY
Income Statement

	Dollars		Component Percentages	
	Year 2	Year 1	Year 2	Year 1
Net sales	$500,000	$200,000	100.0%	100.0%
Cost of goods sold	350,000	120,000	70.0	60.0
Gross profit on sales	$150,000	$ 80,000	30.0%	40.0%
Expenses (including income taxes) .	100,000	50,000	20.0	25.0
Net income	$ 50,000	$ 30,000	10.0%	15.0%

How successful was Year 2?

   Looking only at the component percentages, we see that the decline in the gross profit rate from 40 to 30% was only partially offset by the decrease in expenses as a percentage of net sales, causing net income to decrease from 15 to 10% of net sales. The dollar amounts in the first pair of columns, however, present an entirely different picture. It is true that net sales increased faster than net income, but net income improved significantly in Year 2, a fact not apparent from a review of component percentages alone. This points up an important limitation in the use of component percentages. Changes in the component percentage may result from a change in the component, in the total, or in both. Reverting to our previous analogy, it is important to know not only the relative size of a piece of pie, but also the size of the pie; 10% of a large pie may be a bigger piece than 15% of a smaller pie.

RATIOS A *ratio* is a simple mathematical expression of the relationship of one item to another. Ratios may be expressed in a number of ways. For example, if we wish to clarify the relationship between sales of $800,000 and net income of $40,000, we may state: (1) The ratio of sales to net income is 20 to 1 (or 20:1); (2) for every $1 of sales, the company has an average net income of 5 cents; (3) net income is $\frac{1}{20}$ of sales. In each case the ratio is merely a means of describing the relationship between sales and net income in a simple form.

   In order to compute a meaningful ratio, there must be a significant relationship between the two figures. A ratio focuses attention on a relationship which is significant, but a full interpretation of the ratio usually requires further investigation of the underlying data. Ratios are an aid to analysis and interpretation; they are not a substitute for sound thinking.

Standards of comparison

In using dollar and percentage changes, component percentages, and ratios, the analyst constantly seeks some standard of comparison against which to judge whether the relationships that he has found are favorable or unfavorable. Two such standards are (1) the past performance of the company and (2) the performance of other companies in the same industry.

PAST PERFORMANCE OF THE COMPANY Comparing analytical data for a current period with similar computations for prior years affords some basis for judging whether the position of the business is improving or worsening. This comparison of data over time is sometimes called *horizontal* or *dynamic* analysis, to express the idea of reviewing data for a number of periods. It is distinguished from *vertical* or *static* analysis, which refers to the review of the financial information for only one accounting period.

In addition to determining whether the situation is improving or becoming worse, horizontal analysis may aid in making estimates of future prospects. Since changes may reverse their direction at any time, however, projecting past trends into the future is always a somewhat risky statistical pastime.

A weakness of horizontal analysis is that comparison with the past does not afford any basis for evaluation in absolute terms. The fact that net income was 2% of sales last year and is 3% of sales this year indicates improvement, but if there is evidence that net income *should be* 5% of sales, the record for both years is unfavorable.

INDUSTRY STANDARDS The limitations of horizontal analysis may be overcome to some extent by finding some other standard of performance as a yardstick against which to measure the record of any particular company.[1] The yardstick may be data for a comparable company, the average record of several companies in the same industry, or some other predetermined standard.

When we compare a given company with its competitors or with industry averages, our conclusions will be valid only if the companies in question are reasonably comparable. Because of the large number of *diversified* companies formed in recent years, the term *industry* is difficult to define, and companies that fall roughly within the same industry may not be comparable in many respects. One company may engage only in the marketing of oil products; another may be a fully integrated producer from the well to the gas pump, yet both are said to be in the "oil industry."

Differences in accounting methods also may lessen the comparabil-

---

[1] For example, the Robert Morris Associates publishes *Annual Statement Studies* which contain detailed data obtained from 27,000 annual reports grouped in 223 industry classifications. Assets, liabilities, and stockholders' equity are presented as a percentage of total assets; income statement amounts are expressed as a percentage of net sales; and key ratios are given (expressed as the median for each industry, the upper quartile, and the lower quartile). Measurements within each of the 223 industry groups are grouped according to the size of the firm. Similarly, Dun & Bradstreet, Inc., annually publishes *Key Business Ratios* in 125 lines of business divided into retailing, wholesaling, manufacturing, and construction. A total of 14 ratios are presented for each of the 125 industry groups.

ity of financial data for two companies. For example, the understatement of inventories on the balance sheet of a company using lifo may be so serious as to destroy the significance of comparisons with companies with inventories valued on a fifo basis. Similarly, companies may employ different depreciation methods or estimates of the useful life of substantially similar assets; and the timing of revenue recognition may differ significantly among companies engaged in certain industries. Despite these limitations, studying comparative performances is a useful method of analysis if carefully and intelligently done. Financial analysts often "reconstruct" the financial statements of one company to make them more comparable with the statements of companies using other accounting methods.

Objectives of financial analysis

Business decisions are made on the basis of the best available estimates of the outcome of such decisions. The purpose of financial analysis is to provide information about a business unit for decision-making purposes, and such information need not be limited to accounting data. While ratios and other relationships based on *past performance* may be helpful in predicting the future earnings performance and financial health of a company, we must be cognizant of the inherent limitations of such data. Financial statements are essentially summary records of the past, and we must go beyond the financial statements and look into the nature of the industry, the company's competitive position within the industry, its product lines, its research expenditures, and, above all, the quality of its management.

The key steps in financial analysis are to determine the company's earnings performance and the soundness and liquidity of its financial position. If financial analysis is to be a good predictive tool, we must examine both quantitative and qualitative information and consider the *quality of earnings* and *quality of assets,* as well as trends and amounts.

QUALITY OF EARNINGS Profits are the lifeblood of a business entity. No entity (unless subsidized by government) can survive for long and thus accomplish its other goals unless it is profitable. Continuous losses drain assets from the business, consume owners' equity, and leave the company at the mercy of creditors. For this reason, we are interested not only in the total *amount* of earnings but also in the *rate* of earnings on sales, on total assets, and on owners' equity. In addition, we must look to the *stability* and *source* of earnings. An erratic earnings performance over a period of years, for example, is less desirable than a steady level of earnings. A history of increasing earnings is preferable to a "flat" earnings record.

A breakdown of sales and earnings by major product lines is useful in evaluating the future performance of a company. In recent years many publicly owned companies have broadened their reporting to include sales and profits by product lines, and the SEC now requires such reporting from most companies.

Financial analysts often express the opinion that the earnings of one company are of higher quality than earnings of other similar companies. This concept of *quality of earnings* arises because each company management can choose from a wide variety of accounting principles and methods, all of which are considered generally acceptable. The financial analyst should ascertain whether the accounting principles and methods selected by management lead to a conservative measurement of earnings or tend to inflate current reported earnings by deferring certain costs and anticipating certain revenue. A company's management is often under heavy pressure to report rising earnings, and accounting policies may be tailored toward this objective. We have already pointed out the impact on current reported earnings of the choice between the lifo and fifo methods of inventory valuation and the choice of depreciation policies. In judging the quality of earnings, other appropriate questions are: What has been the effect on earnings of any accounting changes? How much of the net income is attributable to nonrecurring or nonoperating items? The very existence of a concept of *quality of earnings* is evidence that accountants still have some distance to travel in developing a body of accounting standards which will ensure a reasonable comparability of earnings reported by different companies.

QUALITY OF ASSETS AND THE RELATIVE AMOUNT OF DEBT Although a satisfactory level of earnings may be a good indication of the company's long-run ability to pay its debts and dividends, we must also look at the composition of assets, their condition and liquidity, the relationship between current assets and current liabilities, and the total amount of debt outstanding. A company may be profitable and yet be unable to pay its liabilities on time; sales and earnings may be satisfactory but plant and equipment may be deteriorating because of poor maintenance policies; valuable patents may be expiring; substantial losses may be in prospect from slow-moving inventories and past-due receivables; and a high level of debt may expose stockholders to substantial risks in case of a downturn in business.

IMPACT OF INFLATION Financial statements which are prepared in terms of historical costs may not fully reflect the economic resources or the *real income* (in terms of purchasing power) of a business enterprise. The analyst should therefore attempt to evaluate the impact of inflation on the financial position and results of operations of the company he is analyzing. He should raise such questions as: How much of the net income can be attributed to the increase in the general price level? Is depreciation expense understated in terms of current price levels? Is the company gaining or losing from inflation because of the composition of its assets and because its liabilities will be liquidated with "cheaper" dollars? The fundamental issues of dealing with the impact of inflation were discussed in Chapter 14.

Illustrative analysis for Seacliff Company

Keep in mind the above discussion of analytical principles as you study the illustrative financial analysis which follows. The basic information for our discussion is contained in a set of condensed two-year comparative financial statements for the Seacliff Company shown below and on page 547. Summarized statement data, together with compu-

SEACLIFF COMPANY
*Condensed Comparative Balance Sheet**
December 31

Assets	Year 2	Year 1	Increase or (Decrease) Dollars	%	Percentage of Total Assets Year 2	Year 1
Current assets	$390,000	$288,000	$102,000	35.4	41.1	33.5
Plant and equipment (net)	500,000	467,000	33,000	7.1	52.6	54.3
Other assets (loans to officers)	60,000	105,000	(45,000)	(42.8)	6.3	12.2
Total assets	$950,000	$860,000	$ 90,000	10.5	100.0	100.0
Liabilities & Stockholders' Equity						
Liabilities:						
Current liabilities	$147,400	$ 94,000	$ 53,400	56.8	15.5	10.9
Long-term liabilities	200,000	250,000	(50,000)	(20.0)	21.1	29.1
Total liabilities	$347,400	$344,000	$ 3,400	1.0	36.6	40.0
Stockholders' equity:						
6% preferred stock, $100 par, callable at $105	$100,000	$100,000			10.5	11.6
Common stock, $50 par	250,000	200,000	$ 50,000	25.0	26.3	23.2
Paid-in capital in excess of par	70,000	40,000	30,000	75.0	7.4	4.7
Retained earnings	182,600	176,000	6,600	3.8	19.2	20.5
Total stockholders' equity	$602,600	$516,000	$ 86,600	16.8	63.4	60.0
Total liabilities & stockholders' equity	$950,000	$860,000	$ 90,000	10.5	100.0	100.0

*In order to focus attention on important subtotals, this statement is highly condensed and does not show individual asset and liability items. These details will be introduced as needed in the text discussion. For example, a list of the Seacliff Company's current assets and current liabilities appears on page 557.

SEACLIFF COMPANY
Comparative Income Statement
Years Ended December 31

	Year 2	Year 1	Increase or (Decrease) Dollars	%	Percentage of Net Sales Year 2	Year 1
Net sales	$900,000	$750,000	$150,000	20.0	100.0	100.0
Cost of goods sold	585,000	468,800	116,200	24.9	65.0	62.5
Gross profit on sales . . .	$315,000	$281,200	$ 33,800	12.0	35.0	37.5
Operating expenses:						
Selling	$117,000	$ 75,000	$ 42,000	56.0	13.0	10.0
General and administra-						
tive	126,000	94,500	31,500	33.3	14.0	12.6
Total operating						
expenses	$243,000	$169,500	$ 73,500	43.4	27.0	22.6
Operating income	$ 72,000	$111,700	$ (39,700)	(35.6)	8.0	14.9
Interest expense	12,000	15,000	(3,000)	(20.0)	1.3	2.0
Income before income						
taxes	$ 60,000	$ 96,700	$ (36,700)	(38.0)	6.7	12.9
Income taxes	23,400	44,200	(20,800)	(47.1)	2.6	5.9
Net income	$ 36,600	$ 52,500	$ (15,900)	(30.3)	4.1	7.0
Earnings per share of						
common stock	$6.12	$11.63	$(5.51)	(47.4)		

SEACLIFF COMPANY
Statement of Retained Earnings
Years Ended December 31

	Year 2	Year 1	Increase or (Decrease) Dollars	%
Balance, beginning of year	$176,000	$149,500	$26,500	17.7
Net income	36,600	52,500	(15,900)	(30.3)
Subtotal	$212,600	$202,000	$10,600	5.2
Less: Dividends on common stock .	$ 24,000	$ 20,000	$ 4,000	20.0
Dividends on preferred stock	6,000	6,000		
Total dividends	$ 30,000	$ 26,000	$ 4,000	15.4
Balance, end of year	$182,600	$176,000	$ 6,600	3.8

tations of dollar increases and decreases, and component percentages where applicable, have been compiled.

Using the information in these statements, let us consider the kind of analysis that might be of particular interest to: (1) common stockholders, (2) long-term creditors, and (3) short-term creditors. Organizing our discussion in this way emphasizes the differences in the viewpoint of these groups; all of them have, of course, a considerable common interest in the performance of the company as a whole. This approach should be viewed as only one of many that may be used in analyzing financial statements. Furthermore, the ratios and other measurements illustrated here are not exhaustive; the number of measurements that may be developed for various analytical purposes is almost without limit.

Analysis by common stockholders

Common stockholders and potential investors in common stock look first at a company's earnings record. Their investment is in shares of stock, so *earnings per share and dividends per share* are of particular interest.

EARNINGS PER SHARE OF COMMON STOCK As indicated in Chapter 8, earnings per share of common stock are computed by dividing the income available to common stockholders by the number of shares of common stock outstanding. Any preferred dividend requirements must be subtracted from net income to determine income available for common stock, as shown in the following computations for Seacliff Company:

Earnings per Share of Common Stock

		Year 2	Year 1
Earnings related to number of common shares outstanding	Net income	$36,600	$52,500
	Less: Preferred dividend requirements	6,000	6,000
	Net income available for common stock .... (a)	$30,600	$46,500
	Shares of common outstanding, end of year* .... (b)	5,000	4,000
	Earnings per share of common stock (a ÷ b)	$6.12	$11.63

*1,000 shares sold for cash early in Year 2.

Earnings per share of common stock are shown in the income statement below the net income figure. When the income statement includes operations discontinued during the period, the earnings per share of common stock may be reported in the income statement in three amounts as follows: (1) income from continuing operations, (2) income (or loss) from discontinued operations, and (3) net income.

Similar treatment may be appropriate for extraordinary items. The Seacliff Company had no discontinued operations or extraordinary items and therefore the amount earned per share is computed by dividing the net income available for the common stock by the number of common shares outstanding at the end of each year. The computation of earnings per share in more complicated situations was illustrated in Chapter 8.[2]

DIVIDEND YIELD AND PRICE–EARNINGS RATIO The importance of dividends varies among stockholders. Earnings reinvested in the business should produce an increase in the net income of the firm and thus tend to make each share of stock more valuable. Because the federal income tax rates applicable to dividend income are much higher than the rate of tax on long-term capital gains from the sale of shares of stock, some stockholders may prefer that the company reinvest most of its earnings. Others may be more interested in receiving dividend income currently despite the tax disadvantage.

If we compare the merits of alternative investment opportunities, we should relate earnings and dividends per share to market price of stock. Dividends per share divided by market price per share determines the *yield rate* of a company's stock. Net income per share divided by market price per share determines the *earnings rate* of a company's stock. In financial circles earnings performance of common stock is often expressed as a *price-earnings ratio* by dividing the price per share by the earnings per share. Thus, a stock selling for $60 per share and earning $3 per share may be said to have a price-earnings ratio of 20 times earnings ($60 ÷ $3 = 20).

Assume that the 1,000 additional shares of common stock issued by Seacliff Company early in Year 2 received the full dividend of $4.80 paid in Year 2. When these new shares were issued, Seacliff Company announced that it planned to continue indefinitely the $4.80 dividend per common share currently being paid. With this assumption and the use of assumed market prices of the common stock at December 31, Year 1 and Year 2, the earnings per share and dividend yield for the Seacliff Company may be summarized as follows:

---

[2] When shares of stock are issued or retired during the period or when convertible bonds, convertible preferred stock, or options to purchase stock are outstanding, the computation and reporting of earnings per share are much more complicated. In such cases, earnings per share are based on the *weighted average* number of shares actually outstanding during the period; in addition, *fully diluted* earnings per share are presented on the assumption that all convertible securities are exchanged for common stock and that all options to acquire common stock are exercised. For a complete discussion of the complex procedures required under such circumstances, see *APB Opinion No. 15,* "Earnings per Share," AICPA (New York: 1969).

Earnings and Dividends per Share of Common Stock

Earnings and dividends related to market price of common stock	Date	Assumed Market Price per Share	Earnings per Share	Price-Earnings Ratio	Dividends per Share	Dividend Yield, %
	Dec. 31, Year 1 . . .	$125	$11.63	11	$5.00	4.0
	Dec. 31, Year 2 . . .	$100	$ 6.12	16	$4.80	4.8

The decline in market price during Year 2 presumably reflects the decrease in earnings per share. An investor appraising this stock at December 31, Year 2, would consider whether a price-earnings ratio of 16 times earnings and a dividend yield of 4.8% represented a satisfactory situation in the light of alternative investment opportunities open to him. Obviously he would also place considerable weight on his estimates of the company's prospective future earnings and their probable effect on future dividends and on the market price of the stock.

BOOK VALUE PER SHARE OF COMMON STOCK As briefly stated in Chapter 8, the *book value* of a share of stock is equal to the net assets per share. It is computed by dividing the amount of stockholders' equity applicable to a class of stock by the number of outstanding shares of that class. For example, if a corporation has 5,000 shares of a single class of stock outstanding and the stockholders' equity amounts to $150,000, the book value per share is $30. In computing book value, we are concerned only with the number of shares actually outstanding, thus treasury shares are not included.

When a company has two or more issues of stock outstanding, the book value for each class of stock may be computed by dividing the stockholders' equity applicable to that class of stock by the number of shares outstanding. However, book value is generally computed for common stock only, so the question may be stated as follows: How is book value per common share computed when a company has both preferred and common stock? Assuming that no dividends are in arrears on the preferred stock, book value per common share is equal to the total stockholders' equity (exclusive of the call value of the preferred stock) divided by the number of common shares outstanding. The computation of book value per share of common stock for the Seacliff Company is illustrated at the top of page 551.

Book value per share was reduced by $9.35 in Year 2 as a result of dividend payments and the issuance of 1,000 additional shares of common stock at $80 per share, a figure significantly below the book value of $102.75 per share at the end of Year 1; book value was increased by earnings of $6.12 per share in Year 2, thus causing a net decrease of $3.23 in the book value per share.

Book Value per Share of Common Stock

		Year 2	Year 1
Total stockholders' equity		$602,600	$516,000
Less: Equity of preferred stockholders (1,000 shares at call			
price of $105)		105,000	105,000
Equity of common stockholders	(a)	$497,600	$411,000
Shares of common stock outstanding	(b)	5,000	4,000
Book value per share of common stock (a ÷ b).		$99.52	$102.75

Why did book value per share decrease?

Book value does **not** indicate the amount which the holder of a share of stock would receive if the corporation were to be dissolved. In liquidation, the assets would probably be sold at prices quite different from their carrying values, and the stockholders' equity would go up or down accordingly. Book value is occasionally used in judging the reasonableness of the market price of a stock. However, it must be used with great caution; the fact that a stock is selling at less than its book value does not necessarily indicate a bargain.[3] Earnings per share, dividends per share, and prospects for future earnings are usually more important factors affecting market price than is book value.

REVENUE AND EXPENSE ANALYSIS The trend of earnings of the Seacliff Company is unfavorable and stockholders would want to know the reasons for the decline in net income. The comparative income statement on page 547 shows that despite a 20% increase in net sales, net income fell from $52,500 in Year 1 to $36,600 in Year 2, a decline of 30.3%. The **net income as a percentage of net sales** went from 7.0% to only 4.1%. The primary causes of this decline were the increases in selling expenses (56.0%), in general and administrative expenses (33.3%), and in the cost of goods sold (24.9%), all exceeding the 20% increase in net sales.

These observations suggest the need for further investigation. Suppose we find that the Seacliff Company cut its selling prices in Year 2.This fact would explain the decrease in **gross profit rate** from 37.5 to 35% and would also show that sales volume in physical units rose more than 20%, since it takes proportionally more sales at lower prices to produce a given increase in dollar sales. Since the dollar amount of gross profit increased $33,800 in Year 2, the strategy of reducing sales prices to increase volume would have been successful if there had been little change in operating expenses. Operating expenses, however, rose by $73,500, resulting in a $39,700 decrease in operating income.

[3] It is not unusual to find stocks of growth companies selling at 5 or more times book value and the stocks of companies in certain depressed industries selling at 25% or less of book value per share.

The next step is to find which expenses increased and why. An investor may be handicapped here, because detailed operating expenses are not usually shown in published statements. Some conclusions, however, can be reached on the basis of even the condensed information available in the comparative income statement for the Seacliff Company shown on page 547.

The substantial increase in selling expenses presumably reflects greater selling effort during Year 2 in an attempt to improve sales volume. However, the fact that selling expenses increased $42,000 while gross profit increased only $33,800 indicates that the cost of this increased sales effort was not justified in terms of results. Even more disturbing is the increase in general and administrative expenses. Some growth in administrative expenses might be expected to accompany increased sales volume, but because some of the expenses are fixed, the growth should be less than proportional to any increase in sales. The increase in general and administrative expenses from 12.6 to 14% of sales would be of serious concern to astute investors.

Management generally has greater control over operating expenses than over revenue. The *operating expense ratio* is often used as a measure of management's ability to control its operating expenses. The unfavorable trend in this ratio for the Seacliff Company is shown below:

Does a higher operating expense ratio indicate higher net income?

Operating Expense Ratio

		Year 2	Year 1
Operating expenses	(a)	$243,000	$169,500
Net sales	(b)	$900,000	$750,000
Operating expense ratio (a ÷ b)		27.0%	22.6%

If management were able to increase the sales volume while at the same time increasing the gross profit rate and decreasing the operating expense ratio, the effect on net income could be quite dramatic. For example, if the Seacliff Company increased its sales in Year 3 by 11% to $1,000,000, increased its gross profit rate from 35 to 38%, and reduced the operating expense ratio from 27 to 24%, its operating income would then increase from $72,000 to $140,000 ($1,000,000 − $620,000 − $240,000), an increase of over 94%.

RETURN ON TOTAL ASSETS An important test of management's ability to earn a return on funds supplied from all sources is the rate of return on total assets. The income figure used in computing this ratio should be *income before deducting interest expense,* since interest is a payment to creditors for funds used to acquire assets. Income before interest reflects earnings throughout the year and therefore should be related to the average investment in assets during the year. The computation of this ratio for the Seacliff Company is shown on page 553.

Earnings related to investment in assets

Percentage Return on Total Assets

		Year 2	Year 1
Net income		$ 36,600	$ 52,500
Add back: Interest expense		12,000	15,000
Income before interest expense	(a)	$ 48,600	$ 67,500
Total assets, beginning of year		$860,000	$820,000
Total assets, end of year		$950,000	$860,000
Average investment in total assets	(b)	$905,000	$840,000
Return on total assets (a ÷ b)		5.4%	8.0%

This ratio shows that earnings per dollar of assets invested have fallen off in Year 2. If the same ratio were available for other companies of similar kind and size, the significance of this decline could be better appraised.

RETURN ON COMMON STOCKHOLDERS' EQUITY Because interest and dividends paid to creditors and preferred stockholders are fixed in amount, a company may earn a greater or smaller return on the common stockholders' equity than on its total assets. The computation of return on common stockholders' equity for the Seacliff Company is shown below:

Does trading on the equity benefit common stockholders?

Return on Common Stockholders' Equity

		Year 2	Year 1
Net income		$ 36,600	$ 52,500
Less: Preferred dividend requirements		6,000	6,000
Net income available for common stock	(a)	$ 30,600	$ 46,500
Common stockholders' equity, beginning of year		$416,000	$389,500
Common stockholders' equity, end of year		$502,600	$416,000
Average common stockholders' equity	(b)	$459,300	$402,750
Return on common stockholders' equity (a ÷ b)		6.7%	11.6%

In both years the rate of return to common stockholders was higher than the return on total assets, because the average combined rate of interest paid to creditors (both long-term and short-term) and dividends to preferred stockholders was less than the rate earned on each dollar of assets used in the business.

Financing with fixed-return securities is often called ***trading on the equity.*** Results may be favorable or unfavorable to holders of common stock:

1 If the rate of return on total assets is ***greater*** than the average rate of payment to creditors and preferred stockholders, the common stockholders will ***gain*** from trading on the equity.

2 If the rate of return on total assets is *smaller* than the average rate of payments to creditors and preferred stockholders, the common stockholders will *lose* from trading on the equity.

EQUITY RATIO The equity ratio measures the proportion of the total assets financed by stockholders, as distinguished from creditors. It is computed by dividing total stockholders' equity by total assets. The equity ratio for the Seacliff Company is determined as follows:

Equity Ratio

		Year 2	Year 1
Proportion of assets financed by stock-holders	Total assets . . . . (a)	$950,000	$860,000
	Total stockholders' equity . . . . (b)	$602,600	$516,000
	Equity ratio (b ÷ a)	63.4%	60.0%

The Seacliff Company has a higher equity ratio in Year 2 than in Year 1. Is this favorable or unfavorable?

From the common stockholders' viewpoint, a low equity ratio (that is, a large proportion of capital supplied by creditors) will produce maximum benefits from trading on the equity if the rate earned on total assets exceeds the rate of interest paid to creditors; however, a low equity ratio can be very unfavorable if the rate earned on total assets falls below the rate of interest paid to creditors. Furthermore, if a business incurs so much debt that it is unable to meet the required interest and principal payments, creditors may force liquidation or reorganization of the business, to the detriment of stockholders. Because of these factors, the equity ratio is usually judged in the light of the probable stability of the company's earnings, as well as the rate of earnings in relation to the rate of interest paid to creditors.

As we saw earlier in our analysis, trading on the equity from the common stockholders' viewpoint can also be accomplished through the issuance of preferred stock. However, since preferred stock dividends are not deductible for income tax purposes, the advantage to common stockholders will usually be much smaller from issuance of preferred stock than from borrowing.

Analysis by long-term creditors

Bondholders and other long-term creditors are primarily interested in three factors: (1) the rate of return on their investment, (2) the firm's ability to meet its interest requirements, and (3) the firm's ability to repay the principal of the debt when it falls due.

YIELD RATE ON BONDS The yield rate on bonds or other long-term indebtedness cannot be computed in the same manner as the yield rate on shares of stock, because bonds, unlike stocks, have a fixed maturity date and amount. The ownership of a 6%, 10-year bond represents the right to receive $1,000 at the end of 10 years and the right to receive $60 per year during each of the next 10 years. If the market price of this bond is $950, the yield rate on an investment in the bond is the rate of interest that will make the present value of these two contractual rights equal to $950. Determining the effective interest rate on such an investment requires the use of compound interest tables, a discussion of which is reserved to a more advanced coverage of this subject. We can, however, generalize the relation between yield rate and bond price as follows: *The yield rate varies inversely with changes in the market price of the bond.* If the price of a bond is above maturity value, the yield rate is less than the bond interest rate; if the price of a bond is below maturity value, the yield rate is higher than the bond interest rate.

NUMBER OF TIMES INTEREST EARNED Long-term creditors have learned from experience that one of the best indications of the safety of their investment is the fact that, over the life of the debt, the company has sufficient income to cover its interest requirements by a wide margin. A failure to cover interest requirements may have serious repercussions on the stability and solvency of the debtor company.

A common measure of debt safety is the ratio of income available for the payment of interest to the annual interest expense, called *times interest earned.* This computation for the Seacliff Company would be:

Number of Times Interest Earned

		Year 2	Year 1
Operating income (before interest and income taxes) . . . . *(a)*		$72,000	$111,700
Annual interest expense . . . . *(b)*		$12,000	$ 15,000
Times interest earned (a ÷ b)		6.0	7.4

Long-term creditors watch this ratio

The decline in the ratio during Year 2 is unfavorable, but a ratio of 6.0 times interest earned for that year would still be considered quite adequate.

The ability of a company to cover all fixed charges, particularly from a cash flow standpoint, is a useful bit of information to all parties interested in the financial well-being of the company. For this reason the coverage of fixed charges may be expanded to include recurring payments such as lease rentals, property taxes, and contributions to pension and sinking funds.

DEBT RATIO Long-term creditors are interested in the amount of debt outstanding in relation to the amount of stockholders' equity. The *debt ratio* is computed by dividing total liabilities by total assets, as shown for the Seacliff Company at the top of page 556.

Debt Ratio

			Year 2	Year 1
What portion of total assets is financed by debt?	Total liabilities .... (a)		$347,400	$344,000
	Total assets (or total liabilities & stockholders' equity) . . (b)		$950,000	$860,000
	Debt ratio (a ÷ b)		36.6%	40.0

From a creditor's viewpoint, the lower the debt ratio the better, since this means that stockholders have invested the bulk of the funds in the business, and therefore the margin of protection to creditors against a shrinkage of the assets is high.

Analysis by short-term creditors

Bankers and other short-term creditors share the interest of stockholders and bondholders in the profitability and long-run stability of a business. Their primary interest, however, is in the current position of the firm—its ability to generate sufficient cash to meet current operating needs and to pay current debts promptly. Thus the analysis of financial statements by a banker considering a short-term loan, or by a trade creditor investigating the credit status of a customer, is likely to center on the working capital position of the prospective debtor.

AMOUNT OF WORKING CAPITAL The amount of working capital is measured by the *excess of current assets over current liabilities.* Thus, working capital represents the amount of cash, near-cash items, and cash substitutes (prepayments) on hand after providing for payment of all current liabilities. The details of the working capital of the Seacliff Company are shown on page 557.

This schedule shows that current assets increased $102,000, while current liabilities rose by only $53,400, with the result that working capital increased $48,600. There was a shift in the composition of the current assets and current liabilities; cash decreased from 13.9 to 9.8% of current assets, and inventory rose from 41.6 to 46.1%. Inventory is a less liquid resource than cash. Therefore, although the amount of working capital increased in Year 2, the quality of working capital is not as liquid as in Year 1. Although creditors want to see large amounts of high-quality working capital, management must consider that excess amounts of cash are not a productive asset and do not generate a high return.

CURRENT RATIO One means of further evaluating these changes in working capital is to observe the relationship between current assets

SEACLIFF COMPANY
Comparative Schedule of Working Capital
As of December 31

	Year 2	Year 1	Increase or (Decrease) Dollars	%	Percentage of Total Current Items Year 2	Year 1
Current assets:						
Cash	$ 38,000	$ 40,000	$ (2,000)	(5.0)	9.8	13.9
Receivables (net) . . .	117,000	86,000	31,000	36.0	30.0	29.9
Inventory	180,000	120,000	60,000	50.0	46.1	41.6
Short-term prepay-						
ments	55,000	42,000	13,000	31.0	14.1	14.6
Total current assets	$390,000	$288,000	$102,000	35.4	100.0	100.0
Current liabilities:						
Notes payable	$ 50,000	$ 10,000	$ 40,000	400.0	33.9	10.7
Accounts payable . . .	66,000	30,000	36,000	120.0	44.8	31.9
Accrued liabilities . . .	31,400	54,000	(22,600)	(41.9)	21.3	57.4
Total current liabili-						
ties	$147,400	$ 94,000	$ 53,400	56.8	100.0	100.0
Working capital	$242,600	$194,000	$ 48,600	25.0		

and current liabilities, a test known as the **current ratio.** The current ratio for the Seacliff Company is computed below:

Current Ratio

	Year 2	Year 1
Total current assets . . . . (a)	$390,000	$288,000
Total current liabilities . . . . (b)	$147,400	$ 94,000
Current ratio (a ÷ b).	2.6	3.1

Does this indicate satisfactory debt-paying ability?

Despite the increase of $48,600 in the amount of working capital in Year 2, current assets per dollar of current liabilities decreased. The margin of safety (current ratio), however, still appears satisfactory.

In interpreting the current ratio, a number of factors should be considered:

1 Creditors tend to feel that the larger the current ratio the better; however, from a managerial view there is an upper limit. Too high a current ratio may indicate that assets are not being productively used in the business.

2 Because creditors tend to stress the current ratio as an indication of short-term solvency, some companies may take conscious steps to improve this ratio just before financial statements are prepared at the end of a fiscal

period for submission to bankers or other creditors. This may be done by postponing purchases, allowing inventory to fall, and using all available cash to pay current liabilities.

3 The current ratio computed at the end of a fiscal year may not be representative of the current position of the company throughout the year. Since many companies select a fiscal year which ends during an ebb in the seasonal swing of business activity, the current ratio at year-end is likely to be more favorable than at any other time during the year.

Use of both the current ratio and the amount of working capital helps to place debt-paying ability in its proper perspective. For example, if Company X has current assets of $20,000 and current liabilities of $10,000 and Company Y has current assets of $2,000,000 and current liabilities of $1,990,000, both companies would have $10,000 of working capital, but the current position of Company X is clearly superior to that of Company Y. If the current ratio were computed for both companies, the difference would be revealed.

As another example, assume that Company A and Company B both have current ratios of 3 to 1. However, Company A has working capital of $20,000 and Company B has working capital of $200,000. Although both companies appear to be good credit risks, Company B would probably be able to qualify for a much larger bank loan than would Company A.

A widely used rule of thumb is that a current ratio of 2 to 1 or better is satisfactory. Like all rules of thumb this is an arbitrary standard, subject to numerous exceptions and qualifications.

QUICK RATIO Because inventories and short-term prepayments are further removed from conversion into cash than other current assets, a ratio known as the **quick** (or **acid-test**) **ratio** is sometimes computed as a supplement to the current ratio. This ratio compares the highly liquid current assets (cash, marketable securities, and receivables) with current liabilities. The Seacliff Company has no marketable securities; its quick ratio is computed as follows:

Quick Ratio

		Year 2	Year 1
A measure of liquidity	Quick assets (cash and receivables) . . . . (a)	$155,000	$126,000
	Current liabilities . . . . (b)	$147,400	$ 94,000
	Quick ratio (a ÷ b)	1.1	1.3

Here again the analysis reveals an unfavorable trend. Whether the quick ratio is adequate depends on the amount of receivables included among quick assets and the average time required to collect receivables as compared to the credit period extended by the company's short-term creditors. If the credit periods extended to customers and granted by short-term creditors are roughly equal, a quick ratio of 1.0 or better would generally be considered satisfactory.

In recent years, many analysts have made reference to a *liquidity ratio* of corporations as a useful measure of immediate ability to pay short-term debts. This ratio is computed by dividing the total of cash and marketable securities owned by the total current liabilities outstanding.

INVENTORY TURNOVER The cost of goods sold figure in the income statement represents the total cost of all goods that have been transferred out of inventory as a result of sales during the period. Therefore the relationship between cost of goods sold and the average balance of inventory throughout the period indicates the number of times that inventory "turns over" and is replaced each period.

Ideally we should total the inventories at the end of each month and divide by 12 to obtain an average inventory. This information is not always available, however, and the nearest substitute is a simple average of the inventory at the beginning and at the end of the year. This tends to overstate the turnover rate, since many companies choose an accounting year that ends when inventories are at a minimum.

Assuming that only beginning and ending inventories are available, the computation of inventory turnover for the Seacliff Company may be illustrated as follows:

Inventory Turnover

		Year 2	Year 1
Cost of goods sold	(a)	$585,000	$468,800
Inventory, beginning of year		$120,000	$100,000
Inventory, end of year		$180,000	$120,000
Average inventory	(b)	$150,000	$110,000
Inventory turnover per year (a ÷ b)		3.9 times	4.3 times
Average days to turn over (divide 365 days by average inventory turnover)		94 days	85 days

What does inventory turnover mean?

The trend indicated by this analysis is unfavorable, since the average investment in inventories in relation to the cost of goods sold is rising. Stating this another way, the company required on the average 9 days more during Year 2 to turn over its inventories than during Year 1. Furthermore, the inventory status *at the end of the year* has changed even more: At the end of Year 1 there were 93 days' sales in the ending inventory ($120,000/$468,800 × 365 days) compared to 112 days' sales in the ending inventory at the end of Year 2 ($180,000/ $585,000 × 365 days).

The relation between inventory turnover and the gross profit rate may be significant. A high inventory turnover and a low gross profit rate frequently go hand in hand. This, however, is merely another way of saying that if the gross profit rate is low, a higher volume of business is necessary to produce a satisfactory return on total assets. Although a high inventory turnover is usually regarded as a good sign, a rate that is high in relation to that of similar firms may indicate that the company is losing sales by a failure to maintain an adequate stock of goods to serve its customers promptly.

ACCOUNTS RECEIVABLE TURNOVER The turnover of accounts receivable is computed in a manner comparable to that just described for inventories. The ratio between the net sales for the period and the average balance in accounts receivable is a rough indication of the average time required to convert receivables into cash. Ideally, a monthly average of receivables should be used, and only *sales on credit* should be included in the sales figure. For illustrative purposes, we shall assume that Seacliff Company sells entirely on credit and that only the beginning and ending balances of receivables are available:

Accounts Receivable Turnover

		Year 2	Year 1
Are customers paying promptly?	Net sales on credit . . . . (a)	$900,000	$750,000
	Receivables, beginning of year	$ 86,000	$ 80,000
	Receivables, end of year	$117,000	$ 86,000
	Average receivables . . . . (b)	$101,500	$ 83,000
	Accounts receivable turnover per year (a ÷ b)	8.9 times	9.0 times
	Average days to turn over (divide 365 days by receivable turnover)	41 days	41 days

There has been no significant change in the average time required to collect receivables. The interpretation of the average age of receivables would depend upon the company's credit terms and the seasonal activity immediately before year-end. If the company grants 30-day credit terms to its customers, for example, the above analysis indicates that accounts receivable collections are lagging. If the terms were for 60 days, however, there is evidence that collections are being made ahead of schedule. On the other hand, if the sales volume in the last month of the year was unusually large, the average age of receivables as computed above can be misleading.

Summary of ratios and other measurements

The more widely used ratios and other measurements discussed in this chapter and their significance are summarized on page 561.

Ratio or Other Measurement	Method of Computation	Significance
1 Earnings per share of common stock	$$\frac{\text{Net income} - \text{preferred dividends}}{\text{Shares of common outstanding}}$$	Gives the amount of earnings applicable to a share of common stock.
2 Dividend yield	$$\frac{\text{Dividend per share}}{\text{Market price per share}}$$	Shows the rate earned by stockholders based on current market price of stock.
3 Price-earnings ratio	$$\frac{\text{Market price per share}}{\text{Earnings per share}}$$	Indicates whether price of stock is in line with earnings.
4 Book value per share of common stock	$$\frac{\text{Common stockholders' equity}}{\text{Shares of common outstanding}}$$	Measures net assets applicable to each share of common stock.
5 Operating expense ratio	$$\frac{\text{Operating expenses}}{\text{Net sales}}$$	Indicates management's ability to control expenses.
6 Return on total assets	$$\frac{\text{Net income} + \text{interest expense}}{\text{Average investment in assets}}$$	Measures the productivity of assets.
7 Return on common stockholders' equity	$$\frac{\text{Net income} - \text{preferred dividends}}{\text{Average common stockholders' equity}}$$	Indicates the earning power on common stockholders' equity.
8 Equity ratio	$$\frac{\text{Total stockholders' equity}}{\text{Total assets}}$$	Shows the protection to creditors and the extent of trading on the equity.
9 Number of times interest earned (before income taxes)	$$\frac{\text{Operating income}}{\text{Annual interest expense}}$$	Measures the coverage of interest expense (particularly on long-term debt) before income taxes.
10 Debt ratio	$$\frac{\text{Total liabilities}}{\text{Total assets}}$$	Gives the percentage of assets financed through borrowing and the extent of trading on the equity.
11 Current ratio	$$\frac{\text{Current assets}}{\text{Current liabilities}}$$	Measures short-run debt-paying ability.
12 Quick (acid-test) ratio	$$\frac{\text{Quick assets}}{\text{Current liabilities}}$$	Measures the short-term liquidity.
13. Inventory turnover	$$\frac{\text{Cost of goods sold}}{\text{Average inventory}}$$	Indicates management's ability to control the investment in inventory.
14 Accounts receivable turnover	$$\frac{\text{Net sales on credit}}{\text{Average receivables}}$$	Indicates reasonableness of amount of accounts receivable and the effectiveness of collections.

The relevance of any financial statement measurement depends on the direction of its trend and on its relationship to some predetermined standard or industry average. The information available in financial statements is useful in appraising the financial position of a company and in forecasting its earning power. Relationships among reported data can be extremely informative; however, the analyst must be aware that financial statements do not provide all the answers and that other information may be equally important in evaluating the economic well-being of a company. For example, factors which are useful in forecasting the earnings performance of a company include the following: (1) Source of markets for products or services; (2) growth potential for products or services; (3) company's market share in its industry; (4) patent protection for major products; (5) sensitivity to economic fluctuations; and (6) effect of technological, political, economic, and environmental changes on the company's business.

The analyst should recognize that many assets are not reported at current fair value and that not all valuable resources are included in the balance sheet (for example, good management, good credit standing, potential new products, internally developed goodwill, appreciation in the value of assets). Furthermore, the quality of assets must be carefully evaluated. The income statement is a product of matching historical costs with realized revenue for a short span of a company's life and does not depict all changes in the company's economic wealth. The analyst should be fully aware of the limitations of information contained in financial statements, and of the importance of other types of information.

DEMONSTRATION PROBLEM

Given below are the financial statements for the King Company for Year 2 and Year 1, accompanied by miscellaneous additional information.

	Year 2	Year 1
Cash	$ 35,000	$ 25,000
Accounts receivable (net)	91,000	90,000
Inventory	160,000	140,000
Short-term prepayments	4,000	5,000
Investment in land	90,000	100,000
Equipment	880,000	640,000
Less: Accumulated depreciation	(260,000)	(200,000)
	$1,000,000	$ 800,000

	Year 2	Year 1
Accounts payable	$ 105,000	$ 46,000
Income taxes payable and other accrued liabilities	40,000	25,000
Bonds payable—8%	280,000	280,000
Premium on bonds payable	3,600	4,000
Capital stock, $5 par	165,000	110,000
Retained earnings	406,400	335,000
	$1,000,000	$ 800,000
Sales (net of discounts and allowances)	$2,200,000	$1,600,000
Cost of goods sold	1,606,000	1,120,000
Gross profit on sales	$ 594,000	$ 480,000
Expenses (including $22,400 interest expense)	(330,000)	(352,000)
Income taxes	(91,000)	(48,000)
Extraordinary loss	(6,600)	–0–
Net income	$ 166,400	$ 80,000

Cash dividends of $40,000 were paid and a 50% stock dividend was distributed early in Year 2. All sales were made on credit at a relatively uniform rate during the year. Inventory and receivables did not fluctuate materially. The market price of the company's stock on December 31, Year 2, was $86 per share; on December 31, Year 1, it was $43.50 (before the 50% stock dividend) distributed in Year 2.

Instructions Compute the following for Year 2 and Year 1:
(1) Quick ratio
(2) Current ratio
(3) Equity ratio
(4) Debt ratio
(5) Book value per share of capital stock (based on shares outstanding after 50% stock dividend in Year 2)
(6) Earnings per share of capital stock (including extraordinary loss)
(7) Price-earnings ratio
(8) Gross profit percentage
(9) Operating expense ratio
(10) Income before extraordinary loss as a percentage of net sales
(11) Inventory turnover (Assume an average inventory of $150,000 for both years.)
(12) Accounts receivable turnover (Assume average accounts receivable of $90,000 for Year 1.)
(13) Times bond interest earned (before interest expense and income taxes)

SOLUTION TO DEMONSTRATION PROBLEM

	Year 2	Year 1
(1) Quick ratio:		
$126,000 ÷ $145,000	.9 to 1	
$115,000 ÷ $71,000		1.6 to 1
(2) Current ratio:		
$290,000 ÷ $145,000	2 to 1	
$260,000 ÷ $71,000		3.7 to 1

	Year 2	Year 1
(3) Equity ratio:		
$571,400 ÷ $1,000,000	57%	
$445,000 ÷ $800,000		56%
(4) Debt ratio:		
$428,600 ÷ $1,000,000	43%	
$355,000 ÷ $800,000		44%
(5) Book value per share of capital stock:		
$571,400 ÷ 33,000 shares	$17.32	
$445,000 ÷ 33,000* shares		$13.48
(6) Earnings per share of capital stock (including extraordinary loss of $0.20 per share in Year 2):		
$166,400 ÷ 33,000 shares	$5.04	
$80,000 ÷ 33,000* shares		$2.42
(7) Price-earnings ratio:		
$86 ÷ $5.04	17 times	
$43.50 ÷ 1.5* = $29, adjusted market price; $29 ÷ $2.42		12 times
(8) Gross profit percentage:		
$594,000 ÷ $2,200,000	27%	
$480,000 ÷ $1,600,000		30%
(9) Operating expense ratio:		
($330,000 − $22,400) ÷ $2,200,000	14%	
($352,000 − $22,400) ÷ $1,600,000		20.6%
(10) Income before extraordinary loss as a percentage of net sales:		
$173,000 ÷ $2,200,000	7.9%	
$80,000 ÷ $1,600,000		5%
(11) Inventory turnover:		
$1,606,000 ÷ $150,000	10.7 times	
$1,120,000 ÷ $150,000		7.5 times
(12) Accounts receivable turnover:		
$2,200,000 ÷ $90,500	24.3 times	
$1,600,000 ÷ $90,000		17.8 times
(13) Times bond interest earned:		
($166,400 + $22,400 + $91,000) ÷ $22,400	12.5 times	
($80,000 + $22,400 + $48,000) ÷ $22,400		6.7 times

*Adjusted retroactively for 50% stock dividend.

REVIEW QUESTIONS

1 a What groups are interested in the financial affairs of a publicly owned corporation?

b List some of the more important sources of financial information for investors.

2 In financial statement analysis, what is the basic objective of observing trends in data and ratios? What is an alternative standard of comparison?

3 In financial analysis, what information is produced by computing a *ratio* that is not available in a simple observation of the underlying data?

4 Explain the distinction between *percentage change* and *component percentages.*

5 "Although net income declined this year as compared with last year, it increased from 6 to 10% of net sales." Are sales increasing or decreasing?

6 Assume that the Chemco Corporation is engaged in the manufacture and distribution of a variety of chemicals. In analyzing the financial statements of this corporation, why would you want to refer to the ratios and other measurements of companies in the chemical industry? In comparing the financial results of the Chemco Corporation with another chemical company, why would you be interested in the accounting methods used by the two companies?

7 What are the key objectives of financial analysis? What types of non-accounting information may be relevant in evaluating the future profitability of a company?

8 What single ratio do you think should be of greatest interest to:
  a a banker considering a short-term loan?
  b a common stockholder?
  c an insurance company considering a long-term mortgage loan to a manufacturing company?

9 Modern Company earned (after taxes) a 12% return on its total assets. Current liabilities are 10% of total assets and long-term bonds carrying an 8% coupon rate are equal to 30% of total assets. There is no preferred stock. Would you expect the rate of return on stockholders' equity to be greater or less than 12%? Explain.

10 In deciding whether a company's equity ratio is favorable or unfavorable, creditors and stockholders may have different views. Why?

11 Company A has a current ratio of 5 to 1. Company B has a current ratio of 3 to 1. Does this mean that A's working capital is larger than B's? Why?

12 An investor states, "I bought this stock for $50 several years ago and it now sells for $100. It paid $5 per share in dividends last year so I'm earning 10% on my investment." Criticize this statement.

13 Company C experiences a considerable seasonal variation in its business. The high point in the year's activities comes in November, the low point in July. During which month would you expect the company's current ratio to be higher? If the company were choosing a fiscal year for accounting purposes, what advice would you offer?

14 Both the inventory turnover and accounts receivable turnover increased from 10 times to 15 times from Year 1 to Year 2, but net income decreased. Can you offer some possible reasons for this?

EXERCISES

Ex. 16-1 Given below is a condensed balance sheet:

Assets		Liabilities & Stockholders' Equity	
Cash	$ 10,000	Current liabilities	$ 25,000
Accounts receivable	20,000	Long-term liabilities	50,000
Inventory	45,000	Capital stock, $10 par	100,000
Short-term prepayments	15,000	Retained earnings	25,000
Plant assets (net)	100,000		
Other assets	10,000	Total liabilities &	
Total assets	$200,000	stockholders' equity	$200,000

During the latest year, the company earned a gross profit of $160,000 on net sales of $400,000. Accounts receivable, inventory, and plant assets remained relatively constant during the year. From this information, compute the following:

a Current ratio
b Quick ratio
c Equity ratio
d Accounts receivable turnover (all sales are on credit)
e Inventory turnover
f Book value per share of capital stock

Ex. 16-2 The following information is available for the Ford Company:

	Year 2	Year 1
Total assets (40% of which are current)	$800,000	$650,000
Current liabilities	$160,000	$200,000
Mortgage payable, 7%	200,000	100,000
Capital stock, $10 stated value	300,000	300,000
Retained earnings	140,000	50,000
Total liabilities & stockholders' equity	$800,000	$650,000

Dividends of $12,000 were declared in Year 2. Compute the following:
a Current ratio for Year 2 and Year 1
b Debt ratio for Year 2 and Year 1
c Earnings per share for Year 2

Ex. 16-3 Figures for two companies engaged in the same line of business are presented below for the latest year:

	Lowe Company	Highe Company
Net sales (all on credit)	$1,600,000	$1,200,000
Total assets	800,000	400,000
Total liabilities	100,000	100,000
Average accounts receivable	200,000	100,000
Average inventory	240,000	140,000
Gross profit as a percentage of net sales	40%	30%
Operating expenses as a percentage of net sales	30%	18%
Net income as a percentage of net sales	6%	8%

Compute the following for each company:
a Net income
b Net income as a percentage of total assets
c Net income as a percentage of stockholders' equity
d Accounts receivable turnover
e Inventory turnover

Ex. 16-4 Given below is the stockholders' equity for a manufacturing company:

Nonparticipating and noncallable $10 par value cumulative preferred stock, 5%, (dividends two years in arrears)	$ 200,000
Common stock, $1 par	300,000
Paid-in capital in excess of par	600,000
Retained earnings	2,050,000
Treasury stock, at cost, 10,000 shares of common stock	(30,000)
Total stockholders' equity	$3,120,000

a Compute the book value per share of common stock.

b If the debt ratio is 40%, what is the amount of total assets?

c Assuming that the company acquired an additional 90,000 shares of its own common stock at $6 per share, what would be the book value per share of the 200,000 shares outstanding?

Ex. 16-5 The following information relates to the operations of the Lava Corporation:

Sales (60% on credit)	$2,500,000
Beginning inventory, Year 1	350,000
Purchases	2,100,000
Ending inventory, Year 1	?
Ending accounts receivable, Year 1	150,000

Sales are made at 25% above cost. Compute:

a The inventory turnover for Year 1.

b The number of days credit sales in accounts receivable at the end of Year 1. A year equals 365 days.

Ex. 16-6 In the schedule below, certain items taken from the income statements of Ricardo Gonzales, Inc., for two fiscal years ending January 31 have been expressed as a percentage of net sales:

	Percentage of Net Sales	
	Year 2	Year 1
Net sales	100%	100%
Beginning inventory	10	16
Net purchases	68	60
Ending inventory	8	12
Selling expenses	13	15
Administrative expenses	8	9
Income taxes	4	5

Net sales were $1 million in Year 1 and increased by 20% in Year 2. Prepare a comparative income statement in order to determine the change in net income for Year 2 compared to Year 1.

Ex. 16-7 At the end of Year 1, the Zorro Corporation had inventories and short-term prepayments of $84,000, current liabilities of $120,000, and a current ratio of 3 to 1.

The following transactions are completed early in Year 2:

(0) Sold inventory costing $10,000 for $8,000.

(1) Declared a cash dividend, $25,000.

(2) Declared a 10% stock dividend.

(3) Paid accounts payable, $15,000.

(4) Purchased goods on account, $14,750.

(5) Collected cash on accounts receivable, $18,500.

(6) Borrowed cash on short-term note, $40,000.

(7) Issued additional shares of capital stock for cash, $100,000.

(8) Sold temporary investments costing $20,000 for $17,000.

(9) Acquired temporary investments, $12,000.

(10) Wrote off uncollectible accounts, $2,000.

a Compute the amount of working capital and the quick ratio at the end of Year 1.

b Indicate the effect (increase, decrease, none) of each transaction listed above for Year 2 on the current ratio, quick ratio, and working capital. Use the following four-column format (item 0 is given as an example):

Item	Current Ratio	Quick Ratio	Working Capital
0	Decrease	Increase	Decrease

PROBLEMS

16-1 The following information is taken from the records of the Sunset Corporation at the end of Year 1:

Sales (all on credit)	$200,000
Cost of goods sold	120,000
Average inventory (fifo method)	25,000
Average accounts receivable	50,000
Net income for Year 1	20,000
Total assets	250,000
Total liabilities	140,000

The corporation did not declare dividends during the year and capital stock was neither issued nor retired. The liabilities consisted of accounts payable and accrued items; no interest expense was incurred.

Instructions From the information given, compute the following for Year 1:
a Inventory turnover
b Accounts receivable turnover
c Total operating expenses, assuming that income taxes amounted to $7,500
d Gross profit percentage
e Rate earned on average stockholders' equity
f Rate earned on total assets (Use end-of-year total.)

16-2 The Valley Company manufactures and distributes a full line of farm machinery. Given below for Year 1 is the income statement for the company and a common size summary for the industry in which the company operates:

	Valley Company	Industry Average
Sales (net)	$2,000,000	100%
Cost of goods sold	1,440,000	68
Gross profit on sales	$ 560,000	32%
Operating expenses:		
Selling	$ 160,000	7%
General and administrative	180,000	10
Total operating expenses	$ 340,000	17%
Operating income	$ 220,000	15%
Income taxes	100,000	6
Net income	$ 120,000	9%

Instructions
a Prepare a common size income statement comparing the results for the Valley Company for Year 1 with the average for the farm machinery industry.

b Explain fully the significance of the results obtained in the comparative income statement prepared in part **a**.

16-3 The data below are taken from the records of the Ruddy Company at the close of the current year:

Accounts and notes payable	$ 49,300
Accrued liabilities (including income taxes payable)	30,700
Cash	34,000
Inventories, beginning of year	42,300
Inventories, end of year	66,900
Investment in marketable securities	21,000
Operating expenses	107,000
Short-term prepayments	7,500
Income taxes expense (portion has already been paid)	39,400
Purchases (net)	351,600
Receivables, beginning of year (net of allowance)	85,400
Receivables, end of year (net of allowance)	70,600
Sales (net)	526,000

Instructions On the basis of this information, determine the following:
a Amount of working capital
b Current ratio
c Quick ratio
d Inventory turnover and days' sales in inventory
e Accounts receivable turnover and number of days' sales in accounts receivable (Assume a year has 365 days.)
f Rate of gross profit on net sales
g Rate of net income on net sales

16-4 Given below are selected balance sheet items and ratios for the Puzzlement Corporation at June 30, Year 10:

Total stockholders' equity (includes 100,000 shares of no-par value capital stock issued at $6 per share)	$1,000,000
Plant and equipment (net)	$ 470,000
Asset turnover rate per year (sales ÷ total assets)	3 times
Inventory turnover rate per year	6 times
Accounts receivable turnover rate per year	12 times
Gross profit percentage	30%
Ratio of current liabilities to stockholders' equity (there is no long-term debt)	1.2 to 1
Quick ratio (acid-test ratio)	0.8 to 1

Assume that balance sheet figures represent average amounts and that all sales are made on credit.

Instructions From the foregoing information, construct a balance sheet for the Puzzlement Corporation as of June 30, Year 10, in as much detail as the data permit.

16-5 Alex Company and Barnes Company operate in the same industry and are generally comparable in terms of product lines, scope of operations, and the accounting methods used in preparing financial statements. The financial information given below for these two companies (except market price per share of stock) is stated in thousands of dollars and figures are as of the end of the current year:

Assets	Alex Company	Barnes Company
Current assets	$ 97,450	$132,320
Plant and equipment	397,550	495,680
Less: Accumulated depreciation	(55,000)	(78,000)
Total assets	$440,000	$550,000

Liabilities & Stockholders' Equity		
Current liabilities	$ 34,000	$ 65,000
Bonds payable, 8%, due in 15 years	120,000	100,000
Capital stock, no par	150,000	200,000
Retained earnings	136,000	185,000
Total liabilities & stockholders' equity	$440,000	$550,000

Analysis of retained earnings:		
Balance, beginning of year	$125,200	$167,200
Net income for the year	19,800	37,400
Dividends	(9,000)	(19,600)
Balance, end of year	$136,000	$185,000

Market price of capital stock, per share	$30	$61
Number of shares of capital stock outstanding	6 million	8 million

Instructions

a Although market prices for the bonds are not stated, which company's bonds do you think will sell at the higher price per $1,000 bond? Which company's bonds will probably yield the higher rate of return? (You may assume that the safer the bonds, according to your analysis, the lower the yield rate.)

b What are the dividend yield, the price-earnings ratio, and book value per share for the stock of each company? Which company's stock is a better investment?

16-6 Certain financial information relating to two companies, Maine Company and Nevada Company, at the end of the current year, is shown below and on page 571. All figures (except market price per share of stock) are in **thousands of dollars.**

Assets	Maine Company	Nevada Company
Cash	$ 126.0	$ 180.0
Marketable securities, at cost	129.0	453.0
Accounts receivable, net	145.0	167.0
Inventories	755.6	384.3
Short-term prepayments	24.4	15.7
Plant and equipment, net	1,680.0	1,570.0
Intangibles and other assets	140.0	30.0
Total assets	$3,000.0	$2,800.0

Liabilities & Stockholders' Equity	Maine Company	Nevada Company
Accounts payable	$ 344.6	$ 304.1
Accrued liabilities, including income taxes	155.4	95.9
Bonds payable, 7%, due in 10 years	200.0	500.0
Capital stock, $10 par	1,000.0	600.0
Paid-in capital in excess of par	450.0	750.0
Retained earnings	910.0	550.0
Treasury stock (1,000 shares, at cost)	(60.0)	–0–
Total liabilities & stockholders' equity	$3,000.0	$2,800.0
Analysis of retained earnings:		
Balance, beginning of year	$ 712.0	$ 430.0
Net income	297.0	240.0
Dividends	(99.0)	(120.0)
Balance, end of year	$ 910.0	$ 550.0
Market price per share of stock, end of year	$50	$40

Instructions Maine Company and Nevada Company are in the same industry and are generally comparable in the nature of their operations and accounting methods used. Write a short answer to each of the following questions, using whatever analytical computations you feel will best support your answer. Show the amounts used in calculating all ratios and percentages. Carry per-share computations to the nearest cent and percentages one place beyond the decimal point, for example, 9.8%.

a What is the book value per share of stock for each company?

b From the viewpoint of creditors, which company has a more conservative capital structure? Determine the percentage of total assets of each company financed by short-term creditors, long-term creditors, and stockholders.

c What are the price-earnings ratios and the dividend yield on the stock of each company?

d Which company is covering its bond interest by the greater margin?

e Which company has a more liquid financial position?

BUSINESS DECISION PROBLEM 16

Condensed comparative financial statements for Bikina Company appear below and on page 572.

BIKINA COMPANY
Comparative Balance Sheets
At September 30
(in thousands of dollars)

Assets	Year 3	Year 2	Year 1
Current assets	$1,320	$ 870	$1,200
Plant and equipment (net of accumulated depreciation)	7,080	6,630	4,800
Total assets	$8,400	$7,500	$6,000

Liabilities & Stockholders' Equity	Year 3	Year 2	Year 1
Current liabilities	$ 738	$ 684	$ 600
Long-term liabilities	1,572	1,236	1,200
Capital stock, $10 par	4,200	4,200	2,700
Retained earnings	1,890	1,380	1,500
Total liabilities & stockholders' equity	$ 8,400	$ 7,500	$ 6,000

BIKINA COMPANY
Comparative Income Statements
For Years Ending September 30
(in thousands of dollars)

	Year 3	Year 2	Year 1
Net sales	$30,000	$25,000	$20,000
Cost of goods sold	19,500	15,500	12,000
Gross profit on sales	$10,500	$ 9,500	$ 8,000
Operating expenses	9,390	8,425	7,080
Income before income taxes	$ 1,110	$ 1,075	$ 920
Income taxes	510	500	420
Net income	$ 600	$ 575	$ 500
Cash dividends paid (plus 20% in stock in Year 2)	$ 90	$ 155	$ 135
Cash dividends per share	$0.21	$0.37	$0.50

Instructions

a Prepare a three-year comparative balance sheet in percentages rather than dollars, using Year 1 as the base year.

b Prepare common size comparative income statements for the three-year period, expressing all items as percentage components of net sales for each year.

c Comment on the significant trends and relationships revealed by the analytical computations in a and b.

d Would you consider buying this company's capital stock if it is now selling for $11.50 per share? Why?

SEVENTEEN   INCOME TAXES AND BUSINESS DECISIONS

The critical importance of income taxes

Taxes levied by federal, state, and local governments are a significant part of the cost of operating a typical household, as well as a business enterprise. The knowledge required to be expert in taxation has made it a field of specialty among professional accountants. However, every manager who makes business decisions, and every individual who makes personal investments, urgently needs some knowledge of income taxes to make him aware of the tax implications of his decisions. A general knowledge of income taxes will help any businessman to benefit more fully from the advice of the professional tax accountant.

Some understanding of income taxes will also aid the individual citizen in voting intelligently, because a great many of the issues decided in every election have tax implications. Such issues as pollution, inflation, foreign policy, and employment are inextricably linked with income taxes. For example, the offering of special tax incentives to encourage businesses to launch massive programs to reduce pollution is one approach to protection of the environment.

In terms of revenue generated, the four most important kinds of taxes in the United States are *income taxes, sales taxes, property taxes,* and *excise taxes.* Income taxes probably exceed all others in terms of the amounts involved and also exert a pervasive influence on all types of business decisions. For this reason we shall limit our discussion to the basic federal income tax rules applicable to individuals, partnerships, and corporations.

Income taxes are usually determined from information contained in accounting records. The amount of income tax is computed by applying the appropriate tax rates (as set by federal, state, and some local governments) to *taxable income.* As explained later in this chapter, taxable income is not necessarily the same as accounting income even though both are derived from the accounting records. Although taxes are involuntary and often unrelated to benefits received, some degree of control over the amount of tax is usually attainable. Businessmen may legally reduce the amount of taxes payable by their choice of form of business organization, methods of financing, and alternative accounting methods. Thus income taxes are inevitably an important factor in arriving at business decisions.

THE FEDERAL INCOME TAX

The present federal income tax dates from the passage of the Sixteenth Amendment to the Constitution in 1913.[1] This amendment, only 30 words in length,[2] removed all questions of the constitutionality of income taxes and paved the way for the more than 50 revenue acts passed by Congress since that date. In 1939 these tax laws were first combined into what is known as the Internal Revenue Code. The administration and enforcement of the tax laws are duties of the Treasury Department, operating through a division known as the Internal Revenue Service. The Treasury Department publishes its interpretation of the tax laws in Treasury regulations; the final word in interpretation lies with the federal courts.

Originally the purpose of the federal income tax was simply to obtain revenue for the government. And at first, the tax rates were quite low—by today's standards. In 1913 a married couple with taxable income of $15,000 would have been subject to a tax rate of 1%, resulting in a tax liability of $150. Today, a married couple with a $15,000 taxable income (worth far less in purchasing power) would pay over $3,000 in federal income tax.

The purpose of federal income tax today includes a number of goals in addition to raising revenue. Among these other goals are to combat inflation, to influence the rate of economic growth, to encourage full employment, to favor small businesses, and to redistribute national income.

Tax planning

To minimize income taxes is the goal of tax planning. Almost every business decision is a choice among alternative courses of action. For example, should we lease or buy business automobiles; should we obtain needed capital by issuing bonds or preferred stock; should we use straight-line depreciation or an accelerated method? Some of these alternatives will lead to much lower income taxes than others. Tax

[1] A federal income tax was proposed as early as 1815, and an income tax law was actually passed and income taxes collected during the Civil War. This law was upheld by the Supreme Court, but it was repealed when the need for revenue subsided after the war. In 1894 a new income tax law was passed, but the Supreme Court declared this law invalid on constitutional grounds.

[2] It reads: "The Congress shall have power to lay and collect taxes on incomes, from whatever source derived, without apportionment among the several States, and without regard to any census or enumeration."

planning, therefore, means *determining in advance the income tax effect* of every proposed business action and then making decisions which will minimize the income tax burden. Tax practice is an important element of the services furnished to clients by CPA firms. This service includes not only the computing of taxes and preparing of tax returns, but also tax planning.

Classes of taxpayers

In the eyes of the income tax law, there are four major classes of taxpayers: *individuals, corporations, estates,* and *trusts.* Single proprietorships and partnerships are not taxed as business units; their income is taxed directly to the individual proprietor or partners, *whether or not actually withdrawn from the business.* A proprietor reports his business income on his personal income tax return; a partner includes on his personal tax return his share of partnership net income. In addition to his proprietorship income and his share of partnership income, an individual taxpayer's income tax return includes all other income and deductions affecting his tax liability. A partnership must file an *information return* showing the computation of net income for the partnership and the allocation of this income to each partner.

A corporation is a separate taxable entity; it must file a tax return and pay a tax on its annual taxable income. In addition, individual stockholders must report cash dividends received as part of their personal taxable income. The taxing of corporate dividends has led to the charge that there is "double taxation" of corporate income— once to the corporation and again when it is distributed to stockholders in the form of cash dividends.

Special and complex rules apply to the determination of taxable income for estates and trusts. These rules will not be discussed in this chapter.

Cash basis of accounting for individual tax returns

Almost all individual tax returns are prepared on the *cash basis* of measuring income. Revenue is recognized when collected; expenses are recognized when paid. The cash basis is advantageous for the individual taxpayer because it is simple, requires a minimum of record keeping, and often permits tax saving by shifting the timing of revenue and expense transactions from one year to another. For example, a dentist whose taxable income is higher than usual in the current year may decide in December to delay billing patients until January 1, and thus postpone the receipt of gross income to the next year. The timing of expense payments near the year-end is also controllable by a taxpayer using the cash basis. If he has received a bill for a deductible expense item in December, he may choose to pay it before or after

December 31 and thereby influence the amount of taxable income in each year. Further comparison of the cash basis with the accrual basis of income measurement is presented later in this chapter.

Tax rates

All taxes may be characterized as proportional, regressive, or progressive with respect to any given base. A ***proportional*** tax remains a constant percentage of the base no matter how that base changes. For example, a 6% sales tax remains a constant percentage of sales regardless of changes in the sales figure. A ***regressive*** tax becomes a smaller percentage of the base as the base increases. A business license tax of $500, for example, is regressive with respect to sales, since the larger the sales the smaller the license tax as a percentage of sales. A ***progressive*** tax becomes a larger portion of the base as that base increases. The federal income tax is ***progressive*** with respect to income, since a higher tax rate applies as the amount of taxable income increases.

INDIVIDUAL TAX RATES Few generalizations can be made about individual income tax rates since they are frequently changed by legislation. Different rate schedules apply to individual taxpayers, married taxpayers who file ***joint returns,*** married taxpayers filing separate returns, and single taxpayers who qualify as the ***head of a household.*** In computing the amount of the tax, the tax rates are applied to taxable income. The rate schedules below and on page 577 show the personal income tax rates in effect at the time this was written. These rates are frequently changed by Congress.

Tax table for single taxpayers

Unmarried Individuals

Taxable Income	*Tax on Column 1*	*% on Excess*	*Taxable Income*	*Tax on Column 1*	*% on Excess*
$	*$ ....*	*14*	*$ 20,000*	*$ 5,230*	*38*
500	*70*	*15*	*22,000*	*5,990*	*40*
1,000	*145*	*16*	*26,000*	*7,590*	*45*
1,500	*225*	*17*	*32,000*	*10,290*	*50*
2,000	*310*	*19*	*38,000*	*13,290*	*55*
4,000	*690*	*21*	*44,000*	*16,590*	*60*
6,000	*1,110*	*24*	*50,000*	*20,190*	*62*
8,000	*1,590*	*25*	*60,000*	*26,390*	*64*
10,000	*2,090*	*27*	*70,000*	*32,790*	*66*
12,000	*2,630*	*29*	*80,000*	*39,390*	*68*
14,000	*3,210*	*31*	*90,000*	*46,190*	*69*
16,000	*3,830*	*34*	*100,000*	*53,090*	*70*
18,000	*4,510*	*36*	*200,000*	*123,090*	*70*

Example: Find the tax for a *single person* having taxable income of $9,200.

Answer:	
Tax on $8,000 as shown on the rate schedule	$1,590
Tax on $1,200 excess at 25%	300
Tax on $9,200 for a single person	$1,890

Married Individuals Filing Joint Returns

	Taxable Income	Tax on Column 1	% on Excess	Taxable Income	Tax on Column 1	% on Excess
Tax table	$	$	14	$ 40,000	$ 12,140	48
for joint	1,000	140	15	44,000	14,060	50
returns	2,000	290	16	52,000	18,060	53
of	3,000	450	17	64,000	24,420	55
married	4,000	620	19	76,000	31,020	58
taxpayers	8,000	1,380	22	88,000	37,980	60
	12,000	2,260	25	100,000	45,180	62
	16,000	3,260	28	120,000	57,580	64
	20,000	4,380	32	140,000	70,380	66
	24,000	5,660	36	160,000	83,580	68
	28,000	7,100	39	180,000	97,180	69
	32,000	8,660	42	200,000	110,980	70
	36,000	10,340	45	300,000	180,980	70

Example: Find the tax for a *married couple filing a joint return* and having a taxable income of $35,000.

Answer: Tax on $32,000 as shown on the rate schedule	$8,660
Tax on $3,000 excess at 42%	1,260
Tax on $35,000 for a married couple filing a joint return	$9,920

Note that different and lower tax rates are applicable to the taxable income of married taxpayers who combine their income and deductions on a joint return. Certain persons who qualify as the head of a household are entitled to use still another schedule of tax rates. The schedules for heads of households and for married taxpayers filing separate returns are not shown in this chapter.

CORPORATION TAX RATES The corporate tax rate schedule is much simpler than the schedule for individuals. The rates in effect for corporations at the time this was written are shown below. These rates are also frequently changed by Congress.

Corporation	Rate for first $25,000 of taxable income	22%
tax rates	Rate for taxable income over $25,000	48%

In computing the tax, it is often convenient to multiply the entire taxable income by 48% and then deduct $6,500 (26% of the first $25,000 of taxable income which is taxed at only 22%). For example, the tax on $100,000 of taxable income may be determined as follows:

		Method 1	Method 2
Compu-	Rate for first $25,000 of taxable income, 22%	$ 5,500	
tation	Rate for taxable income over $25,000, 48% of $75,000 . . .	36,000	
of income	Tax on entire taxable income of $100,000 at 48%		$48,000
tax for	Less: 26% of $25,000 which is taxed at only 22%		(6,500)
corporation	Total income tax on $100,000 of corporate taxable income	$41,500	$41,500

MARGINAL VERSUS AVERAGE TAX RATES In any analysis of tax costs, it is important to distinguish the *marginal* rate of tax from the *average* rate. This distinction may be illustrated as follows: If a corporation has a taxable income of $100,000, its income tax will be $41,500 ($25,000 × 22% + $75,000 × 48%), an average tax rate of 41.5% of taxable income. On the last dollar of taxable income, however, the tax is 48 cents, since the corporation is subject to a marginal tax rate of 48% on all taxable income over $25,000.

An even wider discrepancy between marginal and average tax rates may exist in the case of individual taxpayers. To illustrate, assume that Clark, an unmarried executive having a taxable income of $32,000, is considering a change to a job that pays $6,000 more per year in salary. Using the illustrative tax rates on page 576, Clark now pays federal income taxes of $10,290, an average of 32% on his taxable income. His *marginal* tax rate on the $6,000 salary increase, however, is 50%. His decision with respect to the new position may well be affected by the fact that he will be able to keep only half of the $6,000 increase in his salary.

INCOME AVERAGING FOR INDIVIDUAL TAXPAYERS Because of the progressive nature of the tax rates, taxpayers whose incomes fluctuate widely from year to year are taxed more heavily than those who receive the same total income in a relatively stable pattern. To illustrate, suppose that two single taxpayers, Jones and Smith, each receive $36,000 in taxable income during a two-year period. Jones receives $4,000 the first year and $32,000 the second, while Smith receives $18,000 in each year. Over the two-year period, Jones would pay $10,980 in federal income taxes while Smith would pay only $9,020. To alleviate this inequity, Congress added a five-year *income-averaging* provision to the tax law which permits a taxpayer with a very large increase in taxable income in a given year to pay taxes at a reduced rate based on his "averaged taxable income" for the most recent five-year period.

INCOME TAX FORMULA FOR INDIVIDUALS

The federal government supplies standard income tax forms on which taxpayers are guided to a proper computation of their taxable income and the amount of the tax. It is helpful to visualize the computation in terms of an income tax formula. The general formula for the determination of taxable income for all taxpayers (other than corporations, estates, and trusts) is outlined on page 579.

The actual sequence and presentation of material on income tax forms differs somewhat from the arrangement in this formula. However, it is easier to understand the structure and logic of the federal income tax and to analyze tax rules and their effect by referring to the tax formula.

General Federal Income Tax Formula for Individuals

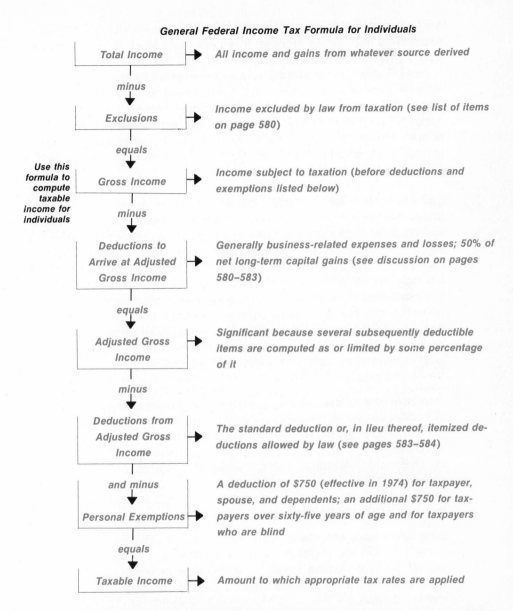

Total Income →	All income and gains from whatever source derived
minus	
Exclusions →	Income excluded by law from taxation (*see list of items on page 580*)
equals	
Gross Income →	Income subject to taxation (*before deductions and exemptions listed below*)
minus	
Deductions to Arrive at Adjusted Gross Income →	Generally business-related expenses and losses; 50% of net long-term capital gains (*see discussion on pages 580–583*)
equals	
Adjusted Gross Income →	Significant because several subsequently deductible items are computed as or limited by some percentage of it
minus	
Deductions from Adjusted Gross Income →	The standard deduction or, in lieu thereof, itemized deductions allowed by law (*see pages 583–584*)
and minus	
Personal Exemptions →	A deduction of $750 (*effective in 1974*) for taxpayer, spouse, and dependents; an additional $750 for taxpayers over sixty-five years of age and for taxpayers who are blind
equals	
Taxable Income →	Amount to which appropriate tax rates are applied

Use this formula to compute taxable income for individuals

TOTAL AND GROSS INCOME Total income is an accounting concept; gross income is a tax concept. *Total income* includes, in the words of the law, "all income from whatever source derived." To determine whether an amount received by an individual taxpayer should be included in total income, one need only ask, "Is it income or is it a return of capital?"

Gross income for tax purposes is all income not excluded by law. To determine whether any given income item is included in taxable gross income, one must ask, "Is there a provision in the tax law excluding this item of income from gross income?'' To identify legal exclusions from gross income, it is necessary to refer to the tax law and sometimes to Treasury regulations and court decisions.

Among the items presently *excluded from gross income* by statute are interest on state and municipal bonds, gifts and inheritances, life insurance proceeds, workmen's compensation and sick pay, social security benefits and the portion of receipts from annuities that represent return of cost, pensions to veterans, GI benefits, compensation for damages, and the first $100 of dividends from corporations ($200 on a joint tax return).

CAPITAL GAINS AND LOSSES Certain kinds of property are defined under the tax law as *capital assets.*[3] Gains or losses from the sale or exchange of such assets are granted special treatment for income tax purposes. Because long-term capital gains generally are taxed at one-half or less than the rates applicable to *ordinary income,* there is a strong incentive for taxpayers to arrange their business and personal affairs so that income will be realized in the form of *capital gains.* The government's efforts to keep such arrangements within bounds have been exceeded only by the collective ingenuity of taxpayers and tax advisers in making income appear in the form of capital gains. In a brief summary, we can only outline the general features of this phase of income taxation.

Amount of gain or loss The tax gain (or loss) from the sale or exchange of capital assets is the difference between the selling price and the *basis* of property sold. Basis rules are complicated; tax basis depends, among other things, on how the property was acquired (purchase, gift, or inheritance), whether it is personal or business property, and in some cases whether it is sold at a gain or at a loss. In general, the basis of purchased property is its cost, reduced by any depreciation that has been allowed in computing taxable income.

Long-term versus short-term Long and short are relative terms: in income taxation the dividing line at present is six months. Long-term capital gains or losses result from the sale or exchange of capital assets held *for more than six months;* short-term from those held six months or less.

The term *net short-term gain* means short-term gains in excess of short-term losses. Net short-term gains must be reported in full and are taxed as ordinary income. Only one-half of long-term gains, reduced by any net short-term losses, are included in adjusted gross income, and the maximum rate of tax on the total gain is generally

[3] Capital assets are defined by exclusion. The Internal Revenue Code states that capital assets include all items of property *except* (a) trade accounts and notes receivable; (b) inventories in a trade or business; (c) real or depreciable property in a trade or business; (d) copyrights, literary, musical, or artistic compositions in the hands of their creator; (e) letters or similar property in the hands of original recipient; (f) government obligations issued on a discount basis and due within one year without interest.

25% of gains up to $50,000.[4] For example, suppose that a taxpayer subject to a marginal tax rate of 30% has a $1,000 net long-term capital gain and no net short-term capital loss. He would include only $500 in adjusted gross income and pay a $150 (30% of $500) tax on the gain. The tax rate applicable to his $1,000 long-term gain is 15%, one-half of his marginal rate.

On the other hand, suppose that the same taxpayer has a marginal tax rate of 70%. If he were to include $500 (one-half of the $1,000 net long-term gain) in adjusted gross income and apply the 70% marginal rate, his tax would be $350, or 35% of the total $1,000 net long-term gain. Instead, he would be entitled to compute his tax on the long-term capital gain at $250 (25% of $1,000). In this case the rate of tax applicable to the long-term capital gain would be *less* than one-half of the taxpayer's marginal rate of tax on other income.

In general, capital *losses,* either long-term or short-term, are deductible only against capital gains. If total capital losses exceed gains, however, individual taxpayers (but not corporations) may deduct capital losses against other gross income up to a maximum of $1,000 in any one year. For example, if an individual incurred a capital loss of $100,000 this year but also had a salary of $50,000, he would have gross income subject to taxation of $49,000. The unused capital loss could be carried forward and offset against capital gains, if any, in future years, or against other income at the rate of $1,000 a year.

Only 50% of a net long-term capital loss can be used in arriving at the $1,000 maximum which can be offset against other income in a single year. In other words, a net long-term capital loss of $2,000 would be required to entitle the taxpayer to take the maximum $1,000 deduction. Although capital losses not deductible in any given year may be carried forward to future tax years, it is apparent that a large capital loss as in the preceding example will not be fully utilized in future years unless the taxpayer is fortunate enough to have a large capital gain.

Long- and short-term capital gains and losses must be combined in a specified way in arriving at adjusted gross income. First, all long-term gains and losses must be offset against each other to produce the *net* long-term gain or loss. Short-term gains and losses must be similarly combined into a *net* short-term gain or loss. The following possible situations may result:

1 Both a net long-term gain and a net short-term gain In this case the two items are treated separately. The short-term gain is included in adjusted gross income and is taxed at regular rates; only one-half of the long-term gain is included in adjusted gross income.

2 Net losses (of either type) greater than net gains (of either type); or both net long-term and net short-term losses In this case the short-term capital

---

[4] The effective maximum tax on net long-term gains in excess of $50,000 may be as high as 35% for taxpayers in the highest tax bracket.

losses are fully deductible up to $1,000, to arrive at adjusted gross income. Only 50% of the net long-term capital loss, up to $1,000, may be deducted in arriving at adjusted gross income. The total deduction for both net long-term and net short-term capital losses cannot exceed $1,000 in any year, but unused capital losses may be carried forward to be deducted in future years subject to the same limitation.

3 Gains (of either type) greater than losses (of either type) Long- and short-term gains and losses must be offset to produce a net capital gain that is either long- or short-term in nature, depending on the characteristic of the larger item.

The foregoing situations are illustrated in the following tabulation.

Case 1

Net LTCG	*$2,000*
Net STCG	*800*

Result: Reported *separately.* All of STCG included in adjusted gross income; one-half of LTCG included in adjusted gross income.

Case 2a

Net LTCG	*$2,000*
Net STCL	*2,900*
Net short-term capital loss . .	*$ 900*

Result: $900 deductible to arrive at adjusted gross income.

Case 2b

Net LTCL	*$ 800*
Net STCL	*3,000*
Total capital loss	*$3,800*

Result: Maximum of $1,000 of short-term capital loss is deductible in current year to arrive at adjusted gross income. Balance ($2,000 STCL and $800 LTCL) carried over to future years.

Case 3a

Net LTCG	*$3,000*
Net STCL	*1,800*
Net long-term capital gain	*$1,200*

Result: $600 (50% of $1,200) included in adjusted gross income.

Case 3b

Net LTCL	*$2,600*
Net STCG	*3,000*
Net short-term capital gain	*$ 400*

Result: $400 included in adjusted gross income in full and taxed as ordinary income.

BUSINESS PLANT AND EQUIPMENT Real or depreciable property used in a trade or business is not a capital asset under the tax law. This means that a net loss realized on the sale or disposal of such property is fully deductible. However, gains on such property held more than six months may be granted capital gains treatment under certain complex conditions. Gains on the sale of assets used in business and held six months or less are taxable as ordinary income.

DEDUCTIONS TO ARRIVE AT ADJUSTED GROSS INCOME The *deductions from gross income* allowed in computing adjusted gross income are discussed below.

1 Business expenses These include all ordinary and necessary expenses of carrying on a trade, business, or profession (other than as an employee). In the actual tax computation, business expenses are deducted from business revenue, and net business income is then included in adjusted gross income.

2 Employees' expenses Some expenses incurred by employees in connection with their employment are allowed as a deduction if the employee is not reimbursed by the employer. These include, for example, travel and transportation expenses, expenses of "outside salespersons," and certain moving expenses.

3 Expenses attributable to rents and royalties Expenses, such as depreciation, depletion, property taxes, repairs, maintenance, interest on indebtedness related to property, and any other expense incurred in connection with the earning of rental or royalty income, are allowed as a deduction. This means that only the *net income* derived from rents and royalties is included in adjusted gross income. (See pages 589–590 for a discussion of statutory depletion allowances on certain royalties.)

4 Losses from the sale of property used in a trade or business The loss resulting from the sale of property used in a trade or business may be deducted against other items of gross income.[5]

5 Net capital losses Up to $1,000 of net capital losses may be deducted in any one year to arrive at adjusted gross income. (See pages 580–582.)

6 Long-term capital gain deduction One-half of the excess of net long-term capital gains over net short-term capital losses is a deduction to arrive at adjusted gross income.

7 Net operating loss carry-over Taxable income may be either positive or negative. If positive income were taxed and no allowance made for operating losses, a taxpayer whose business income fluctuated between income and loss would pay a relatively higher tax than one having a steady income averaging the same amount. Therefore, the tax law allows the carry-back and carry-over of net operating losses as an offset against the income of other years. At the present time a loss must be carried back against the income of the three preceding years, and then forward against the income of the next five years.

DEDUCTIONS FROM ADJUSTED GROSS INCOME An individual taxpayer has an option with respect to *deductions from adjusted gross income.* He may choose to take a lump-sum standard deduction, or he may choose to itemize his deductions, in which case he may deduct a number of expenses specified in the tax law as itemized deductions.

The standard deduction In recent years the standard deduction has been 15% of adjusted gross income, with a maximum deduction of

---

[5] Losses arising from the sale of personal property, such as a home or personal automobile, are not deductible. On the other hand, gains from the sale of personal property are taxable. This appears inconsistent, until one realizes that a loss on the sale of personal property usually reflects depreciation through use, which is a personal expense.

$2,000. For example, if a taxpayer had adjusted gross income of $12,000, his standard deduction would be $1,800 (15% of $12,000); if his adjusted gross income was $25,000, his standard deduction would be only $2,000, the maximum amount allowed.

Deductions *to arrive at adjusted gross income* do not affect the decision to elect the standard deduction. However, itemized deductions (discussed below) are relinquished if the standard deduction is taken. This explains why it is important to know whether a given deduction comes before or after adjusted gross income in the income tax formula.

Itemized deductions   Instead of taking a standard deduction, a taxpayer may elect to itemize his deductions. The major categories of itemized deductions allowable under the law are described below:

1 *Interest.* Interest on any indebtedness, within certain limits.

2 *Taxes.* State and local real and personal property taxes; state income taxes, all sales taxes, and state and local gasoline taxes are deductible by the person on whom they are imposed. No federal taxes qualify as itemized deductions.

3 *Contributions.* Contributions by individuals to charitable, religious, educational, and certain other nonprofit organizations are deductible, within certain limits.

4 *Medical expenses.* Medical and dental expenses of the taxpayer and his family are deductible to the extent that they exceed 3% of adjusted gross income, subject to certain maximum limits, and limits on the deductibility of drugs and medicines. A taxpayer may deduct one-half of his medical insurance costs up to $150 without regard to the 3% exclusion.

5 *Casualty losses.* Losses in excess of $100 from any fire, storm, earthquake, shipwreck, theft, or other sudden, unexpected, or unusual causes are deductible.

6 *Expenses related to the production of income.* In this category are included any necessary expenses in producing income or for the management of income-producing property, other than those deductible to arrive at adjusted gross income. Some examples of *miscellaneous deductible expenses* are union dues, work clothes, professional dues, subscriptions to professional periodicals, investment advisers' fees, legal fees relating to investments, and fees for income tax advice and for preparation of tax returns. Examples of *miscellaneous nondeductible expenses* are the cost of going to and from work, gifts to needy friends, most living expenses, baby-sitting expenses, and the cost of school tuition.

PERSONAL EXEMPTIONS   In addition to itemized deductions, a deduction from adjusted gross income is allowed for *personal exemptions.* One exemption each is allowed for the taxpayer, his spouse, and each person who qualifies as a dependent of the taxpayer. Recently the amount of each personal exemption has been $750. The amount of the personal exemption may be changed by Congress at any time.

The term *dependent* has a particular meaning under law. Briefly but incompletely stated, a dependent is a person who (1) receives over one-half of his support from the taxpayer, (2) is either closely related to the taxpayer or lives in his home, and (3) has gross income during the year of less than the current exemption amount unless he or she is a child of the taxpayer and is under nineteen years of age or is a full-time student.[6]

A taxpayer and his spouse may each claim an additional exemption if he or she is blind, and another exemption if either is sixty-five years of age or over. These additional exemptions do not apply to dependents.

TAX RETURNS AND PAYMENT OF THE TAX Every individual who has gross income in excess of the amount of his own personal exemption (or two exemptions in the case of persons over sixty-five) must file an income tax return within $3\frac{1}{2}$ months after the close of the taxable year. On the calendar-year basis, applicable to most taxpayers, the due date is April 15.

Currently, the payment of federal income taxes is on a "pay as you go" basis. The procedure by which employers withhold income taxes from the wages of employees has been discussed previously in Chapter 13. Without the withholding feature, the present income tax system would probably be unworkable. The high rate of income taxes would probably pose an impossible collection problem if employees received their total earnings in cash and were then called upon to pay to the government a major portion of a year's wages at the end of the year.

To equalize the treatment of employees and self-employed persons, the tax law requires persons who have taxable income in excess of a given amount, from which no withholdings have been made, to file a declaration of estimated income tax and to pay estimated income taxes in quarterly installments. Any under- or overpayment is adjusted when the tax return is filed.

When the tax liability on taxable income has been computed, the final step in computing the amount of tax due is to deduct any allowable *credits* against the tax. Examples of tax credits are: (1) taxes withheld or paid on declared estimates; (2) retirement income credit for taxpayers over 62 years of age; (3) taxes paid to foreign countries on income also taxed by the United States; and (4) the *investment tax credit* on purchase of certain depreciable assets.

COMPUTATION OF INDIVIDUAL INCOME TAX ILLUSTRATED The computation of the federal income tax for Mary and John Reed is illustrated on page 586.

In this example it is assumed that the Reeds provide over one-half the support of their two children. John Reed is a practicing attorney who received $66,000 in gross fees from his law practice, and incurred $30,000 of business expenses. Mary Reed earned $24,400 during the

---

[6] A child under nineteen or a full-time student who qualifies as a dependent in all other respects but who earns over the current exemption amount in any one year has, in effect, two personal exemptions. One may be taken by the taxpayer who claims him as a dependent; the other he will claim for himself on his own personal income tax return.

MARY AND JOHN REED
Illustrative Federal Income Tax Computation
For the Year 19___

Compare with tax formula on page 579

Gross income (excluding $700 interest on municipal bonds):		
Gross fees from John Reed's law practice	$66,000	
Dividends ($15,800 less $200 exclusion)	15,600	
Mary Reed's salary	24,400	
Interest revenue on savings accounts	320	
Long-term capital gain (on stock held more than six months)	800	$107,120
Deductions to arrive at adjusted gross income:		
Operating expenses of John Reed's law practice	$30,000	
Long-term capital gain deduction (50% of $800)	400	30,400
Adjusted gross income		$ 76,720
Deductions from adjusted gross income:		
Itemized deductions	$ 8,720	
Personal exemptions (4 × $750)	3,000	11,720
Taxable income		$ 65,000
Computation of tax (using rates shown on page 577):		
Tax on $64,000 (joint return)	$24,420	
Tax on $1,000 × 55%	550	$ 24,970
Less: Tax credits:		
Withheld from Mary Reed's salary	$ 4,460	
Payments by Reeds on declaration of estimated tax	18,000	22,460
Amount of tax remaining to be paid		$ 2,510

year as a CPA working for a national firm of accountants. During the year, $4,460 was withheld from her salary for federal income taxes. The Reeds received $700 interest on municipal bonds, and $320 on savings accounts. Dividends received on stock jointly owned amounted to $15,800 during the year. During the year, stock purchased several years ago by John Reed for $1,600 was sold for $2,400, net of brokerage fees, thus producing an $800 long-term capital gain.

The Reeds have allowable itemized expenses (contributions, interest expense, taxes, medical costs, etc.) of $8,720. They paid a total of $18,000 on their declaration of estimated income tax during the year.

On the basis of these facts, the taxable income for the Reeds is shown to be $65,000. Since they file a joint return, the tax on this amount of taxable income may be computed from the rate table for married couples, and is $24,970. Taking withholdings and payments on declared estimates into account, the Reeds have already paid income taxes of $22,460 and thus owe $2,510 at the time of the filing of their tax return. If their credits had amounted to $25,000, for example, they would be entitled to a refund of $30.

PARTNERSHIPS

Partnerships are not considered taxable entities by income tax statutes. Under the federal income tax law, partnerships are treated as a conduit through which taxable income flows to the partners. An information return must be filed by all partnerships, showing the determination of net income and the share of each partner. However, certain items of partnership income and deductions are segregated, and each partner is required to treat his share of each of these items as if he had received or paid them personally. In general, segregated items are those granted special tax treatment; they include tax-exempt interest, capital gains and losses, charitable contributions, and cash dividends received. Any salaries actually paid to partners may be deducted in arriving at partnership income, but they must be reported as salaries by the individual partners on their personal income tax returns.

CORPORATIONS

A corporation is a separate taxable entity and is subject to a tax at special rates on its taxable income. Every corporation, unless expressly exempt from taxation, must file an income tax return whether or not it has taxable income or any tax is due.

Corporate taxable income is computed in much the same manner as for individuals, with the following major differences:

1 The concept of adjusted gross income is not applicable to a corporation, since there is no standard deduction or itemized deductions.

2 Corporations are not entitled to the dividend exclusion of $100 allowed to individual taxpayers. Instead a corporation may deduct 85% of any dividends received from other domestic corporations. This means in effect that only 15% of dividends is taxed to the receiving corporation.

3 Corporations may deduct capital losses only to the extent of capital gains. If capital losses exceed gains, the net loss may be offset against net capital gains of the preceding three years (carry-back) or the following five years (carry-forward).

4 Corporations are subject to a maximum tax rate of 30% on net long-term capital gains. A corporation is not entitled to the 50% long-term capital gain deduction. If corporate taxable income (including any long-term capital gain) is below $25,000, a corporation pays the 22% normal tax on the long-term capital gain, rather than the 30% maximum capital gain tax rate.

5 Corporations may deduct charitable contributions only to the extent of 5% of taxable income, computed before the deduction of any contributions. Contributions in excess of the limit may be carried forward for five succeeding years if contributions (including those carried forward) in those years are within the 5% limit.

6 Corporations may deduct organization costs over a period of five years or more.

To illustrate some of the features of the income tax law as it applies to corporations, a tax computation for the Luis Perez Corporation is shown below:

LUIS PEREZ CORPORATION
Illustrative Tax Computation

Revenue:			
Sales			$200,000
Dividends received from domestic corporations			10,000
Total revenue			$210,000
Expenses:			
Cost of goods sold		$118,000	
Other expenses (includes capital loss of $3,000)		50,000	168,000
Income per accounting records			$ 42,000
Add back (items not deductible for tax purposes):			
Capital loss deducted as part of operating expenses*			3,000
Charitable contributions in excess of 5% limit			3,500
			$ 48,500
Special deductions:			
Dividends received credit (85% of $10,000)			8,500
Taxable income			$ 40,000
Tax computation:			
Tax on first $25,000 of taxable income at 22%		$ 5,500	
Tax on taxable income over $25,000 ($15,000 × 48%)		7,200	
Total tax†			$ 12,700

Note difference between income per accounting records ($42,000) and taxable income ($40,000)

*Can be carried back three years and offset against capital gains if any.
†Alternate computation: $40,000 × 48%, or $19,200, less $6,500 = $12,700.

Accounting income versus taxable income

The accountant's objective in determining accounting income is to measure business operating results as accurately as possible, in accordance with the generally accepted accounting principles summarized in Chapter 14. Taxable income, on the other hand, is a legal concept governed by statute. In setting the rules for determining taxable income, Congress is interested not only in meeting the revenue needs of government but in achieving certain public policy objectives. Since accounting and taxable income are determined with different purposes in mind, it is not surprising that they often differ by material amounts.

CASH VERSUS ACCRUAL BASIS OF INCOME MEASUREMENT The *accrual basis* of measuring income has been discussed throughout the preceding chapters of this book, because it is the method used by most business enterprises. Revenue is recognized when it is realized, and expenses are recorded when they are incurred, without regard to the timing of receipt or payment. Any taxpayer who maintains a set of accounting records may elect to use the accrual basis for tax purposes. When the production, purchase, or sale of merchandise is a significant factor in a business, the accrual method is mandatory.

The *cash basis* of measuring income does not reflect income in the accounting sense. Revenue is recognized when cash is received, and expenses are recorded when they are paid. This method is allowed for tax purposes because it is simple, requires a minimum of records, and produces reasonably satisfactory results for individuals not en-gaged in business and for businesses in which receivables, payables, and inventories are not a major factor.

The cash basis allowed for income tax purposes and used on nearly all tax returns by individuals varies in two important ways from a simple offsetting of cash receipts and disbursements.

1 On the revenue side, a cash basis taxpayer must report revenue when it has been *constructively received,* even though the cash is not yet in his possession. Constructive receipt means that the revenue is so much within the control of the taxpayer as to be equivalent to receipt. For example, if a taxpayer has a savings account, for income tax purposes the interest on that account is considered to be constructively received even though he does not draw it out. Similarly, a check received on December 31 is considered to be constructively received even though it is not cashed until January 2.

2 On the expenditure side, the cost of acquiring depreciable property having a service life of more than one year is not deductible in the year of pur-chase. The taxpayer must treat such a purchase as an asset and deduct depreciation in appropriate years. A similar treatment must be given to major prepayments, such as rent paid in advance or insurance premiums which cover more than one year.

The choice between the cash and accrual method, where permitted, rests on the question of tax timing. Taxpayers are motivated to elect the cash basis because it permits postponing the recognition of taxable income and the payment of the tax. In this way they have the interest-free use of funds that would otherwise be paid in taxes.

SPECIAL TAX TREATMENT OF REVENUE AND EXPENSE Even when the accrual method is used for tax purposes, differences between taxable and accounting income may occur. Some differences result from special tax rules which are unrelated to accounting principles.

1 Some items included in accounting income are not taxable. For example, interest on state or municipal bonds is excluded from taxable income.

2 Some business expenses are not deductible. For example, donations to political parties are generally not deductible.

3 Special deductions in excess of actual business expenses are allowed some taxpayers. For example, depletion deductions in excess of actual cost are allowed taxpayers in the oil and mining industries. Currently this *statutory depletion* (or *percentage depletion*) allowance is 22% of the income derived from oil and gas operations.

4 Some business expenses must be treated as capital expenditures for income tax purposes. For example, goodwill may be amortized for accounting purposes; for income tax purposes goodwill is a permanent asset and amortization is not a deductible expense.

In addition, the *timing* of the recognition of certain revenue and expenses under tax rules differs from that under accounting principles. Some items of income received in advance may be taxed in the year of receipt while certain accrued expenses may not be deductible for income tax purposes until they are actually paid in cash.

ALTERNATIVE ACCOUNTING METHODS Various accounting methods result in different net income figures, largely because of difference in the timing of revenue and expense recognition. The tax law permits taxpayers, in some cases, to adopt for income tax purposes accounting methods which differ from those used for financial reporting. For example, it may be advantageous to use accelerated depreciation in the income tax return and straight-line depreciation in the accounting records and financial statements. Businessmen are therefore faced with the option of choosing an accounting method for income tax purposes that will result in minimizing their tax burdens—usually by postponing the tax.

The choice of inventory pricing methods will affect the timing of net income recognition, as we have seen in Chapter 11. One of the reasons for the popularity of the lifo pricing method is that it results in lower net income during periods of rising prices. A peculiarity of the *lifo* tax rules is that **this method must be used in published financial statements if it is elected for income tax purposes.**

The tax law allows the adoption of a variety of depreciation methods in computing taxable income. It will generally be advantageous for a taxpayer to adopt the depreciation method for income tax purposes which results in the largest amount of cumulative depreciation over the shortest period of time.

There are a number of other less common examples of elective methods which postpone taxes. Taxpayers who sell merchandise on the *installment basis* may elect to report income in proportion to the cash received on the installment contract, rather than at the time of sale. The cost of drilling oil wells and preparing wells for production may be charged off as incurred, or may be capitalized and depreciated.

TAXES AND FINANCIAL REPORTING; INCOME TAX ALLOCATION When there are differences between accounting principles and income tax rules, many businesses choose to keep their accounting records on a tax basis as a matter of convenience. In other words, accounting principles give way to tax laws. If the differences are not material, there is no objection to this practice as a means of simplifying the keeping of tax records. When the differences between tax rules and accounting principles are material, however, the result of following the tax law is to distort financial statements. It is clearly preferable to maintain accounting records to meet the need for relevant information about business operations and to adjust such data to arrive at taxable income.

When a corporation follows different accounting methods for book and tax purposes, a financial reporting problem arises. The difference in method will usually have the effect of postponing the recognition of income (either because an expense deduction is accelerated or because revenue recognition is postponed). The question is whether the income tax expense should be accrued when the income is recognized in the accounting records, or when it is actually subject to taxation.

To illustrate the problem, let us consider a very simple case. Suppose the Pryor Company has before-tax accounting income of $200,000 in each of two years. However, the company takes as a tax deduction in Year 1 an expense of $80,000 which is reported for accounting purposes in Year 2. The company's accounting and taxable income, and the actual income taxes due (assuming a tax rate of 40%) are shown below:

	Year 1	Year 2
Accounting income (before income taxes)	$200,000	$200,000
Taxable income	120,000	280,000
Actual income taxes due each year, at assumed rate of 40%		
of taxable income	48,000	112,000

Following one approach, the Pryor Company might simply report in its income statement in each year the amount of income taxes due for that year as computed on the company's income tax returns. The effect on reported net income would be as follows:

		Year 1	Year 2
Company	Accounting income (before income taxes)	$200,000	$200,000
reports	Income taxes actually due	48,000	112,000
actual taxes	Net income	$152,000	$ 88,000

The reader of the Pryor Company's income statement might well wonder why the same accounting income before income taxes in the two years produced such widely variant tax expense and net income figures.

To deal with this distortion between pre- and after-tax income, an accounting policy known as **income tax allocation** has been devised, which is required for financial reporting purposes.[7] Briefly, the objective of the tax allocation procedure is to accrue income taxes in relation to accounting income, whenever differences between accounting and taxable income are caused by differences in the *timing* of revenue or expenses. In the Pryor Company example, this means we would report in the Year 1 income statement a tax expense on the $80,000 ($200,000 − $120,000) of income which was reported for accounting purposes in Year 1 but which will not be taxed until Year 2. The effect of this accounting procedure is demonstrated by the following journal entries to record the income tax expense in each of the two years:

<table>
<tr><td rowspan="7">*Entries to record income tax allocation*</td><td>*Year 1*</td><td>*Income Taxes* ....</td><td>*80,000*</td><td></td></tr>
<tr><td></td><td>*Current Income Tax Liability* ....</td><td></td><td>*48,000*</td></tr>
<tr><td></td><td>*Deferred Income Tax Liability* ....</td><td></td><td>*32,000*</td></tr>
<tr><td></td><td>*To record current and deferred income taxes at 40% of accounting income of $200,000.*</td><td></td><td></td></tr>
<tr><td>*Year 2*</td><td>*Income Taxes* ....</td><td>*80,000*</td><td></td></tr>
<tr><td></td><td>*Deferred Income Tax Liability* ....</td><td>*32,000*</td><td></td></tr>
<tr><td></td><td>*Current Income Tax Liability* ....</td><td></td><td>*112,000*</td></tr>
</table>

To record income taxes at 40% of accounting income of $200,000 and to record actual taxes due.

Using tax allocation procedures, the Pryor Company would report its net income during the two-year period as follows:

<table>
<tr><td></td><td>Year 1</td><td>Year 2</td></tr>
<tr><td rowspan="3">*Company uses tax allocation procedure*</td><td></td><td></td></tr>
</table>

	Year 1	Year 2
Income before income taxes	$200,000	$200,000
Income taxes (tax allocation basis)	80,000	80,000
Net income	$120,000	$120,000

In this simple example, the difference between taxable and accounting income (caused by the accelerated deduction of an expense) was fully offset in a period of two years. In practice, differences between accounting and taxable income may persist over extended time periods and deferred tax liabilities may accumulate to significant amounts. For example, in a recent balance sheet of Sears, Roebuck and Co., deferred taxes of $690 million were reported as a result of the use of the installment sales method for income tax purposes while reporting net income in financial statements on the usual accrual method.

In contrast to the example for the Pryor Company in which income taxes were deferred, income taxes *may be prepaid* when taxable income exceeds accounting income because of timing differences. The portion of taxes paid on income deferred for accounting purposes would be reported as prepaid taxes in the balance sheet. When the income is

---

[7] For a more complete discussion of tax allocation procedures, see *APB Opinion No. 11*, "Accounting for Income Taxes," AICPA (New York: 1967).

reported as earned for accounting purposes in a later period, the *prepaid taxes are recognized as tax expense* applicable to the income currently reported but *taxed in an earlier period.*[8]

ALLOCATION OF INCOME TAXES BETWEEN OPERATING INCOME AND EXTRAORDINARY ITEMS In Chapter 8 we stated that extraordinary gains and losses should be separately reported *net of taxes* in the income statement. This means that the amount of taxes deducted from operating income would be the amount of taxes due *if there were no extraordinary gains or losses.* The tax on any extraordinary gain would be netted against the gain and any tax reduction attributed to an extraordinary loss would be offset against the loss.

To illustrate, assume that the Queen Company has an operating income of $150,000, taxable at 40%, and an extraordinary gain of $250,000, taxable at 30%. The total income tax liability of $135,000 ($60,000 + $75,000) would be reported in the income statement as follows:

An Operating income	*$150,000*
extraordi- Income taxes (actual taxes are $135,000, of which $75,000 is applicable	
nary gain is	
reported net to extraordinary gain)	*60,000*
of taxes Income before extraordinary gain	*$ 90,000*
Extraordinary gain, net of taxes ($250,000 − $75,000)	*175,000*
Net income	*$265,000*

If the entire tax of $135,000 was deducted from operating income, both the income before extraordinary gain and the extraordinary gain would be distorted as illustrated below:

Failure to Operating income	*$150,000*
allocate Income taxes	*135,000*
taxes gives	
a distorted Income before extraordinary gain	*$ 15,000*
picture Extraordinary gain (before taxes)	*250,000*
Net income	*$265,000*

Assume now that instead of an extraordinary gain, the Queen Company had an operating income of $150,000 and a fully deductible extraordinary loss of $120,000. The proper way to report this follows:

A loss of Operating income	*$150,000*
$120,000 is Income taxes (actual taxes are $12,000 as a result of a fire loss of	
reduced to	
$72,000 $120,000)	*60,000*
after tax Income before extraordinary loss	*$ 90,000*
effect Extraordinary loss, net of taxes ($120,000 − $48,000)	*72,000*
Net income	*$ 18,000*

[8] A good example of this treatment is found in the annual report of the Ford Motor Company. A recent balance sheet showed "Income Taxes Allocable to the Following Year," $206.5 million, as a current asset. This large prepaid tax came about as a result of estimated car warranty expense being deducted from revenue in the period in which cars were sold; for income tax purposes, this expense is deductible only when it is actually incurred.

If tax allocation procedures were not followed, the net income of $18,000 would be improperly reported as consisting of income before extraordinary loss of $138,000 ($150,000 − $12,000), less the pre-tax extraordinary loss of $120,000.

TAX PLANNING

Federal income tax laws have become so complex that detailed tax planning has become a way of life for most business firms. Almost all businesses today engage professional tax specialists to review the tax aspects of major business decisions and to develop plans for legally minimizing income taxes. Because it is important for even the nonspecialist to recognize areas in which tax factors may be of consequence, a few of the major opportunities for tax planning are discussed in the following paragraphs.

Form of business organization

Tax factors should be carefully considered at the time a business is organized. As a single proprietor or partner, a businessman will pay taxes at individual rates, ranging currently from 14 to 70%,[9] on his share of the business income earned in any year *whether or not he withdraws it from the business.* Corporations, on the other hand, are taxed on earnings at average rates varying from 22 to 48%. Corporations may deduct salaries paid to owners for services but may not deduct dividends paid to stockholders. Both salaries and dividends are taxed to their recipients.

These factors must be weighed in deciding in any given situation whether the corporate or noncorporate form of business organization is preferable. There is no simple rule of thumb, even considering only these basic differences. To illustrate, suppose that Able, a married man, starts a business which he expects will produce, before any compensation to himself and before income taxes, an average annual income of $50,000. Able plans to withdraw $20,000 yearly from the business. The combined corporate and individual taxes under the corporate and single proprietorship form of business organization are summarized on page 595.

At first glance this comparison suggests that the corporate form of organization is favorable from an income tax viewpoint. It must be noted, however, that the $22,100 ($30,000 − $7,900) of earnings retained in the corporation will be taxed to Able as ordinary income when and if distributed as dividends. On the other hand, if Able later sells his business and realizes these earnings in the form of the in-

---

[9]Effective in 1972, the maximum rate on earned income of individuals is 50%.

Form of Business Organization

	Corporate	Single Proprietorship
Business income	$50,000	$50,000
Salary to Able	20,000	
Taxable income	$30,000	$50,000
Corporate tax:		
22% of $25,000 . . . . $5,500		
48% on excess of $5,000 2,400	7,900	
Net income	$22,100	$50,000
Combined corporate and individual tax:		
Corporate tax on $30,000 income (above)	$ 7,900	
Individual tax—joint return:*		
On Able's $20,000 salary	4,380	
On Able's $50,000 share of business income . . .		$17,060
Total tax on business income	$12,280	$17,060

Marginal notes at left: Which form of business organization produces a lower tax?

* Able's personal exemptions and deductions have been ignored, on the assumption that his other income equals personal exemptions and deductions.

creased value of his capital stock, any gain may be taxed at a maximum of, say, 25%. In either case Able can postpone the payment of tax on retained earnings so long as these earnings remain invested in the business.

If Able decided to withdraw all net income from his business each year, the total tax on corporate net income and on the $22,100 that he would receive in dividends would amount to $21,048, compared to only $17,060 tax paid on the $50,000 of earnings from the single proprietorship. The amount of $21,048 consists of $7,900 corporate tax plus $13,148 tax on personal income of $42,100.

Under this assumption the income tax results under the single proprietorship form of organization are preferable. It is clear that both the marginal rate of tax to which individual business owners are subject and the extent to which profits are to be withdrawn from the business must be considered in assessing the relative advantages of one form of business organization over another.

In an attempt to alleviate the effect of income taxes on the choice of the form of business organization for small businesses, Congress added an elective provision to the tax laws. Under certain conditions, partnerships may choose to be taxed as corporations and small, closely held corporations may choose to be taxed as partnerships.

Planning business transactions to minimize income taxes

Business transactions may often be arranged in such a way as to produce favorable tax treatment. For example, when property is sold under an installment contract, the taxable gain may be prorated over the period during which installment payments are received by the seller. To qualify for this treatment, payments received during the first year must not exceed 30% of the selling price. By arranging the transaction to meet these conditions, a substantial postponement of tax payments may be secured.

Sometimes a seller tries to arrange a transaction one way to his tax benefit and the buyer tries to shape it another way to produce tax savings for him. Income tax effects thus become a part of price negotiations. For example, in buying business property, the purchaser will try to allocate as much of the cost of the property to the building and as little to the land as possible, since building costs can be depreciated for tax purposes. Similarly, in selling a business, the seller will try to allocate as much of the selling price as possible to goodwill, since this is a capital asset. The buyer of the business, however, will want the purchase price to be attributable to inventories or depreciable assets, because the cost of goods sold and depreciation are deductible against ordinary income. Goodwill cannot be amortized for tax purposes. The point is, *any failure to consider the tax consequences of major business transactions can be costly.*

Some examples of provisions of the federal tax laws clearly designed to affect business decisions include (1) accelerated depreciation, (2) additional first-year depreciation of 20% on assets of tangible personal property costing up to $10,000, (3) rapid depreciation on assets "critical to the public interest" such as pollution-control facilities and coal-mine safety equipment, (4) tax-free exchanges of certain types of assets or securities pursuant to a corporate merger, and (5) *investment tax credits* when certain types of depreciable assets are acquired.

Financial planning

Different forms of business financing produce different tax expense. Interest on debt, for example, is fully deductible while dividends on preferred or common stocks are not. This factor operates as a strong incentive to finance expansion by borrowing.

Suppose that a company needs $100,000 to invest in productive assets on which it can expect to earn a 12% annual return. If the company issues $100,000 in 6% preferred stock, it will earn after taxes, assuming a 48% marginal tax rate, $6,240 ($12,000 less taxes at 48% of $12,000). This is barely enough to cover the $6,000 preferred dividend. If, on the other hand, the company borrowed the $100,000 at 6% interest, its taxable income would be increased $6,000 ($12,000 earnings less $6,000 interest expense). The tax on this amount at 48% would be $2,880, leaving income of $3,120 available for common stockholders or for reinvestment in the business. A similar analysis should be made in choosing between debt and common stock financing.

Budgeting

Taxable income computed on the accrual basis is not necessarily matched by an inflow of cash. A healthy profit picture accompanied by a tight cash position is not unusual for a rapidly growing company. Income taxes are a substantial cash drain and an important factor in preparing cash budgets.

DEMONSTRATION PROBLEM

Robert Sandison has been engaged in various businesses for many years and has always prepared his own income tax return. In Year 11 Sandison decided to ask a certified public accountant to prepare his income tax returns.

Early in Year 12, Sandison presented the following tax information for Year 11 to his CPA:

Personal revenue:

Salary from Sandi Construction Company, after withholding of $3,168 and social security taxes of $772	*$ 15,060*
Dividends from Sandi Construction Company (jointly owned)	*16,875*
Drawings from Northwest Lumber Company	*6,000*
Drawings from S & S Business Advisers	*9,600*
Interest income—City of Norwalk bonds	*800*
Interest income—savings account	*950*
Proceeds on sale of stock:	
Sale of stock acquired two years ago for $6,200	*14,200*
Sale of stock held for three months, cost $4,100	*3,400*
Sale of stock held for over six years, cost $3,500	*1,800*

Personal expenses:

Contribution to St. Jerome's Church	*$ 610*
Interest on mortgage, $3,820; on personal note, $900	*4,720*
Property taxes, including $400 on vacant land in Arizona and a special assessment of $500 on residence for street widening	*3,980*
Sales taxes, including $580 paid on purchase of new Cadillac for personal use	*850*
Income taxes paid to state	*1,900*
Medical expenses	*1,100*
Subscription to investment advisory service	*385*

Single proprietorship—wholesale lumber, doing business as Northwest Lumber Company

Sales	*$118,000*
Cost of goods sold	*82,000*
Operating expenses	*38,800*
Drawings by Sandison	*6,000*

Partnership—engaged in business consulting under the name of S & S Business

Advisers:

Fees earned	$ 76,300
Gain on sale of vacant lot acquired four years ago	4,400
Professional salaries and other wages paid	32,400
Supplies expense	3,500
Contributions to charity	1,000
Rent expense	4,800
Miscellaneous business expenses	7,100
Drawings (Sandison, $9,600 and Sims, $6,400)	16,000

Corporation—engaged in construction under the name of Sandi Construction Company:

Customer billings	$230,000
Materials used	70,000
Construction labor	60,000
Officers' salaries expense	25,000
Legal and professional expense	3,500
Advertising expense	2,000
Other business expenses	19,800
Loss on sale of equipment	4,200
Cash dividends paid	22,500

Sandison has a 60% share in the profits of S & S Business Advisers and John Sims has a 40% share. Sandison owns 75% of the stock of Sandi Construction Company. Because of his controlling interest, he is responsible for the preparation of the income tax returns for these organizations.

Sandison is married, has five children, and supports his seventy-nine-year-old mother. He is fifty-five years old and his wife is younger but will not give her date of birth. The oldest child, Bill, is twenty years old and attends school full time. Sandison provides all of his son's support, even though Bill earns approximately $1,400 per year from odd jobs and from investments inherited from his grandfather.

In April of Year 11, Sandison paid $3,100 balance due on his federal income tax return for Year 10. In addition to the income taxes withheld by the Sandi Construction Company, Sandison made four equal payments of $2,000 each on his estimated tax for Year 11.

Instructions

Using the income tax table on page 577, prepare the joint return for Mr. and Mrs. Sandison for last year, showing the amount of tax due (or refund coming). You should also prepare in summary form the information on the partnership tax return for S & S Business Advisers and the corporation income tax return for the Sandi Construction Company. Assume that a personal exemption is $750, that the corporate tax rate is 22% on the first $25,000 of taxable income and 48% on any income in excess of $25,000, and that Sandi Construction Company has not paid any part of its income tax for Year 11.

SOLUTION TO DEMONSTRATION PROBLEM

S & S BUSINESS ADVISERS (a partnership)
Computation of Ordinary Income
For Year Ended December 31, Year 11

Fees earned		$76,300
Operating expenses:		
Professional salaries and other wages	$32,400	
Supplies expense	3,500	
Rent expense	4,800	
Miscellaneous business expenses	7,100	47,800
Ordinary income		$28,500

Ordinary income and other items are to be included in
partners' individual tax returns as follows:

	Sandison (60%)	Sims (40%)
Ordinary income, $28,500	$17,100	$11,400
Gain on sale of vacant lot, long-term capital gain, $4,400	2,640	1,760
Contributions to charity, $1,000	600	400

SANDI CONSTRUCTION COMPANY
Income Tax Return
For Year Ended December 31, Year 11

Customer billings		$230,000
Operating expenses:		
Materials used	$70,000	
Construction labor	60,000	
Officers' salaries expense	25,000	
Legal and professional expenses	3,500	
Advertising expense	2,000	
Other business expenses	19,800	
Loss on sale of equipment	4,200	184,500
Taxable income		$ 45,500
Income tax due: ($45,500 × 48%) − $6,500		$ 15,340

MR. AND MRS. SANDISON
Joint Income Tax Return
For Year 11

Gross income:

Salary from Sandi Construction Company ($15,060 + $3,168 + $772		$19,000	
Dividends from Sandi Construction Company ($16,875, less $200 exclusion)		16,675	
Interest on savings account		950	
Income from S & S Business Advisers, a partnership		17,100	
Net long-term capital gain:			
Stock acquired two years ago	$8,000		
Stock held over six years	(1,700)		
Gain on sale of vacant lot—from partnership return	2,640		
Total long-term capital gain	$8,940		
Less: Short-term loss on stock held for three months	700	8,240	$61,965

Deductions to arrive at adjusted gross income:

Loss incurred by Northwest Lumber Company, a single proprietorship ($118,000 − $82,000 − $38,800)		$ 2,800	
Long-term capital gain deduction (50% of $8,240)		4,120	6,920

Adjusted gross income		$55,045

Deductions from adjusted gross income:

Itemized deductions:

Contributions ($600 from partnership return and $610 to St. Jerome's Church)	$ 1,210	
Interest paid	4,720	
Property taxes ($3,980 − $500)	3,480	
Sales taxes	850	
Income taxes paid to state	1,900	
Subscription to investment advisory service	385	
Total itemized deductions	$12,545	
Personal exemptions (8 × $750)	6,000	18,545

Taxable income for Year 11		$36,500

Computation of tax for Year 11:

Tax on $36,000 on joint return (see page 577)	$10,340	
Tax on $500 excess at 45%	225	$10,565

Less tax credits:

Withheld from Mr. Sandison's salary	$ 3,168	
Payments on declaration of estimated tax ($2,000 × 4)	8,000	11,168

Overpayment of tax for Year 11		$ 603

Notes:

(1) The loss from single proprietorship is properly deducted in arriving at adjusted gross income despite the fact that Sandison withdrew $6,000 from the business.

(2) Sandison's share of ordinary income from the partnership (S & S Business Advisers), $17,100, is fully taxable despite the fact that Sandison withdrew only $9,600 from the partnership.

(3) Sandison's salary from the Sandi Construction Company is included in gross income as $19,000, the gross salary before any deductions.

(4) The ordinary income for the partnership is determined without taking into account the contribution to charity of $1,000 or the long-term capital gain of $4,400. These items are reported by the partners on their personal income tax return on the basis of the profit- and loss-sharing ratio agreed upon by the partners.

(5) The special assessment on residence for street widening, $500, is not deductible in arriving at taxable income.

(6) Medical expenses are less than 3% of adjusted gross income, and therefore none is deductible.

(7) Sandison's son, Bill, qualifies as a dependent even though he earned $1,400 because he is a full-time student.

(8) Interest on City of Norwalk bonds, $800, is not taxable.

REVIEW QUESTIONS

1 List several ways in which businessmen may legally alter the amount of taxes they pay.

2 What is meant by the expression "tax planning"?

3 What are the four major classes of taxpayers under the federal income tax law?

4 It has been claimed that corporate income is subject to "double taxation." Explain the meaning of this expression.

5 Taxes are characterized as *proportional, progressive,* or *regressive* with respect to any given base. Describe an income tax rate structure that would fit each of these characterizations.

6 During the current year Dennison, a bachelor, expects a taxable income of $20,000. Using the tables on pages 576 and 577, determine how much federal income tax Dennison would save were he to get married before the end of the year, assuming that his bride had no taxable income or itemized deductions and that the personal exemption is $750.

7 State in equation form the federal income tax formula for individuals, beginning with total income and ending with taxable income.

8 In computing income taxes, why does it make any difference whether a given deduction may be taken before or after computing adjusted gross income?

9 List some differences in the tax rules for corporations in contrast to those for individuals.

10 Doctor Bame files his income tax return on a cash basis. During the current year he collected $6,300 from patients for medical services rendered in prior years, and billed patients $38,500 for services rendered this year. He has accounts receivable of $8,200 relating to this year's billings at the end of the year. What amount of gross income from his practice should Doctor Bame report on his tax return?

11 Hunt files his income tax return on a cash basis. During the current year $300 of interest was credited to him on his savings account; he withdrew this interest on January 18 of the following year. Hunt purchased a piece of business equipment having an estimated service life of five years in December of the current year. He also paid a year's rent in advance on certain business property on December 29 of the current year. Explain how these items would be treated on Hunt's current year's income tax return.

12 From a taxpayer's viewpoint it is better to have a $10,000 net long-term capital gain than $10,000 of ordinary income; however, ordinary losses are usually more advantageous than net capital losses. Explain.

13 Even when a taxpayer uses the accrual method of accounting, his taxable income may differ from his accounting income. Give four examples of differences between the tax and accounting treatment of items that are included in the determination of income.

14 Under what circumstances is the accounting procedure known as *income tax allocation* appropriate? Explain the purpose of this procedure.

15 List some tax factors to be considered in deciding whether to organize a new business as a corporation or as a partnership.

16 Explain how the corporate income tax makes debt financing in general more attractive than financing through the issuance of preferred stock.

17 Some years ago the Allegheny Ludlum Steel Corporation proposed to discontinue using the lifo method of inventory valuation. This change in accounting method would have resulted in $6,150,000 additional income taxes. Can you give a good reason for this proposed action by Allegheny Ludlum Steel Corporation?

EXERCISES

Ex. 17-1 From the tax tables on pages 576 and 577, compute the tax for each of the following (assume that the 50% limitation on earned income does not apply):

	Taxable Income
a Unmarried individual	$ 13,500
b Unmarried individual	120,000
c Married couple filing joint return	13,500
d Married couple filing joint return	120,000

Ex. 17-2 The Montana Ranches, Inc., reports the following income during Year 1:

Operating income (income before extraordinary items and income taxes)	$550,000
Extraordinary items:	
Gain (long-term capital gain)	250,000
Loss (fully deductible)	50,000

Assume that corporate tax rates are as follows:

On first $25,000 of taxable income	22%
On taxable income over $25,000	48%
On long-term capital gains	30%

a Compute the total tax liability for Montana Ranches, Inc., for Year 1.

b Prepare the lower section of the income statement for the Montana Ranches, Inc., showing income before extraordinary items, extraordinary items net of taxes, and net income.

Ex. 17-3 From the following information for Al Abramson, a married man, compute his taxable income for Year 4:

Total income, including gifts, inheritances, interest on municipal bonds, etc.	*$41,000*
Exclusions (gifts, inheritances, interest on municipal bonds, etc.)	*14,600*
Deductions to arrive at adjusted gross income	*1,400*
Itemized deductions	*5,575*
Personal exemptions ($750 each)	*5,250*
Income taxes withheld from salary	*3,600*

Ex. 17-4 For each of the following cases, determine the amount of capital gain included in adjusted gross income or the capital loss deducted in arriving at adjusted gross income for an individual taxpayer:

	Case 1	Case 2	Case 3
Long-term capital gains	*$32,800*	*$16,800*	*$6,000*
Long-term capital losses	*20,000*	*8,000*	*6,400*
Short-term capital gains	*16,000*	*14,000*	*None*
Short-term capital losses	*4,000*	*23,500*	*520*

Ex. 17-5 Duarte Dredging purchased for $100,000 a machine having an estimated life of 4 years and no salvage value. The owner wants to depreciate the machine on a straight-line basis for income tax purposes but you suggest that he use the sum-of-the-years'-digits method. You also suggest that he invest any amount saved as a result of the postponement of income taxes with a local businessman who pays 10% interest on unsecured loans. Prepare a schedule for the owner showing how much interest he will earn as a result of your plan, assuming that his average marginal income tax rate is 50%.

Ex. 17-6 Ed Cohen, Inc., has used accelerated depreciation and has charged off currently for income tax purposes all research and development costs. On its financial statements it has used straight-line depreciation and has amortized research and development costs over a 5-year period. Taxable and accounting income for the last five years are shown below:

	Year 5	Year 4	Year 3	Year 2	Year 1
Taxable income . . .	*$700,000*	*$600,000*	*$400,000*	*$300,000*	*$200,000*
Accounting income .	*400,000*	*500,000*	*600,000*	*560,000*	*500,000*

Assuming that corporate income is taxable at a flat rate of 45%, compute the net income for the company for each of the five years.

a Based on actual income taxes paid.

b Based on income taxes that would be paid on the income reported for accounting purposes.

Comment on the differences in results obtained in *a* and *b.*

PROBLEMS

17-1 The accountant for the Dallas Corporation determined an income before income taxes of $250,000 for its first year of operations. Some of the items included in the computation of this income are listed below.

(1) Accounts receivable of $3,250 were written off and recorded as uncollectible accounts expense.

(2) Depreciation of $15,000 was recorded using the straight-line method.

(3) Inventories were reported on a fifo basis at $92,500.

(4) Research and development costs of $60,000 will be amortized over a five-year period; amortization of $12,000 was recorded in the current year.

Officers of the corporation are concerned over the large amount of income taxes they must pay on the $250,000 of taxable income and decide to restate taxable income as follows:

(1) An acceptable allowance for uncollectible accounts, after the write-off of $3,250, would be $10,000.

(2) Use of accelerated methods of depreciation would result in depreciation expense of $28,750.

(3) Inventories on a lifo basis would amount to $60,000.

(4) For income tax purposes, research and development costs are to be charged off in full as incurred.

Instructions

a Determine the taxable income of the Dallas Corporation on the revised basis.

b If the tax rates for corporations are 22% on the first $25,000 of taxable income and 48% on any taxable income in excess of $25,000, compute the reduction in the current year's income tax liability for the Dallas Corporation resulting from the accounting changes.

17-2 Case A During the current year Antonio Bravo has total income of $70,000. He has personal exemptions of $5,250, deductions to arrive at adjusted gross income of $5,150, itemized deductions of $7,300, and exclusions from gross income of $1,050.

Case B George Sumner who is an attorney, uses the cash basis of reporting income for federal income tax purposes. During the current year his business net income (computed on an accrual basis) was $95,400. Between the beginning and end of the current year receivables from clients increased by $13,600, and payables relating to operating expenses decreased by $4,800. Included in business income was $900 of interest received on municipal bonds.

Sumner has a personal savings account to which $720 in interest was credited during the year, none of which was withdrawn. In addition to business expenses taken into account in computing the net income of his business, Sumner had $4,380 in deductions to arrive at adjusted gross income. His personal exemptions amounted to $6,750, and his itemized deductions were $1,925.

Instructions For each of the situations described above, determine the amount of the taxpayer's adjusted gross income and his taxable income for the year. Assume that the maximum limit for the standard deduction is $2,000.

17-3 *a* You are to consider the income tax status of each of the items listed below. List the numbers 1 to 15 on your answer sheet. For each item state whether it is *included in gross income* or *excluded from gross income* for federal income tax on individuals,

(1) Cash dividends received on stock of Getty Oil Company.

(2) Value of a color TV set won as a prize in a quiz contest.

(3) Gain on the sale of an original painting.

(4) Inheritance received on death of a rich uncle.

(5) Interest received on Jersey City municipal bonds.

(6) Proceeds of life insurance policy received on death of husband.

(7) Tips received by a waitress.

(8) Value of U.S. Treasury bonds received as a gift from uncle.
(9) Rent received on personal residence while on extended vacation trip.
(10) Share of income from partnership in excess of drawings.
(11) Amount received as damages for injury in automobile accident.
(12) Salary received from a corporation by a stockholder who owns directly or indirectly all the shares of the company's outstanding stock.
(13) Gain on sale of Signal Companies capital stock, held for five months.
(14) Taxpayer owed $1,000 on a note payable. During the current year the taxpayer painted a building owned by the creditor, and in return the creditor canceled the note.
(15) Trip to Hawaii given by employer as reward for outstanding service.

b You are to determine the deductibility status, for federal tax purposes, of each of the items listed below. List the numbers 1 to 10 on your answer sheet. For each item state whether the item *is deducted to arrive at adjusted gross income; deducted from adjusted gross income;* or *not deductible.*

(1) Interest paid on mortgage covering personal residence.
(2) Carry-forward of an unused operating loss from previous year.
(3) Capital loss on the sale of securities.
(4) Damage in storm to motorboat used for pleasure.
(5) State sales tax paid on purchase of family automobile.
(6) Expenses incurred in moving from Arlington to Houston to accept a new position with a different company, not reimbursed by employer.
(7) Travel expenses incurred by employee in connection with his job, not reimbursed.
(8) Cost of traveling to and from home to place of employment.
(9) Fee paid to accountant for assistance in successfully contesting additional personal income taxes assessed by Internal Revenue Service.
(10) Taxpayer does maintenance work on rental property which he owns. This work would cost $500 if the taxpayer hired someone to do it.

17-4 Herman and Harriet Mann are married and have six dependent children. Their income and expenses for the latest year are as follows:

Salary from Piat Associates	$26,500
Consulting fees (net of applicable expenses)	2,500
Dividends (jointly owned)	600
Interest on bonds of State of Washington	180
Casualty loss, interest, taxes, and other expenditures (see list below)	17,000
Long-term capital gains	4,800
Short-term capital losses	2,000
Unused short-term capital loss carry-over from previous year	1,500
Proceeds on insurance policy on life of uncle	25,000

Casualty loss, interest, taxes, and other expenditures:

Theft of furniture on July 20 while on vacation	$ 1,500
Interest paid on loans to buy stocks	2,800
Medical expenses	800
Insurance on home	280
Income taxes withheld from salary	4,060
Miscellaneous deductible expenses	150
Sales taxes	680
Property taxes on home	820
State income taxes	700
Clothes, food, and other living expenses	5,210
Total (as listed above)	$17,000

Instructions Compute the taxable income and the income tax for Herman and Harriet Mann. Use the tax table for married individuals filing joint returns on page 577. Assume that the personal exemption is $750, that the maximum standard deduction is $2,000, and that both Herman and Harriet are fifty years of age.

17-5 Richard Vargo files a joint federal income tax return with his wife Melinda. He owns a hardware business and an apartment building in Arlington. The depreciation basis of the apartment building is $100,000; depreciation is recorded at the rate of 4% per year on a straight-line basis.

Richard and Melinda furnish over one-half the support of their only child, who attends college and who earned $1,600 in part-time jobs and summer work, and of Richard's father, who is seventy-two years old and who has no income of his own.

During the current year Richard and Melinda had the following cash receipts and expenditures:

Cash receipts:

Cash withdrawn from hardware business (sales, $240,500; cost of goods sold, $178,000; operating expenses, $33,600)	$27,600
Gross rentals from apartment building	18,000
Cash dividends on stock owned jointly	1,850
Interest on River County bonds	610
Received from sale of stock purchased two years ago for $6,120	8,420
Received from sale of stock purchased four months previously for $4,160	3,020
Received from sale of motorboat purchased three years ago for $2,995 and used entirely for pleasure	1,695

Cash expenditures:

Mortgage interest on residence	$ 1,142
Property taxes on residence	983
Insurance on residence	140
State income tax paid	1,080
State sales and gasoline taxes	410
Charitable contributions	1,415
Medical expenses	860
Payments on declaration of estimated tax for current year	5,820
Expenditures relating to apartment building:	
Interest on mortgage	4,500
Property taxes	2,950
Insurance (one year)	350
Utilities	1,480
Repairs and maintenance	2,420
Gardening	400

Instructions

a Determine the amount of taxable income Richard and Melinda would report on their federal income tax return for the current year. Assume that the personal exemption is $750.

b Compute the income tax liability for Richard and Melinda, using the rate schedule on page 577. Indicate the amount of tax due (or refund to be received).

17-6 The following information appears in the accounting records of the Victorville Sandstone Corporation for the current year:

Net sales	$2,500,000
Cost of goods sold	1,800,000
Dividends received from a domestic corporation	100,000
Dividends declared by board of directors on common stock of Victorville Sandstone Corporation	200,000
Selling expenses	240,000
Administrative expenses	260,000
Earthquake loss (fully deductible for income tax purposes)	50,000

During the current year, the Victorville Sandstone Corporation incurred $75,000 of sales promotion expenses which were deducted in computing taxable income but which the company has chosen to defer in its accounting records and charge against revenue during the two subsequent years when the benefits of the sales promotion are reflected in revenue. The controller will follow tax allocation procedures in reporting income taxes on the income statement during the current year.

Instructions
a Prepare an income statement for the Victorville Sandstone Corporation for the current year. The company has 100,000 shares of capital stock outstanding. In a separate schedule show your computation of federal income taxes for the year, using the following rate schedule:

First $25,000 of taxable income	22%
On excess over $25,000	48%

b Prepare the journal entry which should be made to record the provision for income taxes and income tax liability (both current and deferred) at the end of the current year. Any tax credit resulting from the full deductibility of the earthquake loss should be offset against the Earthquake Loss account.

BUSINESS DECISION PROBLEM 17

Joseph O'Rourke is in the process of organizing a business which he expects will produce, before any compensation to himself and before income taxes, an income of $60,000 per year. In deciding whether to operate as a single proprietorship or as a corporation, O'Rourke is willing to make the choice on the basis of the relative income tax advantage under either form of organization.

O'Rourke is married, files a joint return with his wife, has no other dependents, and has itemized deductions that average around $6,500 per year.

If the business is operated as a single proprietorship, O'Rourke expects to withdraw the entire income of $60,000 each year.

If the business is operated as a corporation, O'Rourke and his wife will own all the shares; he will pay himself a salary of $35,000 and will withdraw as dividends the entire amount of the corporation's net income after income taxes.

It may be assumed that the accounting income and the taxable income for the corporation would be the same and that the personal exemption is $750. Mr. and Mrs. O'Rourke have only minor amounts of nonbusiness income, which may be ignored.

Instructions

a Determine the relative income tax advantage to Joseph O'Rourke of operating either as a single proprietorship or as a corporation, and make a recommendation as to the form of organization he should adopt. Use the individual (joint return) and corporate tax rate schedules given on page 577.

b Suppose that Joseph O'Rourke planned to withdraw only $35,000 per year from his business, as drawings from a single proprietorship or as salary from a corporation. Would this affect your recommendation? Explain.

SAMPLE
FINANCIAL
STATEMENTS

Financial statements are presented in this appendix for the following publicly owned companies:

Johnson & Johnson

Carnation Company

These financial statements have been audited by eminent international firms of certified public accountants. The report of the independent auditors accompanies each set of financial statements. These particular companies were chosen because they provided realistic illustrations of many of the financial reporting issues discussed in this book.

Johnson&Johnson AND SUBSIDIARIES

Consolidated Balance Sheet at December 30, 1973 and December 31, 1972

(Dollars In Thousands Except Per Share Figures)

Assets

CURRENT ASSETS	1973	1972
Cash and certificates of deposit	$ 60,213	83,324
Marketable securities, at cost which approximates market value (Note 3)	146,609	134,053
Receivables, less allowance for collection losses and discounts $7,829 (1972 $5,935)	223,255	173,026
Inventories (Notes 1 and 4)	269,260	209,286
Expenses applicable to future operations	25,306	18,726
Total current assets	724,643	618,415
MARKETABLE SECURITIES MATURING AFTER ONE YEAR, at cost which approximates market value (Note 3)	66,300	28,769
PROPERTY, PLANT AND EQUIPMENT, at cost less accumulated depreciation and amortization (Notes 1 and 5)	365,136	301,323
OTHER ASSETS	33,013	32,959
Total assets	$1,189,092	981,466

Liabilities and Stockholders' Equity

CURRENT LIABILITIES		
Loans and notes payable (foreign purposes)	$ 15,339	18,101
Accounts payable	86,487	65,204
Federal and foreign taxes on income	57,519	40,176
Other accrued liabilities	77,380	55,877
Total current liabilities	236,725	179,358
LOANS AND NOTES PAYABLE AFTER ONE YEAR (foreign purposes)	31,859	22,694
LONG-TERM LEASE OBLIGATIONS	8,710	8,780
CERTIFICATES OF EXTRA COMPENSATION	25,030	23,066
DEFERRED INVESTMENT TAX CREDIT	6,831	5,867
RESERVE FOR FOREIGN EXCHANGE LOSSES (Notes 1 and 2)	7,517	6,152
MINORITY INTERESTS IN FOREIGN SUBSIDIARIES	4,048	2,671
STOCKHOLDERS' EQUITY (Note 7)		
Capital Stock:		
Preferred Stock—without par value (authorized and unissued 2,000,000 shares)	—	—
Common Stock—par value $2.50 per share (authorized 63,000,000 shares; issued 57,769,134 and 56,665,085 shares)	144,423	141,663
Additional capital	44,339	30,137
Retained earnings	683,719	565,217
	872,481	737,017
Less common stock held in treasury (at cost 245,691 and 246,448 shares)	4,109	4,139
	868,372	732,878
Total liabilities and stockholders' equity	$1,189,092	981,466

See Notes to Consolidated Financial Statements

Johnson&Johnson AND SUBSIDIARIES

Consolidated Statement of Earnings and Retained Earnings

For the 52 Weeks Ended December 30, 1973 and December 31, 1972

(Dollars In Thousands Except Per Share Figures)

	1973	1972
Revenues		
Sales to customers	$1,611,811	1,317,683
Other revenues, principally interest and royalties	28,827	18,886
Total revenues	1,640,638	1,336,569
Costs and Expenses		
Cost of products sold	787,638	650,275
Selling, distribution and administrative expenses (Note 6)	517,396	416,699
Depreciation and amortization of property, plant and equipment (Note 1)	48,951	41,597
Federal and foreign taxes on income (Note 6)	130,076	103,339
Other expenses	8,199	3,953
Total costs and expenses	1,492,260	1,215,863
Net Earnings	148,378	120,706
Retained Earnings At Beginning Of Period	565,217	469,647
Cash dividends paid	(29,876)	(25,136)
Retained Earnings At End Of Period	$ 683,719	565,217
Net Earnings Per Share (Note 1)	$2.59	2.15

Consolidated Statement of Common Stock, Additional Capital and Treasury Stock

For the 52 Weeks Ended December 30, 1973
(Dollars In Thousands)

	Common Stock Issued		Additional Capital	Treasury Stock	
	No. Shares	Amount		No. Shares	Amount
Balance, December 31, 1972	56,665,085	$141,663	$30,137	246,448	$4,139
Stock issued to employees under options exercised and stock compensation agreements	191,547	479	10,823		
Pooling of interests (Note 2)	912,502	2,281	3,319		
Other changes	—	—	60	(757)	(30)
Balance, December 30, 1973	57,769,134	$144,423	$44,339	245,691	$4,109

See Notes to Consolidated Financial Statements

Johnson & Johnson AND SUBSIDIARIES

Consolidated Statement of Changes in Financial Position

For the 52 Weeks Ended December 30, 1973 and December 31, 1972

(Dollars In Thousands)

	1973	1972
Source of Funds		
Net Earnings	$148,378	120,706
Expenses not requiring outlay of working capital:		
Depreciation and amortization of property, plant and equipment	48,951	41,597
Other charges against net earnings	5,987	5,086
Provided from Operations	203,316	167,389
Increase (decrease) in long-term debt—foreign purposes	9,165	11,391
Proceeds from the sales of capital stock under option	6,829	7,846
Proceeds from the sales of property, plant and equipment	5,936	5,955
	225,246	192,581
Use of Funds		
Marketable securities maturing after one year	37,531	12,781
Additions to property, plant and equipment	102,516	76,410
Cash dividends paid	29,876	25,136
Other items—net	6,462	1,770
	176,385	116,097
INCREASE IN CONSOLIDATED WORKING CAPITAL	$ 48,861	76,484
Changes in Components of Consolidated Working Capital:		
Current Assets		
Cash and marketable securities	$ (10,555)	48,643
Receivables	50,229	28,445
Inventories	59,974	18,231
Expenses applicable to future operations	6,580	6,602
	106,228	101,921
Current Liabilities		
Loans and notes payable (foreign purposes)	(2,762)	(1,926)
Accounts payable	21,283	8,711
Federal and foreign taxes on income	17,343	7,078
Other accrued liabilities	21,503	11,574
	57,367	25,437
INCREASE IN CONSOLIDATED WORKING CAPITAL	$ 48,861	76,484

See Notes to Consolidated Financial Statements

Johnson&Johnson AND SUBSIDIARIES
Notes To Consolidated Financial Statements

NOTE 1 Summary Of Significant Accounting Policies
Principles of Consolidation

The consolidated financial statements include the accounts of Johnson & Johnson and subsidiaries. All material intercompany accounts are eliminated.

Assets and liabilities of foreign subsidiaries are translated at approximate year-end rates of exchange except for property, plant and equipment accounts which are translated at the approximate rates of exchange at dates of acquisition. Operating accounts, except for depreciation, are translated at approximate annual average rates. Gains on translation of asset and liability accounts not offset by losses are deferred and included in the Reserve for Foreign Exchange Losses.

Inventories

Inventories are valued at the lower of cost (principally first-in, first-out) or market.

Depreciation and Amortization

Depreciation and amortization of property, plant and equipment are determined generally for book and tax purposes by an accelerated method for domestic companies and principally on a straight-line basis for foreign companies.

Research

Research costs are charged directly against income in the year in which incurred.

Income Taxes

Domestic investment tax credits are amortized over the lives of the related assets.

The Company plans to continue to reinvest its undistributed foreign earnings in expanding its foreign operations and, therefore, makes no tax provision to cover the repatriation of such undistributed earnings. At December 30, 1973, the cumulative amount of undistributed foreign earnings on which the Company has not provided for United States income taxes was approximately $119,000,000.

Earnings per Share

Earnings per share are calculated on the average number of shares outstanding during each year.

NOTE 2 Foreign Subsidiaries

The following amounts are included in the consolidated financial statements for subsidiaries located outside of the United States:

	December 30, 1973	December 31, 1972
Current assets	$251,486,000	181,140,000
Current liabilities	133,125,000	99,729,000
Net property, plant and equipment	133,667,000	92,137,000
Parent company equity in net assets	204,080,000	157,225,000
Excess of equity of parent company over investment	170,089,000	129,229,000
Sales to customers	636,126,000	437,510,000
Net Earnings (after elimination of minority interests)	68,103,000	47,927,000*

*Adjusted to reflect a change in the method of allocating taxes on foreign dividends paid. Previously, such taxes were charged against domestic earnings.

1973 financial results include Dr. Carl Hahn G.m.b.H., which was acquired on a pooling-of-interests basis. The effect on 1973 sales and net earnings was $56,182,000 and $1,775,000, respectively. 1972 consolidated financial statements and 1973 opening retained earnings have not been restated as the effect is not material.

Analysis of the Reserve for Foreign Exchange Losses:

	52 Weeks Ended	
	December 30, 1973	December 31, 1972
Balance Beginning of Period	$6,152,000	5,801,000
Gains on translation of asset and liability accounts	4,118,000	2,131,000
Losses on translation of asset and liability accounts	(2,753,000)	(1,780,000)
Net increase	1,365,000	351,000
Balance End of Period	$7,517,000	6,152,000

NOTE 3 Investments in Marketable Securities

Commencing in 1973 the Company has classified investments in marketable securities maturing after one year and preferred stock held for long-term investment as non-current investments. The 1972 Consolidated Financial Statements have been restated to reflect this classification.

NOTE 4 Inventories

	December 30, 1973	December 31, 1972
Raw materials and supplies	$ 89,370,000	60,438,000
Goods in process	56,018,000	42,007,000
Finished goods	123,872,000	106,841,000
	$269,260,000	209,286,000

NOTE 5 Property, Plant and Equipment

	December 30, 1973	December 31, 1972
Land and land improvements	$ 38,750,000	31,153,000
Building and building equipment	249,688,000	209,401,000
Machinery and equipment	271,010,000	224,355,000
Construction in process	42,703,000	38,954,000
	602,151,000	503,863,000
Less accumulated depreciation and amortization	237,015,000	202,540,000
	$365,136,000	301,323,000

NOTE 6 Income Taxes

Income tax expense consists of:

(Dollars in thousands)

	U.S. Federal	Foreign	Total Federal and Foreign	Domestic State and Local*
Year 1973				
Currently Payable	$69,447	60,620	130,067	9,630
Net Tax Effect—Timing Differences	(3,060)	2,105	(955)	—
Net Deferred Investment Tax Credit	964	—	964	—
	$67,351	62,725	130,076	9,630
Effective Tax Rate	45.6%	47.9%	46.7%	
Year 1972				
Currently Payable	$62,068	41,122	103,190	7,976
Net Tax Effect—Timing Differences	(1,173)	675	(498)	—
Net Deferred Investment Tax Credit	647	—	647	—
	$61,542	41,797	103,339	7,976
Effective Tax Rate	45.8%	46.6%	46.1%	

*Reflected in Selling, Distribution and Administrative Expenses.

NOTE 7 Capital Stock

Stock compensation agreements and options with employees were outstanding at December 30, 1973 under which the Company may be required to deliver shares of common stock. For details see page 24. Common stock equivalents have no material dilutive effects on earnings per share.

During 1973 no shares of the Company were issued under the Johnson & Johnson United Kingdom Executive Share Purchase Plan. As of December 30, 1973, 13,425 shares of the 100,000 maximum authorized under the Plan have been issued.

NOTE 8 Retirement and Pension Plans

The total Company cost (which includes current service cost and amortization of prior service cost at the rate of 10% annually) of the various retirement and pension plans in effect for employees of the Company and certain of its domestic and foreign subsidiaries amounted to approximately $13,310,000 in 1973 and $11,590,000 in 1972. The amounts funded under these plans exceed the actuarially computed value of vested benefits at December 30, 1973.

NOTE 9 Rentals and Leases

Rentals of office and data processing equipment, vehicles and space totalled approximately $20,460,000 in 1973 and $16,507,000 in 1972. Minimum rental commitments under all noncancelable leases were not material.

Accountants' Report

To the Stockholders and Board of Directors of Johnson & Johnson

We have examined the consolidated balance sheet of Johnson & Johnson and subsidiaries as of December 30, 1973 and December 31, 1972, and the related consolidated statements of earnings and retained earnings, common stock, additional capital and treasury stock, and changes in financial position for the fifty-two week periods then ended. Our examination was made in accordance with generally accepted auditing standards and accordingly included such tests of the accounting records and such other auditing procedures as we considered necessary in the circumstances.

In our opinion, the aforementioned financial statements present fairly the financial position of Johnson & Johnson and subsidiaries at December 30, 1973 and December 31, 1972, and the results of their operations and the changes in their financial position for the fifty-two week periods then ended, in conformity with generally accepted accounting principles applied on a consistent basis.

Coopers & Lybrand

New York, New York
February 19, 1974

Common Stock:
Listed New York and Toronto Stock Exchanges
Stock Symbol   JNJ

Transfer Agents:
Morgan Guaranty Trust Company of New York
30 West Broadway, New York, New York 10015

Canada Permanent Trust Company
Canada Permanent Tower
20 Eglinton Avenue West
Yonge Eglinton Center, Toronto, Ontario, Canada

Registrars:
The Chase Manhattan Bank N.A.
1 Chase Manhattan Plaza, New York, New York 10015

Bank of Montreal, Toronto Branch
50 King Street West, Toronto, Canada

Johnson&Johnson AND SUBSIDIARIES

Ten Year Statistical Summary
(Dollars in Thousands Except Per Share Figures)

Johnson & Johnson and Subsidiaries	1973	1972	1971
Income Data			
Sales to customers			
Domestic	$ 975,685	880,173	785,472
Foreign	636,126	437,510	355,013
	1,611,811	1,317,683	1,140,485
Other revenues	28,827	18,886	15,753
Total revenues	1,640,638	1,336,569	1,156,238
Cost of materials and services	790,621	640,795	563,991
Total employment costs	491,409	405,422	351,700
Federal and foreign taxes on income	130,076	103,339	83,747
State and local taxes	31,203	24,710	19,117
Depreciation and amortization of property	48,951	41,597	35,862
Provision for foreign exchange losses	—	—	—
Total costs and expenses	1,492,260	1,215,863	1,054,417
Net Earnings	$ 148,378	120,706	101,821
Per share of common stock[1 and 2]	$ 2.59	2.15	1.82
Percent of sales to customers	9.2	9.2	8.9
Domestic net earnings[3]	$ 80,275	72,779	64,311
Foreign net earnings[3]	68,103	47,927	37,510
Property, Plant and Equipment			
Net investment	$ 365,136	301,323	269,443
Additions during year	102,516	76,410	67,920
Total Assets	$1,189,092	981,466	830,020
Common Stock Information			
Dividends paid per share[1]	$ .53	.45	.43
Taxes per share[1 and 4]	$ 2.81	2.28	1.84
Book value per share at year-end	$ 15.10	12.99	11.10
Shares outstanding (000 omitted)[1]	57,399	56,220	55,879
Stockholders	29,500	28,600	22,700
Employees	49,100	43,300	40,200

[1] Calculated on the average number of shares outstanding during each year.
[2] Common stock equivalents have no material dilutive effects on earnings per share.
[3] The domestic and foreign net earnings for the year 1972 and prior years have been restated to reflect a change in the method of allocating taxes on foreign dividends paid.
[4] Federal and foreign taxes on income; state and local taxes.

1970	1969	1968	1967	1966	1965	1964
705,427	647,724	580,025	514,801	485,872	431,009	384,483
296,608	254,156	221,256	197,529	174,722	145,040	118,785
1,002,035	901,880	801,281	712,330	660,594	576,049	503,268
14,687	13,261	9,053	7,741	5,768	4,302	3,409
1,016,722	915,141	810,334	720,071	666,362	580,351	506,677
499,128	454,590	408,766	372,491	353,889	306,989	269,392
311,376	276,737	245,859	223,076	204,411	180,248	157,538
73,934	70,461	58,714	43,027	38,170	30,708	27,903
16,038	13,663	12,360	10,258	7,482	6,399	5,410
31,784	29,666	25,658	23,200	20,761	19,501	18,086
806	602	1,363	2,072	1,533	2,058	1,529
933,066	845,719	752,720	674,124	626,246	545,903	479,858
83,656	69,422	57,614	45,947	40,116	34,448	26,819
1.51	1.27	1.06	.85	.74	.64	.50
8.3	7.7	7.2	6.5	6.1	6.0	5.3
55,238	48,892	41,248	34,360	30,984	26,697	20,918
28,418	20,530	16,366	11,587	9,132	7,751	5,901
239,160	219,803	195,726	182,278	160,198	137,473	120,123
52,783	55,486	41,975	46,196	44,715	32,215	27,559
706,583	620,054	544,410	476,087	420,810	380,924	319,862
.34	.28	.22	.21	.18	.16	.13
1.62	1.53	1.30	.98	.85	.68	.62
9.57	8.30	7.23	6.32	5.60	5.16	4.67
55,542	54,805	54,573	54,294	53,922	54,228	53,637
19,100	14,300	12,600	11,600	8,800	8,400	7,700
38,200	37,400	35,600	33,500	32,900	29,600	26,600

CONSOLIDATED BALANCE SHEET — CARNATION COMPANY AND SUBSIDIARIES

	December 31	
ASSETS	1973	1972 (Note 8)
CURRENT ASSETS:		
Cash	$ 13,059,007	$ 16,709,283
Short-term commercial obligations, at cost		
(approximately market)	95,613,875	99,058,377
Other marketable securities, at cost (quoted		
market value $14,241,000 and $17,036,000)	5,363,796	5,426,089
Accounts and notes receivable, less provisions of		
$5,196,702 and $4,386,446 for uncollectible accounts—		
Trade	136,273,958	110,644,294
Miscellaneous	14,294,108	10,026,414
Inventories, at lower of cost (principally first-in,		
first-out basis) or market—		
Raw materials and supplies	86,935,246	67,496,696
Finished goods	155,234,648	125,917,167
Prepaid expenses and deposits	8,457,906	6,122,362
Total current assets	515,232,544	441,400,682
NON-CURRENT RECEIVABLES AND MISCELLANEOUS		
INVESTMENTS, at lower of cost or estimated realizable values	8,975,232	9,339,696
INVESTMENTS IN AND ADVANCES TO		
AFFILIATED COMPANIES (Note 1)	14,790,205	7,280,418
PLANT ASSETS, at cost, less accumulated depreciation of		
$179,299,446 and $162,950,725 (Note 3)	199,562,187	191,018,821
EXCESS OF PURCHASE PRICE OF COMPANIES ACQUIRED		
OVER NET ASSETS AT DATE OF ACQUISITION (Note 1)	37,269,456	31,886,456
	$775,829,624	$680,926,073

	December 31	
LIABILITIES	1973	1972 (Note 8)
CURRENT LIABILITIES:		
Indebtedness to banks and others	$21,696,000	$ 24,381,747
Current portion of long-term debt (Note 5)	5,268,556	8,298,494
Trade accounts payable	69,783,363	58,969,885
Other accounts payable and accrued expenses	65,537,610	52,868,053
Income taxes	25,612,453	18,437,629
Total current liabilities	187,897,982	162,955,808
DEFERRED INCOME TAXES (Note 1)	20,667,489	17,549,489
LONG-TERM DEBT (Note 5)	115,213,328	94,963,166
PROVISION FOR STATUTORY SEVERANCE PAY IN FOREIGN COUNTRIES (Note 9)		1,585,000
MINORITY INTERESTS IN SUBSIDIARIES (Notes 1 and 9)	2,884,267	3,600,111
INVESTMENT OF STOCKHOLDERS, represented by (Note 7):		
Preferred stock, no par value—		
Authorized, 2,000,000 shares		
Outstanding, none		
Common stock, $2.00 par value—		
Authorized, 30,000,000 shares		
Outstanding, 17,817,818 shares in 1973 and		
17,787,613 shares in 1972	35,635,636	35,575,226
Other capital, per accompanying statement	39,689,736	38,385,687
Retained earnings, per accompanying statement	373,841,186	326,311,586
COMMITMENTS AND CONTINGENCIES (Note 6)		
	$775,829,624	$680,926,073

CONSOLIDATED STATEMENT OF INCOME

	Year Ended December 31	
	1973	1972 (Note 8)
NET SALES	$1,472,198,191	$1,289,460,653
MISCELLANEOUS INCOME	9,507,716	6,454,758
	1,481,705,907	1,295,915,411
COSTS AND EXPENSES, including provisions for depreciation of $22,957,479 in 1973 and $21,451,014 in 1972 (Notes 1 and 3):		
Cost of sales	1,129,153,820	972,501,530
Selling, general and administrative expenses	213,105,674	202,858,173
Interest expense	9,038,656	8,781,579
Minority interests in net income of subsidiaries	436,406	313,818
Income taxes (including $2,229,000 in 1973 and $2,595,000 in 1972, representing charges equivalent to reduction in income taxes arising from timing differences)	65,100,000	54,032,000
	1,416,834,556	1,238,487,100
NET INCOME	$ 64,871,351	$ 57,428,311
NET INCOME PER SHARE (based on average shares outstanding each year)	$3.64	$3.23

CONSOLIDATED STATEMENT OF OTHER CAPITAL

BALANCE AT BEGINNING OF YEAR:		
Carnation Company, as shown in 1972 annual report	$36,648,318	$48,279,406
Pooled company (Note 8)	1,737,369	1,787,082
	38,385,687	50,066,488
PAR VALUE of 5,815,544 shares of common stock issued in 3-for-2 stock split		(11,631,088)
EXCESS OF FAIR MARKET VALUE OVER PAR VALUE of common stock issued by pooled company	1,304,049	92,496
EXCESS OF PAR VALUE of Carnation common stock (issued in exchange) over book value of common stock of pooled company		(142,209)
BALANCE AT END OF YEAR	$39,689,736	$38,385,687

CONSOLIDATED STATEMENT OF RETAINED EARNINGS

	Year Ended December 31	
	1973	1972 (Note 8)
BALANCE AT BEGINNING OF YEAR:		
Carnation Company, as shown in 1972 annual report	$317,518,782	$277,398,041
Pooled company (Note 8)	8,792,804	7,627,554
	326,311,586	285,025,595
NET INCOME	64,871,351	57,428,311
	391,182,937	342,453,906
DIVIDENDS:		
Cash—$.93 per share in 1973 and		
$.89 per share in 1972	16,327,694	15,589,936
Cash—pooled company	384,668	404,852
Cash in lieu of fractional shares—		
In connection with stock split		147,532
In connection with pooling	65,329	
COST OF COMMON STOCK acquired by pooled company	564,060	
	17,341,751	16,142,320
BALANCE AT END OF YEAR (Note 5)	$373,841,186	$326,311,586

REPORT OF INDEPENDENT ACCOUNTANTS

To the Stockholders and Board of Directors of Carnation Company:

In our opinion, the accompanying consolidated balance sheets and the related consolidated statements of income, retained earnings, other capital and changes in financial position present fairly the financial position of Carnation Company and its subsidiaries at December 31, 1973 and 1972 and the results of their operations and changes in financial position for the years then ended, in conformity with generally accepted accounting principles consistently applied. Our examinations of these statements were made in accordance with generally accepted auditing standards and accordingly included such tests of the accounting records and such other auditing procedures as we considered necessary in the circumstances.

PRICE WATERHOUSE & CO.

Los Angeles, California
February 22, 1974

CONSOLIDATED STATEMENT OF CHANGES IN FINANCIAL POSITION

	Year Ended December 31	
	1973	1972 (Note 8)
Financial resources were provided by:		
Net income	$ 64,871,351	$ 57,428,311
Add (deduct) items not affecting working capital—		
Depreciation and amortization (including excess purchase price).........	23,166,479	21,567,606
Deferred income taxes and investment tax credits	3,616,061	4,177,186
Other items	(320,149)	(420,944)
Working capital provided by operations	91,333,742	82,752,159
Sale of plant assets	3,611,355	1,499,129
Proceeds from long-term borrowings	28,801,057	2,375,791
Decrease in non-current receivables and miscellaneous investments	364,464	1,069,180
Decrease in investments in and advances to affiliated companies		2,314,450
Proceeds from exercise of employee stock options and stock purchase warrants of pooled company	1,364,459	96,036
Other	(395,695)	304,459
	125,079,382	90,411,204
Financial resources were used for:		
Purchase of plant assets	35,610,261	29,592,447
Cash dividends	16,777,691	16,142,320
Payments on long-term debt	8,550,895	8,576,877
Increase in investments in and advances to affiliated companies	7,509,787	
Excess of purchase price of companies acquired over net assets at date of acquisition	5,592,000	
Purchase of treasury shares by pooled company	564,060	
Decrease in statutory severance pay	1,585,000	
Increase in working capital	48,889,688	36,099,560
	$125,079,382	$ 90,411,204

	Increase (Decrease)	
Analysis of changes in working capital:		
Current assets		
Cash	($ 3,650,276)	($ 3,988,193)
Marketable securities and commercial obligations	(3,506,795)	33,597,218
Receivables	29,897,358	18,667,183
Inventories	48,756,031	12,534,481
Prepaid expenses and deposits	2,335,544	1,255,302
	73,831,862	62,065,991
Current liabilities		
Indebtedness to banks and others	(2,685,747)	6,434,371
Trade accounts payable	10,813,478	11,966,711
Income taxes	7,174,824	2,515,755
Other	9,639,619	5,049,594
	24,942,174	25,966,431
Increase in working capital	$ 48,889,688	$ 36,099,560

NOTES TO CONSOLIDATED FINANCIAL STATEMENTS

NOTE 1—Accounting policies:

The major accounting policies and practices followed by the Company and its subsidiaries are as follows:

CONSOLIDATION—The consolidated financial statements include the accounts of the Company and all its subsidiaries; subsidiaries operating outside the United States and Canada are included on the basis of a fiscal year ending September 30.

TRANSLATION OF FOREIGN CURRENCIES—Current assets and liabilities, non-current receivables and long-term liabilities are translated at appropriate year-end rates of exchange; capital assets, intangible assets and related depreciation and amortization are translated at rates of exchange prevailing at the dates of acquisition; and operating statements, except depreciation, are translated at the weighted average rate for the year.

Realized exchange adjustments, which were not material in 1972 and 1973, are recognized in the determination of income as incurred; unrealized exchange gains arising in the current year have been deferred to future years as a reserve for possible unrealized exchange losses and other currency related transactions. Other accounts payable at December 31, 1973 includes such deferred exchange gains aggregating $2,042,000 based on exchange rates at that date. Unrealized gains were not material in prior years. Losses on forward exchange contracts are recognized as they arise; gains are included in income when realized. At December 31, 1973 unrecognized gains on unperformed forward exchange contracts were not significant.

INTERPERIOD ALLOCATION OF INCOME TAXES—Provision is made in the accounts for all major timing differences (primarily accelerated depreciation and franchise taxes) resulting from the recognition of income and expenses in different periods for financial reporting than for tax purposes. There are cumulative undistributed earnings of foreign subsidiaries and affiliated companies at December 31, 1973 aggregating approximately $73,500,000 for which it has not been considered necessary to provide for deferred income taxes as this amount has been or is expected to be reinvested for an indefinite period of time. It is anticipated that undistributed earnings of domestic subsidiaries will not be subject to substantial additional taxes.

INVESTMENT IN AFFILIATED COMPANIES—Investments in all affiliated companies (in excess of 20% ownership) are carried at the Company's equity in underlying assets of such companies.

DEPRECIATION—Depreciation is, in general, provided on a straight line basis over the estimated useful lives of the assets.

INVESTMENT TAX CREDIT—The accumulated reduction in income taxes resulting from application of the investment tax credit is taken into income over the estimated useful lives of the related plant assets.

PENSION COSTS—Pension costs are funded as accrued.

AMORTIZATION OF EXCESS ACQUISITION COSTS—No amortization is provided for costs incurred prior to October 31, 1970 inasmuch as such costs are considered to represent intangible assets with an unlimited life. Costs incurred subsequent to October 31, 1970 are being amortized over forty years from the date of the related acquisition.

NOTE 2—Foreign operations:

After translation of foreign currencies into United States dollar equivalents, the following amounts are included in the consolidated financial statements for that portion of the Company's consolidated operations outside of the United States:

	1973	1972
Net current assets	$ 63,735,427	$41,673,597
Net assets	100,583,716	70,153,391
Net income	13,789,325	11,157,430

Dividends remitted to the Company in United States dollars totaled $316,000 in 1973 and $8,474,000 in 1972.

NOTE 3—Plant assets, less accumulated depreciation:

Plant assets, carried at cost, comprised:

	December 31	
	1973	1972
Buildings	$103,265,386	$ 97,178,440
Leasehold improvements	2,385,206	2,161,029
Real estate improvements	5,329,395	5,166,892
Machinery and equipment	255,883,872	235,253,266
	366,863,859	339,759,627
Less—Accumulated depreciation and amortization	179,299,446	162,950,725
	187,564,413	176,808,902
Land	8,943,209	8,367,903
Construction in progress	3,054,565	5,842,016
	$199,562,187	$191,018,821

The unamortized investment tax credit reserve, aggregating $4,919,752 at December 31, 1973, has been included with accumulated depreciation in the consolidated balance sheet.

NOTE 4—Pension plans:

The Company and its subsidiaries have several pension plans covering substantially all of their employees, including certain employees in foreign countries. The provisions for pension costs aggregated $5,762,000 in 1973 and $6,059,000 in 1972. The Company's policy is, with minor exceptions, to fund pension costs accrued. There are no material unfunded past service costs, and pension funds available are sufficient to cover the present value of vested benefits.

NOTE 5—Long-term debt:

Long-term debt at December 31, 1973, consists of the following:

	Current portion	Long-term
Debentures of various series, 2⅞% to 4%, maturing to 1981	$ 790,000	$ 10,570,000
Bank loans, 4¾% to 8¾%, payable in monthly installments to 1979	1,695,792	3,344,928
4½% long-term notes maturing to 1990	650,000	22,400,000
5% long-term notes maturing to 1991	650,000	23,050,000
7½% long-term notes maturing from 1977 to 1996		25,000,000
5½% subordinated debentures, due in 1978		338,200
4% Convertible Subordinated Debentures, due in 1988 (Note 7)		25,000,000
Other notes payable, 3% to 10½%, with varying maturities to 1985	895,764	2,292,200
Notes payable by foreign subsidiaries, 8% average rate of interest, maturing to 2001	587,000	3,218,000
	$5,268,556	$115,213,328

The indentures and the note agreements under which the debentures, 4½%, 5% and 7½% notes were issued provide for redemption payments each year. Aggregate payments on long-term debt, in each of the five years subsequent to December 31, 1973, are as follows: 1974—$5,269,000; 1975—$4,520,000; 1976—$6,121,000; 1977—$4,404,000; 1978—$6,719,000. In addition, the Company may under certain conditions redeem all or part of the debentures and notes at specified premium rates.

The agreements also contain restrictions as to payment of cash dividends and the acquisition or retirement of common stock. The amount of retained earnings subject to such restrictions at December 31, 1973 was $184,079,000.

NOTE 6—Commitments and contingencies:

The Company and its subsidiaries lease property and equipment used in their operations for terms ranging generally from three to thirty years. Rental expenses for 1972 and 1973 were approximately $6,000,000 and $5,600,000. Rental payments required under long-term leases for the five years subsequent to December 31, 1973, are estimated at $4,482,000 for 1974, $3,763,000 for 1975, $3,023,000 for 1976, $2,273,000 for 1977 and $1,464,000 for 1978. Aggregate rentals for each of the three succeeding five year periods are as follows: 1979-1983, $3,328,000; 1984-1988, $1,541,000; 1989-1993, $505,000. Lease payments required subsequent to 1993 aggregate $734,000.

The Company and/or its subsidiaries are defendants in a number of legal proceedings arising from their day-to-day operations. In the opinion of management, none of the pending cases will have a material effect upon operations of the companies or their financial position.

NOTE 7—Capital stock and other capital:

Transactions in common stock and other capital relate to the statutory merger of Herff Jones Co. in 1973 (see Note 8) and a 3-for-2 stock split in December 1972. In connection with the stock split, authorized shares of common stock were increased to 30,000,000 shares, 5,815,544 shares were issued and other capital was charged for the par value of the additional shares, $11,631,088. Cash was paid in lieu of issuing fractional shares.

Stockholders, at a special meeting in 1972, authorized 2,000,000 shares of a new class of preferred stock, without par value; at December 31, 1973, there were no preferred shares outstanding.

At December 31, 1973 there are 228,825 shares of common stock reserved for conversion of the Company's 4% Convertible Subordinated Debentures due in 1988 and 4,854 shares reserved for stock options and purchase warrants in connection with the statutory merger of Herff Jones Co.

NOTE 8—Mergers and acquisitions:

Effective as of November 8, 1973, the business and assets of Herff Jones Co. were transferred to Carnation Company in a statutory merger of the two companies involving the exchange of 367,993 shares of Carnation stock for the outstanding capital stock and stock purchase warrants of Herff Jones Co.; cash of $65,329 was paid in lieu of issuing fractional shares. This business combination was accounted for as a pooling of interests, and accordingly the consolidated financial statements include the accounts of the companies for the full year. The financial statements for 1972 have been restated for comparative purposes.

Additionally, the Company has made several minor acquisitions involving the purchase of net assets of approximately $15,000,000. These acquisitions have been accounted for as purchases; excess purchase costs over net assets at date of acquisition, aggregating approximately $6,000,000, will be amortized over forty years from the date of the related acquisition.

NOTE 9—Statutory severance pay:

Ownership of a Peruvian subsidiary was reduced to less than 50% and accordingly the company is accounted for on an equity basis rather than a consolidated basis beginning in 1973; an accrual for severance pay of approximately $1,600,000 on the books of this company was included in the consolidated balance sheet at December 31, 1972 with no comparable amount at December 31, 1973.

RECORD OF GROWTH SINCE 1969 ($000 omitted)

SUMMARY OF OPERATIONS	1973	1972	1971	1970	1969
Net sales	$1,472,198	$1,289,461	$1,179,272	$1,081,029	$1,006,271
Income before income taxes	129,971	111,460	102,827	94,412	91,803
Taxes on income	65,100	54,032	51,112	47,522	49,098
Net income	64,871	57,428	51,715	46,890	42,705
Percent to net sales	4.4	4.5	4.4	4.3	4.2
Cash dividends paid	16,712	15,995	15,243	13,804	12,024
Depreciation	22,957	21,451	19,621	17,774	16,146
Capital expenditures	35,610	29,592	36,932	35,558	41,248

YEAR END FINANCIAL DATA					
Current assets	$ 515,233	$ 441,401	$ 381,029	$ 329,979	$ 314,886
Current liabilities	187,898	162,956	136,772	137,920	128,240
Working capital	327,335	278,445	244,257	192,059	186,646
Ratio—current assets to current liabilities	2.74:1	2.71:1	2.79:1	2.39:1	2.46:1
Plant and equipment—net	199,562	191,019	184,644	174,086	159,420
Total assets	775,830	680,926	617,570	554,712	520,224
Long-term debt	115,213	94,963	102,140	76,914	78,396
Stockholders' equity	449,167	400,272	358,890	322,799	300,047
Shares outstanding at year end (Adjusted for stock splits)	17,817,818	17,787,613	17,784,958	17,751,179	17,974,284

PER SHARE (Based on average shares outstanding each year, adjusted for stock splits)					
Net income	$ 3.64	$ 3.23	$ 2.91	$ 2.62	$ 2.38
Dividends	.93	.89	.86	.77	.67
Stockholders' equity	25.20	22.50	20.20	18.06	16.69

Note: In restating the accounts for the Herff Jones merger, 1973 and 1972 were restated on a calendar year basis and the 1971, 1970 and 1969 accounts of Herff were combined on a June 30 basis with the Carnation accounts as of December 31. At December 31, 1971, stockholders' equity has been adjusted to give effect to the short-period operating loss of Herff.

INDEX